FIG. 1.—The Tacarcuna wood quail, gallito del monte fajeado (*Odontophorus dialeucos* Wetmore), found on Cerro Malí and Cerro Tacarcuna, Darién (see page 327). Painting by Walter Weber.

SMITHSONIAN MISCELLANEOUS COLLECTIONS
VOLUME 150, Part 1

THE BIRDS OF THE REPUBLIC OF PANAMÁ

Part 1.—TINAMIDAE (Tinamous) to RYNCHOPIDAE (Skimmers)

By
ALEXANDER WETMORE

CITY OF WASHINGTON
PUBLISHED BY THE SMITHSONIAN INSTITUTION
1981

Library of Congress catalog 66–61601

Copyright 1981 by the Smithsonian Institution

All rights reserved

First printing, 1965
Second printing, 1981

ISBN 0–87474–063–0

Part 2   Columbidae (Pigeons) to Picidae (Woodpeckers)
ISBN 0–87474–064–9   1968

Part 3   Passeriformes: Dendrocolaptidae (Woodcreepers) to Oxyruncidae (Sharpbills)
ISBN 0–87474–122–X   1972

CONTENTS

	Page
Introduction	1
The List of Birds	2
Acknowledgments	4
Order TINAMIFORMES	5
Family Tinamidae: Tinamous; Tinamous	5
Order PODICIPEDIFORMES	24
Family Podicipedidae: Grebes; Somormujos	24
Order PROCELLARIIFORMES	31
Family Diomedeidae: Albatrosses; Albatroses	31
Procellariidae: Shearwaters, Petrels; Pardelas, Petreles	35
Hydrobatidae: Storm Petrels; Paiños	42
Order PELECANIFORMES	48
Family Phaethontidae: Tropicbirds; Aves del Trópico	48
Pelecanidae: Pelicans; Pelícanos	51
Sulidae: Boobies, Gannets; Bobas, Piqueros	55
Phalacrocoracidae: Cormorants; Cuervos Marinos	64
Anhingidae: Snakebirds; Cuervos de Aguja	69
Fregatidae: Frigatebirds; Tijeretas de Mar	72
Order CICONIIFORMES	78
Family Ardeidae: Herons; Garzas	78
Cochleariidae: Boat-billed Heron; Garzota Cuchara	114
Ciconiidae: Storks; Cigüeñas	119
Threskiornithidae: Ibises, Spoonbills; Cocos, Garzas Paletas	122
Order ANSERIFORMES	129
Family Anatidae: Ducks; Patos	129
Order FALCONIFORMES	153
Family Cathartidae: American Vultures; Buitres Americanos	153
Accipitridae: Hawks, Eagles, and Allies; Gavilanes, Águilas, y Especies Afines	171
Pandionidae: Osprey; Águila Pescadora	256
Falconidae: Falcons, Forest Falcons, and Caracaras; Halcones, Halcones del Monte, y Caranchos	259
Order GALLIFORMES	293
Family Cracidae: Curassows and Guans; Pavones y Faisanas	293
Phasianidae: Quails, Pheasants, and Peacocks; Codornices, Faisanas, y Pavos Reales	310
Order GRUIFORMES	334
Family Aramidae: Limpkin; Carrao	334
Rallidae: Rails, Gallinules, and Coots; Cocalecas y Gallinetas de Agua	338
Heliornithidae: Finfoots; Zambullidores de Agua	365
Eurypygidae: Sunbitterns; Abanicos	369

	Page
Order CHARADRIIFORMES	372
Family Jacanidae: Jaçanas; Gallitos de Agua	372
Haematopodidae: Oystercatchers; Ostreros	378
Charadriidae: Plovers; Chorlitos	382
Scolopacidae: Snipe, Sandpipers, and Allies; Agachadizas; Playeros y Aliados	393
Family Recurvirostridae: Avocets and Stilts; Avocetas y Cigüeñuelas.	427
Phalaropodidae: Phalaropes; Falaropos	429
Stercorariidae: Skuas and Jaegers; Gaviotas Salteadoras	433
Laridae: Gulls and Terns; Gaviotas y Gaviotines	438
Rynchopidae: Skimmers; Rayadores	463
Index	467

LIST OF ILLUSTRATIONS

Frontispiece (Figure 1): Tacarcuna wood quail, gallito del monte fajeado. *Odontophorus dialeucos.*

FIGURE *Page*

2. Great tinamou, perdiz de arca, *Tinamus major.* Head shows smooth crown of subspecies of western Panamá 7
3. Crested head of *Tinamus major saturatus,* race of great tinamou found from Canal Zone through eastern Panamá 13
4. Little tinamou, perdiz de rastrojo, *Crypturellus soui* 18
5. Head of pied-billed grebe, buzo, *Podilymbus podiceps,* with large, banded bill 26
6. Least grebe, tigua, *Podiceps dominicus brachypterus,* with slender bill 29
7. Audubon's shearwater, pardela chica, *Puffinus lherminieri,* at entrance of nesting burrow 38
8. Least petrel, golondrina de mar menuda, *Halocyptena microsoma* 46
9. Red-billed tropicbird, rabijunco, *Phaethon aethereus mesonauta* 50
10. Brown pelican, alcatraz, *Pelecanus occidentalis carolinensis* 52
11. Brown booby, piquero moreno, *Sula leucogaster* 57
12. Olivaceous cormorant, cuervo marino, *Phalacrocorax olivaceus olivaceus* 66
13. Anhinga, cuervo de aguja, *Anhinga anhinga leucogaster* 70
14. Magnificent frigatebird, tijereta de mar, *Fregata magnificens,* male, with inflated throat sac 74
15. Agamí heron, garza pechicastaña, *Agamia agami* 96
16. Head of bare-throated tiger-bittern, jorrálico, *Heterocnus mexicanus,* with throat bare from bill to upper foreneck 104
17. Head of banded tiger-bittern, garza tigre rayada, *Tigrisoma lineatum lineatum,* with a line of feathers down the throat, which is bare at sides 107
18. Salmon's tiger-bittern, garza tigre oscura, *Tigrisoma salmoni* 110
19. Head of boat-billed heron, garzota cuchara, *Cochlearius cochlearius* ... 116
20. Head of white ibis, coco blanco, *Eudocimus albus* 125
21. Head of roseate spoonbill, garza paleta, *Ajaja ajaia,* with throat pouch inflated 128
22. Black-bellied tree duck, güichichí, *Dendrocygna autumnalis autumnalis* 133
23. Muscovy duck, pato real, *Cairina moschata* 135
24. Head of American comb duck, pato crestudo, *Sarkidiornis sylvicola,* male, to show the knob on bill 138
25. Foot of blue-winged teal, cerceta ala-azul, *Anas discors,* without a lobe on the hindtoe 141
26. Head of shoveler, pato cuchara, *Spatula clypeata,* male, to show form of bill 146
27. Head of American widgeon, pato calvo, *Mareca americana,* male 147
28. Foot of lesser scaup, pato pechiblanco, *Aythya affinis,* with a distinct lobe on hindtoe 149

FIGURE	Page
29. Masked duck, pato tigre, *Oxyura dominica*, male	151
30. King vulture, rey gallinazo, *Sarcoramphus papa*	155
31. Black vulture, gallinazo, *Coragyps atratus brasiliensis*	158
32. Turkey vulture, noneca, *Cathartes aura*	162
33. Head of turkey vulture, noneca, *Cathartes aura*, with wrinkled skin without papillae on neck	163
34. Head of yellow-headed vulture, guala, *Cathartes burrovianus burrovianus*, with wartlike papillae on neck	169
35. Swallow-tailed kite, gavilán tijereta, *Elanoides forficatus yetapa*	176
36. Plumbeous kite, gavilán plomizo, *Ictinia plumbea*	178
37. Everglade kite, gavilán caracolero, *Rostrhamus sociabilis sociabilis*	181
38. Slender-billed kite, gavilán piquidelgado, *Helicolestes hamatus*	183
39. Head of double-toothed kite, gavilán bidente, *Harpagus bidentatus fasciatus*	185
40. Head of hook-billed kite, gavilán piquiganchudo, *Chondrohierax uncinatus uncinatus*	189
41. Gray hawk, gavilán gris, *Buteo nitidus blakei*	200
42. Large-billed hawk, cuiscuí, *Buteo magnirostris*	212
43. White hawk, gavilán blanco, *Leucopternis albicollis costaricensis*	218
44. Barred hawk eagle, águila de penacho, *Spizaetus ornatus vicarius*	242
45. Marsh hawk, gavilán sabanero, *Circus cyaneus hudsonius*	252
46. Foot of osprey, águila pescadora, *Pandion haliaetus carolinensis*	257
47. Laughing falcon, vaquero, *Herpetotheres cachinnans cachinnans*	261
48. Red-throated caracara, cacao, *Daptrius americanus americanus*	277
49. Bat falcon, halcón cazamurciélagos, *Falco rufigularis petoensis*	284
50. Head of male Central American curassow, pavón, *Crax rubra rubra*	294
51. Crested guan, pava cimba, *Penelope purpurascens aequatorialis*	299
52. Right wing of black guan, pava negra, *Chamaepetes unicolor*, with incised tips of outer primaries	304
53. Crested bobwhite, codorniz, *Colinus cristatus*, male	312
54. Marbled wood quail, gallito del monte jaspeado, *Odontophorus gujanensis*	317
55. Limpkin, carrao, *Aramus guarauna guarauna*, northern subspecies, heavily streaked with white	336
56. Gray-necked wood rail, cocaleca gris, *Aramides cajanea*	342
57. Yellow-breasted rail, cocalequita enana, *Porzana flaviventer flaviventer*	349
58. White-throated rail, carrasqueadora, *Laterallus albigularis*	352
59. Common gallinule, gallineta de agua, *Gallinula chloropus*	358
60. Foot of American coot, gallineta cenicienta, *Fulica americana americana*, with lobed toes	364
61. American finfoot, patico de agua, *Heliornis fulica*	367
62. Sunbittern, abanico, *Eurypyga helias major*	370
63. Head of northern jaçana, gallito de agua castaño, *Jacana spinosa spinosa*	373
64. Wattled jaçana, gallito de agua barbudo, *Jacana jacana hypomelaena*	377
65. American oystercatcher, ostrero blanco, *Haematopus palliatus pitanay*	380
66. Collared plover, turillo, *Charadrius collaris*	388
67. Solitary sandpiper, playerito solitario, *Tringa solitaria*	403

LIST OF ILLUSTRATIONS vii

FIGURE *Page*
68. Black-necked stilt, viuda, *Himantopus mexicanus* 429
69. Skua, salteador grande, *Catharacta skua* 434
70. Right wings of two gulls to show pattern of marking. Upper: Franklin's gull, gaviota de Franklin, *Larus pipixcan*. Lower: Laughing gull, gaviota reidora, *Larus atricilla* 443
71. Head of Sandwich tern, gaviotín patinegro, *Thalasseus sandvicensis acuflavidus* 460
72. Brown noddy, cervera, *Anous stolidus* 461
73. Head of black skimmer, rayador, *Rynchops nigra* 464

THE BIRDS OF THE REPUBLIC OF PANAMÁ, PART 1: TINAMIDAE (TINAMOUS) TO RYNCHOPIDAE (SKIMMERS)

By ALEXANDER WETMORE
Research Associate, Smithsonian Institution

INTRODUCTION

THE long, narrow Isthmus of Panamá, which unites North America on the one hand and South America on the other, is a geographic area outstanding in its interest to biologists in the systematic field as the land connection between these two regions of the Northern and Southern Hemispheres. Present understanding of geologic history indicates that the two areas were separated by open sea in the Tertiary period for a vast space of time that began in the Paleocene epoch and extended toward the end of the Pliocene. For 50 million years South America remained isolated from other lands, while North America had periodic union with Asia through land connections in the present region of Bering Sea. The great diversity in plant and animal life that now marks the Panamanian land bridge is a reflection of invasions from the two adjacent continental areas. Study of present-day distribution, variation, and relationship in any group is of deep interest and valuable in details of scientific information.

The present account is the first installment of a summary of what is known of the birdlife of the area. My personal studies in the field began in 1944 and have continued annually for approximately three months each year since 1946, with laboratory investigation of specimens and a survey of the published works of others who have made contributions in this region.

The number of kinds of birds known from the isthmus is so large, and materials available are so extensive, that completion of the report has required more time than originally contemplated. As there is increasing demand for information on this subject, especially from those engaged in investigation of diseases where species of birds may be suspected as carriers, it has become desirable to present the summary accounts family by family as they are completed in order that the information may be available. This first installment covers the families in systematic sequence from the tinamous, family Tinamidae, through the order that includes the shorebirds, gulls, and their allies. A general account of personal field work, with a review of the studies of other ornithologists, and general discussions of the avifauna will be left for the end.

It may be sufficient here to outline briefly the character of the isthmus as included in the present political boundaries of the Republic of Panamá. The entire Caribbean slope and eastern Darién on the Pacific side are the regions of heaviest rainfall. In the northwest, in the Province of Bocas del Toro, there is no marked break in precipitation for any lengthy period throughout the year. The Pacific slope, from the Costa Rican boundary eastward, has a definite dry season, mainly between the latter part of December and the middle or end of April. Because of this difference the denser forest areas are found on the north and in Darién, where originally tree growth was continuous. On the Pacific side there are extensive areas of open savannas. And forest where found is more open and in part deciduous, so that many trees lose their leaves in dry season. These were the original conditions, now extensively modified over great areas that have been cleared for agricultural use. These changes are most marked from the western boundary in Chiriquí east through the Province of Panamá, where most of the original forest cover is gone, and are proceeding rapidly elsewhere. The main areas that still are primitive lie on the Caribbean drainage in the inland mountain and hill area of interior Bocas del Toro, over the interior hills of San Blas, and on the Pacific side on the mountains and hills of the interior from the eastern end of the Province of Panamá through Darién.

The isthmus in the main is in the Tropical Zone, with subtropical zone forest in the mountain regions of the western half. Additional areas of the latter zone of lesser extent are found along the central spine of the Azuero Peninsula, and in the mountains near the Colombian boundary. Limited Temperate Zone conditions extend across the top of the Chiriquí volcano and on some of the higher ridges to the east in Chiriquí and Veraguas.

THE LIST OF BIRDS

Each family is introduced by a brief general statement on the group as a whole throughout its entire range. This is followed, where necessary, by a key to the species that have been recorded in Panamá, based on the most evident characters of color, size, and form. While this may be of assistance in naming birds in life, it is intended primarily for the identification of specimens in hand. The arrangement in the keys is artificial, and may not follow any order of close relationship. The order of the families is that in my latest revision of the classification for living and fossil birds of the world (Smithsonian Misc. Coll., vol. 139, no. 11, June 23, 1960, pp. 1-37).

References to literature, given in parentheses, are sufficiently complete to allow their consultation if desired. A complete bibliography, and with it a gazetteer of localities, will be included in the final part.

The account of each bird begins with the scientific name, followed by vernacular names in English and in Spanish. Where the species is divided into geographic races, if two or more of these are found in Panamá, general information that applies to all is given under a species heading. This includes brief phrases on characters that may help in identification, and a description. The subspecies follow, each with its scientific name and reference, details of color, size, or form on which the race has been recognized, measurements, range in the Republic, and any other pertinent information. If the nominate form is included among these, reference to this name is given under the subspecies in question. Where this race does not reach Panamá, the species heading carries this reference. In variable species of wide range, where only one of the forms is found all these data are included under the heading with the trinomial scientific name. Vernacular names used apply to the species as a whole. No such names are given to separate subspecies.

Vernacular names have been selected with care, with particular reference to usage in standard works that cover the area. This frequently has involved choice, since in wide-ranging species divided in several geographic races it was early custom to assign such a name to each subspecies, often without regard to its related forms. Modern practice gives vernacular names to the species in its entirety, since the former method was cumbersome and frequently misleading. In the case of migrants from the north, the names used are those of the official A.O.U. check-list (Check-list of North American Birds Prepared by a Committee of the American Ornithologists' Union, fifth edition, 1957). With others, particularly tropical species of wide distribution, names frequently have varied so that a choice has been necessary. The attempt with these has been to select the term most often used, and the one most appropriate. In this, the list proposed by Eugene Eisenmann (The Species of Middle American Birds, Trans. Linn. Soc. New York, vol. 7, 1955) is definitely valuable.

The Spanish names in many instances offer difficulty. Where the species are known to Panamanian countrymen there is no complication, but there are scores of kinds of birds that are not so recognized. With those that range widely in the American Tropics often there are appropriate names available from other Spanish-speaking countries, and these I have taken wherever practicable. Occasionally with birds of obscure habit it has been necessary to propose names both in English and in Spanish, with care that they may be appropriate.

The scientific names follow the International Code of Zoological Nomenclature of 1961 (with certain reservations and some misgiving).

Outlines of range and important records are based on an extended survey of literature and of specimens in museums, in addition to information available from my own work in the field. To avoid misunderstanding it should be explained that many of the names of localities on skins collected by J. H. Batty in Panamá at the beginning of this century are not valid. This is particularly true of skins labeled from islands off the coast of Chiriquí. It is certain that Batty visited Isla Coiba, but a considerable part of the specimens that he labeled as from this island came from the mainland, and data attributing numerous skins to other islands in the area are without question fictitious. (See Wetmore, Smithsonian Misc. Coll., vol. 134, no. 9, 1957, pp. 6-8.)

ACKNOWLEDGMENTS

Throughout my personal field work in the Republic I have had close association with the Museo Nacional of Panamá, through its director, Dr. Alejandro Méndez Pereira, and with the staff of the Gorgas Memorial Laboratory, especially with its former directors, the late Dr. Herbert Clark and his successor, Dr. Carl Johnson, and with Dr. Pedro Galindo, entomologist. This collaboration has continued under Dr. Martin Young, who became the head of the Laboratory in 1964. During my studies on the avifauna of the Republic of Panamá I have had the friendly cooperation of Dr. Eugene Eisenmann, who has placed at my disposal many records of occurrence and other data from his personal notes, in addition to the information in his numerous publications. All have been of major assistance.

The illustrations, presented to show the form in characteristic species in each family, are from the skilful hand of Walter A. Weber.

Governmental authorities of the Republic of Panamá have been uniformly courteous in assistance, especially the officials of the Ministerio de Relaciones Exteriores, through credentials that have recognized the scientific nature of my travels and work. I have to thank especially Coronel Bolívar Vallarino, Comandante Jefe de la Guardia Nacional, for permission to visit Isla Coiba. Authorities of the Panama Canal Zone have been universally helpful, and I owe much to the assistance of the Air Force and of the Department of the Army located in the Canal Zone, especially in transportation to remote areas, accessible without such help with much difficulty if at all. In my travels in the course of my studies, which have taken me widely throughout the Republic, from the Costa Rican border in Chiriquí and Bocas del Toro to the Colombian frontier in Darién and San Blas, I have had courteous and friendly reception everywhere from residents of the country, and I owe much to many for their assistance.

Order TINAMIFORMES

Family TINAMIDAE: Tinamous; Tinamous

The family of tinamous, presumed to be of South American origin, has more than 40 living species in the present range, from southern México south through Central America and South America to the Straits of Magellan. The three found in Panamá, known there universally as *perdices,* are shy inhabitants of forests or thickets, seldom seen as they remain constantly under cover of the ground vegetation. All three are heavy-bodied birds, with long, rather slender necks and small heads. The short tail has its stiffened feathers hidden by the elongated upper and lower tail coverts, so that the body appears short and compact like that of a guineafowl. In traversing their haunts, one occasionally sees a tinamou burst out near at hand with a startling roar of wings, but usually the birds slip away on foot so that their presence is known mainly from their calls. The smallest of the three is the most common, being present universally throughout the Tropical Zone wherever there are thickets or second growth to offer it secure cover. The great tinamou is widely distributed wherever natural forest remains, from sea level to the lower edge of the subtropical zone in the mountains. Though important game birds, these two cannot withstand excessive hunting. The highland tinamou is known only from the subtropical zone forests around the Volcán de Chiriquí, where it is local and far from common.

KEY TO SPECIES OF TINAMIDAE

1. Size large (equal to a small domestic fowl); wing more than 180 mm.; posterior face of tarsus rough, with upper margins of scutes prominent and projecting 2
Size much smaller (equal to a medium-sized pigeon); wing less than 130 mm.; posterior face of tarsus smooth, like the anterior surface.
Little tinamou, Crypturellus soui, p. 17
2. Tarsus strong, with projecting upper margin of posterior scutes sharp and rough; toes, including claws, relatively shorter and heavier, with middle toe and claw less than 40 mm.; general color grayer; throat white or whitish....................Great tinamou, <i>Tinamus major</i>, p. 6
Tarsus more slender with projecting upper margin of posterior scutes prominent but smooth; toes, including claws, longer, more slender, with middle toe and claw more than 45 mm.; general color bright buffy brown, with throat brown (ochraceous tawny).
Highland tinamou, Nothocercus bonapartei, p. 14

TINAMUS MAJOR (Gmelin): Great Tinamou; Perdiz de Arca

FIGURE 2

Tetrao major Gmelin, Syst. Nat., vol. 1, pt. 2, 1789, p. 767. (Cayenne.)

Size of a small domestic fowl, with heavy body, slender neck, and small head.

Description.—Length 400 to 460 mm. Adult (sexes alike), above brownish olive to grayish olive, with narrow, irregular, black bars on back and wing; crown sooty black to chestnut; below grayish white to brownish white, barred heavily on the flanks, and narrowly and indistinctly elsewhere, with grayish black.

Chicks, as they hatch, covered with soft down; chestnut-brown on the body, darker above, paler below, and whitish on the abdomen; flanks barred with whitish; rump and lower back barred with cream-buff; crown paler brown, with a blackish-brown band, lighter in center, extending transversely from eye to eye; a similarly colored band from the base of the bill back through the eye to the ear coverts; sides of the head brownish beneath the eye, grayish above the ear region; chin and throat grayish white.

Juvenile wing quills begin to grow immediately, and the down is replaced quickly by a second plumage of firm feathers, in general appearance like those of the adult, but darker in color, barred less definitely above, but more heavily below, with the dorsal surface sparsely spotted with buff.

An adult male (*Tinamus m. saturatus,* intermediate toward *fuscipennis*) shot near Mandinga, Comarca de San Blas, February 12, 1957, had the iris dark brown; maxilla dusky neutral gray; mandible fuscous, with tip light neutral gray; tarsus and toes neutral gray, except for the roughened scales on the back of the tarsus, which are mouse brown.

The great tinamou, resident in heavily forested areas of the

Fig. 2.—Great tinamou, perdiz de arca, *Tinamus major*. The head shows the smooth crown of the subspecies of western Panamá.

Tropical and lower Subtropical Zones throughout the Isthmus, is much in favor as a game bird because of the meat, white with a slight greenish tint, of the heavy breast. This is delicious in flavor, excelling that of any other bird known to me when properly prepared. Tinamous have been much reduced in number over extensive areas through destruction of their forest cover and through hunting, but some are still found in most extensive tracts of original forest, where they are able to maintain themselves through their secretive habits. In unsettled regions, especially in hill country, they are often common. Occasionally several may be found together, but it is more usual to encounter pairs or single birds. In thinly settled sections they are unsuspicious and, though they seek cover, are not difficult to see; but when much hunted careful approach is necessary to obtain a glimpse of them, as at any alarm they slip quietly away through the ground cover, aided in concealment by the dim light and heavy shadows characteristic of their haunts. Occasionally one that becomes startled will fly, rising at a sharp angle with a roar of wings to 3 to 15 meters from the ground, and then drive swiftly away behind the protective screen of the leaves of the undergrowth and lower branches of the trees. The flight does not continue far, and when once more on the ground it is seldom that the bird will flush again. In areas where they have been little molested rarely one may alight on a large tree limb, but this is unusual. E. A. Goldman in a manuscript note records one such incident, and on one occasion I had one stop briefly on a horizontal tree trunk projecting from the side of a wide barranca. Where the jungle is sufficiently dry it is common to find their dusting places in open areas on the forest floor.

The call note is a tremulous whistle, repeated several times, at first slowly and then, toward the end, more rapidly in slightly higher tone. Though heard in daytime, especially in early morning and late afternoon, their calls come also through the night, carrying to the human listener a feeling of the mystery that surrounds the nocturnal life of the darker hours. Occasionally a tinamou is encountered in night hunting but though the birds may be seen the eyes are so small that it is sometimes difficult to detect their deep red reflection in the beam of the jack light.

The accumulated data indicate a laying season in Panamá that begins in January and extends to July. The available information covers a period of 40 years and comes mainly from the Pacific slope between Chiriquí and Darién and the Atlantic drainage at Barro Colorado Island. It indicates that the breeding period is initiated at the opening of the dry season and continues into the period of rains. It must vary in its period with individual groups of the birds, since so far as is known there is only one brood each season.

The nests that I have seen have been placed against the base of a tree, living or dead, sheltered between the projecting flanges of buttressed roots. The location has been in heavy forest, with the site protected by undergrowth so that it is aside from the more open areas that would be traveled normally by predators. The nest sites invariably were carefully sheltered so that it has been chance that has brought them to my attention. Large dry leaves that have fallen between the roots are molded to line a depression 250 mm. in diameter and about 75 mm. deep in the center. The parent sits close and flushes only at near approach, rising then directly from the nest. Native hunters say that it is always the male that incubates. On the two occasions on which I have shot incubating birds as they roared off on the wing they have been males. One killed two hours after sunrise had the cloaca and lower end of the intestine for a distance of 8 centimeters packed with a bolus of feces almost 2½ cm. in diameter, indicating that it had remained on the nest through the night. The normal clutch seems to be 6 or 7 eggs. The shell of the egg is smooth, with a porcelainlike sheen that reflects light, causing the blue-green color to appear more brilliant than it really is. In fresh eggs the yolk is colored dark orange. The chicks are active and leave the nest within a day or so after hatching. As their wings begin growth at once, the young are able to fly when no larger in body than a brown robin.

Usually this species is known as the *perdiz de arca*, though in the eastern part of the Republic I have heard it called *perdiz de montaña*, and in Bocas del Toro a common name is mountain hen. As one explanation of the first of the names mentioned, I was told an attractive tale of local folklore. According to this, when the Rainbow of Promise appeared in the sky following the Flood, the brilliant colors so frightened the *perdiz* that it flew out in terror from the company of other birds in the Ark of Noah to shelter in the forest, where it has remained hidden ever since!

The species ranges from southeastern México through Central America to western Ecuador, eastern Perú, northern Brazil, and French Guiana. Four subspecies are found in Panamá. In each of these there are two color phases, one of which is grayer, and the other more rufescent, a fact that needs to be borne in mind in identifying specimens.

In the measurements under subspecies, in this and in the other species of the family, tail length has been omitted since the coverts above and below are so intermingled with the rectrices that the correct dimension may not be determined satisfactorily.

TINAMUS MAJOR FUSCIPENNIS Salvadori

Tinamus fuscipennis Salvadori, Cat. Birds Brit. Mus., vol. 27, after Sept. 6, 1895, p. 500. (Escondido River, and San Rafael, Nicaragua = Río Escondido, Nicaragua, restricted by Peters, Checkl. Birds World, vol. 1, 1931, p. 13.)

Characters.—Crown sooty black, usually with a few very small spots or narrow bars of chestnut, particularly toward the nape; averaging darker on the dorsal surface than the other races found in Panamá.

Measurements.—Males (7 specimens from Costa Rica and Bocas del Toro), wing 222-244 (233.3), culmen from base 33.3-37.1 (34.9), tarsus 67.4-74.2 (70.0), middle toe with claw (5 specimens) 36.4-39.4 (37.6) mm.

Females (8 specimens from Costa Rica and Bocas del Toro), wing 224-240 (233.9), culmen from base 32.0-40.0 (36.4), tarsus 71.0-75.8 (72.7), middle toe with claw (7 specimens) 36.0-42.4 (39.3) mm.

Resident in the Tropical and lower Subtropical Zones. From the Province of Bocas del Toro (Changuinola, Almirante, Boquete Trail) eastward on the Caribbean slope across northern Veraguas and western Colón, intergrading with *T. m. saturatus* in the valley of the Río Indio in the Caribbean section of Coclé (El Uracillo) and in Colón. On the Caribbean slope it extends northward through Costa Rica to northern Nicaragua.

It seems certain that birds of this race range into the lower Subtropical Zone in the mountains. There is one skin in the Museum of Comparative Zoology taken at about 600 meters on the Boquete trail back of Laguna de Chiriquí; and another, a typical specimen, in the British Museum (Natural History), received from Enrique Arcé, is labeled "Veraguas" without other information as to locality. It is probable that the latter was taken near the Continental Divide, presumably on the Caribbean side.

Charles O. Handley, Jr., recorded a nest near Almirante, January 23, 1960, with 5 fresh eggs, and another February 13 in which incubation was well advanced. Huber (Proc. Acad. Nat. Sci. Philadelphia, 1932, p 206) reported the dimension of 3 eggs found April 5, 1922, in northeastern Nicaragua, as follows: 59.2×46.4, 61.7×48.8, and 63.2×49.7 mm.

TINAMUS MAJOR CASTANEICEPS Salvadori

Tinamus castaneiceps Salvadori, Cat. Birds Brit. Mus., vol. 27, after Sept. 6, 1895, p. 507, pl. 6. (Southern slope of the Volcán de Chiriquí, Panamá.)

Characters.—Crown chestnut to chestnut-brown; dorsal surface paler.

Measurements.—Males (10 specimens from Costa Rica and Chiriquí), wing 219-232 (227.4), culmen from base 30.8-36.6 (34.4), tarsus 65.4-70.8 (67.7), middle toe with claw (8 specimens) 34.2-40.2 (37.5) mm.

Females (8 specimens from Costa Rica and Chiriquí), wing 221-240 (233), culmen from base 31.7-38.8 (35.6), tarsus 67.4-76.5 (71.3), middle toe with claw (6 specimens) 38.0-40.9 (39.4) mm.

Resident. In forests on the Pacific slope from western Chiriquí through central Veraguas and western Province of Panamá to the Canal Zone, extending into the lower part of the Subtropical Zone to 1,500 meters elevation in Chiriquí (Santa Clara, El Volcán). The extralimital range extends along the Pacific slope west to central Costa Rica (Puntarenas, Río Pirrís).

Intergradation with the subspecies *T. m. saturatus* begins near the original continental divide in the Canal Zone, as is shown by an adult male from Barro Colorado Island that has the feathers of the back of the crown very slightly elongated. Though this appears to be a hint of the nuchal crest that marks *saturatus,* the coloration is that of *castaneiceps.*

Van Tyne (Occ. Pap. Mus. Zool. Univ. Michigan, 1950, pp. 2-4) gives the following data from 2 nests, one of 4 and one of 6 eggs, found on Barro Colorado Island: Size, 56×45 mm. to 62×50 mm.; weight 56.0 to 81.4 grams. He described the color as beryl green.

In examining other races of this tinamou from northern South America one is aware immediately of the close resemblance of *castaneiceps* to *T. m. zuliensis,* the form that is found from the lower Río Sinú Valley in Colombia eastward through the Santa Marta region to eastern and southern Venezuela. The principal characters of difference that mark *castaneiceps* are the somewhat duller reddish brown of the crown, the more buffy, less reddish brown of the hindneck and the sides of the head, and the average darker coloration of the upper surface. In considering the evident close resemblance one has the definite impression that *castaneiceps* and *zuliensis* of today represent the descendants of one stock found formerly throughout the tropical lowland areas from Panamá to Venezuela that has been divided by the intrusion of the much darker *saturatus,* an intrusion permitted through environmental change occasioned by the heavier annual rainfall found in the range of the darker form.

TINAMUS MAJOR BRUNNEIVENTRIS Aldrich

Tinamus major brunneiventris Aldrich, Scient. Publ. Cleveland Mus. Nat. Hist., vol. 7, Aug. 31, 1937, p. 28. (Paracoté, 1 mile south of mouth of Río Ángulo, Veraguas, Panamá.)

Characters.—Generally similar to *Tinamus m. castaneiceps,* but darker above and below; sides of head and crown darker brown (darker than in *T. m. saturatus*).

Measurements.—Males (2 specimens), wing 214, 234, culmen from base 34.0, 34.2, tarsus 67.6, 70.2, middle toe with claw 37.5 mm.

Female (1 specimen), wing 229, culmen from base 34.0, tarsus 69, middle toe with claw 37.1 mm.

Resident. In forests of the Tropical Zone of southern Veraguas adjacent to Golfo de Montijo. Recorded to the lower Río San Lorenzo (east of Bahía Honda), the western slope of the Azuero Peninsula at Altos Cacao (450 meters elevation, between the Río Negro and Río Mariato), and on the slopes of Cerro Montuosa and Cerro Hoya on the central divide.

On Cerro Hoya Handley found it common through the forests to an elevation of 1,000 meters. Little is known of this race other than the few specimens that have been collected.

TINAMUS MAJOR SATURATUS Griscom

Figure 3

Tinamus major saturatus Griscom, Bull. Mus. Comp. Zool., vol. 69, April 1929, p. 150. (Cana, 650 meters elevation, Darién.)

Characters.—Differs from other races in Panamá in having the feathers on the back of the head elongated to form a small crest; crown chestnut as in *Tinamus m. castaneiceps,* but dorsal surface darker, in this like *T. m. fuscipennis.*

Measurements.—Males (14 specimens from Panamá), wing 215-238 (227), culmen from base 32.8-37.5 (35.3), tarsus 64.5-73.1 (69.3), middle toe with claw (6 specimens) 37.4-40.1 (38.6) mm.

Females (12 specimens from Panamá), wing 218-242 (230), culmen from base 33.0-38.5 (35.3), tarsus 66.5-73.3 (69.5), middle toe with claw (6 specimens) 38.1-40.2 (39.5) mm.

Resident. In forest areas on the Pacific slope from the Cerro Azul, eastern Province of Panamá, eastward through Darién; and on the Caribbean side from Madden Lake through the San Blas; ranging upward in Darién into the Subtropical Zone (1,400 meters on Cerro Malí).

Intergradation toward *Tinamus major fuscipennis* is evident in specimens from Cerro Azul, the Río Pequení (Salamanca Hydrographic Station), and Mandinga in the western San Blas. To the eastward this race extends into northwestern Colombia through Chocó to northern Antioquia and Córdoba.

On March 7, 1964, at Tacarcuna Village, Darién, when one of these tinamous flushed in dense undergrowth near the bank of the Río Tacarcuna we found that it had come from a nest beside which rested two chicks a few hours old that proved to be male and female. The nest, the usual shallow depression molded in dried leaves accumulated between two buttressed roots at the base of a large

Fig. 3.—Crested head of *Tinamus major saturatus,* the race of the great tinamou found from the Canal Zone through eastern Panamá.

tree, held the shells of the eggs from which the two had hatched, each divided in half near the center. In general pattern the down in the young birds was warm brown on the upper surface, across the breast, and on the sides, with the throat, foreneck, and abdomen grayish white. The side of the head was darker gray, barred narrowly with dull black. The lower back and rump were paler than the hindneck and upper back. One, which proved to be a male, is somewhat brighter colored, more reddish brown, with lower back and rump basally warm buff tipped with dull brown dotted faintly with dull black. The front half and sides of the crown are grayish white, barred narrowly and indistinctly with dull gray, with the forehead tinged with brown. A narrow black line borders the brown posterior part of the crown and hindneck, and a similar narrow black line leads back from the base of the bill to divide the gray anterior area in two portions. There is also a line of chestnut bordered narrowly above and below with black, that extends across the lores back beneath the eye through the auricular area. In the female chick the anterior crown area is slightly paler brown than the posterior section with only a faint, narrow median line. The brown lateral stripe is restricted on the loral region, and is reduced posteriorly to a brown spot back of the eye. The pattern of the markings in general outline is like that of the male but is only lightly indicated. The differences described need further check to determine whether they indicate two color phases that occur without regard to sex.

A set of 6 eggs of this subspecies taken at the base of Cerro Chucantí in the Serranía de Majé, Province of Panamá, March 10, 1950, measures 62.8×47.3, 62.7×48.2, 61.6×45.9, 60.0×48.4, 58.4×47.0, and 57.6×45.7 mm. Another set, also of 6 eggs, collected at Jaqué, Darién, March 25, 1946, measures 60.3×46.5, 59.4×46.0, 59.0×45.9, 58.5×48.6, 56.8×45.0 and 56.0×43.6 mm. Color in the two sets varies from glaucous-blue to light glaucous-blue. The shells of two eggs from Tacarcuna Village, from which the young described above had hatched, were lumiere blue, a brighter color.

On the Río Cangandí, back of Mandinga, Charles O. Handley, Jr., recorded eggs near hatching May 17, 1959, and a day-old chick, May 21. He found a nest with 4 eggs at the Mandinga airstrip on May 28. Near Armila, San Blas, a male and a female taken February 24 and 25, 1963, were breeding.

Lionel Wafer, surgeon and traveler, undoubtedly refers to this race of the great tinamou in his account of Darién (Isthmus of America, 1699, p. 115) when he writes, "There is also a Russet-colour'd Landbird shap'd not unlike a Partridge; but has a longer Neck and Legs, yet a short Tail. He runs most on the ground, and seldom flies. His flesh is very good meat."

The Cuna Indians at Armila called these birds *pūtū*.

NOTHOCERCUS BONAPARTEI FRANTZII (Lawrence): Highland Tinamou; Perdiz Serrana.

Tinamus frantzii Lawrence, Ann. Lyc. Nat. Hist. New York, vol. 9, 1869, p. 140. (Cervantes, Costa Rica.)

Size of a small domestic fowl; slightly smaller and definitely brighter brown than the great tinamou.

Description.—Length 350 to 400 mm. Adult (sexes alike), crown and sides of head blackish; upper surface dark brown, with the feathers crossed by irregular black bars, so narrow that the two colors blend to produce an olive appearance; wings and lower back more or less spotted with buff; undersurface from the throat to the abdomen cinnamon-buff, with the throat plain, and the rest sparsely barred with narrow lines of black; sides and under tail coverts olive brown, barred with black; abdomen buff, barred with black.

The finer black barring above and the cinnamon-brown throat, with smaller size, smoother posterior surface of the tarsus, and longer middle toe and claw, separate this bird from the great tinamou.

A recently hatched chick in the Museum of Comparative Zoology from Costa Rica (no. 55339) has the crown and hindneck dull black, with partly concealed barring of dull white; rest of dorsal surface mingled rufous and black; sides of head dull black, spotted with white; throat whitish, spotted indistinctly with neutral gray; under surface cinnamon-buff, with foreneck darker and mingled with black. The coloration as a whole is decidedly darker than that of the chick of *Tinamus major*.

José Zeledón on the label of a specimen in the U. S. National Museum noted the following colors of the soft parts in a breeding female taken at La Palma de San José, Costa Rica: Iris brown; base of mandible whitish, rest of bill black; tarsi and toes plumbeous, with a slight olivaceous tint.

Measurements.—Males (8 specimens from Chiriquí and Costa Rica), wing 200-209 (205), culmen from base 31.2-35.4 (33.1), tarsus 66.6-71.3 (69.0), middle toe with claw 48.4-52.0 (50.3) mm.

Females (10 specimens from Chiriquí and Costa Rica), wing 208-233 (220), culmen from base 32.7-36.8 (34.5), tarsus 68.1-74.6 (72.5), middle toe with claw 50.2-55.4 (52.3) mm.

Resident. Through the uppermost Tropical and Subtropical Zone forests of the Volcán de Chiriquí and the higher ridges adjacent. Recorded from 1,400 to 2,000 meters elevation near Boquete, and from 1,400 to 1,800 meters on Cerro Pando, above the Río Chiriquí Viejo. It is found also in subtropical zone forests of central and southern Costa Rica.

The present subspecies, *N. b. frantzii*, a highland bird, is isolated geographically from its nearest relative, *N. b. intercedens* of the western Andes of Colombia, by the central depression of the Isthmus of Panamá. It differs from *intercedens,* and from the three additional races at present recognized from Colombia, Ecuador and Venezuela, as follows: General coloration more buffy, less rufescent, especially on the lower surface; dark color of nape extended down over less than half of hindneck, instead of nearly to the back; under primary coverts plain, or with faint markings on the innermost, instead of appreciably barred throughout.

This is a forest bird that is even more retiring than the great tinamou, so that little is known of it in Panamá, aside from the few specimens that have been taken.

In the Boquete region the Mönniche collection has specimens from Alto de Chiquero, taken between April 19 and May 17, 1933, and Quebrada Velo, August 8, 1939, at elevations of 1,650 to 2,000 meters (Blake, Fieldiana: Zool., vol. 36, 1958, p. 504). In the western area, beyond El Volcán, these tinamous are present in small numbers on Cerro Pando, above Palo Santo, west of the Río Chiriquí Viejo. Two specimens from this area, taken February 18, 1953, and March 6, 1956, have been presented to the U. S. National Museum by Dr. Frank A. Hartman. I had report of this species on the forested ridge above the Quebrada Santa Clara farther to the west, and it is probable that it ranges from 1,400 to 1,800 meters or higher throughout the still unsettled forest section that covers the mountain slopes from Volcán Barú to the Costa Rican border. Available records from Panamá come from the Pacific slope.

Armaguedón Hartmann, who is familiar with this bird in the Tisingal-Santa Clara area, tells me that in April, with the first rains, these birds begin to call, a double note quite different from the whistling of the other two tinamous found in the Republic. As they call usually when moving over the forest floor, it is difficult to approach them because of this movement and of the shelter of low growth in which they live.

My only view of the bird in life has been of one that I flushed above the Silla de Cerro Pando on February 6, 1960. I had hunted slowly out an old logging road and then returned to the main trail, when one rose from scanty cover, where it had hidden within 6 meters of me, and flew 20 meters or so to disappear in a dense thicket. The wings whistled more loudly than in the other species of the family found in Panamá, and the bird appeared very brown.

The little that is known of the breeding habits of the race *N. b. frantzii* comes from a few observations made in Costa Rica. An egg in the U. S. National Museum taken from the oviduct of a bird collected by José C. Zeledón at La Palma de San José (located in the depression between Volcán Irazú and Volcán Barba), on May 1, 1884, is deep glaucous-gray, the smooth surface of the shell reflecting light as usual in birds of this family. It measures

72.6×50.0 mm. While the shell is fully formed, so that the measurements are accurate, the full depth of color had not been developed. Four eggs in the British Museum (Natural History) collected at Estrella de Cartago, Costa Rica, by C. F. Underwood (date unknown) are near myrtle green. They measure 74.2×49.6, 71.2×49.0, 71.3×52.1 and 71.0×48.9 mm. Two other eggs in the same collection ascribed to *N. b. frantzii,* while said by Oates (Cat. Eggs Brit. Mus., vol. 1, 1901, p. 11) to be "of uncertain origin," are listed as purchased from M. Parzudaki, but without other data. They measure 76.6×53.3 and 79.0×52.5 mm. Carriker (Ann. Carnegie Mus., vol. 6, 1910, pp. 377-378) on September 12, 1907, recorded a male accompanied by 5 small chicks, near Ujarrás (de Térraba) near the southern end of the western slope of the Cordillera de Talamanca, Costa Rica.

It is interesting that the eggs of this tinamou are larger than those of the races of the great tinamou, *Tinamus major,* found in Panamá, though the bird itself is slightly smaller in body.

CRYPTURELLUS SOUI (Hermann): Little Tinamou; Perdiz de Rastrojo

Figure 4

Tinamus soui Hermann, Tabl. Aff. Anim., 1783, p. 165. (Cayenne.)

Smallest of the tinamous found in Panamá; size of a large pigeon, with heavy body, very short tail, small head, and slender neck.

Description.—Length 200 to 230 mm. Two color phases, one grayer, the other more buffy or rufescent. Adult, male, general color, bearing this in mind, is grayish brown above, with a dark gray or blackish crown; below clay color to brown, with foreneck and upper breast distinctly gray and throat white.

Female, much more rufescent below, except in the race *modestus,* where the two sexes are nearly alike.

Back of the tarsus is smooth. Males are slightly smaller in body than females.

A downy young (either *C. s. poliocephalus* or *C. s. panamensis*), less than a week old, is chocolate-brown above and on the sides; forehead and indistinct bars on the crown, flanks, and tail buffy brown; throat buffy white; rest of lower surface cinnamon-brown.

This downy stage is followed by a second plumage as follows (description taken from American Museum of Natural History no. 232292, *C. s. panamensis,* ♂ juv., Chimán, Panamá, March 6, 1927): Crown dusky neutral gray, with the feathers ticked with cinnamon on sides; back, tertials, rump, and upper tail coverts dull cinnamon-brown, with a narrow tip and a broad crescent-shaped subterminal spot black; under surface grayish brown, shading toward light olive on the sides, barred strongly but brokenly with black; under tail coverts sepia, tipped with clay color and light cinnamon. This very distinct plumage appears to be retained only briefly before it is replaced by the adult dress. Few examples showing it are found in museum collections.

FIG. 4.—Little tinamou, perdiz de rastrojo, *Crypturellus soui.*

An adult male *C. s. panamensis,* taken at Puerto Obaldía, San Blas, March 15, 1963, had the iris orange; maxilla fuscous black, except the tip which was olive-brown; mandibular rami and gape honey yellow; distal part of mandible dull yellowish brown; tarsus and toes, including claws, dull greenish yellow.

An adult female of the race *C. s. poliocephalus,* taken at Tonosí, Los Santos, March 28, 1957, had the iris light brown; base of mandible brownish (avellaneous) ; maxilla and tip of mandible dark neutral gray; front of tarsus greenish gray, with the margins of the scutes brownish; back of tarsus and toes brownish; claws neutral gray. A male shot at the same time had the tarsal colors duller, more olive green.

The *perdiz de rastrojo* is the most common species of the family and is resident throughout the isthmus from sea level to 1,500 meters elevation. It lives in thickets, in low vegetation, and in the second growth—the *rastrojo*—of abandoned plantations, and along the borders of cultivated fields. Where extensive stands of tall forest still remain it ranges mainly near the banks of streams.

Like the other species of its family it is extremely shy and is seen with difficulty in the dense growths of grass, weeds and brush that it frequents, its concealment being aided by its small size. It has been able to maintain itself in many rather densely populated areas in spite of constant hunting, as it is adaptable in shifting about when clearing for cultivation encroaches on parts of its habitat. On many occasions in small villages I have awakened at night to hear its call where it seemed hardly possible that the birds could exist amid the abundance of dogs, active small boys, and other potential enemies. Often I have heard them in daytime very near at hand, when even the sharp-eyed country boys with me could not see them. I recall in particular one Chocó Indian house in Darién—the usual elevated platform with open sides—where a pair of these tinamous came daily into the matted ground vegetation of the small surrounding plantation. Often they called not more than 12 meters away, but we never had a glimpse of them during a three weeks' stay, though we were certain that they were watching us from the depths of their cover. Rarely one may detect a slight movement as the bird retreats to a more secure location, and still more rarely is one seen walking quietly, or running. In early morning I have come on them in the open at the edge of fields or pastures when they often rise in rapid flight to disappear immediately in nearby cover. The call is a tremulous, whistled note, repeated several times in an insistent tone, with ascending cadence, gaining in strength and rapidity with each repetition, and then falling rather quickly into silence. It is common for others to answer. They call throughout the day, and their regular nocturnal whistling indicates activity at night, though I have never observed one during night-hunting expeditions.

Nesting seems to be irregular throughout the year. I have taken females with ovaries in breeding condition from February through May, and have records from literature of young hatching the middle of July, and a nest with eggs on August 4. Two eggs constitute a set, placed on a few leaves and other dried vegetation in a slight depression on the ground. The site is selected in open brush or near the borders of woodland, and is concealed beneath overhanging leaves and branches. Gross (Ann. Rep. Smiths. Inst. for 1926, 1927, p. 337) describes one incubating bird that allowed him to touch it and that only left the nest when he moved his hands beneath it to feel the eggs. Van Tyne has reported similar experiences. While working at Boca del Río Indio, in western Colón, in 1952, a boy brought me two fresh eggs on February 18. Two more obtained through the same means on February 20 were about two-thirds incubated. In color these varied from pale to light brownish drab. Measurements of these are given under *C. s. panamensis*.

In stomachs that I have examined I have found a variety of seeds and berries with a few bits of small insects, the egg case of a roach, and, in one, bones of a small frog.

Occasionally, in places frequented by washerwomen or others, where the small *perdiz* is little molested, it becomes less shy and may even walk about in the open, but never far from cover. In the Province of Los Santos where sheltering vegetation is frequently too scant during the prolonged dry season to afford protection, country boys said that the *perdiz* often hides beneath piles of the dead leaves accumulated at this time of the year beneath the trees. In this province the birds were called *tapara;* elsewhere they were often known as *perdicita*. The Cuna Indians knew them as *Su-ira*, a term that was in common use for the species among Panamanians and Colombians at Puerto Obaldía.

The species as a whole ranges from northern Oaxaca and southern Veracruz south through the tropical lowlands of Central America to eastern Bolivia and south central Brazil. There is much variation in color in this vast area so that 14 subspecies are recognized, of which 4 are found in Panamá.

CRYPTURELLUS SOUI MODESTUS (Cabanis)

Crypturus modestus Cabanis, Journ. für Orn., 1869, p. 212. (Costa Rica.)

Characters.—Differs from the other races found on the isthmus in having male and female closely similar in color; the entire plumage gray, except for a wash of clay color on breast and abdomen; in general darker colored than the other races of the Pacific slope.

Measurements.—Males (9 specimens from Costa Rica and Chiriquí), wing 121.8-128.5 (124.5), culmen from base 20.0-22.4 (21.0), tarsus 38.0-43.6 (40.0) mm.

Females (6 specimens from Costa Rica and Chiriquí), wing 127.3-135.5, culmen from base 20.3-22.7 (21.6), tarsus 38.8-42.0 (40.3) mm.

Resident. Found widely throughout the Tropical Zone on the Pacific slope in western Chiriquí; recorded in the Subtropical Zone to 1,250 meters near the Río Chiriquí Viejo, west of El Volcán, and to 1,600 meters on Horqueta, above Boquete.

This is the form of western Costa Rica also. Birds from the highlands around the Chiriquí volcano are intermediate toward *C. s. capnodes* of the Caribbean slope. The most eastern specimens seen from Chiriquí are from El Banco, on the lower slopes of the volcano below Boquete. The subspecific status of birds of eastern Chiriquí and western Veraguas is uncertain.

At the Finca Palo Santo, west of El Volcán, on February 15, 1960, I was given the shells of 2 eggs from which the young had just hatched. One of them, brought to the Museum for comparison, agrees in color with the eggs of *C. s. panamensis* collected at Río Indio in western Colón. Skutch (Condor, 1963, p. 225) gives the following measurements of 16 eggs of this race examined near San Isidro del General, Costa Rica: 40.5-45.6×31.8-33.3 mm. He found the complete set to be 2 eggs.

CRYPTURELLUS SOUI CAPNODES Wetmore

Crypturellus soui capnodes Wetmore, Proc. Biol. Soc. Washington, vol. 76, Aug. 2, 1963, p. 173. (Almirante, Bocas del Toro, Panamá.)

Characters.—Darker throughout than *C. s. modestus;* darker reddish brown above with crown blacker; darker below, with the foreneck and upper breast darker gray.

Measurements.—Males (5 from Bocas del Toro), wing 117.4-125.0 (121.9), culmen from base 19.4-21.3 (21.0), tarsus 38.1-40.8 (39.7) mm.

Females (4 from Bocas del Toro), wing 124.0-127.4 (125.5), culmen from base 20.0-22.1 (21.2), tarsus 40.7-42.8 (41.6) mm.

Resident. Local in the tropical lowlands of western and central Bocas del Toro (Zegla, at mouth of Río Teribe; Changuinola; Almirante; Cricamola).

Birds from Cricamola on the Chiriquí Lagoon belong with this race, but begin to show an approach to *C. s. panamensis*. It is probable that *C. s. capnodes* is found in the lower Sixaola Valley in Costa Rica. Specimens from the higher elevations of the mountains around Volcán Barú in western Chiriquí show indication of darker color, but belong with *modestus*.

CRYPTURELLUS SOUI POLIOCEPHALUS (Aldrich)

Crypturornis soui poliocephalus Aldrich, Sci. Publ. Cleveland Mus. Nat. Hist., vol. 7, Aug. 31, 1937, p. 30. (Paracoté, east shore of Montijo Bay, 1 mile south of mouth of Río Ángulo, Veraguas, Panamá.)

Characters.—Compared with *modestus,* male browner above and more cinnamon-buff below; female decidedly different, being rufescent brown on the lower surface.

Measurements.—Males (17 specimens), wing 116.3-126.7 (121.9), culmen from base 19.5-23.0 (21.3), tarsus 35.3-42.1 (38.3) mm.

Females (8 specimens), wing 122.8-134.5 (129.7), culmen from base 20.5-24.6 (22.3), tarsus 38.7-43.4 (40.9) mm.

Resident. Through the Tropical Zone on the Pacific slope, ascending to the lower edge of the Subtropical Zone in the mountains; from western Veraguas (Soná) to the Canal Zone (Empire), and the Province of Panamá, eastward to the lower Río Bayano (Chico; Chepo; San Antonio), including both slopes of the Azuero Peninsula, south to the Tonosí Valley. Isla del Rey, in the Archipiélago de las Perlas.

Birds from Azuero Peninsula are slightly grayer on the crown than those from southern Coclé eastward, but the difference is not sufficient to warrant recognition of two races. The range of *poliocephalus* thus extends over most of the area included by recent authors under the name *panamensis*. Those taken by W. W. Brown, Jr., on Isla del Rey in 1900 and 1904 do not differ from birds of the mainland. It seems possible that the species was introduced there, either by Indians or later, as the bird is one that is kept frequently in captivity.

An egg from the oviduct of a female collected near Chepo, April 6, 1949, has the shell fully formed but lacks the full color and gloss of one completely ready to lay. It measures 41.2×30.4 mm., being slightly smaller than the two sets of *C.s. panamensis* seen.

CRYPTURELLUS SOUI PANAMENSIS (Carriker)

Crypturus soui panamensis Carriker, Ann. Carnegie Mus., Aug. (Sept. 7), 1910, p. 379. (Loma del León, Panamá = Lion Hill, Canal Zone, Panamá.)

Crypturus soui harterti Brabourne and Chubb, Ann. Mag. Hist., ser. 8, vol. 14, Oct. 1914, p. 321. (Vaquería, Province of Esmeraldas, Ecuador.)

Characters.—Decidedly darker than *C. s. poliocephalus* in both sexes (the female being browner on the undersurface than the male);

crown and hindneck blacker; foreneck and upper breast darker gray.

Measurements.—Males (20 specimens from Panamá), wing 117.4-128.0 (122.4), culmen from base 20.0-22.5 (21.1), tarsus 36.9-41.3 (38.4) mm.

Females (20 specimens from Panamá), wing 124.6-138.0 (129.8), culmen from base 20.0-22.6 (21.7), tarsus 37.4-42.2 (40.6) mm.

Resident. Found in the Tropical Zone and lower Subtropical Zone on the Pacific slope from the far eastern area of the Province of Panamá (Río Majé) through Darién; on the Caribbean slope from western Colón, east through the northern Canal Zone, the upper Chagres drainage (Río Boquerón), and San Blas.

Two sets of two eggs each from Boca del Río Indio, western Colón, taken February 18 and 20, 1952, are between pale and light brownish drab in color. One set measures 42.7 × 32.0 and 42.4 × 32.5 mm., the other 43.3 × 32.0, and 43.8 × 33.2 mm. The first was fresh, the second incubated about one-third. At the mouth of the Río Paya, Darién, on February 24, 1959, I found the lower half shells of two eggs evidently recently hatched that are deeper in color than those described above, being near brownish drab.

Van Tyne (Occ. Pap. Mus. Zool., Univ. Michigan, no. 525, 1950, pp. 2-3) records the measurements of three sets of two eggs each found on Barro Colorado, as from 40.7 × 30.5 to 44.0 × 32.0 mm., with a range in weight from 20.4 to 23 grams. He reports the weight of a male bird in breeding condition as 209 grams.

In laboratory examination of six stomachs, the greater part of the food was found to be seeds of a wide variety of kinds, among which grasses of the genera *Panicum* and *Paspalum,* the sedge *Scleria, Amaranthus,* a spurge, oxalis, species of mallow, grape, and passionflower, *Styrax,* and *Solanum* were identified. Smaller amounts of animal food, often only traces, included fragments of a roach, ants, beetles, a bug (heteropteran), and bones of a small frog. Gravel, as a grinding agent, was present in varying amounts, up to 20 percent of the contents.

The name *panamensis* was proposed by Carriker in 1910 to cover the little tinamous of Panamá east of the range of *C. s. modestus.* Griscom (Bull. Mus. Comp. Zool., 1932, pp. 309-310) noted that birds from eastern Panamá were darker and listed them under the name *harterti* Brabourne and Chubb. It has been readily evident that there are two populations in the central and eastern part of the isthmus, but there has been confusion relative to them owing to lack of comprehension of local geography, particularly in the Canal

Zone, coupled with limited material available from the Pacific side in that area. Loma del León, or Lion Hill, the type locality of *panamensis,* now submerged in the northern area of Gatun Lake, was in the lower part of the Río Chagres drainage of the Caribbean slope, about 10 miles south of Colón on the northern coast. It was therefore in the Caribbean area and well removed from the Continental Divide that separates the Chagres Valley from the Pacific. Because of lack of specimens from the Pacific side in the area between Veraguas and the eastern part of the Province of Panamá it has not been recognized that these Lion Hill birds agree in color with the Caribbean and eastern Panamanian population, which is accepted at present as extending south through western Colombia to western Ecuador, the type locality of *harterti.* The name *panamensis* of 1910 has application to this population, previously listed under the name *harterti* of 1914. All birds of the Pacific side between Veraguas and the central part of the Province of Panamá, formerly listed under *panamensis,* are now placed with *poliocephalus* of the Azuero Peninsula, as indicated above.

Order PODICIPEDIFORMES

Family PODICIPEDIDAE: Grebes; Somormujos

The species of this family are among those birds most specialized for life in the water. Their strongly muscled legs, placed far back on the elongated, streamlined body, project at an angle that permits maximum efficiency in swimming. Tail feathers are reduced to hairlike plumes, which may be erected in display, or while swimming in the sun, but otherwise are little apparent. The wings are small but are functional except in one species, *Centropelma micropterum* of Lake Titicaca, Bolivia. The feet, in their adaptation for swimming, have the tarsi compressed, and the flattened toes, joined at the bases in webs, have broad lateral lobes at the ends. One curious circumstance in birds of this family is found in the quantities of feathers invariably present in the large stomach. The body plumage is closely set and abundant, and as the birds preen, feathers are loosened and are swallowed. Often the stomach is filled with these, and the small pyloric lobe leading from the main stomach cavity to the small intestine may have a plug of partly digested feathers. The function concerned is not understood; it is possible that the feather mass aids as padding for the harder fish bones or the chitin of larger insects, until these are digested.

While grebes usually are confused with small ducks, and are called "paticos," they may be recognized by the slender bill. Two of the 20 species that are known are found in Panamá.

KEY TO SPECIES OF PODICIPEDIDAE

ADULTS

1. Bill longer and more slender, plainly colored; size smaller, 200 to 230 mm. long.................................Least grebe, *Podiceps dominicus*, p. 28
2. Bill heavier, with a distinct black band around its center; size larger, 300 to 350 mm. long.............Pied-billed grebe, *Podilymbus podiceps*, p. 25

DOWNY YOUNG

1. Forehead and nape blackish, with a single white or cinnamon line running back to a patch of the same color in the center of the crown.
Least grebe, *Podiceps dominicus*, p. 28
2. Forehead white, with two parallel white lines on either side extending back above the eye; center of crown and band across nape cinnamon.
Pied-billed grebe, *Podilymbus podiceps*, p. 25

PODILYMBUS PODICEPS (Linnaeus): Pied-billed Grebe; Buzo

FIGURE 5

Larger than the least grebe with a heavier bill that is banded broadly through the nostrils with black.

Description.—Length 300 to 350 mm. Grayish to dusky brown above; whitish more or less mixed with gray below, washed lightly with brown on the upper breast and lower foreneck; adult with a prominent black throat patch.

Immature birds, in first plumage, resemble those of the least grebe, but have the sides of the neck spotted instead of streaked. Light streaks remain on the sides of the neck and head until the bird is well grown.

Like the other grebe this species is completely aquatic, and by many it is considered to be a small duck because of this and of its general form. In Panamá it is found on larger ponds and bodies of fresh water, where it is fairly common. It is a wary bird that seldom allows close approach, as it dives at any alarm, swims far under water, and often when it rises shows only the bill and the forepart of the head to allow it to look about while the body remains beneath the surface. Frequently its diving takes it to the shelter of bordering vegetation, or to a distance where it feels completely safe. While fairly strong on the wing it does not take flight readily, in this differing from its small companion. It is unlike that species also in being highly aggressive, so that, except during migration, only pairs or small family groups are found in company.

In the nesting season the male has a loud call, *cow cow cow cow cow* repeated rather slowly, that carries for some distance. It is often given from cover. Males fight savagely and also attack other aquatic birds that may approach their nesting territory. The nests are rounded masses of wet vegetation, pulled together in raftlike form to project a few centimeters above the surface, located amid open stands of water plants.

In Panamá I have noted mated pairs from January to March and

FIG. 5.—Head of pied-billed grebe, buzo, *Podilymbus podiceps*, with large, banded bill.

have seen fully grown immature birds at the same season, indicating a prolonged nesting period. The following notes are from eggs collected in the United States and México. The usual set numbers 5 to 7, but occasionally 10 are found. The pointed oval eggs are faintly bluish white in color, thick-shelled, smooth, or occasionally with small excrescences, and measure 39.0 to 47 mm. long by 28 to 32 mm. wide. Their color is darkened irregularly by stain from wet nest material during incubation.

The species ranges locally from Canada south through Central America and the West Indies, and throughout South America to Chubut in south central Patagonia. Two of the 3 geographic races reach Panamá. The third, *Podilymbus podiceps antillarum* Bangs, of the Greater and Lesser Antilles, differs from the other two mainly in shorter wing ($\male$, 122-126; $\female$, 112.8-114.2 mm.).

PODILYMBUS PODICEPS PODICEPS (Linnaeus)

Colymbus podiceps Linnaeus, Syst. Nat., ed. 10, vol. 1, 1758, p. 136. (South Carolina).

Characters.—Adult, browner on the foreneck and on the sides of the head, and faintly lighter, on the average, on the dorsal surface; juvenile, until nearly grown retains streaks on head and neck, with the background color of this area darker.

Measurements.—Males (13 specimens), wing 124.6-134.3 (129.6), exposed culmen 20.8-23.7 (22.7), tarsus 40.0-43.8 (42.3), middle toe with claw 55.3-57.0 (56.2, average of 7) mm.

Females (18 specimens), wing 115.0-125.7 (120.4), exposed culmen 17.3-20.8 (19.3), tarsus 35.5-41.0 (38.5), middle toe with claw 47.7-54.0 (51.7, average of 14) mm.

Resident. Breeding locally in Bocas del Toro. Migrant elsewhere in western Panamá during the period of northern winter.

Mated birds were seen in February 1958 on one of the temporary water impoundments at Changuinola; and on March 14 I shot a laying female there. Eisenmann (Condor, 1957, p. 249) saw adults and young in juvenile plumage in the same area at the end of June 1956. A skin of this subspecies recorded by Peters (Bull. Mus. Comp. Zool., vol. 71, 1931, p. 302) as a bird of the year, taken December 22, 1927, near Almirante, may have been from the resident stock or a northern migrant. It is probable that this race is the one that nests around the lakes near El Volcán in Chiriquí, where I noted males calling in March 1954; and on February 19, 1960, I saw one, apparently an adult male, that appeared to be guarding a nesting territory. Some of those seen there seemed to be northern migrants, as in 1954 I noted a decrease in their number at the end of the first week in March.

Two immature birds in the British Museum (Natural History) collected by Enrique Arcé in Veraguas, one of them, taken in 1869, marked "Castillo," also are of this race. It is probable that migrants will be found east as far as the Gatun and Madden lake areas.

PODILYMBUS PODICEPS ANTARCTICUS (Lesson)

Podiceps antarcticus Lesson, Rev. Zool., vol. 5, July 1842, p. 209. (Valparaiso, Chile.)

Characters.—The race *antarcticus* differs from typical *Podilymbus p. podiceps* in longer and heavier bill and in larger foot; wing on the average longer; adult somewhat darker on the dorsal surface, particularly on the hindneck; grayer, less brown, on foreneck, upper breast, and sides of head.

Measurements.—Males (13 specimens), wing 130.0-138.0 (132.1), exposed culmen 23.6-26.1 (24.3, average of 12), tarsus 41.3-47.2 (44.7), middle toe with claw 57.1-64.1 (60.7, average of 6) mm.

Females (8 specimens), wing 119.2-131.0 (123.6), exposed culmen 20.6-23.1 (21.9), tarsus 39.4-42.0 (41.5), middle toe with claw 53.3-59.0 (56.4, average of 2) mm.

Resident. Fairly common locally in the Canal Zone on the back waters of Gatun Lake, and on the Río Chagres above Gamboa; grebes seen on Madden Lake probably are of this race. Breeds rarely in the marshes of the Río La Jagua, eastern Province of Panamá, where I collected a fully grown immature bird on June 27, 1953. There is also an immature in first fall plumage in the Museum of Comparative Zoology labeled Tocumen taken July 25, 1936.

The first report of the race for the isthmus is that of Van Tyne (Auk, 1937, p. 379) who shot an adult male in breeding condition at Barro Colorado Island in Gatun Lake on August 5, 1927. I have taken several on the Río Chagres between Gamboa and Juan Mina, where these birds are fairly common.

There are no records as yet in Panamá east of La Jagua. It remains to be learned whether birds that breed at the Ciénaga Macana, near El Rincón, Herrera (that I saw here in March 1948), belong to the present subspecies or to the preceding one.

On January 13, 1961, a pair had pulled together a mass of aquatic plants to serve as the base of a nest opposite the dock at Juan Mina. A few days later this had been destroyed and the birds had moved, disturbed by my traveling in and out in cayucos. By January 18, other mated pairs were scattered through the bays and side channels bordering the main river, but I saw no other nests.

PODICEPS DOMINICUS BRACHYPTERUS (Chapman): Least Grebe; Tigua

FIGURE 6

Colymbus dominicus brachypterus Chapman, Bull. Amer. Mus. Nat. Hist., vol. 12, Dec. 23, 1899, p. 256. (Lomita Ranch, Hidalgo County, Texas.)

Size and general form of a small duck, but with long, slender neck, thin, pointed bill, and feet placed far back on the body; in flight with definite white markings at the ends of the secondaries.

Description.—Length 200 to 230 mm. Adult (sexes alike), dusky gray above, whitish below, with light-colored eyes.

Immature, grayer colored, streaked with white on head and neck. These markings may appear to resemble those of the immature pied-billed grebe, but the bill in the present species is longer and more slender, the depth at the base being one half or less the length.

Iris light orange to yellow; bill dark neutral gray to nearly black, sometimes tipped lightly with yellowish white; tarsus and toes dull black, varying in some to greenish neutral gray on front and inner side of tarsus and on toes; claws dusky neutral gray tipped narrowly with grayish white.

Fig. 6.—Least grebe, tigua, *Podiceps dominicus brachypterus*, with slender bill.

Measurements.—Males (23 specimens), wing 85.5-93.8 (90.7), exposed culmen 19.8-23.5 (21.7), tarsus 30.5-33.8 (32.8) mm.

Females (26 specimens), wing 83.8-91.0 (87.4), exposed culmen 18.2-22.7 (21.1), tarsus 29.3-32.5 (30.9) mm.

Resident. Locally common on fresh-water ponds and lakes throughout the Republic, from coastal areas to 1,200 meters or more in the mountains.

Actual records are as follows: Chiriquí (lakes near El Volcán at 1,250 meters, pond at Palo Santo at 1,280 meters); Bocas del Toro (Changuinola, Almirante); Veraguas (old records at Laguna de Castillo, and Chitra); Los Santos (Pedasí); Herrera (Ciénaga Macana); Canal Zone (Gatun Lake, Gamboa, Juan Mina); Panamá (Río La Jagua); Darién (La Laguna at 850 meters elevation on base of Cerro Malí); Isla Coiba.

Least grebes are especially common on the extensive backwaters of Gatun Lake and the Río Chagres above Gamboa. In Bocas del Toro many frequent artificial ponds made in connection with the banana farms around Changuinola. It is probable that they have increased in number in recent years because of the greater extent of suitable habitat, formed by dams, now available. On large expanses of water least grebes may congregate in groups of a dozen or may remain in scattered pairs. It is common to find them on smaller pools of 50 to 100 meters in extent, where usually they remain in the cover of aquatic vegetation. They seem to fly about to a considerable extent, as I have seen them appear overnight on small ponds in mountain areas several miles distant from larger lakes.

They present an attractive appearance as they swim with head and neck erect, rest in the sun to preen, often rolling far over on the side to reach the breast feathers, or dive alertly in feeding. When approached in a boat they may rise in flight and with wings beating quickly, gather momentum by pattering the feet on the water, and then, when fully under way, fly with neck and feet outstretched. Such flights, barely above the water surface, are of short duration, and usually when the bird alights it dives.

In nesting they arrange a rounded mass of plant materials, anchored to twigs of a submerged tree or amid aquatic vegetation, with the top from 30 to 60 centimeters across, elevated sufficiently so that the eggs, placed in a slight depression in the center, are a few centimeters above the water. Such nest structures may be concealed, or in larger water bodies may be visible for some distance. The nesting season appears to be irregular, for I found half-grown young on Isla Coiba January 14 (1956), eggs at Changuinola March 4 (1958), and fully grown immature birds at Pedasí March 17 (1957). Eisenmann (Condor, 1957, p. 249) records them as breeding in June and July near El Volcán. Information available, mainly from the northern end of the range of this subspecies, indicates that the eggs number 3 to 6 in a set and measure 30 to 38 mm. long by 22 to 25 mm. broad (Bent, U. S. Nat. Mus. Bull. 107, 1919, p. 37). They are dull white in color when laid but become stained immediately to a deep buff from the wet material with which the parent covers them whenever it leaves the nest. One incubating bird that I shot in this act at Changuinola was a male.

Zimmerman (Auk, 1957, p. 390) has recorded what appeared to be courtship display in these grebes seen at the end of April on a forest pond in Campeche. Two birds (apparently male and female, as they differed slightly in size) rested side by side until suddenly they raced across the surface for about a meter with bodies half out of the water at an angle of 45° and then sank down to a sudden stop. After preening and dabbling as though feeding, the display was repeated. Both had the throat patches somewhat distended, and one bird uttered a high-pitched nasal note.

These grebes feed on aquatic life, from insects to small fishes. One taken at La Laguna, Darién, had the stomach crammed with large dragonfly larvae, mixed with fragments of aquatic beetles. The stomach regularly is filled with feathers from the bird itself, that are loosened and swallowed during preening.

The least grebe as a species has a vast distribution from northwestern México and southern Texas south throughout the Americas to Tierra del Fuego, including the Bahama Islands and the Greater Antilles. The present subspecies ranges locally from southern Texas south through México and Central America.

The subspecies *P. d. brachypterus,* compared to *P. d. dominicus* of the Bahama Islands and the Greater Antilles, has the bill slightly smaller and the white color of the secondaries reduced in extent toward the tips of the feathers. The race *P. d. speciosus* Lynch Arribalzaga of South America is similar in size of wing and bill to *brachypterus* but has the white markings on the secondaries extensive, more so than in the typical race *dominicus.*

(The eared grebe, *Podiceps caspicus californicus* Heermann, of western North America is recorded in winter south to Guatemala and also on the eastern Andean lakes of Colombia (De Schauensee, Birds Colombia, 1948, p. 350). It is possible that it may be found as a migrant in Panamá. It resembles the least grebe in slender bill and yellow eye, but is similar to the pied-billed grebe in size.)

Order PROCELLARIIFORMES

Family DIOMEDEIDAE: Albatrosses; Albatroses

Though the narrow wings and general body form of albatrosses are like those of their cousin shearwaters, their much greater size identifies them with no uncertainty. When away from their nesting grounds they are birds of the open seas. Little is known of their occurrence in Panamanian waters. The only records are of vagrants that have been encountered in the Gulf of Panamá. The range of those species that may be expected lies in the Pacific Ocean to the south.

KEY TO SPECIES OF DIOMEDEIDAE

1. Size large, decidedly more than a meter long, body white above and below.
   Wandering albatross, *Diomedea exulans*, p. 33
2. Size smaller, less than a meter long..3
3. Rump white...........Gray-headed albatross, *Diomedea chrysostoma*, p. 32
   Rump dark, barred narrowly with white.
   Galápagos albatross, *Diomemea irrorata*, p. 34

DIOMEDEA CHRYSOSTOMA Forster: Gray-headed Albatross; Albatros Cabecigris

Diomedea chrysostoma J. R. Forster, Mém. Math. Phys. Paris, vol. 10, 1785, p. 571, pl. 14. (South Georgia; designated by Murphy, Oceanic Birds of South America, vol. 1, 1936, p. 516.)

An albatross with head and neck light gray; sides of the bill black.

Description.—Length 700 to 800 mm. Head and neck light gray; upper back dark gray; wings black, with a grayish wash; a dull black mark around eye; under surface, including under side of wings, white.

Iris brown; bill black on the sides, with a bright yellow stripe down the culmen, that is darker on the hook at the tip; a yellow line on the side of the mandibular rami; tarsi and toes bluish gray; claws whitish. (From Murphy, Oceanic Birds S. Amer., vol. 1, 1936, pp. 514-515.)

Measurements (from Murphy, cit. supra, p. 515).—Males (14 specimens), wing 480-555 (510), tail 175-205 (195), exposed culmen 106-122 (114.3), tarsus 79-91 (85.6) mm.

Females (5 specimens), wing 473-523 (504.3), tail 175-199 (189.3), exposed culmen 108-119 (114.7), tarsus 79-89 (84.6) mm.

Accidental. One report on the Pacific coast.

Salvin (Cat. Birds Brit. Mus., vol. 25, 1896, p. 451) records an adult specimen secured by Thomas Bridges on the "Coast of Panama." Salvin and Godman (Biol. Centr.-Amer., vol. 3, 1904, p. 438) list it as "said to have been procured in the Bay of Panama," and Godman (Mon. Petrels, 1910, p. 355) cites the same bird as "obtained by Mr. T. Bridges, near Panama." Griscom (Bull. Mus. Comp. Zool., vol. 78, 1935, p. 291) undoubtedly refers to these sources when he lists the species as "off coast of Chiriquí (once)." The specimen has disappeared. It is not included in a manuscript list of the albatrosses in the British Museum (Natural History) prepared in 1951, nor could I find it in the collections in July 1954. A further search in the museum catalogs in September 1964, did not locate this bird. Thomas Bridges came to Panamá in 1855, where he collected mollusks for several months in the Bay of Panamá, then proceeded to David, where he arrived in January 1856 (Sclater, Proc. Zool. Soc. London, 1856, pp. 138-142). It is possible that the albatross may have been obtained during the sea journey from Panama City to David.

The gray-headed albatross breeds on various islands in the far south, ranges mainly over south temperate seas, and is found casually northward. In considering possible occurrence in Panamá it should be borne in mind that Murphy (Oceanic Birds S. Amer., 1936, pp. 515-516) points out that sight records for the gray-headed albatross may not be accepted, as other species that range along the west coast of South America resemble it closely. He indicates especially that *Diomedea bulleri* and *D. cauta salvini* are so closely similar that they may not be identified except by those familiar with these species with the bird in hand. In *D. bulleri* the raised base of the culmen is decidedly broader back of the nostrils, with a transversely flattened posterior margin. *D. c. salvini* averages somewhat larger and has the bill gray, with the culmen shell ivory and a black spot at the end of the mandible.

DIOMEDEA EXULANS Linnaeus: **Wandering Albatross; Albatros Errante**

Diomedea exulans Linnaeus, Syst. nat., ed. 10, vol. 1, 1758, p. 132. (Cape of Good Hope.)

Largest of the albatrosses to be expected in Panamanian waters, and one of the largest of living flying birds.

Description.—Length about $1\frac{1}{2}$ meters; wing spread about $3\frac{1}{2}$ meters. Adult (sexes alike), wing feathers, and part of coverts blackish; rest of plumage, including under side of wing, white.

Immature, dark brown with white face and throat.

Iris brown; bill salmon-pink (except in breeding season, when it is buffy yellow); tarsi and feet bluish gray (from Murphy, Oceanic Birds S. Amer., vol. 1, 1936, pp. 538, 550).

Measurements (from Murphy, l.c., p. 539).—Males (10 specimens), wing 590-674 (644), tail 186-202 (195), exposed culmen 156-173 (168), tarsus 115-128 (120.7) mm.

Females (4 specimens), wing 585-611 (601), tail 177-200 (187), exposed culmen 157-167 (161), tarsus 111-119 (114) mm.

Accidental. One record for the Bay of Panamá.

Murphy (Condor, 1938, p. 126) reports one captured in August 1937, brought alive to Balboa, where it was photographed by Lee B.

Carr, and then released. He describes it from the photo as "a yearling, with white face and wing-lining."

The species is one of southern range that wanders casually into northern seas. Two races differing in size, particularly of the bill, are recognized. The typical form, *D. e. exulans,* is found in its wanderings in both Pacific and Atlantic oceans. The other race, *D. e. dabbenena,* which is smaller (exposed culmen 144-149, tarsus 108-109 mm.), breeds at Gough Island and in the Tristan da Cunha islands. As this form is known to range in the South Atlantic, probably also in the Indian Ocean, it may be presumed that the record for the Gulf of Panamá is of a bird of the typical subspecies.

DIOMEDEA IRRORATA Salvin: Galápagos Albatross; Albatros Galapagüeño

Diomedea irrorata Salvin, Proc. Zool. Soc. London, 1883, p. 430. (Callao Bay, Perú.)

Differs from other smaller albatrosses in shorter tail, and much larger bill.

Description.—Length, a little less than a meter; wing spread about 2.3 meters. Adult, head and neck white, washed with yellowish buff; above grayish brown, with white markings; below blackish brown freckled with white; bill yellow.

Immature, brown throughout; under wing coverts grayish white.

Iris dark brown; bill yellow (in life), tarsi and feet dull leaden blue (from Murphy, Oceanic Birds S. Amer., vol. 1, 1936, p. 530).

Measurements (from Murphy, l.c., pp. 530-531).—Males (9 specimens), wing 517-551 (542), tail 130-138 (134), exposed culmen 149-156 (152.8), tarsus 99-105 (102.1) mm.

Females (5 specimens), wing 491-555 (528), tail 127-140 (133.8), exposed culmen 137-148 (141.6), tarsus 93-100 (96.6) mm.

Uncertain. Reported as a casual visitor.

Eisenmann (Trans. Linn. Soc. New York, vol. 7, 1955, p. 10) says "ranges north to Panama," and De Schauensee (Birds Colombia, 1952, p. 1141) reports that it "ranges northward to the Gulf of Panama." No definite record is known to me.

This species breeds on Hood Island in the Galápagos group and comes to the offshore waters of South America. De Schauensee, on the basis of information from Robert Cushman Murphy, reports it on the Pacific coast of Colombia between Octavia Rocks and Bahía de Aguacate; hence it may wander casually into the Gulf of Panamá.

Family PROCELLARIIDAE: Shearwaters and Petrels; Pardelas y Petreles

Only one species of this family, a race of Audubon's shearwater that nests on a rocky islet on the coast of Bocas del Toro, is a permanent inhabitant of Panamanian waters. Others have been recorded as ocean wanderers from the outer reaches of the Gulf of Panamá, or casually from nearer the Pacific coast. Most of the reports have been sight records of uncertain status, since not many naturalists have had sufficient experience with the shearwater and petrel group to identify them in life. It is probable that several species will be found regularly, and others casually, when more information is available.

The name *fardela* by which shearwaters are known along the western coast of South America, appears to be a corruption of *pardela,* the usual term in the Spanish language for birds of this group on the coasts of Spain.

KEY TO SPECIES OF PROCELLARIIDAE

1. Tarsus heavier, much compressed; space between nostrils as wide or wider than the nasal openings (genus *Puffinus*) 2
 Tarsus heavier, not compressed; space between nostrils narrow, less in width than the nasal openings (genus *Pterodroma*).
 Dark-rumped petrel, *Pterodroma phaeopygia,* p. 35
2. Tail nearly half the length of the wing, definitely graduated, wedge-shaped.
 Wedge-tailed shearwater, *Puffinus pacificus,* p. 42
 Tail definitely less than half of the length of the wing, rounded, or only slightly graduated ....·........................ 3
3. Under surface white; smaller, wing less than 200 mm.
 Audubon's shearwater, *Puffinus lherminieri,* p. 37
 Under surface gray, or dusky, wing more than 260 mm.
 Sooty shearwater, *Puffinus griseus,* p. 36

PTERODROMA PHAEOPYGIA PHAEOPYGIA (Salvin): Dark-rumped Petrel; Petrel de Rabadilla Oscura

Oestrelata phaeopygia Salvin, Trans. Zool. Soc. London, vol. 9, May 1876, p. 507, pl. 88, fig. 1. (Chatham Island, Galápagos Archipelago.)

A large petrel with sides of the head black.

Description.—Length 400 to 431 mm. Brownish black above; wings and tail black with concealed white patches; forehead and under surface white; sides of head black.

Iris brown; bill black; tarsus and base of toes bluish flesh color; distal part of web and toes, with most of outer toes black.

Measurements (from Murphy, Oceanic Birds S. Amer., vol. 2,

1936, p. 698).—Sexes alike (5 specimens), wing 294-304 (299), tail 134-137 (135.4), exposed culmen 33.0-34.8 (34), tarsus 37.1-39.3 (38.2) mm.

Reported as casual in the Gulf of Panamá. Sight records of Robert Cushman Murphy (Eisenmann, Trans. Linn. Soc. New York, vol. 7, 1955, p. 11).

The bird nests at the Galápagos and wanders toward the coast of South America from off Perú to Colombia. Murphy (in De Schauensee, Birds Colombia, 1952, p. 1142) reports it as found regularly off Malpelo Island, Colombia, to the south of the Gulf of Panamá.

PUFFINUS GRISEUS (Gmelin): Sooty Shearwater; Pardela Sombría

Procellaria grisea Gmelin, Syst. Nat., vol. 1, pt. 2, 1789, p. 564. (New Zealand.)

A shearwater with the size of a small gull; lower surface of body dark in color.

Description.—Length 430 to 460 mm. Blackish brown above, paler on lower surface; under wing coverts white, marked with gray at tips.

Iris brown; bill fuscous or black; outer side of tarsus and outer toes blackish; inner side of tarsus, inner toes and webs bluish neutral gray.

Measurements (from Murphy, Oceanic Birds S. Amer., vol. 2, 1936, p. 667).—Sexes alike (40 specimens), wing 280-309 (293), tail 84.0-99.2 (89.4), exposed culmen 38.0-45.6 (41.7), tarsus 52.5-59.5 (55.4) mm.

Status not certain. Recorded as a visitor in the Gulf of Panamá.

A specimen taken June 8, 1915, by Thomas Hallinan, found floating with several others, all appearing exhausted, near Naos Island at the Pacific entrance of the Panama Canal, was identified originally as *Puffinus tenuirostris* (Hallinan, Auk, 1924, p. 306). The bird, now in the American Museum of Natural History, is, however, the present species (see Serventy and Eisenmann, Emu, 1962, p. 200). Robert Cushman Murphy saw shearwaters of this species near Isla San José on February 21, 1941, a sight record substantiated by specimens that he secured nearby while traveling on the schooner *Askoy*. Another report is that of Robins (Condor, 1958, p. 300), who made scattered sight records on 8 days between July 15 and 26, 1957, from near Isla Taboga through the eastern side of the Gulf to

45 kilometers south southwest of Bahía Piñas. Through the courtesy of Oscar W. Owre I have examined the skin of a male caught by Robins in a dipnet at Isla Camote, on July 25.

Apparently this species, which nests far to the southward, may enter Panamanian waters with some regularity during its wanderings outside the nesting season.

PUFFINUS LHERMINIERI Lesson: Audubon's Shearwater; Pardela Chica

A small shearwater, pure white underneath.

Description.—Length 300 to 330 mm. Blackish brown above, white below; under tail coverts black and white.

Iris brown; bill black, becoming dark neutral gray on mandible, and at base of culmen; outer side of tarsus and outer toes dull black; inner side of tarsus, rest of toes, and webs, flesh color.

Three subspecies of Audubon's shearwater are recorded from Panamá, one a wanderer from its nesting grounds in the Galápagos Islands, one established in a breeding colony on the coast of Bocas del Toro, and the third recorded from a single specimen taken on the Caribbean coast near the Colombian boundary.

PUFFINUS LHERMINIERI LHERMINIERI Lesson

Pufflnus (sic) *Lherminieri* Lesson, Rev. Zool., vol. 2, no. 3, April (May), 1839, p. 102. (Guadeloupe, Lesser Antilles.)

Characters.—Like *P. l. loyemilleri* in color but larger in size.

Measurements.—Males (31 specimens from Bermuda, Bahama Islands, and Lesser Antilles), wing 195-209 (201), tail 83.5-95.0 (88.2), culmen from base 28.1-31.8 (30.0), tarsus 37.8-42.5 (40.2) mm.

Females (29 specimens from Bermuda, Bahama Islands, and Lesser Antilles), wing 193-210 (200), tail 83.7-95.0 (88.9), culmen from base 25.7-31.0 (29.2), tarsus 38.0-41.8 (40.4) mm.

Casual on the Caribbean coast. One record for eastern Comarca de San Blas.

A male in the Herbert Brandt Collection in the museum of the University of Cincinnati was collected by Wedel at Puerto Obaldía on March 10, 1934. The wing measurement of 202 mm. places it with the typical subspecies. The nearest known breeding colony of this form is the one on Crab Cay off Isla Providencia mentioned in the account of the race *P. l. loyemilleri* that follows.

PUFFINUS LHERMINIERI LOYEMILLERI Wetmore

FIGURE 7

Puffinus lherminieri loyemilleri Wetmore, Proc. Biol. Soc. Washington, vol. 72, April 22, 1959, p. 19. (Tiger Rock, Tiger Cays, off Cabo Valiente, Bocas del Toro, Panamá.)

Characters.—Like *P. l. lherminieri* but smaller. Tail longer than in *P. l. subalaris,* 80 millimeters long or more, and flanks white.

Measurements.—Males (6 specimens), wing 185-193 (188), tail

FIG. 7.—Audubon's shearwater, pardela chica, *Puffinus lherminieri,* at entrance of nesting burrow.

80.7-87.7 (85.2), culmen from base 27.1-30.1 (29.3), tarsus 38.4-39.8 (39.3) mm.

Females (5 specimens), wing 185-195 (190), tail 82.8-88.5 (86.3), culmen from base 27.7-31.2 (29.2), tarsus 38.2-40.0 (39.0) mm.

Resident. Breeds on Tiger Rock in the Tiger Cays at the end of the Valiente Peninsula, Bocas del Toro; recorded off the nesting colony and at Puerto Obaldía, Comarca de San Blas.

The Tiger Cays lie in line from 3,000 meters north to 5,000 meters northwest of Cabo Valiente. The outermost, nearly submerged rock, is called Tiger Breaker on the sailing chart (no. 5029, Laguna de Chiriquí). Next is a higher rock bearing a navigation beacon, which is designated Tiger Rock on the chart, and then comes a slightly larger islet that is not named. Following this to the east is a longer island, separated in several sections, which is known to local fishermen as Tiger Rock. At the western end the higher part is nearly divided by a cleft through which storm waves may wash. The shearwater colony is located in burrows at the summit of the eastern sector of this islet, on the steep, landward slope beneath a scattered grove of guarumos and coconut palms, with undergrowth of caña blanca, coarse-leaved grasses, and other herbaceous plants.

The birds were noted here first by Loye Holmes Miller in 1936, during a brief visit to the Chiriquí Lagoon area, where he had quarters on a survey ship of the Hydrographic Office of the Navy. According to notes that Dr. Miller has supplied he was told by a seaman of birds nesting in holes on a rocky island. He visited the site on March 12 and found 4 occupied burrows of Audubon's shearwater with eggs. He collected two skins, a skeleton, and some miscellaneous bones from bodies left by vultures. The specimens, in the collections of the University of California at Los Angeles, attracted no special attention, for it was not realized that they marked a considerable extension of range.

During my work in the Almirante region in 1958 Thomas W. Dunn, through his detailed knowledge gained in fishing these waters, identified the locality shown on the sketch map Miller had furnished. And on February 28, with favorable weather, I crossed from Almirante to the Tiger Cays in a small cayuco driven by an outboard motor. Though a heavy swell prevented our beaching the boat, I landed without difficulty at the cleft on the leeward side of Tiger Rock and within a few minutes had located the shearwaters on the upper slopes of the island. The colony, or the part of it that I examined, covered an area about 10 by 20 meters on the leeward side of the eastern knob near its summit. The occupied section lay midway on the steep slope between the high ridge and the point where there was a nearly vertical descent to the sea. Here there was an accumulation of humus and fine clay, dotted with openings leading into the numerous burrows excavated by the birds. Since the soil was penetrated by tangles of roots of the broad-leaved plants that shaded the surface, the birds had difficulty in digging, as the average length of the burrows was less than three-quarters of a meter. Part, located in pockets where rainwater accumulated, were wet, so that breasts and ends of wings and tails of birds that inhabited them were heavily stained with mud. In nests with proper drainage birds and their eggs were clean. The series of 9 shearwaters collected included 4 males and 5 females, each found with a single egg, except one, and there may have been an egg here that I did not locate. One egg seen lay in a depression beneath some roots with no bird near. All the birds were silent, the only indications of their presence being a few scattered feathers and droppings and the strong shearwater scent. It required an hour and a half to secure the specimens mentioned, when the wind began to freshen, so that I had to leave without exploring the island in detail. It is possible that there are other colonies on adjacent islets, or elsewhere along the coast.

Because of smaller size, I have separated these Panamanian birds as the subspecies *loyemilleri*, named for Loye Holmes Miller, who first discovered them. The wing measurement varies from 185 to 195 mm., compared to 193 to 210 mm. in *Puffinus lherminieri lherminieri*. There are no differences in color.

In addition to the specimens from Tiger Rock, there are two males in the U. S. National Museum from 10 miles off Punta Valiente, taken May 30, 1962, by H. R. Bullis, Jr., and P. Struhsaker. Wedel secured two at Puerto Obaldía, Comarca de San Blas, January 31 and June 22, 1934, which came to the Herbert Brandt Collection now in the museum of the University of Cincinnati.

The 5 eggs that I was able to prepare ranged from fresh to heavily incubated. They are pure white, with the shell slightly pitted, and vary in shape from subelliptical to long subelliptical and long oval. The measurements are 48.3-53.9 × 34.5-36.3 with the average 51.8 × 35.2 mm. Bent (U. S. Nat. Mus. Bull. 121, 1922, pp. 74-75) gives the following dimensions for the eggs of *P. l. lherminieri*: 49.2-57.3 × 34.0-40.8 mm.; average 52.5 × 36.2 mm. The eggs of the newly described race, as well as the birds, thus average slightly smaller.

In the original description of the form of the coast of Bocas del Toro I overlooked one record of the species for the Caribbean area. Cory (Auk, 1887, p. 181) listed Audubon's shearwater among birds collected at Isla de Providencia by Robert B. Henderson "during the winter of 1886-87." Bond (Proc. Acad. Nat. Sci. Philadelphia, vol. 102, 1950, pp. 52-53) during a visit on April 28, 1948, found that the colony was located on Crab Cay off the northeastern coast. Emmet R. Blake of the Chicago Natural History Museum has lent for examination the 10 specimens taken by Henderson on March 12, 1887. Two are downy young, one of them recently hatched. Two of the adults have the tips of the primaries too badly worn and abraded to give an accurate indication of size, and a third has the wing in molt. The 5 remaining vary in length of wing from 195 to 204 mm., which places them within the size range of typical *lherminieri*.

Dr. W. H. Phelps writes me that specimens in the Phelps Collection, taken at their breeding burrows on Gran Roque, in Islas Los Roques, and others secured at sea near Orchila, in Islas Los Hermanos, have wing lengths of 189 to 192 mm. and so agree with *loyemilleri*. Another record to be referred to this race is that of a specimen in the American Museum of Natural History with a wing measurement of 186 mm. taken at sea 100 miles (160 kilometers) off the coast of British Guiana on December 2, 1931.

Enrico Festa secured an Audubon's shearwater on board ship in May 1905 at a point "300 miles" out from the port of Colón (Salvadori and Festa, Boll. Mus. Zool. Anat. Comp. Univ. Torino, vol. 14, no. 339, 1899, p. 13). As no measurements are available the race of this bird is not known.

PUFFINUS LHERMINIERI SUBALARIS Ridgway

Puffinus subalaris Ridgway, Proc. U. S. Nat. Mus., vol. 19, Mar. 15, 1897, p. 650. (Dalrymple Rock, Chatham Island, Galápagos Archipelago.)

Characters.—Similar to *P. l. loyemilleri* of the Caribbean, but with more dark feathers on the flanks, and shorter tail, 68 to 71.8 mm. as compared to 80.7 to 88.5 mm. for the other form.

Measurements (from Murphy, Oceanic Birds S. Amer. vol. 2, 1936, p. 667).—Sexes alike (10 specimens), wing 189-203 (194.8), tail 68-75 (71.8), exposed culmen 24.7-29 (27.7), tarsus 34-37 (36) mm.

Recorded as a visitor. Apparently wanders regularly to the southern area of the Gulf of Panamá.

There are sight records by Murphy (Fish and Wildl. Serv. Spec. Rep. Fisheries no. 279, 1958, p. 104) who recorded many November 24-25 and November 30-December 1, 1956. Robins (Condor, 1958, p. 300) reported them (under the specific name *P. lherminieri*) on July 21, 22, and 23, 1957, from 30 to 40 kilometers southwest of Bahía Piñas. These sight records appear to be validated by a female taken by Horace Loftin at Bahía Piñas, Dec. 20, 1964. There is also a specimen in the U. S. National Museum collected by Charles Fagan on the S. S. *Santa Elisa* while approaching Balboa, about 290 kilometers to the southwest. This would be near lat. 60° 30′ N., about opposite the Gulf of Cupica on the northwestern coast of Chocó, Colombia, and about 80 kilometers south of the Chocó-Darién boundary.

This is the race that breeds at the Galápagos Islands and that is known mainly from that area.

PUFFINUS PACIFICUS CHLORORHYNCHUS Lesson: Wedge-tailed Shearwater; Pardela del Pacífico

Puffinus chlororhynchus Lesson, Traité d'Orn., livr. 8, June 1831, p. 613. (Shark Bay, Western Australia.)

Like the sooty shearwater, but tail longer, wedge-shaped, with the lateral feathers much shorter than those in the center.

Description.—Length 440-470 mm. Dark phase, blackish brown above; grayish brown on under surface, including the under wing coverts; throat somewhat lighter.

Light phase, white from throat to under tail coverts, including under wing coverts; sides gray.

Measurements (from Loomis, Proc. California Acad. Sci., vol. 2, pt. 2, 1918, p. 145).—Males (17 specimens), wing 289-309 (299), tail 129-148 (138), culmen 36.6-41.2 (39.1), tarsus 41.4-48.2 (46.6) mm.

Females (30 specimens), wing 287-311 (298), tail 128-145 (138), culmen 36.6-42.1 (38.9), tarsus 43.8-48.1 (46.0) mm.

Casual visitor. One record off the Pacific coast of southern Darién.

Dr. Robert Cushman Murphy has permitted me to include the only record for this species, based on two specimens that he collected on March 5, 1941, at sea 5 kilometers northwest of Ensenada Guayabo, during the *Askoy* Expedition. The locality is offshore to the south of Jaqué, Darién, a short distance north of the Colombian boundary.

The race *chlororhynchus*, under present understanding of the populations of this shearwater, nests on islands off Australia, at Lord Howe and Norfolk Islands, and at the Seychelles in the Indian Ocean. In the eastern Pacific it breeds on San Benedicto, in the Revilla Gigedo group, off Baja California.

One of the two birds taken is in dark phase, and the other in light phase plumage.

Family HYDROBATIDAE: Storm Petrels; Paiños

Three species of this family reach the Pacific waters off Panamá during wanderings from their breeding grounds, one of them, *Oceanodroma tethys,* coming from the northwestern coast of South America, and the other two, *Loomelania melania* and *Halocyptena microsoma,* from islands near Baja California. Northern and southern groups thus range together in this intermediate area.

It is certain that other kinds will be recorded when more is known of the bird life of the offshore waters. There is now a sight record for a fourth, *Oceanites gracilis,* and probability of several others in Pacific waters. Others may come casually along the Caribbean. (One present sight record in the Gulf of Panamá for *Oceanodroma castro* by C. A. Fleming (Emu, 1950, p. 177) from a steamer July 20, 1948, "approaching the islands in the Bay" appears uncertain.)

KEY TO SPECIES OF HYDROBATIDAE

1. Upper tail coverts white.
    Abdomen black..............Galápagos petrel, *Oceanodroma tethys,* p. 43
    Abdomen white............Graceful storm petrel, *Oceanites gracilis,* p. 45
2. Upper tail coverts dark, like the rest of the plumage.
    Smaller, not more than 150 mm. long.
                                    Least petrel, *Halocyptena microsoma,* p. 45
    Larger, 200 mm. long, or more....Black petrel, *Loomelania melania,* p. 47

OCEANODROMA TETHYS (Bonaparte): Galápagos Petrel; Danzarina

A small petrel, with upper tail coverts and lower rump white; elsewhere dark colored; tail slightly forked.

Description.—Length 140 to 160 mm. Sooty black above; browner on the lower surface and on the wing coverts; lower rump and upper tail coverts white, with dark shafts; some white on the outermost under tail coverts.

Iris brown; bill, tarsus, and toes black.

This is a bird of the Galápagos Islands and the northwest coast of South America that after its breeding season ranges north in the eastern Pacific to waters off northwestern México. As it has been found off Panamá a number of times it appears that it passes regularly through this area though probably, in the main, well at sea.

Two subspecies separated by differences in size currently are recognized with specimens of both recorded within the limits of the present work.

Robins (Condor, 1958, pp. 300-301) saw petrels of this type following the fishing boat on which he traveled July 15 to 26, 1957, from near Taboga to beyond Bahía Piñas, Darién. Dr. Oscar Owre informs me that the specimen recorded by Robins as taken at Bahía Santelmo, Isla del Rey, on July 24, was prepared as a flat skin that could not be preserved permanently so that the race concerned in these records is not known.

Dennis R. Paulson, when a student at the Institute of Marine

Science, University of Miami, in 1961, during a cruise as naturalist on the yacht *Argosy,* A. Glassell owner, found these petrels common from September 6 to 14 in the Bay and Gulf of Panamá, even among the boats anchored off Panama City. Apparently this was the period of their movement from their southern nesting grounds. As noted below one specimen taken was the typical subspecies. Another that came aboard ship in Colombian waters was the race *kelsalli,* so that it appears that both races were in company.

OCEANODROMA TETHYS TETHYS (Bonaparte)

Thalassidroma Tethys Bonaparte, Tagebl. der 29. Versaml. Deutsch. Naturf. Aerzte, Wiesbaden, Beilage, Sept. 25, 1852, p. 89. (Galápagos Islands.)

Characters.—Larger, its greater size indicated by longer wing: Males (3 specimens, from the Galápagos Islands), wing 129.0-132.6 mm.; females (3 specimens from the Galápagos Islands), 132.9-136.0 mm.

Visitor to Pacific waters off Panamá.

This, the nominate race of the species, breeds on the Galápagos Islands, and after the nesting season ranges in the eastern Pacific north to the latitude of southern Baja California, and south to that of southern Ecuador.

A skin in the British Museum (Natural History) collected by the St. George Expedition, with a wing measurement of 129.7 mm., was taken on September 9, 1924, "20 miles south of Panama." Another in the University of Miami Museum, with the wing 129.4, prepared by D. R. Paulson, came to lights on the yacht *Argosy* when near lat. 07° 10' N., long. 79° 04' W., a point due south of the westernmost islands in the Perlas group and about midway on a line from the southernmost point on the Azuero Peninsula to the international boundary between Panamá and Colombia. Though well offshore at the southern end of the Gulf of Panamá, this is within waters that may be regarded as to be included for pelagic species.

OCEANODROMA TETHYS KELSALLI (Lowe)

Thalassidroma tethys kelsalli P. R. Lowe, Bull. Brit. Orn. Club, vol. 46, Nov. 4, 1925, p. 6. (Isla Pescadores, off Ancón, Perú.)

Characters.—Similar to *O. t. tethys,* but smaller, with shorter wing: Males (4 specimens at sea off Perú, Colombia, and Panamá), wing 122.7-125.9 mm.; females (3 specimens at sea off Colombia and Panamá), 123.4-128.0 mm.

Visitor to the Pacific waters of Panamá.

This form breeds on islands off the coast of Perú, where it is reported on Isla Pescadores and Isla San Gallán. Murphy (Oceanic Birds S. Amer., 1936, p. 731) records it as ranging south to the latitude of northern Chile, and his supposition that these birds may come northward as far as Panamá is now verified. A male in the British Museum (Natural History) was taken by the St. George Expedition "near Balboa" on August 22, 1924. Two others of this sex in the American Museum of Natural History were collected by Robert Cushman Murphy, one during the *Askoy* Expedition, 4 miles west of Punta Caracoles, Darién, February 26, 1941, and another south of Punta Dirgado, Darién, September 11, 1937.

Another, a male (now in the American Museum of Natural History), was taken by William Beebe, March 28, 1938, at Banco Hannibal, west of Isla Coiba. Dr. Beebe informed me that the bird came to lights used in the night-collecting of marine animals. (See Beebe, Book of Bays, 1942, pp. 280, 297.)

OCEANITES GRACILIS (Elliot): Graceful Storm Petrel; Golondrina de Mar Chica

Thalassidroma gracilis Elliot, Ibis, vol. 1, no. 4, Oct. 1859, p. 391. (Coast of Chile.)

A small petrel, with upper tail coverts and abdomen white.

Description.—Length about 180 mm. Sooty black; upper tail coverts and abdomen white.

Reported as a casual visitor to the Gulf of Panamá, according to a sight record by Robert Cushman Murphy, cited by Eisenmann (Trans. Linn. Soc. New York, vol. 7, 1955, p. 11).

The typical race, *O. g. gracilis,* known from the west coast of South America from Punta Santa Elena, Ecuador to Valparaiso, Chile, with breeding grounds at present unknown, has the wing 117 to 132 mm., females being larger than males. Another form, *Oceanites gracilis galapagoensis* Lowe, recorded only near the Galápagos Islands, with nesting grounds also unknown, is larger, with the wing 130 to 146 mm.

It is the nominate form that may be expected north to Panamanian waters.

HALOCYPTENA MICROSOMA Coues: Least Petrel; Golondrina de Mar Menuda

FIGURE 8

Halocyptena microsoma Coues, Proc. Acad. Nat. Sci. Philadelphia, March-April (June 30), 1864, p. 79. (San José del Cabo, Baja California.)

Size very small; wholly dark colored.

Description.—Length 145 mm. Plain sooty black. Smallest of the petrels found in Panamá.

Fig. 8.—Least petrel, golondrina de mar menuda, *Halocyptena microsoma.*

Iris brown; bill black; tarsus and toes black.

Measurements (from Murphy, Oceanic Birds S. Amer., 1936, p. 729).—Adult (sexes alike, 11 specimens), wing 118-125 (121), tail 50-56 (53.4), exposed culmen 11-12 (11.4), tarsus 20.5-22 (21.2) mm.

Regular visitor off the Pacific coast.

The least petrel nests in the north near Baja California, on the San Benito Islands off the western coast, and on several small islands in the northern third of the Golfo de California. Bent (U. S. Nat. Mus. Bull. 121, 1922, p. 125) records egg dates from July 2 to 27. While these petrels are common outside the nesting season off Panamá, there are few definite records. Those available are as follows: February 12, 1950, two seen between Isla Pacheca and Taboga (Wetmore); Panamá Bay, March 1888, the second known specimen, taken at night when it flew on board the S. S. *Albatross* (Townsend, Proc. U. S. Nat. Mus., vol. 13, 1890, p. 141); March 14, 1944, half a dozen seen midway between Isla San José and Balboa (Wetmore); March 31, 1962, common in the area to the south of Isla Boná (Wetmore); May 23, 1941, near San José (taken by Robert Cushman Murphy).

Among the petrels seen in the Gulf of Panamá and southward off Darién there may be noted an occasional bird of the present species, known at once from its small size coupled with uniformly dark colors, and rather long, wedge-shaped tail. They fly just above the surface, and may be told from the black petrels by their quicker movements and more erratic fluttering flight, in addition to the size difference. Also they tend to move more in the troughs of the waves. Occasionally they alight for a few seconds while they peck quickly at the water, and then rise easily, twisting and turning, to continue their wandering. Like the black petrel they are not attracted to small boats, for although sometimes I have seen them flying parallel to the course of launches on which I was traveling, they seldom approached nearer than 100 to 200 meters even when crossing in front. I have never had one come within gun range.

On the evening of March 21, 1952, on Isla Taboga, while sitting in the brilliantly lighted, open dining room of the Hotel Taboga overlooking the sea, I saw what I thought was a bat flutter against the white inner wall and drop behind a door. On investigation I found that it was one of these small petrels.

LOOMELANIA MELANIA (Bonaparte): Black Petrel; Golondrina de Mar Negra

Procellaria melania Bonaparte, Compt. Rend. Acad. Sci. Paris, vol. 38, no. 14 (for Apr. 3), 1854, p. 662. (Vicinity of San Francisco, California.)

A petrel of medium size, wholly dark in color.

Description.—Length 200 to 230 mm. Sooty black throughout, somewhat paler on greater wing coverts; tail deeply forked.

Measurements (from Murphy, Oceanic Birds S. Amer., 1936, p. 744).—Adult, sexes alike (from 10 specimens from the California breeding grounds), wing 168-177, tail 80-86, culmen 15-16.5, tarsus 31-34 mm.

Iris brown; bill black; inside of mouth and tongue yellow; tarsus and toes black.

Regular visitor, off the Pacific coast.

The black petrel breeds in the north around Baja California, at Los Corónados and San Benito islands on the northwest coast, and on islands in the northern third of Golfo de California. Bent (U. S. Nat. Mus. Bull. 121, 1922, pp. 157, 158) records eggs from May 30 to July 23, and young in early September. Available dates of occurrence in Panamanian waters are as follows, arranged in order of monthly occurrence (without regard to the year): January 16 to 31 (1960), February 25 (1957), March 14 (1944), March 21, 24 (1952), March 31 (1962), records by the writer; March 24 (1915), specimen taken by Hallinan; July 18, 19, 23, sight records by Robins (Condor, 1958, p. 301); September 8, 9 (1924), specimens in British Museum (Natural History); November (1956), sight records by R. C. Murphy. Apparently the southward movement may start immediately when the first young are on the wing. At the end of March 1952, northward migration may have begun, as on the evening of the 21st one flew into the open, strongly lighted dining room of the hotel on Taboga Island.

(Sight records of petrels in these waters on September 18, 1939, by Fleming, Emu, 1950, p. 177, reported as *Oceanodroma markhami*, may have been of this species.)

In travel by launch in the Gulf of Panamá, black petrels may be noted flying just above the water, moving somewhat erratically from side to side, but at the same time following a fairly direct course. In most instances the view is a distant one since they do not follow boats, and so are encountered only by chance. While they fly low they move less in the troughs of the waves than the fluttering petrel and also have a more direct line of flight. However, they travel with fair rapidity and soon pass from sight. Usually they range well away from land, though I have noted them within 8 kilometers of Balboa. Though most common in the Gulf of Panamá they are found also to the south off Darién.

Order PELECANIFORMES

Family PHAETHONTIDAE: Tropicbirds; Aves del Trópico

The three species of this family have an appropriate English name as they range tropical seas on either side of the Equator around the world. They are gull-like in general form, marked by the long slender plumes of the central tail feathers, which, when fully grown, exceed the length of the head and body. Panamá has the only breeding colony of one species, the red-billed tropicbird, in the whole of Central America.

PHAETHON AETHEREUS MESONAUTA, Peters: Red-billed Tropicbird, Rabijunco

FIGURE 9

Phaëthon aethereus mesonauta Peters, Occ. Papers Boston Soc. Nat. Hist., vol. 5, Apr. 15, 1930, p. 261. (Swan Cay, off Isla Colón, Bocas del Toro, Panamá.)

Gull-like in general form, with greatly elongated central tail feathers.

Description.—Length 760 to 880 mm. (including the fully developed central tail feathers); white, often tinged lightly with pink; upper surface irregularly barred with black; lengthened middle tail feathers, including shaft, white. Plumage firm and compact.

Iris brown; bill red; tarsus and basal half of toes dull yellowish-buff; end of toes, with connecting sections of webs and claws black.

Measurements (from Murphy, Oceanic Birds S. Amer., 1936, p. 798).—Sexes alike (18 specimens from American localities), wing 293-317 (305), tail (normal feathers) 94-115 (105), (central tail feathers 428-658), exposed culmen 60-66 (63.2), tarsus 26-29 (27.8) mm.

Resident. Nests on Swan Cay in the Caribbean off Isla Colón, northeast of the entrance of the pass Boca del Drago. The birds fly out over the sea to feed but apparently do not range far.

Swan Cay, approximately 70 meters long, is a rounded quarter moon in shape, pierced by two openings through one end, and rises 55 meters at the highest point. On the southern side, sheltered from the northeastern trade winds, there is a small sandy beach below a higher level area. Bushes and other vegetation cover the summit, and there is a small clump of coconut palms at the low end. On January 26, 1958, as Thomas Dunn and I, traveling in his fishing boat, approached the island a tropicbird passed high overhead, and presently others circled among the brown boobies that flew out as we came near. The tropicbirds soared easily, with long tail streamers undulating in the wind, graceful and attractive in every way. On the leeward side of the islet several rested on nests placed on narrow ledges on the rock faces above the sea, where they were sheltered by overhang above. Some were low down, a meter or two above the height of maximum storm waves, others higher. I estimated that the colony consisted of 30 to 35 pairs. Scattered birds rested on the water in addition to those that perched on the cliffs, or circled near the island.

The eggs are oval, some broader than others, verging toward short-oval. The shell is pitted, and the ground color is dull white, but in most so solidly dotted with Natal brown to bone brown that the lighter base is almost completely obscured. In some the dots

FIG. 9.—Red-billed tropicbird, rabijunco, *Phaethon aethereus mesonauta.*

are more concentrated at the larger end, and occasional eggs have scattered irregular spots, or are less heavily marked so that the pale base color is seen. Bent (U. S. Nat. Mus. Bull. 121, 1922, p. 188) gives the measurements, taken from 40 eggs, as ranging from 50.5 to 63.2 mm. long by 36.5 to 46. mm. broad, with the average 56.4 by 41.7 mm.

This is the only colony in the western part of the southern Caribbean Sea, the nearest known neighbors of the species being on Los Roques off the north coast of Venezuela, 1,600 kilometers distant. There has been some confusion in published accounts as to the location of Swan Cay. Peters (Bull. Mus. Comp. Zool., vol. 71,

1931, p. 295), who described this race of tropicbird from specimens from this island, was not able to find it on maps available to him, and wrote that it "is said to lie between Isla Bastimentos and Isla Popa," which are two of the islands on the eastern boundary of Almirante Bay. The true location is given in the reference to the original description above.

The red-billed tropicbird is reported to nest on Isla Malpelo, in the Pacific Ocean off Colombia, but apparently does not wander extensively. The only record for the Gulf of Panamá is one seen by Dennis R. Paulson on September 7, 1961, when traveling on the yacht *Argosy* between Balboa and the Pearl Islands.

(The statement by Loye Miller (Condor, 1937, p. 16), that "a single yellow-billed tropicbird (*Phaëthon lepturus*) was seen on the Caribbean coast" between the Canal and the Chiriquí Lagoon, without much question refers to the present species.)

Family PELECANIDAE: Pelicans; Pelícanos

The eight species of pelicans, world wide in distribution through temperate and tropical regions, are heavy-bodied birds, with long bills that support bare throat pouches, used as scoops in capturing their food of fish. While some frequent fresh water for part of the year, the brown pelican, the only species that reaches Panamá, is confined to a salt or brackish-water habitat.

The American white pelican, *Pelecanus erythrorhynchos* Gmelin, has been listed as reaching Panamá in its winter wanderings southward, but this is in error, as the bird is not recorded in Central America beyond Guatemala. (See Hellmayr and Conover, Cat. Birds Amer., pt. 1, no. 2, 1948, p. 116).

PELECANUS OCCIDENTALIS CAROLINENSIS Gmelin; Brown Pelican; Alcatraz

Figure 10

Pelecanus carolinensis Gmelin, Syst. Nat., vol. 1, pt. 2, 1789, p. 571. (Charleston Harbor, South Carolina.)

Large, with a huge pouch, bare of feathers, that extends from the upper foreneck to the end of the long bill.

Description.—Length 1.2 to 1.4 meters. Adult, upper surface, including wings, gray; under surface grayish brown; head white. In breeding dress, the hind neck is very dark brown with a line of white on either side; in winter the neck is entirely white.

Immature, above, including head and neck, dark gray; below white, with sides streaked with brownish gray.

Measurements.—Males (28 specimens from the United States), wing 500-550 (526), tail 123-158 (136), culmen 280-348 (319), tarsus 70-89.4 (80.5) mm.

Females (23 specimens from the United States), wing 483-528 (501), tail 122-153 (136), culmen 280-333 (294), tarsus 68-83.7 (75.7) mm.

Fig. 10.—Brown pelican, alcatraz, *Pelecanus occidentalis carolinensis*.

Iris yellow; bare skin around eye bluish gray; bill dull gray to grayish white spotted irregularly with orange, with the tip of the maxilla and distal half of the mandible dull black, the whole with more or less grayish white exfoliation; pouch dull grayish brown to olive brown; crus, tarsus, toes, and claws black.

Resident. Common along the Caribbean coast; more abundant along the Pacific, especially in Panama Bay. The recorded breeding colonies are as follows: Isla Iguana, on the coast of Los Santos above Punta Mala; islas Pacheca, Pedro González, Señora, and Galera in the Archipiélago de las Perlas; Isla Boná, Isla Chame,

Isla Uravá, islets near Isla Taboguilla, and Isla Taboga, in Panamá Bay.

The brown pelican is one of the most prominent of the sea birds of the Republic, seen constantly along beaches, and found over the open sea among the islands, often to the number of hundreds. Flocks fly in procession over the water, alternately flapping the wings and sailing, in this following the pattern of the one in the lead, so that the change in method of progression flows ripplelike back over the line. Often the birds fly low, almost touching the water, at the proper point over the crest of a long roller where they are aided in support by up draft in the air currents, and so progress with a minimum of effort.

When fish are sighted the birds dive instantly. The neck is extended before reaching the water and the birds submerge completely. Then usually they turn so that as they rise to the surface they face in the direction opposite to that in which they had been flying. If a fish has been captured the bird floats with the tip of the bill down to drain the pouch, when the head is thrown up and the fish swallowed with a gulp. When the pouch is especially full it may be pressed back against the neck to accelerate the flow of water. Often a laughing gull is in attendance to snatch at the food if at all possible, a thievery to which the pelican pays no attention.

In another method of fishing, usually in shallow water, the birds swim with the tip of the bill cutting the surface, and as fish are sighted thrust suddenly at them. Young birds, perhaps not yet fully skilled in diving, often feed by this method in deep water. Where schools of fish remain stationary, pelicans, young and old, rest on the water in close flocks, stabbing at their prey with open bills.

When satisfied they rest in groups, on rocks, or in trees or bushes. Frequently they remain thus at low water, to become more active with change in the tide. On various occasions I have found them fishing at night, even when there was little light.

Pelicans pass constantly across the isthmus, commonly over Gatun Lake, and regularly at other points. The common belief that they have learned to fly the trans-isthmian route by following the canal since it was completed has no foundation. Napoleon Garella (Project Canal travers Istme Panama, 1845, p. 73), who made a survey for a possible canal route in 1844, mentioned pelicans crossing between the head waters of the Río Caimito of the Pacific side, and the Río Paja, tributary to the Río Chagres of the Atlantic slope, and cited their flights to support his location of this pass as the lowest point on the continental divide. Wagner (Abh. Math.-Phys. Cl. Kön. Bayer. Akad. Wiss., vol. 10, 1866, pp. 86, 88) verified these observations of Garella. Pelicans are not restricted in transisthmian journeys to the depression at the Canal Zone, as on occasion they cross elsewhere, even where the land is high. Charles O. Handley, Jr., informs me that on March 15, 1959, while on Cerro Malí, near the head of the Río Pucro in Darién, he saw a flock of 8 pelicans en route from the Atrato basin in Colombia to the head of Río Tacarcuna, bound evidently for the Pacific. They were flying at an elevation of about 2,000 meters.

While brown pelicans fish mainly on salt water they follow channels at the mouths of the larger rivers inland, usually at ebb tide, and may be found then to the head of tidewater.

Nesting is somewhat irregular but appears to come mainly from January to April. On Isla Taboga, in 1952, I found well-grown young on February 3, and later, on March 15, I collected a set of one-fourth incubated eggs. In 1955 they had not yet come to the colony to nest on December 24. In 1960, at Isla Pacheca, several birds were on their nests on January 20, and others were colonized on Isla Galera on January 28. At Isla Boná, March 31, 1962, I noted nearly grown young still in the nest and others only recently on the wing. Maj. Gen. G. Ralph Meyer collected eggs ranging from fresh to slightly incubated on Isla Chame on February 15, 1942, and freshly laid eggs February 21, 1943. The nests are broad, irregular platforms of fair-sized twigs, 400 to 750 mm. across, strongly made, though not especially thick. The 2 or 3 eggs in a set are chalky white, rough-shelled, and usually marked with blood, sometimes heavily when first laid. Stain usually increases as incubation progresses. In form the eggs are somewhat more pointed at either end than subelliptical. Measurements of two sets of two, and two sets of three eggs from islas Chame and Taboga are as follows: Length 72.2 to 76.8 mm.; width 48.8 to 51.4 mm., average 74.4 by 50.2 mm.

Fishermen and others have told me that they know of no nesting colonies of pelicans on the Caribbean coast of Panamá, the nearest to the north of which I have found record being on Isla Contoy, off the coast of Quintana Roo. In the opposite direction, I was informed in 1941 that these birds nested on rocky islets off Santa Marta, Colombia, but I was not able to verify this. However, there may be breeding places nearer at hand, since on February 20, 1958, at Boca del Drago, I saw one young pelican that obviously had not been long away from parental care.

The subspecies *carolinensis* ranges from the southeastern United States along the continental coasts of the Gulf of Mexico and the Caribbean Sea. It is found also on the Pacific side from Guatemala (possibly from southern México) south along the Isthmus of Panamá. Birds from the Pacific side of Panamá usually show an approach in darker color of the hindneck to the race *Pelecanus occidentalis murphyi* Wetmore of the Pacific coast of Colombia and Ecuador, but are to be placed with *carolinensis*.

Pelicans are known locally among fishermen as cuacos. Those who speak English around Almirante call them "Old Joe."

Lionel Wafer (Isthm. Amer., 1699, p. 120) wrote of the pelican that "under the throat hangs a Bag or Pouch, which, when fill'd is as large as both ones Fists. The substance of it is a thin membrane, of a fine grey, ashy Colour. The Seamen Kill them for the sake of these bags, to make Tobacco-pouches of them; for when dry, they will hold a pound of Tobacco; and by a Bullet hung in them they are soon brought into shape." Berthold Seemann (Voy. Herald, vol. 1, 1853, p. 263) describes a deer call that he saw used by hunters in Veraguas made from the wing bone of a pelican "covered at one end with a peculiar kind of cobweb, which forms an instrument that will imitate the cry of a young deer so closely that the old ones, in the belief that some mishap has befallen their kid, repair to the place and are shot."

On the San Blas coast, the Cuna string segments of hollow wing bones of pelicans, usually the ulna, as pendants on necklaces.

Family SULIDAE: Boobies, Gannets; Bobas, Piqueros

The species of this family, like others in the order Pelecaniformes, range worldwide. Gannets are birds of the temperate zones; boobies are found through tropical seas. Four of the 7 living species of the latter group range along Panamanian coasts, confined wholly to salt-water habitat. The family as a whole is an ancient one in avian history, and numerous fossil species have been named from bones found in deposits that range in age throughout the vast reaches of Tertiary time.

KEY TO SPECIES OF SULIDAE

1. Feet red or reddish in all plumages........Red-footed booby, *Sula sula*, p. 63
   Feet greenish, yellow, yellowish, or orange; never red.................. 2

2. Plain sooty brown above, and on throat and upper breast, the latter separated posteriorly from the white or grayish brown lower breast by a definite line......................Brown booby, *Sula leucogaster*, p. 56
White above, or grayish brown, variegated with white.................. 3
3. Tail black........................Blue-faced booby, *Sula dactylatra*, p. 60
Tail grayish, or grayish and white....Blue-footed booby, *Sula nebouxii*, p. 61

SULA LEUCOGASTER (Boddaert): Brown Booby; Piquero Moreno
Figure 11

Adult with neck and upper breast dark, set off sharply from the white of the rest of the under parts.

Description.—Length 660 to 760 mm. Adult, brownish black, with the lower breast and abdomen white.

Immature, dark grayish brown, with the under surface paler, somewhat mottled, usually with a faint indication of the sharply defined line that in the adult separates the white and dark areas of the breast.

Brown boobies, found along both coasts, are more abundant in the Gulf of Panamá than in the Caribbean. To see them it is necessary usually to go offshore, though occasionally they come along the mainland, around rocky headlands, or at the heads of bays. Over the Gulf of Panamá they appear regularly as single birds or small groups that course with set wings, low near the water shifting at intervals in the air currents to rise 10 to 15 meters above the surface. Angular in form, they are streamlined gliders from the tip of the sharp-pointed bill, back over its swelling base and the increasing diameter of the head and the thickened neck, with no appreciable break in outline. This smooth contour swells over the body, and then tapers to termination in the long, pointed tail. The narrow wings, held stiffly without flapping at right angles to the body, are the efficient sail-planes that support the bird, and through slight shifts in angle guide its course and regulate its speed. Only in take-off from the water, or from a perch on land does the booby stroke its wings, and then only to gain sufficient momentum for support on the air currents over which it rides.

Brown boobies live mainly around small offshore islands, on some of which they nest. They rest usually on the face or summits of cliffs or on jumbled rocks above the shore. When the air is calm they remain inactive, but when the wind freshens they range out to feed. In travel by launch through the waters that they frequent one often sees boobies swing briefly near at hand and then, their curiosity satisfied, veer off, intent on their fishing. It is mainly the immature birds that show continued interest, and follow boats for any length of time. Such unsuspicious individuals sometimes ride along near at hand on the favorable air currents generated by the passage of the launch.

When fish are sighted they plunge, often from a fair height,

Fig. 11.—Brown booby, piquero moreno, *Sula leucogaster*.

sometimes directly down, sometimes at an angle. As they surface after a dive they are headed in the same direction as when they entered the water, since they do not turn and reverse as does the brown pelican.

Boobies in their search for food are birds of the sea, the isthmus forming a barrier of land that they do not cross. While the present species is found in both the Caribbean and the Pacific adjacent to the shores, the two oceans are inhabited by subspecies distinct from one another in characters of color.

SULA LEUCOGASTER LEUCOGASTER (Boddaert)

Pelecanus Leucogaster Boddaert, Tabl. Planch. Enlum., 1783, p. 57. (Cayenne.)

Characters.—In this race the adults, male and female, are similar in color. The female differs from that of *S. l. etesiaca* of the Pacific side in having the back, wings, and tail paler brown than the head, neck, and chest.

Iris grayish white; bare skin around eye dull gray, except for the eyelids which are blue; gular pouch, bare skin of forehead and around gape, yellow; base of bill yellow, changing to pale dull grayish brown at tip; tarsus, toes, and webs yellow; claws dull neutral gray.

Measurements (from Murphy, Oceanic Birds S. Amer., 1936, p. 854).—Males (13 specimens), wing 372-391 (381), tail 169-198 (186), exposed culmen 87.8-101.0 (92.7), tarsus 42.0-48.4 (44.3) mm.

Females (10 specimens), wing 384-415 (400), tail 162-198 (180), exposed culmen 91.8-102.0 (96.3), tarsus 45-48 (46.8) mm.

Resident. Fairly common along the Caribbean coast.

The known breeding colonies in Panamá are on the following offshore islands: Swan Key, off Boca del Drago, and islets off the western end of Isla Escudo de Veraguas, Bocas del Toro; Farallón Sucio, off Punta Cacique, between Portobelo and Nombre de Dios, Colón. There is also a breeding colony on Isla Tonel, Colombia, located on the western side of the entrance to the Gulf of Urabá, a few miles beyond the eastern boundary of the Comarca de San Blas. The eggs are like those of *Sula l. etesiaca.*

Downy young of good size were noted March 1, 1958, on the islets at Escudo de Veraguas. Though the birds wander to some extent, and so are seen occasionally off Colón harbor, and elsewhere, they are found more frequently near their nesting colonies. They are common in Almirante Bay and at sea off Boca del Drago.

SULA LEUCOGASTER ETESIACA Thayer and Bangs

Sula etesiaca Thayer and Bangs, Bull. Mus. Comp. Zoöl., vol. 46, June 1905, p. 92. (Gorgona Island, Colombia.)

Characters.—Male strikingly different from that of *S. l. leucogaster,* as the forepart of the head is distinctly gray. Female similar to that of the other race, but with back and wings uniform in color with the head, neck, and chest.

An adult male taken at Pacheca, January 20, 1960, had the iris Marguerite yellow; space around eye dull blue, becoming dull bluish green on the base of rami, and leaden blue on the gular area; base of maxilla dull greenish buff; rest of bill greenish drab, except culmen which was fuscous; feet and tarsi light greenish yellow.

An adult female shot off Isla Cañas, on the same day, had the eye colored as in the male; a large spot in front of the eye dull leaden blue; rest of bare skin around eye, base of bill all around, and gular sac light yellow; bill light avellaneous; tarsus and toes light greenish yellow; webs between the toes bright yellow.

Measurements.—Males (15 specimens), wing 360-384 (370), tail 163-187 (181), culmen from base 82.0-93.3 (88.6), tarsus 44.8-48.0 (45.5) mm.

Females (14 specimens), wing 385-408 (397), tail 182-198 (189), culmen from base 89.6-103.2 (95.8), tarsus 46.8-49.8 (48.2) mm.

Resident. Common along the Pacific coast, particularly in the Gulf of Panamá.

The following nesting colonies are recorded: Isla Boná; Farallón Rock, off the southern side of Isla Taboguilla; Isla Pachequilla, Isla Pacheca, Isla Saboga, and Isla Galera, Archipiélago de las Perlas. Friends who fish in the Gulf of Chiriquí have told me of a colony of boobies on Islas Ladrones, doubtless the piquero moreno, as this is the common one in those waters. Murphy (Vert. SCOPE, 1957, pp. 133-134) reported many near these islands on November 25, 1956. Hellmayr and Conover (Cat. Birds Amer., pt. 1, no. 2, 1948, p. 136) are in error in their inclusion of Isla Chepillo and Isla del Rey in their list of breeding colonies, since these localities are merely records of birds seen many years ago by Bovallius (Rendahl, Ark. Zool., Bd. 12, 1920, p. 10), or where specimens were collected in 1904 by Brown (Thayer and Bangs, Bull. Mus. Comp. Zool., vol. 46, 1905, p. 141).

Three sets of eggs of 2 each, in the U. S. National Museum, collected by Maj. Gen. G. Ralph Meyer, are chalky white, with a slightly roughened surface. The outer chalky deposit completely covers a base color of pale bluish white which is visible only when the shell has been scratched sufficiently to cut through the outer coating. All the eggs are considerably stained. One set with incubation advanced, from Farallón Rock taken December 13, 1942, was placed among rocks on the ground, in a depression about 300 mm.

across, lined with twigs, leaves, and grass stems. Freshly deposited eggs were noted here on another visit on January 23, 1944. Hallinan (Auk. 1924, p. 306) recorded nests with eggs (Dec. 5, 1915) "on a rocky, wooded islet about ¼ mile off shore" from Taboguilla, evidently Farallón Rock. The two additional sets collected by General Meyer were taken April 23, 1944, on Isla Pachequilla, from nests that were depressions in the ground on the level summit of the island. Some were in the open, others among bushes and low trees. In some the depression was partly lined with twigs. The six eggs measure in length 57.9-64.4 and in breadth 38.7-41.8 with an average size of 61.2 × 40.1 mm.

Near Isla Galera I saw immature birds alight on the water and thrust their heads repeatedly below the surface. I could determine no reason for this, unless possibly they were feeding on plankton. Three adult males taken here at 8:30 in the morning seem to have left their sleeping quarters recently, as in all the stomach was empty.

This is the booby most often seen in Panamanian waters, as it outnumbers the blue-footed booby, *S. n. nebouxii*, and is far more abundant than the Caribbean representative of the species.

SULA DACTYLATRA Lesson: Blue-faced Booby; Boba Borrega

Adult white, with black tail.

Description.—Length 750 to 850 mm. Adult, white, with wing feathers, greater wing coverts, and tail black; bare face and throat dark blue.

Immature, upper surface, head, and neck, dark brown, becoming paler on breast, and whitish on abdomen.

This booby, largest of the species of the family reported from Panamanian waters, is known there only from a few sight observations. It has been reported from both coasts so that two subspecies are concerned, but the records need verification by specimens. The two geographic races that should occur differ in size, the supposed color differences in bill and foot color being those that distinguish male and female.

Iris yellow; bare skin of face black; bill orange-yellow at base in males, light red in females, distally horn color in both sexes; tarsus and toes olive-drab in males, plumbeous in females. (From Murphy, Oceanic Birds S. Amer., 1936, pp. 846, 848.)

SULA DACTYLATRA DACTYLATRA Lesson

Sula dactylatra Lesson, Traité Orn., livr. 8, July 11, 1831, p. 601. (Ascension Island, South Atlantic Ocean.)

Larger in size.

Iris yellow; bare skin of face black; and of bill dull brown, with base orange-yellow in male, pale red in female; tarsus and toes dull brown in males, bluish neutral gray in females.

Measurements (from Murphy, Oceanic Birds S. Amer., 1936, p. 846).—Males (9 specimens), wing 406-433 (424), tail 153-173 (166), exposed culmen 92.6-97.2 (95.6), tarsus 53-56.2 (54) mm.

Females (7 specimens), wing 417-440 (429), tail 151-180 (164), exposed culmen 91.6-99.0 (95.7), tarsus 52.0-54.6 (53.4) mm.

Casual visitor to the Caribbean coast.

The only reports are those of sight records by Griscom (Amer. Mus. Nov. 282, 1927, p. 3) who recorded 4 on February 9, 1927, and 30 on February 13, 1924, off Colón harbor. These boobies nest in scattered colonies on islands off northern Yucatán, in the southern Bahamas, the Virgin Islands, the Grenadines, Los Hermanos north of Venezuela, and Los Monjes between the end of the Guajira Peninsula and the island of Aruba. From these breeding places they wander widely through the Gulf of Mexico and the Caribbean.

SULA DACTYLATRA GRANTI Rothschild

Sula granti Rothschild, Bull. Brit. Orn. Club, vol. 13, Oct. 31, 1902, p. 7. (Culpepper Island, Galápagos Islands.)

Similar to *S. d. dactylatra* but averaging larger. The difference, however, appears slight, perhaps too little to be worthy of recognition.

Color of soft parts as in *Sula d. dactylatra*.

Measurements (from Murphy, Oceanic Birds S. Amer., 1936, p. 846).—Males (5 specimens), wing 413-443 (429), tail 172-181 (177), exposed culmen 102.0-104.4 (102.7), tarsus 52.3-58 (55) mm.

Females (6 specimens), wing 427-468 (450), tail 176-189 (183), exposed culmen 102.0-114.5 (106.5), tarsus 54-59 (57) mm.

Reported as a casual visitor in the Gulf of Panamá.

Robins (Condor, 1958, p. 301) recorded one seen in company with brown boobies at sea 30 kilometers off Bahía Piñas, Darién. Dennis R. Paulson recorded others in this same area Sept. 13 and 14, 1961, when traveling on the yacht *Argosy*.

This form is one of probable occurrence as it breeds at Isla de Malpelo, Colombia, about 550 kilometers southwest, as well as in the Galápagos.

SULA NEBOUXII NEBOUXII Milne-Edwards: Blue-footed Booby; Camanáy

Sula nebouxii Milne-Edwards, Ann. Sci. Nat. Zoöl., ser. 6, vol. 13, art. 4, 1882, p. 37, pl. 14. (Pacific coast of America.)

Head and neck gray, mottled with white.

Description.—Length 760 to 860 mm. Adult, back (except for center), wings, and tail, grayish brown, the feathers in the center of the back tipped with white; head and neck gray mottled with white; under surface, upper back, and base of neck, white; central tail feathers white, bordered by gray.

Immature, mottled with dark grayish brown on breast and abdomen.

An adult female taken at Farallón del Chirú had the iris clear yellow, while in another from Isla Villa, not as old, it was light grayish brown, with an indistinct line of Marguerite yellow around the external margin. In both the bill was light greenish gray, shading posteriorly into the grayish blue of the face, bare throat, ramal area, lores, eyelids, and a narrow line on the forehead back of the bill; tarsi and feet light bright blue, with the front of the tarsi, and the basal joints of the toes grayer; claw of middle toe horn color, of other toes neutral gray; bare skin surrounding anus light blue like the webs between the toes.

Measurements (from Murphy, Oceanic Birds S. Amer., 1936, p. 830).—Males (7 specimens), wing 387-413 (403), tail 165-218 (190); exposed culmen 94-106 (99.7), tarsus 47-54 (50.4) mm.

Females (7 specimens), wing 403-426 (416), tail 165-215 (190), exposed culmen 106.0-109.5 (107.5), tarsus 51-57 (55) mm.

Resident. Fairly common in the Gulf of Panamá. Breeding colonies are recorded at Isla Villa, off the coast of Los Santos; Farallón del Chirú, off Santa Clara, Coclé; on Isla Pachequilla (probably also on Pacheca and Galera), Archipiélago de las Perlas; and on Isla Boná. A few pairs probably nest on rocky islets off the western side of Isla Taboguilla.

At Isla Villa on February 28, 1957, a dozen circled off the rocky summit when the birds resting there were alarmed. And at Farallón del Chirú, on the same day, I noted another dozen pairs. With those at this second locality there were a few dark-colored young. Birds seen flying off Riomar, March 15, 1958, are presumed to have come from this same locality. In the Archipiélago de las Perlas, Mrs. Sturgis (Birds Panama Canal Zone, 1928, p. 112) records that "we saw them in considerable numbers in the Pearl Islands on Pacheca and Galera on the ledges of the cliffs." This implies breeding but is not definite; it seems to be the basis for the report of Hellmayr and Conover (Cat. Birds Amer., pt. 1, no. 2, 1948, p. 124) of nesting on these two islands. On two days in January 1960 I found 20 grouped on a cliff edge on Isla Pachequilla, and saw several isolated nesting sites on small ledges on the higher cliffs. Some of these held nearly grown young. The largest colony that I have seen is on Isla Boná, where I observed them in numbers flying off the steep rocky slopes on March 31, 1962. Robins (Condor, 1958, pp. 301-302) in July 1957 found this the most common booby around Isla Camote and Isla Galera and off the coast between Punta Garachiné and Bahía Piñas, Darién. This seems to imply either more extensive breeding colonies than have been reported or that birds that nest elsewhere come to the Gulf of Panamá when food is abundant. I saw one near Isla Pelado, off the mouth of the Río Chimán, on February 15, 1950, but noted no indication of nesting. A specimen in the American Museum of Natural History was taken by Dr. Murphy on the *Askoy* Expedition, at Ensenada Guayabo, southern Darién, on March 2, 1941.

As these boobies circle and swing about they appear very large against the sky. When seen from the side the gray-brown head and neck are outlined clearly from the white breast.

The population found at the Galápagos Islands has been separated by Todd (Proc. Biol. Soc. Washington, 1948, p. 99) as *Sula nebouxii excisa* on the basis of average larger size. Murphy (Oceanic Birds S. Amer., 1936, p. 830), the first to point to this distinction, listed wing measurements as follows:

Pacific coast, 7 males, 387-413; 7 females, 403-426 mm.

Galápagos Islands, 3 males, 406-433; 3 females, 444-448 mm.

The difference is slight but appears valid in the specimens that I have examined.

SULA SULA SULA (Linnaeus): Red-footed Booby; Boba Blanca

Pelecanus Sula Linnaeus, Syst. Nat., ed. 12, vol. 1, 1766, p. 218. (Barbados.)

Adult, white or grayish brown; tail white in both phases.

Description.—Length 660 to 700 mm. Adult, white, with primaries black, washed with gray on the outer webs; or in the darker color phase, grayish brown, with rump and tail white.

Immature, plain grayish brown.

Gular sac black in males, bluish black in females; feet red.

Measurements (from Murphy, Oceanic Birds S. Amer., vol. 1, 1936, p. 862).—Males (9 specimens), wing 362-385 (372.1), tail 206-231 (217), exposed culmen 76.3-85 (81.2), tarsus 32.7-36.9 (33.7), middle toe and claw 66.2-74.5 (69) mm.

Females (7 specimens), wing 378-405 (389), tail 198-215 (207.4), exposed culmen 80.5-86.0 (83.7), tarsus 35-40.3 (37.3), middle toe with claw 70-75.5 (72) mm.

A visitor to the Caribbean coast. Not much is known as to its abundance.

The first record is that of Griscom (Amer. Mus. Nov. no. 282, 1927, p. 3), who reported two in Colón harbor on February 23, 1927. Thomas Imhof informs me that he saw one 5 miles off Colón on February 23, 1943, and I recorded one that was fishing off the mouth of the Río Indio, Colón, to the west of the Canal Zone, on February 20, 1952. In addition to these sight records I have an excellent color photograph of a red-footed booby taken on December 14, 1955, by Mr. and Mrs. Paul Barnard. The bird, in gray plumage with white tail, found on board a ship at Cristobal, was brought to Balboa, photographed, and released there. The U. S. National Museum has an adult female given to me by Charles L. Fagan, when wireless operator on the Grace Line *S. S. Santa Elena,* taken August 27, 1924, in the Caribbean, 300 kilometers N.N.E. of Colón. The species is not known to breed in Panamanian waters, the nearest nesting colony of which there is record being on Half Moon Cay off British Honduras.

Murphy (Oceanic Birds S. Amer., 1936, pp. 861-865) after detailed discussion on the color variations in these boobies does not find clearcut grounds on which to distinguish geographic races. These are to be expected as the species ranges through tropical seas around the world, and other current treatment recognizes separate forms for the Atlantic and the eastern Pacific. The eastern Pacific population, which nests in the Revilla Gigedo Islands, on Cocos Island off Costa Rica, and in the Galápagos, may range casually into the Gulf of Panamá. This Pacific group, described as *Sula sula websteri* by Rothschild, is supposed to differ from typical *Sula s. sula* on the basis of a slightly longer wing. The only report to date is an uncertain one by Mrs. Sturgis (Birds Panama Canal Zone, 1928, p. 111), who says that it is found "about the Pearl Islands" without more definite statement. This reference, however, without much doubt, refers to one of the other boobies.

Family PHALACROCORACIDAE: Cormorants; Cuervos Marinos

The range of the 30 species of this aquatic family covers much of the world, as cormorants have adapted to life in both salt and fresh waters, as well as to a considerable range of temperature. The spread of the family as a whole extends from the far north through temperate and equatorial regions to southern waters. In their modern form cormorants became established before the Middle Tertiary, while ancient allied stocks are recognized in fossil deposits in Paleocene time of more than 60 million years ago.

[PHALACROCORAX BOUGAINVILLII (Lesson): Peruvian Cormorant; Guanáy

Carbo Bougainvillii Lesson, in Bougainville, Journ. Nav. Thétis et Espérance, vol. 2, 1837, p. 331. (Valparaiso, Chile.)

The only present basis for inclusion of this species is a report by Eisenmann (Trans. Linn. Soc., vol. 7, 1955, p. 14) of a sight record "off Darien, once, R. C. Murphy." The guanáy, the principal species concerned in the production of the great guano deposits on the bird islands off the coast of Perú, breeds also in isolated colonies on islands in Chilean waters. In times of change in coastal ocean currents when normal food supplies fail these birds wander widely. They have been found casually north along the Pacific coast of Colombia to Gorgona Island, and to Bahía de Málaga near Buenaventura (De Schauensee, Birds Colombia, 1948, p. 355), and may straggle rarely farther into Panamanian waters.

The species is 700 to 760 mm. long and is marked by pure white breast, with a white patch on the side of the neck, the rest of the body being black, more or less glossed with green.]

PHALACROCORAX OLIVACEUS OLIVACEUS (Humboldt): Olivaceous Cormorant; Cuervo Marino

FIGURE 12

Pelecanus olivaceus Humboldt, in Humboldt and Bonpland, Recueil d'observations zoologie et d'anatomie comparée, vol. 1, livr. 1, 1805, p. 6. (El Banco, Río Magdalena, Magdalena, Colombia.)

Large, dark-colored, with the bill hooked at tip.

Description.—Length 660 to 710 mm. Adult, black; upper surface and wings brownish slate, the feathers edged with black; a white line bordering the gular sac; in breeding dress, head and neck with scattered filamentous white feathers.

Immature, grayish brown; in the first season much paler, some being white on the under surface.

W. W. Brown, Jr., listed colors of an adult female taken March 19, 1904, at Isla del Rey as follows: Iris sea green; gular patch yellow, darker in the center; tarsus black (a color that in the skins includes the toes).

Measurements (from adults taken in the breeding colonies on Isla del Rey and Saboga).—Males (6 specimens), wing 283-298 (291), tail 160-184 (172), culmen from base 58.7-67.4 (63.8), tarsus 53.7-58.9 (57.0) mm.

Fig. 12.—Olivaceous cormorant, cuervo marino, *Phalacrocorax olivaceus olivaceus*.

Females (5 specimens), wing 268-295 (276.5), tail 152-185 (161), culmen from base 55.2-62.5 (59.4), tarsus 53.2-58.0 (56.1) mm.

Resident. Abundant in the Gulf of Panamá, common along the coasts elsewhere, ranging far inland along rivers (even to their head waters), and on Gatun and Madden lakes; seen occasionally on the lakes near El Volcán at 1280 meters elevation and on the Río Caldera near Boquete at about 1200 meters. Nesting colonies are reported on Pacheca and Saboga islands in the Perlas group.

The number of cormorants present on the Gulf varies considerably from season to season, governed apparently by the abundance of the schools of fish that form their food. It seems probable that a part of the great bands that are seen occasionally may be wanderers from other regions in the American tropics. In the early morning of April 4, 1948, at the mouth of the Río Chico, below the La Jagua Hunting Club, tens of thousands flew in lines and irregular bands over the open water of the Gulf. These flocks extended as far as I could see through my binoculars, the total number being far beyond that of the two breeding colonies recorded in the Perlas Islands. Earlier, in February and March 1944, I found flocks of hundreds around Isla San José and Isla Pedro González, which I believed in the main to be the resident population. In contrast to these observations, in the period from January 16 to 31, 1960, when I was working by seagoing launch through the Archipiélago de las Perlas fish were not plentiful, and I recorded only one flock of a hundred cormorants near Isla Contadora, and a few other scattered individuals. Robins (Condor, 1958, p. 302) noted only one during a fishing trip in the Gulf that extended from July 15 to 26, 1957.

Though so grotesque in form that some find them repulsive, cormorants on closer acquaintance show many interesting habits. The great flocks found at times in the Gulf of Panamá are attractive for their numbers alone, as they fly in long lines, 100 to 150 meters above the sea, in search of the schools of small fishes that form their food. When these are sighted the birds circle precipitately down to the water where they swim and dive amid a swarm of swooping frigate birds and laughing gulls, and of plunging pelicans and boobies, while mackerel, amberjack, and other great fishes surge and swirl beneath through the close-packed masses of small fry. No bickering is evident among these active predators, though often I have wondered if there were not frequent collisions that might result in injury, so apparently heedless of one another are the several kinds that join voraciously in the attack.

At a distance the dark forms of cormorants suggest geese by their size and manner of flight. When hunger is satisfied the flocks rest on rocks on the headlands or on sandy beaches where they stand close together in rows, often in the wash of little waves. As others fly in to join these ranks there is often a chorus of the croaking, grunting calls that are the only notes of these birds.

In addition to these flocks, scattered birds are found everywhere along the coasts and inland wherever there is suitable water. While these birds may feed alone, usually they gather in little groups to rest and to sleep—on the coast on trees or rocks along the shore, and inland in dead trees or branches bare of leaves over, or beside, the water. As a boat approaches, these resting birds begin to twist about, until finally they pitch awkwardly into the air where their wings beat heavily to gain momentum for flight, or they plunge beneath the water to appear at a safe distance many meters away.

On the larger rivers as the Tuira and the Chucunaque cormorants are found in hundreds, most of them above the limit of tide. Constantly shifting currents below that point usually keep the streams muddy, so that fish if not actually more abundant are more easily obtained in the clearer waters above. Practically all these cormorants are immature individuals, some in first, and others in second-year plumage, to judge from their color. It is my supposition that many of the young birds from the nesting colonies in the Gulf move to such fresh waters and remain there more or less permanently until ready to breed. One indication of this is that on the upper courses of uninhabited streams young cormorants are often almost stupidly tame, presumably through lack of experience in dangers that would be theirs during more extensive journeys.

On the other hand, it is quite probable that part of the cormorants in these same stages of plumage, found in Bocas del Toro, and elsewhere in western Panamá may be migrants from elsewhere in the Tropics. In crossing from Bocas del Toro to Panamá in a Cessna plane on one occasion I saw one cormorant flying at an elevation of 350 meters across the extensive area of unbroken forest of this part of the Caribbean slope, an indication of wandering that would bring these birds into the remote and isolated waters where they are sometimes found.

The abundance of this species in Panamá attracted the attention of early travelers, even of the buccaneers, as they are one of the birds described in some detail by Lionel Wafer in his account of Darién (Isthm. Amer., 1699, p. 121).

The nesting season appears to come in April, as W. W. Brown, Jr., noted a nest with 6 incubated eggs April 14, 1904, on Isla Saboga (Thayer and Bangs, Bull. Mus. Comp. Zool., vol. 46, 1905, p. 141). On April 24, 1949, in early morning as I watched flocks of cormorants flying down the Río Mamoní, near its mouth at Chepo, a bird near the center of one flock carried a good-sized twig in its bill, while maintaining its proper place in the long line of its companions, indication that the nesting season was near.

According to Bent (U. S. Nat. Mus. Bull. 121, 1922, pp. 262-263) 4 or 5 eggs constitute the normal set. These have a ground color of bluish white concealed beneath a coating of chalky white. In addition usually they are much nest-stained. Measurements range from 47.5-58 × 29-37 mm.

In Venezuela these birds are known as the *cotúa*.

Family ANHINGIDAE: Snakebirds; Cuervos de Aguja

The four species recognized in this family are found throughout the warmer areas of the world, mainly on fresh water. All are similar in slender form, with long, straight bill (in which the edges of the mandibles are finely serrate), narrow head, long, slender neck, and narrow body. Some ornithologists have united this family with the cormorants, presumably on the basis of general resemblances in color and manner of life, but anatomical studies show differences too important to warrant this combination. Among the distinctions, the snakebirds have a peculiar stomach in which there is a separate small lobe at the upper end for the glands found in most other birds in the proventriculus, and a second division at the lower end, in which a series of slender, hairlike processes are clustered around the narrow opening into the intestine. There is also an arrangement in the upperpart of the neck that serves as a trigger to control the head as a spear to impale the fish that form the food. These are peculiar adjustments not found in cormorants, and with other details establish separate family status. It may be noted also that in the snakebirds primaries and secondaries are molted simultaneously as they are in ducks, and so for a period the birds are flightless.

ANHINGA ANHINGA LEUCOGASTER (Vieillot): Anhinga; Cuervo de Aguja

FIGURE 13

Plotus leucogaster Vieillot, Nouv. Dict. Hist. Nat., nouv. éd., vol. 1, Sept. 1816, p. 545. (Florida.)

Long neck, with slender head and long straight bill mark this species, as compared to the cormorant.

Description.—Length 760 to 900 mm. Very slender in form with long, thin neck. Male black, marked prominently on wings and back with grayish white.

Female similar, but with breast, head, and neck, light brown.

For measurements see below.

Fig. 13.—Anhinga, cuervo de aguja, *Anhinga anhinga leucogaster*.

Resident. Found around larger bodies of fresh water in the lowlands, ranging into tidal areas among the mangroves.

The species is most common around Gatun and Madden Lakes, and along the Río Chagres between these two, and is found in fair numbers on the Tuira and Chucunaque Rivers. I have seen it regularly in the Province of Herrera, around the marshes east of Pacora, and have one specimen from the lower Río Jaqué, in Darién. The bird is fairly common also around Changuinola, in Bocas del Toro. Two (now in the British Museum) were collected by Arcé years ago at Laguna de Castillo in southern Veraguas, which is the most western record on the Pacific slope. To date the species has not been reported from Chiriquí, Los Santos, or the Comarca de San Blas.

In ordinary flight the anhinga alternately flaps the wings rapidly several times to gain momentum and then spreads them stiffly while it sails. It is common to see them soaring, alone or in company of other birds, in rising air currents. Their outline against the sky—slender head and neck extended, broad wings and tail—suggests that of a sailplane.

It is common also to see them perched on snags or in dead trees beside the water, and often when approached instead of flying they drop heavily into the water, dive, and disappear. Frequently they swim with the body nearly submerged so that only the slender head and neck are visible, from which habit they are called snakebirds. They fish by diving, during which, unlike most water birds, the outer body feathers become completely soaked. The birds then rest on an open perch with wings wide spread to allow the plumage to dry. On one occasion, on the Río Escotá, near Santa María, Herrera, I shot two for specimens that fell in the river. While we were cutting a long bamboo to retrieve them, both birds became waterlogged and sank, one of them in deep water where it could not be found.

Though the Cuervo de Aguja undoubtedly is resident no nests have been reported yet from Panamá. Elsewhere usually they gather in small colonies though pairs may remain alone.

Information relative to breeding in the southeastern United States from southern Texas to Florida (Bent, U. S. Nat. Mus. Bull. 121, 1922, pp. 230-232) describes the nest as an untidy structure suggestive of that of a heron but more bulky. It is placed rather low in bushes or trees, and is built of sticks, usually with a lining of twigs bearing green leaves. The 3 to 5 eggs are pale bluish white, with a chalky coating that becomes stained brownish or yellowish during incubation. They vary in length from 47 to 57.5 mm. and in breadth by 33 to 37.5 mm. Anhingas often nest in company with herons and ibises.

The species sometimes is known as *cuervo de agua dulce* to distinguish it from the cormorant.

Two geographic races of this wide-ranging bird are recognized at present. The northern form *Anhinga anhinga leucogaster* (Vieillot) of the southeastern United States, south throughout Central America, and of Cuba and the Isle of Pines, has the light band at the tip of the tail narrow and averages smaller.

Males (44 specimens), wing 316-347 (330), culmen from base 74.0-89.9 (81.8) mm.

Females (28 specimens), wing 314-348 (327), culmen from base 70.5-85.0 (77.8) mm.

The typical form *Anhinga anhinga anhinga* (Linnaeus), found in northwestern South America from Colombia to western Ecuador, and east of the Andes south to northern Argentina, has the light tail tip definitely broader and averages larger.

Males (14 specimens), wing 325-365 (341), culmen from base 84.7-98.8 (91.8) mm.

Females (16 specimens), wing 312-361 (335), culmen from base 81.7-91.5 (86.3) mm.

Intergradation between the two begins in Panamá where the birds are intermediate, but nearer *leucogaster,* and continues in northern Colombia, where they are intermediate also but nearer *anhinga.*

The population from western México south to Guatemala appears to average slightly smaller than *leucogaster* from elsewhere and has been named *A. a. minima* by van Rossem (Ann. Mag. Nat. Hist., 1939, p. 439), with type locality Acaponeta, Nayarit. The suggested color characters of the proposed form do not hold. The specimens seen in the present study from the area concerned have been small, but all have been immature birds (including the type) and these usually are smaller than adults. The race is one of questionable validity.

Family FREGATIDAE: Frigatebirds; Tijeretas de Mar

The five species of this family are birds of the warmer seas around the world. All agree in long, angular wings and deeply forked tail, with the differences that separate them specifically found in size, in combination with the location, or absence, of white markings. One species is common along the coasts of Panamá, but another may be expected to come casually along the Pacific.

FREGATA MAGNIFICENS Mathews: Magnificent Frigatebird; Tijereta de Mar

Figure 14

Fregata minor magnificens Mathews, Austr. Av. Rec., vol. 2, no. 6, Dec. 19, 1914, p. 120. (Barrington Island, Galápagos Archipelago.)

Size large; wings long, angular; tail long, deeply forked.

Description.—Length 810 mm. to a meter. Male black, glossed above with violet; throat sac large, bright red in breeding season, shrunken, dull orange at other times.

Female, black, with breast and sides white.

Immature, head and neck white.

Measurements (from specimens from the Pacific coast of Central and South America).—Males (22 specimens), wing 587-648 (622), culmen from base 105.6-116.4 (109.0) mm.

Females (15 specimens), wing 615-695 (648), culmen from base 115.3-135.8 (122.8) mm.

Iris brown; bill dusky neutral gray; tarsus and toes dull black; throat sac of male bright red in the breeding season when capable of inflation, changing to dull orange in the post breeding, contracted state.

Resident. Common along the coasts, particularly in the Bay of Panamá. Often seen soaring far inland; found regularly over the Panama Canal and Gatun Lake.

The known breeding colonies in Panamanian waters are as follows: The western one of two small islets immediately north of Isla Uva, in the Islas Contreras, which lie to the north of Isla Coiba; Isla Iguana, north of Punta Mala; Isla Boná; Farallón del Chirú; Isla Villa; islets near Isla Taboguilla; Isla Chame; Isla Pacheca, Isla Saboga, Isla Cangrejo in the Islas Caracoles (to the north of Isla del Rey), and Isla Galera, in the Archipiélago de las Perlas.

The frigatebird, with its narrow, angular wings and deeply forked tail, is a familiar sight anywhere along the sea, as the birds are constantly on the wing, often high in air. Seen regularly over the coastal towns and cities, they also swing inland, particularly during periods of storm, and so it is not unusual to see one high overhead through some forest opening far distant from the sea. They cross the isthmus constantly from side to side over the canal.

Frigatebirds are notorious for robbing their neighbor terns and boobies of their fish. The brown booby particularly is unfortunate in this, though it often manages to escape. I have seen royal terns and laughing gulls also elude a frigate after a long and agile chase. On the Río Chimán a frigatebird swooped down at a cormorant that had a fish in its bill, but the latter dived instantly and so saved its meal. However, as I have recorded elsewhere, the frigatebirds in the Gulf of Panamá are more often fishermen in their own right, as they swoop regularly over the waves to seize small fishes in their bills, and then swing away without alighting. The birds descend swiftly from a low elevation in the air, glide forward just above the

FIG. 14.—Magnificent frigatebird, tijereta de mar, *Fregata magnificens*, male, with inflated throat sac.

water, then drop the head to snap at fish while the body continues its forward glide, seemingly leaving the head and the long neck behind until it is brought back with its wriggling prey in the bill at the very second when it appears that the bird will be overturned. The bill and sometimes the entire head may be immersed, but neither wing nor body touches the water. Where schools of small fish surface frigatebirds join pelicans and cormorants in voracious attack, remaining always in the air, while their companions plunge and dive amid the larger fish that harass the unfortunate schools beneath the water.

In June 1953 scores of frigates, most of them immature, ranged over the open water at the head of Montijo Bay. As the tide rose the birds followed up the Río San Pablo for some distance. Twice I saw one pick up a sea snake swimming at the surface and carry it, as it twisted and coiled, for a short distance with other frigates in close pursuit, and then finally let it drop. Frank Violette, of long experience in fishing the waters of the Gulf, has told me that when the frigatebird sees large billfish—marlin and sailfish—it watches them as it turns in small circles high in air. He has located such fish frequently by observing this maneuver.

At the end of February 1957 I estimated that a thousand pairs were nesting on Isla Iguana, north of Punta Mala. The birds here occupied most of the island except for a small clearing where two houses were located. Only the pelicans were able to compete with them for nesting sites. Chattering calls came constantly from the birds on their nests. Males had the balloonlike, red throat pouches inflated, and often flew about with bits of grass dangling from the bill.

On February 28 I found between 75 and 100 pairs at Isla Villa and 30 or so at Farallón del Chirú.

Hundreds roost on the steep western slopes of Isla Taboga, but during my visits at various times from December to March I have not noted nests. I believed that the frigatebirds seen around Isla Pelado off the mouth of Río Chimán in February and March 1950 may have nested there, but of this I was not certain. Formerly they were located on the "Fortified Islands" at the Pacific entrance of the Canal.

At Isla Chame near Taboga, on February 15, 1942, Maj. Gen. G. Ralph Meyer collected several eggs, ranging from fresh to three-fifths incubated. The nests were shallow platforms of twigs 300 to 400 mm. in diameter, lined scantily with finer materials, placed 3 meters or so above the ground in the low trees that form groves on the steep slopes of the island, often closely grouped with several in one tree. On a previous visit on February 23, 1941, he had found that several eggs were nearly ready to hatch. On Isla Iguana many of the nests were only 1½ meters or so above the ground, and regularly I walked underneath those higher while the birds watched me within a few meters of my head.

One egg is laid in each nest, its color chalky white, with a slightly roughened shell—sometimes stained with streaks of brown, apparently from blood during laying. In shape they vary considerably from subelliptical and long oval to long elliptical, in the larger shape sometimes somewhat expanded on the larger perimeter. A series of 9 from Isla Chame and 2 from Isla Iguana vary in length from 63.4 to 74.0 and in width from 46.0 to 50.0, with the average 70.1 x47.6 mm.

Back of the sand dunes on the mainland opposite Isla Iguana there is a fresh-water pond, Laguna de la Boca, 250 meters long by 30 to 50 meters wide, and fairly deep. In March 1957, all day long a scattered procession of frigatebirds came from the nesting colony on the island to drink and bathe in the sweet water. The great birds arrived in groups of 4 or 5 to 20, circled the pond, and then came down steeply, like airplanes descending to a landing field. Most of them banked above the surface of the water to straighten out and then as they sailed with set wings dipped the bill, swinging the long neck back beneath as they do in seizing a fish. They rose immediately, usually throwing the head up to swallow. Regularly 2 or 3 dropped lower so that the breast feathers broke the surface. Then, when aloft 15 or 20 meters or more, they sailed with set wings while they shook the body violently and waggled the tail from side to side—an aerial bath. In early morning drinking and bathing were confined to adult males that came in with the throat sac deflated so that it swung loosely from side to side, accompanied by many white-headed immature birds. It appeared that the females then may have been on nest duty. The young birds appeared to bathe more than the adults and were less expert at it, as their breasts often were more deeply submerged. I saw one hit so hard that most of its body went into the water, and it struggled for 3 or 4 wing strokes before it was able to rise. On an earlier occasion on February 20, 1950, I recorded half a dozen drinking at a pool in the Río Chimán, about 12 kilometers inland from the sea at the mouth of the Río Curutú.

The habit of drinking and bathing in fresh water in this species of frigatebird has been noted in literature but seems to have attracted little attention. Bonhote (Ibis, 1903, p. 312) describes small parties that came daily to a fresh-water pond on Little Abaco in the Bahamas where the birds "splashed into the water like swallows." Gifford (Proc. California Acad. Sci., 1913, p. 100) speaks of their visiting the crater lake El Junco at 800 meters elevation on Isla San Cristobal (Chatham Island) in the Galápagos, and the same habit is mentioned by the Conways (The Enchanted Islands, 1948, pp. 164, 165-166) at an upland pond on Isla Santa María (or Floreana) in the same group. The bird on Guadeloupe Island in the West Indies that Noble (Bull. Mus. Comp. Zool., vol. 60, 1916,

p. 364) described as "over a fresh-water pond and diving at intervals for fish" without much doubt had come for water. In a recent observation at a dam on the Río Mulegé, Baja California, bathing without drinking in this species is described in some detail (Kielhorn, Norris, and Evans, Condor, vol. 65, no. 3, 1963 pp. 240-241).

The habit of visiting fresh-water ponds is recorded also for the related Pacific frigatebird *Fregata minor palmerstoni*, as Walter K. Fisher (Condor, vol. 6, no. 3, 1904, p. 60) observed them drinking at a small pond on Laysan Island, in the Hawaiian Bird Reservation.

Proposals to recognize three geographic races of this frigatebird have been based on supposed differences in size. Under this the typical form, alleged to be larger, with longer wing, has been restricted to the Galápagos Islands.

The birds of the Cape Verde Islands, ranging to western Africa have been named *Fregata magnificens lowei* by Bannerman, on the supposition that this population had a much larger bill; and the frigates nesting in the rest of their extensive range in the Atlantic area, including the Caribbean islands, and in the Pacific from Baja California to the coast of Ecuador have been separated by Mathews as *Fregata magnificens rothschildi* on the basis of supposed smaller size. In an extensive series of measurements that I have assembled the suggested differences do not hold, as birds with large and small wing and bill sizes are encountered at random through the entire geographic range. Measurements of birds from the west coast of America are listed above at the beginning of the account of this species. Comparable figures for specimens from the Caribbean area and the western Atlantic are as follows: Males (32 specimens), wing 583-648 (610), culmen from base 106.2-119.3 (111.8) mm. Females (15 specimens), wing 610-672 (636), culmen from base 118.5-132.2 (126.9) mm. Two males from Boa Vista, Cape Verde Islands (type locality of *lowei*) have the culmen 111.0 and 113.9 mm., and in one female this measurement is 129.0 mm. On this basis the species may not be divided with any probability of proper allocation of individuals found away from their breeding grounds.

[*Fregata minor ridgwayi* Mathews, the great frigatebird, which breeds in the Galápagos, and on Isla Cocos, far off the Pacific coast of Panamá, may reach Panamanian waters, though to date it has not been recorded. The adult male of this bird has the back glossy oil green, with a dark-brown band on the wing across the wing coverts. The female has the throat and foreneck whitish or ashy; and in the immature the light-colored head is washed prominently with rusty brown. In *Fregata magnificens,* common in Panamá, the male has a purplish sheen on the back and has no wing band; the female has the throat and foreneck blackish; and the immature has the head plain white. The two species are similar in size.]

Order CICONIIFORMES

Family ARDEIDAE: Herons; Garzas

The numerous species of herons, worldwide in distribution, agree in long legs and long necks, suitable for their type of life in haunts along shores and in shallow waters. They show much diversity in size, from the small least bitterns to the tall great blue and cocoi herons, and equally wide variation in color. Most of them are able to maintain themselves in settled regions, now that their plumage is no longer a commercial item. Only the tiger-bitterns disappear as human settlement increases.

KEY TO SPECIES OF ARDEIDAE

1. Bill longer, 125 mm. or more.. 2
   Bill shorter, not more than 100 mm.................................. 4
2. Larger birds, a meter or more in length, bill strong (genus *Ardea*).... 3
   Medium-sized birds, 750 mm. or less in length, bill very slender, about 150 mm. long......................Agami heron, *Agamia agami,* p. 95
3. Paler, whiter in general appearance; tibia white or gray.
   ....Cocoi heron, *Ardea cocoi,* p. 82
   Darker, decidedly grayer in general appearance; tibia chestnut or chestnut-brown..........................Great blue heron, *Ardea herodias,* p. 80
4. Mainly plain white, white tinged with buff, or white variegated with gray 5
   Definitely darker in color, uniformly dark slate, or with plumage of variegated pattern 9
5. Bill yellow 6
   Bill not yellow 7
6. Larger, length 850 mm. to a meter; pure white.
   ....Common egret, *Casmerodius albus egretta,* p. 88
   Smaller, length 460 to 560 mm., plain white, or with crown and breast buff (in breeding dress)................Cattle egret, *Bubulcus ibis ibis,* p. 93
7. Crown white, white variegated with gray, or slate gray, without elongated plumes 8
   Crown black, with elongated white plumes.
   ....Capped heron, *Philherodius pileatus,* p. 97
8. Bill and tarsi black, toes yellow; plumage entirely white.
   ....Snowy egret, *Egretta thula thula,* p. 89

Bill and tarsi greenish slate; white, with tips of primaries gray; or, in some, plumage variegated with white and gray.

Immature little blue heron, *Florida caerulea,* p. 91

9. Throat completely feathered 10
Throat wholly bare, or feathered only in the central line 19
10. Smaller, wing less than 185 mm.................................... 11
Larger, wing more than 225 mm.................................... 13
11. Coloration in general darker; decidedly larger, wing more than 150 mm. (genus *Butorides*) 12
Coloration in general paler, more buffy; decidedly smaller, wing 100 to 115 mm......................Least bittern, *Ixobrychus exilis,* p. 113
12. Sides of head and neck reddish brown.

Green heron, *Butorides virescens,* p. 83

Sides of head plain gray, or washed with light cinnamon brown.

Striated heron, *Butorides striatus,* p. 86

13. Coloration not predominantly light brown or buffy brown............ 14
Mainly light brown, buff, and buffy brown.

American bittern, *Botaurus lentiginosus,* p. 112

14. Plumage particolored, with variegated pattern...................... 15
Plumage dark throughout; grayish blue, with head and neck washed lightly with chestnut..............Adult little blue heron, *Florida caerulea,* p. 91
15. Body form more robust, bill shorter, 75 mm. long or less............. 16
Body form very slender, bill longer, 90 mm. or more; breast and abdomen white, foreneck slate-gray, or brownish red.

Tricolored heron, *Hydranassa tricolor ruficollis,* p. 92

16. Heavily streaked throughout 17
Without prominent streaks 18
17. Darker; bill more robust; under side of wing dark gray, with under wing coverts prominently streaked with white.

Immature yellow-crowned night heron, *Nyctanassa violacea,* p. 100

Paler; bill more slender toward tip; under side of wing light gray, with spotting on under wing coverts not prominent.

Immature black-crowned night heron, *Nycticorax nycticorax hoactli,* p. 99

18. Sides of head and throat black; breast gray.

Adult yellow-crowned night heron, *Nyctanassa violacea,* p. 100

Sides of head gray; throat and breast white.

Adult black-crowned night heron, *Nycticorax nycticorax hoactli,* p. 99

19. A line of feathers down center of throat, with an elongated bare space on either side 20
Throat completely bare.

Bare-throated tiger-bittern, *Heterocnus mexicanus,* p. 103

20. Tarsus longer, 92 to 115 mm.; bill more slender, with culmen nearly straight toward tip: Adult, with head and neck cinnamon, banded with black: Immature, cinnamon-buff, heavily banded with black; white of abdomen of less amount..Banded tiger-bittern, *Tigrisoma lineatum lineatum,* p. 106
Tarsus shorter, 81 to 91 mm.; bill heavier, with culmen more curved toward tip: Adult, with head and neck black, banded narrowly with cinnamon-buff: Immature, like *Tigrisoma l. lineatum,* but more extensively white on lower breast and abdomen.

Salmon's tiger-bittern, *Tigrisoma salmoni,* p. 109

ARDEA HERODIAS Linnaeus: Great Blue Heron; Garzón Cenizo

The common, widespread species of the two largest of the herons found in Panamá, marked by gray coloration.

Description.—A meter to a meter 3 centimeters in length. Adult, with throat and crown white, the latter bordered with black, and with an elongated crest; neck gray, streaked with black and white; gray above; streaked with black and white below; feathers of tibia rufous brown to light clay color.

Immature, duller in color, with crown black, without white head plumes.

The *garzón cenizo* is found in Panamá in fair numbers during the period of northern winter, and a few are present during the rest of the year. While the majority are northern migrants, some of the specimens available are separable, on the basis of darker dorsal coloration, as another subspecies, which is presumed to be resident, though there is no nesting colony known at present.

Great blue herons are wary birds that keep alert watch and only by chance allow close approach. When ponds formed during the rains begin to evaporate with the clear weather of the dry season, so that small fish are concentrated in shallows, a dozen or more of these herons may gather in fairly close proximity, but it is more usual to find solitary birds. Many of the migrant individuals that come in the period of northern winter appear to wander, while others find suitable habitat and remain in the same area for considerable periods of time.

ARDEA HERODIAS HERODIAS Linnaeus

Ardea Herodias Linnaeus, Syst. Nat., ed. 10, vol. 1, 1758, p. 143. (Northeastern Manitoba.)

Characters.—Lighter gray above.

Common visitor from the north. Present regularly from September to April throughout the lowlands around the larger streams and other bodies of fresh water, ranging inland in Chiriquí to 1,200 to 1,500 meters elevation near El Volcán and Boquete; found also along beaches and in mangroves in coastal areas, including the larger islands: Isla Coiba; Isla Taboga; Isla San José.

Measurements (from Oberholser, Proc. U. S. Nat. Mus., vol. 43, 1912, p. 535).—Males (10 specimens), wing 441-480 (462.7), tail 167-187 (176.6), exposed culmen 123-151.5 (139.5), tarsus 167-205 (183.6) mm.

Females (12 specimens), wing 433-471 (451.2), tail 159-184

(173.7), exposed culmen 127-146 (137), tarsus 157-194 (175.4) mm.
I collected an adult female at Jaqué, Darién, April 8, 1946. There are specimens in the Museum of Comparative Zoology taken in Bocas del Toro, on the Río Changuinola, October 30, 1927; in San Blas at Permé November 15 and 26, and December 9, 1929. (The record by Griscom (Bull. Mus. Comp. Zool., vol. 72, 1932, p. 310) of one from Obaldía apparently was in error, as there is no entry in the museum catalog of a bird from that locality.) Blake (Fieldiana: Zool., vol. 36, 1958, p. 505) reports one from over 1600 meters, above Boquete, November 19, 1946. Other definite records include one banded at Waseca, Minn., May 23, 1925, killed at Gatun, C.Z., the following September (Cooke, Auk, 1946, p. 254). Records during the period of northern winter on Isla Coiba, Isla Taboga, and Isla San José (in the Pearl Islands) probably are of this migrant race, (which may be expected on any of the islands of the Archipiélago de las Perlas).

ARDEA HERODIAS LESSONII Wagler

Ardea Lessonii Wagler, Isis, 1831, col. 531. (Valley of Mexico.)

Characters.—Darker gray above, similar to *A. h. herodias* in size.

Apparently resident, though no breeding records are known; found in small numbers.

Specimen records are as follows: Male, fully adult, in breeding dress, Fort San Lorenzo, Canal Zone, June 21, 1911, and female, immature dress, Río Matisnillo, near Paitilla Point, Panamá, January 20, 1912, E. A. Goldman; female immature, Jaqué, Darién, March 20, 1946, A. Wetmore; male immature, Laguna de Pita, Darién, about August 15, 1893 (Salvadori and Festa, Boll. Mus. Anat. Comp. Torino, no. 339, 1899, p. 11).

With regard to the specimen collected by Festa, preserved in the Instituto e Museo di Zoologia of the University of Torino, Miss Lucia Rossi writes me that the tibia is colored cinnamon-brown, indicating that the bird is of the species *herodias*. In *Ardea cocoi* this area is gray. From the data it is probable that the bird is of the present subspecies.

Other records of interest that may apply to this race are as follows: Imhof (MS. notes) recorded one on the Río Chagres, above Gamboa, June 9, and another near Panamá Viejo, June 20, 1942. Eisenmann (Wilson Bull. 1951, pp. 182, 183) reported birds regularly near the City of Panama between June 17 and July 16 from

1948 to 1950, and recorded others (Smith. Misc. Coll., vol. 117, no. 5, 1952, p. 11) seen occasionally at Barro Colorado Island, from May to August. In 1953 I recorded single birds on the Río San Pablo, below Soná, Veraguas, on June 2 and 11. As an earlier occurrence, in Culebra cut, on May 11, 1921, from a ship in transit through the Canal I saw an immature bird that seemed to be barely grown.

Hellmayr and Conover (Cat. Birds Amer., pt. 1, no. 2, 1948, p. 170) outline the belief held by a number of recent authors that there is no basis for recognition of a Central American race of this heron, but material in the U. S. National Museum, with some specimens seen elsewhere, uphold Oberholser (Proc. U. S. Nat. Mus., vol. 43, 1912, pp. 555-558) in recognition of such a subspecies. This is similar in size to *A. h. herodias* but is darker above in both adult and immature stages, though less sooty than *A. h. fannini*. Specimens of this type are known from southern México through Central America to Darién.

Oberholser has used Wagler's name *lessonii* for this bird, restricting the type locality to the Valley of México. Hellmayr says that the type, in the Munich Museum, is "indistinguishable, in color and size, from birds taken in the eastern United States." If further check upholds this statement a new name will need to be supplied.

Little is known at present of the breeding places of most of the herons of Panamá, though I have been told of heronries in the coastal swamps of Panamá province and Darién.

ARDEA COCOI Linnaeus: Cocoi Heron; Garzón Moreno

Ardea Cocoi Linnaeus, Syst. Nat., ed. 12, vol. 1, 1766, p. 237. (Cayenne.)

Generally similar to the great blue heron, but somewhat smaller and decidedly lighter colored. Feathers of tibia gray in adult and immature.

Description.—A meter to a meter $1\frac{1}{2}$ centimeters long. Adult, crown and sides of the head black, with a narrow median white crown stripe; neck white, with a few streaks of black in front; gray above; extensively black below, with white on breast, legs and under tail coverts.

Immature, white below, narrowly streaked with black.

Measurements.—Males (3 from Darién, Venezuela and Paraguay) wing 421-437 (427.3), tail 161-167 (163.6), culmen from base 129.0-145.2 (137.9), tarsus 170-210 (192) mm.

Females (4 from Colombia, Paraguay, and Argentina), wing 437-445 (440), tail 161-170 (165.5), culmen from base 128.5-148.7 (137.5), tarsus 179-192 (184.5) mm.

Resident. In the lower Río Tuira drainage in Darién; casual (two sight records) near La Jagua, eastern Panamá.

It is possible that Jewel in his account of the great blue heron in Panamá (Auk, 1913, p. 424) examined a bird of this species when he said "on June 9, 1912, a heron was shot on the Gatun River which is clearly another species or at least another form xxx a resident heron in Panama xxx slightly smaller without any rufous on the thighs." As this bird is not listed in the catalog of the Jewel collection in the Academy of Natural Sciences it apparently was not preserved.

The first definite record for the republic (Wetmore, Auk, 1951, p. 525) is of a bird that I saw March 30, 1949, at the Ciénaga Santo Domingo, in the savannas east of Pacora, Province of Panamá. It stood a short distance beyond gun range on an open flat, in company with a dozen great blue herons, some common egrets, and several wood ibises. I watched it for 15 minutes until a distant gunshot startled the group into flight. In February and March 1959 and in January 1964 I found the Cocoi heron so common on the lower tributaries of the main Río Tuira as to indicate a breeding colony somewhere in the great wooded swamps back of the coast, particularly since these birds remained in March after the great blue herons, found with them earlier, had gone in northward migration. A few ranged back along the Río Tuira to the Río Paya, where I secured an adult male March 12, 1959. I recorded them also along the Río Chucunaque to the region between the Tuquesa and Ucurgantí rivers.

As another casual record, on March 27, 1960, I found an adult at the edge of a small channel below the La Jagua Hunting Club and watched it several minutes at a distance of not more than 50 meters. Finally it flew and then began to call, a harsh note that resembled that of the great blue heron but somewhat higher in tone.

The male collected on March 12 on the Río Tuira is small, as indicated by the following measurements: Wing 424, tail 161, culmen from base 129, tarsus 169 mm.

BUTORIDES VIRESCENS (Linnaeus): Green Heron; Martinete

A small, dark-colored heron, with the sides of the neck brown.

Description.—380 to 560 mm. long. Adult, crown and crest black, washed with green; neck chestnut-brown, white in front; above dark greenish, with narrow white edgings in the wings; underparts gray.

Immature, browner, streaked below.

Green herons as a group are found world-wide in warm temperate and tropical areas, including islands in addition to widespread range over the continents.

The many subspecies that are recognized may be segregated in 3 major assemblages, one for Africa, Asia, Australia, and islands in the Indian and Pacific Oceans; one for North America, Central America, and the West Indies; and one for South America. These three, obviously closely related, form a superspecies that many taxonomists treat under one specific name, because of the general similarity found throughout the many forms.

While their close relationship is obvious, at the same time the populations of South America, and of the New World outside that continent, have certain characteristics that distinguish them from those of the Old World. Clearer understanding of them is attained by separating them as morphological entities under 2 specific names—*Butorides virescens* and *B. striatus*—rather than uniting all under one specific heading as *Butorides striatus*.

The *virescens* group is characterized by chestnut to bright rufous brown of the sides of the head and neck, and general darker color of the back, particularly in the adult. Three subspecies in this assemblage are recognized in Panamá.

These small herons are widely distributed wherever there is water, from sandy beaches where they take refuge in the bordering thickets and mangrove swamps, back along the rivers to the smaller tributaries. They watch for food along the water's edge, standing motionless or walking slowly and stealthily. Often they remain quiet except for an occasional downward jerk of the tail until closely approached, and then fly with protesting squawks, the most vociferous of the tropical herons. As small boats pass it is usual for them to climb back among the low branches of trees overhanging the water until they are securely hidden.

Locally they are often called *carga manteca;* on the Río Indio they were known as *coquito*.

BUTORIDES VIRESCENS VIRESCENS (Linnaeus)

Ardea virescens Linnaeus, Syst. Nat., ed. 10, vol. 1, 1758, p. 144. (South Carolina.)

Characters.—Sides of neck dark chestnut-brown; larger; wing, males 176-186 mm., females 172-186 mm. (maximum variation).

Measurements (taken from a small series of migrant birds from México and Panamá).—Males (5 specimens), wing 176-180 (179.1), tail 60.0-66.7 (62.0), culmen from base 58.2-63.8 (60.9), tarsus 50.5-56.0 (53.2) mm.

Females (5 specimens), wing 177-180 (178.7), tail 60.7-65.1 (62.8), culmen from base 59.0-63.0 (61.2), tarsus 51.0-53.5 (52.1) mm.

Common winter visitor from October to April, both on fresh water and along the coasts.

This race breeds from southern Ontario and southern Quebec, south through eastern United States to southern México. Dates of occurrence based on specimens range from September 8, 1932, at Puerto Obaldía, San Blas to April 9, 1911, near Tabernilla, Canal Zone, and May 16, 1927, at Zegla, mouth of Río Teribe, Bocas del Toro.

BUTORIDES VIRESCENS MACULATUS (Boddaert)

Cancroma maculata Boddaert, Tabl. Planch. Enl., 1783, p. 54. (Martinique.)

Neck chestnut-brown as in *B.v. virescens,* though sometimes paler; smaller; wing, males 154-172, females 156-170 mm. (maximum).

Measurements (taken from a small series from Panamá, Colombia, and Haiti).—Males (5 specimens), wing 154-172 (165.8), tail 49.8-62.5 (57.6), culmen from base 55.5-60.5 (58.2), tarsus 45.4-52.7 (49.0) mm.

Females (5 specimens), wing 157-168 (163.4), tail 54.2-60.0 (56.8), culmen from base 55.5-63.0 (58.8), tarsus 45.0-50.6 (48.3) mm.

Resident. Common except in the Archipiélago de las Perlas; most abundant from the provinces of Panamá and Colón westward, but ranging east to Darién, in the lower Río Tuira drainage (Yavisa near the mouth of the Río Chucunaque), and to Permé and Puerto Obaldía, San Blas, near the Colombian boundary. Around the Laguna de Chiriquí, Bocas del Toro, a melanistic phase predominates in which the birds vary from a deep chocolate-brown, that masks the other markings, to normal plumage. This dark phase extends north to Puerto Limón, Costa Rica, and a few of this style are recorded as far east as the eastern part of the Comarca de San Blas.

These smaller, resident birds seem less noisy on the whole than the northern migrants and tend more to skulk and hide rather than to fly for any distance.

On February 25, 1956, I found a nest in the ciénaga near the coast below Las Lajas, Chiriquí, placed in an open-branched bush at an elevation of a meter above the water. The structure, built of twigs, was more substantial than usual among herons. The broad depression in the center held three eggs with incubation begun. These are pale Niagara green, elliptical in form, and measure 37.1×29.0, 37.2×29.3 and 37.5×29.2 mm.

BUTORIDES VIRESCENS MARGARITOPHILUS Oberholser

Butorides virescens margaritophilus Oberholser, Proc. U. S. Nat. Mus., vol 42, Aug. 29, 1912, p. 553. (San Miguel Island = Isla del Rey, Archipiélago de las Perlas, Panamá.)

Similar in size to *maculatus*, but with lower breast and abdomen darker.

Measurements.—Males (3 specimens), wing 161-170 (165.3), tail 51.8-59.5 (55.4), culmen from base 57.6-61.8 (59.8), tarsus 46.7-48.3 (47.6) mm.

Females (3 specimens), wing 162-166 (163.3), tail 57.1-62.7 (59.0), culmen from base 53.8-58.5 (56.4), tarsus 44.0-47.7 (45.6) mm.

Resident in the Archipiélago de las Perlas: Recorded, from specimens identified, on Chapera, Rey, and San José islands: Nest reported on Isla del Rey March 5, 1904 (Thayer and Bangs, Bull. Mus. Comp. Zool., vol. 46, 1905, p. 142).

This race, restricted to the Pearl Islands, is found mainly around the mangrove swamps, where it may seem fairly common, but actually has only a small population because of the limited area of its habitat.

BUTORIDES STRIATUS STRIATUS (Linnaeus): Striated Heron; Chicuaco

Ardea striata Linnaeus, Syst. Nat., ed. 10, vol. 1, 1758, p. 144. (Surinam.)

Butorides striatus patens Griscom, Bull. Mus. Comp. Zoöl., vol. 69, Apr. 1929, p. 156. (Near Panama City, Panamá.)

Like the green heron, but sides of head and neck gray or buff.

Description.—The *striatus* group of South America that ranges into eastern Panamá is marked from the more northern *virescens* of the New World by gray on the sides of the head and neck (a color difference readily seen in life) and by lighter, more grayish green on the back in the adult. In those that have the sides of the neck buff, this color is much paler than the brown found in the forms of *virescens*. The wing length is similar to that of *Butorides virescens maculatus*.

In the immature birds the sides of the head and neck are grayish brown, with a wash of clay color in some individuals.

Measurements.—Males (20 specimens from Panamá), wing 162-173 (168), tail 55.0-64.5 (59.0), culmen from base 53.3-66.2 (60.6), tarsus 44.0-51.6 (48.4) mm.

Females (9 specimens from Panamá), wing 157-169 (161), tail 51.8-59.7 (56.4), culmen from base 57.1-62.8 (59.5), tarsus 44.7-50.0 (47.7) mm.

Resident. Common throughout Darién, ranging west to the eastern side of the Azuero Peninsula, and to western Colón. One record for Puerto Obaldía, San Blas.

Typical gray-necked adult specimens come from near Yavisa on the lower Río Chucunaque, mouth of the Río Paya on the middle Tuira, and Jaqué; also one from Chilar on the Río Indio, western Colón. I have sight records for the Río Chucunaque, from the mouth of the river upstream to the Río Ucurgantí; on the Río Pequení above Madden Lake; in the marshes at La Jagua, in eastern Panamá Province; and at Juan Mina, Canal Zone, on the Río Chagres.

While the only record for the Comarca de San Blas is an immature female in the Brandt collection at the University of Cincinnati, taken by Wedel at Puerto Obaldía, July 3, 1932, there is no reason to suppose that it does not occur in that area regularly, as it is found at Acandí, Chocó, immediately adjacent on the Colombian side of the boundary.

The many records available for the *patens* style of coloration in which the side of the head and neck are buff, include the following: Several from the Province of Herrera on the eastern side of the Azuero Peninsula; one from Guánico Arriba in southwestern Los Santos; Chilar, western Colón; Barro Colorado Island, and Juan Mina, Canal Zone; La Jagua Hunting Club near Chico and Charco del Toro, eastern Province of Panamá; and Jaqué and the Río Jaqué, Darién.

In work on Barro Colorado Island, Van Tyne (Occ. Pap. Mus. Zool. Michigan, no. 525, 1950, pp. 5-6) noted that the breeding season may be either somewhat irregular or of long duration. A male collected on March 7, 1926, had completed the breeding cycle and was in postnuptial molt. Another shot April 11, 1927, was breeding, and a nest with 2 eggs was found July 28, 1925. On August 11 two partly grown young were taken from another nest. The nest with eggs was located "on an isolated stump off the south shore of the island." Other nests on Barro Colorado on March 24 with 3 eggs, and April 28, 1935, with 2 eggs, are recorded by Chapman (Life in an Air Castle, 1938, p. 226). The eggs in color and size resemble those of the resident form of the green heron.

Griscom believed that the herons of this group that he described as *patens* had the legs more brightly colored than in the other species of green heron, but Van Tyne found that this was not true in the specimens that he handled.

Throughout the entire range of *Butorides striatus* from Colombia and Venezuela south to Brazil and Paraguay occasional individuals have a brownish wash, varying from a trace of pinkish buff to vinaceous-buff, over the gray of the head and neck, sometimes also a greater amount of cinnamon to clay color streaking on the lower foreneck and upper breast. A similar type of coloration is prevalent on Isla Margarita off northeastern Venezuela where, as it is coupled with average smaller size, it is recognized as a distinct subspecies, *Butorides striatus robinsoni* Richmond. The brownish coloration in birds of the *striatus* group, as noted, is common in Panamá, west to the eastern side of the Azuero Peninsula on the Pacific slope, and to the lower Río Indio (Chilar) west of the Canal Zone, on the Caribbean side. These birds, separated as *Butorides striatus patens* by Griscom, might be considered a connecting link with the dark, rufescent, brown-necked *virescens* group, since they are found with typical *B.v. maculatus,* and equally typical *B.s. striatus,* if birds exactly like them did not appear at random through the entire South American range of *striatus*. While there may be occasional mixed mating among those herons when they range together, this would not explain the occurrence of the *patens* style of coloration in South America in areas where the *virescens* type does not occur. The supposed race *patens* is regarded therefore as individual variation in typical *Butorides s. striatus.*

CASMERODIUS ALBUS EGRETTA (Gmelin): Common Egret; Garza Blanca

Ardea Egretta Gmelin, Syst. Nat., vol. 1, pt. 2, 1789, p. 629. (Cayenne.)

Definitely larger than any of the other herons of white plumage, with yellow bill, black legs and feet.

Description.—Length 800 mm. to a little more than a meter. Adult, pure white with long crest and dorsal plumes in nesting season.

Measurements.—Males (5 adults, from Florida, Colombia and Paraguay), wing 372-397 (386), tail 146-154 (148), culmen from base 116.5-120.2 (118.2), tarsus 157-175 (166) mm.

Females (5 adults, from Kentucky, North Carolina, Cuba, Colombia, and Paraguay) wing 355-365 (360), tail 137-143 (140), culmen from base 98.7-109.5 (104.3), tarsus 127-147 (138) mm.

Resident in part, and in part a winter visitor from the north. Common along the coasts, and, in the lowlands, inland along open bodies of water; ranging to the smallest offshore islands.

There are records of two banded in Mississippi, one taken near Soná, and the other near Puerto Aguadulce.

In the Archipiélago de las Perlas these herons are common along the shores, where their white plumage stands out in pleasing contrast to the dark rocks on which they rest. They make long flights regularly over the open sea. Robins (Condor, 1958, p. 302) reported one 18 miles south of Taboga, apparently crossing from the Perlas group, and Murphy (Vert. SCOPE, 1956, p. 135) records one on an evidently longer journey 90 miles south of Punta Mala.

In Panamá, as elsewhere, this egret was more abundant in early days, as Rendahl (Ark. Zool., Bd. 12, 1919, p. 6; idem, Bd. 13,1920, p. 13) recorded great flocks seen in 1882 by Dr. C. Bovallius near the Río Pacora, on Isla Chepillo, and on Isla Bayoneta. They are still common, as flocks of two hundred or more may congregate on open lagoons, though it is more usual to see single birds, or two or three in company. In wet pasture lands they are seen regularly around cattle.

Though these herons evidently nest in scattered groups along the coasts, the only colony of record is one on Isla Changamé, off Batele Point west of the Pacific entrance of the Panama Canal. Here on February 15, 1941, Maj. Gen. G. Ralph Meyer found several nests located about 2 meters from the ground, in stands of mangroves and clumps of cactus. The herons had constructed platforms of weed stems 300 to 350 mm. in diameter, loosely placed in the usual style of this family of birds, with a slight depression to hold the eggs. Incubation had begun in two sets of 3 eggs each. He took another set of 2 eggs, with incubation begun, here on February 23, 1941, and on February 15, 1942, one set of 2 eggs, and two of 3 each, with incubation well started. These eggs vary from subelliptical to long elliptical in form, and from Court gray to slightly paler in color. The range of measurement in 11 eggs (4 sets) collected on Changamé is as follows: Length 52.4 to 56.8; breadth 37.1 to 40.0; with an average of 54.6 × 38.9 mm.

EGRETTA THULA THULA (Molina): Snowy Egret; Garceta Blanca

Ardea Thula Molina, Sagg. Stor. Nat. Chili, 1782, p. 235. (Chile.)

This species and the little blue heron in white plumage are similar in size and general appearance, but may be identified in life by differences listed in color of the bill, tarsi and feet.

Description.—Length, 510 to 610 mm.; entire plumage pure white; bill and tarsus black, feet yellow.

Measurements.—Males (6 adults, from Florida, Panamá, Colombia, Venezuela), wing 247-270 (255), tail 86.3-100.0 (90.8), culmen from base 76.6-83.8 (80.2), tarsus 88.5-102.0 (96.5) mm.

Females (7 from Cuba, Haiti, Puerto Rico, Nicaragua, and Panamá), wing 237-257 (241), tail 81.0-92.9 (86.5), culmen from base 76.6-81.8 (77.7), tarsus 88.5-101.0 (93.6) mm.

Resident in part, and in part a winter visitor from the north. Common in the lowlands wherever there is water, from the coastal beaches and mud flats inland, in open marshy areas, and along the larger streams; casual in the lower levels of the subtropical zone, as at the Lagunas de Volcán (elevation 1,280 meters) in western Chiriquí. I found them on Isla Coiba, and Rendahl (Ark. Zool., Bd. 13, 1920, p. 13) records one taken by Bovallius on Isla Casaya (the only record for the Pearl Islands), but they seem less accustomed to wander from the mainland than the little blue heron.

There is record of one banded in Louisiana, and taken subsequently near the mouth of the Río Bayano, and of another marked in Mississippi recovered subsequently at La Jagua.

The snowy egret is less numerous than the little blue heron but is found regularly in suitable haunts, often feeding alone, occasionally in scattered groups of a dozen. However, in February and March 1948, in the coastal region of Herrera, the egret was more common than the little blue heron.

Their usual method of feeding is that common to the family of standing or walking slowly while watching the water or ground attentively. I have seen them occasionally feeding in the wash of waves on the beaches, and once on the Río Chagres near Juan Mina, where schools of minnows rested at the surface in the warm sun of early morning, I saw an egret in flight just above the surface strike repeatedly at the fish. This interesting method appeared successful, as I noted that the heron swallowed after some of its strikes.

In March and April many have the beautiful long plumes on the crown, back, and upper breast that mark the breeding plumage. It is certain that they nest in the republic, though the only definite record at present is a set of 2 eggs collected May 10, 1941, by Maj. Gen. G. Ralph Meyer on Isla Changamé off the Pacific entrance of the Panama Canal. The nest was a shallow platform of twigs placed in a low tree. The eggs, slightly elongated elliptical in shape, in color paler than pearl gray, measure 38.4 × 31.5 and 39.2 × 31.0 mm. Incubation was far advanced. March 28, 1946, I shot a male at Jaqué, Darién, in full breeding plumage, and March 6, 1955, I watched a pair in mating display at the mouth of the Río Chico, which would indicate nesting in those areas.

There is no definite indication that migrants of the subspecies *Egretta t. brewsteri* from western United States, reach Panamá during the winter season. This differs from the typical form in slightly larger size. The specimens I have handled all belong to the typical subspecies.

The genus *Leucophoyx* in which this species has been placed in earlier accounts is not now recognized as distinct from *Egretta*.

FLORIDA CAERULEA (Linnaeus): Little Blue Heron; Garceta Azul (adults), Garceta Blanca (immature birds)

Ardea caerulea Linnaeus, Syst. Nat., ed. 10, vol. 1, 1758, p. 143. (South Carolina.)

A heron of medium size; adult, dark bluish slate; immature, white, sometimes with a mixture of dark gray; bill and legs greenish, which distinguishes them from the snowy egret of similar size.

Description.—Length 510 to 635 mm. Adult, with a reddish-brown wash on head, neck, and upper breast.

Immature, with concealed gray tips on the ends of the primaries.

Measurements.—Males (18 from southeastern United States), wing 255-268 (261), tail 89.3-99.8 (95.7), culmen from base 71.1-82.2 (75.9), tarsus 90.7-102.9 (96.2) mm.

Females (12 from southeastern United States), wing 242-259 (250), tail 84.3-95.2 (91.1), culmen from base 65.4-77.2 (72.4, average of 11), tarsus 80.0-95.7 (88.1) mm.

Common in the lowlands; ranging inland along streams, and, in flooded areas, in open country; at times in dry savannas and pastures; wandering regularly to 1,400 meters or higher in the subtropical zone. Recorded on Isla Coiba and throughout the islands in the Gulf of Panamá.

This heron is most common through the period of northern winter, with abrupt decrease in number in March, so that it is present in lesser abundance from April to October. To date there are no nesting records, and most of the summer individuals seen are in the white immature dress. In fact, birds in this plumage predominate in number throughout the year. There are records of 6 banded in Oklahoma, Mississippi and Florida, and taken subsequently in Panamá, all at Pacific localities near Pedregal, Puerto Aguadulce, Panama City, and

La Jagua. Country people in some sections have a superstition regarding these and some related herons as they say that no one has seen their nests.

While these herons are most abundant on the coastal plain they penetrate into the foothills along the larger streams, even where river currents are fairly rapid. In the Azuero Peninsula in dry season scattered birds range inland along the smallest quebradas, though drought may reduce the water to occasional pools along otherwise dry creek beds, as here small fish are secured with ease. Groups of 15 or 20 sometimes spread along sandy beaches to feed on the abundant mole crabs in the wash of the surf. As each wave recedes the herons run or fly following the water, to snatch at the active crustaceans. When the wash returns the birds come back slowly if the water does not touch their bodies, but fly when the waves rise suddenly. In such activities they suggest huge sandpipers.

It is usual for small groups to gather at night to roost together in some isolated clump of mangroves, or on a small tree or snag standing in water. Such sleeping places may be occupied regularly, and on larger bodies of water flights to them may be noted each evening.

The trematodes *Apharyngostrigea ibis* and *Lypersomum sinuosum*, species described originally from the cattle egret *Bubulcus ibis ibis*, are reported by Caballero and Hidalgo (Rev. Soc. Mex. Hist. Nat., vol. 16, 1955, pp. 29-34) from the intestine of a little blue heron shot at Panamá Viejo, February 21, 1954.

HYDRANASSA TRICOLOR RUFICOLLIS (Gosse): Tricolored Heron; Garza Pechiblanca

Egretta ruficollis Gosse, Birds Jamaica, 1847, p. 338. (Burnt Savanna River, Jamaica.)

A very slender heron, with the lower breast and abdomen white in contrast with darker colors elsewhere.

Description.—Length 560 to 660 mm., with slender neck and body, and long, thin bill. Adult, dark slate gray above and on sides of the neck; lower back and rump white; white below, with foreneck and upper breast streaked with chestnut brown and blackish slate.

Immature, gray on sides of breast and upper surface, with the neck, wing coverts, and back reddish brown.

Measurements—Males (8 from Florida, Cuba, Jamaica and Hispaniola), wing 248-259 (253), tail 81.8-91.8 (87.0), culmen from base 93.8-103.8 (97.5), tarsus 92.0-103.2 (99.2) mm.

Females (7 from Florida, Cuba and Panamá), wing 237-249 (241), tail 78.4-82.8 (80.6), culmen from base 87.0-98.4 (93.7), tarsus 85.5-99.0 (90.8) mm.

Resident in part, and in part a winter visitor from the north. Fairly common in lowland areas, along the lower courses of rivers, and in marshes; seen at the highland lakes near El Volcán, Chiriquí; one specimen in the British Museum (Natural History) taken on Isla del Rey June 26, 1924, by naturalists on the St. George Expedition; one seen on Isleta Málaga, January 29, 1960.

There is record of one banded in South Carolina and taken subsequently on the lower Río Tuira.

In the main these slender herons are solitary, feeding somewhat apart from other species. They are patient fishermen, that stand quietly, or walk stealthily in search of prey, though occasionally I have seen one seize a minnow with a quick dart of the long bill, when the bird was flying low over shallow water.

Though no breeding colonies are on record as yet, it appears certain that they nest in Panamá. Festa collected one on the Río Sabana, Darién, in July 1895. An adult male in full breeding plumage in the collection of the Gorgas Memorial Laboratory was taken on the canal at Boca del Drago, Bocas del Toro, on June 3, 1962. On December 17, 1955, at Juan Mina, Canal Zone, I watched an immature bird, barely grown, fishing about the dock. This bird was completely fearless as it was often within 10 meters of me, in contrast to the wariness of older individuals. It is probable that northern winter migrants come to the Caribbean coast, for in 1958 during the first week in February there was a sudden decrease in their number around Almirante Bay, an indication that part of those observed earlier had begun their return northward.

BUBULCUS IBIS IBIS (Linnaeus): Cattle Egret; Garcilla Bueyera

Ardea Ibis Linnaeus, Syst. Nat., ed. 10, vol. 1, 1758, p. 144. (Egypt.)

Smallest of the white herons found in Panamá, marked from the other small species by the yellow (in breeding season reddish) bill.

Description.—Length 460 to 560 mm. Plumage white, with buff on the crown, more extensive during the breeding season, and found then also on the back and the breast.

Iris yellow; bill yellow; legs dull greenish. In nesting season the bill becomes reddish at the base, and the tarsi also are dull reddish.

Measurements of two taken at La Jagua are as follows: Male, wing 238, tail 86, culmen from base 60.7, tarsus 79.2 mm.

Female, wing 227, tail 83, culmen from base 54.7, tarsus 72.6 mm.

Resident. A recent addition to the avifauna that has increased steadily in number since it was first recorded.

This is a species of the Old World established by unknown means in eastern South America (first recorded in Surinam) that has increased and spread widely in recent years through that continent and northward into the eastern United States. It was first reported for Panamá on August 14, 1954, when Dr. Eugene Eisenmann and Maj. Francis Chapelle saw two at the Mindi dairy, between Fort Davis and Gatun, Canal Zone. Three were observed by Chapelle near María Chiquita, Colón, August 21, and others at the Mindi locality in October, to the number of 14 on October 30 (Eisenmann, Auk, 1955, p. 426). David Fairchild II wrote me at this same period of one seen September 13, 1954, in the eastern suburbs of Panama City. And Karl Curtis sent word of a hundred or so on November 14 walking among the cattle on the savanna at the La Jagua Hunting Club. A local hunter, Baldomiro Moreno, who has worked with me in this region for years, from this date in November found them common near La Jagua each year through the period of rains, but absent during the dry season.

On February 22, 1956, I noted 6 of these egrets near Las Lajas in eastern Chiriquí among cattle in the shallow water of a flooded ciénaga, and saw 2 more on February 24. These were too wild to approach. I saw one at La Jagua on February 22, 1957, and finally on March 20, 1958, Baldomiro and I shot two there, the first specimens of record for the republic. These were nonbreeding birds taken from two flocks of about 25 each that fed among cattle. On March 15, 1958, I saw one in a wet meadow near Antón, Coclé. The following year I recorded the cattle egret on January 31 near Juan Mina, C.Z., and March 19 at El Salto, on the Río Chucunaque, above Yavisa, Darién. I noted half a dozen on April 11 at La Jagua and was told that there were then many through the year. In 1960 on March 23 we recorded one near San Félix, eastern Chiriquí, and 3 near Puerto Vidal, Veraguas. At La Jagua I found about 100 on the marsh on March 27. Charles O. Handley, Jr., recorded one February 29, near Changuinola, Bocas del Toro. On January 9, 1961, four rested in a bush overhanging the Chagres, near Juan Mina. And on January 21, 1962, I saw one with cattle near Guánico Arriba in southern Los Santos.

These early records are given in detail, because of the interest attendant on the increase of the species. It is obvious that the cattle egret now is spread throughout the lowlands of the entire republic. In 1964 hundreds ranged with the herds of cattle along the Río Tuira in the lowlands of Darién near La Palma and El Real. In 1965 it was present in equal number near El Volcán in western Chiriquí. I have identified the head of an immature individual, only recently from the nest, collected in October 1961 at Almirante, Bocas del Toro, for Dr. Conrad Yunkers of the Middle America Research Unit. An adult taken at the same time had the buff of the breeding season on the crown. It is probable that this species, in common with its habit elsewhere, will join nesting colonies of other herons.

These birds often perch on the heads or backs of the cattle among which they feed. The yellow bill marks them instantly from the other herons of similar size.

Some ornithologists have placed the cattle egret under the genus *Ardeola* Boie, type *Ardea ralloides* Scopoli, to which superficially it appears similar. It is found however that the dorsal plumes of the species *ibis* in the adult are hairlike and that the immature is plain white. In *Ardeola* the dorsal plumes have barbs extending nearly to the tips, and the neck and upper breast in the immature are heavily streaked. Differences in the skeleton are of greater importance; e.g., the entire leg in *Ardeola* is much shorter, but the femur and the fibula equal those of the longer-legged *Bubulcus*. The spina externa is very much heavier, though the entire sternum is shorter. Though the humerus in *Ardeola* is definitely shorter, the brachialis anticus depression is larger, and the crista superior reduced. In the skull the anterior part of the palatines is broader. These are part of the differences which in sum maintain the two in separate genera.

AGAMIA AGAMI (Gmelin): Agamí Heron; Garza Pechicastaña
Figure 15

Ardea Agami Gmelin, Syst. Nat., vol. 1, pt. 2, 1789, p. 629. (Cayenne.)

In any plumage known by the elongated, narrow bill, 125 to more than 160 mm. in length.

Description.—Length 660 to 760 mm. Adult, dark glossy green above; deep chestnut-brown below, including sides of neck; sides of head and hindneck black; lower foreneck, and pointed nuchal crest, light bluish gray. In breeding season the ribbonlike feathers of the crest reach a length of 125 mm., and broad ornamental plumes grow from the lower back.

Immature, deep brown above; blackish on crown and back; streaked buff, white, and black below.

Iris light reddish brown; eyelids, and a narrow border around base of mandible, yellow; loral area, and bare space around eye, yellowish green; side of maxilla and mandible, except tip, light blue; ridge of maxilla and tip of mandible black; crus, tarsus, and toes yellow; claws black.

Measurements.—Males (8 specimens), wing 255-272 (265.5), tail 92.5-102.5 (97.4), culmen from base 146.2-163 (153.2), tarsus 94.4-110.8 (105.9) mm.

Females (7 specimens), wing 249-262 (256.7), tail 85.8-98.2 (91.7), culmen from base 125.5-146.8 (136.8), tarsus 83.0-103.0 (93.6) mm.

Fig. 15.—Agami heron, garza pechicastaña, *Agamia agami*.

Resident. Rare, in heavy forest in the Tropical Zone. Records are as follows: Veraguas, taken by Enrique Arcé (Sharpe, Cat. Birds Brit. Mus., vol. 26, 1898, p. 136). Bocas del Toro: Adult, in Gorgas Memorial Laboratory collection, taken on Channel 2, Boca del Drago, June 3, 1962. Canal Zone: Estero west of Salud Point, Barro Colorado Island, seen by Skutch, May 10, 1935; Chiva Chiva, specimen, June 13, 1955; Juan Mina, specimens, January 12, 1949, January 12, 1953. Province of Panamá: Río La Jagua, specimen, February 9, 1951; upper Río Pacora, at 100 meters elevation on the west base of Cerro Azul, specimen, March 28, 1911; Chimán, sight record, March

6, 1927 (L. Griscom); Quebrada Cauchero at 150 meters elevation on Cerro Chucantí, March 8, 1950 sight record. Darién: Mouth of Río Sambú, sight record, February 24, 1927, (L. Griscom); mouth of Río Paya, on the Río Tuira, February 10, 1959, and mouth of Río Tuquesa, on the Río Chucunaque, March 24, 1954, sight records; Río Jaqué, at the mouth of Río Imamadó, April 16, 1947, specimen; Isla del Rey, Archipiélago de las Perlas, May 8, 1900, specimen (Bangs, Auk, 1901, p. 25).

The bird from Cerro Azul, an immature taken by Goldman, was shot at the edge of a stream. The river at that point flowed with considerable fall over a rocky bed through heavy forest where the trees overhung the water. On the Río Jaqué in 1947, rains had formed a narrow, shallow pool in heavy forest along the base of a hill opposite our camp. As I came to this in early morning a dark bird moved on a log resting in the water, and then flew up into the branches. When it flew again I fired, and it fell to the ground amid a cloud of leaves cut by the shot. Its dark colors blended so perfectly with the somber shadows in which I had found it that it seemed truly a bird of the forest, one of the most beautiful and unusual of its family that I have seen. In subsequent encounters I found the haunts just described typical of those sought by this interesting species, a solitary bird whose habits are little known.

Michener (Condor, 1964, p. 77) recorded a colony of a dozen nests in a swamp near Minatitlán, southern Veracruz "built of twigs about 4 to 6 feet above the water level, with water 3 to 4 feet deep." He mentions fresh eggs but gives no further description. An egg in the Museum of Comparative Zoology from the T. M. Brewer collection, labeled "Amazon 1849 Edwards," subelliptical in form, is very pale dull glaucous-blue. It measures 55.8 × 39.5 mm., the length being subject possibly to a minor correction of a fraction of a millimeter as the specimen was end-blown. Schönwetter (Handb. Ool., pt. 2, 1960, p. 92) does not mention color but gives measurements of two eggs as follows: 48.6 × 34.1, and 52 × 38 mm.

PILHERODIUS PILEATUS (Boddaert): Capped Heron; Garza Real

Ardea pileata Boddaert, Table Planch. Enlum., 1783, p. 54. (Cayenne.)

White, with a distinct black crown.

Description.—Length 510 to 590 mm.; adult, white, with back and wings light gray; crown black, except the forehead, which is white; 4 or 5 slender white nuchal plumes that when fully grown are 200 to

230 mm. long. In breeding season the breast, hindneck, and under surface of the wings are light cream-buff.

Immature, paler gray above, so that the bird appears white above and below; nuchal plumes shorter.

Iris yellow; bare space around eye and lores light blue; bill bluish neutral gray, somewhat darker at base, and yellowish white at tip; tarsi and toes bluish neutral gray; claws darker.

Measurements.—Males (6 from Panamá and northern Colombia), wing 267-280 (271), tail 96.0-103.5 (99.1), culmen from base 75.8-81.7 (79.7), tarsus 92.6-98.7 (96.0) mm.

Females (5 from Panamá and northern Colombia), wing 263-274 (269), tail 95.5-101.4 (98.5), culmen from base 76.0-93.0 (82.1), tarsus 92.1-94.8 (93.5) mm.

Resident. Rare; now found mainly in Darién.

Lawrence (Ann. Lyc. Nat. Hist. New York, 1861, p. 301) received one from McLeannan that is listed as taken on the Atlantic slope of the Canal Zone. Collectors for the Malaria Control Service secured an adult female in the Tocumen swamps, east of Panama City, on October 6, 1953; and there is a male in the Havemeyer Collection, in the Peabody Museum at Yale, taken at San Antonio, on the lower Río Bayano, February 23, 1927. Other records are from Darién, mainly on the Río Chucunaque, except for one bird collected April 6, 1922, on the Río Jesús, a tributary of the Sambú (Bangs and Barbour, Bull. Mus. Comp. Zool., vol. 65, 1922, p. 193). The anthropologist J. L. Baer secured 3 near the mouth of the Río Tuquesa, on the Río Chucunaque, March 4 and 5, 1924. In this same region I saw several between March 21 and April 1, 1959, and secured 2 specimens on March 22. One early morning as I moved rapidly on the river in a motor-powered piragua one scrambled up the steep river bank and disappeared in the brush. A few days later I saw one feeding at a heavily shaded forest pool, where it posed with outstretched neck, a strikingly beautiful bird.

Two immature individuals were brought to me, caught alive by country men, who described them as tame and unafraid. In these the tarsi were not quite fully formed, and the primaries were still in growth, so that it is interesting to note that they have the color pattern of adults, including slender nuchal plumes, these being 90 mm. long in one and 115 mm. in the other. The back and wings are paler gray, and the forepart of the body is plain white, without the buff found in breeding adults.

Schomburgk (Fauna Flora Brit. Guiana, 1848, p. 754) says that the nest is built in low trees, and that the bird lays two eggs, but gives no other details.

While this species appears related to the black-crowned night herons, which it resembles in the form of the nuchal plumes, it differs definitely in lack of a well defined immature plumage.

NYCTICORAX NYCTICORAX HOACTLI (Gmelin): Black-crowned Night Heron; Zorro de Agua

Ardea Hoactli Gmelin, Syst. Nat., vol. 1, pt. 2, 1789, p. 630. (Valley of México.)

Adult, crown and back greenish black, white below. Bill more slender than in the yellow-crowned night heron.

Description.—Length 560 to 660 mm. Adult, back and crown glossy greenish black, except forehead and line above eye which are white; wings and tail gray; neck pale gray; below white; two slender, white nuchal plumes, that reach a length of more than 200 mm. in breeding season.

Immature, above grayish brown, streaked heavily with white; below white, streaked heavily with grayish brown, except on the throat and abdomen. Second-year birds are plain gray above, unstreaked.

Measurements.—Males (5 from United States, Panamá, Colombia, and Venezuela), wing 290-307 (298), tail 110.0-117.6 (114.3), culmen from base 70.8-74.3 (72.5), tarsus 71.8-86.5 (78.9) mm.

Females (5 from United States and Colombia), wing 290-298 (293), tail 108.2-114.5 (110.9), culmen from base 70.3-74.6 (73.7), tarsus 74.8-84.8 (81.7) mm.

Resident, and in part a winter visitor from the north. Fairly common in the coastal lowlands.

This night heron was found by Maj. Gen. G. Ralph Meyer on Farallón Rock, off Isla Taboguilla, where there were large young on April 9, 1944; and on Isla Changamé March 16, 1941. I recorded it in the Perlas group on Isla San José, February 21, 1944, and at Isleta Málaga, January 29, 1960. About 30 were seen in the low brush on the summit of Isla Villa, off the coast of Los Santos, February 28, 1957. One in the British Museum was taken on Isla Taboga on September 24, 1924.

There is record of one banded in Michigan, June 26, 1941, that was shot near Río Hato in June 1949.

These herons in the main are nocturnal and during the day remain in dense tree tops in wooded swamps, tall mangroves, or along the lower courses of rivers, and so it is only casually that one is seen as it takes flight heavily when alarmed by human intrusion. From sunset to dark they range out to feed, and I have often recorded them by their harsh calls as, hidden by the darkened sky, they flew past my camp. The note is an explosive *quok,* heronlike in sound, but sufficiently different from others of the family to identify the species.

It is probable that the colony on Isla Villa was on its nesting ground. I believed also that those seen in March 1957, in company with boat-billed herons, on the lower Río Caldera, back of Punta Mala were nesting, and there must be colonies in the swamps at La Jagua from the numbers that are found there. Nests seen on San José Rock, off Naos Island, March 21, 1915, attributed questionably to this species (Hallinan, 1924, p. 308) from the locality more probably were those of the yellow-crowned night heron. The eggs are similar to those of that species. In Darién this species has the same name as the yellowcrown, *huraña,* because of its secretive habits. Near Pacora they were called *chala,* of uncertain meaning but possibly derived from the greenish-black back, in form like a dark-colored chal, or kerchief, often worn by women across the shoulders.

NYCTANASSA VIOLACEA (Linnaeus): Yellow-crowned Night Heron; Huraña

Crown and a streak under eye white, with rest of side of head and throat black; gray underneath in adult; bill strong and heavy.

Description.—Length 510 to 610 mm. Adult, gray, heavily streaked with black above, and indistinctly with whitish on abdomen; side of head and throat black; crown, including the 100 to 150 mm. long nuchal plumes, and streak on the side of head, white.

Immature, brownish gray above and on neck; spotted with buffy white on back and wings; heavily streaked with buffy white on neck; whiter below, heavily streaked with brownish gray, including the throat and abdomen.

The adult has long dorsal plumes extending beyond the tail that are lacking in the black-crowned night heron. There are differences in the skeleton that serve to maintain the two in separate genera.

The *huraña* is found mainly in swampy woodlands in the lowlands, including the taller stands of mangroves, on both sides of the isthmus, and in addition is spread widely through the islands in the Gulf of Panamá. It also reaches Isla Coiba. While the yellowcrown ranges along the larger streams, the majority do not go inland much beyond the head of tidewater, since this is the usual limit of the wet forest that is their haunt. Within these areas they are fairly common, though it is impracticable to judge their number accurately because of difficulty in penetrating their swampy haunts. While they feed at night, they are less nocturnal than the black-crowned night heron as it is common to see them during morning and evening on the seashore, both on rocky headlands, and on mudflats and beaches made bare by ebbing tide. They also are more prone to rest in open trees.

The voice, usually heard as birds pass after dark, is similar to that of the other species but higher in pitch.

Six subspecies are recognized currently in the extensive range of the species from northwestern México and southeastern United States south through Central America and the West Indies to northern and eastern South America. Three of these have been recorded from Panamá, one of them as a migrant wanderer. A second enters the upper Tuira valley from Colombia, and the third is resident along the coasts of the republic.

NYCTANASSA VIOLACEA VIOLACEA (Linnaeus)

Ardea violacea Linnaeus, Syst. Nat., ed. 10, vol. 1, 1758, p. 143. (South Carolina.)

Characters.—Paler gray than *N. v. caliginis,* with more slender bill; depth at nostril 19.0 to 21.9 mm.

Measurements.—Males (30 specimens), wing 281-300 (294), tail 102.0-118.7 (109.2), culmen from base 64.5-75.6 (70.9), depth of bill at nostril 19.0-21.9 (20.8), tarsus 93.6-106.2 (99.4) mm.

Females (22 specimens), wing 271-305 (290), tail 101.1-115.4 (107.8), culmen from base 64.2-75.3 (69.9), depth of bill at nostril 19.4-21.9 (20.8), tarsus 90.5-105.8 (97.1) mm.

Migrant. Found during the period of northern winter: Specimens seen from Bocas del Toro (Bocas del Toro, Nov. 6, 1927; Changuinola, Jan. 21, 1929; Almirante, Feb. 6, 1958; Garay Creek, Almirante Bay, Dec. 19, 1926); Herrera (París, Mar. 4, 1948); San Blas (Permé, Oct. 21 and Dec. 6, 1929); and Isla Cébaco.

This form appears to be fairly common as a migrant on the Caribbean coast of Bocas del Toro. In a preliminary review of the races of this species (Smithsonian Misc. Coll., vol. 106, no. 1, 1946, p. 17) I identified the bird from Garay Creek as *Nyctanassa v. bancrofti,* a race widely distributed through the West Indies. On subsequent examination the specimen proved to be typical *violacea.* There is no record of *bancrofti* from Panamá.

NYCTANASSA VIOLACEA CALIGINIS Wetmore

Nyctanassa violacea caliginis Wetmore, Proc. Biol. Soc. Washington, vol. 59, Mar. 11, 1946, p. 49. (Isla San José, Archipiélago de las Perlas, Panamá.)

Characters.—Dark gray, with thick, heavy bill.

Measurements.—Males (12 specimens), wing 282-299 (290.1); tail 101.7-116.9 (108.7), culmen from base 67.6-81.3 (73.8), tarsus 87.7-101.3 (92.1), depth of bill at nostril 22.2-25.1 (23.4) mm.

Females (2 specimens), wing 288-291 (289.5), tail 101.1-109.0 (105.0), culmen from base 73.7-74.7 (74.2), tarsus 96.5-97.4 (97.0), depth of bill at nostril 22.2-23.5 (22.9) mm.

Resident. From Isla Coiba and southern Veraguas eastward along the Pacific coast (continuing southward along the Pacific littoral of Colombia and Ecuador); and on the Caribbean side from Bocas del Toro to the Comarca de San Blas.

Specimens are recorded on the Pacific side from Isla Coiba; Paracoté, Veraguas; Isla Taboga; Isla San José, Isla Morena, Isla del Rey, and Isla Saboga in the Archipiélago de las Perlas; Fort Kobbe, Río Farfan, and Balboa, Canal Zone; and on the Caribbean coast from Almirante, Bocas del Toro; and Puerto Obaldía, San Blas.

Gen. G. Ralph Meyer found a colony on Isla Changamé near the Pacific entrance of the Canal, where their nests of sticks were placed on the ground, or less than a meter above it in low growths of cactus. In three sets of 3 eggs each, taken February 23 and March 29, 1941, in which incubation had started, the color varies from pale glaucous-green to pale Niagara green, and the shape from elliptical to long elliptical. Measurements of these 9 eggs are as follows: Length 48.0 to 51.5; breadth 33.7 to 37.9; with an average of 49.9 by 36.0 mm.

NYCTANASSA VIOLACEA CAYENNENSIS (Gmelin)

Ardea cayennensis Gmelin, Syst. Nat., vol. 1, pt. 2, 1789, p. 626. (Cayenne.)

Characters.—Closely similar to *Nyctanassa v. violacea* from southeastern United States in slender bill, but averaging darker in color, with the dark streaks on the dorsal feathers narrower.

Measurements.—Males (6 specimens), wing 271-292 (284), tail 101.5-114.8 (109.7), culmen from base 68.4-73.8 (70.2), depth of bill at nostril 19.9-22.0 (21.0), tarsus 97.8-103.0 (99.8) mm.

Females (5 specimens), wing 263-288 (279), tail 97.4-107.8 (101.7), culmen 61.8-71.7 (67.2), depth of bill at nostril 20.3-21.0 (20.5), tarsus 92.7-99.2 (96.6) mm.

Found in eastern Darién, in the Río Tuira Valley; and in eastern San Blas, near the Colombian boundary.

This race is resident in northern South America from northwestern Colombia and Trinidad south to Surinam and northern and eastern Brazil. An adult male from Yavisa, Darién, on the lower Chucunaque is typical of this subspecies. Two adult birds and one in its second year, from the mouth of the Río Paya on the upper middle Tuira, appear somewhat intermediate toward *caliginis,* for although the bill at the nostril is slender it is somewhat more swollen toward the tip. They are, however, to be placed with the South American form. The three birds from the Paya were collected by the staff of the Gorgas Memorial Laboratory on April 11 and 15, 1959, a month after I had left the area. As I did not record the species here during February and March it is possible that they had come into the region from elsewhere subsequent to my departure.

A female collected by Wedel at Permé, May 31, 1929, a bird in a plumage that lacks perhaps a year of being fully adult, agrees with the Paya specimens in slender bill and dark coloration. Another, an adult male, from Puerto Obaldía secured by the same collector Dec. 8, 1931, also is similar.

HETEROCNUS MEXICANUS (Swainson): Bare-throated Tiger-Bittern; Jorrálico

Figure 16

Tigrisoma mexicanus Swainson, in Murray, Encyclopedia of Geography, July 1834, p. 1383. (México.)

Throat and upper foreneck bare of feathers, a character, found even in the young when first hatched, that distinguishes this species in any plumage from the banded tiger-bittern.

Description.—Length 710 to 810 mm. Adult, crown and nuchal crest black; under surface dull cinnamon brown, with the foreneck streaked broadly with black and white; sides of neck and upper surface finely barred with blackish and buffy white, with shaft streaks of dull black on back and wings.

Immature, boldly barred throughout with dull cinnamon-buff and black; sides and under surface of wings white, barred with black.

In an incubating bird at a nest with 3 eggs northwest of Puerto Madero, Chiapas, Walter Dawn (Auk, 1964, p. 231) records colors as follows: Iris deep yellow; bare loral stripe greenish yellow; bare skin of throat bright yellow; tarsus greenish slate.

Measurements.—Males (12 specimens, México to Panamá), wing 330-372 (344), tail 126-142 (136), culmen 100.0-118.0 (111.4), tarsus 104.6-115.0 (111.6) mm.

Females (15 specimens, México to Panamá), wing 316-365 (338), tail 112-153 (131.0), culmen 96.4-112.0 (104.6), tarsus 96.8-114.0 (108.4) mm.

Resident along the Pacific coast from Puerto Armuelles eastward, ranging to Isla Coiba, Isla Canal de Afuera, Isla Cébaco, and the Archipiélago de las Perlas (recorded from Contadora, Chapera, Má-

FIG. 16.—Head of bare-throated tiger-bittern, jorrálico, *Heterocnus mexicanus*, with throat bare from the bill to the upper foreneck.

laga, Bayoneta, and San José). Reported once on the Caribbean coast at Permé, San Blas (specimen, July 25, 1929, in Museum of Comparative Zoology). Found locally in uninhabited areas; rare, or absent, in settled regions.

This interesting heron, long of neck, short of leg, and with bare throat, is now rare in most parts of mainland Panamá; it remains only in sections too remote to be open to casual hunting. In the La Jagua area it is still fairly common as a dozen or more may range in scattered company over marshlands, where tall grass, bushes, and low trees stand in shallow water, or on the open shores adjacent where the birds may walk about. They shelter in swampy woodlands, along the lower courses of the rivers, especially in the taller growths of mangroves. In such localities I have often walked underneath or around them, within 12 or 15 meters, though in the open they are somewhat more wary. It is possible in any event to approach them without much precaution, as the birds are far from shy. This leads to their destruction near regions that become settled as they are easy marks, even for well-aimed sticks and stones.

They move quietly, frequently standing motionless, waiting for the crabs or fish that are their principal sources of sustenance. When flushed they rise with a croaking harsh note, *wok wok wok,* and in late afternoon, or at night, they utter a strange, barking, froglike call. This may be varied to a curious snoring sound, repeated constantly, and at times becoming louder and louder until it is almost a bellow, all notes that carry far in still air.

Nests that I have seen were flattened platforms of sticks, larger than in most herons, placed in trees, as low as 4 meters from the ground. In the Pearl Islands several were located on tree limbs projecting over low cliffs, above water at high tide.

In the latter part of January on Isla Coiba I noted two pairs on a little beach engaged in a display in which they alternately swelled the breast and neck and pointed the bill upward with neck fully extended, in bittern style. In this attitude, because of their short legs, they presented a strange, almost grotesque, appearance. On Isla San José on February 9, 1944, I shot a female about to lay and saw a nest with small young on February 22. A young bird in down was collected here on March 24. Near Chico, Panamá, a nest contained well grown young on March 18, 1949.

The young bird mentioned, taken from the nest, has light grayish white down, except that the longer filaments on the crown are pure white. The brown pinfeathers of the juvenal dress have barely begun growth on the upper surface.

Van Rossem described an egg seen in a nest near San Sebastián, El Salvador as "Dull white, with a greenish tinge, of a rough grain" (Dickey and van Rossem, Birds El Salvador, 1938, p. 83). Dawn (cit. supra, fig. 1) who, in July 1962 photographed one nest and described another, each with 3 eggs, found on the coast of Chiapas, states that the "unspotted eggs ... confirm van Rossem's description." These accounts need to be checked with further observations as eggs of this species in the U.S. National Museum are lightly spotted. The markings are faint and are seen only on close scrutiny.

The set of 2 eggs in question was collected April 20, 1903, near Papayo, Guerrero, by E. W. Nelson and E. A. Goldman. Both are very light pale glaucous-green, marked sparingly and indistinctly with scattered, irregular dots of pinkish buff. They are subelliptical in shape, and measure 56.6×43.5 and 58.1×45.3 mm. Nelson's field notes state that the nest of sticks, slight in structure so that light showed through it from below, was placed about 7 meters from the ground on a fork of a nearly horizontal branch in a mangrove that stood in the open at the shore of a lagoon.

There is a skin in the British Museum from Laguna Castillo, southern Veraguas, taken by Arcé in 1869, and W. W. Brown, Jr. forwarded one from the same province secured on the "Sona River" (the Río San Pablo, near Soná) July 21, 1901 (Bangs, Proc. New England Zoöl. Club, vol. 3, 1902, p. 19). I have recorded them on the lower Río Santa María below París, Herrera, February 24, 1948, at Punta Mala, March 27, 1948, along the Río Caldera at the southern end of the Azuero Peninsula, March 11 and 20, 1957, and have found them regularly in the marshes adjacent to the La Jagua Hunting Club. I took one on April 17, 1949, near the mouth of the Río Bayano, below Chepo, and Griscom reported one seen on March 7, 1927, at Chimán, where I heard them calling at night on several occasions in February 1950. This is the most eastern locality at which they have been recorded on the Pacific side. The report by Chapman (Life in an Air Castle, 1938, p. 226), for Barro Colorado Island, "observed rarely. No specimens" must refer to *Tigrisoma l. lineatum* as *Heterocnus mexicanus* has not been found that far inland.

In connection with the single record for Permé, San Blas, it is of interest to note another in the Chicago Natural History Museum, originally in the collection of C. B. Cory taken March 22, 1881, that is labeled "Mouth of Rio Atrato, Antioquia, Colombia."

TIGRISOMA LINEATUM LINEATUM (Boddaert): Banded Tiger-Bittern; Garza Tigre Rayada

FIGURE 17

Ardea lineata Boddaert, Table Planch. Enlum., 1783, p. 52. (Cayenne.)

Known from the bare-throated tiger-bittern in any plumage by the broad band of feathers down the center of the throat, with a bare space at either side.

Description.—Length 610 to 760 mm. Adult, head, neck, and upper breast chestnut brown, narrowly banded with black, except on the crown; foreneck and breast streaked with white; lower breast and abdomen dull cinnamon; back and wings greenish black, barred and dotted finely with cinnamon.

Immature, bright cinnamon-buff, white on the abdomen and under tail coverts, barred heavily with black; tail black, barred narrowly with white.

FIG. 17.—Head of banded tiger-bittern, garza tigre rayada, *Tigrisoma lineatum lineatum,* with a line of feathers down the throat, which is bare at the sides.

Measurements.—Males (12 specimens, from Panamá and Colombia), wing 276-315 (294.4), tail 101-118 (110.5), culmen from base 93.3-103.7 (98.9), tarsus 93.0-105.5 (99.4) mm.

Females (9 specimens, from Panamá, Colombia and Venezuela), wing 270-305 (291.3), tail 99.5-115.7 (111.0), culmen from base 88.0-98.3 (92.3), tarsus 92.1-106.5 (96.7) mm.

Resident. Found in small numbers in forested areas, on the Caribbean slope from Bocas del Toro to San Blas; and on the Pacific side in Darién in the Tuira-Chucunaque Valley (Laguna de Pita; above Yavisa; El Real) where it ranges upward on the slopes of Cerro Pirri to 550 meters (Cana).

In Bocas del Toro specimens are recorded from Changuinola, Almirante, and Cricamola (Peters, Bull. Mus. Comp. Zool., vol. 71, 1931, p. 307). C. O. Handley, Jr., collected an adult on Cayo Agua, February 14, 1963. From near the line of the Panama Railroad, McLeannan forwarded specimens a hundred years ago, and W. W. Brown, Jr. secured one at Lion Hill in March 1900 (Bangs, Proc. New England Zoöl. Club, vol. 2, 1900, p. 15). Goldman collected one on February 23, 1911, on the Río Indio, near Gatun, Canal Zone, and I have one taken January 14, 1955, at Juan Mina. I saw several near Mandinga along the San Blas coast in January and February 1957 and collected one January 28. It is probable that it ranges locally eastward along this coast as we have specimens taken in Colombia in the Atrato area. In Darién, Festa secured two immature birds at the Laguna de Pita in August 1895. There is one in the American Museum of Natural History from near Yavisa, and I shot one at the mouth of the Río Tuquesa on the Chucunaque on March 27, 1959, and one near El Real February 16, 1964. Goldman secured one at 550 meters elevation near Cana March 14, 1912, this being the highest point at which the bird is recorded. (The locality "Tocoumé" or Tocumen on a specimen collected by E. André in the American Museum of Natural History in which the original label is missing is believed to be in error as the bird is not known in the savanna area.)

This tiger-bittern is found along the forested banks of the larger streams and in swampy forests and mangroves, usually alone except in the nesting season, or when recently grown young still remain with the parents. They live more in forests than the *jorrálico*, and in contrast to that species seem always to seek shade. They are found along the banks of streams, sometimes those of small size. Occasionally they range along small, dry quebradas in regions of low hills.

As the birds rise when alarmed they call, *quok quok quok,* like the bare-throated species, a sound that also resembles the note of a night heron but is louder and deeper in tone. I have heard birds that were not frightened give another note, harsh and long drawn out, *quoh - h - h - h, quoh - h - h - h.* They also have a strange groaning call, harsh in tone, a sound that carries far, particularly since it is heard mainly during the quiet air of night.

The stomach of the bird shot on the Tuquesa contained a partly armored fish of good size.

There is little known of their breeding. A nest of the closely allied race *T. l. marmoratum* is described as a crude platform, rather small compared to the size of the bird, with 2 eggs grayish blue in color, dotted and blotched lightly with dull red. These measured 48×65 mm. (Guimarães Sobrinho, Rev. Mus. Paulista, vol. 17, 1932, p. 918).

Rossi (Univ. Buenos Aires Fac. Cienc. Ex. Nat., Contr. Cient. Ser. Zool., vol. 1, no. 2, 1958, pp. 38-41) in a study of the breeding of this race in the zoological gardens in Buenos Aires, records 14 nestings each with 3 eggs.

He describes the ground color as "celeste claro" (clear sky blue), marked with dots and small blotches of brown and violet. Measurements in 12 eggs were 58.3-61.2×44.1-45.8 mm.

The species sometimes is called *garza vaca* or *pájaro vaca* (or in Venezuela *vaco*), through a fancied resemblance of its calls to the lowing of cattle.

TIGRISOMA SALMONI Sclater and Salvin: Salmon's Tiger-Bittern; Garza Tigre Oscura

FIGURE 18

Tigrisoma salmoni P. L. Sclater and Osbert Salvin, Proc. Zool. Soc. London, June 1875, p. 38, fig. 2. (Medellín, Antioquia, Colombia.)

A tiger-bittern with bill shorter and heavier at the point than that of *T. l. lineatum*; adult blacker.

Description.—Length 560 to 660 mm. Adult, similar to *Tigrisoma l. lineatum,* but head and neck black, banded narrowly with cinnamon-buff.

Immature, also like *T. l. lineatum,* but more extensively white on the lower surface, including the under wing coverts.

An adult female taken on February 28, 1964, on the north fork of the Río Pucro, Darién, had the iris yellow; loral area black, except for the upper margin and the area immediately in front of the eye, which are bright yellow; rest of bare area above and behind eye green, including the posterior margin of the eyelids; central section of the edge of the upper eyelid black; tip of bill horn color; rest of maxilla black, except for the cutting edge from below the nostril to the gape, which is yellowish green, and a narrow margin on the nasal operculum which is dull green; line of the gonys and lower edge of the side of the mandibular rami yellowish green, brighter toward gape; rest of side of mandible black; bare skin at base of mandible and on sides of throat bright yellow; crus, posterior face of tarsus, and lower part of sides of toes dull green; front of tarsus and top of toes dull fuscous brown; claws greenish neutral gray, becoming yellowish at tips.

Fig. 18.—Salmon's tiger-bittern, garza tigre oscura, *Tigrisoma salmoni*.

Another female, not quite in full adult plumage, taken February 23, had all the bare skin on the side of the head yellow except for a narrow line of fuscous across the loral area, another on the edge of the upper eyelid, and a line of bluish green above the eye. The side of the mandible also was more extensively yellow along the lower half.

Measurements.—Males (5 from Panamá and Chocó, Colombia), wing 274-292 (285.6), tail 106.0-117.6 (109.7), culmen from base 86.4-91.4 (88.9), tarsus 81.2-93.8 (90.0) mm.

Females (6 from Panamá and Chocó, Colombia), wing 265-288 (279), tail 106.0-114.0 (108.4), culmen from cere 74.7-83.0 (78.7), tarsus 79.0-88.0 (84.8) mm.

Resident. Locally fairly common, in the humid tropical lowlands, ranging to the subtropical zone in Darién; recorded from Bocas del Toro (Río Changena, 750 meters elevation); the Caribbean slope of Coclé (El Uracillo); Colón, in the upper Chagres Valley (Salamanca and Peluca hydrographic stations); Darién (Tacarcuna village and head of Río Pucro on Cerro Tacarcuna); and San Blas (Ranchón, Puerto Obaldía).

The species was first recognized from Panamá from an adult male that I collected February 29, 1952, on the Río Uracillo, above the town of that name in the foothills of the Caribbean slope of Coclé. On February 21, 1961, I secured another, an immature bird, on the Río Boquerón a short distance below the Peluca hydrographic station. Collectors for the Gorgas Memorial Laboratory shot an immature female at 750 meters elevation on the Río Changena, Bocas del Toro, on September 9, 1961.

My first bird rose from the open bank of a small quebrada and flew into the forest beyond, where its dark coloration concealed it so perfectly that I looked for several minutes in the dim light before I saw it again, though it stood on an open limb. The area was one where fog lay long in early morning, and the low vegetation was seldom dry. I saw others here on February 24 and March 4, and on the latter date approached another adult closely as it crouched on a branch, motionless except for an occasional flick of the tail. In handling the male I found a pair of long, continuous powder-down tracts on the side of the breast, the extent being impressive as there was no division in the entire length. A smaller pair lay on either side of the flanks.

The immature bird taken on the Boquerón ranged along the gravel bars in the river, and sheltered in the trees above when alarmed.

In February 1964 two were collected among several seen along the head of the Río Pucro at about 1,300 meters elevation on the slopes of Cerro Tacarcuna. One of these had the stomach filled with the small armored catfish (family Loricariidae), abundant in these streams, of the kind called *wakupu* by the Cuna Indians, who prize them as food. The other had eaten a large aquatic waterbug. I saw an immature individual at about 600 meters elevation on the Río Tacarcuna on March 14.

I have found no account of the nest and eggs of this species.

Identification of the first two specimens mentioned led to critical examination of the tiger-bitterns in the American Museum of Nattural History and the Museum of Comparative Zoology, with discovery of other skins that had been identified as *T. l. lineatum*, including one from Tacarcuna, Darién, taken March 28, 1915, in the collection first named. Of the others, in Cambridge, one taken March 11, 1936, comes from the old Salamanca hydrographic station, now abandoned, near the upper end of Madden Lake. Those taken by Wedel at Puerto Obaldía and Ranchón, San Blas, had been recorded erroneously by Griscom (Bull. Mus. Comp. Zool., vol. 72, 1932, p. 311) as *T. lineatum*. It is evident that *T. salmoni* ranges locally through the more humid forest areas of the republic.

Birds of this species from southeastern Perú and western Bolivia have been separated by Sztolcman as the race *brevirostre* on the basis of shorter bill. This, however, needs further consideration since bill measurements in those I have examined, including several others from Colombia and Venezuela in addition to those cited above, cover the sizes alleged to mark the race that it is proposed to recognize.

BOTAURUS LENTIGINOSUS (Rackett): American Bittern; Avetoro Pasajero

Ardea lentiginosa Rackett, in Pulteney, Cat. Birds, Shells, and Plants Dorsetshire, ed. 2, May 1813, p. 14. (Parish of Piddletown, Dorsetshire, England.)

A heron of medium size, mainly buffy brown, with a prominent black stripe on the side of the upper neck at the base of the head.

Description.—Length 560 to 660 mm. Mixed buff and brown above, with back and wings finely spotted and lined with blackish; throat white, with a black patch on either side at the base of the neck; below buff streaked with yellowish brown.

Accidental, as a migrant from the north. One record for the Canal Zone.

The only report of this North American species is that of a bird that McLeannan secured when he was stationed at Lion Hill (Lawrence, 1862, p. 478). The specimen, in the American Museum of Natural History, is marked 1862, with indication that it was received from McLeannan, but no further data.

The bittern has been found several times in Costa Rica, but that apparently is its usual southern limit during its migrations. Normally it frequents open, grassy, fresh—or brackish—water marshes.

[The pinnated bittern, *Botaurus pinnatus*, somewhat blacker above than the American bittern, with the neck barred heavily with slaty black, is recorded from Costa Rica and Colombia. It is possible that it may be found in grassy marshes along the Caribbean Coast of Panamá.]

IXOBRYCHUS EXILIS (Gmelin): Least Bittern; Garza Enana

Smallest of the herons, easily recognized by its size—less than half that of the little green heron, or *martinete*—and by its buffy color.

Description.—Length 250 to 330 mm. Male, with back and crown black; sides of head, neck and wings chestnut; greater wing coverts buff; underparts buffy white.

Female, brown, with the under surface streaked with buff.

The least bittern frequents fresh-water marshes where it remains hidden in tall grass and rushes, though toward evening it may appear in the open to fly across channels to some feeding place. At other times they flush rarely, even when closely approached. The few records come from around Barro Colorado Island and from the Chagres marshes near Juan Mina. Two races are found, one a winter migrant from the north, the other, of South American affinity, a resident.

IXOBRYCHUS EXILIS EXILIS (Gmelin)

Ardea exilis Gmelin, Syst. Nat., vol. 1, pt. 2, 1789, p. 645. (Jamaica.)

Characters.—Side of head buff.

Winter visitor from the north.

The only certain records are of two females, one that I took in the marshes opposite the dock at Juan Mina on January 31, 1959, and another, now in the Academy of Natural Sciences of Philadelphia, collected on September 13, 1913, at Mount Hope, Canal Zone, by L. L. Jewel.

IXOBRYCHUS EXILIS ERYTHROMELAS (Vieillot)

Ardea crythromelas (sic) Vieillot, Nouv. Dict. Hist. Nat., nouv. éd., vol. 14, Sept. 1817, p. 422. (Río Paraguay.)

Characters.—Differs from typical *exilis* in having the side of the head rufous-brown, like the stripe over the eye and along the side of the crown.

Measurements.—Males (2 from Panamá), wing 106.5, 109.0, tail 39.6, 41.9, culmen from base 43.2, 42.9, tarsus 39.0, 41.8 mm.

Females (2 from Panamá), wing 109.8, 114.4, tail 36.4, 42.9, culmen from base 42.8, 44.8, tarsus 41.5, 44.7 mm.

These figures indicate that the size agrees with that of the typical race *I. e. exilis.*

A male taken on January 13, 1961, had the following colors: Inner edge of iris bright yellow, outer ring reddish orange; base of culmen wood brown, changing at level of nostrils to dusky neutral gray; cutting edges of maxilla and mandible honey yellow; loral area honey yellow, with a line of buffy yellow above and below; space around eye honey yellow; crus, tarsus and toes honey yellow, tinged with neutral gray on the front of the tibio-tarsal joint and of the tarsus; claws wood brown tipped with dark neutral gray.

Resident. Recorded only in fresh-water marshes, along the lower Chagres.

The few records are as follows: A female in the Salvin-Godman collection in the British Museum, sent by McLeannan from Lion Hill, Canal Zone; another, a male, in the American Museum of Natural History, marked 1863, from the same source, but without more detailed data, a bird in first fall plumage, with the back feathers margined lightly with rufous. In addition to these I have collected two in the marshes bordering the Río Chagres near Juan Mina, a female on January 10, and a male on January 13, both in 1961.

Least bitterns are fairly common between Gamboa and Juan Mina but remain closely under cover and so are seldom seen. In January as the breeding season approaches they begin to call, a low, drawling *kwuh-h-h-h,* repeated at brief intervals, given while the birds remain concealed in the marsh growth. In early morning, and more regularly in late afternoon, they move about to feed, and then may fly a few meters low down in the open, but immediately drop into cover. I have had one call at dusk within 10 meters and still not be able to see it. One that I shot had a small fish in the stomach, and this appears to be their principal food.

Family COCHLEARIIDAE: Boat-billed Heron; Garzota Cuchara

The single species of this family ranges in the Tropical Zone lowlands from northern México (Sinaloa on the west, Tamaulipas on the east) south through Central America to northern Argentina. Two of the three races recognized are covered in the present report, a very pale one of South America that ranges from southwestern Darién southward, and a very dark one, found in southwestern Costa Rica and most of Panamá, that enters Colombia on the northwestern shores of the Gulf of Urabá. The third, *Cochlearius cochlearius zeledoni* (Ridgway), of México and most of Central America, is paler gray above than *C. c. panamensis* of Panamá, but otherwise is similar. These birds suggest night herons in general appearance but are marked at once by the broad bill—less than twice as long as it is wide—from which the family takes its name. In the adult a crest of broad, loose feathers extends a third of the way down the neck and the dorsal feathers are elongated to the level of the rump.

The characters that set these birds off as a distinct family compared to the true herons (Ardeidae) are found in the enlarged bill, which is a scoop instead of a spear, and in the considerable structural changes in the mouth and skull that accompany this. There are four pairs of powder-down patches instead of the three of true herons. The bill at hatching is short, triangular, broad at the base, and tapers rapidly to a blunt point, an appearance quite different from that of true herons of the same age. A downy specimen of this age of the race *Cochlearius cochlearius zeledoni* from southern Veracruz, with an egg tooth present on both maxilla and mandible is dull white below, pale gray above, and brownish black on the crown.

COCHLEARIUS COCHLEARIUS (Linnaeus): Boat-billed Heron; Garzota Cuchara

FIGURE 19

A heronlike bird of medium size, with a heavy bill in which the breadth is more than half the length.

Description.—Length 480 to 510 mm. Adult, forehead and forecrown white; rest of crown, broad, elongated nuchal plumes, and a patch on upper back, blackish slate; rest of upper surface, including sides of neck, gray; breast, abdomen, and under tail coverts, cinnamon-brown; sides and flanks slaty black.

As stated under the family heading, this species suggests the night herons in general, though distinct from them in many ways. During the day boatbills remain in roosts in mangrove swamps, or in inland localities, in trees over small streams or ponds. They fly readily when approached, but usually merely to heavier cover nearby. Though they may rest in the sun in early morning, they are nocturnal in general, as they are active and feed mainly at night. I have found them often while night-hunting, usually as they stand or walk in shallow ripples in the rivers, where they scoop at aquatic animals rather than spear at them in heron style. Usually they are so wary that they take flight with protesting squawks as soon as the beam of the lamp touches them, unless the light is a very weak one. Once, on the Río Majé, I came on one that was so intent on its fishing that I was able to watch it close at hand for several minutes, but when I turned on a flashlight for a better view it flew instantly with protesting calls. The eye shine is faint, and is orange in color. They often scold loudly at night, the usual call resembling that of the night herons but in higher tone.

Fig. 19.—Head of boat-billed heron, garzota cuchara, *Cochlearius cochlearius*.

They nest in small colonies. The nest is described as a loosely made structure of sticks, placed in a tree, often over water. The eggs, 2 to 4 in a set, short to long subelliptical in form, are pale bluish white, spotted lightly with pale brown, mainly at the larger end. The colors fade somewhat with age in museum collections so that they may appear whiter, with some of the spotting so indistinct as to be seen only on close examination.

COCHLEARIUS COCHLEARIUS COCHLEARIUS (Linnaeus)

Cancroma Cochlearia Linnaeus, Syst. Nat., ed. 12, vol. 1, 1766, p. 233. (Cayenne.)

Characters.—Adult, pale gray above and on the sides of the neck; upper breast and all of foreneck pure white.

Immature, back and wing coverts cinnamon-buff; underparts white washed with buff on lower foreneck and sides.

Measurements.—Males (3 from northern Colombia), wing 272-281 (276), tail 108.6-115.1 (111.1), culmen from base 79.0-86.9 (82.9, average of 2), tarsus 78.0-84.2 (81.5) mm.

Females (5 from Darién and northern Colombia), wing 259-266 (263), tail 102.5-107.6 (105.7), culmen from base 67.0-75.4 (70.4), tarsus 75.0-82.7 (78.7) mm.

Resident on the Río Jaqué, in southeastern Darién.

This form of South America is so markedly different from the race of the rest of Panamá in its much lighter color—light gray on the back, and pure white on the foreneck and side of the head, in the adult—as almost to suggest a separate species.

On the Río Jaqué, in April 1947, the boatbills were fairly common near our camp located at the mouth of the Río Imamadó. They were nocturnal, coming out at dusk to walk in the shallows over gravel bars along the Imamadó, and the Río Chicao, or flying down to the broader waters of the main river. One evening I sat in the end of our large piragua that rested half in the water, to write the day's notes, while a pleasant breeze kept mosquitoes away. The river was in flood from a heavy rain that had come in late afternoon, and when it became too dark to write I sat quietly, watching the water and the forest border beyond. At full dark I had an indistinct view of a large bird that approached with fluttering, wavering flight, in search of a suitable spot to alight, appearing white, like an immature little blue heron, or an egret. It stopped 10 meters away on a gravel bar and stood quietly, until we turned a flashlight on it, when the light revealed a boatbill watching the water intently. The bird took flight almost instantly when the light beam touched it. A few nights later I waited here for a possible shot until it had become so dark that I was about to leave. Suddenly I had an indefinite view of a broad-winged bird passing with steadily beating wings that I thought must be an owl. A hasty shot at the almost invisible target, a splash as it dropped in the river, and a moment later the boatbill was in my hand.

We sometimes saw as many as half a dozen while night-hunting but always found them so wild that they flew immediately when they saw our light, even at a considerable distance. Often I heard them calling in a low tone, *qua qua qua,* as they flew away. In skinning the one taken I was impressed by the considerable development of the muscles of the sides of the head and in the palatal area.

Interestingly enough, the bird here proved to be the South American form that has not been reported previously in Central America. The indication is that *C. c. cochlearius* ranges along the Pacific coast only to the Río Jaqué, since *C. c. panamensis* is found in the Tuira drainage a short distance to the north.

Two sets of 3 eggs each of *C. c. cochlearius* in the U. S. National Museum, collected by G. D. Smooker, on July 14 and August 5, 1935, on the Caroni River, Trinidad, are almost white, tinged weakly with pale glaucous blue, with a few very faint spots and irregular markings of cinnamon. They vary from subelliptical to long subelliptical in shape and show the following measurements: 49.9×35.5, 50.0×35.3, and 52.5×35.7; 46.9×36.4, 50.5×37.4, and 53.5×36.6 mm.

The species is one that soon disappears as the countryside is developed for increasing human occupancy.

COCHLEARIUS COCHLEARIUS PANAMENSIS Griscom

Cochlearius zeledoni panamensis Griscom, Amer. Mus. Nov. no. 235, Nov. 18, 1926, p. 11. (Corozal, Canal Zone, Panamá.)

Characters.—Adult, darker throughout than *C. c. cochlearius*, with the side of the head and neck and the back and wings dark gray; lower foreneck and breast light grayish brown.

Immature, much darker above and below than the same stage in typical *cochlearius*.

Measurements.—Males (4 from Panamá), wing 266-282 (275), tail 95.7-107.8 (102.1), culmen from base 75.5-81.6 (78.9), tarsus 77.0-81.5 (78.5) mm.

Females (4 from Panamá and Chocó, Colombia), wing 260-269 (265), tail 94.4-104.2 (97.6), culmen from base 72.5-81.0 (75.9), tarsus 65.0-76.8 (72.9) mm.

Resident. Found in the tropical lowlands throughout the Republic, except on the Río Jaqué, southwestern Darién.

These birds must occur along the lower river courses in Chiriquí and the Pacific side of Veraguas, as they range into southwestern Costa Rica, but the only definite report of them in that area to date is the ancient record of one taken by Arcé at Mina de Chorcha, east of David, Chiriquí (Salvin, Proc. Zool. Soc. London, 1870, p. 218). In the Azuero Peninsula I found them along the Río Escotá near Santa María, and picked up a weather worn skull at Alvina, in Herrera. Farther south, near tidewater on the Río Caldera back of Punta Mala, in March 1957, I located a colony of 20 to 30, that had young fully grown but not long out of the nest. Some of the country people here, who called these birds *bocacho,* had a superstition that they were evil because of their ugly appearance due to the broad bill. In Bocas del Toro they are recorded from Changuinola and Almirante (Peters, Bull. Mus. Comp. Zool., vol. 71, 1931, p. 305), and in the swamps at Boca del Drago. Farther east I found one at Chilar, western Colón, March 11, 1952, and there are records for both slopes in the Canal Zone, from Corozal, Balboa, Pedro Miguel Locks, Juan Mina, Lion Hill, Gatun, and Colón. Goldman secured one at Portobelo June 1, 1911. Wedel collected one at Permé, and C. O. Handley, Jr. secured one female on the Quebrada Venado, back of Armila, San Blas. These are representative of this race which extends beyond to Acandí, across the boundary in Colombia. Griscom (Bull. Mus. Comp. Zool., 1932, p. 311) was in error when he said that the subspecies *panamensis* "is devoid of the slightest rusty tinge" above, since a wash of dark reddish brown is of common occurrence in birds through Panamá.

On the Pacific side, Karl Curtis informed me that a colony nests in the rainy season in the swamps near the La Jagua Hunting Club. In 1949 I secured two from the Río Mamoní, a short distance above Chepo, and in February and March 1950, I noted several on the lower Río Chimán and at Charco del Toro on the Río Majé. In 1959 I saw them on the lower Río Tuira, between Pinogana and El Real, and found others on the Río Chucunaque near the mouth of the Río Tuquesa. This is the most inland point at which they have been reported. One collected by Goldman near Gatun had the stomach filled with shrimps.

An adult female, shot on March 9, 1957, on the Río Caldera, below Pedasí, Los Santos, had the following colors of the soft parts: Iris wood brown; maxilla black, except the area of the nostrils (below the operculum) which is dull yellow; cutting edge and upper side of mandible dark neutral gray, lower margin and gonys dull yellow; lower eyelid, except as noted, and lores neutral gray; spot on anterior lower lid (adjacent to lores), and a line beside the feathering above the eye greenish yellow; gular sac back to base of rami dull yellow, with a few spots of neutral gray; posterior fourth of gular sac dull brownish gray; tarsus, crus, and toes greenish yellow. An immature male, taken at the same time, had the iris duller brown, no dark spots on the gular pouch, the front of the tarsus dull grayish brown, and the posterior face, the crus, and the underside of the toes light yellowish green.

Other adults that I have examined as museum specimens have the whole bill and the gular pouch back to the gape black, which appears to be the color of the mating season.

Family CICONIIDAE: Storks; Cigüeñas

The family is worldwide in its distribution. The two species recorded in Panamá, like herons, range in marshes and around lagoons. Only the wood ibis is found regularly in the Republic.

KEY TO SPECIES OF CICONIIDAE

Smaller, wing less than 500 mm. long; bill decurved toward end, with the tip rounded.................................Wood ibis, *Mycteria americana*, p. 120

Larger, wing more than 600 mm. long; bill straight to slightly recurved toward end, with the tip pointed.....................Jabiru, *Jabiru mycteria*, p. 120

JABIRU MYCTERIA (Lichtenstein): Jabiru; Garzón Soldado

Ciconia mycteria Lichtenstein, Abh. K. Akad. Wiss. Berlin, Phys. Kl., 1816-1817 (1819), p. 163. (Northeastern Brazil.)

Of very large size, with heavy, recurved bill; head and neck bare, except for a tuft of downy feathers on the nape.

Description.—A meter 200 mm. to a meter and a half tall; wing 630-650, bill 305-335 mm. Adult, head and neck bare of feathers; upper part of neck black, lower third orange red; plumage white.

Immature, dark gray, or brownish; in older stage with underparts, tail, upper tail coverts, and rump, white.

Casual straggler.

The only published record is that of a male shot by Hasso von Wedel at Cricamola, Bocas del Toro, August 11, 1927 (Peters, Bull. Mus. Comp. Zool., vol. 71, 1931, p. 304).

Baldomiro Moreno, a local hunter, has described one to me that he saw on the La Jagua marshes, his only view of this bird. The species is found widely from southern México to northern Argentina.

MYCTERIA AMERICANA Linnaeus: Wood Ibis; Gabán

Mycteria americana Linnaeus, Syst. Nat., ed. 10, vol. 1, 1758, p. 150. (Northeastern Brazil.)

Large size, coupled with bare head and upper neck, and decurved bill, distinguish this from other wading birds found in Panamá.

Description.—Length 860 mm. to nearly a meter. Adult, white; flight feathers and tail black, with a sheen of dark green (seen with the bird in hand); head and neck without feathers.

Immature, head and neck scantily feathered, grayish brown; rest of plumage like adult but duller in color.

Measurements.—Males (6 from Florida, México, and Panamá), wing 453-492 (476), tail 155-166 (158), culmen from base 215-235 (227), tarsus 194-213 (203) mm.

Females (6 from México, Nicaragua, Costa Rica, Panamá, and Colombia), wing 435-455 (446), tail 143-150 (148), culmen from base 190-205 (196), tarsus 175-192 (183) mm.

Resident. Seen regularly in extensive marsh areas in the lowlands;

wanders during the dry season, attracted to any aquatic haunt available when pools and channels begin to dry.

These great birds are found regularly about ciénagas and the channels of extensive marshes, sometimes alone, sometimes in flocks. The most western record on the Pacific coast is that of two that I saw near Remedios, Chiriquí, January 30, 1955. Aldrich (Scient. Publ. Cleveland Mus. Nat. Hist., vol. 7, 1937, p. 36) found them in February 1932 around a drying lagoon near the head of Montijo Bay. And in Herrera in February and March 1948 I noted occasional birds along the middle and lower courses of small streams, or on the partly dry lagoons of the coastal plain. On March 10 we found a flock of 75 at Ciénaga de Buho and admired their flight as they moved to perch in distant trees along the Río Escotá. A female shot from a large tree standing in dry scrub back of the open playa at Alvina, near the mouth of the Río Santa María, had the ovaries so far developed that it appeared that the laying season was near. On January 17 and 20, 1963, I recorded a number on the salinas below Aguadulce, Coclé.

The wood ibis comes at intervals around Changuinola and Almirante. It is seen occasionally along the Chagres (Fort San Lorenzo, January 1, 1955) and around Gatun Lake, as one was taken in this area by McLeannan (Lawrence, Ann. Lyc. Nat. Hist. New York, vol. 7, 1861, p. 334). And one is recorded along the coast of San Blas at Obaldía (Griscom, Bull. Mus. Comp. Zool., vol. 72, 1932, p. 311). In the lowland marshes between the Pacora and Bayano Rivers, on the Pacific side, I have found them regularly. In seasons like that of 1958, when the channels through the marsh remained full of water, several hundred were present, and in other years I have found dozens gathered on the drying ciénagas. I have record of them also at Chimán, on the Río Chucunaque at the mouth of the Tuquesa, and in the Tuira Valley near El Real and at the mouth of Río Paya.

While no colonies are on record, the wood ibis undoubtedly nests in wooded swamps near the Chico and Bayano Rivers and also in the great swamps on the northern shores of Golfo de San Miguel and the lower Tuira.

They appear ungainly when perched in trees because of the bare head and neck, more attractive as they move or stand about channels or pools, and magnificent when flocks pass on the wing, especially when they circle in ascending air thermals. On occasion I have seen them soaring with groups of hawks and vultures.

The species is known commonly to the countryman in Panamá as the *grulla,* or crane.

Family THRESKIORNITHIDAE: Ibises, Spoonbills; Cocos y Garzas Paletas

This group of long-legged wading birds lives in the same haunts as the herons and in general shares their habit of life. Ibises are marked by their long curved beaks, the spoonbill by its broad bill, much widened at the tip. The family as a whole is one of numerous species throughout the temperate and tropical world. The white ibis and spoonbill range widely in Panamá; the Cayenne ibis is local. The other species listed come as stragglers.

KEY TO SPECIES OF THRESKIORNITHIDAE

1. Bill slender, decurved; not enlarged at tip............................ 2
   Bill flat, straight, much widened at tip..Roseate spoonbill, *Ajaia ajaja*, p. 127
2. Wholly black with a sheen of green, or brownish black................ 3
   White, or parti-colored 4
3. Middle toe with claw, equal to the tarsus or longer; a pronounced nuchal crest....................Cayenne ibis, *Mesembrinibis cayennensis*, p. 124
   Middle toe with claw decidedly less than tarsus; no pronounced nuchal crest..........................Glossy ibis, *Plegadis f. falcinellus*, p. 124
4. Throat wholly bare....................White ibis, *Eudocimus albus*, p. 125
   Throat feathered in center, bare at sides.
   White-throated ibis, *Theristicus c. caudatus*, p. 126

MESEMBRINIBIS CAYENNENSIS (Gmelin): Cayenne Ibis; Corocoro

Tantalus cayennensis Gmelin, Syst. Nat., vol. 1, pt. 2, 1789, p. 652. (Cayenne.)

A short-legged, dark-colored ibis, with a bushy crest.

Description.—Length 480 to 530 mm. Upper surface black, with a sheen of bronze green; a greenish black, bushy crest on the back of the head; below dull black.

An adult male, taken at Mandinga, had the soft parts colored as follows: Iris light brown; bare frontal area, and most of the bill, dull greenish gray; tip of bill light fuscous; bare skin around eye, lores, extreme base of mandible, and bare throat, deep neutral gray; crus light brownish white; tibio-tarsal and tarso-phalangeal joints bluish neutral gray; rest of tarsus and toes dull vetiver green.

Measurements.—Males (5 from Panamá, Colombia, and Brazil), wing 263-300 (280), tail 127-155 (138), culmen from base 104.5-118.5 (112.6), tarsus 61.8-63.5 (62.4) mm.

Females (4 from Panamá, Colombia, and Brazil), wing 280-289 (283), tail 131-148 (142), culmen from base 103.0-113.0 (108.5), tarsus 56.8-62.2 (59.5) mm.

Resident. Tolerably common around Almirante Bay, Bocas del Toro, and on the Río Chucunaque, Darién; casual elsewhere.

The Cayenne ibis is a heavy-bodied bird, found in the depths of wooded swamps, that comes out along shaded channels to walk along the shores or rest in the trees above. Formerly it ranged on the Atlantic slope of the Canal Zone, where McLeannan secured specimens along the line of the railroad, but it has not been recorded there since that time. One of these old skins in the British Museum is labeled "Lion Hill." In Bocas del Toro this ibis is found in fair numbers in the wet forests back of Boca del Drago, where it is seen especially along the old canals. Handley in 1962 and 1963 found it common in the swamps of Isla Bastimentos. A few range in the mangrove swamps of Quebrada Nigua and Río Occidente, but here they remain inside. And so their presence is known mainly from their mellow, rolling calls, heard at sunrise and dusk. Wedel shot one at Chiriquicito on April 18, 1928 (Peters, Bull. Mus. Comp. Zool., vol. 71, 1931, p. 304).

On February 15, 1957, I found one in the wet forest bordering the lower Río Mandinga in the Comarca de San Blas. With advance of the dry season the swamp was drying, leaving small pools with many fishes, where the bird had been feeding, as indicated by its muddy bill. There is one in the Chicago Natural History Museum from Obaldía in the extreme eastern San Blas. Collectors for the Gorgas Memorial Laboratory secured one on September 15, 1958, in the San Antonio Swamp, east of Pacora, the only record for this area.

On the Río Chucunaque in March 1959 these ibises were fairly common from the mouth of the Río Canglón to the Ucurgantí and I collected one for a specimen. I saw them regularly around pools in the quebradas, or in swampy woods where they walked about rather quickly with nodding head, probing in soft mud, often clear to their eyes. So long as I remained quiet they had little fear, as one fed within 15 meters of me. At such times a casual ray of the sun at the proper angle displayed the glossy green of back and crest attractively. I heard one calling briefly near Pinogana but saw none above that point on the Río Tuira. They are known locally in Darién as Coco Roto, and around Almirante as Coco Quam.

Schönwetter (Handb. Ool., pt. 2, 1960, pp. 104, 107), describes the eggs as deep olive-green. Most are without markings, but some have fine brown or blackish spots or irregular lines on the larger end. The average size is 62.5 × 42.6 mm. Nehrkorn (Kat. Eiersamml., 1899, p. 229) gives the measurements of 2 spotted eggs collected by Hauxwell in Perú as 52-53 × 37-38.5 mm. I have seen no description of the nest.

PLEGADIS FALCINELLUS FALCINELLUS (Linnaeus): Glossy Ibis; Morito

Tantalus Falcinellus Linnaeus, Syst. Nat., ed. 12, vol. 1, 1766, p. 241. (Lake Neusiedl, Austria.)

An ibis with smoothly feathered head, that is dark in color throughout.

Description.—Length 460 to 560 mm. Adult, in the hand, above shining bronzy green, with purplish reflections; lower parts chestnut. At any distance, in life, they appear black.

Immature, upper surface duller, lower surface dark grayish brown; head and neck streaked with white.

Iris brown; bare lores purplish black; bill fuscous brown; tarsus and toes greenish-brown.

Measurements.—Males (5 from southeastern United States and Hispaniola) wing 275-286 (279.6), tail 97.9-104.0 (101.0), culmen from base 127.5-136.6 (131.3), tarsus 99.2-112.0 (103.1) mm.

Females (5 from southeastern United States and Hispaniola) wing 252-260 (257.4), tail 90.3-94.5 (92.5), culmen from base 100.4-108.1 (102.7), tarsus 78.0-88.0 (81.8) mm.

Casual wanderer. One record, March 18, 1949, a specimen taken near the La Jagua Hunting Club east of Pacora.

On March 18, 1949, three fed together over the drying muddy bed of Ciénaga Campana. After watching them for a few minutes I flushed them in order to drop one at long range. Presumably this small flock may have been migrant from one of the known breeding colonies in the Greater Antilles, though one may speculate on the possibility of nesting groups elsewhere.

I was told that dark-colored ibises (called *coco negro*) are found at times in this region, but it seems probable that these were the Cayenne ibis. It seems probable also that the white-faced glossy ibis, *Plegadis chihi* (Vieillot), may occur here.

While there has been much uncertainty relative to identification of immature specimens of the two species of glossy ibises I have found them to be readily separable. In *P. f. falcinellus* back, wings, and tail are deep oil green, and the entire dorsal surface appears darker and blacker. In *P. chihi* back, wings, and tail are lighter green with a distinct brassy sheen, and the dorsal surface is lighter, more dark brownish gray.

The type locality listed above has been designated by Hellmayr and Conover (Cat. Birds Amer., pt. 1, no. 2, 1948, p. 265).

EUDOCIMUS ALBUS (Linnaeus): White Ibis; Coco Blanco

FIGURE 20

Scolopax alba Linnaeus, Syst. Nat., ed. 10, vol. 1, 1758, p. 145. (South Carolina.)

Differs from other ibises found in Panamá by white undersurface of the body.

Description.—Length 560 to 610 mm. Adult, white; tips of outermost primaries black, with a sheen of steely blue.

Immature, upper surface, head, neck, and upper breast streaked with grayish brown.

FIG. 20.—Head of white ibis, coco blanco, *Eudocimus albus*.

Iris bluish white; bare skin of head orange-red; bill orange-red with terminal third olive; tarsus and toes rosy flesh-color; claws black (Dickey and van Rossem, Birds El Salvador, 1938, p. 89).

Measurements.—Males (5 from southeastern United States) wing 279-285 (282.6), tail 107.1-119.8 (112.1), culmen from base 145.4-163.0 (155.1), tarsus 90.3-102.5 (95.9) mm.

Females (5 from Florida) wing 260-268 (265), tail 93.3-104.8 (98.6), culmen from base 118.5-130.0 (125.6), tarsus 83.8-88.0 (85.5) mm.

Resident. Tolerably common locally in the coastal swamps on the Pacific side: Found on Isla Coiba; and in the Archipiélago de las Perlas (islas San José, Pedro González, Rey, Víveros, Pacheca).

The most western record on the mainland is for the head of Montijo Bay where Aldrich (Scient. Publ. Cleveland Mus. Nat. Hist., vol. 7, 1937, pp. 36-37) found them common in 1932. There is a specimen from Isla Coiba in the British Museum collected on the St. George Expedition in 1924; and I recorded them there in fair number in 1956. There were numbers near the coast in the Province of Herrera in 1948, and several on the mudflats at Puerto Salado, below Aguadulce, Coclé, Jan. 25, 1963. Other recent records are from Farfan Beach, Canal Zone (specimen September 28, 1953), and of one seen near Panama City (J. M. Abbott, March 7, 1942). Hallinan (Auk, 1924, p. 307) shot one on Isla Taboguilla December 5, 1915. I have seen them regularly in the marshes near the La Jagua Hunting Club, and in 1950 found them common near Chimán, where they ranged inland on the Río Chimán to the Río Curutú. Several were seen at Majé, Panamá in 1950, and others near El Real, Darién in 1964. The first formal record for Panamá is that of 3 on the Río Sabana, Darién, reported by Salvadori and Festa (Boll. Mus. Zool. Anat. Comp. Univ. Torino, vol. 14, no. 339, 1899, pp. 2, 12).

White ibises are found in tidal ponds in mangroves, and also around ciénagas and shallow waters on the flats, but do not go far inland. They sleep in the coastal swamps, and may be seen in small flocks flying to and from such roosts in morning and evening. The immature birds sometimes allow close approach, but adults are more wary.

On June 7, 1941, Maj. Gen. G. Ralph Meyer found a colony on Isla Changamé at the Pacific entrance of the Panama Canal and took 6 sets of 2 eggs each, which are now in the National Museum. The nests were shallow platforms, 175 to 200 mm. in diameter, made of twigs and weed stems, with some leaves in the lining, placed on the tops of cactus and stunted trees. The eggs are subelliptical, dull white to buffy white, marked with chocolate to cinnamon-brown, changing to lilac where the pigment is overlaid by a deposit of shell. Some are heavily blotched, mainly around the larger end, others are spotted finely throughout. These 12 eggs range in length from 52.1 to 61.0 mm., and in width from 35.5 to 38.8 mm., with the average 56.7×37.3 mm.

THERISTICUS CAUDATUS CAUDATUS (Boddaert): White-throated Ibis; Bandurria Común

Scolopax caudatus Boddaert, Tabl. Pl. Enl., 1783, p. 57. (Cayenne.)

An ibis with heavy body and short legs; a prominent white patch in the wing, that otherwise is dark in color.

Description.—Length 710-760 mm. Head and neck white, with crown and lower foreneck brownish buff; back dark gray; wings black with a large white patch across the center; coverts light gray; below, including underside of wings and tail, black.

In specimens of the closely similar subspecies *Theristicus c. hyperorius* Todd that I collected in Paraguay I recorded the colors of the soft parts as follows: Iris light red; bill and bare skin on head dull black, except for lower eyelid which was pale purplish blue; tarsus dull red, somewhat paler on toes; claws dull black.

Measurements.—Males (4 from Colombia), wing 385-394 (391), tail 193-203 (198.7), culmen from base 131-149 (143.5), tarsus 80.0-83.3 (81.5) mm.

Females (2 from Colombia), wing 383, 387, tail 190, 197, culmen from base 130.6-141.0, tarsus 77.1, 78.6 mm.

Casual wanderer from South America: One record, near Pacora, Panamá.

The species ranges from Colombia and Venezuela to northern Argentina.

Through Karl Curtis the U. S. National Museum has received one of these birds killed by Baldomiro Moreno, September 18, 1950, from a flock of four on the savannas near San José, beyond Pacora. The specimen was roughly skinned by Baldomiro, and was prepared for me by Ratibor Hartmann, of the Gorgas Memorial Laboratory. The record is the first for Central America. Another was reported to me by Baldomiro as seen on the same savanna in November, 1958.

AJAIA AJAJA (Linnaeus): Roseate Spoonbill; Garza Paleta
FIGURE 21

Platalea Ajaja Linnaeus, Syst. Nat., ed. 10, vol. 1, 1758, p. 140. (Rio São Francisco, eastern Brazil)

An ibislike species, with flattened bill, broadly expanded at the tip.

Description.—Length 710 to 810 mm. Bill broad, flat, expanded at the tip. Adult, pink, with lesser wing coverts and tail coverts light red; crown bare.

Immature, whiter; crown feathered, except on the forehead.

Measurements.—Males (5 from México, El Salvador, Colombia, and Argentina), wing 347-365 (353.4), tail 93.0-101.5 (95.1), culmen from base 156-173 (167.4), tarsus 106.6-111.6 (108.7) mm.

Females (4 from Florida, Louisiana, Colombia and Argentina), wing 332-357, tail 86.8-97.6 (93.4), culmen from base 150-177 (158.7), tarsus 96.5-116.6 (103.8) mm.

Resident. Found along the Pacific coast; now uncommon.

The spoonbill still remains in remote areas of extensive swamps, though in reduced numbers. It is reported from near Puerto Armuelles, where it was recorded in November 1929 (McClellan, Proc. California Acad. Sci., vol. 23, 1938, p. 256), across to Darién, where I saw one near the mouth of the Río Tuquesa, March 27, 1959. I have seen it also near the mouth of the Río Vidal in western Veraguas (June 8, 1953, March 25, 1965) and at the Ciénaga de Buho, near Santa María, Herrera (March 10, 1948). It is found regularly in the swamps around the lower Río Chico and the Río La Jagua, though it is necessary to go far across from the La Jagua Hunting Club to see it. Here I collected two on March 21, 1958. There is said to have been a small colony of them until about 1930 in

FIG. 21.—Head of roseate spoonbill, garza paleta, *Ajaja ajaia*, with throat pouch inflated.

mangroves at the mouths of small streams in the Cocolí area in the Canal Zone.

The birds seem to be restricted to the Pacific slope, as the only record for the Caribbean side is of one at Gatun, Canal Zone, in November, 1911 (Jewel, Auk, 1913, p. 424).

Spoonbills feed around ponds where they walk through the shallows, swinging the bill from side to side to cut the mud and water, and so to sift out mollusks and other food.

They are known to many of the country hunters as the *pato cuchara*.

Order ANSERIFORMES

Family ANATIDAE: Ducks; Patos

This family, of world-wide distribution and many kinds, has 14 species in Panamá, of which 5 are resident and 7 come as migrants during the period of northern winter. There are 2 others that appear to be of accidental occurrence through stray individuals. Habitat for these birds is somewhat restricted since the species concerned frequent broad reaches of fresh or brackish waters. They have been best known on the Pacific slope, though now numbers of the migrants come to the artificial ponds made in recent years in the extensive cleared areas between the Changuinola and Sixaola rivers on the Caribbean side.

The isthmus, particularly along the Pacific is a regular flyway for those that pass to South America in their migrations. Duck hunting is a favored sport and numbers are killed each year.

KEY TO SPECIES OF ANATIDAE

1. Hind toe without a lobe.. 2
   Hind toe with a lobe... 14
2. Lower end of tarsus with reticulate scales.......................... 3
   Lower end of tarsus with transverse scales.......................... 5
3. Neck black; forepart of head white; sides heavily barred.
   White-faced tree duck, *Dendrocygna viduata*, p. 130
   Neck not black; no white on head; sides plain or longitudinally streaked 4
4. No white in wing; mainly cinnamon brown, with elongated feathers on sides and flanks............Fulvous tree duck, *Dendrocygna b. bicolor*, p. 131
   A prominent white patch in wing; breast gray; abdomen black.
   Black-bellied tree duck, *Dendrocygna a. autumnalis*, p. 132
5. Space around eye partly bare, usually with colored caruncles.
   Muscovy duck, *Cairina moschata*, p. 134
   Space in front of eye feathered...................................... 6
6. A ridge or flat-sided tubercle on upper surface of bill near base.
   American comb duck, *Sarkidiornis sylvicola*, p. 137
   Bill without a ridge or projecting tubercle on upper surface.......... 7
7. Bill greatly broadened at tip............Shoveler, *Spatula clypeata*, p. 145
   Bill not broadened at tip... 8
8. Larger, 460 mm. or more long; bend of wing without a prominent blue patch 9
   Smaller, not more than 380 mm. long; bend of wing with a prominent blue patch 11
9. Bill smaller, not more than 38 mm. long; a prominent white patch on wing.
   American widgeon, *Mareca americana*, p. 146
   Bill larger, 50 mm. or more long; no white patch in wing............. 10

10. Tail elongated, with the feathers sharply pointed; wing speculum green in male; gray in female.......................Pintail, *Anas acuta*, p. 140

   Tail rounded; wing speculum deep, shining blue in both sexes.

   Mallard, *Anas p. platyrhynchos*, p. 139

11. A prominent white crescent on forepart of head in front of eye.

   Blue-winged teal, *Anas discors*, male, p. 141

   No white mark on forepart of head............................... 12

12. Plumage cinnamon or chestnut brown, above and below.

   Cinnamon teal, *Anas cyanoptera septentrionalium*, adult male, p. 144

   Blackish above edged with buffy white, lighter below, mottled in appearance throughout 13

13. Bill slightly smaller, 37-41 mm. long.

   Blue-winged teal, *Anas discors*, female, p. 141

   Bill slightly heavier, 41-44 mm. long.

   Cinnamon teal, *Anas cyanoptera septentrionalium*, female, p. 144

14. Smaller, wing less than 150 mm.; tail longer, with narrowed feathers, the extended feet not reaching to its end.

   Masked duck, *Oxyura dominica*, p. 150

   Larger, wing more than 175 mm.; tail shorter, with broader feathers, the extended feet reaching to its end................................. 15

15. Wing speculum white............Lesser scaup duck, *Aythya affinis*, p. 148

   Wing speculum gray............Ring-necked duck, *Aythya collaris*, p. 150

DENDROCYGNA VIDUATA (Linnaeus): White-faced Tree Duck; Jacamillo

Anas viduata Linnaeus, Syst. Nat., ed. 12, vol. 1, 1766, p. 205. (Cartagena, Colombia.)

Forepart of head white; sides black barred with white.

Description.—Length 380 to 430 mm. Head white to behind level of eyes; posterior area of head, sides of neck, center of breast, abdomen, lower back, wings, and tail black; foreneck white in some, or black with a spot of white in the center in others; a brown band around lower neck, upper breast, and upper back; sides buffy white barred with black; upper back fuscous lined with buff.

Iris brown; bill black; tarsus bluish gray; toes darker; claws black.

Measurements.—Males (4 from Venezuela, Brazil, Paraguay, and Argentina), wing 206-229 (218), tail 56.5-63.4 (60.7), culmen from base 47.0-49.0 (48.0), tarsus 49.5-56.7 (54.3) mm.

Females (4 from Panamá, Venezuela, and Argentina), wing 207-228 (215), tail 60.5-64.4 (62.2), culmen from base 43.8-49.3 (46.6), tarsus 49.8-53.7 (51.7) mm.

Resident. Formerly fairly common, now rare; recorded from the Canal Zone, and from the marshes near the Río Pacora and the Río La Jagua.

Little is known regarding this species in Panamá. Griscom (Bull. Mus. Comp. Zool., vol. 78, 1935, p. 296) records it with the statement "Canal Zone (1 shot)," without further detail. There are two specimens in the U. S. National Museum from the marshes near Pacora, Panamá, one taken on July 30, 1928, by J. A. Weber, and one collected July 20, 1931, by Rex Benson.

The species seems always to have been local in occurrence, since it was not reported by early naturalists and collectors except as noted. Karl Curtis informs me that in the early 1930's there was an invasion of hundreds of these ducks in the La Jagua area and that they nested there in cover of tall grass in the pastures, in company with the black-bellied tree duck. Elsewhere they are reported as nesting in hollow trees. The 8 to 12 eggs are described as yellowish or ivory white, with a size range from 42 to 51 mm. long by 34 to 41 mm. broad. In the records of the La Jagua Hunting Club, Herbert Clark recorded 40 shot in 1940, 9 in 1941, 4 in 1942, and one in 1943, an account that indicates their steady decline in number. None have been seen in recent years.

The species is known locally as the *jacamillo,* from the form of the head markings that suggest a bridle. It has been recorded elsewhere in Central America only in Guanacaste, Costa Rica (at Bebedero).

DENDROCYGNA BICOLOR BICOLOR (Vieillot): Fulvous Tree Duck; Yaguaso Colorado

Anas bicolor Vieillot, Nouv. Dict. Hist. Nat., nouv. éd., vol. 5, Dec. 1816, p. 136. (Paraguay.)

Under surface plain cinnamon-brown; with prominent stripes of buff and black on the elongated flank feathers.

Description.—Length 460 to 480 mm. Head, upper neck, and under surface cinnamon-brown, deeper in color on crown and sides; a black streak down hind neck, and a band of dull white, lined finely with black, on the middle of foreneck; back, wings, and tail black, the back barred broadly with cinnamon brown; lesser wing coverts rufous brown; upper tail coverts buff; sides and flanks with prominent, elongated feathers, each with a broad central stripe of buff, bordered narrowly with black.

Measurements.—Males (4 from Colombia and Argentina), wing 215-219(217), tail 49.0-58.0 (53.7), culmen from base 44.9-50.0 (47.6), tarsus 52.2-57.5 (55.3) mm.

Females (3 from Argentina), wing 203-218 (208), tail 49.0-58.2 (52.4), culmen from base 45.5-48.0 (47.0), tarsus 51.5-56.5 (54.2) mm.

Accidental visitor. The only record is of one shot by Karl Curtis in the La Jagua marshes, in eastern Panamá province on June 14, 1936 (Griswold, Auk, 1936, p. 457).

The specimen, in the collections of the Museum of Comparative Zoology, is an adult bird in slightly worn plumage. The species is found in northwestern Colombia and may be expected to wander casually into Darién.

DENDROCYGNA AUTUMNALIS AUTUMNALIS (Linnaeus): Black-bellied Tree Duck: Güichichí

FIGURE 22

Anas autumnalis Linnaeus, Syst. Nat., ed. 10, vol. 1, 1758, p. 127. (West Indies.)

A prominent white patch in the wing; sides and abdomen black.

Description.—Length 430 to 460 mm. Crown, lower neck, upper breast, and back rufescent brown; sides of head, and upper neck light gray; throat white; lower back, abdomen, flight feathers, and tail black; a band of brownish gray across breast; lesser wing coverts brownish buff; middle coverts gray; greater coverts, and bases of central primaries prominently white; under tail coverts streaked with white.

Measurements.—Males (5 from Panamá and northern Colombia), wing 217-235 (227), tail 60.4-76.0 (67.1), culmen from base 47.5-57.5 (50.7), tarsus 55.1-57.2 (56.2) mm.

Females (5 from Panamá and northern Colombia), wing 222-237 (226), tail 59.0-70.5 (64.0), culmen from base 46.6-50.0 (48.5), tarsus 52.0-56.0 (54.9) mm.

Resident. Tolerably common; recorded on the Pacific slope from western Chiriquí (Divalá), Veraguas (Soná), Herrera (lower Río Santa María, Ciénaga Macana), eastern Panamá (Tocumen, Pacora, Río La Jagua); Darién (specimen in U. S. National Museum without definite locality); and, on the Caribbean side, in the eastern San Blas (Permé, Obaldía).

Lawrence (Ann. Lyc. Nat. Hist., vol. 8, 1863, p. 13) recorded one received from McLeannan; Salvin had a specimen from the same source (Salvadori, Cat. Birds Brit. Mus., vol. 27, 1895, p. 161) and saw two tame birds kept by McLeannan at Lion Hill (Sclater and Salvin, Proc. Zool. Soc. London, 1876, p. 374). Festa, also, obtained a pair alive in Panama City (Salvadori and Festa, Boll. Mus. Zool. Anat. Comp. Univ. Torino, vol. 14, no. 339, 1899, p. 13).

These attractive ducks are found along the lower courses of the larger rivers, in the brackish waters back of the mangrove swamps, and about fresh-water lagoons.

In the early morning of March 4, 1948, on the Río Santa María, above the mouth, I saw about 20 resting on an open sandbar exposed by low tide, some asleep and some preening. From a distance they resembled small geese. Later, as the water level rose with the incoming tide, the flock took flight toward distant mangrove swamps. One

FIG. 22.—Black-bellied tree duck, güichichí, *Dendrocygna autumnalis autumnalis*.

taken a few days later, an immature bird, came flying slowly past me at the Ciénaga Macana, as I stood in water to my waist, and alighted on a growth of water hyacinth. I waded slowly toward it through the sticky mud, expecting each moment that it would fly, but it stood watching with head erect, flicking its wings alternately until I was close enough for a shot. In June 1953 I noted these ducks regularly in pairs on the Río San Pablo, below Soná, Veraguas; a female taken on June 2 was about to lay. Here they rested on sandbanks and also perched in trees.

From 1936 to 1942 records of the La Jagua Hunting Club show this species as one of importance as game until at the very end of the period it showed great decrease in number. A few still remain, as I saw several here at the end of June 1953. They are subject to little hunting pressure now during May and June, as that period marks the usual end of the shooting season.

Little is known of their nesting in Panamá except that the eggs are reported from hollows in trees. Karl Curtis was told of one nest with 25 in a hollow stub at the Ciénaga Macana. In color the eggs are ivory-white. Measurements given by Schönwetter (Handb. Ool. pt. 2, 1960, p. 124) for the species as a whole (without regard to geographic races) are as follows: 44-58 × 29-42 mm.

These ducks are popular as captives and, kept usually in pairs, live well in a domesticated state. Young birds may be tethered by a cord tied about the neck or to one leg, but they soon become tame so that they are allowed to range in freedom among the usual domestic fowl. In view of the regular commerce that existed with the Spanish mainland in the eighteenth and early nineteenth centuries it is quite probable that captive ducks of this species recorded in Jamaica by Gosse in 1847, and by March in 1866, may have come in part from Panamá.

A northern race, *Dendrocygna a. fulgens* Friedmann, with the breast, foreneck, and back deeper reddish brown, that ranges from Costa Rica north to southern Texas, may come to extreme western Panamá, but to date it has not been recorded.

CAIRINA MOSCHATA (Linnaeus): Muscovy Duck; Pato Real

FIGURE 23

Anas moschata Linnaeus, Syst. Nat., ed. 10, vol. 1, 1758, p. 124. (Brazil.)

Largest of the ducks found in Panamá; brownish black, with a greenish sheen.

Description.—Length, male, 760 to 840 mm., female 580 to 610 mm. Male, with a prominent crest, and fleshy reddish caruncles over the eye and at the base of the bill; grayish black underneath; blacker above with a sheen of green, particularly on the wings, changing to violet on the upper back; under side of wing and wing coverts white, the latter forming a prominent patch.

Female, similar but duller, with caruncles on head reduced or absent.

Immature, duller in color, with white in wing reduced to a few feathers in the greater coverts.

An adult male that I shot in Paraguay had the soft parts colored as follows: iris cream-buff; nail on mandible and maxilla dark neutral gray; remainder of tip of bill dark drab gray, washed on the margin with brown; spots behind nostrils, line of culmen, and central part of mandibular rami, pale drab gray; band around bill in front of nostrils, base of bill, and bare skin on side of head, black; caruncles black at base, purplish vinaceous at tip; tarsus and toes black.

FIG. 23.—Muscovy duck, pato real, *Cairina moschata*.

Measurements.—Males (5 from México, Costa Rica, Colombia, Paraguay, and northern Argentina), wing 363-404 (385), tail 182-198 (191), culmen, from frontal feathering, 66.6-76.6 (69.9), tarsus 63.2-70.0 (66.3) mm.

Females (5 from México and Colombia), wing 293-326 (308), tail 142-167 (153), culmen, from frontal feathering, 52.0-59.5 (54.8), tarsus 45.9-55.0 (51.2) mm.

Resident. Fairly common locally on the Pacific slope in eastern Panamá (Río La Jagua, Río Chico, Río Chimán, Río Majé), and Darién (Laguna de Pita, Río Tuira, Río Jaqué); Isla Coiba.

The only published record that refers to the Canal Zone is that of Osbert Salvin in 1863, who said of it (Sclater and Salvin, Proc. Zool. Soc. London, 1864, p. 373), following his brief visit at Lion Hill, "Common in the swamps of the low forests." Karl Curtis has informed me that he found these ducks common on the lower Chagres and along its tributary the Río Indio below Gatún in early days on the Isthmus, but through hunting, and as the formation of Gatun Lake flooded out their haunts, they have become rare.

The *pato real* in Panamá is the duck most prized by hunters and the one that is universally known. It is curious, therefore, that the definite information available on its distribution, as outlined above, covers a somewhat limited area. It is probable that it ranges also along the Caribbean coast.

These ducks frequent small channels or swampy places in wooded areas, where they range singly or in small groups. I have seen them flying morning and evening, sometimes high in air, but more often low, above water. On Isla Coiba at sunrise one morning half a dozen passed along the shore of Bahía Damas, the only time that I have seen them over salt water. At the La Jagua Hunting Club they are found in fair abundance. From 1936 to 1943 the number shot annually ranged from 13 (in 1936) to 79 (in 1939). One evening here, as I was writing notes by lamp light, one, apparently confused by the light, flew against the side of the house.

Males often are nearly double the size of females and are decidedly heavier. The late Dr. Herbert Clark weighed 65 shot at La Jagua and recorded the heaviest as $7\frac{1}{4}$ pounds ($3\frac{1}{4}$ kilos). Phillips (Nat. Hist. Ducks, vol. 1, 1922, p. 57) reports males with a maximum weight of 4 to 5 kilos, and females of $2\frac{1}{2}$ kilos.

The nesting season appears to be in June, as on June 28, 1953, at La Jagua I was told of a female seen with 11 newly hatched young. The eggs are laid in hollows in trees, rarely amid rushes, on a scanty amount of down from the parent bird. The setting is usually 8 or 9, occasionally more, perhaps when 2 females join. The eggs are glossy white with a buffy tinge, oval in form. Schönwetter (Handb. Ool., pt. 2, 1960, p. 125) gives the range of measurement as 56.5-67.5 × 42.7-48.0 mm.

In two stomachs of males taken in the Canal Zone March 14, 1920, one held many remains of a thick-shelled seed that was not identified. The other was filled with fragments of seeds of some species of pickerelweed (Pontederiaceae) and a few of a sedge (*Fimbristylis*).

I have recorded a wing bone of this species from deposits of Late Pleistocene age at El Hatillo, west of Pesé, Herrera, where it was found by C. Lewis Gazin, during excavations in the fossil beds of this area (Wetmore, Wilson Bull., vol. 68, 1956, p. 327).

SARKIDIORNIS SYLVICOLA Ihering and Ihering: American Comb Duck; Pato Crestudo

FIGURE 24

Sarkidiornis sylvicola Ihering and Ihering, Cat. Fauna Brazileira, vol. 1, Aves Brazil, 1907, p. 72. (Northeastern Brazil.)

A very large duck with a rounded comb on the base of the bill in the male; back, sides, and spots on head and neck, black; elsewhere white.

Description.—Length, male 610 mm., female 500 to 540 mm. Male, with a fleshy comb on the bill, 35 by 50 mm. in the adult, smaller in the immature; feathers on back of head and upper hindneck curled, forming a slight crest; center of crown, hindneck, and scattered spots over sides of head and upper neck, black with a violet sheen; sides, back, wings, and tail black, with a sheen varying from blue and violet to green and bronzy green; rest of plumage white.

Female, without the comb or crest; sides grayish brown; more heavily spotted on head, and barred on back and sides of lower neck.

The species may be confused by hunters with the *pato real,* as the two are about the same size. Males of the comb ducks are easily told by the rounded, compressed ridge rising from the base of the bill over the nostrils, this being very large in adults, and of fair size in immature individuals. The females lack the comb but may be recognized by the white underparts and the blackish spotting on the white of the neck and sides of the head.

"Bill dull lead color; iris black or very dark brown; legs and feet dirty yellowish green." (Phillips, Nat. Hist. Ducks, vol. 1, 1922, p. 77.)

Measurements.—Males (4 from Panamá, Venezuela, and Paraguay), wing 327-365 (348), tail 129-135 (131), culmen from base 56.3-69.9 (63.3), tarsus 69.3-76.1 (73.5) mm.

Female (1 from Paraguay), wing 301, tail 116, culmen from base 48.3, tarsus 52.8 mm.

Resident. Tolerably common on the Río Chucunaque in Darién; casual on the Río La Jagua, eastern Panamá.

The first record of this species for the isthmus was an immature male taken March 30, 1949 (Wetmore, Auk, 1951, p. 526; the date given as "May 29" in the original reference is in error). A band of 5 comb ducks, according to native hunters, had appeared on the marshes on the Río La Jagua, at the end of March 1949, and a few days later on March 30 Baldomiro Moreno, our helper, shot one near the La Jagua Hunting Club while night-hunting for *pato real*. This was an immature male, with the comb small, very fat, and the testes in resting stage. Later, on May 20 and 21, Karl Curtis saw three comb ducks together and one flying alone.

In Darién, on March 27, 1959, on the Río Chucunaque, near the mouth of the Río Tuquesa, one that proved to be an adult male flew

FIG. 24.—Head of American comb duck, pato crestudo, *Sarkidiornis sylvicola*, male, to show the knob on the bill.

overhead and presently returned to perch on an open branch in the top of a tall guarumo. In silhouette and in manner of flight the bird was so like the muscovy duck that I did not recognize it until it alighted, when I could see the large comb on the bill and the white underparts. In the tree the bird jerked and craned the extended neck as the male Muscovy does when nervous or excited. I was told that they were regular in occurrence here, but few seemed to distinguish them from the ordinary *pato real*. Little is known of their habits anywhere within their extensive range in South America.

It is probable that the species will be found from time to time in marshy areas adjacent to the lower Río Bayano and the Río Chico, particularly in dry seasons when scarcity of water may make it necessary for them to wander from their usual haunts.

Schönwetter (Handb. Ool., pt. 2, 1960, pp. 113, 114) remarks that eggs of the genus are cream-colored and smooth. He gives the dimensions of 2 eggs of *S. sylvicola* (p. 125) as 58.4-60.6×43.2-43.6 mm.

ANAS PLATYRHYNCHOS PLATYRHYNCHOS Linnaeus: Mallard; Ánade Real

Anas platyrhynchos Linnaeus, Syst. Nat., ed. 10, vol. 1, 1758, p. 125. (Sweden.)

A large duck; male head green, and a white collar around neck; female mottled brown, with blue wing speculum, bordered on both sides by a line of white.

Description.—Length 560 to 660 mm. Male, head and neck bright green, with a narrow collar of white; back brownish; rump, and upper and lower tail coverts, black, the middle upper coverts curled upward at the end; wing speculum bright blue, bordered with white on either side; breast chestnut brown; rest of under surface gray.

Female, mottled dusky and brown, with the wing speculum like that of the male.

Measurements (from Delacour, Waterfowl World, vol. 2, 1956, p. 42).—Males, wing 260-270, tail 82-95, culmen 50-56, tarsus 40-44 mm. Females, wing 240-270, tail 80-90, culmen 43-52, tarsus 38-42 mm.

An accidental visitor. Migrant from the north.

The only report of this species that is at all definite is of "one seen" by Jewel (Auk, 1913, p. 424) on one of the lakes near Miraflores, Canal Zone, on Nov. 26, 1911. Other notices in literature refer to Lawrence (Ann. Lyc. Nat. Hist. New York, 1863, p. 13) in an account of birds collected by McLeannan, where the mallard is included with the statement that this species was one of "a few satisfactorily determined from a list furnished by him, without specimens—such for instance as the King Vulture, Musk Duck, Mallard, Brown Pelican, etc. I omit many others named in the list, as they require to be more positively identified."

Karl Curtis informs me that in over 40 years of hunting he has never seen a mallard, though from time to time female pintails have been brought to him on the supposition that they were the species under discussion. North of Panamá, the mallard comes regularly to southern México and is reported casually to Nicaragua and Costa Rica.

ANAS ACUTA Linnaeus: Pintail; Pato Rabudo

Anas acuta Linnaeus, Syst. Nat., ed. 10, vol. 1, 1758, p. 126. (Sweden.)

Of medium size, with long, slender neck, and pointed tail; wing speculum bronze green or grayish brown with a bronze sheen.

Description.—Length 580 to 710 mm. Male, head and hindneck grayish brown; back gray, finely lined with black; long scapulars and tertials black, bordered with gray; wing coverts brownish gray; long, pointed middle tail feathers black; foreneck and under parts white; sides barred finely with black; under tail coverts black, speculum bronze green.

Female, blackish brown, spotted and streaked with buff; below dull white mottled with brown; speculum grayish brown with a sheen of bronze green; tail pointed, but shorter than in the male.

Measurements (from Delacour, Waterfowl World, vol. 2, 1956, p. 131).—Males, wing 254-287, tail 172-209, culmen 48-59, tarsus 39-44 mm.

Females, wing 242-266, tail 114-127, culmen 45-50, tarsus 38-42 mm.

An irregular winter migrant. At times abundant.

Published reports of this duck are based mainly on its inclusion by Lawrence (Ann. Lyc. Nat. Hist. New York, 1863, p. 13) in a list of birds sent to him without supporting specimens by James McLeannan. The records of the La Jagua Hunting Club segregated ducks killed by species beginning in 1936. The pintail appears first in 1938 when 45 were shot, and figures annually to the end of the record in 1943, when 47 were taken. There seem to have been few present in 1941 when only 3 were shot, and in 1942 when 6 were killed. In 1949 at La Jagua I saw one killed by Baldomiro Moreno on March 12, when the flight was nearly at end. Earlier they had been common. Moreno caught one alive while night hunting on March 29, probably a cripple. One banded by Ian Cowan at Murphy Lake, 150-mile House, Kamloops District, British Columbia, August 1, 1954, was reported by Karl Curtis as killed at the La Jagua Hunting Club on December 15 in the same year. There are 5 additional returns of banded birds from La Jagua and of 9 others from Bocas del Toro Los Santos, and Coclé. On January 2, 1955 I saw one at a pozo above La Jagua, and learned that several thousand had been present through December. On January 8 I was told that thousands of ducks, including many pintails, rested on bars at the mouth of the Río Chico. The birds continued to be abundant through January, and Karl Curtis told me that 10 were shot February 2. Pintails have been reported there in greater or lesser number annually since that time.

They come also to fresh-water impoundments near Changuinola, but I have no detail as to their abundance in this area.

ANAS DISCORS Linnaeus: Blue-winged Teal; Cerceta Ala-azul

FIGURE 25

Small size and grayish-blue patch on the shoulder distinguish this teal from other ducks found in Panamá.

Description.—Length 340 to 380 mm. Male, head and neck dark gray, blacker on crown, with a broad white patch on the side of the forepart of the head; upper surface blackish, with edgings of buff

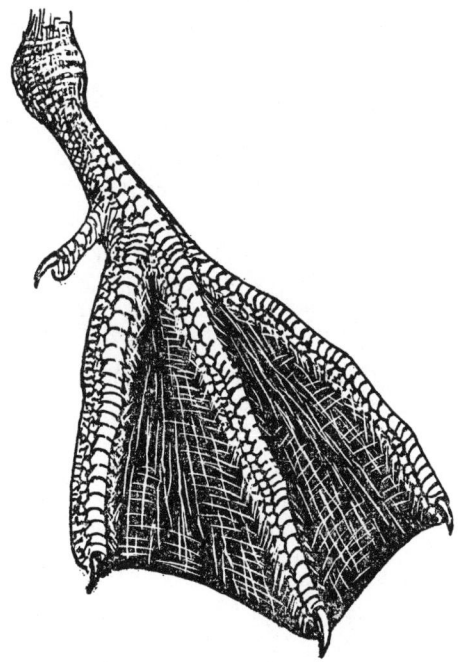

FIG. 25.—Foot of blue-winged teal, cerceta ala-azul, *Anas discors*, without a lobe on the hindtoe.

and dull gray; lesser and middle wing coverts and a line on the tertials grayish blue, forming a prominent patch; primary coverts broadly white at ends, black at base; speculum deep green; under tail coverts black, with a white patch on flanks; rest of lower surface dull rusty brown, barred and spotted with black, the feathers white basally.

Female, duller, marked by grayish-blue shoulder patch; no white on head or flank; under surface mottled with dull white, dull buff, and dull black; exposed culmen 37-41.5 mm.

Common winter visitor; most abundant of all ducks; found wherever there are fresh-water ponds, and along the larger rivers, from sea level to lakes and pools in mountain areas.

Two geographic races are represented among those that come to Panamá.

Records of the 121 banded blue-winged teal that have been reported from Panamá all came from the interior range of the typical subspecies and cover the suitable lowland areas in the Republic, but more especially such well-known shooting localities as the mouth of the Río Tuira in Darién, the La Jagua marshes in eastern Province of Panamá, the marshes near Río Hato and Aguadulce, Coclé, the area from París, Herrera to Las Tablas, Los Santos, and the vicinity of Pedregal in western Chiriquí. The returns indicate a considerable flight from the north during October, with a few earlier as shown by dates of birds killed in Chiriquí, September 12, and in Coclé, September 19. Seven of the reports are of birds shot more than 2 years after having been banded, one having lived for 4 and another for 5 years.

ANAS DISCORS DISCORS Linnaeus

Anas discors Linnaeus, Syst. Nat., ed. 12, vol. 1, 1766, p. 205. (South Carolina.)

Characters.—The typical subspecies is somewhat lighter in color than *Anas d. orphna*.

Measurements (from Stewart and Aldrich, Proc. Biol. Soc. Washington, 1956, pp. 31-32).—Males (25 specimens), wing 173-193 (181.9), tail 59.5-71.5 (64.6), culmen 37.5-42.0 (39.9), tarsus 30-35 (32.2) mm.

Females (15 specimens), wing 167-183 (174.5), tail 59.5-70.0 (64), culmen 37-40 (38.9), tarsus 30-33 (31.4) mm.

Migrant from the north. The abundant form in Panamá.

Records of actual occurrence, assumed to be the typical race, are as follows:

Chiriquí: Lakes at 1,280 meters, near El Volcán; Las Lajas (one Feb. 15, 1956).
Bocas del Toro: Changuinola, abundant; Almirante (specimen, Oct. 27, 1960).
Veraguas: Laguna del Castillo (Salvin, Proc. Zool. Soc. London, 1870, p. 219).
Herrera: Ciénaga Macana, Ciénaga de Buho.
Los Santos: Punta Mala.
Coclé: Puerto Aguadulce.
Colón (western): Río Indio.
Canal Zone: Mindi, Gatun Lake, Gamboa, Juan Mina, Chiva Chiva Lakes.

Panamá (eastern): Pacora, Río La Jagua, Chico, El Llano, Chimán, Río Curutú, Charco del Toro on Río Majé.
Darién: Pinogana, Boca de Cupe.
San Blas: Mandinga, Puerto Obaldía.
Isla Coiba: Several seen in January 1956; reported to be regular in occurrence.

I have male and female specimens taken on the Río La Jagua near Chico, March 15, 1949. An albino was killed here by Gil Hulcher on April 17, 1949. One banded at Lanz Lake, Rock County, Nebraska, on July 30, 1955, was killed at the head of tidewater on the Río Tonosí, below Tonosí, Los Santos, on February 22, 1958.

The main flight from the north arrives in the latter half of October, and the birds remain in numbers until the latter part of April. Early records of fall arrival are as follows: September 18, 1945 (specimen in Museo Nacional, from Puerto La Chorrera); September 22, 1931 (Puerto Obaldía, San Blas, specimen in Carnegie Museum); September 23, 1928 (Changuinola, specimen, Peters, Bull. Mus. Comp. Zool., vol. 71, 1931, p. 307); October 14, 1911 (Canal Zone, Jewel, Auk, 1913, p. 424); October 15, 1915 (Gamboa, Hallinan, Auk. 1924, p. 307).

At the La Jagua Club I have noted regular evening flights from the latter part of March into April and have observed these also in the last week of March near the head of tidewater on the Río Majé. I believe that these were birds passing northward from wintering grounds in South America. Karl Curtis recorded 3 of these teal flying at La Jagua on May 20 and 21, 1949, an unusually late date. The occasional bird found there through the period of northern summer is undoubtedly a cripple from the winter shooting. The flight in 1959, 1960 and 1961 was reported to be unusually small, undoubtedly a reflection of the reduced numbers found these years in the north.

About ponds and lakes blue-winged teal range in small bands that feed by dabbling in the shallows, and then rest and preen on some secluded shore. Where not disturbed they become very tame, and in travel on the rivers I have had flocks fly ahead of my piragua repeatedly, often for considerable distances. Hundreds have been reported on occasion from the seashore near the mouth of the Río Pacora. The largest concentrations that I have recorded personally have been on the impounded waters of flooded fields near Changuinola.

On two occasions I have seen these teal alight on the open sea, once off Punta Mala, where a bird rose to fly through a host of circling terns, and once at high tide off Panamá Viejo.

Much of the hunting of all kinds in Panamá to date has been through jack-lighting at night, which, so far as ducks are concerned, requires more skill than may be supposed. Men wait in complete dark at pools favored by ducks, with head lamp and gun in readiness. When the birds arrive they alight with an audible spatter and disturbance in the water. As the headlight is flashed the gun must fire instantly, since the birds rise in the second that the light appears and are gone. Some become expert at this, but others never learn the proper coordination. The annual kill at the La Jagua Hunting Club has ranged from 85 in 1938 to 257 in 1942 and 173 in 1943.

ANAS DISCORS ORPHNA Stewart and Aldrich

Anas discors orphna Stewart and Aldrich, Proc. Biol. Soc. Washington, vol. 69, May 21, 1956, p. 31. (Elliott, Dorchester County, Maryland.)

Characters.—The dark markings blacker; head and neck darker gray; averaging darker throughout.

Measurements (from Stewart and Aldrich, cit. supra).—Males (8 specimens), wing 180-193 (186.1), tail 61.0-69.5 (66.4), culmen 35.0-43.5 (41.0), tarsus 30.5-34.5 (32.0) mm.

Females (3 specimens), wing 168.5-180.0 (173.2), tail 59.5-65.5 (63.3), culmen 39.0-41.5 (40.0), tarsus 30.5-33.0 (31.5) mm.

Winter visitor from the north. Rare.

The only record for Panamá is a male shot by Rudolfo Hinds near Almirante, Bocas del Toro, March 25, 1960.

This subspecies, marked by darker colors, nests in brackish waters along the Atlantic seaboard from Nova Scotia south to northeastern North Carolina. In migration it has been reported in Cuba and in Venezuela.

ANAS CYANOPTERA SEPTENTRIONALIUM Snyder and Lumsden:
Cinnamon Teal; Cerceta Colorado

Anas cyanoptera septentrionalium Snyder and Lumsden, Occ. Pap. Royal Ontario Mus. Zool., no. 10, Aug. 10, 1951, p. 16. (2 miles south of Jensen, Utah.)

Similar in form and color of shoulder to the blue-winged teal; male reddish brown, without white mark in front of eye; female differs from blue-wing only in faintly longer bill.

Description.—Length 340 to 380 mm. Male, in size and form like the blue-winged teal but reddish brown, with blackish rump and tail, and markings of black on the back; wing coverts grayish blue.

Female, so like the female blue-winged teal that it may be identified with difficulty; bill usually averaging longer, 40.8 to 44.1 mm.

Measurements (from Snyder and Lumsden, cit. supra, p. 12).—Males (41 specimens), wing 176-194 (184.9), tail 64-77 (71.2), culmen 39-47 (43.9), tarsus 30-34 (32.2) mm.

Females (personal records, 12 specimens), wing 172-181 (176.1), tail 59.0-69.8 (64.5), culmen 40.8-44.1 (42.1), tarsus 31.0-32.1 (31.7) mm.

Winter visitor. Abundance not known.

Griscom (Bull. Mus. Comp. Zool., vol. 78, 1935, p. 296) reported it as "Canal Zone (1 shot)" without giving details as to the source for his statement. The only definite occurrences are of 3 banded birds, 2 from California and Utah killed at the Río La Jagua January 20, 1955, and January 7, 1956, and one from Idaho, taken near Chame November 8, 1957. Karl Curtis informs me that he shot one at La Jagua in the month of June, which may have been a bird that did not move northward in spring with the other ducks, but also raises the interesting possibility that it may have been a wanderer from one of the populations of this species found in South America.

SPATULA CLYPEATA (Linnaeus): Shoveler; Pato Cuchara
Figure 26

Anas clypeata Linnaeus, Syst. Nat., ed. 10, vol. 1, 1758, p. 124. (Southern Sweden.)

Differs from all other ducks found in Panamá in the form of the bill, which is narrow at the base and much widened toward the tip.

Description.—Length 460 to 510 mm. Male, head, neck, and back black, the head with a sheen of green; lateral tail feathers white, central ones black; wing coverts light blue; speculum green, bordered with white anteriorly; upper breast white; lower breast, sides, and abdomen chestnut brown, with white on the flanks.

Female, brown, mottled with buff; blue wing patch and broad bill tip as in the male.

Measurements.—Males (5 from eastern United States), wing 232-239 (237), tail 76.0-85.4 (80.5), culmen 60.5-71.0 (66.9), tarsus 35.8-40.7 (38.2) mm.

Females (5 from eastern United States), wing 221-226 (223.2), tail 74.6-88.7 (79.8), culmen 59.5-61.8 (60.5), tarsus 34.7-37.7 (36.1) mm.

Winter visitor. Tolerably common at times, but irregular in appearance.

W. W. Brown, Jr., obtained a female at David, Chiriquí, October 16, 1900 (Bangs, Auk, 1901, p. 358; reported as from "Divala" by Griscom, Bull. Mus. Comp. Zool., vol. 78, 1935, p. 297, through a slip of the pen). I was told that shovelers were shot occasionally near Changuinola, Bocas del Toro. The records of the La Jagua Hunting Club list 2 killed in 1940 and 9 in 1943. At times they have been fairly common there. In recent years, Karl Curtis shot a male there in January 1953 and another (sex not stated) on February 3, 1955; and I secured a female there on January 14, 1962.

Fig. 26.—Head of shoveler, pato cuchara, *Spatula clypeata*, male, to show form of bill.

MARECA AMERICANA (Gmelin): American Widgeon; Pato Calvo
Figure 27

Anas americana Gmelin, Syst. Nat., vol. 1, pt. 2, 1789, p. 526. (New York.)

A medium-sized duck with small bill; male with white crown.

Description.—Length 460 to 540 mm. Male, crown white; a green stripe behind eye; rest of head light buff, sprinkled with small dots of black; upper surface light brown with fine lines of black; a prominent white patch on the wing; speculum green, bordered by black; rump, undertail coverts, and tail black; breast and sides pinkish brown; a prominent patch on either side of the flanks; under wing coverts white. Bill short and small.

Female, head dull white, finely spotted with blackish brown; blackish brown above, lined with dull brown; speculum black; a white or grayish patch on the wing; upper breast and sides brown; lower breast and abdomen white; bill like that of male.

Measurements.—Males (5 from southeastern United States), wing 253-260 (255.4), tail 98.2-126.5 (110.1), culmen 35.0-37.6 (35.9), tarsus 36.9-38.8 (37.9) mm.

Females (5 from Alaska to California and Maryland), wing 233-245 (240.6), tail 85.6-96.0 (90.3), culmen 32.7-36.7 (34.1), tarsus 35.3-37.2 (36.4) mm.

Irregular winter visitor. Fairly common some years on the Pacific side in the Canal Zone and eastern Panamá province; more common near Changuinola, Bocas del Toro.

In 1958, near Changuinola, I recorded 15 to 20 scattered over a broad lagoon on January 17, and a hundred or more in the same water on January 30. I was told that many were shot here each year. Charles O. Handley, Jr., recorded one on the Río Changuinola at the mouth of the Río Teribe on March 7, 1960. Griscom (Bull. Mus. Comp. Zool., vol. 78, 1935, p. 297) reported "Canal Zone (once)," a record based probably on the head of a female in the Lawrence collection, collected by McLeannan in 1863. December 10, 1955, I

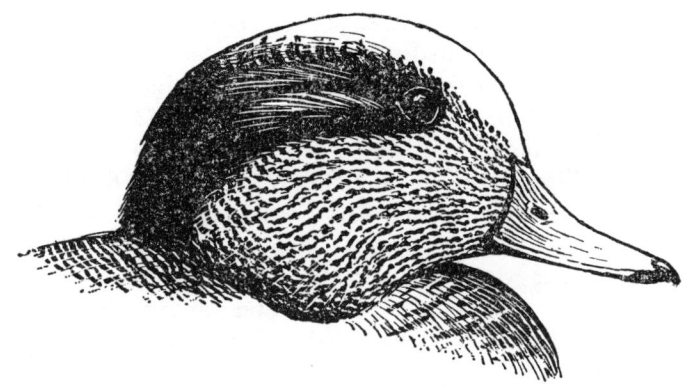

FIG. 27.—Head of American widgeon, pato calvo, *Mareca americana,* male.

saw an adult male near Juan Mina, Canal Zone, resting in a little bay at one side of the main stream of the Río Chagres, and on January 1, 1956, I noted 3 at the Miraflores lakes beyond Fort Clayton. In 1957 the birds were more common, as I saw a number at the lakes last mentioned on January 13 and 21 and February 24. On January 10, 1961, I shot a male on the Chagres at Juan Mina, which appears to be the second complete specimen record for the isthmus.

At the Río La Jagua Karl Curtis shot one during a hunt in 1935, and another January 15, 1938 (Bond and de Schauensee, Acad. Nat. Sci. Philadelphia, Mon. 6, 1944, p. 27). According to Mr. Curtis two were killed there in 1954. There is record of one banded as a duckling in Saskatchewan July 27, 1956, that was taken in southern Los Santos, in December, 1957.

In summary, it appears that these ducks come in fair numbers from time to time but may not be present each year.

AYTHYA AFFINIS (Eyton): Lesser Scaup; Pato Pechiblanco
FIGURE 28

Fuligula affinis Eyton, Mon. Anatidae or duck tribe, June, 1838, p. 157. (North America.)

Of medium size, with white wing speculum; young males, and females with white in front of eye.

Description.—Length 380 to 410 mm. Adult male, head and neck black, with faint purplish sheen; upper back, breast, rump, wings, upper and under tail coverts, and tail black, often with a brownish wash; center of back and scapulars lined narrowly with black and white; wing speculum white, bordered with black.

Female and immature male, forepart of head, breast, and abdomen white; rest of plumage brownish black, except for the white wing speculum, like that of the male.

Measurements.—Males (5 from southeastern United States), wing 193-200 (197), tail 51.8-54.5 (52.6), culmen 39.6-42.9 (41.1), tarsus 33.9-36.0 (35.0) mm.

Females (5 from the United States), wing 185-191 (187.4), tail 48.0-51.0 (49.6), culmen 36.6-40.0 (38.2), tarsus 33.0-34.8 (33.6) mm.

Regular winter visitor. Tolerably common on larger bodies of fresh water, seen occasionally on salt water; arrives from the north about the middle of November, and remains through March. Recorded as follows:

Chiriquí: Lakes near El Volcán.
Bocas del Toro: Changuinola, Almirante.
Veraguas: Laguna del Castillo (Salvin, Proc. Zool. Soc. London, 1870, p. 219).
Canal Zone: Gatun Lake, Gamboa, Juan Mina, Chiva Chiva Lakes.
Panamá (eastern): Panamá Viejo; Río La Jagua.
Isla Coiba (lagoon at Cativu).

Three records of banded birds include one each from Almirante Bay, Río Hato, and La Jagua.

Lesser scaups are diving ducks that frequent ponds and lakes of quiet water and are seldom seen where tidal and other currents are changeable and rapid. They have the sociable habits common to most species of their family, and so it is usual to see them in small flocks. Single individuals may become separated during feeding periods, when the birds dive constantly, but later, when all are at rest, they group again, on open water, or, if in some place where they are not disturbed, at the water's edge. I have found them regularly on the lakes at 1280 meters elevation near El Volcán, Chiriquí, and I shot a female here on February 15, 1960. They come regularly also to the artificial lakes in the banana farms near Changuinola, where I recorded them in January 1958.

The main body of these ducks in Panamá winters on Gatun and Madden Lakes and on the broad stretches of water on the Río

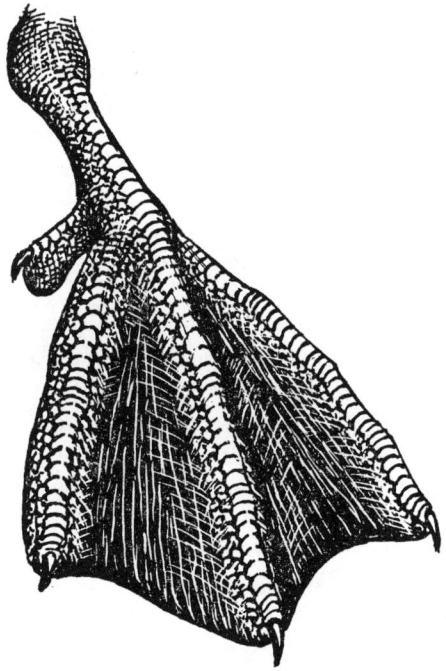

FIG. 28.—Foot of lesser scaup, pato pechiblanco, *Aythya affinis*, with a distinct lobe on the hindtoe.

Chagres above Gamboa. Here they are hunted regularly and become quite wild. There are usually a few on the small lakes in the Pedro Miguel, Chiva Chiva area, and a few come with other ducks in the marshes along the Río La Jagua, where from one to a dozen may be shot annually, though the water areas here in the main are too shallow to attract ducks that feed by diving. I recorded five on a small lagoon at Cativitel on Isla Coiba, January 14, 1956. Once, on December 31, 1955, I saw five on the salt water of the bay offshore from Panamá Viejo, but this is unusual.

AYTHYA COLLARIS (Donovan): Ring-necked Duck; Pato de Collar

Anas collaris Donovan, Brit. Birds, vol. 6, 1809, pl. 147, and text. (Lincolnshire?, England. Found in Leadenhall Market, London.)

Size of lesser scaup duck but with gray wing speculum; a light colored ring around bill back of tip; male with dark back.

Description.—Length 410 to 460 mm. Male, head and neck black with a sheen of purple; an indistinct chestnut collar on neck; back and upper breast black; lower breast and abdomen white; wing speculum gray; bill bluish gray, with two white rings and a black tip.

Female, head, neck, and upper parts dull brown; lower breast and abdomen white; speculum and light-ringed bill as in the male.

Measurements.—Males (5 from southeastern United States), wing 185-199 (191.4), tail 54.8-57.0 (54.8) culmen 43.7-46.4 (45.0), tarsus 34.3-35.9 (34.9) mm.

Females (5 from southeastern United States), wing 173-183 (178.8), tail 50.8-57.3 (54.0), culmen 42.2-46.7 (44.2), tarsus 32.1-35.4 (33.6) mm.

Winter visitor from the north. Not common.

This is a migrant from North America, that was first formally recorded for Panamá from a male seen on a lake at the Río Caimito near Red Tank in the Canal Zone on February 25, 1951, by Dr. and Mrs. Robert Scholes (Condor, 1954, p. 166). I saw several on the Río Chagres near Juan Mina in January and again in December 1955, and noted one near Pedro Miguel on January 7, 1960. Karl Curtis informs me that they have been shot from time to time along the Río La Jagua.

The species, here near the southern limit of its winter migration, is little known in Panamá because of its general similarity to the Lesser Scaup Duck.

OXYURA DOMINICA (Linnaeus): Masked Duck; Pato Tigre

FIGURE 29

Anas dominica Linnaeus, Syst. Nat., ed. 12, vol. 1, 1766, p. 201. (Hispaniola.)

A small, mottled-brown duck, with heavy neck, and tail usually elevated when on the water; a prominent white patch in the wing.

Description.—Length 320 to 360 mm. Male, head and throat black; neck, upper surface, and sides chestnut-brown, the two last mentioned streaked with black; wings and tail black, with a large white patch on the wing coverts; under surface dull brownish buff.

Female, dull black above, spotted and barred irregularly with brownish buff; sides of head and under surface buffy brown, with a black line through the eye, and another on the side of the head from the gape back over the ear coverts; breast and sides mottled with black; a prominent white wing patch.

Immature male resembles the female but is more extensively black on the crown.

Measurements.—Males (5 from Panamá), wing 136.2-138.0 (137.2), tail 75.2-79.0 (77.1), culmen from base 31.1-33.9 (32.0), tarsus 26.1-27.6 (27.0) mm.

Fig. 29.—Masked duck, pato tigre, *Oxyura dominica*, male.

Females (5 from México, Panamá, and Venezuela), wing 132.0-139.0 (136.4), tail 74.0-79.2 (76.5, average of 4), culmen from base 30.8-34.2 (32.0), tarsus 25.7-27.9 (26.9) mm.

An adult male, taken December 12, 1955, had the iris reddish brown; base of the maxilla light blue, shading to light greenish blue toward the tip; nail, space immediately behind, and culmen, to and including the nostrils, and a few irregular, scattered spots over the rest of the bill, black; tip of mandible flesh color; mandibular rami pale grayish blue, with a line on either side of the tip, spots toward the base, and the bare skin between, black; tarsi and toes, including the nails, greenish olive-brown.

Resident. In the tropical zone in suitable fresh waters; locally fairly common.

Recorded as follows:

Veraguas: Pacific slope (specimen in British Museum collected by Arcé).
Herrera: Ciénaga Macana.
Canal Zone: Río Chagres between Gamboa, Juan Mina, and Santa Rosa; Miraflores lakes.
Panamá (eastern): Río La Jagua.
Darién: Laguna de Pita (Salvadori and Festa, Boll. Mus. Zool. Anat. Comp. Univ. Torino, vol. 14, no. 339, 1899, p. 13).

The masked duck is an inhabitant of fresh-water ponds and the quiet waters of the larger streams, where there are extensive growths of aquatic plants that make suitable shelter. Usually two to a dozen or more are found together in small pools or in open stands of floating vegetation where they remain quiet or seek cover. If they have not been disturbed by shooting often they are tame and allow fairly close approach. At such times they remain quiet, with neck drawn in, even when boats pass close at hand, as they are camouflaged against their background, if indeed they are not actually hidden. Their flight is swift and strong, with the white patch in the wing showing prominently. As they rise from open water they may splatter along for 4 or 5 meters to gain momentum, but they also go straight up as readily as teal. In alighting they come in a few feet above the surface, bank, back stroke into the wind, and then drop with a plump into the water, where they bob up and down for a few seconds, often without moving forward appreciably. Both methods—that of arising and that of alighting—are practical adaptations to a water surface covered with floating or submerged vegetation. On the wing masked ducks suggest their relative, the ruddy duck (*Oxyura jamaicensis*), as they have the same bulky head, thickened neck, and short, rounded form. Flight in the two is equally strong, but masked ducks rise more easily from the surface of the water. While they are active on the wing they hide regularly among standing water plants. Sometimes when approached they submerge quietly, and then usually disappear completely, even where the plant cover appears too sparse to give them protection.

Little is known as yet concerning their nesting. The egg in the Barnes collection described by Bent (U. S. Nat. Mus. Bull. 130, 1925, p. 162) may be of doubtful identity since, with a measurement of 63.0 by 45.8 mm., it appears to be too large. Schönwetter (Handb. Ool., pt. 2, 1960, p. 116) describes the eggs as cream-colored, with a roughened shell, and (pt. 3, 1961, p. 133) gives the measurements of 9 specimens as 59-63 ×44-47.4 mm. which also seems over large. Bond (Checkl. Birds West Indies, Third Suppl., 1958, p. 3, fig. 1) lists 5 eggs from Cuba as decidedly smaller and smoother shelled than those of the Ruddy Duck, in color pale buff to buffy white, subelliptical in form, with measurements 53.7-55.6 × 40-41.6 mm. Persons living near the haunts of the *pato tigre* in Panamá say that it makes a nest among rushes and that it lays 4 to 6 eggs. At Juan Mina Enrique van Horn told me that he had seen a parent with 5 young about the first of December 1955. On December 12 I shot a male in breeding condition that had the intromittent organ much enlarged, with blackish, spiny papillae around the base.

The skin over the neck and upper breast in these birds is loose, thickened with fatty tissue, and full as it is in the ruddy duck, and like that species the syrinx in the male is simple without the enlarged bulb found in males of most ducks. The esophagus, when inflated with air, has an elongated sac near the center that is 25 mm. in diameter. The trachea is enlarged at the upper end, and there is a small elliptical aperture here on the ventral surface that opens into a rounded, thin-walled sac, about 10 mm. in diameter when inflated. There is also a somewhat larger extension that opens from another aperture on the dorsal surface of the trachea. Evidently these have some relation to a similar larger sac found in the male ruddy duck (Wetmore, Proc. U. S. Nat. Mus., vol. 52, 1917, pp. 479-482). These openings in the trachea of the masked duck were described many years ago by von Pelzeln (Orn. Brasiliens, 1870, p. 321) who, however, seems not to have detected the air-sacs into which they led.

Call notes have been described for the masked duck, but in my experience with these birds they have been silent. They are hunted to some extent, but they do not fly as much as the true game species. Shooting, however, has reduced their numbers.

At present the masked duck is recorded from the Caribbean drainage only on the Río Chagres. It is probable, however, that it is found near Changuinola, in Bocas del Toro, as these birds are known to wander extensively.

Order FALCONIFORMES

Family CATHARTIDAE: American Vultures; Buitres Americanos

The birds of this family, of large size, known everywhere as carrion-eaters, have the head and neck bare, or with only a scanty growth of short down or hairlike feathers. The seven living species are found only in the Americas, where they range from temperate regions in the far north and far south, and the higher mountains, throughout the warmer central areas, with their greatest abundance in the vast extent of the Tropics. Four of the seven kinds are known from Panamá, where they are seen so constantly that often they attract little attention. Three, the Gallinazo, the Noneca, and the Cacicón are readily recognized, while the fourth, the Guala is usually confused with the Noneca because of general similarity in form in these two species.

KEY TO SPECIES OF CATHARTIDAE

1. Larger; head relatively short and heavy; commissure shorter, with the posterior angle of mouth located below, or very slightly behind, the nostril; bill shorter, not more than two-thirds the length of the head; eye light colored, yellowish white in adult, grayish white in immature.
King vulture, *Sarcoramphus papa*, p. 154
Smaller; head relatively longer and more slender; commissure much longer in relation to the rest of the head, with the posterior angle of the mouth located farther back, almost beneath the eye; bill longer than the head; eye dark, reddish brown, or brown................................. 2
2. Tail square ended; legs longer, feet extending beyond end of tail when bird is flying; head completely black in life.
Black vulture, *Coragyps atratus*, p. 157
Tail rounded; legs shorter, feet not reaching end of tail during flight; head red or orange in life... 3
3. With small but prominent wartlike processes on sides of neck; head mainly orange, yellow and blue in life.
Yellow-headed vulture, *Cathartes burrovianus*, p. 168
Sides of neck smooth, head mainly red in life.
Turkey vulture, *Cathartes aura*, p. 161

SARCORAMPHUS PAPA (Linnaeus): King Vulture; Rey Gallinazo

FIGURE 30

Vultur Papa Linnaeus, Syst. Nat., ed. 10, vol. 1, 1758, p. 86. (Surinam.)

Largest of the vultures found in Panamá; adult, white with black wings; immature at a distance appears wholly black.

Description.—Length 710 to 810 mm. Adult, head and neck bare, except for a pattern of black hairlike feathers on head; a conspicuous, irregularly lobed caruncle on cere; bare skin of head, upper neck, and crop, variegated with yellow, orange, and black; a dark gray ruff around lower neck; flight feathers, rump, and tail black; elsewhere white with a buffy tinge on back and shoulders.

Immature, caruncle on bill small, often not developed; plumage throughout blackish brown, with increasing age gradually becoming white on breast and abdomen.

Aldrich (Scient. Publ. Cleveland Mus. Nat. Hist., vol. 7, 1937, p. 37) gives the following description of the soft parts in an adult: "Nape (greatly thickened and wrinkled skin) yellow; posterior auricular region flesh color washed with purplish red; sides of throat reddish orange; middle of throat yellowish orange; area of thickened and greatly wrinkled skin on side of head running in a reverse S-shaped curve from nape to angle of jaw, reddish orange on dorsal

Fig. 30.—King vulture, rey gallinazo, *Sarcoramphus papa.*

fourth, bluish gray on adjoining fourth (on same plane with eye), and gray on remaining (central) half; crown reddish orange; ring around eye red; remainder of sides of head purplish red; cere and caruncle orange; anterior two thirds of bill dull red; posterior third black; iris white."

A female living in the New York Zoological Park weighed 3 kilograms (Conway, Auk, 1962, p. 275).

Measurements.—Males (10 from México, Costa Rica, and Colombia), wing 490-525 (503), tail 207-227 (215), culmen from cere 32.1-38.8 (35.2), tarsus 93-103 (98.6) mm.

Females (2 from México), wing 490-497 (493), tail 213-217 (215), culmen from cere 33.5-34.0 (33.7), tarsus 100-106 (103) mm.

Resident. Found in small number throughout the Isthmus, from coastal areas to 1200 to 1500 meters elevation in the mountains; recorded from all of the provinces and territories, and on Isla Coiba. The total population is not large.

The usual sight of this species is of one soaring high above the earth, when its greater size and, if it is an adult, the conspicuous black and white pattern separate it instantly from other vultures that may be in the air. Rarely two appear in the same area of sky, and on a few occasions I have seen as many as four.

The *rey gallinazo* comes to carrion with the other vultures, when its larger size dominates the scene, so that the smaller species usually wait in the background until the king vulture leaves. It is this circumstance that has given the species its local names in Panamá of *cacique* and *cacicón*. Once, however, at Ana Luz, below Chepo, I saw one feeding at a carcass amid an avid swarm of black vultures.

When attracted by a prospect of food king vultures sometimes descend from high in air with great rapidity, and a roaring of wings that may be startling, particularly in heavy forest where the view of the sky is cut off by the high tree crown. At our camp at Quebrada Cauchero, on the base of Cerro Chucantí, one made such a descent when it spotted our trays of specimens spread out to dry on a pole rack in our tiny clearing. Occasionally I have come across one perched at rest in forest, when the bird peered down through light-colored eyes, with head depressed to the level of the shoulders or below. On Isla Coiba they were especially tame as they were not disturbed, so that I approached one within 12 meters without alarming it, but this is unusual.

In spite of the wide range of this species, from central México through Central America and South America to northern Argentina, little is known of its nesting. An egg in the collections of the U. S. National Museum, laid by a bird in captivity in the National Zoological Park on April 7, 1920, is unusual, for though elliptical in its central outline it is definitely bluntly pointed at both ends. It is dull white, unmarked, and has a slightly roughened, granular shell. It measures

91.4×60.8 mm. This is similar to the dimensions of 92×60 mm. given by Swann for one from "South America" (locality not listed) in the British Museum.

The Penards (Vog. Guyana, vol. 1, 1908, p. 357) state that the nest is in a hollow tree or rock fissure, and that one egg is laid. This they describe as oval, white or dirty white, with somewhat shining, roughened shell, in size 92×63 mm. Col. L. R. Wolfe has a single egg in his collection, collected many years ago in northeastern Perú, and formerly in the collection of J. Parker Norris, Jr. This is rounded oval, dull white in color, with a very finely pitted shell, and measures 89.4 by 64.2 mm (Ool. Rec., 1951, p. 18). Norris (Ool. Rec., 1926, p. 25) lists another from nothern Bolivia taken in October 1874, with a dimension of 92.5×65.0 mm.

On February 19, 1954, on Barro Colorado Island I saw a young bird, only a week or two on the wing, perched in a large tree near the laboratory building. It must have been reared near at hand. In January 1957 Carl Koford found a young bird in down, with wings nearly developed but the tail still rudimentary, living on the forest floor, also on Barro Colorado. This bird was kept under observation until it was able to fly.

Heck (Zool. Gart., vol. 27, pt. 6, 1963, p. 296) in a report of a breeding pair in captivity at the Catskill Game Farm gives the incubation period to hatching for single eggs as 56 and 58 days.

CORAGYPS ATRATUS BRASILIENSIS (Bonaparte): Black Vulture; Gallinazo

FIGURE 31

Cathartes brasiliensis Bonaparte, Consp. Gen. Avium, vol. 1, pt. 1, 1850, p. 9. (Rio de Janeiro, Brazil.)

Tail square-ended and short, so that in flight, when the legs are extended back, the toes project beyond the end.

Description.—Length 560 to 660 mm. Adult, black throughout, except on the under side of the central webs of the outer primaries, which are white, and form a prominent light patch on either wing when the bird is in the air; head and neck without feathers, black, the skin much wrinkled.

Juvenile, when hatched, with down pale cinnamon-buff over the body, changing to olive-brown on the nape and the back of the neck, and dark neutral gray from the center of the crown forward.

Measurements.—Males (17 from México, Panamá, Colombia, Venezuela, British Guiana, and Surinam), wing 386-410 (401), tail

Fig. 31.—Black vulture, gallinazo, *Coragyps atratus brasiliensis*.

160-195 (174), culmen from cere 21.8-23.7 (22.8), tarsus 69.5-82.0 (77.9) mm.

Females (23 from México, El Salvador, Panamá, Colombia, Trinidad, British Guiana, Perú, Brazil, and Bolivia), wing 388-413 (400), tail 160-181 (170), culmen from cere 21.0-24.6 (23.0), tarsus 71.8-82.0 (77.1) mm.

Resident throughout the isthmus, except in the very high mountains, found mainly in settled areas; absent or rare in regions of unbroken forest. Isla Coiba; islas Pacheca, Saboga, Bayoneta, Señora, Pedro González, and San José, in the Archipiélago de las Perlas; Isla Taboga; Isla Gobernadora.

The black vulture, recognized throughout tropical and subtropical America as an efficient scavenger, is one of the prominent species in settled areas, found singly or a few together around country houses or congregated in dozens about abattoirs or refuse dumps near villages. They enjoy protection in general through recognition of their efficient services in disposal of offal, though in recent years there has been consideration of the possibility that they may be carriers of some animal diseases as they move from carcasses of dead animals to rest near living ones in corrals and farmyards. These are matters that are under special study.

Where black vultures become unusually tame they often enter familiarly in patios, or come near buildings, where care must be used to prevent their thievery of meats or other human food. And it is necessary always, where they have become more or less domestic, for the naturalist to guard his specimens. In some village areas, where there is dependence on rain water caught by drain spouts from buildings, these vultures are distinctly troublesome when abundant, as their droppings may pollute the metal roofs, and so wash into the cisterns.

In flight these birds flap the wings rapidly several times, spread them stiffly to glide, then flap again, a method of alternately different movements that serves to identify them at any distance from the steadily soaring turkey vultures. However, black vultures also are adept at soaring in rising air currents without change to flapping wings. In such a manner they often continue for long periods, sometimes rising until they may be barely seen against the sky.

Keen vision is proverbial among vultures as they detect sources of food at distances that seem almost incredible. In work on the San Blas coast at Mandinga, in 1957 I saw none of this species until one morning I spread bodies of small birds that I had skinned for specimens on the old abandoned air strip in order to secure a check on the forms of turkey vultures present. At noon I saw first one black vulture and then another in descent at a sharp angle from high in air, and walked out to find that 9 had arrived, and that all of the meat had been eaten. During the month that I lived there I saw only one other bird of this species.

Near the coast black vultures watch the beaches for dead fish cast up by the waves. If tide is rising so that the waves wash over their feet they may seize small bits of such refuse and pull it back away from the water. About large carcasses dozens congregate with much scrambling, jostling, and fighting, in which the black vultures by force of number often crowd out the turkey vultures. Only when the king vulture, the *cacicón,* arrives do they fall back. The rapidity with which a band of black vultures will strip a dead horse or cow to bare bones and shreds of hide is remarkable. Often when a feeding group is disturbed one or two scramble out of the body cavity where they have been concealed amid the ribs.

At abattoirs groups of black vultures gather as animals are killed. On such occasions they run and hop about in much excitement while forced to wait, often holding the tail partly erect over the back, an odd attitude that gives them the appearance in outline of huge rails. It is then that the hissing sigh that is their usual note is most often heard. Though ordinarily aggressive when a number are together I have seen a laughing gull refuse to give way to a single vulture that attempted to seize a bit of fish on which the gull was feeding.

Animal carrion is the main sustenance of the black vulture, but on occasion it takes vegetable food. At Almirante they fed on ripe avocados in trees growing beside the houses, and when the fruits tumbled to the ground descended to finish them there. I have seen them eating scraps of the soft meat of coconuts (*pipas*) that had been drained of fluid and cast aside. And they also eat the oily pulp covering the seeds of some of the palms.

In the Canal Zone dozens gather in evening to roost in the trees on the slopes of Ancon Hill, and many soar for hours here in the strong air currents, particularly during the dry season. Elsewhere I have observed scattered individuals or small groups coming to roost in coconut and other tall palms. At La Jagua one season two slept on a dead stub, where they were exposed to the strong sweep of the wind. At Panamá Viejo in evening many come out from the city to roost in palms and other trees.

While silent in the main, I have heard them utter a low, guttural note, *croo-oo-oo croo croo,* varied to a husky aspiration, *hwuh-h-h,* repeated several times.

The eggs, normally 2 in number, are laid in a hollow log, a hole in a tree base, under matted vegetation in low rastrojo, or, in hill country, in cavities among rocks. There is no nest lining. On Isla Coiba in 1956 convicts working in the fields reported that the vultures had begun to nest the middle of January. On March 20, 1961, at La Jagua I found two half-grown young in a dense stand of spiny pita at the border of forest beside the marsh. They ran out when poked with a stick, but immediately scuttled back under the cover of their spiny shelter. At Soná, Veraguas, I saw young recently on the wing at the beginning of June.

The eggs are fairly smooth, white with a very faint bluish or greenish tinge, ordinarily spotted rather heavily with chestnut brown. Three sets of 2 each in the U. S. National Museum, collected on the island of Trinidad, of the same tropical race of black vulture that is found in Panamá, vary from subelliptical to long elliptical in form, and from 70.9×48.1 mm. to 74.0×51.2 mm. in size. A single egg from La Jagua, Panamá, taken on January 13, 1962, laid on the ground in a huge cavity in the base of a large tree, measures 69.9× 51.0 mm.

The typical subspecies of black vulture, *Coragyps atratus atratus* (Bechstein) differs from the tropical race in larger size, with a wing measurement in both sexes ranging from 414 to 445 (average 426) mm. The tropical subspecies, which is the one of Panamá, found from southern México to southern Brazil, has the wing 386 to 413 (401) mm. The two are alike in general form, and in color, except that in the tropical race the light area on the under wing is somewhat more extensive, and is whiter, so that it appears slightly more prominent. (For further discussion, see Wetmore, Smithsonian Misc. Coll., vol. 145, no. 1, 1962, pp. 1-4.) While it has been suggested that the Black Vulture may be migratory (Eisenmann, Wilson Bull., 1963, pp. 244-249) through Panamá, my personal observations do not verify this supposition.

In northern South America this species is called *zamuro*.

CATHARTES AURA Linnaeus: Turkey Vulture; Noneca
FIGURES 32, 33

Tail long so that in flight the feet do not project beyond end; wings longer, more pointed.

Description.—Length 635 to 760 mm. Adult, dull black in general, with more or less of a bluish gloss above; the wing coverts edged with dark brown; under surface of wings grayish white, beyond the black under wing coverts; bare head and upper neck of adult red, marked with transverse yellow lines in the resident race *ruficollis,* entirely red in the two forms that come to Panamá as migrants from the north.

Immature birds have the neck, and to less degree the head, covered with short, grayish black down, except for an irregular mark of dull white on either side of the back of the head. Juvenile: Nestlings when hatched are covered with soft white down.

Soaring turkey vultures, a constant feature of open skies throughout tropical America, are more in evidence in open country but are seen regularly also where forest cover remains. On the wing their graceful evolutions, performed with a minimum of obvious effort, constantly please the eye, but birds at rest, in hunched position with featherless heads protruding, are completely without esthetic attraction. Their food is carrion, like that of their companion species, and

FIG. 32.—Turkey vulture, noneca, *Cathartes aura*.

they are found regularly at large carcasses, usually a bit apart from the jostling confusion of any mob of black vultures. The turkey vulture takes fresher flesh when available and swings and circles for hours, now high, now low, in its search for recently dead bodies of animals of any kind, large or small. Sea beaches at changing tides are examined, and in recent years their highway patrol gives them constant small supplies of food in the bodies of animals killed by automobiles.

Three geographic races of this species found on the isthmus are described in detail beyond, one of them resident and the other two present as visitors. The two visitors, which are migrants from the north, have the bare skin of the head completely red in life. In the resident form there are several lines of yellow across the nape, and usually an irregular ivory-yellow spot in the center of the crown.

FIG. 33.—Head of turkey vulture, noneca, *Cathartes aura*, with wrinkled skin without papillae on the neck.

The migrants arrive from the north during October and continue to pass during November, often in tremendous flocks (see Loftin, Caribbean Journ. Sci., vol. 3, 1963, pp. 63-64). While many remain on the isthmus, thousands pass farther south into northwestern South America. The return flight north begins in February, and continues through March and early April, forming a notable addition to the great migratory flight of the Swainson's and broad-winged hawks. At Chimán on March 1, 1950, I estimated that about 15,000 passed in the hour before sunset, an indication of the vast numbers concerned. In these travels the turkey vulture moves mainly as a sail plane, soaring by means of supporting air currents, with a minimum of the greater muscular effort required by flapping flight. In this the trade winds that blow steadily from the northeast through the dry season are the main means of assistance, aided by the rising thermals generated by the heat of the sun. These migrant movements in Panamá were reported first by Frank M. Chapman (My Tropical Air Castle, 1929, pp. 147-148; Auk, 1933, pp. 30-34) in his observations at Barro Colorado Island. In the course of my studies I have found that the main lines of flight are not isthmus-wide at random but follow a definite pattern. Most of the birds that come from South America cross from the lower Atrato basin in Colombia to the Pacific side of Panamá in eastern Darién. Then they travel northwest, between the sea and the inland mountains, quartering against the steady northeast trade winds, a course that they follow until they reach the central, low depression crossed from sea to sea by the Canal Zone. Here the vultures move across Gatun Lake, and then swing over the Caribbean slope, turning gradually northwestward again, to continue over Bocas del Toro, and on to Costa Rica. They travel sometimes in small, separated bands of 25 to 400 or more individuals, but during the period of greatest movement join in continuous lines in which thousands pass during the course of an hour. The flights vary from 150 to 500 meters or more above the earth, with the birds moving steadily forward, supported by slightly bowed, stiffly held wings that carry them steadily without flapping. Occasionally they encounter rising thermals in which they may circle, sometimes to gain altitude, but ordinarily they pass quickly and silently across the sky.

So far as I have observed, the movement is entirely by day, and at dusk the vultures come down to sleep in open trees, where they remain in companies. Periods of rain, when the wind drops or changes direction, may leave them stranded. This happens particularly in the heavier rainfall found along the north coast. At Almirante in early morning I have seen several hundred perched near together in dead trees during rains that held the birds motionless for hours. Not until past noon did the heat of the sun build up the necessary rising air currents to enable them to move. There is no pause for feeding in these migrations, but regularly some of the birds drop down to open stretches along the rivers to drink.

In addition to the main line of flight that I have described in detail I have seen small groups moving north near Jaqué on the coast of Darién. Small flights in the Tonosí valley near the southern end of the Azuero Peninsula may be indication that turkey vultures, like numerous small birds, may cross the open Gulf of Panamá from the Chocó or adjacent Darién. Small groups pass north through Chiriquí.

At present data on movement during the southward flight that begins in October are not available in detail.

While this species is usually known as *noneca* in Panamá, it is called also *aura, aura tiñosa,* and by some *catana.*

CATHARTES AURA AURA (Linnaeus)

Vultur Aura Linnaeus, Syst. Nat., ed. 10, vol. 1, 1758, p. 86. (Veracruz, México.)

Characters.—Under surface brownish black; wing coverts edged with brown; definitely less dark throughout than *C. a. ruficollis;* head in life entirely red.

Measurements.—Males (21 specimens), wing 462-495 (478), tail 226-249 (238), culmen from cere 22.8-25.1 (22.6), tarsus 58.8-64.5 (62.4) mm.

Females (12 specimens), wing 471-495 (482), tail 231-251 (241), culmen from cere 22.7-25.9 (24.1), tarsus 58.6-66.5 (62.5) mm.

Migrant. Common, October to April, through the isthmus.

Birds with the wholly red heads that mark this race and the next, *C. a. meridionalis,* are recorded in my notes throughout the republic. Museum specimens of the subspecies *aura* have been examined from Empire and Barro Colorado Island, Canal Zone; Alhajuela, Panamá; Jaqué, Darién; and Isla San José, Pearl Islands.

CATHARTES AURA MERIDIONALIS Swann

Cathartes aura meridionalis Swann, Syn. Accipitres, pt. 1, Sept. 28, 1921, p. 3. (Santa Marta, Magdalena, Colombia.)
Cathartes aura teter Friedmann, Proc. Biol. Soc. Washington, vol. 46, Oct. 26, 1933, p. 188. (Riverside, California.)

Characters.—Similar in color of plumage and of bare head to *C. a. aura,* but larger, as indicated by longer wing.

Measurements.—Males (25 specimens), wing 487-528 (509), tail 237-268 (253), culmen from cere 22.2-26.6 (24.5), tarsus 60.6-65.1 (63.7) mm.

Females (16 specimens), wing 495-526 (511), tail 245-272 (259), culmen from cere 24.0-26.3 (25.2), tarsus 62.5-67.6 (64.9) mm.

Migrant. Common, October to April, throughout the republic.

As stated above, birds with wholly red heads are recorded in my notes from all of the political divisions. Museum specimens of the race *C. a. meridionalis* have been examined from Paracoté, at the head of Montijo Bay, Veraguas; Empire and Barro Colorado Island, Canal Zone; Puerto Obaldía, San Blas; and Isla San José in the Pearl Islands.

The type of Swann's race *meridionalis* from Colombia named in 1921 is a migrant bird from western North America (see Wetmore, Smithsonian Misc. Coll., vol. 146, no. 6, Aug. 14, 1964, p. 4.)

CATHARTES AURA RUFICOLLIS Spix

Cathartes ruficollis Spix, Avium Spec. Nov. Brasiliam, vol. 1, 1824, p. 2. (Interior of Baía and Piauí, Brazil.)

Characters.—Borders of wing coverts very dark brown; under surface of body decidedly black; in life, head and neck dull red with several transverse lines of greenish white or dull yellow on back of head; adult usually with an irregular area of yellowish white in center of crown.

Adults shot in the latter part of March had the general color of cere, head and upper part of the neck dull red; 8 narrow, raised ridges across the back of the head and upper hindneck pale bluish to pale greenish white; an irregular area in center of crown dull ivory white, that in one bird measured 16 mm. wide; tarsus dull grayish white, dull red on front when first killed, but fading immediately until only a faint reddish tinge remained; toes dull brownish white; claws black.

Measurements.—Males (18 specimens), wing 476-508 (490), tail 235-265 (254), culmen from cere 21.9-24.3 (23.2), tarsus 60.0-64.9 (62.4) mm.

Females (21 specimens), wing 475-509 (491), tail 235-264 (247), culmen from cere 22.3-26.6 (23.7), tarsus 60.4-68.0 (63.8) mm.

Resident throughout the republic from the Costa Rican border eastward to Colombia.

Definite records of birds with the typical head marking are as follows:

Chiriquí: Alanje, Boquete, San Félix, Remedios, Guabalá.
Veraguas: Puerto Vidal, Soná, lower course of Río San Pablo.
Coclé: El Valle.
Canal Zone: Gamboa, Juan Mina.
Panamá: Río La Jagua, Chepo, Chimán.
Darién: mouth of Río Tuquesa on the Río Chucunaque, Boca de Paya, Jaqué, Río Jaqué.
San Blas: Mandinga.
Isla Parida; Isla Coiba; Isla Taboga; Isla San José.

Turkey vultures (of any of the races) are not common in the Archipiélago de las Perlas. Murphy (Auk, 1945, p. 116) has reported them at Isla Pacheca, and in addition to the record listed for Isla San José I have seen them (without knowledge of the subspecies) on Saboga, Chapera, Cañas, Rey, Bayoneta, and Pedro González.

The identification of a turkey vulture collected May 12, 1944, on Isla San José in the Pearl Islands as this subspecies (Wetmore,

Smithsonian Misc. Coll., vol. 106, no. 1, Aug. 5, 1946, pp. 24-25) was interpreted then as a record of a wanderer from some nearby South American area, since that was the known range of this race at the time. Others of this subspecies were found in Darién two years later, and in subsequent seasons the race *ruficollis,* little by little, was traced westward across the isthmus. As I have found it within 30 kilometers of the Costa Rican border, below Alanje in western Chiriquí, it seems probable that it may range farther north in Central America. The records listed are of birds collected, and of others observed close at hand so that the head marking was seen clearly. It remains to determine the identity of the resident subspecies of the Caribbean coast in western Colón and Bocas del Toro.

While these birds have the usual habit of the species of feeding on carrion, I was interested to find the crop of one killed at La Jagua late in March filled with bright yellowish-orange pulp from the large fruits of the spiny-trunked corozo palm. I was told that this was a common source of food for vultures. The bird that I examined personally was of the resident race *ruficollis*. It is not certain that migrant *aura* from the north shares this habit.

Though there is no detailed information regarding the breeding of this race in Panamá, other than that I was told that they used hollows in tree trunks on, or very near, the ground, it is assumed that nesting here is like that elsewhere in the range of the race. In general, two eggs are laid on whatever natural accumulation of decayed wood, humus, or earth there is in the hollow selected as a nest shelter. Occasionally one egg or three may be encountered. In color the eggs are dull white to creamy white, marked more or less heavily with spots and blotches of light to very dark brown.

The young of *ruficollis,* when fully grown and able to fly, have head and bill dull black, the former covered with short, blackish down, except for the spot of dull white on either side of the nape. When nestling turkey vultures are approached they often assume a grotesque attitude, with arched neck, head bent down so that the bill touches the breast, and partly feathered wings spread, while they utter a peculiar cat-like hiss. At intervals the tip of one wing is struck sharply against the ground, and the note changes to a rough growl, the sound and the note coming abruptly in startling fashion. The vocal efforts of adult birds are limited to low, barely audible hissing sounds.

CATHARTES BURROVIANUS BURROVIANUS Cassin: Yellow-headed Vulture; Guala

FIGURE 34

Cathartes Burrovianus Cassin, Proc. Acad. Nat. Sci. Philadelphia, vol. 2, no. 8, 1845, p. 212. (Near Veracruz Llave, Veracruz, México.)

In flight generally similar to the other turkey vulture, but near at hand seen to have the bare skin of the side of the head bright orange, becoming somewhat duller on neck; crown bluish gray.

Description.—Length 530 to 590 mm. General appearance like that of the red-headed turkey vulture, but more brownish black on lower surface; definitely smaller, and of lesser bulk; neck with numerous small but prominent papillae, easily seen in fresh specimens, and readily evident on close examination in dried skins. In life the ruff on the neck comes higher on the back of the neck than in the red-headed species, a distinction between the two that often is lost when the birds are prepared as museum specimens, as the position of the ruff may be shifted by stretching or contraction.

In two young recently from the nest (collected near Soná) I found that a few papillae had begun development. Now that these two have been preserved as museum specimens the caruncles are seen best under a lens.

The following color notes were made from an adult female taken at the Ciénaga Macana, Herrera, March 17, 1948: Iris red; cere, forepart of crown to center of eyes, nape, back of head, and throat, dull orange-red; center of crown dull bluish gray; sides of head, from posterior loral space back through the space around the eye and the ear, including the area to below the gape, bright orange; lores greenish yellow; spot in front of eye and slightly above it dull bluish gray; sides and front of neck, including the area covered by papillae dull orange-red. Another taken at the same time had the colors somewhat duller. An adult female, near breeding, shot March 24, 1961, at La Jagua, was more brilliantly colored, as indicated by the following: Iris orange red; center of crown indigo, in an irregular triangle with the apex forward, bordered narrowly on either side by pale greenish blue; side of head down over the mandibular rami, and including the loral area, bright orange; bare foreneck, including the prominent caruncles, dull orange; back of head dull blue, crossed by 3 irregular rows of caruncles which are dull orange; bill dull ivory white; crus dull yellowish white; front of tarsus dull greenish gray; rest dull white; toes fuscous black; claws fuscous.

Measurements.—Males (6 from Panamá, Colombia and northwestern Venezuela), wing 432-454 (445), tail 195-218 (204), culmen from cere 19.6-23.3 (21.5), tarsus 52.4-59.1 (56.9) mm.

Females (7 from Panamá, Colombia, and northwestern Venezuela), wing 444-459 (449), tail 193-214 (199), culmen from cere 21.1-24.0 (22.5, average of 6), tarsus 56.0-60.0 (57.9) mm.

Resident. Locally common, on the Pacific slope, from Chiriquí through Veraguas and Coclé to the eastern section of the Province of Panamá, including the eastern side of the Azuero Peninsula in Herrera and Los Santos.

Fig. 34.—Head of yellow-headed vulture, guala, *Cathartes burrovianus burrovianus,* with wartlike papillae on the neck.

This species is found in more open areas near the largest streams, and near marshes, particularly during the dry season. In the period of rains it spreads with the greater extent of the open swampy areas that form its haunts.

When seen near at hand it may be known by the extensive yellow on the sides of the head and neck, while in the hand the prominent papillae on the neck, in addition to the head colors mentioned, identify it readily. In flight at any distance, when the colors are not visible, it may not be distinguished from the other species. For a time I thought that these birds were lighter colored on the underside of the wing, but this has proved to be a variable matter in both species.

The first report of the yellow-headed vulture as a bird of Panamá came in the dry season of 1948 when Watson M. Perrygo and I were in the field on the eastern side of the Azuero Peninsula. On March 17, during routine collecting, we shot 3 turkey vultures at the Ciénaga Macana, near the small settlement of El Rincón, not far from the lower course of the Río Santa María. In life they had seemed somewhat small, and in the hand the peculiar head markings brought to mind at once the yellow-headed vultures that I had known in the distant Chaco of northern Argentina and western Paraguay. The head colors were recorded on Kodachrome film within an hour through the assistance of Richard Stewart of the National Geographic Society. Subsequent studies of vultures in museum collections led to their identification in the Academy of Natural Sciences of Philadelphia with Cassin's ancient type specimen of *Cathartes burrovianus*. Since this recognition of its presence the bird has been found regularly on the Pacific slope of Panamá. Thus far it has been seen in the savannas and the sections adjacent to them, east to the region near the Río La Jagua. It is possible that it may occur also in Darién in the extensive swamps adjacent to the lower Río Sabana and the Río Tuira.

In the open marshes toward the Río Chico, below the La Jagua Hunting Club in dry season I have recorded them constantly, sometimes to the number of 20 to 30 in a day. As they are never disturbed here they are not wild. Often I have walked very near them as they rested quietly in low, leafless trees. These lower areas around lagoons containing water are their regular haunt, and their occurrence on the higher savannas comes mainly during the period of rains.

They have the same graceful flight as the red-headed species, but on the whole seem more sedentary and less given to soaring at great altitudes. Fish seem to be a regular food, sought in drying pools, and they seem to come to mammal carcasses infrequently. One that I shot at La Jagua had fragments of fish in the crop, so fresh that they had evidently been taken alive. Once, near David, I saw one flying with a large dead lizard in its bill to prevent being robbed of its meal by black vultures, one of the few occasions on which I have seen a vulture of this genus carrying anything.

Little is known of their nesting in the Republic. Near the Río San Pablo a short distance below Soná on May 14, 1953, I found a pair with two young, only recently able to fly, that rested in an open-branched tree. Early the following morning the young were not seen on my arrival, but at my first shot at another bird both came flying to the same tree. Evidently the nesting place was somewhere near. In the hand, I found that both had the neck and back of the head covered with down as usual in this genus. A white band crossed the back of the head, the down above and below this being dull, dark brown. This mark is lost soon, since in older birds, that are obviously immature, as indicated by the soft feathering that remains on the head and neck, the back of the head is uniform in color.

No records of the eggs of this northern race of the species have come to my attention.

In Panamá it is only an occasional hunter, like Baldomiro Moreno, who recognizes these birds as different, and these few merely know them as another kind of *noneca,* the name for the red-headed species. In Colombia they are called *guala.* The typical form is recorded in the lowlands from eastern México, to Honduras and Panamá, and across northern Colombia to northwestern Venezuela. *Cathartes b. urubitinga,* found from the llanos of eastern Colombia and the lower Orinoco valley in Venezuela south to the southern Chaco in Argentina is larger, with the wing in adult males from 454-493 (474.5), and in adult females 461-501 (484) mm.

Family ACCIPITRIDAE: Hawks, Eagles, and Allies; Gavilanes, Águilas, y Especies Afines

The members of this family, worldwide except in Antarctica in their distribution, are numerous in tropical America, where many live in heavy forests. These species range through the high tree crown, or the intermediate branches below, and seldom descend lower. Other kinds that inhabit more open lands usually secure their food on or near the ground.

The reputation of the family as predators on domestic fowls comes from those that are hunters of birds and small mammals and that on occasion come to capture chickens. The majority of the hawks found in Panamá, however, are harmless, as their food is large insects, crabs, frogs, lizards, snakes, and the mice and rats that abound about cultivated fields. It is unfortunate that few persons distinguish these from the predatory kinds, so that all are regarded with disfavor and are killed at every opportunity. For this reason, and also through the extensive clearing of forests, most of the family now are rare. Only a few of the forest inhabitants have been able to adapt their lives to the scattered tracts of second growth that now furnish the main forest cover over extensive areas.

It should be noted that many of the species resident in the Tropics are far more sedentary than their relatives of the temperate zones.

They are active when feeding, particularly when caring for young, but at other times may remain quietly on some perch for long periods and so escape attention. Only part of the tropical species appear to soar with any regularity in the open air above the forest.

In addition to the resident kinds a few others come during the northern winter. Among these the migrant flocks that pass over the isthmus twice each year, en route to and from winter homes in South America, form one of the spectacular sights of the bird world.

KEY TO SPECIES OF ACCIPITRIDAE

1. Tail long and deeply forked.. Swallow-tailed kite, *Elanoides forficatus*, p. 175
   Tail not deeply forked.. 2
2. Side of maxilla with two deep notches on margin separating two distinct toothlike projections.
   Double-toothed kite, *Harpagus bidentatus fasciatus*, p. 184
   Side of maxilla not double-toothed on margin....................... 3
3. Tarsus short and heavy; length less, or only slightly more, than middle toe with claw 4
   Tarsus proportionately longer; length decidedly more than middle toe with claw 8
4. Maxilla narrow, in proportion to its width at base, the tip produced in a slender, elongated hook... 5
   Maxilla not excessively slender or elongated in proportion to its width at base 6
5. Tail long, more than 150 mm.; wing more pointed, distance between tips of longest primaries and longest secondaries more than 80 mm.
   Everglade kite, *Rostrhamus sociabilis sociabilis*, p. 180
   Tail short, less than 140 mm.; wing rounded, distance between tip of longest primaries and longest secondaries 50 mm. or less.
   Slender-billed kite, *Helicolestes hamatus*, p. 182
6. Inner webs of outer primaries chestnut.
   Plumbeous kite, *Ictinia plumbea*, p. 177
   Inner webs of outer primaries without chestnut...................... 7
7. Tarsus less than 40 mm.; bill strongly compressed, with narrow, elongated tip...........Hook-billed kite, *Chondrohierax uncinatus uncinatus*, p. 188
   Tarsus 42 to 51 mm.; maxilla swollen laterally, with tip broader and less elongated...........Cayenne kite, *Leptodon cayanensis cayanensis*, p. 186
8. Head conspicuously crested... 9
   Head not conspicuously crested..................................... 13
9. Size very large, wing more than 500 mm.; feet unusually strong and powerful........................Harpy eagle, *Harpia harpyja*, p. 249
   Size smaller, feet normal in size................................... 10
10. Tarsus feathered to the toes....................................... 11
    Tarsus bare except at upper end.
    Crested eagle, *Morphnus guianensis*, p. 246
11. Under surface white, without dark markings.
    Black-and-white hawk-eagle, *Spizastur melanoleucus*, p. 244
    Under surface mainly black, or white barred with black............. 12

FAMILY ACCIPITRIDAE

12. Under surface of body black, or blackish slate.
    Black hawk-eagle, *Spizaetus tyrannus serus,* p. 240
    Under surface white, barred more or less with black; head and neck marked with chestnut......Barred hawk-eagle, *Spizaetus ornatus vicarius,* p. 241
13. Size large and robust, wing 490 mm. or more.
    Solitary eagle, *Urubitornis solitaria solitaria,* p. 238
    Size smaller, wing under 450 mm................................. 14
14. Feathers from auricular region around forepart of head elongated to form a distinct facial ruff........Marsh hawk, *Circus cyaneus hudsonius,* p. 251
    Without a facial ruff; feathers of side and forepart of head not distinctly elongated 15
15. Outer toe conspicuously shorter than inner toe; tibiotarsal joint capable of forward and backward flexure.
    Crane hawk, *Ischnosceles caerulescens,* p. 253
    Outer toe as long as, or longer, than inner toe; tibiotarsal joint capable only of forward flexure 16
16. Under side of toes finely and sharply spiculate.
    Black-collared hawk, *Busarellus nigricollis nigricollis,* p. 227
    Underside of toes normal, sometimes roughened, but never sharply spiculate 17
17. Lesser and middle wing coverts chestnut-brown..................... 18
    Lesser and middle wing coverts not prominently chestnut-brown........ 20
18. Size small, wing less than 150 mm.
    Tiny hawk, *Accipiter superciliosus fontanier,* immature, brown phase, p. 192
    Size large, wing more than 300 mm................................ 19
19. Wings cinnamon-rufous tipped with black.
    Savanna hawk, *Heterospizias meridionalis meridionalis,* p. 223
    Wings fuscous, more or less buffy white or white on inner webs.
    Harris's hawk, *Parabuteo unicinctus harrisi,* p. 226
20. Breast, abdomen, and tibia white, finely and evenly barred with black.
    Barred hawk, *Leucopternis princeps,* p. 222
    Posterior under surface not as in 20............................... 21
21. Under surface plain dark gray, with the tibia barred with white.
    Plumbeous hawk, *Leucopternis plumbea,* p. 221
    Under surface not plain gray; tibia not barred...................... 22
22. Upper surface mainly pure white except for black-tipped wings and tail.
    White hawk, *Leucopternis albicollis costaricensis,* p. 217
    Upper surface with little, if any, white............................. 23
23. Entire under surface pure white.
    Semiplumbeous hawk, *Leucopternis semiplumbea,* p. 220
    Lower surface not plain white..................................... 24
24. Tarsus decidedly longer, more than 115 mm., so that the outstretched feet reach nearly to end of the tail.
    Greater black hawk, *Buteogallus urubitinga,* p. 229
    Tarsus shorter, less than 100 mm................................. 25
25. Smaller, wing less than 350 mm.................................. 26
    Larger, wing more than 360 mm................................... 35
26. Very small, wing less than 150 mm.
    Tiny hawk, *Accipiter superciliosus fontainier,*
    adult and immature, light phase, p. 192
    Larger, wing more than 160 mm................................... 27

27. Tibia russet to cinnamon, without bars; under surface without bars or streaks, buffy white to cinnamon-buff (immatures), or dark gray (adults).
Bicolored hawk, *Accipiter bicolor bicolor*, p. 190
Tibia not plain russet or chestnut without bars, under surface streaked or barred, or if plain, black to slate-black............................ 28
28. Loral area heavily feathered... 29
Loral area bare except for scattered bristles........................ 31
29. Smaller, wing 160 to 210 mm.; form slender, head small; tarsus and toes long and slender.....Sharp-shinned hawk, *Accipiter striatus velox*, p. 194
Larger, wing more than 240 mm.; form robust, head large; tarsus and toes larger, heavier 30
30. Upper surface black, or brownish black, without definite streaks on the crown; under surface black, or white, usually plain, but in some with a few narrow dusky streaks on the sides.
Short-tailed hawk, *Buteo brachyurus*, p. 202
Brownish gray, or grayish brown above, more or less mottled with cinnamon and white, especially on the crown; below barred with white and dull brown, or white more or less streaked with dusky.
Broad-winged hawk, *Buteo platypterus platypterus*, p. 204
31. Much larger, wing more than 325 mm., tarsus more than 80 mm.
Lesser black hawk, *Buteogallus anthracinus*, p. 232
Decidedly smaller, wing less than 260 mm.; tarsus less than 75 mm...... 32
32. Ground color clear gray, barred with white on lower surface, and mottled and barred above with dusky gray.
Gray hawk, *Buteo nitidus blakei*, adult, p. 199
Ground color not clear gray... 33
33. Back and wings sooty black, with crown buffy white streaked narrowly with black; tibia plain buff..Gray hawk, *Buteo nitidus blakei*, immature, p. 199
Back and wings not sooty black, tibia not plain buff.................. 34
34. Head, back, and wings grayish brown, lined and mottled with white and buff; lower surface white, streaked with sooty brown; tibia barred narrowly with dusky.
Gray hawk, *Buteo nitidus blakei*, immature, second stage, p. 199
Head, back, and wings plain grayish brown; breast, abdomen, and tibia cinnamon, barred with white; foreneck and upper breast dark gray.
Large-billed hawk, *Buteo magnirostris*, p. 211
35. Tail not more than half as long as wing.
White-tailed hawk, *Buteo albicaudatus hypospodius*, p. 195
Tail more than half as long as wing................................. 36
36. Three outer primaries distinctly emarginate, or notched, on inner web.
Swainson's hawk, *Buteo swainsoni*, p. 208
Four outer primaries distinctly emarginate or notched on inner web.... 37
37. Black above and below, including under wing coverts; the under surface in immature birds lightly spotted with white.
Zone-tailed hawk, *Buteo albonotatus*, p. 197
Upper surface of tail cinnamon-brown, with a black subterminal band (adult); or grayish, or blackish-brown, barred narrowly with dusky black (immature)............Red-tailed hawk, *Buteo jamaicensis*, p. 206

FAMILY ACCIPITRIDAE

ELANOIDES FORFICATUS YETAPA (Vieillot): Swallow-tailed Kite; Gavilán Tijereta

FIGURE 35

Milvus yetapa Vieillot, Nouv. Dict. Hist. Nat., nouv. éd., vol. 20, May 30, 1818, p. 564. (Paraguay.)

The long, deeply forked tail identifies this species at a glance from any other hawk.

Description.—Length 500 to 630 mm. Adult, wing coverts and back very dark green; outer scapulars, wings, and tail dark gray, the longer feathers with a greenish sheen; inner scapulars, head, neck, and whole of under surface, including the under wing coverts, pure white.

Immature, head and upper breast streaked narrowly with blackish brown.

Measurements (From Friedmann, U.S. Nat. Mus. Bull. 50, pt. 11, 1950, p. 90).—Males, wing 405-447 (418), tail 298-330 (318), culmen from cere 19-20 (19.6), tarsus 31.5-33.0 (32.4) mm.

Females, wing 390-427 (411), tail 275-326 (304), culmen from cere 19.5-21.0 (20.2), tarsus 32.0-33.5 (32.3) mm.

Found throughout the Republic in the tropical and lower subtropical zones, where it nests; fairly common. Possibly migrant in part after breeding, but from present information this is not certain.

These are birds of graceful, soaring flight that remain for long periods on the wing. Though they eat lizards, and are reported to take birds, nestlings, and eggs, they also feed extensively on insects of a considerable variety of kinds. Skutch (Condor, 1965, p. 236) saw them eating small insects which they captured in their feet while on the wing. As the kite continued to circle it lowered the head and brought the foot forward to place the small morsel of food in its mouth.

The eggs of the swallow-tailed kite, with smooth shell, are white to creamy white, marked with dark brown or chestnut in an irregular pattern that varies from fine spots to heavy blotches. Two eggs constitute the usual set, though 4 have been recorded. Schönwetter (Handb. Ool., pt. 3, 1961, p. 154) records the measurements of 4 of this race as 45.1-47.4 × 35.0-37.1 mm. One in the U. S. National Museum received from Col. L. R. Wolfe, collected in Sucre, Venezuela, April 24, 1935, is elliptical in form, and in color faintly creamy white, heavily marked with brown. It measures 47.9 × 39.5 mm.

A female that I collected at the lakes near El Volcán March 6, 1954, was about to lay.

Though all of the specimens taken in Panamá that I have examined are of the race *yetapa*, it is probable that birds of the typical sub-

Fig. 35.—Swallow-tailed kite, gavilán tijereta, *Elanoides forficatus yetapa*.

species *Elanoides forficatus forficatus*, marked by dark blue instead of dark green upper back and scapulars, may form part of those that are recorded over the isthmus. This race, which nests in southeastern United States, moves southward in winter as far as Ecuador, but little is known of its winter range.

ICTINIA PLUMBEA (Gmelin): Plumbeous Kite; Gavilán Plomizo
FIGURE 36

Falco plumbeus Gmelin, Syst. Nat., vol. 1, pt. 1, 1788, p. 283. (Cayenne.)

Long wings, notched tail, and plain gray color mark this species, usually seen soaring at the edge of forest.

Description.—Length 290 to 350 mm. Adult, head, neck, upper back, and under surface, including under surface of wings, gray; lower back, wings, and tail black, with a slight sheen of gray; distal half of inner webs of primaries cinnamon-brown; tail with two broken bands of white.

Immature, upper surface dull black; head and neck with feathers edged narrowly with white; back and wings with feathers tipped lightly with buff, or buffy white; primaries tipped more widely with white; tail with three prominent white bands; under surface white, streaked heavily with dusky neutral gray; under wing coverts dark neutral gray, edged and tipped with white and buffy white.

Iris deep red; bill black; cere dusky neutral gray; tarsus and toes orange-yellow; claws black.

Measurements (from Friedmann, U.S. Nat. Mus. Bull. 50, pt. 11, 1950, p. 126).—Males, wing 270-313 (298), tail 123-167 (148), culmen from cere 15.5-18.0 (16.6), tarsus 37.0-42.4 (38.5) mm.

Females, wing 274-320 (307), tail 139-161 (145), culmen from cere 16.0-19.5 (17.1), tarsus 34-42 (37.7) mm.

Migratory, fairly common. Breeds in areas of open forest throughout the lowlands. Arrives from early February to the beginning of March, and remains through September, occasionally into October. Found on San José, Trapiche, Pedro González, and Rey Islands in the Perlas group.

Early arrival dates: Cerro Pirre, February 7, 1961; San Félix, February 21, 1956; Chimán, February 26, 1950; Armila, San Blas, February 27, 1963; El Uracillo, February 28, 1952; Boca de Paya, March 2, 1959. Late dates of occurrence: Cocolí, Canal Zone, August 1, 1955 (specimen in U.S. National Museum); Barro Colorado Island, Canal Zone, August 17, 1927, (Van Tyne, in Eisenmann, Smithsonian Misc. Coll., vol. 117, 1952, p. 14); Isla San José, latter part of September (Morrison, in Wetmore, Smithsonian Misc. Coll., 106, no. 1, 1946, p. 26); Almirante, Bocas del Toro, October 10, 1960, male collected by R. Hinds.

While not abundant this kite is widely distributed and so is seen with fair regularity. It is found about groves and open stands of trees, so that cultivated areas where there is older rastrojo are favorable to it. In sections of dense forest it may be encountered along the borders but it does not appear to penetrate into the interior though it may sweep high overhead in its soaring evolutions. Open

FIG. 36.—Plumbeous kite, gavilán plomizo, *Ictinia plumbea*.

pastures with scattered trees are favored localities, and it is in such areas that I have found them on the eastern side of the Azuero Peninsula, as far down as the Río Caldera, back of Punta Mala. I have seen them at 900 meters elevation above El Valle, and Griscom records a breeding bird from Cana (Bull. Mus. Comp. Zool. vol. 69,

1929, p. 158), which appears to be near the upper limits of the range.

These kites, like the related Mississippi kite of the north, feed mainly on insects. Orthoptera are favored items; beetles and occasionally dragonflies are taken. In the latter part of the dry season when cicadas are abundant they are picked off expertly while the bird is on the wing, and often eaten while the hawk continues its flight. They are said to eat lizards, but this I have not observed. Small birds show no fear of these kites.

Plumbeous kites are ready to nest when they arrive on their breeding grounds and mate immediately. Those taken at this time have the body encased in fat, this being true particularly of the females. They spend much time on the wing, soaring gracefully, and at rest select exposed perches, the open branches of the *guarumo* (*Cecropia*) being especially favored. In the air the long, pointed wings suggest those of a falcon. They present a dark silhouette until the sun strikes them at the proper angle, when the light-colored head sometimes appears almost white. The distinct notch in the tip of the tail may be seen as they turn.

The nest is a fair-sized structure of sticks deeply cupped, located rather high in trees. Seven sets of one egg each of this species, presented to the U.S. National Museum by Col. L. R. Wolfe, collected at Guanoco, Sucre, Venezuela, are dull white, with a very finely granulated shell, without markings. They are broad oval to nearly elliptical in form and measure as follows: 42.6-45.0 × 34.0-37.9 mm. Eggs of these birds become much soiled as incubation proceeds which may account for reports of those with distinct markings.

The young at hatching are covered with white down.

The closely allied Mississippi kite, *Ictinia misisippiensis* (Wilson), which nests now from northeastern Kansas, Tennessee, and South Carolina south to northern Texas, Louisiana, and northern Florida, also is migrant but with a winter range as yet not clearly known. It is recorded through eastern and southern México and once in eastern Guatemala. Aside from this, 3 specimens are reported taken far to the south, December 14, 1944, and February 26, 1942, at Colonia Nueva Italia, Villeta, southern Paraguay (Blake, Auk, 1949, p. 82) and Mocoví, Chaco, northern Argentina, Jan. 6, 1904 (Eisenmann, Auk, 1963, p. 74). I have felt certain that some of the migrant flocks I have seen on the Pacific side of Panamá were the Mississippi kite, but have not been able to substantiate this belief with specimens. On April 14, 1949, while I was walking over an open savanna on the western end of Cerro Carbunco, northwest of Chepo, a flock of 25 circled in ascending spirals barely beyond gun range. They rose rapidly and finally whirled to disappear over the crest of the ridge. Watson Perrygo and I, both of us familiar with the two species concerned, watched them closely and were satisfied that they were the Mississippi kite. On March 20, 1950, at Charco del Toro on the Río Majé, between 300 and 400 kites that I believed to be the northern bird rushed past, swerving about with roaring wings, ahead of a heavy rain. And on April 7, 1959, at Las Cumbres, outside of Panama City, I watched a flock of 75 shifting in formation as they beat against the strong tradewind, that also seemed to be this species.

Fully adult birds of the Mississippi kite are similar to the other species in size, and in general gray and black color but lack the broken white bar in the tail. The bright brown of the inner webs of the primaries, prominent on all of these feathers in the plumbeous kite, is restricted to a few small, hidden spots on a few of the innermost feathers. The toes are dusky instead of yellow like the tarsus.

ROSTRHAMUS SOCIABILIS SOCIABILIS (Vieillot): Everglade Kite; Gavilán Caracolero

FIGURE 37

Herpetotheres sociabilis Vieillot, Nouv. Dict. Hist. Nat., nouv. éd., vol. 18, Dec. 1817, p. 318. (Corrientes and Río de la Plata.)

Of medium size, black, with or without buff streaks on lower surface; rump and base of tail white; bill very slender, much curved.

Description.—Length 390 to 430 mm. Adult male, black to blackish slate; feathers of forehead, throat, and lower eyelid white basally; tail coverts, both above and below, white; tail with concealed base white, bordered distally by an indistinct band of mouse brown, and with end brown tipped with dull white; under surface of primaries and secondaries, with indefinite bars of grayish white.

Adult female, somewhat browner black; throat and breast streaked lightly with buff; elsewhere with feathers in part edged lightly with dull cinnamon.

Immature, fuscous above, with indistinct edgings of cinnamon-buff; crown with indistinct streaks of dull cinnamon; forehead and superciliary buffy white, streaked with fuscous, the superciliary much broader above ear region; crown and nape feathers white basally; under surface buffy white, with shaft lines fuscous on throat and foreneck; lower breast and sides heavily streaked with fuscous; a band of nearly solid fuscous across upper breast; under wing coverts tipped broadly with rufous.

The very slender, much hooked bill, and equally slender claws, coupled with the white rump and base of tail, are diagnostic. The outermost primary is definitely notched, the next 4 sinuate in decreasing amount.

FIG. 37.—Everglade kite, gavilán caracolero, *Rostrhamus sociabilis sociabilis*.

Measurements.—Males, wing 325-341 (332.5), tail 164-182 (172.1), culmen from cere 24.5-26.5 (25.2), tarsus 49-54 (51.5) mm.

Females, wing 338-350 (342); tail 167.5-188 (175); culmen from cere 24-25 (24.6), tarsus 47-51 (49) mm.

Rare. The only record is that of a female, in full immature dress, taken by Wedel on March 22, 1929, at Permé, San Blas.

This kite frequents fresh-water marshes where it feeds on the large apple snails (*Pomacea*). It is rare in southern Central America.

HELICOLESTES HAMATUS (Temminck): Slender-billed Kite; Gavilán Piquidelgado

FIGURE 38

Falco hamatus Temminck, Nouv. Rec. Planch. Col., livr. 11, June 1821, pl. 61. (Pará, Brazil.)

Generally similar to the Everglade kite, but wings less pointed; tail short and without white; bill and claws slender, much curved.

Description.—Length 380 to 410 mm. Adult, dark gray throughout, becoming blackish on head and neck.

Immature, somewhat paler gray, with wing coverts, secondaries, and upper tail coverts tipped narrowly with brown, buff or white; webs of remiges barred narrowly on the lower surface with white and light gray; under tail coverts tipped and barred with white or buffy white; tail sooty black, tipped and barred with white.

The female listed beyond, collected February 24, 1959, had the eye bright golden-yellow; base of mandible, gape, cere, and bare skin in front of eye, reddish orange; margin of eyelid dusky neutral gray, bordered, adjacent to the feathering, by a narrow line of reddish orange; base of gonys dull yellowish buff; rest of bill black; tarsus and toes reddish orange; claws black.

Measurements.—Male (1 from Darién), wing 265, tail 113.0, culmen from cere 25.5, tarsus 50.8 mm.

Females (5 from Darién, Ecuador, Venezuela, and Brazil), wing 272-285 (279), tail 120.4-132.4 (129.2), culmen from cere 26.7-27.7 (27.3), tarsus 46.0-51.0 (48.8) mm.

Resident. Rare; recorded only in the Tuira Valley, Darién, near the mouth of the Río Paya.

This is a little known species of tropical South America, known in Panamá only from the Paya region of Darién. On February 24, 1959, I found one, a female perched over a shaded pool in a forest quebrada, near the point where the small stream came down a bed broken by rock exposures into the Río Tuira. The bird flew a short distance to another perch, where it continued to give a low mewing call of a single note. It ranged at intermediate levels, well below the heavy tree crown of the high forest. There were numerous shells of the apple snail (*Pomacea zeteki* Morrison) scattered about along the sandy shore of the quebrada, which I assumed the kite had shared with the limpkins that ranged in the same area. Later I received another of these kites that had been taken in 1958 in this same section by collectors for the Gorgas Memorial Laboratory. These are the first reports of the species outside South America (see Wetmore, Smithsonian Misc. Coll., vol. 145, no. 1, 1962, p. 11).

Haverschmidt (Auk, 1959, p. 35), in Surinam, found a nest placed on a strong branch of a huge cotton-tree growing in a coffee plantation. The nest, rather small, was made of sticks, in the form usual among tree-nesting hawks. The single nestling was "mouse brown, with a dirty white stripe over the back: its head was dirty white with a mouse brown triangle on top. Soft parts were as follows: iris black; bill glossy black, with the white egg tooth still on the upper

FIG. 38.—Slender-billed kite, gavilán piquidelgado, *Helicolestes hamatus*.

mandible; cere and sides of bill orange yellow; inside of mouth reddish pink; feet orange yellow with claws glossy black." Eggs of this interesting species are not yet known.

The slender-billed kite in general form and food habits is a forest-inhabiting counterpart of the Everglade kite of open marshlands. The forest bird differs in heavier form, and in relatively shorter and more rounded wings, in which the primaries project less beyond the secondaries. The tail also relatively is shorter. A more interesting distinction is found in the immature plumage, which resembles the plain color of the adult rather closely, while the Everglade kite at this age differs decidedly in heavily streaked pattern. Amadon (Amer. Mus. Nov. no. 2166, 1964, pp. 3-4) after discussion of these matters, in view of the general resemblance, suggests union of the two under the older genus name *Rostrhamus* since they have no other close relatives. It appears plausible to believe that the two have related ancestry. But it would appear that *hamatus* is the more conservative, perhaps more like the ancestral stock, from its smaller population. Pending information on its internal anatomy, particularly the skeleton, I prefer here to emphasize the differences by listing the two in separate genera.

HARPAGUS BIDENTATUS FASCIATUS Lawrence: Double-toothed Kite; Gavilán Bidente

FIGURE 39

Harpagus fasciatus Lawrence, Proc. Acad. Nat. Sci. Philadelphia, vol. 20, 1868 (April-May, 1869), p. 429. (Guatemala.)

The irregular, double-toothed margins toward the tip of the maxilla and mandible serve to identify this species in any plumage from other hawks found in Panamá.

Description.—Length 290 to 330 mm. Male, above, including side of head, dull gray; wings and tail blackish, the latter with whitish tip, and 3 broken cross bars, the uppermost concealed by the tail coverts; throat and upper foreneck white, streaked with dull gray and grayish black; upper breast chestnut brown at sides, gray, barred indistinctly with chestnut brown, in center; lower breast and abdomen barred narrowly with white, and more broadly with gray bordered narrowly with chestnut; under tail coverts and under wing coverts white; under surface of wing barred broadly with white.

Female, somewhat browner gray above; upper breast chestnut-brown, with scant indication of bars; lower surface elsewhere barred broadly with chestnut brown, with gray edging reduced, and white bars prominent.

Immature, grayish above, with the concealed feather bases white on head, back, and coverts; below white, streaked broadly on breast, and barred irregularly on sides and abdomen, with fuscous.

I recorded the colors of the soft parts in a female of the typical *H. b. bidentatus,* taken in Venezuela, as follows: Iris orange-red; maxilla black, except for a dull gray area extending across the posterior tooth and the base of the tomium behind; mandible dull gray; cere dull greenish; tarsus and toes bright yellow; claws black.

Measurements.—Males (5 from Panamá), wing 200-204 (201.8), tail 132.8-140.0 (137.4), culmen from cere 15.1-17.3 (16.1), tarsus 41.5-44.3 (42.8) mm.

Females (4 from Panamá), wing 207-216 (211.7), tail 139.1-149.7 (144.7), culmen from cere 15.4-16.4 (16.0), tarsus 40.5-43.8 (42.6) mm.

Resident. Tolerably common in forested areas throughout the mainland; Isla Coiba. (There are no definite records for the provinces of Coclé or Los Santos, but I feel quite certain that the bird is found there.)

Primarily this is a bird of forested areas, where it is encountered not only in heavy stands but also where the tree growth is fairly open.

FIG. 39.—Head of double-toothed kite, gavilán bidente, *Harpagus bidentatus fasciatus.*

It is thus able to find suitable cover in second growth and comes also into groves and lines of trees that border fields, pastures, and streams in savanna country. Because of its small size it is little molested, and so usually it is not especially wary. Often I have seen them close at hand, perched low down in leafy branches. They also come to low perches in the open in cultivated fields. They feed mainly on lizards and large insects that they capture in the trees, when necessary climbing, walking, or hopping actively along sloping branches in pursuit. While these kites are attracted occasionally by squeaking, the small forest birds show no fear at their presence, though they may scold or dart at them. I have never seen them attack a bird.

On March 26 and 27, 1955, at the base of Cerro Chame I found a pair at the foundation of a nest of small sticks placed in a crotch 12 meters from the ground in open forest. The location, within 15 meters of a trail, was open without any screen of leaves or branches for concealment. Laughlin (Condor, 1952, pp. 137-139) described a completed nest found on Barro Colorado Island on June 29, 1951, as made of twigs, shallow, and placed over 20 meters from the ground, in a crotch in a tall cedro espinoso (*Bombacopsis fendleri*), where it was concealed from above but not from the side. The female began incubation on July 3. The male drove at a large woodpecker, at white-faced monkeys, and Aracari toucans, and chased them away, but a Swainson's toucan was seen to intimidate the female and take one egg. A few days later the nest was found deserted. The egg, seized by the toucan "appeared whitish speckled with brown," which agrees with published descriptions of the eggs of the related *Harpagus diodon* of South America.

The double-toothed kite is silent in the main except when nesting, when they utter high-pitched calls, in shrill intonation like those of other small hawks.

While these kites are found most often in the tropical zone, they range in Chiriquí to 1,300 meters in the forested valleys. I was interested to collect one in heavy forest on Isla Coiba.

The typical form, *Harpagus bidentatus bidentatus* (Latham), which ranges from eastern Colombia, east of the Andes, Venezuela, and Trinidad to eastern Bolivia and south central Brazil, is less heavily barred on the lower surface.

LEPTODON CAYANENSIS CAYANENSIS (Latham): Cayenne Kite; Gavilán Cabecigris

Falco cayanensis Latham, Index Orn., vol. 1, 1790, p. 28. (Cayenne, French Guiana.)

In the hand these hawks differ from any others found in Panamá by the short, heavy tarsus, which is 42 to 50 mm. long, feathered for nearly half its length. In life the gray head, dark back, banded tail and light-colored undersurface are diagnostic.

Description.—Length 450 to 525 mm. Adult, head gray, paler on the foreneck and throat; rest of upper surface dark gray with a bluish cast; primaries and secondaries with very faintly indicated lighter gray bands; tail blackish, tipped narrowly with grayish white, with 2 narrow bands of light gray, and a third broken one of variable extent, more or less concealed by the upper tail coverts; under surface white, with a tinge of gray; flanks and tibia spotted and streaked with dark gray; under wing coverts grayish black; undersurface of wing blackish banded with grayish white.

Immature in light phase, crown and upper surface brownish black; tail with two bands of brownish gray, and a broad tip of light brown;

forehead, sides of head, ring around hind neck, and under surface, including under wing coverts, white. The head is entirely white in some, except for a small area in the center of the crown.

Immature in dark phase, the upper surface, head, throat, and upper breast black; rest of the lower surface white, heavily streaked with black. In some the white streaking extends also over the foreneck and upper breast.

An adult female taken near Mandinga, Comarca de San Blas, on February 8, 1957, had the iris hazel brown; cere and extreme base of maxilla neutral gray; rest of maxilla, and sides of mandible for distal half, including the tip, dark neutral gray; bare space on side of head, including eyelids, space above eye, lores, gape, base of mandible, distal half of gonys, side of maxilla below nostril, and inside of the nares, including the outer edge of the operculum, light bluish gray; tarsus pale neutral gray; scutes of toes light neutral gray; under side of toes brownish white; claws black.

Measurements.—Males (5 from Panamá and northern Colombia), wing 292-302 (297), tail 199-215 (206), culmen from cere 23.6-25.0 (24.3), tarsus 43.0-49.6 (45.9) mm.

Females (5 from Panamá and northern Colombia), wing 307-326 (314), tail 218-242 (228), culmen from cere 24.5-26.6 (25.4), tarsus 42.0-44.0 (42.9) mm.

Resident. Fairly common in forested areas in the tropical and subtropical zones. Records to date do not include Colón, or Coclé, where the species should be found, nor is it reported from the eastern side of the Azuero Peninsula, or from any of the larger islands.

While a species that is widely spread through the isthmus, it is comparatively little known, since it ranges in the high tree crown of the forests where it is concealed in the leafy canopy. Although most frequent in unbroken forest, in the savanna country on the Pacific slope it comes in lesser number into the lines of trees along the banks of streams and marshes, as around La Jagua.

Cayenne kites soar regularly and are observed sometimes in early morning on tall dead stubs, but on the whole they are seen mainly by chance through some small opening in the high leafy cover. Toward the end of the dry season they begin to call, a loud *kek kek kek kek,* repeated at short intervals, a sound that carries far. At such times they rest on high dead branches that look out over the forest. Others widely separated, to the number of two or three, may answer. Though one that I followed and shot proved to be a female, it is my assumption that the call is given by both sexes. I have heard the note from near sea level on the San Blas coast to 2,000 meters elevation above Cerro Punta. The immature bird in dark phase—black above and white heavily streaked with black below—is especially striking in appearance, since it is so different from the adult in light phase.

The stomach of one taken at Cana was filled with 55 pupae and 38 adults of a wasp (*Odynerus pachyodynerus*) with a few bits of an ant (*Azteca* sp.). Haverschmidt (Condor, 1962, p. 154) in Surinam reports them as eating a variety of insects. In one he found a frog and in another the shell of a small bird's egg.

Schönwetter (Handb. Ool., pt. 3, 1961, p. 155, pl. 6, fig. 7) gives the measurements of 3 eggs from Trinidad as 53.4-54.3×42.2-45.0 mm. His plate illustrates an egg that is elliptical in form, and plain white in color. Haverschmidt (Journ. f. Orn., 1964, p. 66) considers the identification doubtful as the measurements appear small for a bird of this size.

Specimens from southern Brazil, Paraguay, and Bolivia to northern Argentina are larger (wing in a male from the Paraguayan Chaco 355, tail 250 mm.), as indicated by Hellmayr and Conover (Cat. Birds Amer., pt. 1, no. 4, 1949, p. 25), and are to be recognized, according to Hellmayr, as *Leptodon c. monachus* Vieillot, described as *Sparvius monachus* Vieillot, Nouv. Dict. Hist. Nat., nouv. éd., vol. 10, June, 1817, p. 341. ("Bresil")

CHONDROHIERAX UNCINATUS UNCINATUS (Temminck): Hook-billed Kite; Gavilán Piquiganchudo

Figure 40

Falco uncinatus Temminck, Nouv. Rec. Planch. Col., livr. 18, Jan., 1822, pls. 103, 104. (Baía, Brazil.)

The large, somewhat compressed, strongly hooked bill is the important character on which to recognize this species; in its dark and light color phases it varies greatly in color.

Description.—Length 380 to 420 mm. Adults, dark phase, from dark gray to fuscous-black, with a broad white band across the center of the tail, which has a gray end, bordered narrowly at the tip with white; concealed bases of the feathers back of the center of crown and of the nape white. Adults, light phase, fuscous-black above, grayish on the sides of the head and wing, and barred broadly below with buffy white and bright brown (the latter color bordered with dark gray below); under side of wings barred with white; the tail band gray.

Immature in dark phase, two bands across the tail, and the tip buffy white; narrow tips of cinnamon above and below, and the bases of the feathers of the under surface prominently white. Immature, light phase, white to buffy white below, with a light band across the hind neck, more or less barred with fuscous below; 3 tail bands of brownish gray.

An immature bird in dark phase, taken at Juan Mina on January 14, 1955, had the iris dull Marguerite yellow; maxilla and anterior half of cutting edge of mandible dusky neutral gray; rest of mandible, anterior one-fourth of loral space, and cere, dull yellowish green; remainder of loral space, and bare eye ring, light vetiver green; gape,

FIG. 40.—Head of hook-billed kite, gavilán piquiganchudo, *Chondrohierax uncinatus uncinatus*.

and a bare spot above lores, orange; tarsus and toes yellow; claws black. An adult in complete dark phase taken at 200 meters elevation in the Cerro Azul along the upper Río Pacora differed in having the iris bluish gray.

Measurements.—Males (6 from Panamá and Colombia), wing 272-290 (281), tail 177-195 (185), culmen from cere 26.7-31.5 (29.7), tarsus 34.6-39.9 (37.1) mm.

Females (5 from Panamá and Colombia), wing 272-285 (280), tail 179-193 (186), culmen from cere 30.0-30.9 (30.3), tarsus 33.5-39.5 (36.5) mm.

Resident. In forested areas in the tropical and lower subtropical zones. Recorded to date from Chiriquí (Boquete, El Volcán); Veraguas (Arcé specimen without locality); eastern Panamá (lower slopes of the Cerro Azul); Isla Saboga, and Isla Pedro González,

Archipiélago de las Perlas. Known from the Caribbean slope only in the lower Chagres Valley, where it has been taken at Madden Dam, Juan Mina, Gamboa, Barro Colorado Island, and near Lion Hill.

This is a forest species, found ordinarily on wooded slopes above streams, often in hill country. It is a sedentary bird that perches in the middle branches, or in the tree crown, though it comes lower at times, even to the ground, when it is in search of the large land snails that are a major source of its food. The hooked bill tip often is worn, apparently from extracting these animals from the shell. Once I had one clamber along a branch and then fly a few feet toward me, attracted by the squeaking sounds that I was using to decoy other birds. In the hand this kite seems slight in body, with feet especially weak for a hawk, particularly when these are contrasted with the heavy bill. Birds in dark phase may be confused with the crab hawk, until it is noted that the tail is longer, the body form more slender, and the legs and feet shorter and weaker.

The type locality has been designated as Baía by Hellmayr and Conover (Cat. Birds Amer., pt. 1, no. 4, 1949, p. 27).

Haverschmidt (Journ. f. Orn., 1964, pp. 64-66) describes a nest in Surinam found in mid-April that was placed about 10 meters from the ground in a shade tree over coffee. The shallow structure built of dry twigs held two young covered with white down with a slight reddish wash on the head, back, and wings.

Schönwetter (Handb. Ool., pt. 3, 1961, p. 155, pl. 6, fig. 8) records 2 eggs of this bird from Trinidad with measurements of 53.5-53.7 × 40.4-40.6 mm. The specimen figured (in color) is white (apparently with a light tinge of buff) spotted and blotched rather lightly with brown. In form it is slightly pointed oval.

ACCIPITER BICOLOR BICOLOR (Vieillot): Bicolored Hawk; Gavilán Pantalón

Sparvius bicolor Vieillot, Nouv. Dict. Hist. Nat., nouv. éd., vol. 10, June 21, 1817, p. 325. (Cayenne.)

A long-tailed, slender-bodied bird-hunter, gray in the adult, white or buff underneath in the immature; end of tail rounded.

Description.—Length 350 to 420 mm. Adult, crown and upper hindneck sooty black; wings and tail fuscous-black, the latter with 3 brownish crossbars; rest of upper surface slate-gray; sides of head slate; below pale neutral gray, becoming lighter on lower abdomen, and white on lower tail coverts; tibia chestnut; under wing coverts mixed white and chestnut; under wing surface dull neutral gray to dull black, barred heavily with white; tail bars white on under side.

Immature, head black, becoming brownish on cheeks; above fuscous; under surface from nearly white in some individuals to ochraceous in others, the paler ones with an indistinct whitish or buffy ring on hindneck.

An adult female, taken on Isla Coiba, had the following colors: Iris orange; base of maxilla below nostril, and base of mandible, neutral gray; rest of bill black; cere dusky neutral gray; edge of eyelids honey yellow; rest of the bare skin about the eye, and on the loral area, dull yellowish green; tarsus and toes yellow; claws black.

Measurements.—Males (5 from Panamá and northern Colombia), wing 202-211 (207), tail 166-173 (170), culmen from cere 14.6-15.5 (14.9), tarsus 59.9-64.1 (61.7) mm.

Females (5 from Panamá and northern Colombia), wing 234-240 (237), tail 177-189 (184), culmen from cere 16.7-19.5 (18.1), tarsus 67.3-69.3 (68.4) mm.

Resident. Rare; widely distributed, but not recorded from Los Santos and Herrera on the eastern side of the Azuero Peninsula, Coclé, or San Blas. Found on Isla Coiba.

This is another forest species, a hunter of small birds, that may be more common than appears from the few seen, since a fair number have been collected over a period of one hundred years.

In Chiriquí it has been taken from Boquete across the southern slopes of the volcano to Bugaba, near the Costa Rican boundary, as well as near San Félix in the eastern part of the province. Salvin (Proc. Zool. Soc. London, 1870, p. 215) received skins from Arcé shot at Chitra and Calovévora in Veraguas. These are records that may not be duplicated as most of the lowland forest cover in these provinces now is gone. At Paracoté, Aldrich (Scient. Publ. Cleveland Mus. Nat. Hist., vol. 7, 1937, p. 42) shot an immature male as it crossed an open field with direct flight, alternately beating the wings and gliding. Lawrence received one from McLeannan, taken somewhere along the Panama Railroad, and there is one in the National Museum from the same source marked Frijoles. Imhof (manuscript notes) recorded one in the Madden Forest Reserve May 31, 1942. In Bocas del Toro, von Wedel collected one (Peters, Bull. Mus. Comp. Zool., vol. 71, 1931, p. 311) near Almirante, and Mönniche one at Cedral near 1,500 meters elevation on the Holcomb Trail. Loye Miller secured one near Cricamola on August 31, 1936 (specimen at the University of California in Los Angeles).

The only records for the eastern area are of a male taken at San Antonio on the lower Río Bayano east of Chepo (Havemeyer collection in the Peabody Museum at Yale), and specimens from 600 meters elevation near Cana, Darién. The species has been reported most often in the western part of the republic.

On Isla Coiba on January 17, 1956, a female, attracted by the calls of a wounded thrush, came dashing in through low branches to a perch a few feet from me. This bird had the double ovary, usual in the genus *Accipiter*, with indication in the left lobe that the bird had laid rather recently. The right ovary was about one-third the size of the other. A few days later, on January 23 a prisoner brought me an immature male that had begun the molt to adult dress on back, tertials and tail.

Capt. Vivian Hewitt (Ool. Rec., 1937, pp. 13-14) reports an egg collected in the "Rio Orinoco District" in Venezuela, as white with slight rust-colored streaks. It measured 38.0×32.7 mm. The nest, on which the bird was seen, was small and cup-shaped, built of sticks and lined with a few leaves, placed near the end of a branch about 15 meters from the ground. Schönwetter (Handb. Ool., pt. 3, 1961, pp. 143, 160) records a single egg from western Ecuador as pale bluish gray, sparingly spotted with dark brown. The measurement is given as 46.5×35.2 mm. (As this egg, in the Pässler collection, is so different from the one reported by Hewitt it is possible that it is wrongly identified.)

ACCIPITER SUPERCILIOSUS FONTAINIER Bonaparte: Tiny Hawk; Gavilancito Enano

Accipiter Fontainier Bonaparte, Compt. Rend. Acad. Sci. Paris, vol. 37, 1853 (not earlier than Nov. 28), p. 810. (Santa Cruz, Sierra Nevada de Santa Marta, Colombia.)

Smallest of the hawks found in Panamá.

Description.—Length 200 to 250 mm. Adult, crown and hindneck dull black; upper back dark neutral gray; rest of upper surface fuscous; tail with 4 dull black bars, the interspaces fuscous-brown, a concealed spot of white at base; side of head gray, streaked indistinctly with dull white; under surface white, barred narrowly with fuscous, except the throat and foreneck, which vary in marking from a few narrow shaft streaks to plain white; under wing coverts white, lightly barred with dark neutral gray; under surface of primaries and secondaries white basally, dull light gray distally, heavily barred with fuscous.

Immature (dark phase), above fuscous-black; tail with 5 dark bars, tipped narrowly with black; under parts buff, barred with buffy brown.

Immature (rufous phase), crown fuscous; rest of upper surface hazel brown, with concealed areas of dull brown and white bases; tail hazel barred with black; below white, barred with light brown, and washed with bright hazel on under side of wing, sides, center of breast, and outer side of tibia.

An adult male, taken on the Río Tuira, had the iris bright orange-red; rim of eyelids, bare skin around eyes, lores, cere, gape, and mandibular rami, bright yellow; maxilla (except base), and extreme tip of mandible, dusky neutral gray; base of maxilla below nostril, and rest of mandible dull buffy white; tarsus and toes yellow, the toes slightly brighter; claws black.

Measurements.—Males (3 from Panamá and northwestern Colombia), wing 130.3-132.5 (131.5), tail 86.7-92.9 (89.9), culmen from cere 10.8-11.5 (11.1), tarsus 40.8-42.2 (41.3) mm.

Female (1 from Panamá), wing 149.7, tail 105.7, culmen from cere 12.7, tarsus 45.0 mm.

Resident. Rare; found in forested areas in the tropical zone.

This is a little-known species, small in size, that has been recorded seldom. McLeannan collected one early in his work, that is presumed to have come from near Lion Hill (Lawrence, Ann. Lyc. Nat. Hist. New York, vol. 7, 1862, p. 462). Arcé secured one a few years later near Santiago, Veraguas (Salvin, Proc. Zool. Soc. London, 1867, p. 158). Hasso von Wedel shot a male at Obaldía, San Blas (Griscom, Bull. Mus. Comp. Zool., vol. 72, 1932, p. 313). There is an immature bird (a female from its size), not previously reported, in the National Museum, collected on February 10, 1889, by H. T. Heyde in forest on the Atlantic slope in the Cascajal area of northern Coclé.

I have found the species twice, first on February 22, 1959, in heavy forest at Boca de Paya, on the Río Tuira, Darién. I was watching small birds moving among leaves a few feet over my head, when one of these little hawks swooped in, seized one of them and then flew to a perch 50 meters distant, holding its prey in its feet. I shot the hawk immediately, and as it fell the little bird flew away, apparently unharmed.

On March 9, 1961, on the Río Pequení above the Candelaria Station, I had a similar experience when one of these small hawks seized an arrocero immediately in front of me and alighted with it on a branch. My companion, who was ahead, shot, and again the little bird, its prey, flew away unharmed. The hawk was another male, somewhat younger, as there were still two chestnut feathers with dusky bars in the scapulars of one side. The colors of the side of the head and of the tarsus also were slightly duller than in the adult.

Nothing is known of the nesting of this subspecies. Eggs of the closely allied typical form *Accipiter s. superciliosus* (Linnaeus) from Minas Geraes, Brazil, are described by L. R. Wolfe (Ool. Rec., 1936, p. 84) as pale bluish white, with a greenish tinge when viewed against a strong light. One egg has a wash of light brown over the large end, and scattered streaks and spots of this color elsewhere. The other two in the set appear unmarked until viewed against the light as mentioned, when small specks of reddish scattered through the shell may be seen. They measure 36.1×29.0, 36.6×29.1, and 39.0×29.0 mm. Capt. Vivian Hewitt (Ool. Rec., 1937, p. 13), in Venezuela, flushed one of these hawks from a hole in a tree while climbing to a nest of a *Busarellus*. Both nests were empty but two weeks later he found that the small accipiters had abandoned the hole, and had taken over the nest of the larger hawk. The single egg that both parents guarded was plain white without markings, and measured 35.0×27.5 mm.

The typical race *superciliosus*, found from eastern Colombia, east of the Andes, and Venezuela, south through eastern Brazil to Misiones in northeastern Argentina, differs only in slightly less heavy barring on the undersurface, with the dark bars grayer, less black. Size is the same in both races. The subspecies found in Panamá ranges from Nicaragua south through Central America and Colombia west of the eastern Andes to western Ecuador.

ACCIPITER STRIATUS VELOX (Wilson): Sharp-shinned Hawk; Gavilancito de Paso

Falco velox Wilson, Amer. Orn., vol. 5, 1812, p. 116, pl. 45, fig. 1. (Philadelphia, Pennsylvania.)

Similar in form to the bicolored hawk, but smaller, darker and with a definite pattern of streaks or bars on the lower surface; end of tail square.

Description.—Length 250 to 350 mm. Adult, above slate gray, darker on the crown; feathers of nape with concealed white bases; underparts cinnamon-brown, spotted and barred with white; tail tipped with white, with 4 blackish bands; under tail coverts white; under wing coverts white, spotted and barred with fuscous; under wing broadly barred with blackish.

Immature, above fuscous, darker on the head, narrowly edged with tawny; scapulars and tertials with concealed white spots; lower surface white or pale buff streaked and spotted with fuscous and dull brown.

Measurements.—Males, wing 162-178 (171), tail 134-152 (140.8), culmen from cere 9.5-11 (10.3), tarsus 46-54 (49.9) mm.

Females, wing 195-210 (200), tail 150-179 (165.6), culmen from cere 10.5-14 (12.7), tarsus 45-58.5 (54.9) mm.

Migrant from the north to western Panamá; rare.

Arcé secured one on the Volcán de Chiriquí (Salvin, Proc. Zool. Soc. London, 1870, p. 216); Mrs. Davidson collected a male February 15, 1934, at 650 meters on Horqueta, above Boquete (Davidson, Proc. California Acad. Sci., vol. 23, 1938, p. 256), preserved in the California Academy of Sciences. There is one in the Mönniche collection in the Chicago Natural History Museum taken at about the same elevation at Quiel, above Boquete, October 24, 1937 (Blake, Fieldiana: Zool., vol. 36, 1958, p. 505). A specimen in the British Museum, "obtained through Boucard from Panama" (Salvin and Godman, Biol. Centr-Amer., vol. 3, 1897, p. 50) probably was collected by Arcé. Stone (Proc. Acad. Nat. Sci. Philadelphia, 1918, p. 249) was in error in listing this species from the Canal Zone.

The sharp-shinned hawk undoubtedly is more regular in occurrence than the few records indicate. While I have not taken specimens, I saw this species near Cerro Punta, Chiriquí on March 7, 1955, when one circled a hundred meters in the air at sunrise near our house, and again the following day when I recorded one flying at the edge of the forest above the village. Near Monagrillo, Herrera, on February 25, 1948, I saw one close at hand in thick brush, and on March 15, 1957, near Pedasí, Los Santos, one circled over the pastures near the Río Pedasí for several minutes.

The sharpshin ranges in brushy areas, or in forest, often in undergrowth. In hunting the small birds that form its food it may dash across the borders of fields or pastures.

BUTEO ALBICAUDATUS HYPOSPODIUS Gurney: White-tailed Hawk; Gavilán Tejé

Buteo hypospodius Gurney, Ibis, ser. 3, vol. 6, no. 1, Jan. 1876, p. 73, pl. 3. (Medellín, Antioquia, Colombia.)

Adult in light phase, white underneath, with dark head, dark wing tips, and a dark band at the end of the tail.

Description.—Length 500 to 610 mm. Adult, above mainly slate gray, including the sides of the head, the feathers of upper back with concealed white bases; lesser wing coverts cinnamon, with scapulars tinged with the same; outer webs of primaries and tips black; lower back, rump, and upper tail coverts white, barred with dark gray, tail coverts in some plain white; rectrices white, becoming gray on the outer webs of the outer feathers, with black subterminal band, and a white tip; sides of throat and breast gray; rest of under surface white, barred more or less on sides with gray to brownish gray; under wing coverts white, barred narrowly with gray to brownish gray.

There is also a dark phase in which the under parts are gray to slate color, edged with white.

Immature, above black to fuscous-black; hindneck with concealed white and buffy edgings on back; below streaked more or less with buffy white; upper tail coverts buffy white, barred irregularly with cinnamon brown; under wing coverts barred with black and buffy white; tail light gray, edged with dull black, and with many narrow bars of fuscous.

Measurements (from Friedmann, U. S. Nat. Mus. Bull. 50, pt. 10, 1950, p. 234).—Males, wing 404-430 (416.4), tail 194-207 (200.6), culmen from cere 23.5-27.5 (25.0), tarsus 92.0-95.0 (93.7) mm.

Females, wing 423-450 (438.8), tail 198.5-211 (201.4), culmen from cere 25.5-28.5 (27.5), tarsus 84.5-93.0 (87.1) mm.

Resident. Rare; recorded from Calovévora and Chitra, Veraguas (Salvin, Proc. Zool. Soc. London, 1870, p. 215); Cricamola, Bocas del Toro (female in University of Cincinnati Museum, taken by von Wedel October 15, 1936). There are sight records from the western Province of Panamá; at El Espino (near the boundary of Coclé) and Cerro Campana; also at París, Herrera; and on Isla Taboga.

On March 4, 1948, I recorded one soaring near the Río Santa María, northeast of París, Herrera. In March 1951 I saw a pair on several occasions soaring in strong wind across the southern slopes of Cerro Campana. They often hung poised for several minutes over one spot, usually with partly closed wings. Once as one remained in that fashion I could see a small bird held in one foot. Occasionally one of these birds came down to perch on a rock at the crest of a ridge, but they were wary and never allowed close approach. On March 24, 1951, I recorded a pair that flew up from perches on rocks on a high ridge above the Río Calabozo at El Espino.

On Christmas day, 1955, on Isla Taboga a great ascending thermal that formed over the hill slopes early in the forenoon drew scores of brown pelicans, frigatebirds and vultures that came from afar to soar over the island. Among them I saw a white-tailed hawk that presently drifted away toward Cerro Cabra on the opposite mainland.

It was my impression that the bird had come over from that area for a time attracted by the soaring flock.

In the air the adults appear white underneath, with dark head sharply outlined from the lower foreneck, dark wing tips, and a dark band at the end of the tail. It would be difficult if not impossible to distinguish those in dark stage of plumage from other species of black colored hawks.

The Spanish name, *gavilán tejé,* is given in imitation of the high-pitched double-noted, accented call, uttered often as the bird circles high in air.

While there is no description of the breeding of this hawk in Panamá, elsewhere in the range of this race, which extends from southern Texas through México and Central America to northern Colombia and Venezuela, the nest is a structure of sticks placed in low trees in open country. Bent (U. S. Nat. Mus. Bull. 167, 1937, p. 218) says that the set includes 1 to 3 eggs, in color dull white to pale bluish white, some spotted with dull brown, clay color, or buff and some plain, without markings. Measurements vary from 52.7-65×42.2-50 mm., with the average 58.9×46.5 mm. The downy young, with the body dull buffy brown, whiter underneath, becoming dull sepia on the head with a dull black mark through the eye, are quite different in appearance from those of other species of the larger hawks.

BUTEO ALBONOTATUS Kaup: Zone-tailed Hawk; Gavilán Negro

[*Buteo*] *albonotatus* Kaup, Isis von Oken, 1847, Heft 5 (May), col. 329. (México.)

Black, with under surface of wing banded with white.

Description.—Length 450 to 550 mm. Adult, black, with many of the feathers white, or partly white, basally; some individuals with a wash of slate color on back and breast; lores and forehead white, with blackish shaft streaks; tail, above tipped narrowly with white, and banded with 5 or more indistinct gray bands; below, grayish to white, banded narrowly with neutral gray; under surface of primaries and secondaries neutral gray, barred with white; under wing coverts black.

Immature, sooty brown to black, spotted irregularly with white on lower surface; tail with numerous bands.

In the hand it may be noted that four outer primaries are distinctly notched at the tip. The other species of the genus *Buteo* found in Panamá that are black or dark-colored below have only 3 of the outer primaries cut on the inner margin.

Iris dark brown; eyelids and bare space above dull gray; bill dull neutral gray at base, shading to dusky neutral gray, or dull black, toward tip; cere and gape yellow; tarsus and toes yellow; claws black.

Measurements.—Males (4 from Costa Rica, Panamá, Colombia and Venezuela), wing 365-394 (378.7), tail 190-205 (199), culmen from cere 20.6-21.5 (21.0), tarsus 66.0-69.0 (68.1) mm.

Females (6 from Panamá, Colombia and Venezuela), wing 385-421 (404.3), tail 197-219 (208.5), culmen from cere 23.4-24.5 (23.8), tarsus 70.6-80.5 (74.8) mm.

Status not certain. Rare; 6 specimens known from Panamá.

W. W. Brown, Jr. collected male and female on Isla del Rey on March 6 and 11, 1904 (which are in the Museum of Comparative Zoology). A female in the U. S. National Museum was shot on November 9, 1953, on the K-6 Road, near Cerro Galera, Canal Zone. Hasso von Wedel secured a female at Permé, San Blas, August 27, 1929 (specimen in the Museum of Comparative Zoology) and two others at Puerto Obaldía, August 14, 1931, and January 13, 1932 (now in the Brandt collection at the University of Cincinnati).

Material that I have seen does not justify separation of the two races that have been recognized in most reports that include this bird. The slaty wash supposed to mark a northern subspecies, in the series seen has been confined to fully adult individuals, as shown by the few broad light tail bands. The blacker individuals throughout the range mainly are those with the narrow, multiple tail bands of the immature. Wing measurements indicate a possible separation, in which there is a larger population in North and Central America, and a slightly smaller one in northern South America. The material seen, however, does not demonstrate this clearly. It is possible that the mixing of larger and smaller individuals found in tropical America is due to an invasion of northern migrants, and that the same mixing in the north may be due to faulty sex determination.

If two forms are recognized, five of the specimens recorded from Panamá, viz., the male (wing 375 mm.) and the female (wing 403) from Isla del Rey, the female (wing 415) from Permé, and the two from Obaldía (wing 394 and 402) appear to come within the smaller, southern group under the name *Buteo albonotatus abbreviatus* Cabanis. These might be residents. The fourth, the female from the Canal Zone (wing 421 mm.), which is decidedly larger, then would be regarded as a migrant of typical *Buteo albonotatus albonotatus* from the north.

BUTEO NITIDUS BLAKEI Hellmayr and Conover: Gray Hawk; Gavilán Gris

Figure 41

Buteo nitidus blakei Hellmayr and Conover, Cat. Birds Amer., pt. 1, no. 4, Aug. 1949, p. 160. ("Pozo del Rio Grande" = El Pozo de Térraba, 150 meters elevation, Costa Rica.)

Distinguished in the adult by dark bands on the light gray back, and the gray-banded under surface.

Description.—Length 370 to 420 mm. Adult, upper surface light gray, paler on crown and hindneck, marked abundantly with rather narrow bands of darker gray, and with shaft lines of black; tips of primaries black, and of secondaries white; upper tail coverts and lower rump feathers black, tipped with white; tail black, with a broad subterminal band and narrow tip white, in some individuals with another band of white above the center; throat white; side of head grayish white, marked obscurely with pale gray; lower surface of body, including the sides and axillars, white, barred heavily with neutral gray; under tail coverts white; under surface of wing white, changing through grayish white to dark neutral gray on tips of primaries, with widely separated, narrow bars of neutral gray on the under wing coverts, as well as on the flight feathers.

Immature, crown and sides of head cream-buff to cinnamon-buff, more or less streaked with fuscous; above fuscous with the feathers edged with russet, more heavily on the wing coverts, which are blotched basally with white and rufous brown; primaries black at tips, pale rufous barred with black and with blackish brown shafts elsewhere; secondaries tipped with cinnamon; upper tail coverts light buff; tail black tipped with white, barred with 3 paler bands of brownish gray; below cinnamon-buff, streaked and spotted broadly with brownish black; tibia and under wing coverts cinnamon-buff; under surface of primaries and secondaries pale pinkish buff, barred narrowly with dull black.

The pattern of the immature in life suggests that of the immature broad-winged hawk, but the markings on the lower surface are much heavier, and the upper surface is decidedly black. Usually the crown is much paler, though in some it is heavily streaked.

A male in immature dress taken near Armila, San Blas, March 1, 1963, had the colors of the soft parts, as follows: Iris light brown; cere and gape light honey yellow; side of maxilla at gape, lower half of mandibular rami, and extreme base of gonys light green; rest of maxilla and tip of mandible black; middle of mandible dull neutral gray; tarsus and toes bright yellow; claws black.

Measurements.—Males (4 specimens), wing 234-240 (237), tail 147-150 (148); culmen from cere 20.0-22.0 (20.9), tarsus 66.2-70.0 (68.8) mm.

Females (5 specimens), wing 244-255 (249), tail 149-160 (164), culmen from cere 20.8-23.3 (22.1), tarsus 67.5-73.0 (70.5) mm.

Fig. 41.—Gray hawk, gavilán gris, *Buteo nitidus blakei*.

Resident. Found locally in forested areas through the tropical zone, to 1,200 meters in Chiriquí (Barriles); apparently most common on the Pacific slope.

The species has not been recorded to date from Bocas del Toro nor from Darién, though it should be found. A specimen taken by Mrs. Davidson Terry at Barriles is the only record for Chiriquí. They are fairly common in northern Herrera, and range to the southern end of the Azuero Peninsula, below Pedasí.

This handsome hawk spends much of its time in the higher levels of forest trees, where usually it flies from behind cover, and so it is not easily seen. Its apparent greater abundance on the Pacific slope may be due to the more open cover in that area which permits clearer view. The species is less common than the large-billed hawk and also is much more retiring. The larger feet with longer claws, as well as the heavier body indicate also that it is a more active predator. Mice, rats, lizards, and frogs are recorded as its food. It also preys on small birds to some extent. Sometimes these hawks have decoyed to the distress calls that I use in hunting.

Near Mandinga, San Blas, at the end of January a pair were building a nest in the upper branches of a dark-leafed tree a hundred meters from our house, and were active in this until our departure on February 15. The usual call was a loud *kree-ee-ah,* with additional whistled notes, in general like those of the crab-hawk, but definitely higher in tone. Sometimes when I approached quietly one of the birds that I believed to be the male would alight on an open limb in a gray-barked jobo tree, which his color matched perfectly. Here he rested with body inclined forward, and vibrated the tail steadily from side to side, a movement that emphasized the black-and-white markings of the tip. The nest, which we were unable to reach because of the size of the tree, appeared to resemble that of other tree-building hawks, in that it was constructed of small sticks. On February 7 I saw one of the birds fly to it bearing a freshly broken, leafy branch.

Wolfe (Ool. Rec., 1938, p. 50) describes a set of 2 collected by Austin Paul Smith, May 2, 1923 in the Province of Guanacaste, Costa Rica as lightly marked with light brown. They measure 42.5 × 36.3, and 43.6 × 37.2 mm. The ground color in eggs of this species varies from dull white to bluish white, usually plain, rarely spotted with brown.

This subspecies was first described by Harry Kirke Swann in 1922 as *Asturina nitida costaricensis*. With its transfer to the genus *Buteo* this name is preoccupied by *Buteo jamaicensis costaricensis* Ridgway, dated 1874. It was renamed *blakei*, therefore, by Hellmayr and Conover, as indicated in the heading above. The type locality cited by Swann as "Pozo del Rio Grande, Bornea" (= Boruca) has been followed by other authors but needs correction. The type specimen, a male in the Museum of Comparative Zoology, was collected in 1906 by C. F. Underwood at Pozo del Rio Grande, a point at about 150 meters elevation, according to Bangs (Auk, 1907, pp. 287, 290).

It now is known as El Pozo de Térraba, according to information received from Dr. Paul Slud. Boruca is a hill town at about 450 meters, located some distance farther inland. Bangs in his list of types (Bull. Mus. Comp. Zool., vol. 70, 1930, p. 189) merely quoted what Swann had written, but with correction of the spelling of Boruca, as he cites the locality as "Boruca, Pozo del Rio Grande," without realizing that the two geographic terms represented two distinct places.

BUTEO BRACHYURUS Vieillot: Short-tailed Hawk; Gavilán Cola Corta

Buteo brachyurus Vieillot, Nouv. Dict. Hist. Nat., nouv. éd., vol. 4, Dec., 1816, p. 477. (Cayenne.)

A small hawk. In black phase, black with short, white-banded tail. In light phase, white below, with a wash of cinnamon on sides of breast.

Description.—Length 370-460 mm. Adult, dark phase, black to brownish black throughout, with a slight indication of grayish wash on the upper back; forehead and anterior part of lores narrowly white, with the feather shafts black; back part of crown and upper hindneck with concealed white bases; upper tail coverts with hidden bars of white; longer outermost under wing coverts dark neutral gray, the rest and the axillars black; central area of flight feathers marbled with white and pale gray; tips of primaries dull gray; tips of secondaries dull mouse gray; shafts of flight feathers black above white underneath, except for the tips which are dark brown; upper surface of tail with 5 or 6 dull brownish gray bands; tail with a narrow, indistinct terminal band of mouse brown, tipped faintly with grayish white.

Adult, light phase, above dark grayish brown; white on forehead and anterior lores more extensive than in dark phase; primaries and secondaries dull black; tail with 6 somewhat irregular black bands across the gray-brown feathers, which are tipped with brownish black, and margined lightly with white to grayish white; sides of head and neck brownish black, changing to dull cinnamon on sides of upper breast; under surface elsewhere pure white; under wing white, except for neutral gray spots on the ends of the longest outermost under coverts, and the tips of the primaries which are blackish brown; inner primaries and secondaries white to light gray banded with light neutral gray to mouse brown.

Iris brown; bill black, becoming slate gray at base of mandible; cere yellow; tarsus and toes yellow; claws black.

Measurements.—Males (5 from México, Panamá, and Venezuela), wing 269-299 (281.6), tail 137-148 (144.8), culmen from cere 16.8-19.6 (18.1), tarsus 54.4-61.0 (57.9) mm.

Females (5 from México, Nicaragua, Costa Rica, and Panamá), wing 299-313 (307.6), tail 151-171 (158.2), culmen from cere 19.0-21.0 (20.2), tarsus 57.0-62.7 (59.2) mm.

Resident. Rare, in the more open lands.

Little is known of this species in Panamá, where the few records for it over a period of nearly one hundred years are widely scattered. In Veraguas, Enrique Arcé secured two at Calovévora and another at Calobre (Salvin, Proc. Zool. Soc. London, 1870, p. 215; Salvin and Godman, Biol. Centr.-Amer., vol. 3, 1900, p. 72). W. W. Brown, Jr., en route to Chiriquí, shot one at Soná, July 25, 1901 (Bangs, Proc. New England Zoöl. Club, vol. 3, 1902, p. 20). In Bocas del Toro, Hasso von Wedel collected a female at Changuinola, November 5, 1928 (Peters, Bull. Mus. Comp. Zool., vol. 71, 1931, p. 311). In the Canal Zone, Hallinan secured one at Gatun, February 11, 1909. Brown shot a male near Panama City, May 4, 1904 (Thayer and Bangs, Bull. Mus. Comp. Zool., vol. 46, 1906, p. 214), Wedel one at Permé, San Blas (Griscom, Bull. Mus. Comp. Zool., vol. 72, 1932, p. 314), and another, a female in light phase, at Puerto Obaldía, San Blas, June 16, 1933 (in the museum of the University of Cincinnati).

I have found this species only in northern Herrera, where Perrygo and I collected one on February 26 near Portobellilo, and another March 8, near Santa María, both in 1948. The first was flying along a line of trees bordering a lane in open country. The second was among large trees in gallery forest. In general appearance on the wing these birds were similar to other small hawks of the same genus. They seem however, to be more aggressive, as one taken was killed as it stooped swiftly at a brown robin that had come to feed on berries. Hallinan records that the one he collected had killed two lizards, and that it had fragments of a small bird in its stomach.

While the range of this species includes the vast area of tropical America from México through Central America and South America to northeastern Argentina, its nesting is known principally from the population isolated in Florida. Here the birds build open nests in trees often high above the ground. Bent (U. S. Nat. Mus. Bull. 167, 1937, pp. 256-257) says that the usual set is of two eggs, with a range in number from one to three. These are plain pale bluish white in some, or dull white, spotted or blotched in varying degree with brown. Measurements vary from 48.6-57.5 × 40.3-45.5 mm.

BUTEO PLATYPTERUS PLATYPTERUS (Vieillot): Broad-winged Hawk; Gavilán de Paso

Sparvius platypterus Vieillot, Table Encycl. Meth., Orn., vol. 3, 1823, p. 1273. (Philadelphia, Pennsylvania.)

A medium-sized, heavy-bodied hawk; adult with side of head, foreneck and upper breast cinnamon-brown; immature white underneath streaked with grayish brown.

Description.—Length 340 to 410 mm. Adult, above grayish brown to dull black, the feathers edged lightly with grayish white to cinnamon-buff; forehead and lores white; crown feathers edged lightly with dull white; nape with concealed feather base white; primaries and secondaries tipped lightly with dull white; upper tail coverts and lateral rump feathers tipped and barred broadly with white; tail blackish brown to black, with two broad bars of grayish white, a grayish brown band near the end and white tip; side of head below eye blackish, edged with light gray, becoming browner over the ear region, and continuing thus down the side of the neck; throat white to buffy white streaked with dull black; under tail coverts white to buff, immaculate or lightly marked with light brown; rest of lower surface, including the feathered part of legs, banded irregularly with broad marks of wood brown, edged somewhat with dull gray and white; under wing coverts buffy white, marked lightly with light brown, with the longer, outermost feathers tipped and barred lightly with grayish and brownish black; under wing feathers white, becoming gray and finally black at tips of primaries; under surface of secondaries barred with dark gray and wood brown. Some individuals are whiter below and blacker above, and some browner above and below, with others in intermediate stage between these two styles.

Immature, blackish brown above, with the partly concealed feather bases white so that this lighter color appears abundantly in spots and streaks; below white to buffy white, streaked lightly to heavily with brownish black; under wing surface whiter than in the adult.

Rarely an individual shows a dark phase that is almost black, so that it resembles the short-tailed hawk, but may be told by the smaller feet, with the middle toe without the claw shorter than the bare portion of the tarsus in front.

Measurements (from Friedmann, U. S. Nat. Mus. Bull. 50, pt. 10, 1950, p. 309).—Males, wing 244-277 (262.8), tail 148.0-173.5 (159), culmen from cere 17-20 (18.2), tarsus 57.5-65.5 (62.3) mm.

Females, wing 265-296 (282.8), tail 155-185 (171), culmen from cere 17.1-20.5 (19.3), tarsus, 59-66.4 (62.8) mm.

Winter visitor from the north and passage migrant. Common; found throughout the mainland; recorded on Isla Coiba, and on islas Taboga, Taboguilla, Uravá, Gobernadora and Cébaco.

The broad-wing apparently is averse to long flights over water, as though it passes regularly in migration into South America as far as northern and eastern Venezuela, to reach these regions it moves over land through Central America and Colombia. It has not been recorded to date for the Archipiélago de las Perlas, though it crosses islands immediately adjacent to the mainland. In 5 weeks in the field on Isla Coiba I recorded only half a dozen.

These hawks appear from the north in October and remain until April. Early dates of arrival are October 7, 1953, near Pacora (specimen in U. S. National Museum), October 12 to 14, 1942, flights over Chorrera (T. A. Imhof, notes), October 19, 1929, Permé, San Blas (Griscom, Bull. Mus. Comp. Zool., vol. 72, 1932, p. 313). The main flight northward from wintering grounds in South America passes through the isthmus during the month of March. On March 31, 1950, I observed hundreds near Chimán, and on April 1, 1955, I recorded numbers mingled with a great flight of Swainson's hawks over Pedro Miguel. The major migration ends abruptly. A few late records for single birds during April are as follows: April 4, 1946, at Jaqué, Darién; April 6, 1950, Barro Colorado Island; April 19, 1901, near Boquete, Chiriquí (Bangs, Proc. New England Zoöl. Club, vol. 3, 1902, p. 20).

One banded in Maine July 5, 1938, was taken the following December near Los Santos.

Though groups of broad-wings often move alone, the major flights usually are in company with Swainson's hawks and follow the pattern described for that bird. The total number, however, is less than that of the larger species, and on the whole the broad-wing movement is less spectacular. Those that remain on the isthmus during the northern winter are spread singly through forested areas, including lines of trees through cultivated lands, and older stands of second growth. Sometimes they may come out briefly to soar in the company of native hawks, but usually they are seen perched among open branches, in or below the tree crown. In the mountains in the cool air of early morning often they are seen resting in the sun in dead trees standing in the pastures. Birds taken in March for specimens may be heavy with fat.

In Panamá these hawks feed extensively on large Orthoptera and to some degree on lizards. They appear regularly on freshly burned lands, and then become so much blackened that they may be difficult to recognize. Chapman (Life in an Air Castle, 1938, p. 126) saw one capture an immature ani, but this must be unusual, as I have never seen one show any interest in the abundant small birds when these chance to appear near, and conversely the forest birds ordinarily pay little or no attention to the hawks. The exceptions usually are tropical kingbirds and *Myiozetetes similis* that pursue large birds of any kind, even to turkey vultures that pass too near.

BUTEO JAMAICENSIS (Gmelin): Red-tailed Hawk; Guaraguao

Falco jamaicensis Gmelin, Syst. Nat., vol. 1, pt. 1, 1788, p. 266. (Jamaica.)

This is a species found throughout North America, from near the limit of tree growth in the far north south to Panamá and the Greater Antilles. In this extensive range 8 subspecies have been recognized of which two are known from the Republic, one as a resident in the mountains of Chiriquí and Veraguas and another as a casual migrant. Details regarding these are covered under the two headings that follow.

BUTEO JAMAICENSIS COSTARICENSIS Ridgway

Buteo borealis var. *costaricensis* Ridgway, in Baird, Brewer, and Ridgway, Hist. N. Amer. Birds, Land Birds, vol. 3, 1874, pp. 258 (in key), 285. (Costa Rica.)

A large, broad-winged hawk with rufous brown tail in the adult. The inner webs of the four outermost primaries are incised toward the tip.

Description.—Length 470 to 570 mm. Adult, crown and hindneck hair brown to black, with the concealed feather bases white; rest of upper surface blackish brown; tail russet to cinnamon-brown, with a narrow black subterminal band; upper tail coverts cinnamon, barred irregularly with dusky, and tipped with white; sides of head, neck, and upper breast hair brown, edged or washed with dull cinnamon; foreneck and breast white, streaked lightly with hair brown; abdomen, sides, flanks, and tibia cinnamon-brown; under tail coverts cinnamon-buff; tibia sometimes lightly barred with dull black; under wing coverts cinnamon-brown, becoming white on outer edge, with the longest outermost coverts dusky neutral gray, forming a large, prominent spot; under side of flight feathers dull white, freckled with pale gray, tipped with dusky neutral gray, and with 2 or more bars of the same color. There are two color phases, one that is almost entirely white below, with a few cinnamon buff bars on the tibia, and one that is more rufescent on the under surface than the detailed description above.

Immature, like the adult, but with crown indistinctly lined with white; tail grayish cinnamon-buff, with many narrow hair brown crossbars; tibia whitish, barred with reddish brown; under wing coverts mainly white.

The bright brown color of the upper surface of the tail in the adult fades decidedly before the feathers are molted, as the birds perch and soar much at hours when they receive the full force of the tropical sun.

Measurements (from Friedmann, U. S. Nat. Mus. Bull. 50, pt. 10, 1950, p. 266).—Males, wing 368-377 (372.2), tail 207.0-216.5 (213.6), culmen from cere 25.0-26.7 (25.4), tarsus 87.0-90.5 (88.6) mm.

Females, wing 397-410 (402.2), tail 222-239 (229.2), culmen from cere 26.0-28.0 (26.8), tarsus 85.0-95.3 (87.1) mm.

Resident. Tolerably common in the subtropical and temperate zones in the higher mountains of Chiriquí and Veraguas; found casually east to the Canal Zone.

There is indication that formerly, when lowland forests in Veraguas were extensive, these hawks came down the mountain slopes into the tropical zone, as there is a specimen in the British Museum collected by Arcé marked Castillo. Arcé secured specimens also in the mountains of Veraguas near Chitra and Calobre. Red-tailed hawks that are supposed to be this race are seen casually east as far as the lowlands of the Canal Zone. The only specimen presumed to come from this area is one in the British Museum, sent to Salvin by McLeannan when he was stationed at Lion Hill (Sclater and Salvin, Proc. Zool. Soc. London, 1864, p. 369). J. M. Abbott informs me that he saw a red-tailed hawk at Fort Clayton, February 1, and another near Pedro Miguel on March 3, 1942. Dr. and Mrs. Scholes recorded one along the Chiva Chiva trail back of Fort Clayton on December 23, 1951 (Condor, 1954, p. 166). It is my supposition that these were probably wanderers of the subspecies found in the western mountains.

Most of the specimen and other records refer to the mountains of Chiriquí, which is the main area of present day occurrence. Here the birds may be noted over the higher slopes of the volcano, and also on the mountains that adjoin the main Volcán Barú. One was taken at Boquete by W. W. Brown, Jr., and a series by Mönniche at Chiquero, Horqueta, and Lérida, in that same area. A skin in the California Academy of Sciences was taken by Mrs. Davidson on December 24, 1929, at Barriles across the Río Chiriquí Viejo from Cerro Pando. I have recorded them from time to time over Pando, near Santa Clara (Chiriquí), near Sereno on the Costa Rican boundary, and at 2,100 meters elevation above Cerro Punta. Wedel shot one near Changuinola, Bocas del Toro, December 9, 1928 (Peters, Bull. Mus. Comp. Zool., vol. 71, 1931, p. 310).

Usually they are seen soaring high in air, turning in circles, and occasionally uttering a shrill, screaming call. As they tilt a bit in the air currents a view of the bright brown color of the tail makes their identification certain.

The nesting of this subspecies has not been recorded.

BUTEO JAMAICENSIS CALURUS Cassin

Buteo calurus Cassin, Proc. Acad. Nat. Sci. Philadelphia, vol. 7, no. 7, Jan.-Feb. (May 22), 1855, p. 281. (Fort Webster, Rio Mimbres, New Mexico.)

Adult, in normal phase, like *B. j. costaricensis,* but blacker above; below washed with pale buff to pale cinnamon; tibia barred definitely with bright brown. In melanistic phase, the bird is blackish brown above and below, with the under tail coverts marked with cinnamon; wings white to gray underneath. Some in the dark phase have the head, hindneck, and upper back edged with cinnamon.

On the whole they are like the resident subspecies, but in normal dress are darker, and much darker in the black phase.

Casual wanderer from farther north. One record, a bird in the British Museum, shot by E. Arcé in 1870 on the southern slopes of Volcán de Chiriquí.

This darker race of the species nests from Alaska and northern Canada south through the western United States to Baja California and New Mexico. In winter some wander south to Guatemala, casually as far as Nicaragua.

BUTEO SWAINSONI Bonaparte: Swainson's Hawk; Irol

Buteo Swainsoni Bonaparte, Geogr. and Comp. List, 1838, p. 3. (Fort Vancouver, Washington.)

A large hawk, variable in color, similar in form to the red-tail, but with three outer primaries incised at the tip.

Description.—Length 450 to 550 mm. Adult, pale phase, upper surface dark grayish brown to fuscous, the feathers with narrow edgings of grayish white to cinnamon; forehead and lores white, the former streaked with grayish brown; feathers of nape with concealed white bases; lateral upper tail coverts white to tawny, barred with grayish brown; secondaries fuscous, tipped lightly with white to cinnamon; primaries dull black, with outer webs toward tips more or less grayish; rectrices brownish mouse gray, tipped with grayish or buffy white, with 9 or 10 bars of dull black; throat white, streaked with grayish brown to dull black; sides of the head dull black; upper breast grayish brown to light russet, with narrow black shaft lines; rest of under surface buffy white, varying from nearly immaculate, to spotted and barred irregularly with grayish brown to tawny; tibia barred with cinnamon; under wing coverts white to buffy white with the longer outer ones dark gray to dull black, forming a distinct spot; elsewhere spotted lightly with grayish brown to cinnamon.

Rufous phase, entire under surface washed with light brown, barred narrowly with russet; concealed nape patch buffy.

Black phase, body throughout dull black to brownish black; under tail coverts buffy, barred with fuscous.

Immature, blackish above, with forehead extensively white; crown and hindneck broadly streaked with white, and rest of upper surface heavily and irregularly spotted with white; below buffy white, with a fuscous area on breast. Birds in the first year vary from this to individuals with under surface fuscous-black spotted with tawny.

As the description indicates there is much variation in color. In life the lighter individuals are marked by the dark breast. The blacker ones suggest the zone-tailed hawk, but usually they will be seen in migrant flocks with their lighter colored companions, while the other species is found alone or in pairs, and is very rare. In the hand it will be seen that 3 outer primaries are notched near the tip, in which Swainson's hawk resembles the white-tailed hawk. From that species Swainson's hawk differs in having the tarsus definitely less than 80 mm. long, while in the other this measures 85 to 95 mm.

Measurements (from Friedmann, U. S. Nat. Mus. Bull. 50, pt. 10, 1950, pp. 297-298).—Males, wing 362-406(383.6), tail 185-214 (204.6), culmen from cere 20.5-24.9 (22.1), tarsus 63.1-72.6 (68.2) mm.

Females, wing 375-427 (404.6), tail 193.6-234.0 (214.6), culmen from cere 20.5-25.7 (23.7), tarsus 61.5-76.4 (70.6) mm.

Migrant from the north. Seen usually in flocks, en route to or from a winter range in South America.

The southward flight begins in the latter part of September (Sept. 28, 1940) and continues through October (Oct. 22, 1911). The northward movement starts in early February (Feb. 3, 1952), with the main migration in March and the beginning of April (large flocks Apr. 2, 1950). A few continue to pass through early April. Some remain on the isthmus during the northern winter, as indicated by 2 skins in the U. S. National Museum, one taken near Gatun, Canal

Zone, December 18, 1910, and another obtained near Pacora November 28, 1958. The main flight seems to pass along the Pacific slope and the central mountains from Darién to Chiriquí. In 1952 I saw a flock at El Uracillo, Coclé, on the upper Río Indio, but did not note them at the mouth of the river on the Caribbean coast. There is no present record for Bocas del Toro, nor for Herrera or Los Santos. I have seen them on Taboga and Taboguilla, but not in the Pearl Islands.

The great flocks of these migrant hawks constitute one of the notable sights for the ornithologist in this part of the world. While other species, principally the broad-winged hawk and turkey vulture, with scattered ospreys, marsh hawks and peregrine falcons may join, half at least of these migrants are the present species. At times they are seen in an endless line that moves high across the sky, until one tires of watching. Or the birds may pass rapidly in groups of a hundred to several thousand, that pause to circle in some rising air thermal, and then move swiftly until they disappear. In full migration across the open savanna several such flocks may appear in view simultaneously. On other days single birds and small groups pass more leisurely at intervals. On various occasions when examining some high-flying bird with binoculars I have seen large flocks of hawks passing so high above the earth that they were not visible to the unaided eye.

The bands pause at night to sleep on some forested hill slope or other spot where they will not be disturbed. While I have noted their roosts in Panamá only in trees, in Costa Rica and in El Salvador flocks are recorded also as spending the night on the ground on open ridges in the hills. They do not appear to stop for food, at least in the isthmian part of their journey. Occasionally one or two alight on the ground in the savannas, or on a rock on an open hillside, and sometimes small flocks may pass low overhead, but ordinarily they move far beyond gunshot above the earth. For this reason few persons recognize that they are hawks, and those who see them ordinarily call them *iroles* or *pájaros del norte*. The Cuna Indians call the moon that approximates our month of September *kigini* or hawk, because of the regularity with which these annual flights appear. The local name *irol* applies to this species in the main, though the great mixed flocks of Swainson's hawk and broadwings usually are called *iroles* without understanding that two kinds are concerned.

Like the turkey vultures these hawk flights move mainly by sailing with set wings, propelled by favoring air currents. I recall one especially interesting flight seen in the latter part of March over the forest at Charco del Toro on the Río Majé. In early morning scattered Swainson's hawks that appeared to have slept nearby came over the trees in steadily increasing number, until two groups each of a thousand or more were wheeling in circles 500 meters apart. Suddenly the two bands joined immediately overhead, giving me an extraordinary view. As I looked up through the rapidly moving segments of their spirals the air seemed completely crowded with the rapidly turning birds. This continued for 15 minutes until the entire flock moved rapidly to a higher elevation in a favorable air current with which they disappeared. Such flights are the more impressive as there is no sound of calling from any of the birds.

BUTEO MAGNIROSTRIS (Gmelin): Large-billed Hawk; Cuiscuí

FIGURE 42

Falco magnirostris Gmelin, Syst. Nat., vol. 1, pt. 1, 1788, p. 282. (Cayenne.)

A small hawk with the wing feathers partly rufous, and the foreneck and upper breast gray.

Description.—Length 330 to 370 mm. Adult, above brownish gray, darker and grayer on the crown and sides of the head; upper breast and foreneck gray; throat feathers bordered with white or buffy white to produce streaks; upper tail coverts buffy white, barred broadly with black; tail with 4 heavy black bars, the uppermost concealed by the upper tail coverts, the light bars rufous, or light gray, according to the race; lower surface white to buffy white, barred heavily with cinnamon brown to buffy brown, the bars edged more or less prominently with gray; under wing coverts white to warm buff, spotted irregularly with cinnamon; primaries and secondaries cinnamon buff to rufous, barred heavily with black, with the tips black; lower surface of these feathers lighter in color.

Immature, like adult, but with more or less brown as a wash or streaks in the gray of the upper breast.

The iris in adult birds is yellow; bare skin above eye and across loral area greenish yellow; bare edge of eyelid honey yellow; cere, gape, and base of mandibular rami dull orange; a small area on side of maxilla (behind the "tooth," and below the level of the nostril) and central area of mandibular rami dull neutral gray; rest of bill black; tarsus and toes light orange yellow; claws black. (Colors taken from specimens of the race *B. m. petulans.*)

This is the most commonly seen hawk of the tropical zone, found mainly in open country, and noted frequently in rows of trees along fences in pastures and cultivated lands and also in more open stands of second growth. In forested areas it avoids the deep shade of the lower levels but ranges across the high forest crown, where the undulating upper surface of the leafy canopy affords an open hunting ground suited to the life of a bird that elsewhere inhabits open fields and savannas.

Fig. 42.—Large-billed hawk, cuiscuí, *Buteo magnirostris*.

The customary perch when at rest is shaded above but open at the sides, so that the bird has clear view of its surroundings. The species ranges mainly in lowland areas, from the landward side of the mangrove swamps inland through the more open slopes of the hill country. As clearing for farms has progressed it has become more common at higher elevations, and now is seen regularly in the lower subtropical zone in Chiriquí up to elevations of over 1,200 meters.

Usually these hawks show little fear, in many places being almost foolishly tame, so that they are easy to approach, and they come regularly to the squeaking sounds that the hunter makes to attract small birds. Often they betray their presence by high-pitched, querulous calls, repeated slowly, in imitation of which they are called cuiscuí.

Following periods of rain, they sometimes rest in early morning with partly spread wings and tail to enjoy the agreeable warmth of the sun. In general they are of sluggish habit spending much time at rest, making short flights only when disturbed. Though they may soar in small circles, they do not rise high, and usually only continue for brief periods.

Their principal food is composed of lizards, large Orthoptera, and other insects, but may include an occasional small bird, usually a young one, or a mouse. People living in the country complain that individuals that range near houses capture small chicks, the only damage that may be ascribed to them, as otherwise they appear harmless.

The species is one of those found throughout much of the tropical area of the Americas from México to northern Argentina. There is considerable variation in color in different sections, so that different authorities have recognized between 15 and 20 races in the entire range. Four of these subspecies are found in the Republic of Panamá.

The species *magnirostris* uniformly has the webs of the primaries and secondaries rufous, and so is readily known. It has been placed by some authorities in a distinct genus *Rupornis,* which however appears to have no trenchant characters when the many species of the broad *Buteo* group are considered.

Double ovaries are common in these birds, and undoubtedly have led to the marking of some females in museum collections as males by preparators not familiar with this condition. One female that I took near Alanje, Chiriquí, March 3, 1960, had the right ovary dormant, though of fair size, and ova in process of development in the one on the left side.

BUTEO MAGNIROSTRIS ARGUTUS (Peters and Griscom)

Rupornis magnirostris arguta Peters and Griscom, Proc. New England Zoöl. Club, vol. 11, Aug. 30, 1929, p. 46. (Almirante, Bocas del Toro, Panamá.)

Characters.—Distinctly brownish gray above and on foreneck and upper breast; pale tail bands gray, or with slight rufous edging on either side, adjacent to the black bands; light bars on lower surface deeper buff.

The measurements are similar to those of the next race, *B. m. petulans.*

Resident. Fairly common in Bocas del Toro, from the Costa Rican border through Changuinola and Almirante to Cricamola; Isla Colón, Isla Cristobal, Isla Pastores.

This is a form of southern Central America from eastern Honduras south to Costa Rica, that reaches its most southerly point in the lowlands around the Laguna de Chiriquí.

A female taken along the Changuinola Canal on February 20, 1958, was nearly ready to lay.

Kennard and Peters (Proc. Boston Soc. Nat. Hist., vol. 38, 1928, p. 449) record the eye in the adult as varying from barium yellow to cinnamon buff and pinard yellow; and in the immature as russet.

BUTEO MAGNIROSTRIS PETULANS van Rossem

Buteo magnirostris petulans van Rossem, Condor, vol. 37, no. 4, July 15, 1935, p. 215. (Lion Hill, Canal Zone, Panamá.)

Characters.—Differs from *B. m. argutus* in grayer coloration: less brownish on upper surface, foreneck, and upper breast; light tail bands entirely or mainly rufous; light interspaces on lower surface white to very pale buff.

Measurements.—Males (8 specimens), wing 205-215 (209), tail 132-151 (144), culmen from cere 16.5-17.5 (17.1, average of 6), tarsus 55.0-64.5 (60.5) mm.

Females (16 specimens), wing 215-227 (221), tail 141-163 (153), culmen from cere 17.8-20.2 (19.2, average of 15), tarsus 60.0-66.5 (63.5) mm.

Resident. Pacific slope, from Chiriquí, where it ranges to 1,200 meters in the mountains, eastward to the southern shores of Golfo de San Miguel (Garachiné) in the lowlands of Darién; on the Caribbean side from northern Coclé (El Uracillo) east through the Province of Colón and the Canal Zone; Isla Parida; Isla Coiba; Isla Taboguilla; Isla Iguana, off the coast of Los Santos. Intergrades with the race *insidiatrix* on the lower Río Tuira. Birds from the lowlands below Pacora and Chepo have the light tail bands grayer, less rufous, and thus tend toward *insidiatrix,* but otherwise agree with *petulans,* and are placed with that race.

As I have seen no specimens from eastern Bocas del Toro, or from the Caribbean slope of Veraguas, this area is omitted in the range given above. On the Pacific side this race extends throughout the Azuero Peninsula, where I have specimens from the southern end at Tonosí and Pedasí. Six skins from Isla Coiba agree with the series from the mainland. Hawks of this species seen on Isla Taboguilla are assigned here on basis of probability. I have not recorded it on Isla Taboga, where it is probable that it has been killed off through the long period of extensive settlement on this island.

An occupied nest seen on January 21, 1956, on Isla Coiba was placed about 12 meters from the ground in a tree of moderate size that stood in a second-growth thicket. A hawk was noted carrying nesting material on March 8, 1948, near Santa María, Herrera, and in the month of April I have seen them regularly in pairs in the Pacora-Chepo area.

While the usual name for these hawks throughout the republic is cuiscuí in imitation of the call, near Soná they were called guiño.

This subspecies was known long under the name *ruficauda,* from *Asturina ruficauda* Sclater and Salvin (Proc. Zool. Soc. London, 1869, p. 133). With the location of this form in the genus *Buteo* this is preoccupied by *Accipiter ruficaudus* Vieillot, 1807, which is a synonym of *Buteo jamaicensis borealis* (Gmelin). Accordingly the race under discussion was named *petulans* by van Rossem as indicated in the citation in the heading.

BUTEO MAGNIROSTRIS INSIDIATRIX (Bangs and Penard)

Rupornis magnirostris insidiatrix Bangs and Penard, Bull. Mus. Comp. Zoöl., vol. 62, April, 1918, p. 36. (Bonda, Magdalena, Colombia.)

Characters.—Differs from *B. m. petulans* in lighter gray of dorsal surface, with the light-colored tail bands dark gray, in some with a faint tinge of cinnamon-buff; whiter below on the light interspaces, with the dark bands grayer, less rufescent, varying from buffy brown to warm brown, occasionally brighter sayal brown centrally.

Measurements. (The series measured is mainly from northern Colombia).—Males (19 specimens), 207-219 (213.3), tail 135-157 (147.5), culmen from cere 16.4-19.9 (17.6), tarsus 60.0-65.0 (62.8) mm.

Females (14 specimens), wing 217-234 (222.0), tail 138-164 (147.1), culmen from cere 17.3-19.8 (18.6), tarsus 57.8-67.8 (63.6) mm.

Resident. Caribbean slope throughout the Comarca de San Blas (Mandinga; Permé; Armila; Obaldía); on the Pacific side on the Río Chucunaque (mouth of Río Tuquesa), and the middle Río Tuira and its tributaries (Pucro, Boca de Paya). Birds from the lower Chucunaque (Yaviza), and the lower Tuira (Marragantí; El Real) are intermediate toward *petulans.*

I did not find these birds at Jaqué, Darién, in 1946 and 1947, and there are no present records for the species on the Pacific coast south of Garachiné. To the south and east this race ranges across northern Colombia and northern Venezuela. It is fairly common along the Chucunaque and the Tuira, less so in the western area of the San Blas coast. When perched near at hand it is possible to note the gray bands on the tail, which are a field mark to distinguish this race from *petulans* of farther west, in which these marks are rufous.

Todd and Carriker (Ann. Carnegie Mus., vol. 14, 1922, p. 155) describe two eggs of this race, collected at Bonda, Magdalena, Colombia, by H. H. Smith, April 13 and 18, 1898, as "dull grayish white, specked and blotched with pale chocolate, sparsely over the small end, more thickly about the middle, while the large end in one is palely washed and mottled with chocolate over the greater part of the surface; in the other, the large end is more heavily washed with a much darker shade of chocolate and heavily streaked with lines of dark umber. They measure 42.5×35 and 42×34, the eggs being oval."

J. Parker Norris, Jr. (Ool. Rec., vol. 6, 1926, p. 36), had one egg of this subspecies, taken from a nest about 10 meters from the ground in an upright crotch in tree in "semi-savanna country" near La Tigrera above Santa Marta, Colombia. The egg, described as "brownish-white marked with an indistinct cap of pinkish brown at the large end," measured 45.5 by 36.3 mm.

Sets that I have seen of other subspecies from Tamaulipas, México (*B. m. griseocauda*), and from Rio Grande do Sul, Brazil (*B. m. magniplumis*), were of two eggs each.

The type locality in the original description was given as "Santa Marta Mountains." The race was described from a female taken by W. W. Brown, Jr., in the Museum of Comparative Zoology labeled, "Colombia (Santa Martha) Mts. January 16, '98." From what is known regarding the itinerary of the collector, on the date in question he was located at Bonda, a village a few miles east of Santa Marta.

BUTEO MAGNIROSTRIS ALIUS (Peters and Griscom)

Rupornis magnirostris alia Peters and Griscom, Proc. New England Zoöl. Club, vol. 11, Aug. 30, 1929, p. 48. (San Miguel, Isla del Rey, Archipiélago de las Perlas, Panamá.)

Characters.—Similar to *B. m. petulans* but averaging slightly larger; foreneck and breast slightly darker gray; white edgings on throat feathers reduced, with little or no mixture of buff; dark bars on lower surface averaging broader and darker brown; light bars whiter; light tail bands grayer, less rufous.

Measurements.—Males (7 specimens), wing 210-222 (215), tail 142-161 (150), culmen from cere 18.2-20.3 (19.0, average of 6), tarsus 62.1-67.2 (64.1) mm.

Females (2 specimens), wing 226-234 (230), tail 156-160 (158), culmen from cere 19.5-19.8 (19.6), tarsus 66.0-69.1 (67.5) mm.

Resident. Found in the Archipiélago de las Perlas, where it is recorded from Isla del Rey, Isla Cañas, Isla San José, and Isla Pedro González.

The birds were fairly common on Isla San José in 1944, but on visits to the other islands on which they are reported I have found them in smaller numbers. Like the races of the mainland, they range around clearings in inhabited areas, and where forests persist rest in the better-lighted upper branches in the tallest trees.

At times I saw yellow-green vireos scolding them. As I have not observed this regularly elsewhere, it is an indication that this race may be more predatory on the nests of neighbor birds than seems to be the case on the mainland, where the lizards and large insects that are its usual food are more abundant.

B. m. alius, in larger size and grayer tail bands, shows approach to the subspecies *insidiatrix* of the northern coast of Colombia.

LEUCOPTERNIS ALBICOLLIS COSTARICENSIS Sclater: White Hawk; Gavilán Blanco

FIGURE 43

Leucopternis ghiesbreghti costaricensis W. L. Sclater, Bull. Brit. Orn. Club, vol. 39, April 9, 1919, p. 76. ("Carillo" = Carrillo, Costa Rica.)

Of medium size; white, with black-tipped wings, and black-banded tail.

Description.—Length 470 to 510 mm. Adult, pure white, with primaries and secondaries black, the latter tipped broadly with white; a broad black subterminal bar on the tail; some black mottling or streaking on the wing coverts and tertials; under surface of wing mainly white, with ends of flight feathers black, barred above the tips with light gray.

Immature, with narrow shaft lines of black on the crown and more black in the wings.

In two adult males I recorded the following colors: Iris brown; bare skin around eye greenish slate; tip of bill dark neutral gray to black; base clear light gray; cere greenish gray; tarsus and toes dull light yellow, with the scutes on the inner side of the front of the tarsus tinged centrally with pale neutral gray; claws black.

Measurements.—Males (11 specimens from Honduras, Costa Rica, and Panamá), wing 336-358 (346), tail 209-226 (215), culmen from cere 25.1-29.0 (26.6), tarsus 82.0-93.3 (85.8) mm.

Females (3 specimens from Panamá), wing 350-377 (367), tail 215-231 (221), culmen from cere 27.5-28.9 (28.1), tarsus 83.8-87.5 (85.4) mm.

Resident. Fairly common in forested areas in the tropical zone of both slopes; less often in the lower subtropical zone; to 1,250 meters

FIG. 43.—White hawk, gavilán blanco, *Leucopternis albicollis costaricensis*.

elevation in Chiriquí (Bajo Mono, near Boquete), Veraguas (Cordillera de Tolé), on the high divide at 900 meters at Cavulla, on the base of Cerro Viejo, head of Río Mariato, western slope of the Azuero Peninsula, and Coclé (above El Valle); Isla Cébaco.

This beautiful bird, one of the most attractive of its family, when observed resting on some dead stub in early morning sun appears pure white, and it is only on close scrutiny, or as it flies, that the black pattern of wings and tail is seen. In the forest, which is its normal haunt, ordinarily it rests below the high tree crown, where its colors in the play of light and shadow as seen from below are far from conspicuous. And often the birds stand on huge, sloping limbs that are covered with epiphytes, completely hidden from underneath.

In such wild, unsettled areas as the forests adjacent to the Río Chucunaque these hawks show little fear, and on several occasions I have had them fly down to perch near at hand in order to watch me with evident curiosity, often with a low mewing call, *kee-ee wee*. This note is heard also when they rise to soar above the trees, when against the sky their white plumage often appears gray.

Foremost in my recollections of the species is of an early morning flight by helicopter across the lower slopes of Cerro Pirre, back of El Real, in Darién, when in a quarter hour I counted 20 of these beautiful birds, singly or in pairs soaring over the forest far below us—moving silhouettes of white, dark wing tips on either side, against the deep green of the unbroken forest underneath.

Their food is taken from such small mammals as mice, rats, and small opossums, and from lizards, snakes, frogs, and large Orthoptera. Small birds do not seem troubled by their presence, and I have never seen the hawk pay much attention to them. Van Tyne (Occ. Pap. Mus. Zool. Michigan, no. 525, 1950, p. 6) records the basiliscus lizard as regular prey.

Chapman (Trop. Air Castle, 1929, pp. 60-61), on March 9, 1929, found a nest on Barro Colorado Island placed in the top of a tall tree. One of the pair rested beside it with a leafy green twig in its bill. A female shot by E. A. Goldman near Gatun on February 3, 1911, was nearly ready to lay.

The preference of this species is for forested areas in rolling hill country, and it originally appears to have been distributed throughout the republic, except in the extensive savannas of the central and western areas of the Pacific slope. I have not found it in the open scrubs of the lowlands on the eastern side of the Azuero Peninsula, or in the swampy woodlands near the coast. As land has been cleared for cultivation these birds have disappeared.

The body plumage is long and heavy, and there is much under down, so that these birds appear much larger in body than is actually the case. This may be a protective device since, though tropical temperatures may not register low in terms of degrees on a thermometer, when the air is humid it often becomes chill. As the animals that form the food of the *gavilán blanco* usually are large enough so that one constitutes a meal, or as smaller prey is so common that it is easy to capture several, the hawk after eating may remain inactive for considerable periods, and so need this insulation. The plumage is so dense, in fact, that it serves almost like a protective armor that guards the body against injury by the pellets in a shot gun charge when the birds are at any distance.

LEUCOPTERNIS SEMIPLUMBEA Lawrence: Semiplumbeous Hawk; Gavilán Cenizo

Leucopternis semiplumbeus Lawrence, Ann. Lyc. Nat. Hist. New York, vol. 7, Jan. 1861, p. 288. (Along the Panama Railroad, Caribbean slope, Canal Zone, Panamá.)

A small gray species, with black, white-banded tail, and white lower surface; bill and feet orange.

Description.—Length 310 to 350 mm. Adult, upper tail coverts and tail black, latter with a white subterminal band; in some specimens a second more or less complete white band below the upper tail coverts; rest of upper surface dark gray, usually darker on the head, with indistinct shaft lines of black; below white, including the under wing coverts; a few narrow shaft lines of grayish black on throat and foreneck; tips of primaries and secondaries on under surface light gray, barred and tipped with blackish gray; rest of under wing white.

Juvenile, breast and sides of throat with narrow dark gray shaft stripes.

A male taken near Chimán on February 23, 1950, had the iris bright yellow; cere, side of premaxilla, gape, and base of mandible to symphysis deep orange; sides of maxilla at base and mandible in front of symphysis for one-third its length dull honey yellow; rest of bill dark neutral gray; tarsus deep orange; claws dark neutral gray. Another male shot at Boca de Paya, Darién, on March 8, 1959, was similar in bill, eye, and tarsus, and in addition I noted that the edge of the eyelids, lores, and the bare skin above the eye were orange-yellow and that the skin beneath the feathers on the underside of the wing (including the patagium), foreneck, abdomen, and knee was dull yellow.

There is a prominent powder down patch across the thigh.

Measurements (from Friedmann, U. S. Nat. Mus. Bull. 50, pt. 10, 1950, p. 384).—Males (7 specimens), wing 165-184 (179), tail 127-137 (132.4), culmen from cere 18-20 (19.2), tarsus 55-64 (60.1) mm.

Females (14 specimens), wing 183-202 (195.2), tail 126-148 (135.7), culmen from cere 18-21 (20), tarsus 57-66 (61.6) mm.

Resident. Local in forested areas in the tropical zone; recorded on the Pacific slope from Veraguas eastward through Darién, and on the Caribbean side from Bocas del Toro east through the Comarca de San Blas (Permé, Armila, Puerto Obaldía), including the Chagres Valley (Quebrada Peluca on the Río Boquerón).

There are no reports from the Azuero Peninsula, and the only one from Veraguas is of a specimen without locality collected by Arcé

(Salvin and Godman, Biol. Centr.-Amer., vol. 3, 1900, p. 84). I saw two soaring over a forested ridge on the approach to El Valle, Coclé on June 22, 1953. On the Pacific side of the isthmus the bird is found mainly in Darién but is nowhere common. It is dependent on forest cover and so disappears when the land is cleared.

These small hawks have little fear, and most of those I have seen have been attracted when I was calling smaller birds. Then they sometimes utter a low, mewing call. Occasionally I have observed one resting in the morning sun along a Darién river as I passed in a piragua, when their clear white-and-dark-gray plumage, with orange feet and base of bill, made a beautiful contrast with the green of the leafy background. On the Río Jaqué one flew past carrying a small jungle rat that slipped from its feet and dropped as the bird perched. At the mouth of the Quebrada Peluca on the Boquerón one scrambled actively along the stream bank in pursuit of small frogs. Near Armila, San Blas, one was caught in a mist net set in heavy forest.

Nothing is known of the nesting habits.

LEUCOPTERNIS PLUMBEA Salvin: Plumbeous Hawk; Gavilán Azul

Leucopternis plumbea Salvin, Ibis, ser. 3, vol. 2, pt. 3, July 1872, p. 240, pl. 8. (Ecuador.)

Medium size; gray, with black wings and tail.

Description.—Length 350 to 370 mm. Wings and tail black, the latter with a subterminal white band and a faintly paler tip; elsewhere gray, paler below with faintly indicated black shaft lines; tibia and lower abdomen barred with white; concealed white and white freckling on sides, upper abdomen, and lower breast; under surface of wing white, with tips of primaries dull black, barred on the outer half with white to grayish white.

Measurements.—Males (6 from Panamá), wing 219-232 (225), tail 131.3-150.0 (139.5), culmen from cere 20.2-22.1 (21.4), tarsus 68.1-72.9 (70.8) mm.

Females (3 from Panamá and Colombia), wing 233-245 (237.8), tail 139-157 (136.9), culmen from cere 21.0-22.5 (21.5), tarsus 66-74 (69.8) mm.

Resident. Rare; in forested areas in the tropical zone.

I have found the following records from Panamá. One marked Panamá without locality and one labeled Veraguas (taken by Arcé) in the British Museum; one from Natá, Coclé, in the U. S. National Museum, collected on the Río Chico by Heyde and Lux, January 7, 1889; and two from Permé, San Blas, in the Museum of Comparative

Zoology, obtained by Hasso von Wedel. In the Brandt Collection at the University of Cincinnati there are 5 males taken by Wedel at Puerto Obaldía, San Blas, in 1931 and 1933. In addition to these, near Armila, San Blas, on March 4, 1963, one of C. O. Handley's assistants brought me an adult male shot in heavy forest. This bird had the iris brownish orange; cere and base of bill below the level of the nostril, the gape, and the mandibular rami orange; a small area on the base of the maxilla, in front of the orange, and the base of the gonys neutral gray; anterior part of bill black; tarsus and toes orange yellow; claws black.

Apparently this species ranges in forest in a manner similar to that of the more common *Leucopternis semiplumbea*. It is probable that through clearing of its normal cover it is no longer found in the western part of the Republic.

LEUCOPTERNIS PRINCEPS Sclater: Barred Hawk; Gavilán Rayado

Leucopternis princeps P. L. Sclater, Proc. Zool. Soc. London, Oct. 1865, p. 429, pl. 24. (Tucurriqui, Costa Rica.)

Leucopternis princeps zimmeri Friedmann, Auk, vol. 52, Jan. 8, 1935, p. 30. (San José de Sumaco, northeastern Ecuador.)

Black above and on foreneck; closely barred black and white on rest of lower surface.

Description.—Length 550 to 590 mm. Adult, upper breast, throat, head, and entire upper surface black, with a faint bloom of gray through narrow edgings of this color at the ends of many feathers; plumage with a concealed base of white, particularly on crown and hindneck; band across tail, and hidden bars on inner secondaries, white; lower surface, (except upper breast), including edge of wing, under wing coverts, and under tail coverts, white, barred narrowly with numerous bands of black; under surface of wings gray, marbled with white, barred distally and tipped with dark neutral gray.

Immature, like the adult but with wing coverts narrowly tipped with white.

Kennard made the following record of the soft parts from a male taken on the Boquete Trail, March 12, 1926: "Bill chrome yellow and tea green; iris dark chocolate; tarsus chrome yellow" (Kennard and Peters, Proc. Boston Soc. Nat. Hist., 1928, p. 449).

Measurements.—Males (3 from Costa Rica and Panamá), wing 347-360 (354.3), tail 185-220 (199.7), culmen from cere 28.7-30.8 (29.5), tarsus 80.5-98.3 (91.2) mm.

Females (5 from Costa Rica and Panamá), wing 352-381 (368), tail 191-218 (201.8), culmen from cere 29.2-33.3 (31.4), tarsus 95.0-96.5 (95.5) mm.

Resident. Rare; found in heavy forest in the Subtropical Zone; recorded in western Chiriquí from Quiel, above Boquete, at 1,500 meters elevation on the slopes of the volcano, and also near Boquete; in Bocas del Toro, on the Río Changena at 750 meters, and on the Boquete Trail at 950 meters; in Los Santos, on Cerro Hoya at 1,200 meters; and in Darién, on Cerro Pirre, at 1,500 meters on the head of Río Limón.

These are the only certain reports. The record in literature for a specimen in the American Museum of Natural History, obtained from J. H. Batty, marked "Isla Cebaco," an island of low elevation off the mouth of Montijo Bay on the coast of southern Veraguas, is certainly erroneous, like many others in collections that Batty sent to Rothschild. The species is known only from the subtropical zone, and the specimen probably came from near Boquete.

Nothing is known to me of the nesting of this handsome species or of its habits beyond the fact that it is a forest inhabitant. The species ranges in mountain areas from Costa Rica through Panamá and western Colombia to Ecuador.

Herbert Friedmann (Auk, 1935, p. 30), with limited material, found that 4 seen from Ecuador appeared smaller than 6 others from Costa Rica and Panamá and separated the southern group on this basis under the name *Leucopternis princeps zimmeri*. Additional material that I have seen from Panamá does not support the size difference described, as the bird appears variable in dimensions throughout the range.

HETEROSPIZIAS MERIDIONALIS MERIDIONALIS (Latham):
Savanna Hawk; Gavilán Acanelado

Falco meridionalis Latham, Index Orn., vol. 1, 1790, p. 3. (Cayenne.)

Description.—Length 460 to 500 mm. A savanna species of reddish brown plumage, with black tail banded with white. Adult, crown rufous-brown, with shaft lines of black edged with gray; sides of head brownish gray, with shaft lines of neutral gray bordered narrowly with buff; hind neck cinnamon, barred narrowly with dark neutral gray, becoming brownish gray on upper back, edged with cinnamon bordered with dark neutral gray, and finally on rest of back brownish gray, edged irregularly with cinnamon to buff; wing coverts rufous-brown, the middle and greater series dark gray basally; primaries and secondaries rufous-brown tipped with black, changing to brownish gray on inner secondaries, barred more or less on inner webs with black; upper tail coverts variegated black and cinnamon-brown, tipped with white; tail black, with tip and a broad central bar white; under surface cinnamon-brown to cinnamon-buff, with foreneck lined indistinctly with shaft streaks of neutral gray; the rest, including sides and axillars, barred narrowly with black; tibia and under tail coverts rufous-brown, the latter tipped with buff; under surface of wing cinnamon, barred irregularly with black; under wing coverts cinnamon, tipped with buffy white along the edge of the wing.

Immature, "birds during their first season are very dark brown, almost black, save for more or less white on the under surface and some rufous in the primaries and greater coverts. During the second year the amount of rufous in the wings is increased and invades more or less of the underwing surface as well as the lesser wing coverts. In the third year the under parts and head become rufous, barred below, save on the throat, with blackish, but the back remains fuscous brown. In fully adult plumage, apparently in the fourth year, the upper back assumes an ashy shade" (Wetmore, U. S. Nat. Mus. Bull. 133, 1926, p. 114).

Measurements.—Males (10 specimens), wing 375-396 (388.8), tail 176-200 (188.1), culmen from cere 23.0-24.5 (23.7), tarsus 98.7-112.4 (106.7) mm.

Females (5 specimens), wing 375-403 (388.6), tail 170-193 (180.2), culmen from cere 23.0-25.8 (24.6), tarsus 97.0-105.0 (102.3) mm.

Resident. Fairly common on the tropical savannas of the Pacific slope from Veraguas (Soná) through Coclé to near the lower Bayano (below Chepo) in the eastern section of the Province of Panamá. Casual in western Chiriquí (Dolega, sight record), Bocas del Toro (Changuinola, sight record, Eisenmann, Condor 1957, p. 250) and Comarca de San Blas (Permé, Griscom, Bull. Mus. Comp. Zool., vol. 72, 1932, p. 313).

This is a hawk of open lands, restricted, however, to the lowlands, as there are no reports for it on the elevated open grass slopes of the mountains. It is especially common on the savannas east of Pacora, where it ranges to the last of the prairies at Ana Luz, near the Río Bayano below Chepo. On the eastern side of the Azuero Peninsula I have noted it in the region between Parita, París, and Santa María, in the Province of Herrera. And on March 27, 1948, near Punta Mala, in southern Los Santos, I found feathers of one that had been killed recently. Occasionally one is seen on Albrook Field and Howard Field in the Canal Zone.

In early morning I have observed these hawks walking about on the ground, standing very tall on their long legs and moving easily and gracefully. The top of the head at such times often appears almost white in the rays of the rising sun. This is one of the hawks (known collectively to the countryman as *bebe humo*) that follows grass fires to feed on large insects and lizards flushed, killed, or injured by the flames. These, with rats and mice, seem to constitute the principal items of food. Birds, except for an occasional aggressive kingbird or fork-tailed fly-catcher, pay little attention to them, and so it would appear that they are not active in molesting them.

The Penards (Vog. Guyana, vol. 1, 1908, p. 391) describe the nest in Surinam as made of sticks and twigs, placed in trees at elevations ranging from high to low. The one or two eggs in a set are described as white with a few reddish-brown spots and blotches. An egg that I saw in the possession of Dr. Carlos Lehmann, collected at Maicao, in the Guajira Peninsula of Colombia, April 15, 1941, before it was blown was light blue, with a few small scattered spots of light cinnamon. Schönwetter (Handb. Ool., pt. 3, 1961, p. 163) gives variation in the measurements of 15 eggs as 55.5-64.0 × 46.0-48.2 mm.

As a species this bird ranges in open country from western Panamá, Colombia, and Venezuela south to Argentina. No differences in color are evident when specimens of similar age are compared, but in the far south, in northern Argentina, the birds are appreciably larger. There has been some uncertainty regarding this since an occasional specimen of large size has been taken in the more northern parts of South America, but these I believe are winter migrants from the southern limits of the range, as they stand out in size among those that appear to be resident. As an example of this, 10 specimens from northern Colombia from Bolívar, Magdalena, and the Guajira have wing measurements of 379 to 403 mm. One that I shot at Maicao in the Guajira on April 14, 1941, in the same area in which I secured two of the smaller birds, has the primaries worn at the tip but still measures 418 mm. The date represents the nonbreeding period in the far south, and I regard this bird as a migrant of the following form.

The southern race, *Heterospizias meridionalis rufulus* (Vieillot), with wing 418 to 452 mm., on the basis of present data is the breeding race from southern Paraguay and Rio Grande do Sul, Brazil, to the provinces of Córdoba and Santa Fé, Argentina. In the northern subspecies, *Heterospizias m. meridionalis,* which ranges from Panamá south to Bolivia, northern Paraguay, and southern Brazil (north of the southeastern state of Rio Grande do Sul) the wing measurement ranges from 379 to 412 mm. Intergradation comes apparently in northwestern Argentina, from Tucumán northward, and in central

Paraguay. Kirke Swann recognized the two forms and in 1921 named the southern one *australis,* a name, however, that is antedated by *rufulus* Vieillot of 1816.

Plótnick (Hornero, 1956, pp. 136-139), in a study of the osteology, has established that *Heterospizias* is a genus of the subfamily Buteoninae and not of the Accipitrinae, where it has been placed by Peters and others. This I find fully verified on examination of skeleton material available.

PARABUTEO UNICINCTUS HARRISI (Audubon): Harris's Hawk; Gavilán Andapié

Buteo Harrisi Audubon, Birds Amer. (folio), vol. 4, 1837, pl. 392. (Between Bayou Sara and Natchez, Mississippi.)

A black hawk with white rump and tail tip that differs from others with this color pattern in the rufous markings on the back and wings.

Characters.—Length 480 to 560 mm. Adult, above fuscous-black; forehead and superciliary streaked with white; nape feathers white basally; wings dull black, with outer webs of primaries and ends of secondaries edged with grayish white; lesser and middle wing coverts rufous; greater coverts, back, and rump feathers edged or tipped with rufous; tail black, with base, including upper tail coverts and tip, white; below dull black; feathers of throat and sides of head edged with white to produce streaks; legs and flanks rufous, mottled indistinctly with white; under tail coverts buffy white; under wing coverts cinnamon, mottled with white, more heavily toward outer edge of wing; a prominent patch of white near center of underside of primaries, extending to their bases, with indistinct light barring toward tips.

Immature, fuscous above, with indistinct barring, edging, and streaking of cinnamon-buff, especially on wings; lesser and middle coverts rufous more or less variegated with black; superciliary cinnamon-buff; throat white, lined with fuscous; undersurface white to cinnamon-buff, streaked and spotted heavily with dull black; legs and flanks buffy white, barred narrowly with dull rufous; under surface of tail grayish white, barred narrowly with blackish brown; rump, upper tail coverts, and upper surface of tail as in adult, but with a narrow margin of cinnamon-buff above the white tail tip.

Measurements (from Friedmann, U. S. Nat. Mus. Bull. 50, pt. 10, 1950, p. 371).—Males, wing 318-331 (323); tail 215-262 (234), culmen from cere 24-28 (26.3), tarsus 84-90 (86.2) mm.

Females, wing 325-370 (358.4), tail 213-243 (232.5), culmen from cere 25-29 (26.7), tarsus 80-92 (87) mm.

Rare; status not certain.

The little that is known of this interesting species, which is found elsewhere from southern Texas south through México and Central America to Colombia and western Ecuador, is embodied in 3 brief records. Arcé collected one in Veraguas (Salvin, Proc. Zool. Soc. London, 1867, p. 158), that was recorded as from Santa Fé. From the habit of the species elsewhere it is probable that it was taken in the open country below, toward San Francisco. Bovallius secured a male near Pacora on March 4, 1882 (Rendahl, Ark. Zool., Bd. 12, 1919, p. 9). Hasso von Wedel collected a female near Almirante, Bocas del Toro, November 24, 1927 (Peters, Bull. Mus. Comp. Zool., vol. 71, 1931, p. 310). It seems probable that the species in Panamá is a wanderer from elsewhere in its extensive range.

In northeastern Columbia I have found these handsome birds in open country where the savanna lands were interspersed with scattered brush and low trees. The call is a harsh scream suggestive of that of the red-tailed hawk.

BUSARELLUS NIGRICOLLIS NIGRICOLLIS (Latham): Black-collared HAWK; Gavilán de Ciénaga

Falco nigricollis Latham, Index Orn., vol. 1, 1790, p. 35. (Cayenne.)

Adult, at rest marked by black breast band against the brown body and white throat; in flight the blackish wings show in contrast with the brown body, and the breast band is prominent.

Description.—Length 480 to 510 mm. Adult, head, including throat and sides, white, with the crown washed with buff to cinnamon-buff, and blackish shaft streaks; a black half-collar across lower foreneck; body, above and below, russet to chestnut-brown, with heavy shaft-lines of black on back, upper and under wing coverts, and tertials; wings black, with faint cinnamon tips on secondaries; tail black, barred basally with rufous, and tipped with cinnamon-buff; a light spot that varies from white to cinnamon-buff at base of outermost primaries on under side.

Immature, paler, more buffy on under surface, with indistinct black shaft lines, and faint russet bars on the paler tibia; upper tail coverts and secondaries dull russet, barred with black.

Iris reddish brown; gape, including margins of both maxilla and mandible, the bare bases of the mandibular rami, and the base of the gonys, neutral gray; bill and cere dull black; tarsus and toes drab to flesh color, with a tint of gray; claws black.

Measurements (from Friedmann, U.S. Nat. Mus. Bull. 50, pt. 10, 1950, p. 412).—Males (8 specimens), wing 358-383 (378.1), tail 157-182 (171.9), culmen from cere 26-30 (27.9), tarsus 72-84 (80.1) mm.

Females (7 specimens), wing 380-405 (392.3), tail 175-183 (180.4), culmen from cere 28-30.5 (29.3), tarsus 78-89 (85.3) mm.

Resident. Local, in small numbers, in the tropical lowlands on the Pacific slope, from Veraguas to Darién, including northern Herrera. The only record for the Caribbean side is of a male taken at Lion Hill, Canal Zone, by W. W. Brown, Jr., in March, 1900 (Bangs, Proc. New England Zoöl. Club, vol. 2, 1900, p. 15).

This handsome bird is found around lowland marshes, in small openings in swampy woodlands, and along the larger rivers. Though it ranges widely from southern México through Central America to eastern Bolivia and Brazil, there have been only a few records of it in Panamá. Salvin received one from Arcé, taken in Veraguas, without definite locality (Salvin and Godman, Biol. Centr.-Amer., vol. 3, 1900, p. 86). On March 10, 1948, I saw one at the Ciénaga de Buho beyond Santa María, Herrera, where the bird rested in the sun on an open stub standing at the border of the marsh. On April 1, 1949, we shot a male at the nearly dry Ciénaga Campana east of Pacora and saw another in this same area on April 4. The only locality at which I have seen them in any number is along the Río La Jagua.

In Darién, Festa collected one at Laguna de Pita in August 1895 (Salvadori and Festa, Boll. Mus. Zool. Anat. Comp. Torino, vol. 14, 1899, p. 10). The National Museum has a female taken by J. L. Baer on the Río Chucunaque near Yavisa on March 20, 1924. Farther up this same river I saw one on March 27, 1959, near the mouth of the Río Tuquesa. The bird rested in an open tree over a pool in swampy woodland.

The tarsus in this species is rather short, while the toes are exceptionally long, with long, strongly curved, sharp-pointed claws. The pads on the underside of the toes are armed with conical, sharply pointed papillae, and the tip of the maxilla is long, strongly curved, and sharply pointed. The main food appears to be fish, so that it is intriguing to find that in the strong, curved claws and spiculate toe pads this hawk is the counterpart of the fish-feeding osprey, though the hindtoe does not have the peculiar development found in that species. In other characters than those mentioned the bird is similar to related species of its subfamily, the Buteoninae. The plumage, especially, is like that of other hawks, with none of the waterproof qualities found in the osprey, as in its fishing it becomes water soaked on the legs, and at times on the body.

The Penards (Vog. Guyana, vol. 1, 1908, pp. 401-402) state that in Surinam this species breeds principally during the season of heavy rains. The nest, of small sticks, may be located in high trees, though near the coast it may be placed at lower elevations in mangroves. The nest may be used for several years, when it may become very large as the pair add more material to it annually. The eggs, one, seldom two, in shape are bluntly oval or rounded. The ground color varies from dull whitish or yellowish to a bluish or greenish tint, with spots and blotches of cinnamon, reddish brown, and lilac-gray, the pattern varying from almost plain to heavily marked. The average size is 59 by 45 mm. Kreuger (Ool. Rec., 1963, p. 6) gives a similar description of a set of two taken on the Demerara River, British Guiana, April 2, 1927. These measured 58.2 × 45.2 and 56.2 × 45.2 mm.

BUTEOGALLUS URUBITINGA (Gmelin): Greater Black Hawk; Cocolino

Like the lesser black hawk in color, but larger; legs longer.

Description.—Length 510 to 590 mm. Adult, dull black throughout, with a faint slaty cast, and indistinct dark-gray markings in the form of shaft lines in crown, edgings on back, and broken bars on primaries and secondaries; feathers of nape white basally; tibia and edge of wing barred narrowly and irregularly with white; underside of wing dull black, except for faintly indicated gray bars.

Immature, brownish black above and on sides of head, with crown and hindneck streaked and edged with cinnamon-buff, this color forming an indistinct superciliary streak; back, wing coverts, and secondaries edged indistinctly with cinnamon; upper tail coverts buff; tail brownish black, barred, narrowly and irregularly, and mottled, with brownish gray to white, changing to cinnamon-buff on inner webs; below cinnamon, whiter on the throat, streaked and spotted with dull black; tibia white, barred irregularly with black, underwing buff to cinnamon-buff, spotted on the under coverts, and tipped on the axillars, with dull black; primaries and secondaries tipped with brownish black, and barred narrowly and irregularly with the same color.

In what appears to be a second-year plumage, the buff is paler, often white, and the black markings on the undersurface are much more extensive; above mainly dull black, except for white to buffy white streaks on the head; tail tipped broadly with black, barred narrowly, and mottled, with the same color.

I have recorded the soft parts in the race *azarae* of Paraguay and northern Argentina, as follows (Wetmore, U. S. Nat. Mus. Bull. 133, 1926, p. 110) : Iris dark brown; bill black, except for the base of the mandible, and the space below the nostril on the maxilla, which are light gray; cere and gape chamois; tarsus and toes dull yellow; claws black. The head and foot colors are definitely duller than in *Buteogallus anthracinus.*

Two subspecies, similar in size but differing in color pattern in the tail, are found in Panamá.

Plumages of this species and those of *Buteogallus anthracinus* are so similar, in both adult and immature, that close attention to detail is required to separate them. This is true particularly in their identification in life. With adult birds of the present species close at hand, the white barring on the tibia may be visible, and in any stage the longer legs may be noted, as well as the blacker bill, and more slaty color of the side of the head. These colors, however, are less strongly marked in immature individuals.

The two black hawks under discussion differ in certain structural details which have led to allocation of the larger one in a separate genus, *Hypomorphnus* of Cabanis. Amadon (Auk, 1949, p. 54) questioned the validity of this separation, and in a later paper (Amadon and Eckelberry, 1955, p. 68) he gave some further discussion in which he listed both species under the genus *Buteogallus.* The structural differences between the two may be summarized as follows:

GREATER BLACK HAWK: Tarsus longer, more than 110 mm.; space between the broad, undivided plates at the front of the lower end, and those on the base of the middle toe, longer, measuring 20 mm. or more; the intermediate scutes graduated progressively from larger to those much smaller; loral area, the anterior region of the forehead adjacent to the cere, and the chin more heavily feathered; wing more rounded, the primaries less than 20 mm. longer than secondaries.

LESSER BLACK HAWK: Tarsus shorter, less than 100 mm.; space between the broad, undivided plates at the front of the lower end and those on the base of the middle toe shorter, measuring 12 mm. or less; the intermediate scutes larger, with the transition from larger to smaller abrupt, without gradual change in size; loral area, anterior region of the forehead, and chin scantily feathered; wing more pointed; primaries from 40 to 70 mm. longer than the secondaries.

Buteogallus aequinoctialis of eastern South America, type species of the genus *Buteogallus,* agrees with the lesser black hawk in the form of the scutes on the lower end of the tarsus and in length of wing tip, but the loral area is more nearly bare, as it has only a line of hairlike filaments at the anterior margin. *Buteogallus gundlachii* of Cuba, however, bridges the gap between the two groups as in its tarsal characters the distal space at the lower end in front breaks up into a series of small scutes, more extensive in length than in *anthracinus*, but less than in *urubitinga*. In addition, *B. gundlachii* has a longer wing tip like *anthracinus*, and agrees in heavier feathering of the anterior part of the head with *urubitinga*. From this summary it is evident that separation of the four species in two genera is not warranted.

BUTEOGALLUS URUBITINGA RIDGWAYI (Gurney)

Urubitinga ridgwayi Gurney, List Diurnal Birds Prey, 1884, pp. 77, 148. (Guatemala, Chiapas, and Sinaloa = Cobán, Alta Verapaz, Guatemala, designated by Hellmayr and Conover, Cat. Birds Amer., pt. 1, no. 4, 1949, p. 181.)

Characters.—Tail in adult white, with a broad black terminal band, and a second narrower one of the same color above the center.

Measurements.—Males (9 from Panamá), wing 363-377 (369), tail 221-250 (231.8), culmen from cere 29.0-32.6 (30.6, average of 8), tarsus 114.8-125.0 (121.3) mm.

Females (5 from Panamá), wing 360-391 (371), tail 227-245 (234), culmen from cere 32.0-34.0 (32.9), tarsus 114.7-120.0 (117.1).

Resident. Tolerably common in the tropical zone, rarer in the lower subtropical zone in western Chiriquí. On the Caribbean coast from the Costa Rican boundary to Bahía Caledonia, San Blas; on the Pacific side from western Chiriquí to Darién (specimens seen from the mouth of the Río Canglón on the Chucunaque, and Boca de Paya on the Tuira).

These are woodland birds of the more open areas, and in heavy forest they are found mainly near the larger streams. Adults usually range in pairs, which rise to soar in the manner common to many of their family. At such times they often appear completely black against the sky, their rounded wings and broad tails giving them a square-cut outline. Immature individuals, in streaked dress, usually are found alone.

Frogs form a principal source of food, and the birds in search of them rest regularly on low perches, or on the ground, near small pools and along stream banks, often in open pastures and fields. Lizards also, particularly the basilisk, are eaten.

Nests that I have seen have been located in large forest trees from 12 to 20 meters from the ground, where they were inaccessible. They were built of sticks, placed in a crotch, sometimes amid large limbs where only the rim was visible from below. Nests containing young were noted at the Ciénaga Macana, near París, Herrera, March 17, 1948, and near the Río Pacora, above Pacora, Panamá, April 21, 1949. No description of the egg of this form is known to me.

The screaming call, something like that of the red-tailed hawk, but clearer, less harsh, and therefore more pleasing in its usual utterance, has four notes, of which the first two are given quickly, and the last two in slower, drawn out syllables. In imitation, the bird has the country name of *cocolino*.

The race *ridgwayi* ranges north through Central America to northern México.

BUTEOGALLUS URUBITINGA URUBITINGA (Gmelin)

Falco Urubitinga Gmelin, Syst. Nat., vol. 1, pt. 1, 1788, p. 265. (Pernambuco, fide Pinto, Cat. Aves Brasil, pt. 1, 1938, p. 76.)

Characters.—Tail in adult white, with a single broad subterminal black bar. Size as in *B. u. ridgwayi*.

Resident at the eastern end of the Comarca de San Blas (recorded from specimens taken at Permé and Puerto Obaldía by Hasso von Wedel).

This is the form of extensive range in South America that enters the Republic from Colombia along the northeastern coast.

Schönwetter (Handb. Ool., pt. 3, 1961, p. 145) states that the eggs in general are like those of species of the genus *Buteo,* with some plain in color and others marked sparingly to heavily with reddish brown, varied to lilac. Measurements are 57.4-61.2 × 47.0-49.4 mm.

BUTEOGALLUS ANTHRACINUS (Deppe): Lesser Black Hawk; Gavilán Cangrejero

Slaty black, with base of bill and loral area orange yellow.

Description.—Length 430 to 510 mm. Adult, black, with more or less of a slaty wash; upper tail coverts tipped with white; tail banded rather broadly across center and tipped with white; feathers of crown white at base; upper back and hindneck white mixed with buff at base in varying amount, in some absent; under wing with bases of primaries mottled with white.

Immature, fuscous; cheeks, and indefinite streaks on head, hindneck, and upper back, white, often mixed with cinnamon-buff; innermost primaries and secondaries more or less cinnamon on inner webs, barred with black; tail barred, narrowly and irregularly, and tipped with white; throat white, with shaft lines of fuscous; under tail coverts and tibia white barred with fuscous; breast and abdomen white, blotched heavily with fuscous; under wing buffy white, barred irregularly with fuscous except for the dark tips of the primaries. The amount of the light markings underneath varies, some having the fuscous color restricted to heavy streaks, others appearing quite black. Many show a rufescent phase in which the light markings are cinnamon instead of white or buffy white.

As stated in the account of the greater black hawk, care is necessary to separate that species and the present one unless the birds are seen clearly. The lesser black hawk has the cere, base of the bill, and the loral area distinctly orange-yellow, which is a definite field mark. Though less in evidence in birds in immature dress this area still appears more yellowish in good light. The fully adult bird lacks the white barring on the feathered part of the leg of the larger species. This barring however is present in the immature.

In Panamá the lesser black hawk in the main is a bird of the coastal areas, found especially in mangroves, and in the swampy woodlands adjacent to the poorly drained lands inland that are affected by tide waters. On the larger rivers they range farther into the interior but here live along the streams. It is the most common hawk in these areas. Crabs form a principal source of their food, and their presence seems to govern the range of the *cangrejero*.

The call is a series of whistled notes, high in pitch, heard especially when nesting, quite different from the voice of the *urubitinga* group. In feeding usually they perch low down where they have clear view of the ground on which crabs may be expected. And at times I have seen them on open sand or mud bars along the rivers. One in such a situation suddenly ran to a nearby log and seized a crab lurking beneath it. This agile habit is customary with them. Often I have found the feet of those taken for specimens coated with sand or mud.

They soar regularly and in the air present an outline of rounded wings and rather short tail. In early morning with the sun low in the sky the yellow cere may be seen if the birds are not too high in the air. When the pale immature bird joins the adults as they circle the contrasts in color and pattern are interesting. The young bird at such times shows two rounded light patches at the center of each of the wings.

The main nesting season appears to begin in February and seems to be in full course in March, as adult birds then were found in pairs. I saw them carrying sticks for building and have noted nests under construction in the edge of mangrove swamps, usually at an elevation of about 12 meters, but I was not successful in obtaining eggs. Paired birds are especially noisy at this time, and so their high-pitched calls—repetitions of single notes—are heard regularly, a pleasing sound during long afternoons in camp when I was occupied with notes and specimens.

Usually they were tame, since, as stated above, they have few human intruders in their swampy haunts. On occasion in a cayuco I have passed within 10 meters of birds that were watching for food, without disturbing them. They spend much time on low perches and often have not been at all alarmed when I stopped nearby for a few minutes to share their cool shade. At low tide they come out to rest on rocks or open beaches and mud flats. Immature birds frequently were curious, particularly when I was calling to attract small birds. While the principal food as noted is crabs, I have had some complaint from persons living at the borders of swamps that these hawks sometimes took small chicks. Mangrove warblers and other swamp inhabiting species, however, were not at all nervous when these hawks were nearby, indicating that they are not regularly predatory on small birds.

Individual variation in depth of color and in extent and kind of lighter markings is so great that there has been uncertainty as to the population groups that may be recognized. From examination of over 200 specimens I find only two that appear valid, aside from the bird of the island of Cuba which it appears appropriate to treat as a separate species, *Buteogallus gundlachii*.

The nominate race, *B. a. anthracinus,* marked by larger size, ranges from southern Arizona, southern New Mexico, and southern Texas south through tropical México (except the coast of Chiapas) and Central America to Panamá (except for the lowlands along the Pacific coast), and across northern Colombia and northern Venezuela to northwestern British Guiana, including also the islands of St. Vincent and Trinidad. A decidedly smaller form *B. a. bangsi,* is found along the Pacific in the mangrove swamps and adjacent lowlands from northwestern Perú to Chiapas. Both races occur in Panamá. Measurements that serve to separate them are given in the accounts of the subspecies that follow.

BUTEOGALLUS ANTHRACINUS ANTHRACINUS (Deppe)

Falco anthracinus W. Deppe, Preis—Verz. Säugeth. Vög. Amphibien, Fische u. Krebse, Deppe u. Schiede Mexico gesammelt., 1830, p. 3. (Veracruz.)
Urubitinga anthracina cancrivora A. H. Clark, Proc. Biol. Soc. Washington, vol. 18, Feb. 21, 1905, p. 63. (Barrouallie, St. Vincent.)

Characters.—Larger, shown mainly in length of wing.

Measurements (from the entire geographic range).—Males (33 specimens) wing 354-378 (363), tail 173-216 (200), culmen from cere 23.5-28.8 (26.2, average of 32), tarsus 84.0-93.8 (88.4) mm.

Females (36 specimens), wing 365-398 (377), tail 190-226 (208), culmen from cere 25.2-30.5 (27.7), tarsus 83.5-94.0 (89.3) mm.

An adult male from Mandinga, taken on January 29, 1957, had the iris wood brown; cere orange; base of mandible and bare area below nostril to gape light orange; rest of bill neutral gray; loral area, and bare skin above eye, chrome yellow; lower eyelid dull whitish; tarsi and toes chrome yellow; claws black.

Resident. Fairly common in the tropical lowlands, mainly near the coast, from Bocas del Toro to eastern San Blas; in Darién along the Chucunaque and Tuira Rivers, above the influence of tide, and in hill country near the coast; Isla Coiba.

Three females from Isla Coiba, with the wing 364, 369, and 370 mm. respectively, belong evidently with this form, an isolated colony on this large, remote island.

Birds from the Caribbean slope from western Colón to western San Blas are somewhat smaller but come within the lower limit of size given above. Birds in immature plumage throughout the range often are smaller than adults, a fact that should be kept in mind in identification, as some may approach or equal the size found in adults of the smaller race. At Jaqué, in eastern Darién, the race *bangsi*, in typical small form is common in the mangrove swamps at the mouth of the Río Jaqué, but an adult female that I shot on a high rocky headland above a sand beach along the coast toward Colombia is certainly the larger race.

The eggs are described by Bent (U. S. Nat. Mus. Bull. 167, 1937, p. 26) as dull white, spotted sparingly with various shades of brown, with the shell finely granulated. Some have the markings much reduced so that they appear almost plain white. The range of measurements is 50-66.5 × 42.3-48.3 mm. In the northern limit of the range, from southern Arizona to southern Texas, the birds may have from one to three eggs in the nest, but in tropical areas a single egg is usual, increased rarely to two.

BUTEOGALLUS ANTHRACINUS BANGSI (Swann)

Urubitinga anthracina bangsi Swann, Syn. Accipitres, pt. 2, Jan. 3, 1922, p. 98. (San Miguel = Isla del Rey, Archipiélago de las Perlas, Panamá.)

Characters.—Similar in color to *B. a. anthracinus* but definitely smaller.

Measurements.—Males (17 specimens), wing 325-348 (337), tail 176-213 (189), culmen from cere 23.6-28.8 (26.2), tarsus 80.0-90.0 (86.6) mm.

Females (9 specimens), wing 337-363 (348), tail 186-212 (197), culmen from cere 25.6-29.1 (27.2), tarsus 85.7-92.4 (88.1) mm.

An adult female taken at Chimán on February 16, 1950, had the iris hazel; cere orange; base of mandible, loral area, and eyelids orange yellow; base of maxilla, and center of mandible, duller yellow; rest of bill neutral gray; tarsus and toes orange yellow; claws black.

Resident. Common in the swamps of the Pacific coast, particularly in the mangroves, from western Chiriquí (Estero Rico below Alanje, Las Lajas); Veraguas (Puerto Vidal, Río San Pablo below Soná, Paracoté); Los Santos (Tonosí, Punta Mala, Pedasí, Puerto Mensabé, La Honda); Herrera (París, lower Río Santa María); Coclé (Puerto Aguadulce); Panamá (La Jagua, Chico, Chepo, Chimán, Majé); and Darién (El Real, Aruza, mouth of Río Jaqué); Isla Parida; Isla Bolaños; Isla Brincanco, in the Contreras group; Isla Canal de Afuera; Isla Cébaco; Archipiélago de las Perlas (San José, Rey, Cañas, Bayoneta, Málaga, and Contadora islands).

Below Chepo and in the drainage of the Río Chico these hawks range for some distance in swampy areas inland from the coastal mangroves. The same is true in the lowlands of Chiriquí where these smaller birds are found back to Bugaba. Possibly occasionally, they wander inland, as Goldman collected an immature bird of very small size on the upper Río Pacora in the lower levels of the Cerro Azul.

In the mangroves bordering the Estero Salado, below Aguadulce, Coclé, I saw one at its nest on January 25, 1963, an early date. The site was a crotch in a large dead tree 15 meters from the ground. Seen from below, the structure was a considerable accumulation of twigs and small branches half again taller than the bird that rested beside it. On Isla Parida these birds were in pairs during the first week of February.

These hawks were especially common in the swamps bordering the Río Pocrí, at Puerto Aguadulce. Here one swooped at a floating dowitcher that I had shot, but a heavy load at 70 meters, though it did no harm, caused the hawk to veer away. A little later, however, one seized another dowitcher that I had killed and escaped with it to the shelter of the mangroves.

Clearly marked color differences that have been alleged to separate this form from *B. a. anthracinus* are not verified in the considerable series that I have had available, the only character being that of lesser size. These smaller birds are found in Pacific coastal areas in mangroves, and in the swampy woodlands immediately inland, from the mouth of the Río Tumbes in northwestern Perú, and the Gulf of Guayaquil (Puna Island), Ecuador, north along the coast of Colombia (Nuquí), and Central America to Chiapas. Those from Perú, Ecuador and southwestern Colombia have the central area of the inner primaries and the secondaries heavily marked with cinnamon-brown (cross-banded with black) that forms a prominent patch on the folded wing. These are the race *Buteogallus a. subtilis* Thayer and Bangs, described from Gorgona Island, Colombia. Birds from Panamá and from the coast of Colombia south to Nuquí, Chocó, have the general coloration of the wing more uniform as the cinnamon is restricted or almost absent. These may be recognized as a slightly different subspecies, *bangsi* Swann. Intergradation is presumed to take place along the Colombian coast below Buenaventura. The type of *bangsi*, though marked as a male, has a wing length of 363 mm. so that it must be a female.

Monroe (Occ. Pap. Mus. Zool. Louisiana State Univ. no. 26, 1963, pp. 1-5) has described a northern race *rhizophorae* from El Salvador and Honduras, which differs in the adult in lack of rufous or buff on primaries and secondaries. As no intergradation in wing size between *anthracinus* and the coastal population is evident he treats the smaller birds as a distinct species under the name *subtilis*. The suggestion is interesting and one that requires careful consideration in further field studies.

Amadon (Nov. Colombianas, vol. 1, no. 1, Sept. 1, 1961=1963, p. 358) has identified specimens of *subtilis* from Tumbes, northwestern Perú, which marks an extension in range southward to this point. An early report for this locality is that of Taczanowski (Proc. Zool. Soc. London, 1877, p. 745), who, under the name of "*Urubitinga schistacea* (Sund.)," lists two males and a female from Santa Luzía, Perú. In his Ornithologie du Pérou (vol. 1, 1884, pp. 109-110) he describes these specimens in careful detail. Sundevall's name properly refers to another hawk of similar color pattern now known as *Leucopternis schistacea* (Sundevall). It appears evident that Taczanowski made his error in identification through reference to

Sharpe's account in volume 1 of the Catalogue of Birds in the British Museum (1874, p. 216), where the genus name *Urubitinga* is used for the species *anthracina* Lichtenstein and *schistacea* Sundevall. The description given by Taczanowski is detailed and complete and agrees fully in color and in small size with the race currently known as *subtilis*. This is substantiated by his quotations from Stolzmann and Jelski, collectors of his specimens, who describe the birds as found in the mangroves in the delta of the Río Tumbes, where they fed on crabs, and were almost stupidly tame.

URUBITORNIS SOLITARIA SOLITARIA (Tschudi): Solitary Eagle; Águila Solitaria

Circaëtus solitarius Tschudi, Arch. Naturg. vol. 10, Bd. 1, 1844, p. 264. (Río Chanchamayo, Perú.)

Of eagle size, dark gray, with tail banded with white.

Description.—Length 600 to 800 mm. Adult, dark slaty gray; upper tail coverts tipped with white; tail black, tipped narrowly with white, and with a broad central band of white, mixed with neutral gray on some of the feathers; feathers of hindneck basally white; primaries and secondaries banded indistinctly with paler gray; outermost primaries banded with grayish white, more prominently toward base.

Immature, back and wings fuscous, edged on back with cinnamon, and with indistinct grayish and buff mottling on the middle and greater coverts; crown fuscous; rest of head and under surface, including under tail coverts, buff to whitish buff, streaked with fuscous; a fuscous-black patch on breast; tibia fuscous, barred lightly with cinnamon; under surface of wing cream buff, with heavy fuscous markings on the under wing coverts.

Measurements.—This species is so rare that it has been difficult to assemble comparable measurements since most records in literature do not indicate whether the wing size given is taken from the chord or from the wing flattened. Some figures apparently include a mixture of the two. The notes that follow I have made personally, with the wing measured on the chord.

Males (3 specimens), wing 490-506 (496), tail 219-227 (222), culmen from cere 38.2-41.5 (39.8), tarsus 125.1-127.5 (126.1).

Female (one specimen), wing 513, tail 255, culmen from cere 44.0, tarsus 120.2 mm.

Four additional birds with sex not marked have the wing 492-500, tail 254-260, culmen from cere 39.5-40.0, and tarsus 122.6-129.8 mm.

Resident. Rare, in areas of heavy forest.

The species is one that is little known. The only definite records are two birds in immature dress in the British Museum taken by Arcé at Calobre, Veraguas, one in 1869 and the other in 1870. On April 14, 1949, as I descended a narrow, open ridge from the higher slopes of Cerro Carbunco, northwest of Chepo, an adult eagle that I was certain was this species crossed directly in front of me. At my shot it pitched down the steep slope above the Río Tranca. We could not see where it struck because of the trees that blocked our view, and though we searched long and carefully we were unable to find the bird because of the rough and broken contours of the steep descent. From its size, relatively short tail, and color, I felt certain of the identification.

Published accounts usually state that this eagle has a short bushy crest, though actually the feathers on the back of the head are not lengthened more than they are in related hawks that are regarded as not crested. Amadon (Auk, 1949, pp. 53-56) has placed *Urubitornis* as a synonym of *Harpyhaliaetus*. And Hellmayr and Conover (Cat. Birds Amer., pt. 1, no. 4, 1949, pp. 199-200) go further, as they list *solitarius* as a subspecies of *Harpyhaliaetus coronatus*. Friedmann (U. S. Nat. Mus. Bull. 50, pt. 10, 1950, p. 415) has called to attention the similarity of *solitaria* to the greater black hawk, *Buteogallus urubitinga,* and it is my own opinion that affiliations of *solitaria* are closer with *Buteogallus* than they are with *Harpyhaliaetus*. It resembles the greater black hawk in proportionate length of the feathering on the back of the head, in rounded wing tip, in tarsal scutellation, particularly at the lower end, and also in the reduction of feathering on the side of the head. The much larger *Harpyhaliaetus coronatus* has a distinct crest of narrow, elongated feathers, and appears completely different in other ways.

In view of these differences, I prefer to maintain *Urubitornis* as a separate generic entity pending further information. The internal structure of the two groups as yet is not known.

A larger race, *Urubitornis solitaria sheffleri* van Rossem, recognized from the mountains of southeastern Sonora, with the wing in the male 530, and in the female 552 mm., is said to have heavier tarsi and toes, to be darker in the adult, and to have a definite subbasal white band across the outer rectrices. This latter mark in typical *solitaria* is indicated only as a grayish brown trace.

In the original description of *solitaria,* cited in the heading above, Tschudi listed this species only as from Perú, which is the type locality given in most of the current accounts. In his Fauna Peruana, Ornithologie, 1845-1846, p. 94, he states that he had only one specimen taken in the heavy forests of Chanchamayo, which therefore is the definite locality. Tschudi (p. xiii) locates the Río Chanchamayo as a stream in northern Junín that joins the Río Paucartambo to form the Río Perené.

SPIZAETUS TYRANNUS SERUS Friedmann: Black Hawk Eagle; Águila Crestuda Negra

Spizaetus tyrannus serus Friedmann, Smithsonian Misc. Coll., vol. 111, no. 16, Feb. 28, 1950, p. 1. (Río Indio, near Gatun, Canal Zone, Panamá.)

A black, crested eagle, with relatively long tail.

Description.—Length, 570 to 680 mm. Head with a prominent, rather bushy crest of numerous broad-ended feathers, without the considerably elongated central plumes found in *Spizaetus ornatus;* tarsi feathered nearly to the toes; tail three-fourths as long as wing or more. Adult, black, with feathers of crown, crest, throat, and upper back white basally; tail with 3 broad bars and narrow tip that are gray above, white underneath; under tail coverts and legs barred heavily with white, the latter to the lower end of the tarsus; sides usually barred lightly with white; under wing coverts marked extensively with white; under surface of primaries and secondaries with wide white bars.

Immature, brownish black; crown streaked widely with white to deep buff; lower back, rump, and upper tail coverts barred with white; breast brown, with black shaft streaks, the feathers edged and tipped with white; lower breast, abdomen, sides, legs, and under tail coverts barred with white.

Measurements.—Males (5 from Costa Rica, Panamá and Colombia), wing 371-383 (378.2), tail 291-312 (302.8), culmen from cere 27.3-30.2 (28.4), tarsus 78.1-86.0 (82.0) mm.

Females, (3 from Panamá and Venezuela), wing 390-393 (391.2, average of 2), tail 296-311 (303), culmen from cere 29.5-30.3 (30.0), tarsus 84.6-92.0 (87.9) mm.

According to L. L. Jewel (Stone, Proc. Acad. Nat. Sci. Philadelphia, 1918, p. 250) a female taken at Gatun, February 4, 1912, had the "iris bright orange, bill blue-black, cere slaty, toes yellow."

Resident. Uncommon, in areas of heavy forest, mainly in the tropical zone, but recorded in western Chiriquí to 1,650 meters.

Definite records are as follows:

CHIRIQUÍ: Lérida, May 20, 1933 (Blake, Fieldiana: Zool., vol. 36, 1958, p. 507).

VERAGUAS: Calobre (Salvin, Proc. Zool. Soc. London, 1870, p. 215).

BOCAS DEL TORO: Changuinola, Sept. 29, 1927; Fruitdale, Nov. 18, 1928 (Peters, Bull. Mus. Comp. Zool., vol. 71, 1931, p. 309).

CANAL ZONE: Near Cerro Galera (K-6 Road), Oct. 26, 1953; Gamboa, 1957, and Nov. 20, 1961 (specimens in U. S. Nat. Mus.); Barro Colorado Island, sight records June 28, 1949 (Eisenmann, Smithsonian Misc. Coll., vol. 117, no. 5, 1952, p. 16), May 5, 1953 (Wetmore); Lion Hill, March 1900 (Bangs, Proc. New England Zoöl. Club, vol. 2, 1900, p. 15); Gatun, Feb. 4, 1912 (Stone, cit. supra), Jan. 28 and Mar. 4, 1911 (E. A. Goldman).
COLÓN: Peluca Hydrographic Station, on Río Boquerón, Feb. 27, 1961.
COMARCA DE SAN BLAS: Puerto Obaldía (Hellmayr and Conover, Cat. Birds Amer., pt. 1, no. 4, 1949, p. 208).

Goldman secured his first specimen near Gatun as it sat in the top of a tall tree eating an iguana. His second one circled over him in early morning as he was ascending the Río Indio, near Gatun. A pair that I saw high in air above Barro Colorado Island were easily identified by the long tail and dark color; and with binoculars I could see the light markings on wing and tail.

The present subspecies ranges from southeastern México through Central America to northern and western Brazil. The typical race, *Spizaetus tyrannus tyrannus* (Wied), of eastern and southeastern Brazil, according to Friedmann in his description of *serus,* is larger. Another difference in the typical race is found in the lesser amount of white on the under wing coverts, and in the narrower barring on the legs, a character, however, that is variable, as immature individuals of both subspecies have more white than the adults.

When I came to Isla Coiba on January 6, 1956, Capitán Juan A. Souza, Director of the Colonia Penal, showed me the partly decomposed feet of a hawk, kept as curiosities from a bird killed the week before my arrival. These had the tarsi feathered, and appeared to be blackish in color. Because of their condition I could detect no markings, nor was I able to preserve them. I believed that they came from a hawk eagle, probably from *Spizaetus tyrannus,* but of this I was not certain. Some of the guards and convicts seemed to know this group of hawks but I did not succeed in finding it.

SPIZAETUS ORNATUS VICARIUS Friedmann: Barred Hawk Eagle; Águila de Penacho

FIGURE 44

Spizaetus ornatus vicarius Friedmann, Journ. Washington Acad. Sci., vol. 25, no. 10, Oct. 15, 1935, p. 451. (Near Manatee Lagoon, British Honduras.)

A crested eagle, with undersurface white, heavily barred.

Description.—560 to 630 mm. Tarsi feathered nearly to the toes; head crested with the central feathers narrow and elongated. Adult, crown, including crest, black; filamentous feathers of loral area white at base, with elongated shafts black; sides of head and neck to sides of upper breast rufous brown, forming a ring around the hind neck that becomes darker until it merges with the black back; lesser, middle, and greater wing coverts black, tipped narrowly with white; primary

FIG. 44.—Barred hawk eagle, águila de penacho, *Spizaetus ornatus vicarius*.

coverts mouse brown basally, tipped with black; primaries and secondaries mouse brown, banded indistinctly with dull black, with inner primaries and outer secondaries tipped lightly with white; upper tail coverts brownish gray, with a black terminal band, and narrow tip of white; tail brownish gray, with 4 black cross bands, and narrow tip of white; a black line below the brown on the side of the head; under surface, including under wing, white; throat and foreneck pure white, elsewhere banded heavily with black.

Immature, head and neck white, washed more or less with cinnamon; mainly mouse gray above and white below, with black bars restricted to sides, legs, tail, and undersurface of wing.

An adult male taken at the mouth of Río Tuquesa, Darién, March 27, 1959, had the iris bright yellow; loral area (bare except for bristles) bluish gray; bill black, except for neutral gray shading on side of maxilla at base (below the level of the upper margin of the nostril), and on side of mandible at base; toes yellow basally, shaded distally with greenish; claws black.

Measurements (adapted from Friedmann, U. S. Nat. Mus. Bull. 50, pt. 10, p. 446).—Males, wing 338-349 (340), tail 244-268 (255.6), culmen from cere 25.5-29 (27.1), tarsus 87-92 (89) mm.

Females, wing 353-388 (377.8), tail 266-290 (281.6), culmen from cere 27-31.5 (30), tarsus 89.5-100 (94.1) mm.

Resident. Uncommon, in regions of heavy forest, ranging from the lowlands to above 1,500 meters in the mountains of Chiriquí and Darién.

Though these birds are widely distributed there are no records as yet from the Azuero Peninsula.

I have seen this handsome hawk soaring over an opening made by a fallen tree on Barro Colorado Island (Feb. 8, 1950), and there is a specimen from that reserve in the University of Michigan Museum, taken on August 17, 1927, by J. Van Tyne. One in the U. S. National Museum from near Gamboa, C. Z., was collected November 25, 1960, by N. Gale and C. M. Keenan. Near Chepo, on April 26, 1949, one shot by W. M. Perrygo was lured within range by calls to attract smaller birds. A living individual presented to the National Zoological Park by Dr. H. M. Mitchell was captured on the Río Maestra, eastern Panamá, in January 1961. In the woodland along the Río Chucunaque, near the Tuquesa, a pair ranged in one section of forest, hunting usually through the middle branches, below the tree crown. I shot the male here on March 27, 1959. Goldman collected one at over 1,500 meters elevation at the head of Río Limón on Cerro Pirre on April 19, 1912. H. von Wedel secured one March 4, 1938 (sex not marked), "24 miles inland" from Cricamola, Bocas del Toro, and a female June 15, 1932 at Puerto Obaldía, San Blas.

The nest and eggs have not been reported in literature that I have seen. They are said to feed on reptiles, but also take birds. On the Río Pucro in Darién I saw one capture a ringed kingfisher (*Megaceryle torquata*).

In the original description of this race, through a typographical error, the type, taken by Morton E. Peck, was listed as from "Manatol" Lagoon. Stephen M. Russell informs me that Peck's field notes state that the bird was collected "in the pine ridge near Manatee Lagoon." Mr. Russell writes that tall rainforest and pinelands are found in this area. The former is the usual habitat of this eagle.

The subspecies *vicarius* is found from southern México through Central America and northern South America to western Ecuador. In northern Colombia it ranges eastward across northern Antioquia to western Guajira (to Riohacha). The typical subspecies, *Spizaetus ornatus ornatus* (Daudin), which has the brown of the head and neck brighter, more rufous, is found from eastern Colombia, east of the eastern Andes, Venezuela, and Trinidad, south to Bolivia, northern Argentina, and southern Brazil.

SPIZASTUR MELANOLEUCUS (Vieillot): Black-and-White Hawk Eagle; Águila Blanca y Negra

Buteo melanoleucus Vieillot, Nouv. Dict. Hist. Nat., nouv. éd., vol. 4, Dec. 1816, p. 482. (Guiana.)

Crest short and bushy, like that of *Spizaetus tyrannus;* tarsus feathered nearly to the toes; readily identified by the white under surface and black back.

Description.—Length 460-580 mm. Adult, loral area, a very narrow line above the eye, a small spot on either side of the upper breast, posterior half of crown, crest, back, and wings black; primaries edged, in part, with grayish brown; tail mouse brown, with 4 black bands, and a white tip; under surface, including under side of wing, except as noted beyond, pure white; tips of primaries, and indistinct bands on inner webs above end, dull black; tips of secondaries gray.

Immature, upper surface black mixed with brownish gray; lesser and middle wing coverts tipped with white.

An adult female taken near Chepo on April 22, 1949, had the iris light orange-yellow; maxilla and mandible to symphysis black; cere, base of mandible, and entire gape bright orange, shading anteriorly to dull yellow toward the mandible; bare eyelids dull greenish gray; feet bright yellow; claws black.

Measurements (adapted from Friedmann, U. S. Nat. Mus. Bull. 50, pt. 10, 1950, p. 439). Males, wing 340-386 (364.6), tail 230-245

(238.5), culmen from cere 24.5-28.0 (25.9), tarsus 72-84 (77) mm. Females, wing 394-423 (411.7), tail 230-253 (242), culmen from cere 26-30 (28), tarsus 88-99 (93.4) mm.

Resident. Rare, in forested areas from the tropical lowlands to 1,650 meters elevation in the mountains of Chiriquí.

Though this handsome hawk eagle ranges from southern México to northeastern Argentina and southern Brazil it seems uncommon throughout this vast area, since it is known mainly through scattered reports.

The few records for Panamá are as follows:

> CHIRIQUÍ: Above Boquete, at Lérida, June 10, 1936, and Velo, May 26, 1932, Sept. 1, 1939 (Blake, Fieldiana; Zool., vol. 36, 1958, p. 506).
>
> VERAGUAS: Specimen in British Museum, without specific locality, taken in May 1874 by Arcé.
>
> BOCAS DEL TORO: Banana River, Dec. 10, 1927 (Peters, Bull. Mus. Comp. Zool., vol. 71, 1931, p. 309); Cricamola, Sept. 4, 1936, specimen at University of California in Los Angeles, taken by Loye Miller.
>
> CANAL ZONE: Near Lion Hill, specimen taken by McLeannan, 1863, in British Museum; Barro Colorado Island (Chapman, My Tropical Air Castle, 1929, p. 401).
>
> PANAMÁ PROVINCE: La Jagua, Jan. 25, 1958, F. A. Hartman (identified from kodachrome slides; specimen not preserved); Chepo, April 22, 1949, female; Charco del Toro, Río Majé, March 28, 1950 (sight record, Wetmore).

The bird shot on April 22, 1949, was secured in the hills at Camarón, near the Río Mamoní above Chepo. It came with considerable force through high forest to strike at Araçari toucans that chattered and dashed about in the branches, much excited. Another was seen the following year in heavy forest above the head of tidewater on the Río Majé. The contrasted black and white colors made both of these individuals conspicuous even in the dark shadow beneath the dense leaves of the forest canopy.

Nothing appears to be recorded regarding the nest. Schönwetter (Handb. Ool., pt. 3, 1961, p. 170) gives the dimensions of 3 eggs as 60.1-62.4 × 49.9-53.3 mm., but includes no details regarding color or marking. Kreuger (Ool. Rec., 1963, p. 6) reports two sets of 2 eggs each, both collected in British Guiana on April 27, 1927, and in March, 1928. He describes the ground color as cream-white spotted with dark brown, gray-lilac, and light brown, varying in extent of marking from heavily spotted to sparingly marked. Size in one set is given as 62.4 × 47.5 mm., and 62.2 × 48 mm.

From external characters this species is separated generically from *Spizaetus* by the outermost or first primary longer than the innermost or tenth, instead of the reverse. The whole wing appears more pointed, the tail is relatively shorter, the cere proportionately larger, and the bristly feathering of the lores more abundant.

MORPHNUS GUIANENSIS (Daudin): Crested Eagle; Águila Moñuda

Falco guianensis Daudin, Traité Elém. Compl. Orn., vol. 2, May 1800, p. 78. (French Guiana.)

Size large; head crested; tail nearly as long as wing; body form slender; varying from white underneath to lightly banded with cinnamon, or in some heavily banded with black.

Description.—Length 710 to 830 mm. Adult, light phase, crown, sides of head, basal crest feathers, hindneck, and band across lower foreneck and upper breast gray; crown feathers streaked and spotted with dark neutral gray; elongated central crest feathers white at base, black on tips; upper surface black, with rump and upper tail coverts white; wing coverts tipped and mottled with gray; primaries and secondaries mottled obscurely with gray; tail black, with white tip and 3 broad cross bands of gray, mottled with mouse brown; throat white; lower surface from gray breast band to under tail coverts white, with narrow bars of cinnamon, lined with gray; under surface of wing white, becoming gray on the outer half of the primaries, which are gray banded with black.

Immature, crown, sides of head, crest, and under surface white, washed with pale gray on crown and upper breast; upper surface dull black, with wing coverts freckled with white and gray, and wings with irregular gray bars spotted with black; under surface of wings as in adult.

Dark phase, crown and sides of head dark gray; above black, with the wing coverts tipped lightly with white, and the wings faintly freckled with gray; tail banded with gray, mottled with black, and tipped with white; breast band black; rest of lower surface, including under wing coverts white, barred heavily with black. (The dark individuals are less common.)

A male, in dark phase, taken on the Cerro Azul, had the following colors: Iris hazel; bill dull black; cere and loral area (bare except for scattered bristles) dark neutral gray; tarsus and toes dull yellow; claws black.

Measurements (from specimens from Panamá, Colombia, and the upper Amazon).—Males (7 specimens), wing 425-449 (437), tail 340-380 (364, average of 5), culmen from cere 30.1-33.6 (32.6, average of 6), tarsus 105.2-117.7 (110.9) mm.

Females (5 specimens), wing 450-477 (464), tail 373-407 (381), culmen from cere 34.7-37.7 (36.0), tarsus 108.1-116.2 (113.4) mm.

Resident. Rare, in regions of heavy forest.

The available records are as follows:

> CHIRIQUÍ: Boquete, Mar. 15, 1960 (sight record, Wetmore).
> BOCAS DEL TORO: Changuinola, Banana River (Peters, Bull. Mus. Comp. Zool., vol. 71, 1931, p. 309).
> COCLÉ: Head of Río Guabal, Caribbean slope (sight record, Wetmore).
> CANAL ZONE: Lion Hill (taken by McLeannan, specimen in British Museum); Barro Colorado Island, March 30, 1936 (specimen in American Museum of Natural History), Feb. 8, 1950 (dark phase), and May 5, 1953 (sight records, Wetmore).
> PANAMÁ: Quebrada Carriaso on Pacific slope of the Cerro Azul (head waters of Río Pacora); dark phase, April 25, 1949; Chepo, March 18, 1911.
> DARIÉN: Mouth of Río Imamadó on the Río Jaqué, April 8 and 11, 1947 (dark phase; sight records, Wetmore).
> COMARCA DE SAN BLAS: Permé and Puerto Obaldía (Griscom, Bull. Mus. Comp. Zool., vol. 72, 1932, p. 315); male and female, Puerto Obaldía, Dec. 10, 1931, and March 28, 1932 (specimens in Brandt collection, University of Cincinnati); Puerto Obaldía, Feb. 17, 1963 (sight record, Wetmore).
> ISLA COIBA: Jan. 15 and 22, 1956 (sight records, Wetmore).

As this is a species that lives in tall forest, it is seen mainly by chance, and probably it is more common than the few records indicate. In my own experience I have observed it at Boquete soaring high over the valley, when the long tail and short wings served to identify it at sight. This is the only report for Chiriquí at present. On Isla Coiba one rested on an open perch below the top of a tall tree, where it was seen first by the keen eye of Vicente, my companion. It perched quietly, with raised crest. Others were seen here soaring high over the forest.

On April 25, 1949, my last day afield for that season, I had gone up the Río Pacora into the eastern part of the Cerro Azul and had continued higher on foot along the Quebrada Carriaso, to an elevation of about 350 meters, in an area that at the time was little troubled by human intrusion. I noted tracks of tapir, deer, and jaguar at intervals along the stream, and smaller forest creatures appeared in the undergrowth and in the trees. Toward noon I found it necessary to return to meet my companions at the jeep, left near the main river. But first, reluctant to leave, I tried calling once more. A few small birds were attracted, then a hummingbird, and then this beautiful eagle came swiftly into a little open space above me, circled expertly, opening and closing the long tail, and then smashed through slender branches to a perch only 12 meters distant, where it turned its head quickly to search for the source of the distress call that I was making. As I raised the gun it looked directly at me, and a second later it was on the ground. Its motions were rapid and certain, a true bird of prey. This was a fine example of the dark phase.

Earlier, on April 8, 1947, on the upper Río Jaqué, I had a clear view of one, also in dark phase, as on set wings it crossed a small clearing in the forest. Another was seen here in the forest a few days later.

The dark phase of this attractive eagle in its fully colored form, with heavy black barring across the lower surface of the body below the black upper breast, presents a decidedly different appearance from the paler coloration seen in most individuals. Gurney, who received a specimen of this kind from Ecuador, believed it to represent a distinct species and described it as *Morphnus taeniatus* (Ibis, 1879, p. 176). For some time the few known came from South America, where the bird ranges south to Bolivia and to Misiones in northeastern Argentina. A specimen in the American Museum of Natural History from Ecuador has the lower surface from the lower breast to the under tail coverts barred somewhat sparingly with black, and another from the same country has the axillars and flanks heavily barred, while elsewhere on the under parts the markings are reduced to scattered flecks of black. These appear to bridge over to the paler, more common style.

Lehmann (Caldasia, no. 7, 1943, pp. 172-175) has described and figured a specimen from the Río Juradó, Chocó, that is almost entirely blackish brown beneath, with few light markings, which, as an extreme manifestation of melanism, strengthens the supposition that the *taeniatus* style is merely a color variant.

The nesting of these birds is little known. The Penards (Vog. Guyana, vol. 1, 1908, p. 409) were told that the nest was made of sticks placed in the tallest trees. Kreuger (Ool. Rec., 1963, pp. 5-6) describes a single egg in his collection from "Polaro" (=Potaro), British Guiana as "deep cream with large pale yellow-brown spots, richly dispersed round the larger end of the egg, with finer small spots spread over the rest of the surface. Additionally a few pale lilac-gray, smaller-sized spots are visible." The measurements are 73.7 × 53.4 mm. The *águila moñuda* is said to feed on the smaller monkeys, large birds, and iguanas. Dr. Lehmann states that the call is somewhat similar to that of the greater black hawk.

HARPIA HARPYJA (Linnaeus): Harpy Eagle; Harpía

Vultur harpyja Linnaeus, Syst. Nat., ed. 10, vol. 1, 1758, p. 86. (México.)

The largest and most powerful of the eagles; general form and appearance like that of *Morphnus guianensis,* but much greater in size; head with a prominent, double-pointed crest; tail long; wings relatively short and rounded; feet very strong and powerful.

Description.—Length, 950 mm. to more than a meter. Adult, head all around, including throat, smoke gray; bushy crest darker, blacker, with elongated central feathers that often are erected in a double point; upper surface black, with a wash of bluish gray; rump and upper tail coverts narrowly tipped with white; wing coverts and scapulars tipped with white or pale gray; outer primaries black; inner primaries and secondaries mottled with gray and dull black; tail with 4 black bands, separated by 3 that are grayish white, and tipped with white; upper breast black; rest of under surface (except for the gray throat) white, with sides streaked, and tibia barred, with black; under wing coverts white, with large, irregular spots of black; bases of flight feathers pale gray; tips dull black, barred with white; under surface of tail grayish white, barred narrowly with black.

Immature, head, neck, and under surface white; crest black mottled with gray, and tipped with white; above mottled gray and black; tibia lightly barred. The weight of a living male in the New York Zoological Society collection is given as 4.6 kilograms (Conway, Auk, 1962, p. 275). A male collected March 8, 1963, near Armila, San Blas weighed 4.53 kilos. Fowler and Cope (Auk. 1964, p. 209) record the weight of living birds in a male as 4.8 kilos and in two females as about 7.6 kilos.

The iris in the male last mentioned was orange; cere and bill black; tarsus and toes yellow; claws black.

Measurements (from Friedmann, U. S. Nat. Mus. Bull. 50, pt. 10, 1950, p. 434).—Males, wing 543-580 (556.5), tail 372-412 (392), culmen from cere 41.5-54 (48.3), tarsus 114-120 (115.8) mm.

Females, wing 583-610 (587.6), tail 417-420 (418), culmen from cere 46-63 (53), tarsus 118-130 (123) mm.

Resident. Rare, in areas of heavy forest.

This great eagle, usually acknowledged as the most powerful of its group in the entire world, ranges through the forested lowlands of tropical America from southern México to northern Argentina. A hundred years ago it was fairly common in Panamá, as McLeannan, station master on the Panama Railroad, on the Atlantic side, told Osbert Salvin that he saw them regularly in the forests (Sclater and Salvin, Proc. Zool. Soc. London, 1864, p. 368). Definite records however are relatively few. The Museum of Comparative Zoology received two from Almirante, Bocas del Toro, shot April 15, 1923, and March 26, 1924, by H. S. Blair, division manager for the Chiriqui Land Co., and one from Banana River, taken on April 21, 1928, by Wedel (Peters, Bull Mus. Comp. Zool., vol. 71, 1931, p. 309). There is a male in the Brandt Collection at the University of Cincinnati received from Wedel, labeled Almirante Bay, March 21, 1939. Charles O. Handley, Jr., had report of one 7 kilometers southwest of Changuinola, February 26, 1960, and received the skull of one shot on the Río Teribe in October 1962.

In the Canal Zone these birds have been recorded occasionally on Barro Colorado Island, and McLeannan collected one near Lion Hill. The newspaper *Star and Herald* of Panamá published an account and a photograph of one killed by a hunter in the Bohío area on September 14, 1951, that judged from the picture was a fully grown immature individual. It was reported to have had a wing spread of 6 feet 5 inches (nearly 2 meters). An older bird, brought to Dr. Alejandro Méndez P., Director of the Museo Nacional in Panamá, was killed on November 11, 1951, by Adolfo Arias Espinosa on the farm of Dr. Adolfo Arias near the Río Pacora, beyond Pacora. A sight record is of one flushed from a low perch in dense brush near the Río Camarón, west of La Campana, Panamá, March 9, 1951. Apparently it was hunting the marmosets that were numerous in the area. H. von Wedel secured a male at Miel, on the boundary at Puerto Obaldía, San Blas, June 15, 1934 (in the Brandt Collection at the University of Cincinnati).

The harpy is reported to prey on the smaller monkeys and sloths, to attack smaller deer, and also to capture macaws and other large birds. The one taken near Armila, San Blas, shot by a hunter employed by C. O. Handley, Jr., had fur and claws of a young two-toed sloth in its stomach. While the flight appears rather slow and heavy, this perhaps is misleading, because of its large size and heavy body. The feet and legs are muscular and heavy, far more so than in any other of the eagles.

Joseph Parker Norris, Jr. (Ool. Rec., vol. 7, 1927, pp. 25-26), has published an account of two eggs in his collection obtained by Rodolphe M. de Schauensee and James Bond at "Costanhal, near the Rio Apehu" in Brazil in 1926. De Schauensee informs me that the locality is near the Belém-Bragança Railroad, about 85 kilometers east of Belém. The nest was placed on the bottom limb next to the trunk of a huge tree about 35 meters (111 feet) from the ground. It was made of large sticks and was lined with the hair of sloths. A fresh egg taken here on April 27, white without markings, although badly nest stained, measured "2.80×2.35 inches, or 71.12× 69.9 mm." (The final figure should be corrected to 59.69, which is the equivalent of 2.35 inches.) On a second visit, on May 9, another egg, with incubation begun, was secured that measured "76.71× 57.15 mm." This also was stained, but Norris believed that it was marked also with blotches of light brown. Fowler and Cope (l.c., pp. 260, 262) describe two nests examined in British Guiana built in forks in tall silk-cotton trees. They were bulky structures from 1.2 to 1.3 meters in diameter placed at about 40 meters from the ground, above the level of the surrounding forest canopy.

Five eggs in the U. S. National Museum were laid by a captive bird at the National Zoological Park between 1946 and 1951, 4 in the month of July and 1 in August. These are white, somewhat nest-stained (but without markings) with a finely granulated shell. They are short subelliptical to nearly elliptical in shape and measure as follows: 73.4×60.5, 77.4×62.2, 78.0×62.1, 78.0×62.3, and 78.1×60.2 mm.

This species is often called *aguilucho*.

CIRCUS CYANEUS HUDSONIUS (Linnaeus): Marsh Hawk; Gavilán Sabanero

FIGURE 45

Falco hudsonius Linnaeus, Syst. Nat., ed. 12, vol. 1, 1766, p. 128. (Hudson Bay.)

Marsh hawks, in any plumage, are distinguished from all others of the family by the small but distinct semicircular ruff of feathers with decurved tips that extends from the sides of the base of the head forward and around across the lower throat; and by the white patch on the lower rump and upper tail coverts, prominent when the birds are in flight.

Description.—Length, 450 to 530 mm. Adult male, upper surface, throat, and upper breast pale gray, washed above more or less with brown to produce indefinite streaks on crown and hindneck; rest of under surface white, barred indefinitely with gray on upper breast, and barred and spotted lightly with cinnamon elsewhere; tips of flight feathers black; rest of under wing surface white, barred and spotted lightly with gray; rump and upper tail coverts white; tail gray, barred rather indefinitely with grayish brown.

Adult female, fuscous-brown above, with feathers of crown, hindneck, back, and wing coverts edged with buffy brown to cinnamon;

below cinnamon-buff, except for foreneck and extreme upper breast which are fuscous-brown; sides streaked with dark brown to rufous; under wing surface strongly barred with grayish brown.

Immature, like female but browner.

Migrant from the north. Tolerably common; found on open lands from sea level to the slopes of the higher mountains.

FIG. 45.—Marsh hawk, gavilán sabanero, *Circus cyaneus hudsonius*.

Present from late October to April. Early dates of arrival: October 16, 1929, Permé, San Blas (Griscom, Bull. Mus. Comp. Zool., vol. 72, 1932, p. 316); October 21, 1935, Puerto Obaldía, San Blas (specimen in Museum of Zoology, University of Michigan, taken by Wedel); October 20, 1961, near Penonomé, Coclé (Loftin, Carib. Journ. Sci. 1963, p. 64); October 26, 1927, Cocoplum, Bocas del Toro (Chapman, Auk, 1931, p. 120). Late dates of departure: April 4, 1948, near Chico, Panamá; Balboa, C. Z., April 10, 1942 (T. Imhof, field notes); Canal Zone, April 18, 1911 (Jewel, Auk, 1913, p. 426); April 27, 1949, Pacora, Panamá.

There is record of one banded as a nestling in Kansas on June 15, 1951, that was taken in southern Los Santos, near Tonosí, on December 3, 1953.

Usually the marsh hawk is seen in graceful flight low over open fields or grassy marshes, where it quarters the ground in search of the mice, small birds, and lizards on which it feeds. At any movement in the grass it pounces quickly, with long legs and sharply armed toes fully extended to reach through the open grass cover. It may rise with its prey in its feet, but then drops back to the ground in some open area where it has clear view around while it eats.

During March those that have wintered farther south are in passage northward, and then the birds are more common. Those noted in this movement travel in the great flocks of Swainson's and broad-winged hawks. As the majority pass before the end of the month, only a few are seen during April.

ISCHNOSCELES CAERULESCENS (Vieillot): Crane Hawk; Guiño

Sparvius caerulescens Vieillot, Nouv. Dict. Hist. Nat., nouv. éd., vol. 10, June 1817, p. 318. (Cayenne.)

Size medium; slate to grayish black; tail long, black, with two broad white or buff bands; legs long and slender; feet small, with outer toe decidedly shorter than inner one; tibiotarsal joint flexible both forward and backward.

Description.—Length 430 to 500 mm. Adult, slate gray to blackish slate; primaries and secondaries dark neutral gray; tail black, becoming gray at the end, tipped with white, with two broad bands of buff or white, often variegated with gray; under tail coverts banded with white, or buff; legs and abdomen plain or banded narrowly with white; under wing slaty black, banded narrowly with white on under wing coverts, and with a prominent white band across the outer primaries.

Immature, upper throat, forehead, superciliary line, and streaks on side of head and crown white; a brownish wash over the blackish upper surface; upper tail coverts banded with white; abdomen and legs banded with buff. The eye in the immature is reddish brown to orange (Dickey and van Rossem, Birds El Salvador, 1938, p. 130).

Hellmayr and Conover (Cat. Birds Amer., pt. 1, no. 4, 1949, p. 227) point out that *Geranospiza* Kaup, 1847, in current use for this group of birds, is antedated by *Ischnosceles* Strickland, Ann. Mag. Nat. Hist., ser. 1, vol. 13, no. 86, June 1844, p. 409, type, *Falco gracilis* Temminck. Under the rules of nomenclature Strickland's name is not invalidated by *Ischnoscelis* Burmeister, 1842, for a genus of Coleoptera.

Two subspecies (*I. c. niger* and *I. c. balzarensis*) are found in the Republic, one in the west and the other in the east.

These are hawks of slender form that range along the borders of streams, usually in more open woodland. The exceptionally long legs are most noticeable when they are seen on the ground, as then they stand very erect, almost as though on stilts. In the hand, the broad scutes on the front and back of the tarsus are smooth, and in part may appear fused in one long plate. The outer toe, definitely shorter than the inner one, is also slightly shorter than the hind toe.

The flight is direct and rather slow, performed by a succession of rapid wing-beats, followed by a short sail with the wings held fully extended. At La Jagua, toward evening, one came occasionally to rest on an open branch, where, in the steady trade wind, it bent forward until the body was nearly horizontal. The food appears to be mainly frogs, lizards, and small snakes for which it may search on the ground at the open borders of streams. They also clamber about rather awkwardly in open trees, bending far over to examine the under side of the limbs. I have observed small flycatchers pursuing them, but the hawks have paid no attention to these attacks.

The nesting of these birds in Panamá has not been reported but should not differ from that of related subspecies. Two eggs of *I. c. livens* (Bangs and Penard), a form of northwestern México, in the Museum of Comparative Zoology, taken at Álamos, Sonora, on February 9, 1888, by M. A. Frazer are chalky white, without gloss, with a very faint bluish tinge. They are oval in form and measure 50.0×39.6, and 51.0×39.2 mm. The collector described the nest as about 10 meters from the ground, placed insecurely on a tangle of small thorny branches growing from two larger limbs. It was built of small sticks, lined with others still smaller, and was so flimsy that the eggs were visible through the bottom. The tree stood in a small grove in the bottom of an arroyo. Two other sets of two, and one with a single egg, in the W. J. Sheffler collection, taken near the Hacienda Guiracoba, in southeastern Sonora, were in nests built of small sticks, vine stalks and weed stems, lined with finer materials including twigs with green leaves, located high in trees growing along nearly dry washes. The eggs, described as plain white, have the following range in measurement: $50\text{-}53 \times 38\text{-}43$ mm. (Sutton, Wilson Bull., 1954, pp. 241-242).

Hewitt (Ool. Rec., vol. 17, 1937, p. 12) records a single egg of the typical race *I. c. caerulescens* from southern Venezuela also as white, without gloss, with measurements of 47.5×38.5 mm. The nest, of small sticks lined with "dry leaves and a few feathers from the breast of the bird," was an open cup about 25 centimeters across located near the end of a branch 25 meters from the ground.

ISCHNOSCELES CAERULESCENS NIGER Du Bus

Ischnosceles niger Du Bus, Bull. Acad. Roy. Sci. Lett. Beaux Arts Belgique, vol. 14, pt. 2 (for August) 1847, p. 102. (México.)

Adult, blackish slate; tail bands white, occasionally with the upper one faintly tinged with buff; slightly larger. Wing, male 290-305, female 310-332 mm.

Iris "bright red; the cere, eyelids, and mouth corners dull gray; the bill black with bluish cast; the tarsi and toes orange or redorange; the claws black" (Sutton, Wilson Bull., 1954, p. 237).

Measurements.—Males (5 from México, Guatemala, and western Panamá), wing 290-305 (299.8), tail 215-240 (230.2), culmen from cere 18.6-19.9 (19.3), tarsus 81.0-90.0 (84.2) mm.

Females (4 from México and western Panamá), wing 310-332 (316.3), tail 233-247 (237.6), culmen from cere 20.0-21.5 (20.5), tarsus 88.0-93.4 (90.1) mm.

This subspecies is found from north-central México through the tropical lowlands of Central America to central Panamá.

Resident. Tolerably common; found locally, in western Panamá, east to the Canal Zone.

Records for this race follow:

CHIRIQUÍ: Divalá, Nov. 24, 1900 (Bangs, Auk, 1901, p. 358).
VERAGUAS: Mina de Chorcha (Salvin, Proc. Zool. Soc. London, 1870, p. 216).
HERRERA: El Rincón; Santa María.
CANAL ZONE: Atlantic slope, near the railroad (Lawrence, Ann. Lyc. Nat. Hist. New York, vol. 7, 1861, p. 289); Barro Colorado Island.

Birds from the Canal Zone and Herrera show intergradation toward the next race.

ISCHNOSCELES CAERULESCENS BALZARENSIS (W. L. Sclater)

Geranospiza caerulescens balzarensis W. L. Sclater, Bull. Brit. Orn. Club, vol. 38, March 4, 1918, p. 45. (Balzar, Provincia de Guayas, Ecuador.)

Adult like *Ischnosceles caerulescens niger* but grayer; pale bars on tail tinged with buff; size somewhat smaller.

Measurements.—Male (1 from northwestern Colombia), wing 279, tail 217, culmen from cere 18.2, tarsus 73.0 mm.

Females (8 from Panamá and Colombia), wing 288-298 (290), tail 218-237 (229), culmen from cere 19.2-20.4 (20.1), tarsus 81.7-87.0 (83.3) mm.

Resident. Found locally from the eastern sector of the Province of Panamá eastward.

Records are as follows:

PANAMÁ: Río La Jagua, Chico.
DARIÉN: Río Tuira (Chapman, Bull. Amer. Mus. Nat. Hist., vol. 55, 1926, p. 223).
SAN BLAS: Permé (Griscom, Bull. Mus. Comp. Zool., vol. 72, 1932, p. 316); Puerto Obaldía, July 18, 1933 (Specimen in the Brandt collection at the University of Cincinnati).

Family PANDIONIDAE: Ospreys; Águilas Pescadoras

The ospreys, specialized for capturing their food of fish, are widespread through the great continents of the world and as marginal populations range in the Bahamas in the West Indian area and to distant islands of the Pacific, in addition to an extensive distribution through the East Indies. The single species is divided into 5 geographic races, distinguished by differences in size and in extent of dark markings, but all unmistakably ospreys wherever they are found.

PANDION HALIAETUS CAROLINENSIS (Gmelin): Osprey; Águila Pescadora

FIGURE 46

Falco Haliaëtos carolinensis Gmelin, Syst. Nat., vol. 1, pt. 1, 1788, p. 263. (South Carolina.)

Size large, wings long and pointed; under surface and side of head white, with a prominent dark streak through the eye. Found over or near water.

Description.—Length, 510 to 610 mm. Adult, forecrown, hindneck, streak through eye, and rest of upper surface deep brownish black; rest of crown and under surface white, with a band of rufous-brown spots across the upper breast.

Immature, crown streaked with brownish black; feathers of dorsal surface tipped conspicuously with white.

Outer toe reversible so that it may be directed forward or back; undersurface of toes with sharp spicules; undersurface of claws rounded, instead of grooved as in other hawks; tarsus strong; leg with short compact feathers. In the hand ospreys have a strong, oily, fishy odor.

Measurements (from Friedmann, U. S. Nat. Mus. Bull. 50, pt. 11, 1950, p. 529).—Males (15 specimens), wing 462-498 (477.4), tail 199-220 (208.8), culmen from cere 31-34 (32), tarsus 58-63 (60) mm.

Females, wing 488-512 (503.7), tail 212-240 (225.4), culmen from cere 32-36 (35), tarsus 58-68 (63.3) mm.

Migrant. Tolerably common along the coasts and on larger bodies of water.

Ospreys arrive from the north in October and November and leave in March and April. A few remain in Panamá through the period of northern summer but do not nest.

The osprey is found along the coasts, about the mouths of rivers, and inland regularly along their lower courses to the head of tidewater. On the larger streams where there are wide stretches of open water favorable for fishing it goes farther. I have recorded it on

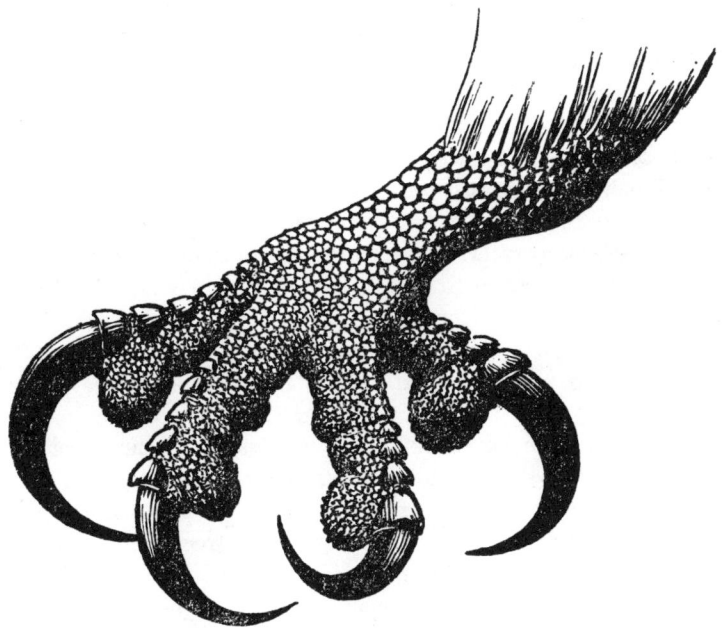

Fig. 46.—Foot of osprey, águila pescadora, *Pandion haliaetus carolinensis*.

the Tuira to the mouth of the Río Paya, on the Chucunaque to the Río Canglón, and far inland on the Río Boquerón, the Río Pequení and the Río Pucro. It comes also to the lakes near El Volcán, and is seen regularly on Madden and Gatun Lakes. They are recorded also at Isla Coiba, and Isla Coibita; Isla Taboga, and Isla Taboguilla; and in the Archipiélago de las Perlas at Isla San José, Isla del Rey, Isleta Málaga, and Isla Saboga. On October 11, 1940, I saw one at sea 60 kilometers north of Cristobal in flight to the south out of sight of land.

The osprey feeds on fishes, captured near the surface of the water. It flies slowly about at a moderate elevation, occasionally pausing to hover, until prey is sighted, when it drops swiftly with long legs extended. The grasp of the long, sharp claws is aided in holding the slippery prey by the horny spicules on the underside of the toes. If the bird has been successful in capture it rises and flies to an open perch in a tree, carrying the fish head forward, grasped with its feet one behind the other. As it comes to the perch one foot is released to grasp the limb. In feeding on the larger fish flesh is stripped and the head, bones, and body are discarded. As the bird comes regularly to favored resting places these discards accumulate on the ground below when not carried away by scavengers. The birds feed as indicated on both salt and fresh water, and may go some distance from land as around the off-shore islands of Isla Villa on the coast of Los Santos, and Farrallón del Chirú, near La Venta, Coclé. On the Río Chimán near the mouth of the Curutú I saw one carrying a bird the size of a small pigeon in its feet, a highly unusual occurrence and one seldom recorded.

Occasionally ospreys rest on a gravel bar, usually so that they may bathe. Near Fort Amador one came at low tide to a small islet exposed by the falling water, walked with short mincing steps for a little distance, and then began to splash its breast and wings in the wash of small waves.

The call, that I have heard only occasionally in Panamá, is a high-pitched, whistled note, repeated several times, that carries for some distance.

Migrants are seen occasionally in company with the great flights of Swainson's hawks. At such times the osprey may stop to rest in open country at a distance from water. I have observed one, for example, perched briefly in a huge dead tree in an inland area near El Uracillo on the Atlantic side of Coclé, and another in a similar situation on one of the ridges at the base of the Cerro Azul.

There are 3 records at present of ospreys banded in the north as nestlings, one from New York State recovered near Jaqué when 2 years old, one from New Jersey marked in July and killed at La Jagua the following December, and one from Maryland with the date of June 23, found near Tonosí on October 4 of the same year.

Near Jaqué on March 20, 1946, one showed heavy molt in the flight feathers of both wings. One taken here a week later appeared about to begin migration as it was extremely fat. Some of the birds that I have seen in summer were in very worn plumage, suggesting that they had not returned north because of an abnormal physiological state.

This species, in addition to the usual name is known locally as the *gavilán de playa* and the *águila de mar*.

Family FALCONIDAE: Falcons, Forest-Falcons, and Caracaras; Halcones, Halcones del Monte, y Caranchos

Members of this family are found throughout the world with the exception of the Antarctic Continent, as residents, or on oceanic islands as birds of passage during migration. The true falcons take living prey regardless of the rapidity through which bird or mammal may attempt escape, and because of their skill the larger species have been trained by man as hunters for hundreds of years. Other kinds, more secretive, but skilled in their hunting, are inhabitants of the forest, where they watch from lookout stations and kill when hungry; or skulk low in undergrowth, with equal success in the capture of living prey. A few descend to any flesh living or dead, and so are scavengers; fewer still are insect eaters.

Representatives of all these types are found among the 12 species recorded from the Republic of Panamá, one of the hunters being especially active in the capture of snakes.

KEY TO SPECIES OF FALCONIDAE

1. Edge of maxilla straight or slightly sinuated, never with a sharp projecting angle or toothlike process 2
   Maxilla with a distinct sharp, toothlike process near tip; mandible notched to receive this (genus *Falco*) 8
2. Head with a distinct crest 3
   Head not crested 4
3. Breast and tibia white or buffy white; crest short and bushy.
   Laughing falcon, *Herpetotheres cachinnans*, p. 260
   Breast and tibia black, or dark brown more or less streaked.
   Caracara, *Caracara plancus*, p. 271
4. Wing tip longer; longest primaries more than 70 mm. longer than secondaries 5
   Wing tip rounded; longest primaries exceeding secondaries by less than 40 mm. (genus *Micrastur*) 6
5. Head fully feathered except on lores and eyelids; lower surface mainly buff....... Yellow-headed caracara, *Milvago chimachima cordatus*, p. 274
   Throat and sides of head with feathering scanty or absent; bare skin red in life; plumage black, with white abdomen.
   Red-throated caracara, *Daptrius americanus americanus*, p. 276
6. Smaller; wing not more than 180 mm.
   Barred forest-falcon, *Micrastur ruficollis interstes*, p. 268
   Larger; wing more than 200 mm. 7
7. Wing less than 240 mm.; tail definitely shorter than wing.
   Slaty-backed forest-falcon, *Micrastur mirandollei*, p. 264
   Wing more than 250 mm.; tail equal to wing, or longer ....
   Collared forest-falcon, *Micrastur semitorquatus naso*, p. 266

8. Back and tail bright cinnamon-brown, barred, more or less, with black.
   Sparrow hawk, *Falco sparverius sparverius*, p. 291
   Back and tail gray, dark brown, or nearly black 9
9. Larger; wing more than 300 mm.
   Peregrine falcon, *Falco peregrinus anatum*, p. 280
   Smaller; wing less than 290 mm., usually much less 10
10. Breast white, or buffy white, streaked with black, or brownish black.
    Pigeon hawk, *Falco columbarius*, p. 288
    Breast black, usually banded with white 11
11. Side of head black, but with a distinct white, or buffy white superciliary.
    Aplomado falcon, *Falco femoralis femoralis*, p. 287
    Side of head black with no light colored superciliary stripe............ 12
12. Larger; wing more than 240 mm.; feet stronger, middle toe without claw
    as long as tarsus........Orange-breasted falcon, *Falco deiroleucus*, p. 281
    Smaller; wing less than 225 mm.; feet weaker, middle toe without claw
    shorter than tarsus.........Bat falcon, *Falco rufigularis petoensis*, p. 283

HERPETOTHERES CACHINNANS CACHINNANS (Linnaeus): Laughing Falcon; Vaquero

FIGURE 47

Falco cachinnans Linnaeus, Syst. Nat., ed. 10, vol. 1, 1758, p. 90. (Surinam.)

A falcon with bushy crest, long tail, and short rounded wings, that in life appears black on the side of the head and back, white on the crest and lower surface.

Description.—Length, 430-470 mm. Adult (sexes alike), sides of head, back, wings, and tail fuscous-black; the tail with 4 or 5 bands of white, that in some individuals are only spots; rest of head and under surface white, the bushy crest, streaked narrowly, more or less, with fuscous-black; under surface of wings light buff, with dusky spots on the under wing coverts, and indistinct bars on the primaries and secondaries. In some the white of head and lower surface is washed more or less with buff.

Immature, feathers of back and wings, including wing coverts, edged narrowly with buffy brown; some individuals with sides, tibia, and under tail coverts streaked and spotted lightly with cinnamon-buff and fuscous.

Iris dark brown; cere and gape yellow; rest of bill black; tarsus and toes deep olive-buff; claws black.

Measurements (birds from Costa Rica, Panamá, and Colombia).—Males (12 specimens), wing 252-276 (265), tail 186-216 (200), culmen from cere 21.2-26.1 (22.4), tarsus 59.8-63.8 (61.3) mm.

Females (12 specimens), wing 255-268 (260), tail 185-207 (194), culmen from cere 22.5-26.1 (23.5), tarsus 59.8-63.5 (61.2) mm.

Resident. Throughout the tropical zone, locally common, but in recent years rare or absent from the more heavily settled regions (including the Canal Zone); ranging to 1280 meters in the lower subtropical zone (Palo Santo, El Volcán) on the Pacific slope in Chiriquí.

The strange calls of this interesting species of the falcon family are the usual indication of its presence, as the birds themselves may be seen infrequently, especially in heavily forested areas. Though

FIG. 47.—Laughing falcon, vaquero, *Herpetotheres cachinnans cachinnans.*

they are not particularly wary, it is usual for them to rest on high, open perches that many times are concealed from observation by leafy cover below. At rest they stand erect, the bushy crest causing the head to appear large. During flight the short, rounded wings, which beat rapidly, and the long tail present an unusual silhouette. The loud calls, heard most often in morning and evening, as well as through the night, in still air carry distances of more than a kilometer. They begin with a single note, repeated rather slowly, increase in tempo, and change to a loud *gua kow*, uttered more and more rapidly. Presently a companion may join when the two may call, sometimes alternately, sometimes in unison, for 10 minutes or more, a strange, weird concert, startling to one who hears it for the first time without knowing its author. Some complain of its loudness but to me it has always been one of the more pleasing among the stranger tropical sounds. Near at hand paired birds utter lower cackling or chuckling calls that often are quite amusing to the human ear.

Snakes form the principal food of this species, and in their capture they are most adept. I recall particularly a pair near our little house above Concepción, in western Chiriquí, that once or twice daily flew past with the limp form of a snake dangling from the feet. One came regularly with its prey into the dead top of a tree on the slope immediately below us, where it called until another, that I believed to be a grown young one, came scrambling up to seize the food and carry it down into the leafy cover below. The parent then usually stood erect with flaring crest, while it called vociferously for several minutes. Often one or both carrying prey flew past uttering guttural, chattering notes that we found entertaining through their resemblance to low-voiced human laughter. On several occasions I saw a chimango hawk following as the laughing falcon passed with its dangling prey, and once one came tailed by a group of half a dozen parakeets, all chattering excitedly. These sights were of daily occurrence, but in over two weeks during which I covered miles of the surrounding terrain, I myself did not see a single serpent. In the stomach of one that I collected near Alanje, Chiriquí I found the end of the tail of a coral snake that Dr. Doris Cochran identified as *Erythrolamprus aesculapii*.

Those who have seen this hawk hunting have told me in detail of how it alights on the ground and spreads one wing whose stiff feathers fend off the strikes of an aggressive snake until the falcon can seize it in one foot near the head and so hold it until it is killed.

Though this falcon is one of wide distribution, there is little information as to its nesting habits. In southeastern Sonora W. J. Sheffler found it using cavities in cliffs and from one nest collected a young bird several days old. This was covered with light brownish-buff down, paler on the chin and throat, and darker on the upper surface, with a "black facial mask and collar around the nape" like the similar markings of the adult plumage (Sheffler and van Rossem, Auk, 1944, pp. 141-142). The first authentic egg, sent to Col. L. R. Wolfe (Ool. Rec., vol. 18, 1938, p. 77) from Horqueta, Paraguay, was "clear white, fairly well marked around the large end with flakes and splashes of rich reddish-chestnut and a few flecks of light red scattered over the remainder. Size 56.5 × 45.6 mm." Later, in Tamaulipas, Wolfe (Condor, 1954, p. 161) flushed a laughing falcon from a cavity in a large tree and saw another broken stub where the birds were said to nest. In the same account he describes an egg taken in San Luis Potosí from a natural cavity where it lay without lining other than the debris usual in such openings. This egg, subelliptical as shown in an accompanying illustration, had the ground color entirely concealed by a "wash of dark chocolate brown and a few splashes of burnt umber, but there are a few streaks of lighter yellowish brown where the pigment is thinner." It measured 58.0 × 44.6 mm.

There is an egg in the U. S. National Museum collections, long attributed to the collared forest-falcon (*Micrastur semitorquatus*) that was collected by John Xántus on the "Nishpa Río" in Michoacán in April 1863. This is between subelliptical and oval and between cinnamon-buff and clay color in ground color, irregularly washed and blotched with chestnut-brown, thickened in occasional irregular spots until it appears almost black. It measures 59.2 × 43.3 mm. Under date of April 19, 1863, Xántus wrote to Prof. S. F. Baird from the mountains of southern Michoacán that he had collected an egg of the "vaco" from "the hollow top, about 5 feet in the trunk" of a large wild fig tree. He attributed the nest to the collared forest-falcon which he had collected at or near this point, but in evident error. Though the nest and eggs of the latter are unknown, in the numerous specimens of this species that I have handled there has been no evidence whatever of feather wear that is inevitable in any hole-nesting bird with such a long tail. The site, the common name, the form, and color of the egg are those of the laughing falcon.

There has been uncertainty as to the geographic variation found in these birds, so that the number of subspecies recognized by different authors has varied from two to six. The main difficulty has come from lack of understanding of the considerable amount of individual variation both in color and size. After examination of more than 125 specimens I still find it reasonable to recognize the three races that I outlined in a study of more than 20 years ago (Wetmore, Proc. U. S. Nat. Mus., vol. 95, 1944, pp. 35-38). These are *Herpetotheres cachinnans chapmani* Bangs and Penard, which is more grayish brown above, with the edgings of the dorsal feathering of the immature lighter, brighter brown, found from México to northern Honduras and El Salvador; *H. c. cachinnans* (Linnaeus), darker, blacker above, with the edgings in the immature darker, more chestnut brown, that ranges from Honduras to Perú and central Brazil; and *H. c. queribundus* Bangs and Penard, which is lighter, more grayish brown above than *chapmani*, with the edgings in the immature paler and grayer than in either of the other two races. This extends from eastern Bolivia and eastern Brazil south to Chaco and Misiones in northern Argentina.

Size as a distinction between subspecies is not reliable. And the presence of a wash of buff over the white of the head and lower surface that some students have used to separate one supposed race has no value, as this color appears in some specimens in all the groups outlined above. It is found more frequently in wet areas so that the color may be intensified through stain from damp vegetation.

MICRASTUR MIRANDOLLEI (Schlegel): Slaty-backed Forest-Falcon; Halcón Gateador

Astur mirandollei Schlegel, Mus. Pays-Bas, Astures, 1862 (after Sept.), p. 27. (Surinam.)

Micrastur mirandollei extimus Griscom and Greenway, Bull. Mus. Comp. Zoöl., vol. 81, May 1937, p. 418. (Permé, San Blas, Panamá.)

In form the adult suggests the similar stage of the collared forest-falcon, but is smaller, with a shorter tail, dark gray back, and no light band across the hindneck. The immature is marbled with gray and buffy white on the lower surface.

Description.—Length, 400-450 mm. Adult, dark slate gray above, and on the side of the head; tail blacker, with tip and 3 narrow bands, sometimes indistinct, of white or buffy white; below white or buffy, in some lined narrowly with black; under side of wing white or buffy white, barred with dark gray.

Immature, similar, but with breast and foreneck mottled and lined with dark gray. In some heavily marked individuals a dark gray band crosses the breast.

An adult male, from Armila, San Blas, shot on March 7, 1963, had the iris verona brown; bare skin on side of head, cere, and base of the bill forward to a point in front of the nostril yellow; anterior half of bill black; tarsus and toes yellow; claws black.

An immature male, taken at Juan Mina on January 11, 1961, had the iris wood brown; base of maxilla along cutting edge to level of anterior end of nostril neutral gray; rest dark neutral gray, except the lower half forward of the nostril, and the hooked tip, which, with the lower mandible and gape, were bright yellow; line on side of mandibular rami neutral gray; free edge of eyelids bright yellow; rest of bare skin on side of head, including the lores, neutral gray; tarsus and toes bright yellow; claws black.

Measurements.—Males (1 from Costa Rica, 8 from Panamá), wing 218-231 (224), tail 175-199 (188), culmen from cere 20.0-23.0 (21.1), tarsus 75.7-80.5 (78.3) mm.

Females (3 from Panamá), wing 224-229 (227), tail 189-196 (191), culmen from cere 21.3-21.9 (21.5), tarsus 74.5-79.9 (77.0) mm.

Resident. Rare, in the tropical zone in regions of heavy forest. The few records based on specimens are as follows:

Coclé: El Uracillo.
Canal Zone: Caribbean slope along the railroad (McLeannan); Gamboa, Apr. 4, 1962 (Hayward), Juan Mina, Jan. 11, 1961 (Wetmore)
Panamá: Puerto San Antonio, on the lower Río Bayano; Charco del Toro, on the Río Majé.
Darién: Jaqué.
San Blas: Permé, Obaldía.

There is one in the British Museum marked "Panamá" that is said to have been collected by Arcé.

The bird is little known. In my own experience, in which I have come across it on six different occasions, I have found it always on low perches in forest, with one exception only, at La Jagua, when, during a lull in a rainstorm, one rested briefly in an open tree top. Those I have taken, attracted by my bird calls, have dashed in to perch very near at hand. One was so intent on prospective prey that it followed my companion as he moved away to a proper distance for a shot. Those taken had eaten birds except for one which had the crop filled with remains of a green snake. Near Jaqué I saw one carrying a lizard. This locality, in Darién, is the only place where my Panamanian helpers have known the bird. They called it *halcón* (or *gavilán*) *gateador,* and I was told that sometimes it hunted on foot on the forest floor, where, on occasion, it could run more rapidly than a dog. This is verified by the one taken at Armila, San Blas, which was on the ground.

The body, on the open areas between the feather tracts, including the underside of the fleshy part of the wings and the wing membranes, is covered heavily with white down, as is common in many forest-inhabiting hawks. Nothing is recorded of the breeding of this species, except the usual statement of Indians in South America that it nests in tall trees.

The characters ascribed to a supposed race *extimus* from Panamá prove to be those of individual variation.

MICRASTUR SEMITORQUATUS NASO (Lesson): Collared Forest-Falcon; Halcón del Monte Collarejo

Carnifex naso Lesson, Écho du Monde Savant, vol. 6, ser. 2, no. 46, Dec. 15, 1842, col. 1085. (Realejo, Nicaragua.)

A large, long-tailed hunting falcon, inhabitant of dense jungle, with plain (adult) or widely barred (immature) breast.

Description.—Length, 460-560 mm. Adult (sexes alike), upper surface brownish black to black, with a line of the same color on the side of the head, and down the base of the foreneck; upper tail coverts and long tail barred and tipped rather narrowly with white; under surface, cheeks, and a narrow collar across the hindneck, either white or cinnamon-buff, the latter varying from pale to dark; under surface of wings barred with white and dark brownish gray.

Immature, crown, side of head, hindneck, and side of neck blackish brown; rest of upper surface very dark dull brown, with the feathers, including the wing coverts, tipped or barred brokenly with dull buff; tail and upper tail coverts black, barred and tipped with white as in the adult; under surface white, or occasionally buffy, barred broadly with brownish black; under surface of wing as in the adult. In an older stage the upper surface is as in the adult, with the breast and sides white or buff lightly streaked with brownish black.

Dark phase (rare): In the full stage the entire plumage is dark brownish slate, with narrow, sometimes partly indistinct, bars above and below on the posterior half of the body; varying from this to brownish black above and on foreneck and breast, with dark bars predominating on the rest of lower surface. In these unusual melanistic plumages the tail has the usual light bars, but with the white obscured, so that they may appear gray.

An adult male, taken on the Río Pequení, had the iris light wood brown; bare skin around eye, over loral area, and back of cere, dull green; mandibular rami, and base of maxilla below nostril, also dull green, with a spot of dull honey yellow in the center of the base of the rami; bare skin across base of gonys, and in center of chin area, also dull honey yellow; rest of bill black; tarsus and toes bright yellow; claws black.

Measurements (birds from México, Guatemala, Honduras, and Panamá).—Males (7 specimens), wing 251-263 (260), tail 247-275 (261.7); culmen from cere 19.7-23.2 (21.4), tarsus 85.3-97.4 (88.6) mm.

Females (4 specimens), wing 270-279 (274), tail 270-288 (281), culmen from cere 23.6-24.1 (23.8), tarsus 86.5-95.0 (90.1) mm.

Many museum specimens have the sex wrongly marked, so that the differences in size that exist between male and female are obscured.

Resident. Not common, in forested areas of the tropical zone; found less often to 1600 meters in subtropical woodlands in Chiriquí (Quiel, Finca Lérida). Not recorded to date, though probably present, in Coclé, Los Santos, and Colón.

This is a hunting falcon of the forests, where it lives under cover and is little seen. My main observations of it have been when calling to attract small birds, as occasionally a forest-falcon has come swiftly through the undergrowth to alight near at hand. Their savage hunting spirit was illustrated especially by one on the Río Tuira that was carrying a bird and that flew ahead of me several times, until finally I lost it in dense undergrowth. A short time later as I called to attract hummingbirds the hawk came dashing in to perch a few feet distant where a charge of shot soon put it in my hand. I was interested to find the crop crammed with bits of bird flesh to the amount of a good-sized cupful, but still it had come precipitately at the prospect of another kill.

The principal food appears to be lizards and birds. The hawk seems usually to tear off the flesh, as I have found only flesh and internal organs without bones or feathers in the crop and stomach of the dozen or so that I have handled in the field. Once, at La Jagua, in late afternoon, one rested for some time on a stub at the border of forest, my only observation of this falcon in the open. A pair of Wagler's woodpeckers that had a nest hole on the underside of a slanting limb lower down were much excited but took care to remain on perches where, though near, they were safe. Occasionally I have seen one of these hawks in swift pursuit of small parrots or other birds in the forest, or engaged in hunting *faisanas* (chachalacas) through the tree tops in early morning. The latter bird is recognized as a favored quarry throughout the range of the falcon, an indication of its fierce strength, as such prey is as large and heavy as the hawk itself. On one occasion in northern Herrera while stalking *faisanas* that were moving rapidly through the branches I made right and left kills with a double-barreled gun, to find that one bird was a chachalaca and the other a forest-falcon that also was hunting the other species.

Van Rossem (Dickey and van Rossem, Birds El Salvador, 1938, pp. 133-134) describes the voice as a series of loud calls, *hah hah hah*, uttered deliberately, in tone like the laughing falcon but without the change to rapid tempo common with that species. I have heard this in Panamá, but have not actually seen the bird calling.

There appears to be no definite report of their breeding. Indians in Surinam told the Penards that these hawks made large nests of sticks, twigs, and similar materials in trees during the little dry season. On Barro Colorado Island F. W. Loetscher, Jr., recorded two grown young resting in a tree on July 20, 1949.

While there is much individual variation in color in this species, differences that may be correlated with geographic range are slight. Birds from México south through Central America to Darién, recognized as the race *naso,* average blacker above, and in the immature stage usually have the dark barring on the under surface somewhat heavier. The population of Panamá is especially black. This subspecies extends into northwestern Colombia, and according to Hellmayr and Conover, (Cat. Birds Amer., pt. 1, no. 4, 1949, p. 244) ranges south to western Ecuador. Typical *M. semitorquatus semitorquatus* of Vieillot, with type locality in Paraguay, in the adult is more brownish black above, especially on the head. Immature birds are slightly lighter colored above, and usually are less heavily barred below. This race extends from northern Antioquia (Tarazá) and Bolívar (probably also from Córdoba) in northwestern Colombia east through Venezuela, and south to northern Argentina and southern Brazil.

Many persons do not distinguish between the adults of this species and the laughing falcon because of their similarity in color and in color pattern.

MICRASTUR RUFICOLLIS INTERSTES Bangs: Barred Forest-falcon; Halcón del Monte Rayado

Micrastur interstes Bangs, Auk, vol. 24, no. 3, July 1907, p. 289. (La Estrella, Cartago, Costa Rica).

A small forest-falcon with rounded wings and long tail, dark gray above and narrowly barred black and white below; immature a miniature of the collared forest-falcon.

Description.—Length 320-350 mm. Adult, grayish black above; tail black, with 2 or 3 narrow bars and tip white; wings like back, or in some brownish black; chin white; side of head and foreneck dark gray; rest of under surface and under wing coverts barred narrowly with grayish black and white; under surface of flight feathers dark gray, banded narrowly and irregularly with white.

Immature, brownish black above, with head, hindneck, and tail, blacker, the latter with 5 narrow bars and tip white; a narrow white collar around base of hindneck; underneath white or buffy white, with a narrow line of grayish black or gray down the sides of the base of the neck, a band that in some is united across the center; rest of under surface barred sparsely and irregularly with grayish black; wing coverts white or buffy white; under surface of flight feathers as in adult.

An adult female taken, on February 28, 1964, at 1,350 meters on Cerro Tacarcuna, Darién, had the iris dull orange; bare skin on side of head and the gape bright yellow; cere dull greenish brown clouded with fuscous; maxilla black except cutting edge back of nostril, which is bright yellow changing to dull neutral gray on the projecting tooth; tip of mandible dull neutral gray; rest dull yellow; tarsus and toes bright yellow; claws black.

Measurements.—Males (8 from Panamá), wing 158-167 (165), tail 142-159 (151), culmen from cere 13.7-15.6 (13.9), tarsus 58.1-64.8 (61.9) mm.

Females (6 from Panamá), wing 170-175 (172), tail 147-164 (155), culmen from cere 14.1-16.3 (15.6), tarsus 61.0-65.3 (63.1) mm.

Resident. Locally fairly common, in tropical and lower subtropical zone forests, to 1,350 meters in the mountains; not recorded from the eastern side of the Azuero Peninsula.

This interesting member of its genus is fairly common in forested areas, mainly along the Pacific slope, though its presence is detected usually through its calls, as the bird is shy and is seldom seen. It ranges to some extent in the lowlands but is more frequent in hill country, probably because it is in such areas that suitable forest cover still remains. I have found it especially over the lower mountains in Chiriquí to 1,500 meters, and there are similar records for it in Veraguas at Calobre and Calovévora (Salvin and Godman, Biol. Centr.-Amer., vol. 3, 1901, p. 111). Formerly, when the lowlands in these provinces were heavily forested, it ranged lower, as there is one record for Divalá (Bangs, Auk. 1901, p. 358), but suitable cover in those areas has long been gone. I have recorded it on Cerro Campana and have found it regularly from the Cerro Azul to Darién. Formerly it ranged through the Chagres Valley on the Caribbean slope, where it was taken by McLeannan at Lion Hill a hundred years ago and by Jewel at Agua Clara and Gatun in 1911 and 1912. It was found on Barro Colorado Island in the period of Chapman's studies but does not appear to have been recorded there since. The only other report for it on the Caribbean side is of two taken by Wedel near the Colombian boundary at Permé.

These hawks frequent low perches in the undergrowth, where they remain concealed and usually slip away unseen at any approach. As stated above, their presence is known mainly through their call, a querulous, single note, sometimes a low *keh-h-h* and at others a louder *keow*, repeated at short intervals, most commonly in early morning at sunrise or soon after. I have found it useless to attempt to stalk them as they fly so noiselessly and low that they may not be seen. When I have been calling small birds one of these falcons has come frequently to perch near at hand, though they remain shy and fly into cover at any sudden movement. It appears that they hunt to some extent on the forest floor as occasionally I have seen them fly up from such situations. Immature birds are seen sometimes on open perches where they afford a clear view. In such circumstances their color and color pattern invariably suggest the much larger collared forest-falcon.

They appear to feed mainly on small birds and to some degree on lizards. Worth (Auk, 1939, p. 310) saw one take a nestling blue-black grosbeak from the nest. Jewel (Stone, Proc. Acad. Nat. Sci. Philadelphia, 1918, pp. 248-249) found remains of slugs, batrachians, and small lizards in the stomach of one taken near Gatun.

The variations in this species from the gray-backed populations of the north to the brown birds of the south are highly interesting. With considerable more material than was available to Hellmayr and Conover (Cat. Birds Amer., pt. 1, no. 4, 1949, pp. 249-252) it appears to me to be appropriate to recognize two races in the area from México to northern Colombia. While there is some variation, adult birds from southern México to Nicaragua have the dark barring spaced more widely on the posterior lower surface, so that they appear whiter, and also usually have more or less of a cinnamon wash on the foreneck and upper breast. These are *Micrastur ruficollis guerilla* Cassin. Adults from Costa Rica and Panamá through western Colombia to western Ecuador, the race *interstes,* have the black barring underneath more evenly spaced throughout, average darker above, and in only an occasional individual is there a cinnamon wash on the foreneck.

A few individuals throughout the entire northern area of the range, that includes both these races, display a faint brownish tinge on the head and back, a hint of the fully brown coloration in these areas that prevails through the main part of the South American range.

FAMILY FALCONIDAE

CARACARA PLANCUS (Miller): Caracara; Carancho

Falco Plancus J. F. Miller, Var. Subj. Nat. Hist., pt. 3, 1777, pl. 17. (Tierra del Fuego.)

A long-legged, strong-bodied hawk, with black crest and red bare side of head, that in flight appears dark underneath, with prominent white patches on throat, base of tail, and near the tips of the wings.

Description.—Length, 490 to 520 mm. Adult, crown, with slightly elongated crest, black; a dull white band across upper hind neck that merges below on upper back with an area of fuscous-black barred with white; wings, lower back, rump, breast, upper abdomen, tibia, sides, under wing coverts, and end of tail brownish black to black; a prominent white patch, somewhat broken by grayish brown bars and edgings, across the middle of the flight feathers; foreneck white; upper breast buffy white, barred and spotted with brownish black; lower abdomen and under and upper tail coverts white; basal three-fourths of tail white, with many narrow grayish brown bars.

Immature, lower foreneck, and upper breast buff, lined with buffy brown; breast and upper abdomen dark brown, streaked indistinctly with buffy white; upper back brown tipped and streaked with dull white, with narrow shaft lines of fuscous brown.

Iris dull orange; cere and bare skin on side of head dull red; line of culmen, cutting edge, distal third of maxilla, and tip of mandible dull white; base of both mandibles bluish gray; tarsus and toes yellow; claws black.

The *carancho* is a forceful bird, alert, with direct, strong flight performed with steadily beating wings. It is both a scavenger and a predator, seen often in pairs, frequently alone, always using care to avoid too close human approach, whether at rest on some tree that gives it outlook, walking on open ground, or in flight toward some distant point.

Dead fish in a drying pool, an injured bird unable to escape, the bodies of lizards and rats killed by autos along a highway, small chickens and ducks that stray too far afield, turtles, rabbits, other small mammals, all are food to this aberrant falcon. It also comes to larger carrion and about slaughterhouses for waste, but usually it is wary. Farmers are inclined to shoot the carancho on sight, particularly where sheep are herded, as the birds are relentless in their attacks on newborn lambs.

The bulky open nest, made of sticks, weed stems, dried rushes, and like materials, is placed in a tree in some secluded area. The two or three eggs have the white ground color nearly or wholly concealed by a wash of warm brown, mingled with blotches, irregular spots, and lines of chestnut and darker shades of brown. There is much variation in marking, and occasionally eggs are merely lightly spotted, or, rarely, nearly plain. At first view of a series the variation is so great as to give the impression that several species must be represented. Bent (U. S. Nat. Mus. Bull. 170, 1938, p. 130) gives the average size as 59.4×46.5 mm. (taken principally from eggs collected in Texas and Florida).

The rattling, clattering call of these birds, almost mechanical in its sound, is heard mainly in the nesting season.

Near Pacora, *caranchos* are called *guaraguo,* a name that applies properly to the red-tailed hawk.

Caracaras are found from Baja California, southern Arizona, New Mexico, Texas, Florida, and Cuba, south throughout the Americas to Tierra del Fuego and the Falkland Islands. South to northern Brazil the back and rump are plain blackish brown to black, and the upper tail coverts also are plain or lightly barred at the side. From south of the Amazon River southward the back, rump, and upper tail coverts are barred with grayish white. The difference described is definite but is one of degree, and the birds throughout agree in form, habits, and voice. Though the two styles have long been regarded as separate species, the present-day tendency to unite them as one is here accepted. The two intergrade in Brazil in the area immediately south of the Amazon River.

Two subspecies, slightly different in depth of color, are found in Panamá.

The generic name *Caracara* used here follows acceptance of this name in the last edition of the A.O.U. Check-list of North American Birds (1957, p. 116). *Polyborus* proposed in 1816 by Vieillot (Anal. Nouv. Orn. Élém., p. 22) with "Caracara, Buff.," which is *Falco brasiliensis* Gmelin, as its only species and therefore its type, was long the accepted genus for the caracaras. Buffon's name "Caracara" is based on a bird described by Marcgrave in his História Natural do Brasil published in 1648, with an illustration in the stilted form common in works on natural history of that period. In a study of the original paintings from which the figure was reproduced Adolf Schneider (Journ. Orn., 1938, pp. 93-94, fig. 3) found that the Caracara of Marcgrave actually is the harrier known currently as *Circus buffoni* (Gmelin). The generic name *Polyborus,* 1816, thus becomes a synonym of *Circus* Lacépède, 1799. The next available name for the group formerly called *Polyborus* is *Caracara* Merrem (in

Ersch u. Gruber, Allg. Encycl. Wiss. Künste, vol. 15, 1826, p. 159). Amadon (Auk, 1954, pp. 203-204) has cited a personal communication from Stresemann who "would prefer to declare the drawing as unidentifiable" in order to avoid this change. But examination of the figure reproduced by Schneider shows definitely that it is a harrier. While the drawing, like most of its day, is crude, the evident ruff on the side of the small head clearly indicates a harrier, and the barring on the under tail coverts is characteristic of *Circus buffoni*. This species ranges widely in northern and eastern South America from Colombia, Venezuela, and Trinidad to central Chile, Argentina, and much of Brazil. Specimens are recorded from Pará and from Espiritu Santo to the north and south of the area where Marcgrave traveled, a point that Stresemann seems to have overlooked in his comment that no harrier had been recorded from the region concerned. There seems to be no reason to reject the identification.

CARACARA PLANCUS AUDUBONII (Cassin)

Polyborus Audubonii Cassin, Proc. Acad. Nat. Sci. Philadelphia, vol. 17, no. 1, Jan.-Mar. (Aug. 7) 1865, p. 2. (Florida.)

Characters.—Dark markings browner; back, wings, breast, sides, and tibia, brown to dark fuscous.

Measurements.—Males (4 from México and western Panamá), wing 355-403 (388), tail 201-233 (216), culmen from cere 31.5-32.6 (32.1), tarsus 86.4-94.1 (91.0) mm.

Females (6 from México and western Panamá), wing 374-401 (387), tail 201-228 (215), culmen from cere 31.0-33.3 (32.3), tarsus 88.2-95.6 (91.4) mm.

Resident. Pacific slope, in the tropical lowlands, from western Chiriquí (Alanje, Bugaba) east to near the western boundary of the Canal Zone; Isla Taboga.

In the range outlined caracaras appear to be most common on the drier, eastern side of the Azuero Peninsula, where they range to the southern end near Punta Mala. The record for Taboga, of one seen on a high grass-grown ridge, may have been a straggler from the mainland.

CARACARA PLANCUS CHERIWAY (Jacquin)

Falco cheriway Jacquin, Beytr. Gesch. Vögel, 1784, p. 17, pl. 4. (Aruba, Netherlands Antilles).

Characters.—Dark markings blacker; back, wings, breast, sides, and tibia fuscous-black to black.

Measurements.—Males (5 from Panamá and Colombia), wing 352-385 (366), tail 170-205 (191), culmen from cere 29.8-31.7 (30.5), tarsus 87.5-92.8 (90.2) mm.

Females (4 from Colombia and Venezuela) wing 355-388 (376), tail 180-210 (198), culmen from cere 30.1-33.7 (31.8), tarsus 88.3-95.5 (91.2) mm.

Resident. On the Pacific slope, in the tropical lowlands, from Tocumen east to Chimán and the Río Majé; Archipiélago de las Perlas (Isla Pacheca).

While "Darién" is usually cited as a northern locality in the range of this race, I have no record in Panamá to the east and south of the mouth of the Río Majé, though it is probable that these birds range to the Golfo de San Miguel. I have not found caracaras above the gulf along the Río Tuira, nor did I encounter them along the coast to the south at Jaqué. The only record for the Pearl Islands is of 2 taken on Pacheca by W. W. Brown, Jr., on April 14, 1904.

This race of the *carancho* is common in the savanna country east of Panama City, particularly between Pacora and Chepo where they may be recorded during most days afield. The nesting period begins toward the close of the dry season, as the birds pair at the beginning of March.

Near the mouth of the Río Chico I saw one make passes at a cormorant resting on a mud bar, until finally the latter scrambled into the water. At La Jagua turtles lay their eggs in holes dug in the slopes above the marsh. Caracaras search out these nests, scrape them open with their feet, break the eggs and eat the contents. The wrinkled, parchment-like shells beside the hole where they were laid are a common sight.

MILVAGO CHIMACHIMA CORDATUS Bangs and Penard: Yellow-headed Caracara; Chimango

Milvago chimachima cordata Bangs and Penard, Bull. Mus. Comp. Zoöl., vol. 62, Apr. 1918, p. 35. (Isla del Rey, Archipiélago de las Perlas, Panamá.)

A small hawk with buffy-white head and undersurface (streaked below in the immature) and barred tail, found in open country, regularly about cattle. In flight the markings of the underside of the wing often show as a light bar.

Description.—Length, 400 to 430 mm. Adult, head, hindneck, and undersurface, including the under wing coverts, warm buff to buffy white; slender filaments fringing eyelids, and a narrow streak on the side of the head behind the eye, brownish black, wings and back fuscous-black, the back, scapulars, and inner wing coverts margined indistinctly with grayish white; lower rump mixed buffy white and fuscous-black, with a few irregular spots of the latter color on the central feathers of the buffy upper tail coverts; tail barred with buff and brownish gray to black, the dark bands equal in width to the pale ones, with a broad subterminal band of fuscous-black, and a narrow tip of white; under surface of wing buffy white, barred narrowly, and tipped broadly with brownish black.

Immature, with head, neck all around, breast, and sides streaked with fuscous; under wing coverts barred with the same color; tip of tail banded like the central portion.

Measurements.—Males (8 from Panamá), wing 265-287 (278), tail 177-201 (188), culmen from cere 21.5-23.5 (22.6), tarsus 50.4-54.2 (51.8) mm.

Females (4 from Panamá), wing 272-288 (282), tail 183-198 (189), culmen from cere 21.7-24.1 (22.7, average of 3), tarsus 51.0-52.2 (51.3) mm.

Resident. Fairly common in the tropical lowlands of the Pacific slope, from western Chiriquí (Alanje) east to the lower Río Bayano (El Llano), including the Azuero Peninsula, and the Archipiélago de las Perlas (reported from Pacheca, Saboga, Rey, Cañas, Víveros, La Vivienda, Pedro González, Trapiche, and San José islands); ranging upward to 600 meters in western Chiriquí (Buena Vista above Concepción).

These are birds of savanna lands bordered by trees and open scrub, that are not found in the more humid Caribbean lowlands or in Darién. As the forests are cleared they spread to some degree through country formerly not suited to them. In January 1961 I saw one at Gatuncillo on the Río Chagres between Juan Mina and the dam. They are found constantly feeding on the ground around cattle and often fly up to perch on the backs of grazing or resting beasts, where ordinarily their great companions pay no attention to them. On occasion I have seen one fluffing and arranging its feathers as it sat on the hip bone of a cow at rest on the ground. At La Jagua one early morning one alighted on the back of a resting bull where it moved along to its head in search of ticks, particularly around its ears. Later other bulls were less complaisant, for when two birds came they switched their tails and moved their heads to drive the hawks away.

The flight is direct but not swift, divided between flapping and sailing, and seems rather weak for a bird of this family. They are scavengers to some degree, and in addition eat such small animal prey as is available—large insects, small birds (including young), lizards, and small mammals. Though they are not regularly aggressive I saw one stoop at a groove-billed ani which hid on the ground at the base of a low stub, on which the hawk perched to look for its prey. Immediately it was attacked so fiercely by a fork-tailed flycatcher that the hawk ducked and turned about repeatedly in such confusion that the ani escaped unnoticed. Country people complain that caracaras take young chickens. I have noticed them lingering about more powerful hawks that were carrying prey or feeding, and have seen them eating bits of flesh that I have discarded in the preparation of specimens. In the Pearl Islands it is common to see them along the beaches, half running, half flying in pursuit of the abundant crabs. Their notes are harsh, including some high pitched, and some that are squalling sounds.

The nest, of good size, built of sticks is placed in trees. Two eggs constitute the usual set. Col. L. R. Wolfe (Ool. Rec., vol. 18, 1938, p. 37) describes eggs of the typical race from Brazil and Paraguay as varying "from deep red, red smeared with dark mahogany, and brown to light yellowish-brown." Schönwetter (Handb. Ool., pt. 3, 1961, p. 186) gives the measurements of 5 eggs of the race *cordatus* as $41.2\text{-}46.0 \times 33.3\text{-}38.2$ mm.

In the Pearl Islands these birds are known as the *aguirre*, in the southern Azuero Peninsula they were called *guaracho*, and in Coclé province I heard them called *gavilán garrapatero*.

This northern race of the species, found from Panamá through Colombia and Venezuela to northern Brazil, differs in the adult from *Milvago chimachima chimachima* (Vieillot) of the region south of the Amazon River in the marking of the tail in which the dark bars are definitely wider and heavier, with the white marks equal to the dark ones or narrower. In *M. c. cordatus* the dark tail bars are appreciably narrower. Also, *cordatus* averages slightly darker buff on the head and underparts, a character, however, that is not completely definitive since this color may fade as the feathering becomes worn. The immature *cordatus* has the markings on the lower surface browner.

DAPTRIUS AMERICANUS AMERICANUS (Boddaert): Red-throated Caracara; Cacao

FIGURE 48

Falco americanus Boddaert, Table Planch. Enl., 1783, p. 25. (Cayenne.)

Easily identified by the bare bright red or orange-red skin on the throat and side of the head and the black-and-white plumage.

Description.—Length 490 to 560 mm. Adult (sexes alike), throat, upper foreneck, and side of head, around and directly behind the eye, bare except for scattered, slender, filamentous feathers, which are arranged in a line from the bill down the center of the upper neck, are scattered over the lores, and across the lower eyelid, and form a stronger fringe along the free border of the upper eyelid; lower border of breast, abdomen, flanks, tibia, and under tail coverts

Fig. 48.—Red-throated caracara, cacao, *Daptrius americanus americanus*.

white; auricular region, and side of upper neck behind it, with the feathers white basally, producing faint light lines (absent in some specimens); elsewhere black, and a faint sheen of dull green.

Immature birds are said to lack the light lines on the sides of the head, but this is not certain.

A male, taken at El Uracillo, Coclé, February 28, 1952, had the iris deep red; bill honey yellow; cere, gape, and base of mandible dark neutral gray, extending forward irregularly into the brighter color of the tip; bare skin of throat and side of head deep red; an area of marguerite yellow on lower eyelid, concealed when the eye is open; tarsus and toes coral red; claws black.

Another male, from Armila, San Blas, March 2, 1963, had the iris reddish orange; cere, gape, and mandibular rami light blue; rest of bill bright yellow; bare skin of throat and side of head orange-red; tarsus and toes bright reddish orange; claws black.

A female from the mouth of the Río Tuquesa, Darién, March 22, 1959, otherwise similar, had the tarsus and toes orange red.

Measurements.—Males (10 from Panamá), wing 340-355 (346), tail 229-248 (239), culmen from cere 24.0-26.7 (25.6, average of 8), tarsus 52.0-57.5 (54.1) mm.

Females (7 from Panamá), wing 331-362 (344), tail 227-258 (243), culmen from cere 22.9-27.9 (25.5, average of 6), tarsus 53.4-60.0 (56.2) mm.

Resident. Locally fairly common in forested areas in the tropical zone. Found to 600 meters on Cerro Pirre, at 1000 meters and more rarely to 1500 meters on Cerro Malí, the highest elevations on the isthmus at which it has been reported. Not recorded from the Pacific slope in Coclé, Herrera, or Los Santos.

A first acquaintance with this interesting forest species of the falcon family is certain to come through its loud, raucous calls of *cao ca cao, ca ca cao, kee yow-w-w*, with other variations. The birds frequently range in groups of half a dozen but are found in pairs toward the end of the dry season. At a distance their cawing, croaking calls in their harsh, explosive tones sometimes suggest the notes of macaws, but near at hand they are like nothing else heard in the forest. Only in amount of noise produced do they suggest those of the laughing falcon, whose calls have a certain musical intonation entirely lacking in the present species. At times when a pair of red-throated caracaras has lingered in the trees near my forest camps their harsh, continued racket has passed the amusing stage to become a bit annoying.

These birds range through the tree crown, flying rather heavily with quickly flapping wings, which then are set to sail for short distances when they have sufficient momentum. In places remote from settlement, where ammunition is too valuable to use except to kill game, the *cacao* is often tame and so curious that it may fly down within a few meters to watch any human intruder, always with a steady repetition of its calls. The bird is one that is widely known through its noisy habits, and its notes are the base of several names.

The common one of *cacao* in imitation of its calls is usual from Costa Rica south through northern South America. Another appellation from the same source is *deslenguado,* often abbreviated to *'lenguado,* explained as given because of resemblance to the uncouth sounds made by persons who have lost their tongues, a name that may date back to the early period when this was a punishment for certain crimes. Another term, heard in Bocas del Toro, is *hablador,* whose derivation is readily understood. The Cuna Indians at Armila called it *pai kä kä,* apparently in imitation of its uncouth calls. The *cacao* also is one of the birds of ill omen called *pájaro brujo*—wizard or sorcerer bird—which superstition says, may bring misfortune if killed.

The food of the *cacao* is mainly the larvae of wasps and bees, and apparently includes also quantities of the adults of the abundant little black stingless bees, obtained by tearing open the nests of these species. Some of my specimens have had the crop and stomach crammed with these insects, and often when I have handled them when freshly killed I have noted the sweetish odor common to many kinds in these groups of Hymenoptera. That they are also fruit eaters is indicated by one that had the stomach filled with seeds and other remains of small drupes.

The breeding habits are unknown. The badly worn wing and tail tips on some of the specimens I have examined may be indication that they place their eggs in holes, though related species in southern South America build nests. One female that I collected on the Río Chucunaque in Darién, on March 21 held an egg nearly ready for the shell.

Daptrius americanus as a species ranges from Chiapas in southern México south through Central America and South America to Bolivia and southern Brazil. Two races have been recognized that currently have been treated as meeting in central Panamá. The only distinction is in size, the more northern group being larger. The specimens that I have been able to examine indicate that while two forms may be accepted the ranges assigned need adjustment northward. There is no appreciable difference in size between male and female, and so the two sexes may be considered together. Birds from Guatemala and Costa Rica (11 specimens) with the wing from 360 to 375 mm. are *Daptrius americanus guatemalensis* (Swann), a form that ranges from the Pacific slope in Chiapas and Guatemala to southern Costa Rica, where there is intergradation with typical *americanus.* The link between the two is not a continuing cline, as some have supposed, since from Panamá southward the wing of *Daptrius ameri-*

canus americanus, while smaller, varies from 325 to 360 mm. regardless of location in the vast region that it inhabits. Occasional individuals in this population range slightly larger to 363 mm. though these larger specimens are uncommon.

FALCO PEREGRINUS ANATUM Bonaparte: Peregrine Falcon; Halcón Peregrino

Falco Anatum Bonaparte, Geogr. and Comp. List, 1838, p. 4. (Egg Harbor, New Jersey.)

A large hawk (largest of the falcons found in Panamá), with long pointed wings; a broad black stripe on the side of the head below and behind the eye.

Description.—Length, male 390 to 430 mm., female 440 to 500 mm. Adult, head, including cheeks, and hindneck black, the crown washed with gray; back, wing coverts, and secondaries, light gray, with faint, irregular crossbars of darker gray and fuscous, and shaft lines of black; primaries black, washed lightly with gray, with a white line around tip; under surface white to buffy white, with throat, foreneck, and upper breast immaculate, or with a few dark lines; elsewhere, including tibia and under wing, barred narrowly with fuscous-black; under side of primaries barred with dark gray and white.

Immature, brownish black above, with the feathers edged very narowly with brownish white; tail with indistinct broken crossbars of dull buffy white; primaries black; side of head and throat white, with a bold band of black on the cheeks; underneath white to buff, streaked heavily with dull brown to fuscous-black; under wing buffy white, with irregular blotches and cross bars of fuscous; under surface of primaries dark gray, with narrow bands of dull buffy white.

The tarsus is short and the foot large, the middle toe being as long as the tarsus.

Measurements (from Friedmann, U.S. Nat. Mus. Bull. 50, pt. 11, 1950, p. 652).—Males, wing 301-327 (314.2), tail 138-154 (145.1), culmen from cere 18-21 (19.6), tarsus 46-54 (50.6) mm.

Females, wing 340-376 (356.3), tail 167-192 (178.9), culmen from cere 20-25 (23.4), tarsus 50-57 (54.4) mm.

Migrant and winter visitor from the north. Fairly common; mainly in the lowlands; Isla Coiba; Isla Taboga; Archipiélago de las Perlas (San José, Contadora).

Peregrines arrive in October (Oct. 14 earliest date), and remain through April, occasionally later (May 3, Changuinola; May 5, Barro Colorado Island).

Single birds are seen regularly during the periods of migration, moving southward in October and November, and toward the north in March and April. A fair number remain through the months of northern winter, when they may be found frequently around the Bay of Panamá. Their migrations appear to follow the main line of movement of other hawks, viz., along the Carribbean coast to the Canal Zone, and the Pacific littoral from there southward. On March 1, 1950, at Chimán I recorded 4 in a great migration flight of thousands of turkey vultures and Swainson's hawks. While it is certain that the halcón peregrino visits all the political divisions, it has not been formally reported from the San Blas, or from Chiriquí, undoubtedly owing to the absence of interested observers in coastal areas at the proper seasons.

The duck hawk universally is one of the most spirited hunters of its family, feeding on birds, mainly of aquatic species that it captures at rest or in flight with ease. Often they stoop at birds in play, and rarely may become excited enough to kill when they are not hungry. On Isla Coiba I saw one drop on a laughing gull, cripple it, and then leave it. At La Jagua on one occasion a large female swung past the head of one of my helpers as he waded a muddy lagoon to retrieve an ibis, coming so close as to make him throw up an arm; but each time the falcon turned without actually striking him, to stoop at a blue-winged teal or at one of the numerous jaçanas nearby. Obviously it was intent on my specimen, so finally I decoyed it by imitating its cackle and waving a red handkerchief, and added it to my bag for the day. On another day at the mouth of the Rio Chico a duck hawk carried off a willet that I had shot before we could get to it. On other occasions I have seen two heckling a pair of black crab hawks, and others swooping at soaring turkey vultures which swerved and turned to avoid them.

FALCO DEIROLEUCUS Temminck: Orange-breasted Falcon; Halcón Pechicastaño

Falco deiroleucus Temminck, Nouv. Rec. Planch. Col., livr. 59, June 25, 1825, pl. 348. (Ilha de São Francisco, Santa Catharina, Brazil.)

Color and color pattern that of the bat falcon, but bird larger, more robust.

Description.—Length, 300-350 mm. Adults, entire upper surface and side of head dull black, with back, wing coverts, rump, and upper tail coverts margined with dark gray; tail with tip and narrow cross bands white; foreneck white, bordered on either side by an irregular line of cinnamon; upper breast, abdomen, tibia, and under tail coverts cinnamon-brown; middle and lower breast and sides black, barred with white and buff; under wing coverts black with irregular spots of white and buff; under surface of wing dark gray, barred with white.

Immature, similar, but upper surface with narrow edgings of buffy brown, except that secondaries and scapulars are tipped with white; foreneck buffy white; breast, tibia, and under tail coverts barred heavily with buff; under wing coverts heavily spotted with buff.

Measurements.—Males (3 from México, Costa Rica, and Perú), wing 244-249 (247), tail 115-130 (120.4), culmen from cere 18.1-19.2 (18.6), tarsus 39.6-41.2 (40.2) mm.

Females (3 from Brazil, Perú, and Paraguay) wing 265-284 (277.6), tail 133.5-145.7 (138.3), culmen from cere 21.6-23.0 (22.2), tarsus 44.6-47.8 (46.2) mm.

Resident. In the tropical zone, very rare.

The present specimen records for Panamá known to me are of a male, now in the British Museum, collected at Bugaba, Chiriquí, in 1869 by Enrique Arcé; and another skin labeled Chiriquí in the Rothschild Collection.

Little known. The species has been reported at scattered points from Veracruz south through Central and South America to Paraguay and northern Argentina.

Griscom's inclusion of Veraguas in his check-list (Bull Mus. Comp. Zool., vol. 78, 1935, p. 302) apparently was based on sight records that he made during his travels through that area. In an earlier account on the birds of Guatemala (Bull. Amer. Mus. Nat. Hist., vol. 64, 1932, p. 164) under this species he wrote that in "western Panama the bird nests in church towers and belfries in the hearts of towns and cities." Later he informed Eugene Eisenmann that his observations were made in Santiago and Las Palmas. The records seem so unusual that they require confirmation, especially since the bat falcon, so similar in markings, is the species found frequently in the plazas of such towns.

On March 29, 1957, along the highway 18 kilometers west of Penonomé, as I drove slowly one of these falcons crossed close in front of my jeep and swung into the shelter of a grove along a small stream. When it swerved from side to side I had a clear view of the back, and saw the under surface less plainly. My impression was of a beautifully marked and graceful bird, similar to a bat falcon but of larger size.

The close superficial resemblances of this species to the bat falcon have led to some uncertainties as to its classification. The proportions of the foot, where the middle toe with its claw is definitely longer than the tarsus, place it near the duck hawk. The form of the tail also agrees with that of *Falco peregrinus* as the central feathers are very slightly longer than the outer ones so that the form is slightly tapered when folded. However, the supposition that *deiroleucus* is merely a tropical form of *Falco peregrinus* is not to be accepted.

Coltart (Ool. Rec., vol. 26, 1951, p. 43) has described two nests, one with 2 eggs and one with 3, from Trinidad, "collected by G. D. Smooker on 21st April, 1930, and 28th March 1937. One nest was 30 feet up in a knot hole in a ceiba tree, whilst the other was in the hollow at the base of a palm branch about 40 feet up. The eggs have a whitish or yellowish ground, more or less obscured by smears and blotches of browny-red and dark-red with a few darker superimposed blotches." They measure 43.0 × 35.0; 42.2 × 34.7, and 40.5 × 34.5; 41.7 × 35.3; 39.7 × 34.5 mm.

FALCO RUFIGULARIS PETOENSIS Chubb: Bat Falcon; Halcón Cazamurciélagos

FIGURE 49

Falco rufigularis petoensis Chubb, Bull. Brit. Orn. Club, vol. 39, Nov. 30, 1918, p. 22. (Peto, Yucatán.)

A small, heavy-bodied falcon that in life appears black, with white or buff throat, cinnamon abdomen and tibia, (some with a cinnamon band on upper chest); breast and sides barred narrowly with white and buffy white.

Description.—Length, 230 to 270 mm. Adult (sexes alike), head, including cheeks, and hindneck black; back, wing coverts, tertials, rump, and upper tail coverts black basally, tipped and washed with dark gray; primaries and secondaries black, the inner primaries and secondaries in fresh plumage edged narrowly at the tip with white; tail black, tipped narrowly with white; throat and foreneck white or buff, often cinnamon-buff at sides and across chest; breast and sides black, barred narrowly with white to cinnamon-buff; abdomen, tibia, and under tail coverts dark cinnamon; under wing coverts black, spotted and barred with white and buff; undersurface of primaries, secondaries, and tail barred very narrowly with white.

Immature, like adult but blacker above, and with under tail coverts barred broadly with cinnamon-buff.

Iris dark brown; cere greenish yellow; bare orbital region brighter yellow; base of mandible neutral gray; rest of bill black; tarsus and toes yellow; claws black.

FIG. 49.—Bat falcon, halcón cazamurciélagos, *Falco rufigularis petoensis*.

Measurements.—Males (9 from Panamá), wing 180-191 (185.2), tail 86.8-96.2 (90.4), culmen from cere 10.8-12.1 (11.5), tarsus 31.6-33.8 (32.7), middle toe with claw 35.5-37.8 (36.4) mm.

Females (4 from Panamá), wing 209-221 (214.7), tail 97.8-106.5 (103.0), culmen from cere 13.8-14.6 (14.2), tarsus 34.6-39.0 (37.0), middle toe with claw 38.4-42.0 (40.8) mm.

Resident. Locally fairly common, throughout the Tropical Zone. Recorded in Chiriquí in the uplands to Boquete and the Cordillera de Tolé, and in Veraguas near Santa Fé, but found mainly below 800 meters elevation; Isla Coiba; Isla Taboga; Isla San José.

This handsome falcon is the species of its genus most frequently seen on the isthmus, as, in addition to its usual resting places on stubs projecting above the forest canopy, it comes regularly to the dead trees that stand in pastures and other clearings.

Rarely I have seen one soaring in favorable thermals in company with turkey vultures. In Soná, in May and June 1953, I recorded one or two daily, toward sunset, when they came to hawk over the plaza for flying beetles and other large insects, and a little later as darkness approached to capture some of the numerous bats. They are so amazingly quick in the air that few are the flying creatures that may elude them. On the coast of Darién I saw them pursuing dragonflies and verified the capture of these insects when I found one in the stomach of a falcon that I had shot. Cicadas also are taken. On Barro Colorado Island Chapman (My Tropical Air Castle, 1929, pp. 240-241) recorded them feeding on moths. The small birds around them, myriad in number, are a principal item in their food, particularly when they are feeding young. William Beebe (Zool., vol. 35, 1950, pp. 69-86) has published a graphic account of observations made at Rancho Grande in the coast range of northern Venezuela of a pair that he watched for over five months, while they mated and reared two young. As the birds lived within a hundred meters of his laboratory windows he was able to identify many items of their food. These included 33 mammals of 5 species, 163 birds of 56 species, 19 insects of 14 species, a lizard, a snake, and a frog. Most of the insects were butterflies, among them a morpho and a swallowtail. The mammals, aside from one mouse, were bats. The hunting skills of these swift-flying falcons are illustrated well in the kinds of birds taken, which in addition to wood warblers, tanagers, and finches included 17 swallows of 5 kinds, 34 hummingbirds, ranging from tiny emerald hummers to large hermits, and 26 swifts of 8 species. This last amazing item included 3 collared swifts, large, heavybodied birds, capable of great speed in flight, with wings nearly as long as those of the falcon which captured them. The male falcon regularly brought food for his mate and later for her to feed to the young. Birds usually were prepared for eating by careful plucking, with feathers discarded, except casually for some of the more firmly attached wing quills.

I have noted that bat falcons protest disturbance of their nesting areas frequently with cackling notes *ke ke ke ke,* which suggest those of the duck hawk in tone. And males harass passing large birds, especially the larger hawks, darting at them angrily.

The bat falcon nests in hollows in trees, where the eggs are placed on whatever material has been deposited by chance—usually decayed wood fragments, perhaps with a few wind drifted leaves or twigs. At Barro Colorado Island on March 23, 1955, a falcon of this species of good size that I supposed was a female rested beside a hole near the top of a tall stub that stood in the water 50 meters from shore. I assumed it to be a nest cavity, for the bird turned to peer into it at intervals, and she spread wings and tail in threat when a pair of red-fronted parrots circled to alight. A Wagler's woodpecker, marooned in a hollow branch 10 meters above, protested his immolation from time to time but did not dare move except to thrust out his head to call for a few seconds. A nest, with two small young, found by J. P. E. Morrison on Isla San José on May 12, 1944, was in a hollow 12 meters from the ground. The nest described by Beebe was at an elevation of approximately 15 meters, perhaps a little more. The eggs in a set of 3 in the U.S. National Museum, collected near Victoria, Tamaulipas, México, on April 11, 1908, by F. B. Armstrong, are short-subelliptical, with a pinkish white ground color almost completely covered by a blotchy wash of clay color that changes in some areas around the larger end to deeper brown. They measure 39.0×31.3, 40.3×32, and 40.8×32.1 mm. They were taken from a hole in a tree about 10 meters from the ground.

A juvenile only a few days old, from the nest on Isla San José, is completely covered with white down except for the loral area and the space around the eyes. Beebe describes the three in the nest that he had under study as creamy white when about a week old.

Disagreement as to the recognition of a northern subspecies of the bat falcon has resulted from misunderstanding of variation due to age. Immature individuals are blacker than full adults, the difference in the two age groups being most pronounced in the area from northern Colombia north through Central America. When adult specimens are compared it is found that birds from this northern region are lighter, grayer above, in particular on the head than those from Venezuela and northern Brazil. The northern population may be separated from typical *F. r. rufigularis* as the race *petoensis*. The nominate race is found from the base of the eastern Andes of Colombia east through Venezuela to Trinidad, and south to northern Bolivia, and northern Brazil.

FALCO FEMORALIS FEMORALIS Temminck: Aplomado Falcon; Halcón Azulado

Falco femoralis Temminck, Planch. Col., livr. 21, April 1822, pl. 121. (Brazil)

Of medium size, with light throat and upper breast; a heavy black patch on lower breast and sides, in some partly divided by pale markings at center.

Description.—Length, 315 to 360 mm. Adult (sexes alike), upper surface very dark gray, in some with faint shaft lines of black, with a light wash of brown; rump, and upper tail coverts paler, barred with white; primaries black, edged lightly with white; secondaries tipped prominently with white; tail black, barred and tipped narrowly with white; forehead, a narrow broken line over the eye, that broadens behind and joins with the companion line of the opposite side as a narrow band across the hindneck, white or buff; a broad band through eye to side of neck, and moustachial stripe black; cheeks, throat, foreneck, and upper breast white or pale cinnamon-buff; sides and lower breast black, barred narrowly with white; abdomen, tibia, and upper tail coverts cinnamon, with this color mingled with the black in the central line of the lower breast; under wing coverts buff to pale cinnamon, streaked and barred with black; under surface of remiges dark neutral gray, barred broadly with white.

Occasional birds have the lighter markings cinnamon throughout.

Immature, blacker above, with a wash and edgings of brown; rump, and upper tail coverts like back; upper breast streaked heavily with black.

Iris brown; cere and bare space around eyes yellow; base of mandible and sides of maxilla yellowish; rest of bill slate, becoming black at the tip, and along the culmen; tarsus and toes yellow; claws black.

Measurements (specimens from Colombia, Venezuela, and northern Brazil).—Males (12 specimens), wing 226-240 (233), tail 142-159 (149), culmen from cere 14.0-15.9 (15.0), tarsus 40.6-43.2 (41.9) mm.

Females (15 specimens), wing 245-273 (258), tail 155-186 (167), culmen from cere 16.9-18.9 (17.9), tarsus 41.3-48.8 (45.2) mm.

Resident. Rare, in the lowland savannas: Recorded from Coclé (near Aguadulce), Veraguas, Herrera (París, Potuga), and the Canal Zone (Barro Colorado Island).

This is a falcon little known in Panamá that lives in savanna country bordered by groves. It was first recorded for the Republic by Griscom (Amer. Mus. Nov. no. 280, 1927, p. 1) from one taken by Benson near Aguadulce. Hellmayr and Conover (Cat. Birds Amer. pt. 1, no. 4, 1949, p. 316) in a table of measurements list a male and a female from Veraguas, without indication of specific locality. (Their statement in the range should read western, instead of eastern, Panamá.) In Herrera on March 2, 1948, I saw three in an open pasture near Potuga, two of them in mating play. One stooped gracefully at a plumbeous kite. Two days later I recorded another near París. On March 10, 1957, I saw a falcon along the beach dunes near Pedasí, Los Santos, that I believed to be this species, but I was not wholly certain of the identification. On February 19, 1954, I watched one that circled over the shore of Barro Colorado Island, at Salud Point.

The typical form of this species is found in open savanna or semi-arid plains regions from Panamá, Colombia, Venezuela, and Trinidad south through eastern South America to Tierra del Fuego. A northern form *Falco femoralis septentrionalis,* distinguished by lighter-gray upper surface, with the breast solid black, and somewhat larger size, breeds from southern Arizona, southwestern New Mexico, and southern Texas south through México and ranges casually to Guatemala. While there is little definite information on the nesting of the bird of Panamá, that of the northern subspecies just mentioned is known. According to Bent (U. S. Nat. Mus. Bull. 170, 1938, pp. 96-97) the nest is a platform of twigs lined with grass, placed in a low tree. Some pairs in southern Arizona are said to have used old nests of the white-necked raven, which are of similar form to those made by the falcons. The eggs, usually 3, are oval, "white, creamy white, or pinkish white. This is usually nearly, or quite, covered with small spots or minute dots of russet, cinnamon-rufous, or other bright browns." Some are less heavily marked, so that they show the ground color. The average is 44.5×34.5 mm.

Aplomado falcons are bird hunters, doves and quail being common food. They also take lizards and mice.

FALCO COLUMBARIUS Linnaeus: Pigeon Hawk; Halcón de Paso

Size that of the bat falcon; streaked underneath and on head; upper surface gray in adult, brownish gray to sooty gray in immature.

Description.—Length, 275 in male, to 340 mm. in female. Male, gray above, streaked with dull black on crown and hindneck, with heavy shaft streaks of black on wing coverts, back, and upper tail coverts; wings black, with secondaries and inner primaries tipped lightly with white; tail black, barred widely with light gray, and tipped with white; undersurface white to buffy white, with sides of head, breast, sides, abdomen, tibia, and under tail coverts streaked heavily with black to brownish black; under wing coverts white to buffy white, streaked and spotted with dull black; undersurface of primaries and secondaries dark neutral gray, barred broadly with white.

Female, similar to male but much browner above, except on the rump and upper tail coverts; light markings on under side of wings more buffy; under parts washed with buff.

Immature, similar to the female but browner above, with feathers of back edged with rusty.

While these falcons, American representatives of the Old World merlin, spread widely in migration from their nesting grounds, which extend from the limit of tree growth in the far north south to the more northern United States, comparatively few reach the Isthmus and northern South America. They are true falcons that feed mainly on birds, regularly killing doves that are their equal in size.

The few records for Panamá are divided between two subspecies that differ in color, but are similar in size.

FALCO COLUMBARIUS COLUMBARIUS Linnaeus

Falco columbarius Linnaeus, Syst. Nat., ed. 10, vol. 1, 1758, p. 90. (South Carolina.)

Characters.—Darker above.

Measurements.—Males (10 specimens), wing 182-194 (187.6), tail 114-125 (121.1), culmen from cere 12-13 (12.6), tarsus 36-41 (37.7) mm.

Females (10 specimens), wing 206-215 (209.7), tail 130-140 (135.8), culmen from cere 13.5-15.0 (14.2), tarsus 38-42 (40.2) mm.

Winter visitor from the north. Rare; recorded from Chiriquí, Veraguas, the Canal Zone, and eastern San Blas; Isla San José.

The specimens listed by Salvin and Godman (Biol. Centr.-Amer., vol. 3, 1901, p. 120) from Chiriquí, and Calobre, Veraguas, taken by Arcé, and from Lion Hill, Canal Zone, collected by McLeannan, now in the British Museum, I have identified as the typical subspecies in accordance with treatment by Griscom (Bull. Mus. Comp. Zool., vol. 78, 1935, p. 303). H. von Wedel sent a female to Herbert Brandt, taken at Puerto Obaldía, San Blas, November 3, 1931. This bird is now in the U. S. National Museum.

On February 9, 1944, in forest on Isla San José a pigeon hawk struck a pale-vented pigeon in flight and knocked it down almost at my feet. At the same instant it saw me and rose to perch on a branch where I shot it. The pigeon, actually larger in body than the falcon, lay bleeding under one wing, with most of its tail feathers torn out while I retrieved the hawk, and then, as I returned, recovered sufficiently to fly away. The falcon is an adult female of the eastern subspecies, marked by its darker color.

I recorded a pigeon hawk on the Río Escotá, near Santa María, Herrera, on March 8, 1948, and one at Panamá Viejo, Panamá, February 2, 1952. The records are listed here, though the subspecies is uncertain.

FALCO COLUMBARIUS BENDIREI Swann

Falco columbarius bendirei Swann, Bull. Brit. Orn. Club, vol. 42, no. 265, Feb. 2, 1922, p. 66. (Fort Walla Walla, Washington.)

Characters.—Lighter, grayer above.

Measurements.—Males (10 specimens), wing 186-198 (192.6), tail 124-129 (125.2), culmen from cere 12-13 (12.1), tarsus 36.5-40.0 (39.1) mm.

Females (10 specimens), wing 206-215 (210.2), tail 135-142 (139.6), culmen from cere 14-15 (14.2), tarsus 39-42 (40.7) mm.

Winter visitor from the north. Rare.

The three records for this western subspecies are as follows: A female came at sunset on April 15, 1946, to rest in the top of a tall tree standing beside our quarters near the air strip at Jaqué, Darién. We had been occupied through the day in packing in readiness for a plane to call for us early the following morning so that guns and ammunition were not available. As Perrygo and I watched the bird with longing eyes, and the wish that we had it, Tom Watson, Air Force sergeant, an expert marksman, brought it down with his service rifle from a distance of 90 meters. I expected to retrieve broken bits of skin and feathers, but instead I found that with careful aim he had creased the falcon across the back of the neck and the head so that it was only slightly marked. Two additional specimens in the Brandt Collection at the University of Cincinnati were taken by H. von Wedel—a female at Bocas del Toro, September 29, 1938, and another (from its size, probably a male) secured at Puerto Obaldía, San Blas, October 16, 1934.

This western form, the breeding race from Alaska across to northern Saskatchewan, and south to Oregon and Idaho, has been reported previously in migration only to southern México. It is slightly paler in color in adult and immature than the eastern race, with the paler markings in the female and immature more buff. The specimen from Jaqué is a female of the previous season. It is probable that the race equals the typical one in its southward limits, as there is another in the U. S. National Museum taken by M. A. Carriker, Jr., on the high páramo of the Sierra Nevada de Santa Marta in northern Colombia.

FALCO SPARVERIUS SPARVERIUS Linnaeus: Sparrow Hawk; Cernícalo

Falco sparverius Linnaeus, Syst. Nat., ed. 10, vol. 1, 1758, p. 90. (South Carolina.)

A small falcon, reddish brown on back and tail, with a spot of the same color on the center of the crown.

Description.—Length, 245 to 270 mm. Male, top of head and hindneck dark gray, with a patch of chestnut brown in the center of the crown; back, rump, and tail cinnamon-brown, the back barred with black; primaries and secondaries black, the latter tipped with gray; wing coverts gray spotted with black, very heavily at the bend of the wing; tail cinnamon brown, with a broad subterminal band and a few lateral spots of black; outer web of outer rectrix, and terminal half white, barred broadly with black; tip of tail white or buffy white; side of head white, with a black vertical band below the eye, and another over the auricular region; breast and sides cinnamon to buffy white, spotted more or less with black; throat, abdomen, and under tail coverts white to buffy white; under wing coverts white, spotted with black; under surface of flight feathers dull gray barred boldly with white.

Female, similar, but with wing coverts cinnamon-brown like the back; entire upper surface from the upper back to the end of the tail barred heavily with black; breast and sides streaked broadly with buffy brown to brownish gray.

Measurements.—Males (10 specimens), wing 178-187 (182.2), tail 120-130 (125.8), culmen from cere 12.0-12.5 (12.1), tarsus 38-40 (38.5) mm.

Females, wing 187-195 (191.9), tail 125-136 (131.4), culmen from cere 12-13 (12.7), tarsus 37-40 (38.5) mm.

Winter visitor throughout the isthmus. Locally fairly common. Arrives about the middle of October (Oct. 11, 1936, above Boquete; Oct. 14, 1953, Pacora; Oct. 16, 1929, Permé), and remains until the latter part of March or early April (Apr. 8, 1949, Chepo; Apr. 1, 1954, Aguadulce; Mar. 30, 1955, Chico); Isla Coiba; Isla San José.

As the sparrow hawk ranges in open country it is most common in the savannas of the Pacific slope from southern Chiriquí to Chepo, including the eastern side of the Azuero Peninsula. Although heavily forested areas do not afford it suitable habitat, its annual travels soon bring it to any extensive clearings, and so it may be found in any part of the Republic. In 1952 I saw none in the recently made farms along the Río Indio in western Colón, from its mouth to the foothills in the Caribbean corner of northern Coclé. But in the older plantation areas in Bocas del Toro, between Almirante and the Costa Rican border, the bird has been common during the period of northern winter for many years. As it is a species adapted to northern climates its zonal range is broad, particularly on the more open Pacific side of the mountains. In Chiriquí I have found sparrow hawks from the coastal area near San Félix and Las Lajas to near 2,000 meters elevation above Cerro Punta; in other words, from the tropical to the temperate zones. Occasionally I have recorded one in park areas in Panama City, Balboa, and Ancon.

The birds are solitary and select what commanding perches may be available on dead trees, shrubs, or failing such higher points, on boulders, or termite hills, as stations from which to watch for food. Telephone poles along the highways and fence posts in cultivated lands are favored stations.

Their food is largely the grasshoppers (Acrididae) common in their haunts, varied with small lizards, and an occasional mouse, rarely a bird. Though they stoop frequently at flying swallows or at other small species at rest in open tree tops, and also at larger hawks this is in play. They often hover with rapidly moving wings a few meters above the earth in their watch for food.

The call, heard rather seldom from these migrants, is a rapidly uttered *killy killy killy*.

In March when the annual burnings—the candelas—clear pastures and areas where the trees have been felled for cultivation sparrow hawks become much stained from feeding over the blackened ground. I recall in particular one that I stalked for half an hour in careful approach on the supposition that it was some strange, dark-plumaged species with which I was not familiar.

While the sparrow hawk is not known to winter farther south than eastern Panamá the number that reach this distant section is larger than has been understood, since in March as they start the return northward there is definite increase in the number found on the eastern savannas near Pacora and La Jagua. Once, on March 20, 1949, while night-hunting in a jeep in this area I flushed a sparrow hawk from a sleeping place on the ground on the open plain. It is probable that some cross into Colombia in northern Chocó, as the birds have been found in some numbers at Permé and Obaldía in the Comarca de San Blas near the boundary.

Order GALLIFORMES

Family CRACIDAE, Curassows and Guans; Pavones y Faisanas

These are birds of the warmer climatic areas of the Western Hemisphere, found mainly in the tropical zone, but there are a few kinds of limited distribution that are adapted to life in colder subtropical and even temperate zone areas. All have a fowl-like form, with heavy body, small head, long neck, and rounded wings, and in most the tail is elongated. While they live in part on the ground, they are mainly arboreal, with a foot adapted for perching, since the somewhat elongated hind toe is on the level of the three in front. The nearly 50 species now recognized are divided among 11 genera, of which 4, each with a single species, are found in Panamá. All are held in high regard as food and game birds.

One member of the genus *Ortalis* ranges north to southern Texas, while to the south several are found as far as the northern provinces of Argentina. Fossil species of Tertiary age are known from the north-central United States in Nebraska and South Dakota and also from Florida. The greatest variety among living species is found in northern South America.

KEY TO THE SPECIES OF CRACIDAE

1. A prominent crest, in which the ends of the feathers curl forward; size large..............Central American curassow, *Crax rubra*, p. 293
   Crest short, with feathers straight; size smaller..................... 2
2. Breast prominently streaked with white.
   Crested guan, *Penelope purpurascens*, p. 298
   Breast without prominent streaks................................. 3
3. Color, including wings, mainly black.
   Black guan, *Chamaepetes unicolor*, p. 303
   Color brown and gray; primaries chestnut.
   Gray-headed chachalaca, *Ortalis cinereiceps*, p. 305

CRAX RUBRA RUBRA Linnaeus: Central American Curassow; Pavón

FIGURE 50

Crax rubra Linnaeus, Syst. Nat., ed. 10, vol. 1, 1758, p. 157. (Western Ecuador.)

Size of a turkey, with heavy body, and long narrow crest in which the feathers are recurved at the tip; male, body black; female body cinnamon-brown.

Description.—Length, male 870 to 920 mm; female 780 to 840 mm. Male, black, with a very faint greenish sheen, except on abdomen, flanks, and under tail coverts, which are white; tail in some tipped narrowly with white, in others plain.

Female, brown phase, feathers of head, including the crest, throat, and neck (front and back), white in center, tipped with black; back, wings, rump, and upper tail coverts deep cinnamon, the wings barred narrowly and indefinitely with black; tail with alternate bars

FIG. 50.—Head of male Central American curassow, pavón, *Crax rubra rubra*.

of buff and black, mixed with cinnamon-brown, tipped with buff; upper breast deep cinnamon-brown; lower breast cinnamon; abdomen, flanks, and under tail coverts cinnamon-buff; under surface of wing cinnamon-brown barred narrowly with black.

Female, dark phase, lower neck, above and below, and upper back black to brownish black; tail black, or black mottled with deep cinnamon; inner primaries and secondaries like tail, but barred narrowly with white or buff.

Male, iris dark brown; bare areas on side of head dull black; lower eyelid dull yellow; cere, tubercle, and base of maxilla light yellow; base of mandible dull yellow; rest of bill neutral gray, shading to black at tip; tarsus and toes neutral gray; claws brownish white.

Female, like male, except the cere, which is dark neutral gray; and the bill, which is neutral gray at base, shading to black at outer end.

Measurements.—Males (6 from Panamá), wing 360-411 (377), tail 309-340 (326), culmen from cere 27.2-33.4 (30.9), tarsus 121.2-131.8 (124.7) mm.

Females (7 from Panamá), wing 333-370 (354), tail 304-338 (322), culmen from cere 24.8-30.8 (28.2), tarsus 107.1-121 (114.6) mm.

Resident, in the tropical and lower subtropical zones, in regions of heavy forest; found only in unsettled sections. As of 1960, distributed in the more remote areas of the Caribbean slope from Costa Rica to Colombia. On the Pacific slope in southeastern Veraguas, south of Soná; in the forests of the western side and interior hills of the Azuero Peninsula; and locally from the Cerro Azul through Darién to the Colombian boundary; recorded to 1,900 meters on Volcán Barú, Chiriquí; and to 1,450 meters in the mountains of Darién (Cerro Malí, Cerro Tacarcuna).

The great *pavón* is one of the prized game birds of the Panamanian forests, formerly widely distributed, but a species that soon disappears as settlement increases and its haunts become accessible. It remains now only in remote areas.

In the western part of the republic the species is distributed through the lowland forests of the Caribbean slope, though it has disappeared in the cultivated regions. Hasso von Wedel sent a female to the Museum of Comparative Zoology taken near Almirante on February 16, 1929 (Peters, Bull. Mus. Comp. Zool., vol. 71, 1931, p. 297), but in 1958 I heard of it only in distant inland sections in that region. To the eastward, in 1952, there were still a few along the Río Indio in Colón and northern Coclé from Chilar inland to the Río Uracillo, but here they ranged only at a distance from the scattered fincas.

Salvin and Godman (Biol. Centr.-Amer., vol. 3, 1902, p. 273) write that the curassow was noticed by Mr. Champion "on the Pacific slope of the Volcan de Chiriqui, but specimens were not preserved," a report that is indefinite at best. The female collected by W. W. Brown, Jr. (Bangs, Proc. New England Zoöl. Club, vol. 3,

1902, p. 21), on April 20, 1901, labeled "Boquete, 5000 feet," probably was taken on the Caribbean slope to the north and at a lower elevation. In Chiriquí a few range the slopes of Volcán Barú back of El Volcán.

Karl Curtis told me that years ago he shot them in the wooded country then found in western Veraguas between the Río Virá and the Río Tabasará. In June 1953 I recorded a few near the Río San Pablo at Guarumal and La Isleta in southern Veraguas. Aldrich (Scient. Publ. Cleveland Mus., vol. 7, 1937, pp. 51-53) shot a pair at about 600 meters elevation on Cerro Viejo, on the western side of the Azuero Peninsula, but saw no others. These are the only records for Veraguas, and are the only definite reports of the bird for the Pacific slope west of the Canal Zone.

Farther east the curassow in early days was widespread, and in uninhabited regions it still is fairly common. A hundred and more years ago McLeannan sent specimens taken near the railroad on the Atlantic side to the Smithsonian and to Salvin. The last recorded in the Canal Zone area were on Barro Colorado Island in 1926. Chapman (Life in an Air Castle, 1938, p. 224) wrote of them regretfully "rare; I have seen only a feather." In eastern Colón Goldman collected one on Cerro Bruja back of Portobelo, June 6, 1911.

In the Comarca de San Blas (as of 1957) curassows ranged from Mandinga eastward. And during my work near Chepo in 1949 they were still present in the lower forests near the Río Mamoní and on Cerro Carbunco. In 1950 they were fairly common along the Río Chimán and were common in the great forests of the southern slopes of the Serranía de Majé. Through Darién they have disappeared near the settlements, and where Indians live along the rivers, but persist in wilder lands where there are no inhabitants. Festa in 1895 (Salvadori and Festa, Boll. Mus. Zool. Anat. Comp. Univ. Torino, vol. 14, no. 339, 1899, pp. 9-10; and 1909, p. 22) found them near the Río Lara and the Río Cianatí, above the Gulf of San Miguel, but Barbour in 1922 (Bangs and Barbour, Bull. Mus. Comp. Zool., vol. 65, 1922, p. 195) noted them as very rare in the Sambú region. He prepared one specimen at Jesucito. In 1959 they were still common on the middle Tuira and near the Chucunaque, and I saw them in 1961 on the slopes of Cerro Pirre. In 1963 they were common inland from Armila in the eastern San Blas. Obviously the species is one that is steadily on the road to disappearance.

Usually curassows range in pairs that, following the nesting season, may be accompanied by grown young for a brief period. While they are tree inhabitants that range into the high leaf crown, they descend to the ground to feed, and, at the borders of streams, to drink. Males call regularly, a curious sound, subdued in tone, but with fair carrying power, that may be imitated by the syllable *oom-m-m-m,* uttered with closed lips, and prolonged. The note is ventriloquial, therefore difficult of orientation, in particular to know whether the bird is on the forest floor or in trees. If on the ground it often moves ahead under cover of the undergrowth until it may slip aside and hide. I have also heard a low, excited *quit quit* from them, apparently the note of the female. When startled they rise heavily but rapidly so that they are killed only by a quick shot. In taking off from high trees they gain swift speed immediately, alternately flapping and then sailing with set wings. Though they may not fly far, usually they hide so that they are not seen again.

The nesting season in eastern Panamá must come in the rainy season, as in February and March near Chimán, and in the area to the eastward, I noted numerous immature birds that were fully grown. And from February to April the males were calling regularly. Little is known in detail of their nesting except that they build a flimsy structure of sticks, lined with green leaves, in trees 6 to 30 meters from the ground, in which 2 eggs are laid. Two single eggs are in U. S. National Museum, collected by José Zeledón in Costa Rica, one at Pirrís, April 10, 1883, and one near San José in 1887. Both are subelliptical and creamy-white, with roughened, pitted shells. They measure 91.0 × 72.4 and 90.6 × 64.5 mm. A third collected by Charles Sheldon on April 22, 1904, in northern Veracruz, 75 miles south of Tampico, measures 95.2 × 64.7 mm., and is similar to the others. A notation on the label with this specimen indicates a "spoiled egg left in nest." The structure is not described. In the Museum of Comparative Zoology there are two, presented by Karl Curtis, laid in confinement in the Canal Zone, that measure 88.7 × 64 and 95.3 × 62.6 mm.

When the eggs hatch, the down-covered chicks are said to tumble out of the nest to the ground and to grow under the care of both parents. The wings develop rapidly, and when still quite small the young birds fly readily to escape danger. Curassows feed on drupes borne by trees and shrubs, often descending to pick up those that have fallen to the ground. Females sometimes are called *pava rubia* from their color.

A male and a female taken back of Armila on March 13, 1963, each weighed 3.8 kilograms (8½ lbs). It is widespread belief that while the flesh is excellent the bones must not be given to dogs, as they may cause the animals to go mad. Apparently this notion has come down from early contact with Indians, since Wafer (Isthmus Amer., 1699, p. 116) writes that the "Indians either throw the Bones of the *Corrosou* into the River, or make a Hole and bury them, to Keep them from their Dogs, being thought unwholesome for the Dogs to eat; and the Indians say they will make the Dogs run mad."

The Cuna Indians at Armila called this species *sihgi* (pronounced with the g hard).

Crax rubra rubra ranges from northern México south through Central America to the Atrato Basin, the Baudó Mountains of northwestern Colombia, and western Ecuador. A subspecies, *C. r. griscomi*, distinguished by smaller size, with the wing in the male 325 to 355 and in the female 320 to 330 mm., is restricted to Isla Cozumel off the coast of Quintana Roo.

PENELOPE PURPURASCENS AEQUATORIALIS Salvadori and Festa: Crested Guan; Pava Cimba

FIGURE 51

Penelope aequatorialis Salvadori and Festa, Boll. Mus. Zool. Anat. Comp. Torino, vol. 15, no. 368, Feb. 19, 1900, p. 38. (Río Peripá, western Ecuador.)

Form slender, pheasantlike, with long, thin neck, bare reddish-colored throat, small bushy crest, and long tail; size of a small hen turkey.

Description.—Length, 720-800 mm. Adult (sexes alike), crown, sides of head, and hindneck dark clove brown, with a slight bronzy sheen; upper back, wings, and outer tail feathers blackish brown, with a distinct sheen of dark green; middle of back to upper tail coverts dark russet; lower foreneck, breast, and sides like back, but feathers edged broadly with black; abdomen, flanks, tibia, and under tail coverts dull chestnut; under wing coverts like back.

Immature, like adult, but with wing and tail feathers washed with rufous-brown, and mottled with blackish brown.

A young chick in the Museum of Zoology at the University of Michigan, found on Barro Colorado Island by J. Van Tyne on April 19, 1926, with wings large enough to permit flight, and developing tail, but otherwise in down, is colored as follows: Forehead, line over eye, crop region, foreneck, rump, and area of lesser wing coverts sayal brown; line on either side of crown, extending down either side of hindneck, pale olive-gray; rest of crown black; hindneck blackish brown; upper back basally pale neutral gray, tipped lightly with sayal brown; greater wing coverts mouse brown, tipped with black, with sayal brown down filaments still adhering to the tips; wing quills chaetura drab; throat whitish, with the feathers tipped indistinctly with pale neutral gray, producing a faintly mottled appearance; breast and abdomen dull white; sides, flanks, and tibia dull sayal brown, with the down mottled somewhat with neutral gray at the base; tail feathers chaetura drab, tipped with sayal brown, barred indistinctly with black.

FIG. 51.—Crested guan, pava cimba, *Penelope purpurascens aequatorialis.*

Adult, iris dark red; cere, bare skin of side of head, and chin slaty black; bare throat somewhat dull light red; bill black; front of tarsus, and top of toes dull dark red; back of tarsus, and claws black.

Measurements.—Males (5 from Panamá), wing 350-368 (356), tail 320-365 (344), culmen from cere 33.5-35.5 (34.8), tarsus 87.0-91.0 (89.0) mm.

Females (5 from Panamá), wing 333-349 (342), tail 330-348 (341), culmen from cere 32.0-36.5 (33.9), tarsus 84.0-90.8 (85.7) mm.

Resident in forested areas in the tropical and lower subtropical zones; absent only from the open savannas of the Pacific slope, and from the lowlands of the eastern side of the Azuero Peninsula. Fairly common where hunting pressure is not too great. Though sought for food and for sport, for reasons not clear this species often remains in suitable country after the larger curassow has disappeared.

The only positive records for Chiriquí are of specimens collected by W. W. Brown, Jr., one taken at Divalá, December 8, 1900 (Bangs, Auk, 1901, p. 356), and 5 from "Boquete and Caribbean slope 4000 to 7000 feet" in April and June 1901 (Bangs, Proc. New England Zoöl. Club, vol. 3, 1902, p. 21). Those listed from the Caribbean slope are to be allocated to Bocas del Toro, leaving some uncertainty as to actual occurrence in the Boquete area. The birds must have been rare in this western sector, as the species was not included in the Mönniche collection from the Boquete region. It may be noted also that Arcé secured no specimens in his work in Veraguas and Chiriquí, though Karl Curtis informs me that about 1912 he found these birds plentiful in the area where Puerto Armuelles now is located. On the Pacific slope of Veraguas I found a few in 1953 in lowland forests along the Río San Pablo at Congal and Guarumal near Soná, and Aldrich (Scient. Publ. Cleveland Mus., vol. 7, 1937, p. 53), in 1932, recorded them as not uncommon away from plantations on the western side of the Golfo de Montijo. Handley found them abundant in 1962 on Cerro Hoya to an elevation of 1,000 meters. None are known from the eastern lowlands of the Azuero Peninsula or from the region through the Pacific slope of Coclé and the western sector of the Province of Panamá. Karl Curtis informs me that in his early years he found them on Ancon Hill, back of the Gorgas Hospital, and that they were common also years ago in timbered areas above the Río La Jagua. In my work since 1946 along the Cerro Azul and from there eastward through Darién I have found them common in wilder areas, except that I did not record them anywhere on the lower Río Jaqué. It is probable that hunting by the Chocó Indians and other residents along that stream has killed them. They are common in the mountains of Darién to 1000 meters elevation, and in lesser numbers range to 1450 meters (Cerro Malí, Cerro Tacarcuna).

In the Caribbean forests these birds are found throughout the Republic from the Costa Rican boundary to Colombia in sections where they have been free from overhunting. From Bocas del Toro, there are specimens in the Museum of Comparative Zoology from the Boquete Trail and from Guabo. A female in the U. S. National

Museum was taken on the Río Changena. McLeannan collected them a hundred years ago along the railroad near Lion Hill, but since his day the only reports for the Canal Zone come from Barro Colorado Island where a few remain. While the crested guan ranges in forested level lands, it is most frequent in hill country where it ascends regularly to 1,000 meters, though more common lower down.

They are more active than the bigger curassows and are less timid. Their food in large part is such forest drupes as wild figs and mangabé berries, which they seek in the high trees and for which also they descend to the ground when there are many fallen, dropped from their own feeding, and from that of parrots, toucans, and other birds. Guans range regularly at times on the forest floor, often making considerable scratchings to uncover food.

They are seen in pairs, or, where common, as many as 6 or 8 may be found together. When disturbed on the ground they mount immediately into the trees, flying with noisy wings, and then run actively along the larger branches, taking flight again through and over the tree crown. In the air they move with neck outstretched, alternately sailing with wings stiffly spread, and flapping quickly after a short distance to maintain momentum. It is common in such movements to see them sail off from some high point to cross a wooded valley, and in regions where the trees are tall birds moving through the tree crown often fly across clearings 75 meters or more above the ground. When not frightened they walk gracefully along the inclined branches, but at an alarm they may freeze motionless among the leaves, standing erect, or crouched on a branch with neck extended, when it is most difficult to make them out in spite of their size and their long bodies. In the more open gallery forests when wind is not blowing I have found it profitable at such times to watch the leaf shadows on the ground as it possible to detect slight head movements of hidden birds that otherwise would remain unnoted. In our field work we often use whistles that produce a variety of sounds, some shrill and penetrating, others gabbling or moaning to attract such species as forest hawks and high-canopy hummingbirds. The *pava cimba* finds these sounds disturbing, and frequently betrays its presence by calling in reply. Occasionally, particularly with shrill eagle calls, they may become much excited, when I have had them run out on open limbs, or even descend to the ground to strut about with spread wings within a few meters of my feet.

Their usual note is a yelping call that is repeated excitedly, often for several minutes. Another louder sound with a strange resonant quality may be heard especially toward sunset from birds resting on open perches high above the ground. An approaching storm, with the mutter of thunder, may excite them to this response. Where two or three join they produce a ringing jungle melody most pleasing to the ear.

Their meat has been frequent camp fare in remote areas, particularly when supplies were low. It is rather dark, and tough unless cooked for some time, and is best when broiled, or cut up and cooked again with rice. Fully grown, these birds are heavy-bodied and of good flavor.

In spite of their extensive range little is known of their breeding. In mating males display among open branches where they fly slowly, but with rapidly beating wings that produce a loud rattling, drumming sound. They are said to build platforms of sticks in trees well above the ground as is usual among their relatives. The only egg that I have seen is one from the closely related northern race, taken by E. W. Nelson and E. A. Goldman from the oviduct of a female shot on Cerro Tancítaro, Michoacán, on March 2, 1903. This is fully formed and has the dull white to faintly creamy white color and the roughened, finely pitted shell common in species of its family. It is between subelliptical and oval and measures 77.0×56.0 mm. Leopold (Wildlife of Mexico, 1959, p. 208), in his account of this northern subspecies, gives Helmuth Wagner as authority for the statement that 2 eggs constitute the normal set and that "these are dull white and measure approximately 75 by 51 mm." Schönwetter (Handb. Ool., pt. 4, 1961, p. 204) gives the measurements of 3 eggs of the race *aequatorialis* as $70\text{-}72 \times 48.3\text{-}50$ mm. The nesting season of the race found in Panamá seems to be similar to that of the *pavón*, as I have taken nearly grown immature birds in February and March.

The present subspecies, marked by chestnut-brown rump, upper and under tail coverts, and lower abdomen, ranges from Nicaragua and Costa Rica through Panamá and western Colombia to western Ecuador. An allied race, *P. p. brunnescens*, which is more brownish on the back and wings, with a less greenish sheen on the crown and upper back, is found from the Santa Marta region in Colombia to the Maracaibo Basin in Venezuela. In the typical race, *Penelope p. purpurascens*, distributed from southern México to Honduras, the rump, upper and under tail coverts, and lower abdomen are dull dark brown, much darker and blacker than in the subspecies found in Panamá.

CHAMAEPETES UNICOLOR Salvin: Black Guan; Pava Negra

FIGURE 52

Chamaepetes unicolor Salvin, Proc. Zool. Soc. London, June 1867, p. 159. (Calovévora, Veraguas, Panamá.)

Breast and abdomen brownish black; elsewhere black.

Description.—Length 620 to 690 mm. Adult (sexes alike), three outermost primaries narrowed at the tip, the third from the outside less so than the outer two; breast, abdomen, and sides fuscous-black, with the feathers edged faintly with olive; elsewhere black with a sheen of greenish olive.

Immature, outermost primary falcate at tip, second and third from outside narrowed and slightly sinuate at tip; otherwise like adult.

Male, iris red to reddish brown; bill black, with a black ring surrounding the nostril; a dark neutral gray line along the center of the cere from the base of the horny maxilla to the feathers; cere elsewhere light blue, shading into dark violet-blue on the bare lores and side of the face, including the basal half of the mandibular ramus; bare area around eye dusky neutral gray; tarsus and toes light brick red; claws black.

Female, like male.

Measurements.—Males (3 from Chiriquí), wing 276-303 (292.3), tail 244-277 (263.6), culmen from cere 18.5-19.6 (19.0), tarsus 70.7-74.5 (73.0) mm.

Females (5 from Chiriquí), wing 275-294 (284), tail 250-260 (254), culmen from cere 18.0-19.0 (18.4), tarsus 70.9-73.7 (71.8) mm.

Resident. Uncommon, in the subtropical and upper tropical zones of the mountains of Chiriquí and Bocas del Toro, ranging from 1,500 to 2,500 meters, except on the Boquete Trail in Bocas del Toro where it is reported down to 450 meters.

This interesting species was found first by Arcé at Calovévora, on the Caribbean slope of Veraguas beyond Santa Fé, and later in eastern Chiriquí in the Cordillera de Tolé. Brown collected males above Boquete in March 1901, and in 1926 Kennard secured several in Bocas del Toro on the trail leading to Boquete from Chiriquicito. Later it was found to be fairly common on slopes above Boquete, where Mrs. Davidson secured males on January 27, 1933, at Quiel, and on Horqueta on February 12, 1934. The Mönniche collection included a series taken at Bajo Mono, Lérida, and on the Río Caldera, and several collected in this same region by Rex Benson in 1931 are now in the U. S. National Museum.

The *pava negra* in the main is a bird of the higher mountains, but it ranges in lesser numbers in the upper tropical zone forests. I have seen it in life only on the slopes of Cerro Picacho, where it still remains in small numbers. Above Cerro Punta in March 1955 I noted feathers where one had been killed by hunters.

While heavy bodied the birds move and fly easily through the trees much in the manner of the *faisana* (*Ortalis cinereiceps*). In February I noted them in pairs, some of them accompanied by

FIG. 52.—Right wing of the black guan, pava negra, *Chamaepetes unicolor*, with incised tips of outer primaries.

grown young. In my limited observation they have been always in trees, never on the ground. The call of the male is a single note that suggests that of the *pavón* but without the resonant tone usual in the latter bird. They are reported to be one of the best of their family for the table, and therefore are sought by hunters.

The trachea in both male and female is straight and enters the thoracic cavity without convolutions. The tube in the male is slightly wider than in the female. Nothing is known of the nest and eggs.

This species is found only in the mountains of Costa Rica and of western Panamá.

ORTALIS CINEREICEPS (Gray): Gray-headed Chachalaca; Faisana

Pheasantlike with long neck, small head, and long tail; head gray; primary feathers chestnut.

Description.—Length 480 to 580 mm. Adults (sexes alike), head and upper neck gray; lower hindneck, wing coverts, back, rump, and upper tail coverts grayish brown; tail grayish to greenish brown, tipped with dull white or buffy white; primaries cinnamon; secondaries like back, but with inner webs cinnamon; lower foreneck and upper breast grayish brown; lower breast, sides, and flanks grayer; center of abdomen white to grayish white; under tail coverts grayish brown; under wing coverts cinnamon to grayish brown.

The *faisana* is the only species in its family that is able to adapt to the changed conditions brought by human settlement, since it is not dependent on primitive forest cover for habitat as are its relatives. It is found throughout the tropical lowlands of the Isthmus wherever there are groves or tracts of *rastrojo* that offer cover. When these are cleared the birds retreat but spread again wherever thickets begin to cover abandoned fields. In heavy forest the *faisana* ranges along the more open borders of streams, or over the high tree crown, as it seeks the sun rather than the deep shadows favored by many forest species. They are interesting birds, graceful in movement as they walk along sloping branches, and equally attractive when resting quietly, either standing, or with the legs bent so that the body rests on some perch grasped firmly in the feet. They feed on small fruits borne on the higher tree branches, and also range constantly on the ground, where their presence may be indicated by scratchings that often are as extensive as those made by domestic fowls.

Faisanas are most active in early morning and late afternoon. Toward the middle of the day they walk or fly back into some cover where people do not regularly penetrate, and to which they return quickly at any disturbance. The flight, with neck outstretched and tail partly open, begins with quickly beating wings to gain momentum, then a sail, the two methods alternating until they are safe behind tree cover. On the ground they run rapidly with head erect and partly spread tail.

On the Pacific side they are found regularly in tracts of low, dense *monte* where the trees may not be more than 6 to 10 meters tall. Elsewhere, in better watered sections, with tall trees, they rest in early morning in the high, open branches of guarumos in the warmth of the rising sun. Where they are not hunted they become quite tame. It is usual to find several in company, and where they are common a flock may contain ten or a dozen birds.

The notes of this bird are a series of whistling, squeaking calls interspersed with harsher chattering sounds, usually uttered rapidly as though the bird was much excited. These notes have limited carrying power, and in this, as well as in sound, they are quite different from the loud calls of the related species *Ortalis vetula* to the north and *O. ruficrissa* in Colombia, which may be heard easily at a distance of a kilometer. The account by Beebe (Book of Bays, 1942, p. 268) of a bird call heard on board a yacht anchored in Bahía Honda that he attributed to the *faisana* must refer to some other kind.

The species of this genus, as a group, build flimsy nests of twigs, grass, and weed stems, usually with a lining of a few green leaves, in low trees. The usual set of eggs is three. They are dull white, with a distinctly roughened shell that often shows many pits. Measurements for a series of 10 by Skutch (Wilson Bull., 1963, p. 265) show the following range: 55.6-61.9 × 38.1-42.5 mm. (As the locality for Skutch's observations is stated to be the Térraba valley in southwestern Costa Rica it is presumed that these are of the subspecies *Ortalis c. cinereiceps*.)

The trachea in the male has the form usual in the genus, in which it passes down the front of the neck to the furculum, makes a loop down the right side of the body between the skin and the pectoral muscles, and then returns to enter the thorax, where it divides in the usual manner in two bronchi that lead to the lungs. In an immature male, barely grown, taken at Almirante on January 20, 1958, the loop had formed only far enough to fill the fork of the furculum. In another older bird, taken at Mandinga on February 5, 1957, the loop extended halfway down the length of the pectoral muscle, and in a bird that appeared to be fully adult, from near the mouth of the Río Pacora April 3, 1949, the trachea reached to the point of the keel on the sternum.

While this species has been treated regularly as conspecific with *Ortalis garrula,* a bird with chestnut head and upper neck, found in northern Colombia from near the Río Sinú east to the western base of the Sierra Nevada de Santa Marta information now available indicates that it is distinct. De Schauensee in connection with his description of the race *chocoensis* (Not. Nat. no. 221, 1950, pp. 2-3) listed two females from Tierra Alta, Córdoba, one with the rufous head of typical *garrula,* and the other with the gray head of the race *mira,* which he interpreted as evidence of intergradation at that point. In our collections also there is one from Tierra Alta, and another from Nazaret to the west of the Sinú, both of which in head color are typical *garrula*. All specimens in the considerable series that I have seen are clearly gray or brown on the head and neck with no appearance of intergradation. The single gray-headed specimen recorded from Tierra Alta may indicate that the two are found together. After a review of the information available it seems desirable to regard the complex as a superspecies, with two closely allied species. The northern one found in Panamá will be called *Ortalis cinereiceps*.

Four slightly differentiated races may be recognized in *cinereiceps* of which three are found in Panamá. The distinctions are in variation in depth of color. Size seems variable regardless of area, the individual differences in dimension commonly noted apparently being due to age. The three forms of the Isthmus are treated in detail beyond. The fourth, *Ortalis cinereiceps chocoensis* described by de Schauensee (cit supr., p. 2), from the Río Jurado, Chocó, in extreme northwestern Colombia, is a very dark race, that resembles *frantzii* of the Caribbean slope of southern Central America, but has the foreneck grayer, less olive-brown, and the gray of the head paler and not extended as far down on the hindneck. The tail tip also is paler. It is probable that this form will be found in southeastern Darién as it is known in Colombia near the boundary, on the Río Jurado, and at Unguía.

ORTALIS CINEREICEPS CINEREICEPS Gray

Ortalida cinereiceps G. R. Gray, List Spec. Birds Coll. Brit. Mus., pt. 5, Gallinae, 1867, p. 12. (Isla del Rey, Archipiélago de las Perlas, Panamá.)
Ortalis struthopus Bangs, Proc. New England Zoöl. Club, vol. 2, 1901, p. 61. (Isla del Rey, Archipiélago de las Perlas, Panamá.)
Ortalis garrula olivacea Aldrich, Sci. Publ. Cleveland Mus. Nat. Hist., vol. 7, Aug. 31, 1937, p. 53. (Paracoté, Veraguas, Panamá.)

Characters.—Palest in general color of the 3 forms found on the Isthmus; compared to the race *mira* grayer, less brownish, on the lower surface, with the center of the abdomen nearly white; light tips on tail nearly white; head, on the average paler gray.

A female taken at Juan Mina January 18, 1961, had the iris wood brown; bill fuscous-brown, shading to neutral gray at tip; tarsus and toes plumbeous; claws fuscous.

Measurements.—Males (6 specimens from Panamá), wing 205-212 (206), tail 221-242 (231), culmen from base 24.2-29.0 (26.7), tarsus 63-74.1 (68.7) mm.

Females (4 specimens from Panamá), wing 198-206 (203), tail 226-256 (236), culmen from base 23.4-26.4 (25.4), tarsus 61.7-64.0 (62.9) mm.

Resident. Fairly common in the tropical lowlands of the Pacific slope from the Costa Rican boundary through Chiriquí and Veraguas, including both sides of the Azuero Peninsula; east locally to the lowlands beyond Pacora, La Jagua, and the mouth of the Río Chico; found on the Pacific side of the Canal Zone (Farfán), and also in the middle Chagres drainage between Madden Dam and Juan Mina; Isla del Rey, in the Archipiélago de las Perlas; formerly on Isla Pedro González.

This race ranges north on the Pacific slope in southwestern Costa Rica.

The type of *cinereiceps*, which I have examined in the British Museum, received from the *Herald* expedition in a collection made by Kellett and Wood, is marked, owing to some confusion, as from the "north-west coast of America." Aldrich (Scient. Publ. Cleveland Mus., vol. 7, 1937, p. 55) appropriately has designated Isla del Rey as the type locality. The bird formerly was common there, but in January, 1960, when I collected one near Ensenada, I was told that now few were found. W. W. Brown, Jr., in 1900 secured one from a native that had been taken on Isla Pedro González. In 1944 I failed to find them there, and have assumed that all have been killed on that relatively small island. Though these birds have been known long from the Archipiélago de las Perlas it is possible that the faisana may have been introduced there from the mainland, perhaps by Indians.

ORTALIS CINEREICEPS FRANTZII Cabanis

Ortalida Frantzii Cabanis, Journ für Orn., vol. 17, May 1869, p. 211. (Eastern Costa Rica.)

Characters.—Head dark gray; undersurface including the center of the abdomen washed heavily with brown; decidedly dark above; light tips on end of tail cinnamon-buff; decidedly darker throughout than the other races found in Panamá.

A chick of this race from Costa Rica (U.S.N.M. 64989), apparently less than a week old, has the crown, side of the head, lower back, and rump sooty brown; upper back dull chocolate-brown; hindneck and bend of wing cinnamon-buff; wing dusky gray with the outer edge and tips of the growing remiges cinnamon, and the downy coverts tipped with cinnamon-buff; throat, lower breast, and abdomen white;

upper breast cinnamon; lower breast and sides cinnamon buff; legs and under tail coverts with the down dusky basally.

Measurements.—Males (8 specimens from Costa Rica and Panamá), wing 199-208 (203), tail 208-227 (218), culmen from base 24.3-26.8 (26.2), tarsus 62.3-68.3 (66.5) mm.

Females (3 specimens from Costa Rica), wing 190-194 (192), tail 205-214 (210), culmen from base 23.2-26.8 (24.5), tarsus 61.0-65.3 (63.1) mm.

Resident. Fairly common in the tropical lowlands of western Bocas del Toro from the Costa Rican boundary to the valley of the Río Changuinola. Birds from the western side of Bahía Almirante (Water Valley, Isla Cristobal) east along the Laguna de Chiriquí (Cricamola, Guabo) show intergradation with *O. c. mira*.

To the north this race extends through the Caribbean lowlands of Costa Rica to northeastern Nicaragua.

The only definite record of the breeding of this form is that of Huber (Proc. Acad. Nat. Sci. Philadelphia, vol. 84, 1932, p. 207), who found a nest near the Eden Mine in northeastern Nicaragua on May 27, 1922. The 3 eggs were placed on a small structure of decaying vegetation on the top of a stump hidden in a clump of bushes in an open pasture. The eggs, with the roughened, pitted surface usual in this genus, were creamy white, much stained from the damp nest material. They measured 50.4 × 36.8, 51.5 × 36.6, and 52.0 × 37.7 mm. A chick in the Chicago Natural History Museum a little over 2 weeks old, collected by von Wedel at Cricamola, July 1, 1937, also indicates a nesting season in May.

In 1958 I found small flocks of these birds in Water Valley in the edge of mangroves and along the border of the woodland behind, and also noted them near Punta Rodríguez on Isla Cristobal.

ORTALIS CINEREICEPS MIRA Griscom

Ortalis garrula mira Griscom, Bull. Mus. Comp. Zoöl., vol. 72, no. 9, Jan. 1932, p. 318. (Ranchón, San Blas, Panamá.)

Characters.—Similar to *O. c. frantzii* in brownish wash on breast and foreneck, but definitely paler, with the head somewhat lighter gray; above paler brown; tail tipped with buffy white.

An adult male taken near El Llano on the lower Río Bayano, February 5, 1962, had the iris warm brown; eyelids and bare skin on side of head dusky neutral gray; bare area on sides of throat rosy red; bill neutral gray; tarsus and toes neutral gray; claws black.

Measurements.—Males (9, including one from Acandí, Chocó), wing 198-225 (213), tail 221-253 (241), culmen from base 25.6-29.8 (27.8), tarsus 64.9-74.5 (70.1, average of 8) mm.

Females (7, including one from Acandí, Chocó), wing 193-207 (201), tail 217-244 (226), culmen from base 23.1-28.6 (26.2), tarsus 64.4-68.2 (65.6) mm.

Resident. Fairly common in the tropical lowlands of the Caribbean slope, from near central Bocas del Toro through western Colón (Río Indio), and the lowlands of extreme northern Coclé (El Uracillo) to the Colombian boundary. At the Cerro Azul this race ranges across to the Pacific slope in the lowlands near Chepo, and continues eastward to the Río Majé, formerly at least along the Río Chucunaque (mouth of Río Tuquesa, specimen 1924), and the Golfo San Miguel (Laguna de Pita, specimen 1895).

Possibly hunting by Indians has reduced or eliminated the *faisana* in parts of Darién, as I did not find it on the Chucunaque-Tuira drainage in 1959. There were none in the region of the Río Jaqué in 1946 and 1947, and none have been reported from the Cerro Pirre area.

In the Canal Zone *faisanas* are fairly common on Barro Colorado Island, mainly near the lake shore, and are found in sheltered localities elsewhere from the lower Chagres Valley to the headwaters of that stream. At Juan Mina, where the divide is low, the population seems nearer *cinereiceps*. At Mandinga in the San Blas I found them common through tracts of rastrojo.

A female taken on the Río Chimán on February 20, 1950, was nearly ready to lay.

Family PHASIANIDAE: Quails, Pheasants, and Peacocks; Codornices, Faisanes, y Pavos Reales

This family of many species, found under natural conditions throughout temperate and tropical regions, is best known through the domestic fowl, the most valuable bird in a commercial sense in the world. In Panamá the Phasianidae are represented by five handsome species of the group of quails, four of these, the wood quails, forest inhabitants, and the fifth found in low coverts near the savanna lands of the Pacific slope in the western part of the Republic. Only three are sufficiently common to be considered game birds, and these are present in limited numbers that cannot survive any extensive hunting.

KEY TO SPECIES OF THE PHASIANIDAE

1. Size small, wing less than 105 mm.; undersurface strongly spotted and barred with buff, brown, and black.
   Crested bobwhite, *Colinus cristatus*, p. 311
   Larger, wing more than 110 mm.; undersurface plain, or with less conspicuous pattern; if barred, these markings not present on lower foreneck and upper breast.. 2
2. Smaller, wing less than 120 mm.; head without a distinct crest; 10 rectrices.
   Banded wood quail, *Rhynchortyx cinctus*, p. 330
   Larger, wing more than 120 mm.; head with a distinct bushy crest; 12 rectrices (*Odontophorus*)... 3
3. Breast, sides, and crest plain cinnamon-brown.
   Rufous-breasted wood quail, *Odontophorus erythrops melanotis*, p. 325
   Breast and crest more or less variegated............................. 4
4. Throat black, streaked with white; rest of lower surface distinctly spotted with white or buff......Spotted wood quail, *Odontophorus guttatus*, p. 322
   Not as in 4.   5
5. Breast black, in some mixed with brown barred with white; throat white, or white mixed with black.
   Black-breasted wood quail, *Odontophorus leucolaemus*, p. 328
   Breast grayish brown, finely barred, spotted, or marbled with dull black, buff, or grayish white.. 6
6. Foreneck and throat gray to grayish brown, with many fine cross bars of white to grayish white.
   Marbled wood quail, *Odontophorus gujanensis*, p. 316
   Foreneck white with a broad central band of black mixed with rufous brown.
   Tacarcuna wood quail, *Odontophorus dialeucos*, p. 327

COLINUS CRISTATUS (Linnaeus): Crested Bobwhite; Codorniz

FIGURE 53

Tetrao cristatus Linnaeus, Syst. Nat., ed. 12, vol. 1, 1766, p. 277. (Curaçao.)

A small quail, with form rounded and compact, short tail, and head with pointed crest.

Description.—Length 190 to 200 mm. Male, crown white or buff shading to gray on the crest and back, bordered posteriorly by brown more or less lined with black; sides and back of neck black, spotted with white; rest of upper surface finely mottled with gray, brown, and black; tertials spotted with black, with the inner borders black; foreneck in some white, in others chestnut; under surface buff to chestnut, spotted with white and barred with black; ear coverts white or buffy white.

Female, similar, but crown black in front, brown behind, including the crest, with sides buff lined narrowly with black; throat buff to white with the feathers bordered and tipped narrowly with black.

Crested bobwhites are found in small coveys in thickets and along the edge of woodlands bordering fields and savannas in the western part of the Pacific slope. They are shy birds that often run, rather than fly, and remain so well hidden that few persons become familiar with them in the wild. Occasionally on less frequented country roads a little flock may scurry quickly across in front of a car, but ordinarily it is useless to try to follow them as they move rapidly and hide even where there seems to be scanty cover. My best views of them have been in early morning when they have come out from their usual

FIG. 53.—Crested bobwhite, codorniz, *Colinus cristatus,* male.

cover. On many occasions on open trails I have stopped my jeep and have remained without moving, while a dozen or so came fearlessly about. Then they walked or ran, often crouching, with a continuous murmur of soft quail notes like those of bobwhites of related species found through the extensive range of the genus from Canada to northern South America. In feeding they peck strongly and rapidly to expose whatever might be concealed in the ground, be it soft or hard.

When startled they may fly, but seldom more than 10 meters, to the nearest cover, where they drop instantly out of sight, and then usually disappear so that they may not be seen again. These short flights though rapid are not strong. Once I saw a three-quarter-grown bird that could not rise over a 6-meter bank, at the abrupt angle necessary from its point of take-off. Bobwhites usually are more common than the small numbers ordinarily seen may indicate, as may be learned following heavy rains that soak the vegetation, as then they tend to feed more in the open.

Males begin to call toward the end of January, a 3-noted whistle, *ah-bob-white,* in a tone familiar to those who know the quail in the eastern half of the United States, but uttered much more rapidly. I have assumed that like the northern species males of those found in Panamá whistle until they have found a mate and then cease, since I have heard them rather infrequently in relation to the amount of time that I have traveled in their haunts. The mating season may vary locally, as I have recorded males calling as early as January 29 (near Bejuco) and as late as June 20 (near Penonomé).

In addition to this whistle of the males, both sexes have a variety of soft calls that serve to hold together the individuals that compose the little flocks. A louder sound, high-pitched and rather querulous, resembles the syllables *ka kwee, ka kwee,* heard often when a covey has become scattered.

They appear to nest at the beginning of the rainy season, as I saw young nearly grown near Soná at the end of May.

Schönwetter (Handb. Ool., pt. 4, 1961, p. 223) says that eggs of *Colinus cristatus,* as represented by the typical race *C. c. cristatus,* and the subspecies *leucotis* and *sonnini,* all of northern South America, are cream-colored, spotted and blotched, often very heavily, with shades of brown. While those of the Panamanian race are not at present known, it seems probable that they are similar.

As a species *Colinus cristatus* has an isolated colony with two subspecies in the western half of the Pacific slope in Panamá and then appears again in northwestern Colombia to range through Venezuela, and south to northern Brazil, including the islands of Aruba, Curaçao, and Margarita. Two subspecies are found in Panamá, and in the South American range 7 additional races are recognized. All agree in form of the crest and general size but differ in details of depth and extent of the color found in their plumage. All live in open regions of scrub and savanna with limited rainfall. The populations of western Panamá thus are isolated from the range of their close relatives by the great forests of Darién and the Atrato basin. It seems curious that these quail are not known in the savanna country between the city of Panamá and the lower Río Bayano.

An allied species, *Colinus leucopogon,* found from Guanacaste in western Costa Rica northward through western Nicaragua, western

Honduras, and El Salvador to western Guatemala, is generally similar in form but has a much shorter crest, a completely white superciliary stripe, and much darker cheeks, while in the male the throat is mainly black, instead of bright brown. It is said also to lay white eggs like those of most other species of *Colinus*.

In Panamá these birds are known usually as *perdiz*, since most persons do not distinguish them as of a different family from the small tinamou. The correct name is *codorniz*.

COLINUS CRISTATUS PANAMENSIS Dickey and van Rossem

Colinus leucotis panamensis Dickey and van Rossem, Condor, vol. 32, no. 1, Jan. 20, 1930, p. 73. (Aguadulce, Coclé, Panamá.)

Characters.—Black markings restricted so that the dorsal surface is grayish brown, and the breast bright brown, rather than black. Compared to *Colinus c. mariae* the coloration throughout is decidedly brown.

A male taken at El Potrero, Coclé, March 7, 1962, had the iris brown; bill black; tarsus and toes light brownish gray; with the claws slightly darker.

Measurements.—Males (12 specimens), wing 92.3-97.3 (94.1), tail 50.0-54.5 (52.1), culmen from cere 12.7-14.0 (13.2), tarsus 27.6-31.6 (29.4) mm.

Females (9 specimens), wing 91.0-100.5 (95.8), tail 47.0-54.8 (51.4), culmen from cere 13.0-14.0 (13.5), tarsus 28.3-31.4 (30.2) mm.

Resident. Lowlands of the Pacific slope in western Veraguas from 10 kilometers west of Soná eastward (Santiago, near Santa Fé) through Coclé (El Valle, El Copé, El Potrero, Aguadulce, Penonomé, Río Hato) and the adjacent area of the western sector of the Province of Panamá (El Espino, San Carlos, Bejuco) to the valley of the Río de la Mona at the south base of Cerro Campana; south on the eastern side of the Azuero Peninsula through Herrera (Santa María, Potuga, El Barrero, París, Parita, Monagrillo, Chitré) and Los Santos, (Los Santos, Mensabé) to Pedasí, Los Asientos, and the lower Tonosí Valley.

I have found this race most common in Herrera. In 1948 dozens trapped for the market were sold for 10 cents each. It was common in Parita to see them alive in small cages that were suspended near the household kitchens to protect them from dogs and other marauders until they were wanted for the table.

(Two specimens from the H. Bryant collection in the American Museum of Natural History labeled as from the Panama Railroad Line collected by "Jas McLellan" undoubtedly have erroneous data, as the quail has not been known to range so far to the eastward.)

COLINUS CRISTATUS MARIAE Wetmore

Colinus cristatus mariae Wetmore, Smithsonian Misc. Coll., vol. 145, no. 1, June 26, 1962, p. 5. (7 kilometers south of Alanje, Province of Chiriquí, Panamá.)

Characters.—Definitely darker throughout; blacker on the back and wings; black markings on the lower surface more extensive, particularly on the upper breast and the lower foreneck.

Measurements.—Males (6 specimens), wing 92.6-95.3 (93.7), tail 46.3-52.3 (49.2), culmen from cere 12.7-13.9 (13.2), tarsus 27.9-29.1 (28.5) mm.

Females (3 specimens), wing 92.0-96.1 (94.0), tail 45.7-50.0 (48.4), culmen from cere 12.4-13.4 (12.8), tarsus 27.2-29.4 (28.5) mm.

Resident. Western Chiriquí from the southern slopes of the Volcán de Chiriquí near Boquete (El Salto, 1,350 meters elevation), and El Francés (1,000 to 1,100 meters near El Banco) down to the coastal plain near the sea below Alanje (Martina, Paja Blanca).

On my first brief views of these birds on the sandy plain below Alanje the much darker color, compared to the quail of Veraguas and Coclé, was immediately evident, though it was several days before I was successful in shooting a pair for specimens. The birds ranged, as usual with this species, in small coveys in open lands where thickets offered cover, but nowhere did they seem abundant. When I encountered them, usually in driving a jeep along roads deep in sand, they flew a few feet or ran among low bushes where they disappeared instantly and seldom were seen again, even where the cover was of limited extent. Later I found one covey in the sloping fields at El Salto above Boquete, where the birds flew a short distance and hid in low bushes where we tramped about for some time without success in seeing them again. These observations were made in the first half of March when the bands included young birds from half to three-quarters grown.

This western population of the crested bobwhite has a decidedly restricted distribution, as it was not found by the early collectors in Chiriquí. The oldest specimens that I have seen, sent to Rothschild by H. J. Watson, were taken at El Francés below Boquete in 1895. Apparently they were not common here, for Watson's further collections do not seem to have included others. The only published record of specimens of the race *mariae* seems to be that of Hellmayr and Conover (Cat. Birds Amer., pt. 1, no. 1, 1942, p. 252), who in their account of the subspecies *panamensis*, of Veraguas and Coclé, listed two of Watson's skins from El Francés.

My two from near Alanje are definitely blacker than those from the higher elevations. It appears that the maximum depth of pigmentation in this race is found in the coastal lowlands.

I have named this subspecies for Mrs. Robert A. Terry who, as Mary E. McLellan Davidson, through her early field work added much to our knowledge of the birds of Chiriquí.

[COLINUS VIRGINIANUS Linnaeus: Bobwhite; Codorniz Norteña

Members of the Río Hato Rod and Gun Club are reported to have imported a number of bobwhite quail from the United States for release in the savanna country near the Río Hato military base. At present there is no information as to the success of this experiment.

This species in general body form is like the native quail but is larger and does not have the prominent crest of the *codorniz* (*Colinus cristatus*). The throat in the adult male is white, and in the female plain buffy brown without dark spots or streaks. The wing in males measures from 106 to 119 mm., in females from 103 to 118 mm.]

ODONTOPHORUS GUJANENSIS (Gmelin): Marbled Wood Quail; Gallito del Monte Jaspeado

FIGURE 54

Tetrao gujanensis Gmelin, Syst. Nat., vol. 1, pt. 2, 1789, p. 767. (Cayenne.)

A forest quail with undersurface brown, mottled and barred lightly with black, buff, and dull white.

Description.—Length, 230 to 285 mm. Adult, crown crested, brown; neck all around and upper back brown or gray, finely barred with black; wings, wing coverts, and scapulars brown, barred with buff, buffy white, and black, with heavy blotches of black, the concealed web of the scapulars lined with gray; lower back and rump brown, barred brokenly with brown and buff; tail similar but darker; side of head and chin chestnut; flight feathers fuscous, with broken bars of buffy brown on outer webs; throat gray, barred with dull white; lower surface brown to grayish brown, barred brokenly and spotted with black, buff, and buffy white, more prominently on the under tail coverts; under wing covers gray mottled with white.

There is much individual variation in depth of color and in amount of barring.

These elusive birds, inhabitants of forests, are found in areas of irregular terrain, especially in hill country where they live on the ground in the cover of undergrowth. Usually they range in small flocks of 6 or 8 individuals, rarely more, as the bands have the appearance of family groups. These shelter often about a fallen tree, or a steep broken slope may be attractive where they walk about quietly, often to the accompaniment of low calls that barely are heard by the human ear. At an alarm they crouch and hide, and I

FIG. 54.—Marbled wood quail, gallito del monte jaspeado, *Odontophorus gujanensis*.

am sure that often I have passed near such little bands without being aware of their presence. If I chance directly upon them there is immediate alarm, in which one or two may fly suddenly, with a startling roar of wings, and dart away low for 60 or 80 meters, and then alight to run, while others dash off under cover on foot. In such manner the entire flock scatters and disappears in a flurry of excited chirping calls to hide so effectively that it is seldom that one is seen again. In dense cover they crouch with head forward as they run, but when the forest floor is fairly open they scurry off with head and neck erect and feathers compressed, making them appear so slender that it is somewhat of a surprise to note their heavy bodies when a shot brings one to hand. When all is quiet the birds call softly until they are assembled again. In uninhabited areas, where they are more common, and may be tame, a male sometimes steps out with crest raised, head erect, and feathers fluffed to bow quickly with extended neck.

Sometimes I have found them feeding beneath berry-bearing trees on the drupes dropped or knocked down by other birds or by monkeys. It is common to observe their scratchings on the forest floor, often over considerable areas. Rarely in early morning I have seen them venture out on an open sand bank to the edge of a river to drink.

Their presence and abundance are known mainly from their loud, rapid calls heard most often at dusk or at dawn, occasionally on moonlight nights, and less often in the earlier hours of the forenoon. The notes may be written *perro-mulato, perro-mulato,* repeated without a break, sometimes for several minutes for a total of several hundred times. These notes, audible for half a kilometer or more, give them their common country name of *perro mulato*—mulatto dog —throughout the whole of eastern Panamá. Others, mainly those living along the Caribbean, have likened the notes to *corcoro-vado,* and from this call them *corcorovado.* In 1963 in the eastern San Blas, where I heard them frequently, the call there seemed nearer to this rendition than to the other with which I had been long familiar at numerous localities on the Pacific slope. In addition they are known everywhere by the common appellation of *gallito monte.* The Cuna Indians call them *ūcūrū.*

Chapman (My Tropical Air Castle, 1929, pp. 275-276) found from observations of two captive birds, presumed to be a pair, that the call heard so commonly is a duet, in which the two alternate in perfect time. In Chapman's rendition of the call as *corcoro vado* the second bird was responsible for the last two syllables. Some observations of my own verify this, as at Boca de Paya in Darién one evening I heard one wood quail start with a loud *Mu-u-u-latto* repeated several times until suddenly the call changed to the usual *perro mu-u-latto,* undoubtedly when a companion joined. In 1963, near Armila, San Blas, when the female of a pair was taken for a specimen, the remaining bird called *corcoro*—for several evenings, until in a week or so this changed again to the full *corcoro-vado* so that we believed that another mate had been obtained.

The species has a wide distribution from southwestern Costa Rica through Panamá to northern Colombia and Venezuela, and south, east of the Andes, through Ecuador and Perú to eastern Bolivia and Brazil. Two geographic races are found in Panamá.

ODONTOPHORUS GUJANENSIS MARMORATUS (Gould)

Ortyx (*Odontophorus*) *marmoratus* Gould, Proc. Zool. Soc. London, pt. 11, no. 124, Dec. 1843, p. 107. ("Santa Fe de Bogotá," Colombia.)

Odontophorus guianensis panamensis Chapman, Bull. Amer. Mus. Nat. Hist., vol. 34, May 27, 1915, p. 363. (Line of Panama Railroad.)

Odontophorus guianensis panamensis Chubb, Ibis, ser. 11, vol. 1, no. 1, Jan. 8, 1919, p. 26. (Lion Hill, Canal Zone.)

Odontophorus guianensis chapmani Griscom, Bull. Mus. Comp. Zoöl., vol. 69, no. 8, Apr. 1929, p. 153. (Cana, Darién.)

Characters.—Neck all around and upper back gray (varying from light to dark); white on throat and upper foreneck more extensive.

A male taken at Mandinga, San Blas, February 12, 1957, had the iris wood brown; bill dusky neutral gray, very slightly paler at the base of the gonys; eyelids, lores, and skin beneath the gape, dull orange; tarsus and toes neutral gray, with a small area of light neutral gray on the front of the tarsus, below the proximal joint.

Another male shot at Frijolito, Panamá, near the Canal Zone boundary differed slightly in having the iris russet brown; bill dull black; bare skin around eye and on lores light orange; tarsus and toes neutral gray; and claws black.

Measurements.—Males (17 from Panamá), wing 137.0-149.2 (143.8), tail 56.8-71.5 (65.0), culmen from cere 17.0-19.8 (18.8), tarsus 41.2-48.1 (45.1) mm.

Females (4 from Panamá), wing 136.7-140.8 (137.3), tail 57.0-63.6 (61.1), culmen from cere 16.1-17.8 (16.9), tarsus 40.8-41.8 (41.4) mm.

Resident. In the Tropical Zone lowlands, from the Caribbean slope of Coclé (El Uracillo), western Colón (Chilar), and the Canal Zone (Lion Hill, Barro Colorado Island, Juan Mina) east throughout forested areas on both slopes to the Colombian boundary, ranging to 500 meters on Cerro Chucantí, and to 1,000 meters on Cerro Pirre; fairly common in areas remote from human settlement.

One in the British Museum was taken near Lion Hill by Mc-Leannan (date not recorded). In May 1904 W. W. Brown, Jr. shot two near Panama City (Thayer and Bangs, Bull. Mus. Comp. Zool., 1906, p. 214); on September 3, 1911, and February 22, 1912, Jewel collected males near Gatun (Stone, Proc. Acad. Nat. Sci. Philadelphia, 1918, p. 242); and in January or February 1921 M. J. Kelly took one near Gamboa that he prepared as a mount for exhibition in the Everhart Museum of Scranton, Pa. Formerly these wood quail were reported regularly on Barro Colorado Island but now are rare, my last record being of one that called at dusk from the forested slope above the laboratory on May 5, 1953. My only other recent record for the Canal Zone area was on January 14, 1961, when, as I landed from a cayuco on the forested bank of the Chagres at Guayabalito, above Juan Mina, a pair ran off across the forest floor. To the eastward in forested regions the birds remain fairly common, as they still find shelter on steep hill slopes that have not yet come under cultivation. I have noted them in such locations in numerous localities from above Chepo and Chimán eastward through Darién, and at Mandinga on the San Blas coast.

M. A. Carriker, Jr., collecting for the U. S. National Museum in Colombia at Unguía, northern Chocó on March 2, 1950, flushed a female from a nest at the foot of a large tree in the forest. There was one egg. This is oval, glossy white, with a very faint buffy tint, and measures 36.0 × 26.7 mm. Another egg, taken from the oviduct of a female shot at the Hacienda Belén, in northeastern Antioquia, Colombia, March 24, 1948, is also oval, but is pure white without gloss (owing probably to a shell deposit still incomplete). It measures 36.3 × 27.7 mm. This description and the dimensions correspond to those given by Oates (Cat. Eggs Brit. Mus., vol. 1, 1901, p. 69) for 2 eggs collected by Salmon at Remedios, Antioquia. Schönwetter (Handb. Ool., pt. 4, 1961, p. 224) says that occasionally eggs of this form are finely spotted, or more rarely heavily marked with brown. He gives the measurements of 6 as 35-38.6 × 27.0-28.0 mm.

Four-fifths of the contents of the stomach and crop of one taken at Cana consisted of the broken fragments of starchy seeds, with a few harder ones that may have helped in grinding the others. In addition there were remains of a dozen or more millipeds, 6 ants, 2 roaches, a spider, and bits of beetles and beetle larvae.

In any series of these birds there is much range in marking from those very dark to others much lighter, and from those definitely barred to others that show finely marbled markings, but these appear to be purely individual variations. Our series of 21 from Panamá and 28 from northern Colombia, most of them recently taken, confirms the final conclusions of Chapman (Amer. Mus. Nov. no. 380, 1929, p. 5) and Griscom (Bull. Mus. Comp. Zool., vol. 72, 1932, pp. 319-320), based on older material, that the bird of Panamá must be recorded under the name *marmoratus* described by Gould from a Bogotá trade skin. This subspecies, therefore, has a range extending from central Panamá across northern Colombia (through the lower valleys of the Atrato, Sinú, Cauca, and Magdalena Rivers), and along the eastern base of the eastern Andes, into northwestern Venezuela.

A chick, a male recently hatched, collected by Bernard Finestein at 900 meters on the slopes of Cerro Malí, Darién, on February 26, 1959, is darker than burnt umber above and on the legs and under tail coverts, with a tint of cinnamon on the bases of the down on the sides of the head and the upper neck, where it forms an indefinite, rather broad line; less distinctly cinnamon on the wings; a narrow line of buffy white from the base of the wing to the rump on either side; below dull buffy white, barred indistinctly with neutral gray on the throat and foreneck; breast and sides dull brownish black; center of lower breast and abdomen dull white.

An older male that I secured at Jaqué, Darién, on April 6, 1946, has short, narrow stripes of cinnamon buff on the breast, and the upper fore neck grayish brown, with faint basal markings of grayish white.

ODONTOPHORUS GUJANENSIS CASTIGATUS Bangs

Odontophorus castigatus Bangs, Auk, vol. 18, no. 4, Oct. 1901, p. 356. (Divalá, Chiriquí, Panamá.)

Characters.—Neck, all around, and upper back brown; with less white on throat and upper foreneck than *O. g. marmoratus*.

Measurements.—Males (6 specimens from Panamá) wing 139-148.8 (142.6), tail 61.2-71.0 (65.3), culmen from cere 17.8-19.5 (18.6), tarsus 43.0-46.3 (44.6) mm.

Females (3 from Panamá), wing 137.8-144.8 (142.1), tail 56.2-61.0 (59.5), culmen from cere 16.9-17.3 (17.1), tarsus 43.1-44.6 (43.9) mm.

Iris brown; tarsus lead color (from label of a male, collected by W. W. Brown, Jr.).

Resident. Tropical Zone of western Chiriquí; known in Panamá from early collections made at Divalá and Bugaba; no recent records.

The race was described originally from 7 specimens taken at the end of 1900, near Divalá, by W. W. Brown, Jr. Arcé had obtained a pair earlier at Bugaba (Salvin, Proc. Zool. Soc. London, 1870, p. 218) which came to the British Museum in the Salvin-Godman collection. Bangs (Proc. New England Zoöl. Club, vol. 3, 1902, p. 22) received 3 males taken by Brown at Bugaba in July 1901, the latest published report of this race in the republic.

This form of the marbled wood quail has most of its range in southwestern Costa Rica, as it barely enters Panamá. An early report of it from "Veragua" (Sclater and Salvin, Nomen. Avium Neotrop., 1873, p. 138) refers to the skins sent by Arcé from Bugaba.

The two lowland areas from which it has been recorded, both in or near the drainage of the Chiriquí Viejo river system, formerly heavily forested, have been cut over until little of the original cover remains. It seeems doubtful that any are still to be found in the Republic.

Two specimens in the American Museum of Natural History, sent originally by J. H. Batty to the Rothschild collection, have data that are not to be trusted, as they are labeled "Isla Cebaco" with the dates February 4 and 5, 1902. Probably they are Arcé skins from somewhere on the mainland.

ODONTOPHORUS GUTTATUS (Gould): Spotted Wood Quail; Gallito del Monte Pintado

Ortyx guttata Gould, Proc. Zool. Soc. London, pt. 5, no. 56, 1837 (Feb. 13, 1838), p. 79. (Bay of Honduras.)

Odontophorus Veraguanensis Gould, Athenaeum, no. 1490, May 17, 1856, p. 620. ("Near David, in Veragua," Panamá.)

Odontophorus veraguensis Gould, Proc. Zool. Soc. London, pt. 24, no. 307, Aug. 13, 1856, p. 107. (Boquete, Chiriquí.)

A forest quail with under surface grayish brown or dull cinnamon spotted with white; throat black, streaked with white.

Description.—Length, 230-275 mm. Adult male, (in gray-brown phase) crown brownish black, with the elongated crest feathers bright cinnamon-buff, except for the darker tips; side of head grayish brown, with a streak of chestnut, mixed slightly with black from beneath the eye back over the ear coverts to the side of the neck; hindneck and upper back mottled olive-brown and gray, with shaft lines of white; a few black feathers mixed with chestnut forming a narrow indefinite collar across hindneck; lower back, rump, and upper tail coverts finely mottled with grayish brown and olive; wing coverts similar, but with small spots of mixed black and buffy white; tertials and inner secondaries with bold, irregular black spots, barred narrowly with chestnut-brown, and lined with buffy white; flight feathers fuscous, the outer webs of the secondaries with narrow, irregular bars and spots of buff to cinnamon; tail dull black, with faintly indicated bars and spots of cinnamon; throat and foreneck black, streaked narrowly with white; lower surface grayish brown with small elongated spots of white bordered narrowly with black; upper breast, sides and flanks washed with warm brown; under tail coverts dull chestnut-brown, banded indistinctly with black; under wing coverts dark grayish brown.

Female, similar but with exposed crown feathers brown, and the longer ones at rear duller brown.

An erythristic phase is common in both sexes in which the concealed crest feathers vary from cinnamon to chestnut, the upper surface is brighter colored, and the ground color of the lower surface is cinnamon brown to snuff brown. This variant, found throughout the range, was supposed to be a distinct species for many years. In Panamá it was long recorded under the name *Odontophorus veraguensis* Gould.

Chick in down, center of crown and occiput, and middle of the back russet; forehead and side of crown buff to ochraceous-buff; rest of upper surface dark ochraceous-buff, mottled with dusky; under surface buff, mixed with olive-gray. This natal down is followed by a grayish brown plumage, with narrow elongate streaks that terminate in enlarged spots of white narrowly edged with black on breast, sides, back, and wing coverts.

The chick is paler colored than that of *O. gujanensis* or *O. erythrops,* the former being very dark, almost chocolate-brown above, and the latter cinnamon-brown. (The description of the downy young given under *Odontophorus erythrops melanotis* in Friedmann, U. S. Nat. Mus. Bull. 50, pt. 10, 1946, p. 371, is taken from a specimen of *O. guttatus.*)

Adult, iris light brown; bill dark neutral gray to black; bare lores neutral gray; eyelids dull greenish gray; tarsus and toes dull green, with the claws fuscous.

A juvenile female, three-fourths grown, had the iris hazel; cere, base of maxilla, and mandible fuscous; rest of maxilla light chestnut-brown; tarsus and toes dull greenish gray.

Measurements.—Males (11 from Chiriquí), wing 134.7-144.1 (140.4), tail 55.7-68.5 (62.2), culmen from cere 16.2-18.5 (17.3), tarsus 42.8-46.8 (44.5) mm.

Females (11 from Chiriquí), wing 134.1-141.5 (136.0), tail 53.8-65.6 (58.7), culmen from cere 15.3-17.8 (16.3), tarsus 40.2-44.3 (42.9) mm.

Resident. Fairly common in the subtropical zone in western Chiriquí from Cerro Horqueta across the slopes of the Chiriquí Volcano, Cerro Picacho, and Cerro Pando to the highlands on the Costa Rican boundary, mainly from 1,250 to 2,100 meters; recorded at 1,100 meters at El Banco. Confined in Panamá, according to available records, to the Pacific slope.

To the north this species ranges through the mountains of Central America to southern México.

These quail are found in small bands on forested slopes where locally they may be fairly common, as to the present time they have not been hunted extensively. They are secretive like the lowland species, and hide at any alarm, but on the whole appear less wary. When approached one or two may fly a few feet, but most run rapidly away with head erect and crests raised. Their feet make a rapid pattering sound on dry leaves that I have heard sometimes when the birds were hidden from me in the undergrowth. Often they hide and remain so quiet that I have had a band secreted within 30 meters for a period of 15 minutes, until chance brought me nearer, forcing them to run.

Their presence in the forest often is indicated by their scratchings, which are roughly circular, 30 centimeters or more across, with the leaves cleared so that the ground is bare. Where the forest floor is level such depressions may be spread over an area several meters across.

The calls of this species will be recognized at once by those familiar with the *perro mulatto* of the lowlands in the eastern part of the Republic, as the two are similar in excited, rapid tone. The present species, however, has more variation in its notes. The usual series of phrases may be rendered as *wheet-o-wet-to-wheo-who*, repeated steadily with the terminal syllables sometimes changed to *to-whao*. Variation in tone, and occasional confusion in utterance, that I have noted has indicated that the call was a duet similar to that characteristic of the lowland species. They call mainly at sunrise, and for a short space afterward, and it is then that their numbers become known. At times, I have heard half a dozen groups on as many separate wooded slopes.

When alarmed they give low trilling notes as they become excited and run away, and when a flock has been scattered they utter mournful whistles, similar to calls of some of the trogons, to unite the little band again.

Schönwetter (Handb. Ool., pt. 4, 1961, p. 224; pt. 5, 1961, p. 267) indicates that the eggs are creamy white, sometimes spotted with brown. He gives the measurements of 6 as 39.2-40.5 × 28.5-29.7 mm.

Recently hatched chicks were taken near El Volcán March 10 and 25, 1965.

ODONTOPHORUS ERYTHROPS MELANOTIS Salvin: Rufous-breasted Wood Quail; Gallito del Monte Pechicastaño

Odontophorus melanotis Salvin, Proc. Zool. Soc. London, pt. 3, 1864 (Feb., 1865), p. 586. (Tucurrique, Costa Rica.)

Odontophorus melanotis coloratus Griscom, Amer. Mus. Nov. no. 280, Sept. 10, 1927, p. 3. (Guaval, Río Calovévora, northern Veraguas.)

A forest quail with chestnut-brown breast and sides.

Description.—Length, 220-260 mm. Male, crown chestnut-brown, with the longer crest feathers tipped or washed with fuscous-black; hindneck and upper back dull black to brownish black, mottled finely with dull buff or cinnamon-buff; lower back, rump, and upper tail coverts browner, also mottled, and with indistinct spots and broken bars of black; wing coverts and scapulars dark grayish brown, mottled lightly and spotted irregularly, with black, and lined with cream-buff, the scapulars with heavy cross bands of black; flight feathers fuscous; outer webs of primaries with irregular bars of cinnamon; outer webs of secondaries with heavier, mottled bars of mixed grayish buff and cinnamon-buff; tail dull cinnamon-brown, mottled and barred indistinctly with dull black; sides of head, throat, and sides and front of neck dull black, with a faintly indicated band of chestnut on the side of the head; breast and sides cinnamon-brown, merging with the black of the throat through an over wash of chestnut, the hidden centers of the feathers of the sides mottled finely with black; feathers of the abdomen fluffy, blackish basally, tipped with cinnamon-buff; tibia, flanks, and under tail coverts dull black, barred and tipped with cinnamon-buff.

Female, without black on the throat or sides of the head.

Chick, chestnut-brown above, dark cinnamon to cinnamon-buff below. The bird molts immediately into a plumage that resembles that of the adult but has the crest feathers duller, and the back with prominent white to buffy white lines. Below it is heavily spotted and barred with black.

Birds taken at Cricamola have the iris in a male marked as dark red brown, and in a female as coffee brown. The feet in both are said to be blue black; bare skin around eye purplish in male, bluish black in female; bill black; tarsus and toes blue-black.

Measurements.—Males (6 from Panamá) wing 138.8-147.8 (143.3), tail 42.7-59.6 (51.7), culmen from cere 18.1-20.0 (18.9), tarsus 42.6-47.0 (45.9) mm.

Females (6 from Panamá), wing 139.8-149.4 (143.1), tail 49.8-52.8 (50.9), culmen from cere 18.0-18.8 (18.3), tarsus 43.8-47.1 (45.7) mm.

Resident. Rare, local in distribution in tropical zone and lower subtropical zone forests, ranging on Cerro Pirre to 1,600 meters. Not known from the Pacific slope west of the Cerro Azul, except for two reports from the southern side of Veraguas.

While this species is one of wide distribution there is little knowledge of it in Panamá other than the few specimens that have been collected. The only records for the Pacific slope of western Panamá are of one sent by Arcé to Salvin (Proc. Zool. Soc. London, 1867, p. 161), marked as from near Santiago, and another in the American Museum collected near Santa Fé on March 31, 1925, by Benson. From Bocas del Toro Wedel sent specimens to the Museum of Comparative Zoology taken between March 21 and 30, 1928, at elevations of 450 to 1,000 meters, on the Boquete trail, back of the Laguna de Chiriquí. Another was secured near Cricamola on February 15 and one at Guabo on April 10 (Peters, Bull. Mus. Comp. Zool., vol. 71, 1931, p. 297). There are two others in the Conover Collection of the Chicago Natural History Museum from Cricamola taken by Wedel on September 7, 1936, and October 25, 1937. Benson and Gaffney secured a pair at Guaval, on the Río Calovévora in Caribbean Veraguas which Griscom described as a distinct race *coloratus*. This, however, proves not to differ from *O. e. melanotis*.

Goldman on March 22 and 25, 1911, collected 4 females at 750 meters near the head of the Río Pacora on Cerro Azul, another on June 8 at 600 meters on Cerro Bruja, Colón, and a male on April 24, 1912 at 1,600 meters on Cerro Pirre in Darién. Hasso von Wedel on February 1, 1933, shot a male at Puerto Obaldía, San Blas that came to the Conover collection. The latest report of the species is an adult male, prepared by C. O. Handley, Jr., that was captured by a dog beside a forest trail on Cerro Azul, January 27, 1958.

Goldman left a manuscript note in which he described their scratchings as similar to those of other gallinaceous birds and says that the birds he collected were visible for a few seconds only as they ran with outstretched necks beneath the undergrowth. On Cerro Bruja one allowed him to approach closely. The only other observation on habits that I have seen is that of C. W. Richmond (Proc. U. S. Nat. Mus., vol. 16, 1893, p. 524) on the Río Escondido, eastern Nicaragua, where a flock of a dozen "flew into surrounding trees and afterward off into the woods, two or three at a time." The indication is that birds of this species may be less wary than their close relatives.

Schönwetter (Handb. Ool., pt. 4, 1961, p. 224; pt. 5, p. 267) says that one egg available was marked like the spotted eggs of *Odontophorus gujanensis marmoratus* and gives the measurements as 37.6 × 27.9 mm.

Individual variation in depth of color, especially on the lower surface, is considerable in the series seen both from Costa Rica and Panamá, so much so that there is no apparent basis for recognition of more than one race in this area.

ODONTOPHORUS DIALEUCOS Wetmore: Tacarcuna Wood Quail; Gallito del Monte Fajeado

FIGURE 1, FRONTISPIECE

Odontophorus dialeucos Wetmore, Smithsonian Misc. Coll., vol. 145, no. 6, Dec. 16, 1963, p. 5. (1,450 meters elevation, 6½ kilometers west of the summit of Cerro Malí, Serranía del Darién, Darién, Panamá.)

Upper foreneck white, with a broad central band of black, mixed with rufous-brown.

Description.—Length, 220 to 250 mm. Male, crown black mottled lightly with rufous and spotted finely with white; superciliary streak white; a mottled brown band across the hindneck, becoming cinnamon-buff where it joins the superciliary on either side; back brownish olive, barred and mottled with sooty black and cinnamon; inner secondaries and wing coverts snuff brown, finely marked with buffy white; tertials marked heavily with black; upper foreneck white, with a broad central band of black mixed with rufous-brown; rest of lower surface dull buffy brown to tawny olive, darker on flanks and under tail coverts, mottled with sooty black and buffy white.

Female, brighter brown on the lower surface.

Immature, like female, but with black band across foreneck broader so that it covers most of the area to the base of the bill; white of lower segment duller.

Measurements.—Males (3 specimens), wing 128.8-131.4 (129.9); tail 50.1-54.0 (52.5); culmen from base 19.8-20.0 (19.9); tarsus 45.2-47.6 (46.6) mm.

Females (4 specimens), wing 125.6-132.0 (130.9); tail 46.4-50.4 (47.8); culmen from base 19.4-20.0 (19.7); tarsus 44.5-49.2 (46.5) mm.

Resident. In the subtropical zone of the southern end of the Serranía del Darién; known at present from Cerro Malí and Cerro Tacarcuna.

The three specimens from which this interesting wood quail was described were collected by Dr. Pedro Galindo of the Gorgas Memorial Laboratory near a camp at 1,450 meters elevation located 6½ kilometers west of the summit of Cerro Malí. A young female came first to hand on June 5, 1963, followed by an adult pair two days later.

Among its relatives *Odontophorus dialeucos* resembles most *O. strophium* of the subtropical zone of the mountains of central Colombia. This also has a white upper foreneck banded broadly with black across the center but differs in the presence of a narrow black collar below the lower white neck band and in being rufous and cinnamon on the breast and sides, with prominent white spots and shaft lines. Its crown is fuscous-brown and its whole upper surface is rufescent with prominent black markings. The darker bird of Darién is an interesting contrast in its plainer pattern.

In February and March of the following year we found these birds fairly common on the slopes of Cerro Malí and Cerro Tacarcuna from 1,200 to 1,450 meters. They ranged in pairs and little flocks of six or eight in undergrowth, and were not wild since they had had no hunter contact. While they were birds of the forest floor, once one flew to a perch in a small tree 5 meters above the ground. When disturbed they gave the low, rapid calls common to other wood quail when approached.

ODONTOPHORUS LEUCOLAEMUS Salvin: Black-breasted Wood Quail; Gallito del Monte Pechinegro

Odontophorus leucolaemus Salvin, Proc. Zool. Soc. London, June 1867, p. 161. (Cordillera de Tolé, eastern Chiriquí, Panamá.)

Odontophorus smithianus Oberholser, Proc. Biol. Soc. Washington, vol. 45, Apr. 2, 1932, p. 39. (San Joaquin de Dota, Costa Rica.)

Odontophorus smithians "Oberholser" Griscom, Auk, vol. 50, July 6, 1933, p. 298. (Lapsus for *smithianus*.)

A forest quail with black breast and white throat (white sometimes much reduced).

Description.—Length, 220 to 240 mm. Adult (sexes alike), above, including the crest, dark cinnamon-brown, very finely barred with black to produce a mottled appearance; scapulars and inner secondaries spotted and barred boldly with black; flight feathers fuscous; outer web of primaries faintly spotted with cinnamon; outer webs of secondaries heavily mottled with dark cinnamon and dull black; tail dull black, with numerous narrow indefinite bars of cinnamon and cinnamon-buff; sides of head, malar region, lower foreneck, and breast black, the breast barred narrowly with white; throat and upper foreneck white; abdomen dull fuscous with faint tippings of cinnamon; sides, flanks, tibia, and under tail coverts like the upper surface but brighter brown; shorter under wing coverts like back, longer ones fuscous like flight feathers.

There is much variation in color in which the upper surface may be blacker, and the white of the throat much reduced or nearly absent; or both upper and lower surface, including much of the breast, are brighter brown. The supposed species *smithianus* was described from birds in the blacker phase.

Immature birds have the tip of the bill cinnamon to buffy brown, while in the adult it is black.

Measurements.—Males (10 from Panamá and Costa Rica), wing 117.9-130.1 (124.6), tail 44.2-58.6 (49.1), culmen from base 14.7-17.5 (16.3), tarsus 44.5-48.0 (45.9) mm.

Females (7 from Panamá and Costa Rica), wing 125.0-129.7 (127.2), tail 46.2-50.2 (48.2), culmen from cere 14.6-17.2 (15.6), tarsus 43.2-45.5 (44.1) mm.

Resident. Rare, in the subtropical zone of Chiriquí, Veraguas, and Bocas del Toro; recorded from 1,350 to 1,600 meters elevation.

This distinct species was named by Salvin from a female taken by Arcé in the Cordillera de Tolé, which is in eastern Chiriquí under present political boundaries, though recorded originally from "Veragua." Arcé later sent Salvin (Proc. Zool. Soc. London, 1870, p. 217) a specimen from Calovévora, Veraguas, and also one to Gould from Chitra (Salvin and Godman, Biol. Centr.-Amer., vol. 3, 1903, p. 311). In western Chiriquí Bangs (Proc. New England Zoöl. Club, vol. 3, 1902, p. 22) received specimens taken by W. W. Brown, Jr., near Boquete and also on the Caribbean slope beyond, which would place them in Bocas del Toro. In the American Museum of Natural History collection there is one specimen from Boquete, taken by Watson, another collected by Arcé at Chitra, and two taken at this same point at over 1,000 meters, December 30 and 31, 1925, by Benson. Mönniche (Blake, Fieldiana: Zool., vol. 36, 1958, p. 508) secured a male at Camp Cilindro on July 14, 1933, and a female at Camp Holcomb on June 26, 1933, both on the Caribbean side of the divide in Bocas del Toro. These last are the latest records for the species in Panamá.

There is a skin in the U. S. National Museum collected by Heyde and Lux labeled "Natá, Coclé," a lowland locality where this species would not be found. It is possible that the collectors secured it in a journey that they made into the subtropical zone beyond La Pintada.

The black-breasted wood quail ranges in the highlands to eastern and northern Costa Rica, but other than specimens that have been taken little is known of it. Carriker (Birds of Costa Rica, 1910, pp. 388-389) wrote of it in Costa Rica that like "all other species of the genus it is an inhabitant of the forest, congregates in small coveys, and keeps to the thickest parts of the jungle." Oberholser (Proc. Biol. Soc. Washington, 1932, p. 41) cited observations by Austin Paul Smith, who found it an elusive inhabitant of steep, heavily wooded slopes in Costa Rica where the "birds were noisy early in the morning during March and April."

RHYNCHORTYX CINCTUS CINCTUS (Salvin): Banded Wood Quail; Gallito del Monte Menor

Odontophorus cinctus Salvin, Ibis, ser. 3, vol. 6, no. 23, July 1876, p. 379. (Veraguas, Panamá.)

Odontophorus spodiostethus Salvin, Ibis, ser. 4, vol. 2, no. 8, Oct. 1878, p. 447. (Veraguas.)

Odontophorus rubigenis Lawrence Mss., Richmond, Proc. U. S. Nat. Mus., vol. 16, Oct. 4, 1893, p. 525. (Panamá.)

Rhynchortyx cinctus hypopius Griscom, Bull. Mus. Comp. Zoöl., vol. 72, no. 9, Jan. 1932, p. 320. (Puerto Obaldía, San Blas.)

A small forest-quail, with upper breast plain gray (male) or plain brown (female); head not prominently crested; bill heavy.

Description.—Length 170 to 200 mm. Male, crown and hindneck dark brown, very faintly spotted with buff and black; upper back dark gray, slightly mottled with buff, the feathers tipped more or less with brown; lower back paler gray, washed with buff, barred lightly and indistinctly with darker gray, and spotted with cinnamon-buff and black; uppermost lesser wing coverts black, barred narrowly with cinnamon; rest of wing coverts brownish gray, with irregular bars and spots of buff and black; tertials and innermost secondaries spotted boldly with black and barred with cinnamon; flight feathers fuscous; outer webs of primaries spotted faintly with buff; outer webs of secondaries with irregular spots and broken bars of cinnamon-buff; rump, upper tail coverts, and tail dull cinnamon, with shaft lines of black and mottling of fuscous; band from eye back over ear coverts dark grayish brown; side of head, including a broad superciliary line and the malar area, cinnamon; throat mixed white and light gray; foreneck and upper breast dark gray; lower breast cinnamon-buff; sides dull gray, mottled and washed with buff and cinnamon-buff; abdomen and tibia white; flanks and under tail coverts cinnamon-buff, barred with black; shorter under wing coverts brownish black, spotted faintly with white.

Female, browner above; a dull black stripe over eyelids and auricular region; superciliary and a spot on lores buffy white; throat white; foreneck and upper breast brown, with the feathers more or less gray basally; lower breast and sides white, barred heavily with black.

Downy young, (3 to 6 days old from Darién, collected March 26, 1915 by W. B. Richardson, A. M. N. H. 135313) down of crown, back, rump, and tail chocolate brown; line through eye across auriculars brownish black; throat, malar region, lores, and an indistinct line along side of crown dull cinnamon-buff; line from eye back above auricular region buff; lower foreneck, side and back of neck, upper breast, and upper back bright buffy brown; sides, flanks, and tibia dark gray; lower breast and abdomen white.

An adult female taken near Armila, San Blas, March 4, 1963, had the iris warm brown; cere and mandible neutral gray; base of culmen mouse brown; rest of maxilla black; tarsus, toes, and claws dull bluish gray.

Measurements.—Males (16 from Panamá), wing 112.0-119.5 (115.3), tail 38.0-49.1 (42.7), culmen from cere 14.7-16.0 (15.3), tarsus 32.7-36.7 (34.3) mm.

Females (7 from Panamá), wing 108.0-114.7 (111.7), tail 38.1-45.6 (42.3), culmen from cere 13.6-16.1 (14.6), tarsus 32.0-35.5 (33.1) mm.

Resident. Rather rare in forested areas of the tropical and lower subtropical zones; reported from Veraguas, and from western Province of Panamá (sight record on Cerro Campana); recorded mainly from the eastern half of the isthmus from eastern Colón (Cerro Bruja), eastern Panamá (Río Pequení, Chepo, Cerro Chucantí), Darién (Cerro Sapo, Cerro Malí), and San Blas (Mandinga, Armila, Puerto Obaldía).

The first specimens of this bird collected by Arcé came to Salvin through the dealer Boucard labeled "Veragua," without more definite locality. The sexes are so different that they were named as two distinct species and were so regarded until their identity was established by Hartert (Nov. Zool., vol. 9, 1902, pp. 600-601). Hellmayr (Proc. Zool. Soc. London, 1911, p. 1207) finally determined that the bird described as *cinctus* in 1876 was the female and that *spodiostethus,* named two years later, was based on the male sex.

The little known of this wood quail relates to the few localities in the eastern half of Panamá at which it has been taken. On the Pacific slope I secured a male on April 9, 1949, on a low hill at Zanja Limón on the Río Mamoní back of Chepo. In February 1950, we saw two in forest along the Río Chimán near the mouth of the Río Corotú. And on March 13 and 14 we secured specimens on the Cerro Chucantí, where they were found to elevations of 500 meters. In Darién Barbour and Brooks, in April 1922, collected 7, including 2 downy young, on Cerro Sapo, and Galindo secured two on Cerro Malí, a female at La Laguna at 1100 meters June 10, 1963, and a male on Cerro Malí at 1450 meters June 7, 1963. Goldman shot one April 18, and another May 3, 1912 at 1400 meters on Cerro Pirre. I saw one at Boca de Paya on the Río Tuira on March 13, 1959.

In the Caribbean drainage Griswold (Proc. New England Zoöl. Club, vol. 15, 1936, p. 101) recorded them on the Río Pequení above the old Salamanca Hydrographic Station. Goldman shot a male on June 7, 1911, at 600 meters on Cerro Bruja, and at Mandinga, in the Comarca de San Blas, Florentino, a native hunter, shot one for me in the forest immediately back of our little house. I saw another near here on February 14. H. von Wedel collected a series at Puerto Obaldía and Permé in 1930.

In addition to the specimen records W. M. Perrygo on March 21, 1951, flushed several in heavy forest on Cerro Campana.

These birds range in the same forests as the larger marbled wood quail. Perhaps because of their smaller size they seem often to hide, even when near at hand, rather than fly or run, and because of this habit they may be more common than the few observations that have been published indicate. In the heavy cover that they frequent it is only by chance that I have come onto them so directly as to cause them to fly. Near the mouth of the Paya early one morning one flushed near the border of a small clearing and flew so swiftly that it was in the cover of the bordering woodland before I could bring my gun around, the only time that I have seen one in the open. In their forest cover sometimes they run aside for a meter or two and sometimes fly for a few meters above the undergrowth, and then with set wings scale down again to the ground.

The claws of this species are quite small for birds of this family, indication that it may not share the scratching habit common in the related genus *Odontophorus*.

The typical subspecies has been found rarely north on the Caribbean slope of Costa Rica (recorded from Villa Quesada). It is more frequent in northwestern Colombia in Córdoba, northern Antioquia (Tarazá) and southern Bolívar (Volador). A much darker race *R. c. australis* Chapman is found on the Pacific slope in the Province of Chocó. An adult female from Cerro Pirre is somewhat intermediate toward this race. *Rhynchortyx cinctus hypopius* Griscom, described from the eastern San Blas, through the additional specimens now available is not separable, as the characters described from the original series are merely those of individual variation.

George N. Lawrence received a specimen from Panamá marked "Dec. 1879" with "Wallace" indicated as collector (A. M. N. H. no. 45162) that apparently he believed to be new as the label bears the name *"Odontophorus rubigenis"* in Lawrence's handwriting. Evidently he then found Salvin's description of the bird in the Ibis for 1878, as he added this reference on the label. Richmond inadvertently quoted Lawrence's manuscript name with descriptive data in comparing this specimen with one that he collected in eastern Nicaragua, and so the name *rubigenis* needs to be included in synonymy.

Schönwetter (Handb. Ool., pt. 4, 1961, p. 224; pt. 5, 1961, p. 268) describes 3 eggs of *R. c. australis* of northwestern Colombia as white without markings, with measurements 29.6-30.0×23.5-23.8 mm. The female taken at Armila, March 4, 1963 contained a nearly developed egg.

[**PHASIANUS COLCHICUS** Linnaeus: Ring-necked Pheasant; Faisán Común

Phasianus colchicus Linnaeus, Syst. Nat., ed. 10, vol. 1, 1758, p. 158. (Rion, formerly Phasis, Georgian S. S. R.)

In September 1959, Pablo Brackney released 80 pheasants on his property at Palo Santo near El Volcán, Chiriquí. These were birds about 5 months old that had been reared in a pheasantry near Panama City. Corn had been planted as food and cover for them, and in February and March of the following year many were present, as I heard males crowing regularly. One nest had been found at that time and the eggs taken and placed under a hen, as the area was to be burned, but they were lost. On March 18, 1960 Mr. Brackney saw one brood of young chicks. By 1963 they had multiplied and had begun to spread into adjacent areas. But in 1965 I was told that all had been shot by hunters. One had been killed about November, 1959, near Santa Clara, 25 kilometers west toward Costa Rica.]

[Family NUMIDIDAE: Guineafowl; Gallinas de Guinea

The seven living species of this family are native in Africa, including Madagascar and the Cape Verde Islands, with one extending to southwestern Arabia.

The guinea, or guinea-hen, common now in poultry yards, was known in the period of the Roman Empire, though the present-day domestic stock stems from birds brought to Europe from Africa by Portuguese traders during the fifteenth century. In the beginning the guinea-hen was known as the bird of Turkey, that geographic name being applied widely to Moslem countries from Africa eastward. In the writings of early naturalists it became confused with the larger turkey introduced from America a little later, which finally inherited the original name, and the bird from Africa became the guinea.

NUMIDA MELEAGRIS GALEATA Pallas: Guinea-hen, Gallina de Guinea

Numida galeata Pallas, Spic. Zool., vol. 1, fasc. 4, 1767, p. 13. (Based on the domesticated fowl: Murphy, Bull. Amer. Mus. Nat. Hist., 1924, pp. 264-265, suggested Bathurst, at the mouth of the Gambia River, as type locality.)

According to the records of La Jagua Hunting Club, 27 guineafowl were released at the clubhouse at 4:30 a.m. on June 11, 1933. The birds, obtained through Mr. Van Reed of Port-au-Prince, Haiti, from wild stock naturalized in that island, came in three lots on May 14, 25, and 31 of the year in question to Capt. William Ancrum at Balboa Heights. Karl Curtis informs me that some were seen from time to time through the following year, but that eventually all disappeared. There is no record of their nesting.

The species has been known as a game bird in the wild in Hispaniola for more than 200 years, and it was hoped that it might have become established in the woodlands that border the Río La Jagua marshes.]

Order GRUIFORMES

Family ARAMIDAE: Limpkin; Carrao

The single living species of this family ranges in the New World from the Okefinoke Swamp in southeastern Georgia through Florida and the Greater Antilles, and from south central México through Central America and South America to northern Argentina and southern Brazil. The relationships of the family are with the cranes and the trumpeters. Bones of two fossil species described from Oligocene deposits in South Dakota, and of a third from Middle Miocene beds in Nebraska, are indication of former diversity in the group and of its long history in the Americas. Bones of the living species have been found in Pleistocene deposits in several localities in Florida.

ARAMUS GUARAUNA (Linnaeus): Limpkin; Carrao

FIGURE 55

Form ibislike, but with shorter, heavier, nearly straight bill; blackish brown, with white streaks on the neck, and in some races on the body.

Description.—Length 580 to 630 mm. Adult (sexes alike), forehead and lores grayish brown; crown blackish brown, paler on the forehead; throat white; neck black to dark gray, streaked with white; body olive-brown, more or less streaked with white, the amount varying in the different subspecies (see beyond).

Downy young, chin dull white; throat and upper foreneck, an indistinct superciliary, malar region, and upper abdomen dull white, with the downy plumes tipped lightly with buffy brown; elsewhere dull brown, darker above and paler below.

Iris brown; bill grayish brown, almost black at the tip, with the base reddish brown on the mandible, and dull buff on the maxilla; tarsus and toes dull olive-black; claws darker, nearly black.

The limpkin is so rare in its occurrence in Panamá that its presence there has been overlooked until recent years. On the Isthmus these birds are found mainly along the lower courses of larger rivers where the forested banks are low so that they may be flooded in periods of high water. Their presence may be detected by the empty shells of large apple snails left on muddy shores, as these form their main food supply. In early morning limpkins may be found in the open, but at any alarm they retreat to the shelter of forest and there remain concealed. In other parts of their extensive tropical and subtropical range they come out in open marshes, but there is little suitable habitat of that type in Panamá, except in the banana farms of Bocas del Toro. Here limpkins are found occasionally on cleared lands that have been flooded.

To secure their food limpkins wade in shallow water probing with the bill. When an apple snail is found it is carried to the bank, and set in the mud with the opening upward. The bird, with partly opened bill tip, with quick dexterity then removes the horny operculum that protects the snail, when the mollusk is pulled out and swallowed.

Limpkins walk rather slowly, with constantly twitching tail, and a curious undulating tread that gives the impression of lameness or limping, from which the common name of limpkin is derived. Their flapping flight is performed with head and neck extended, and feet and legs projecting behind, in the manner of a crane. Where not hurried they often show an attractive mannerism in the air in which open wings are raised to a 45° angle and then brought down to body level, suggestive of the flight method of many of the larger butterflies.

As they move about they utter low clucking notes and then may burst out in loud calls of *car-r-r-rao car-r-r-rao,* from which they

Fig. 55.—Limpkin, carrao, *Aramus guarauna guarauna,* northern subspecies, heavily streaked with white.

derive their usual common name among those few of the country people that recognize them. To most they are not distinguished from the ibises, or *cocos.* The loud call, often mingled with harsher sounds, is given sometimes in flight, and also may be heard at night.

In the adult male limpkin the trachea, as it descends the neck, is elongated, and below the center is folded in a tight double loop on the right hand side. It then continues to enter the thorax, where it divides in the usual matter in two bronchi. The loop is not found in females, and I have found it absent also in males that I assumed to be immature. Apparently it is this stage that has misled some early authorities who have stated that such convolutions were not present in this species.

The nests of limpkins are masses of vegetation placed on tangled branches, or growths of vines. In areas of extensive marsh land they are built on mats of saw grass. The 4 to 8 eggs are ovate, with a slightly glossy, smooth shell, buff to olive-buff, with blotches of drab and brown.

Two of the recognized subspecies are found in Panamá.

ARAMUS GUARAUNA GUARAUNA (Linnaeus)

Scolopax guarauna Linnaeus, Syst. Nat., ed. 12, vol. 1, 1766, p. 242. (Cayenne.)

Characters.—White stripes confined to the sides of the head and neck, with a few on the lower surface and rarely on the wing coverts, partly concealed by darker feather ends; darker olive-brown; smaller.

Measurements.—Males (5 from Panamá and Colombia), wing 301-309 (305.2), tail 122.8-138.8 (129.1), culmen from base 104.6-116.8 (111.2), tarsus 109.6-126.8 (117.2) mm.

Females (3 from Panamá and Colombia), wing 290-291 (290.3), tail 122.2-129.7 (127.0), culmen from base 101.5-107.0 (104.7), tarsus 106.0-114.7 (109.4) mm.

Resident. Rare; found in the Canal Zone on the middle Río Chagres (above Juan Mina) and in Darién on the middle Río Tuira (Boca de Paya), and the lower middle Río Chucunaque (mouth of Río Ucurgantí).

The first report for Panamá was of a male taken by Festa at the Laguna de Pita near the mouth of the Río Tuira in August 1895 (Salvadori and Festa, Boll. Mus. Zool. Anat. Comp. Torino, vol. 15, 1900, p. 42). At Juan Mina on the Río Chagres on several occasions Enrique van Horn described to me an ibislike bird that I was certain must be a limpkin. In January 1958 he shot one for Dr. Frank Hartman, who in the course of his studies prepared it as a skin that he presented to the U. S. National Museum. The following year I found the empty snail shells left by these birds scattered over a muddy shore beneath overhanging bushes. And on January 28, 1958, I secured one for a specimen.

Later in the same season I collected a female on February 18 at our camp where the Río Paya enters the Tuira; and during the following month I noted one from time to time on the Paya immediately above its mouth. Collectors for the Gorgas Memorial Laboratory took another here on April 15. On the Chucunaque one was reported to me on March 21.

Hellebrekers (Zool. Med. Nat. Hist. Leiden, vol. 24, 1942, p. 245) gives the following description of a set of 6 eggs from Surinam in the Penard collection: "Ground: light buff . . . some eggs with a very slight greenish tinge. Spots: yellowish brown, sayal brown . . . especially at the large end, and purplish under markings. Average measurements in mm: 56.1 × 44.2."

On both the Chagres and the Tuira the limpkin ate the local apple snail *Pomacea zeteki* Morrison.

ARAMUS GUARAUNA DOLOSUS Peters

Aramus pictus dolosus Peters, Occ. Pap. Boston Soc. Nat. Hist., vol. 5, Jan. 30, 1925, p. 144. (Bolsón, Guanacaste, Costa Rica.)

Characters.—Olive-brown, with breast, sides, and wing coverts heavily streaked with white; back similarly marked but less heavily; secondaries with broad, partly concealed, white shaft streaks; larger.

Measurements (from Peters's original description).—Males (4 from México and Costa Rica), wing 315-333 (324), culmen 123-127 (125.7), tarsus 126-135 (131.5) mm.

Females (3 from México, British Honduras, and Costa Rica), wing 300-308 (304), culmen 102-115 (109.3), tarsus 117-119 (117.6) mm.

Status uncertain, rare. Recorded from western Bocas del Toro.

A male in the Chicago Natural History Museum was taken by Hasso von Wedel at Cricamola, Bocas del Toro, April 15, 1937. The only other probable occurrence of this race is a limpkin that I saw on the shore of an impoundment of water in the banana farms at Changuinola on January 24, 1958, a bird that I stalked without success. This subspecies ranges regularly from the lowlands of south central México and Honduras south to Costa Rica. To date it has not been recorded in Guatemala.

Schönwetter (Handb. Ool., pt. 5, 1961, p. 306) gives the measurements of one egg of this race from México as 58.0 × 45.6 mm.

Family RALLIDAE: Rails, Gallinules, and Coots; Cocalecas y Gallinetas de Agua.

Rails are found throughout much of the world, even on oceanic islands, absent only in arctic regions. Typically they are marsh inhabitants, with certain groups, the coots and gallinules, that swim and feed like ducks in open waters. Some others have adapted to dry land conditions, and may range in upland country, though these seem to require access with regularity to water. The 9 species found in Panamá are widely distributed and may be locally common, but are so retiring that little is known in detail of their manner of life.

FAMILY RALLIDAE

KEY TO THE SPECIES OF RALLIDAE

1. Flanks plain, without bars.. 3
2. Flanks barred with black and white............................ 10
3. Smaller, wing less than 130 mm.
   Uniform crake, *Amaurolimnas concolor guatemalensis*, p. 339
4. Larger, wing more than 150 mm................................. 5
5. Without a prominent frontal shield above the base of the bill; bill longer than the head (genus *Aramides*).................................... 7
6. With a prominent frontal shield above the base of the bill; bill not longer than the head.. 8
7. Head and neck gray, somewhat darker on the occiput; under wing coverts cinnamon-brown, barred with black.
   Gray-necked wood rail, *Aramides cajanea*, p. 341
   Head and upper neck chestnut-brown; under wing coverts black, barred with white (in some partly mixed with cinnamon).
   Rufous-crowned wood rail, *Aramides axillaris*, p. 346
8. Toes with prominent lateral membranes or lobes on each joint; frontal shield small, not extended on forehead back of the eyes.
   American coot, *Fulica americana americana*, p. 363
   Toes without lateral membranes or lobes; frontal shield large, much expanded on forehead, and extended back to center of eyes or farther... 9
9. Bill stouter; nostril small, its width about one half its length; feathering in front of eye terminated in a nearly straight vertical line along the base of the bill; adult brilliant green and blue; immature with more or less blue on wings........Purple gallinule, *Porphyrula martinica*, p. 360
   Bill more slender; nostril elongated, its length much more than twice its width; feathering in front of eye projecting at an angle on the base of the bill; coloration slate gray, black on the head.
   Common gallinule, *Gallinula chloropus*, p. 357
10. Back mixed brown and black, streaked narrowly with white (genus *Porzana*)... 11
    Back plain reddish or grayish brown, without streaks (genus *Laterallus*) 12
11. Larger, wing 100 mm. or more; space in front of eye black or dark gray.
    Sora, *Porzana carolina*, p. 350
    Smaller, wing 70 mm. or less; a prominent white line from base of bill to above eye..Yellow-breasted rail, *Porzana flaviventer flaviventer*, p. 348
12. Sides of neck and breast gray; rump and upper tail coverts black barred narrowly with white..........Gray-breasted rail, *Laterallus exilis*, p. 355
    Sides of neck and breast reddish brown; rump and upper tail coverts black or brownish black, without bars.
    White-throated rail, *Laterallus albigularis*, p. 351

AMAUROLIMNAS CONCOLOR GUATEMALENSIS (Lawrence): Uniform Crake; Rascón Castaño

Corethrura Gautemalensis (sic) Lawrence, Proc. Acad. Nat. Sci. Philadelphia, June 1863, p. 106. (Guatemala).

A rail of medium size, rufescent-brown on lower surface; olivaceous-brown above.

Description.—Length, 200-210 mm. Adult (sexes alike), olivaceous-brown above, more rufescent on the scapulars; side of head grayish brown; under surface rufous brown, lighter on the throat, darker on the sides and under tail coverts; wings fuscous, margined with brown; under wing coverts grayish brown to nearly black, washed lightly with rufous brown.

Immature, duller, more grayish brown on lower surface.

Iris orange-brown; side of maxilla, to a point anterior to nostril, and mandibular rami, dull yellowish green; rest of bill dusky neutral gray; bare skin adjacent to gape, and along the base of the mandible, dull grayish purple; front of tarsus and toes fuscous; sides and back of tarsus somewhat reddish brown; crus light reddish brown; distal end of claws dark neutral gray.

Measurements.—Males (4 from Panamá), wing 110.9-118.0 (114.3), tail 39.0-43.2 (41.8), culmen from base 25.5-28.2 (26.6), tarsus 40.8-42.9 (41.5) mm.

Females (3 from Panamá and Nicaragua), wing 110.0-114.0 (111.5), tail 44.7-46.7 (45.3), culmen from base 26.2-26.5 (26.3), tarsus 39.8-42.4 (41.3) mm.

Resident. Tropical zone, rare; recorded from Chiriquí (without definite locality); Bocas del Toro (Almirante); San Blas (Mandinga); Darién (sight record, El Real); and Isla San José, Archipiélago de las Perlas.

There is a female from Chiriquí in the American Museum of Natural History (Chapman, Bull. Amer. Mus. Nat. Hist., vol. 36, 1917, p. 217). H. von Wedel collected one at Almirante, Bocas del Toro, on August 5, 1927, and I shot two there on February 15 and March 5, 1958. At Mandinga, San Blas, I secured another on January 28, 1957. The record for Isla San José is of a female taken August 23, 1944 by Dr. J. P. E. Morrison. On January 23, 1964, I had a brief view of one at the edge of a road leading through marshy land near El Real, Darién.

The first one that I found at Almirante was in a dense thicket at the border of a banana plantation. My companion saw it move in the dark shadows, and after a few minutes, during which we remained partly hidden, it came furtively to peer at me. The second bird lurked half concealed under the ground cover at the border of a swampy spot. The one taken at Mandinga was in second growth at the border of a small quebrada.

The only published record of the egg that I have seen is that of Nehrkorn (Kat. Eiersamml., 1899, p. 202), who described one from

Guatemala, as reddish gray with a few small spots of violet and rust brown, and measurements of 34×31.5 mm. According to Schönwetter (Handb. Ool., pt. 5, 1961, p. 316) this egg has disappeared. (The measurements are quoted incorrectly by Schönwetter as 33× 26.5 mm.)

When I identified the collections made on the islands of San José and Pedro González, in the Archipiélago de las Perlas (Wetmore, Smithsonian Misc. Coll., vol. 106, no. 1, 1946), I made no mention of two eggs brought from San José by Dr. J. P. E. Morrison, after I had left the island, as at that time I was not wholly certain of their identity. Through familiarity with the avifauna of Panamá that has come since I am certain now that they are of the present species. They were brought by one of the work force for the Chemical Warfare Service on September 1, 1944, with the statement that they had been found in a low nest, but no other information. Their form is somewhat pointed short subelliptical, with the slightly glossy shell smooth. The color is pale buff with a faint cinnamon cast, marked sparingly with small scattered spots of chestnut brown, that appear violet or grayish blue when overlaid by a thin deposit of shell. Though one is broken, measurements may be made from both as follows: 32.7×27.3 and 32.6×26.5 mm.

There is a study skin of this race in the British Museum (Natural History) from the Salvin-Godman collection with the data "Guatemala (McLeannan)," cited in this same form by Sharpe (Cat. Birds Brit. Mus., vol. 23, 1894, p. 88), in which either the locality or the collector is in error, since McLeannan worked only in Panamá.

ARAMIDES CAJANEA (Müller): Gray-necked Wood Rail; Cocaleca Gris
FIGURE 56

Large size, gray head and neck, brown breast, and black abdomen mark this species.

Description.—Length 325 to 350 mm. Adults (sexes alike), head and neck gray, brownish on the crown; throat white to light gray; upper back and scapulars olive-green; breast, sides, and wings cinnamon-brown; lower back, rump, tail, flanks, and abdomen black; tibia dark, somewhat brownish, gray; under wing coverts cinnamon barred with black.

Downy young, head, foreneck, and upper breast sayal brown, with an indefinite line of deep mouse gray extending up the upper breast onto the foreneck; hind neck, wings, and rest of body, dull black, somewhat brownish black on under surface.

Iris red; bare skin around eye, and gape dull red; base of bill yellow to level of nostrils, changing there to light green for terminal half; gape red; crus, tarsus and toes red; claws grayish brown.

Though wood rails are widely distributed, and are as widely known, they are so secretive that their presence is recognized mainly from their calls heard in morning, evening, and during the early hours of

FIG. 56.—Gray-necked wood rail, cocaleca gris, *Aramides cajanea.*

night. Their range is governed by suitable cover to afford concealment, as they are found from the borders of mangrove swamps inland throughout the tropical zone, and in places they may follow streams to the lower edge of the subtropical zone at elevations up to 1,300 meters. In hill country they often range on slopes where forest is not too high to points that are far from water. On Isla San José in the Pearl Islands, and on Isla Coiba, I heard them or noted their tracks regularly in the drier upland areas.

They are found in pairs, except for limited periods when they may be accompanied by young. In the dry season on the eastern side of the Azuero Peninsula I have seen them regularly in early morning in the open trails, walking about like chickens. The tail is held at an angle, and the birds move stealthily, with the head held forward. At any alarm their slow steps change instantly to a rapid run and they disappear. Aside from this I have had only an occasional glimpse of one at the edge of mangroves, or along some stream, though often their presence has been known from their calls. These are loud, with a curious halting cadence, and rise and fall in sound with the individual syllables. They may continue for several minutes. Regularly the notes are uttered as a duet, with two birds alternating in their utterance. At a distance the sound is melodious and pleasing, but near at hand low, rattling, clacking notes intermingled completely spoil the agreeable effect.

The names by which they are known are taken mainly from imitation of their calls, the usual one being *cocaleca.* Sometimes this is shortened to *coclé,* or varied to *chilico,* or *chilicote.* English-speaking Panamanians in the province of Bocas del Toro call them mangrove hens, a name obviously of Jamaican origin. And those American hunters near the Canal Zone, who know them, refer to them as the king rail. The name *cocaleca,* obviously derived from the call notes, is also applied to other rails, even to those of small size.

In upland areas on occasion I have eaten the bodies of those that I have shot for specimens, but birds taken in the mangrove swamps, where their main food is crabs, often have an offensive odor.

Though they move about at night, usually in the hour or two immediately after sunset, or in periods of bright moonlight, they also sleep, as I have come across them occasionally while night-hunting. They rest two or three meters above the water, or above the ground in the brush adjacent to a stream or swamp, often in exposed situations, and may be so dazed by the jack light that I have caught them by hand. I have seen captive birds in possession of native boys tethered in a curious way by a slender cord of tough bark fastened to the bill through the open nostrils, which are perforated naturally from side to side.

In addition to small crabs they eat roaches and other large insects and often have the stomach crammed with small seeds and the remains of drupes. George Shiras, 3d (Nat. Geogr. Mag., Aug. 1915, p. 174), had them come regularly at night to his cameras set with flashlight powder, regardless of whether the bait used was meat or fruit.

ARAMIDES CAJANEA CAJANEA (Müller)

Fulica cajanea P. L. S. Müller, Vollstand. Natursyst. Suppl. Register-Band, 1776, p. 119. (Cayenne.)

Characters.—Averaging somewhat larger; darker in color, above and on the under surface.

Measurements.—Males (8 from Panamá), wing 172-192 (182.2), tail 57.8-71.8 (62.9), culmen from base 51.0-58.3 (53.2), tarsus 70.0-81.0 (75.8) mm.

Females (9 from Panamá), wing 174-184 (179.1), tail 57.5-67.1 (63.8), culmen from base 50.0-54.1 (52.0), tarsus 69.0-81.6 (75.2) mm.

Resident. Coastal lowlands throughout the Republic, mainly in the larger river valleys; found locally in the subtropical zone; in Chiriquí a few range to 1,000 to 1,300 meters on the southern and western mountain slopes; in Los Santos to 1,000 meters on Cerro Hoya; in Darién to 1,400 meters on Cerro Malí: Isla Coiba; Isla Cébaco; reported on Isla Parida.

The open nest of these birds is built of twigs, dried weed stems, and similar materials placed in a bush or low tree over or near water, at an elevation of a meter to 5 or 6 meters above the surface. Usually it is well concealed, and when seen may not be distinguished from other masses of dried vegatation left amid the branches by flood waters. The well formed inner depression normally holds 3 to 5 eggs. Belcher and Smooker (Ibis, 1935, p. 282) record exceptional sets of 6 and 7. A set of 3 in the U. S. National Museum taken by Smooker on the Caroni River, Trinidad, on September 3, 1931, vary from subelliptical to oval and are somewhat glossy, with a very slightly roughened shell. Two are pale cream color, while the third is pale buff. All are marked sparingly with small spots of cinnamon, chestnut, and lavender, mainly near the larger end. They measure 46.7 × 33.3, 46.8 × 32.4, and 46.8 × 33.5 mm. Belcher and Smooker state that some eggs are marked with "scrawlings and hair lines of brown."

These rails are hunted to some extent but are not common enough to be regarded as game birds.

Three that I secured on Isla Coiba are equal in size to typical *cajanea* of the mainland, but are slightly darker. Occasional mainland specimens, however, approach their color closely. The tendency toward deepened pigmentation, common in birds resident on Coiba, thus is indicated, but not sufficiently to warrant recognition by name.

ARAMIDES CAJANEA LATENS Bangs and Penard

Aramides cajanea latens Bangs and Penard, Bull. Mus. Comp. Zoöl., vol. 62, Apr. 1918, p. 41. (Isla del Rey, Archipiélago de las Perlas, Panamá.)

Characters.—Averaging smaller than typical *cajanea* and definitely paler in color, especially on crown, neck, and under surface; brown of breast and sides more cinnamon-buff, less rufous.

Measurements.—Males (2 specimens), wing 168, 173; tail 57.5, 59.7; culmen from base 50.0, 51.8; tarsus 68.2, 69.0 mm.

Females (2 specimens), wing 161.0, 172.0; tail 57.5, 63.8; culmen from base 51.0, 51.5; tarsus 67.0, 70.3 mm.

Resident. Archipiélago de las Perlas (Isla del Rey, Isla Víveros, probably Isla de Cañas, and Isleta Málaga).

This race is known from the four specimens of the type series in the Museum of Comparative Zoology collected on Isla del Rey in February and March 1904 by W. W. Brown. The statements of characters and the measurements given above are from my personal examination of these birds. Rendahl (Ark. Zool., 1920, p. 22) listed a female taken on Isla Víveros, on April 4, 1882, by Carl Bovallius, that is unquestionably this race as the bird is said to be paler on the head, neck, and underparts, when compared with skins from Surinam and Baía. From January 21 to 23, 1960, I heard wood rails calling on several occasions on Isla Cañas, which is separated from the eastern side of Rey by a very narrow channel; and at Isleta Málaga, immediately east of Isla Bayoneta, heard others on January 29. It is probable that these records refer to the race *latens* since the islands listed lie on the same shallow submarine platform that surrounds Isla del Rey.

ARAMIDES CAJANEA MORRISONI Wetmore

Aramides cajanea morrisoni Wetmore, Proc. Biol. Soc. Washington, vol. 59, Mar. 11, 1946, p. 50. (Isla San José, Archipiélago de las Perlas, Panamá.)

Characters.—Similar in small size to *A. c. latens*, but gray of hindneck clearer, less brownish, and also darker; back, wing coverts, and scapulars darker, more olivaceous green.

Measurements.—Males (6 specimens), wing 165-179 (174.3), tail 54.1-64.2 (58.3), culmen from base 46.8-58.7 (52.5), tarsus 64.2-71.0 (67.6) mm.

Females (6 specimens), wing 161-173 (166.5), tail 54.5-56.8 (54.9), culmen from base 48.0-51.9 (49.8), tarsus 62.7-70.0 (66.5) mm.

Resident. Fairly common; islands of San José and Pedro González, Archipiélago de las Perlas.

During field work on Isla San José in 1944 I found these rails common but so shy that, though I heard them constantly, it was only on occasion that I had a glimpse of one in the undergrowth of the forest. They were recorded in my notes almost daily but mainly from their calls, or from their tracks, seen in the dust of trails and roadways. During February and March they ranged in pairs. Later in the season, as construction work concerned with a field laboratory for chemical tests spread, they became more accustomed to human presence through the many workmen engaged on roads and trails, and were less timid. After my departure, Morrison, who remained on the island, secured a dozen adults and one young bird in down taken July 22.

This race is like the form of Isla del Rey in small size, but in the series from the two islands available, *morrisoni* differs definitely in darker color. It should be noted that San José and Pedro González are separated from the shallow bank around Isla del Rey by depths of 12 to 15 meters or more.

ARAMIDES AXILLARIS Lawrence: Rufous-crowned Wood Rail; Cocaleca Cabecicastaña

Aramides axillaris Lawrence, Proc. Acad. Nat. Sci. Philadelphia, June 3, 1863, p. 107. (Barranquilla, Colombia.)

Smaller than the gray-necked wood rail, with head and neck rufous-brown.

Description.—Length 250-280 mm. Adults (sexes alike), head, upper hindneck, foreneck, and breast rufous-brown; throat white; lower hindneck and extreme upper back gray; back and scapulars olive brown; wings chestnut; rump, tail, flanks, and under tail coverts black; center of abdomen grayish brown; under wing coverts white, barred with black.

Immature, neck and breast grayish brown.

A male taken on January 19, 1963, at Puerto Aguadulce had the iris orange-brown; bill greenish gray, darker toward the tip, with the side of the maxilla behind the nostril, and the base of the mandible shading from this grayer shade to dull honey yellow which becomes true honey yellow on the lower half of the base of the mandible; crus, tarsus and toes dull red; claws black.

Measurements.—(From Ridgway and Friedmann, U. S. Nat. Mus., Bull. 50, pt. 9, 1941, p. 125).

Males (18 from México and Colombia), wing 163-174 (169), tail 53-63 (58.3), exposed culmen 39.5-46.0 (43.7), tarsus 52.5-63.0 (59.5) mm.

Females (13 from México and Panamá), wing 145.5-170.0 (163.6), tail 47.0-62.5 (57.3), exposed culmen 37.5-46.0 (42.2), tarsus 50.0-60.5 (57.6) mm.

Resident. Known in Panamá from the mangrove swamps near Almirante, Bocas del Toro, and the Río Pocrí, at Puerto Aguadulce, Coclé.

Hasso von Wedel collected two females, one adult and one immature, on January 14 and 15, 1929, on the Quebrada Nigua, across from Almirante. On January 27, 1958, as I sat at the landing place on the south side of Water Valley, to skin out a heron that threatened to spoil, one of these rails came quietly across the mud of the swamp to watch me. In the hand this proved to be an immature female, still gray underneath, but with head and neck partly changed to the chestnut of the adult.

In January 1963 I was interested to find this species in the mangroves bordering the Río Pocrí at Puerto Aguadulce and to learn that local hunters were familiar with it as a species distinct from the larger *cocaleca*. On my first fleeting view of one I noted what seemed unusually dark coloration but attributed this to the dark shadows in which it ran. Male and female were taken at this same point on January 19 and 22 as they came out to the water's edge at low tide. Mannerisms in walking, in jerking the tail, and alert though furtive posture were like those of the companion species. From what I was able to learn the *cocaleca cabecicastaña* is confined to the mangroves and does not wander far from their shelter. Though specimens have been reported from the Nicoya Peninsula in Costa Rica, and from Nuquí in northwestern Chocó in Colombia, this is the first report from the Pacific side of the republic. Nothing more is known of the species in Panamá. (The records in Ridgway and Friedmann, cited above, for David and Lion Hill refer to *Aramides c. cajanea*.)

Belcher and Smooker (Ibis, 1935, p. 283) in Trinidad record the nest as "an open bowl of small twigs, lined with weed-stems, dead leaves, and, finally, with green bamboo leaves. One was at about ten feet from the ground in a small tree, the other on a dead stump overhanging the river, six feet above the water. The clutch in each case was five." They describe the color and form of the eggs as like those of *Aramides c. cajanea*.

Schönwetter (Handb. Ool., pt. 5, 1961, p. 317; pt. 6, 1962, p. 343) gives the size of ten eggs that he has examined as ranging from $43\text{-}47 \times 31\text{-}36.1$ mm.

PORZANA FLAVIVENTER FLAVIVENTER (Boddaert): Yellow-breasted Rail; Cocalequita Enana

FIGURE 57

Rallus flaviventer Boddaert, Table Planch. Enl., 1783, p. 52. (Cayenne.)

Smallest of the rails in Panamá; crown dull black, with a white line over the eye.

Description.—Length 120 to 130 mm. Adult (sexes alike), top of head and nape, and a streak through eye dull black; line from base of bill over eye white; side of head pale gray or pale buff; feathers of back, scapulars, and tail black or brownish black centrally, with wide borders of buff to dark cinnamon-buff, and narrow shaft lines of white; lesser wing coverts brown, with faint tips of white; a streak of black, with the feathers tipped with white, on the central, middle, and greater coverts; wings in some barred heavily with black and white; throat, upper foreneck, upper breast, and abdomen white, with a strong wash of buff to cinnamon buff on lower foreneck, upper breast, and adjacent sides; sides of lower breast, abdomen, flanks, and under tail coverts barred heavily with black and white.

Immature, with indefinite bars of dark neutral gray on neck and breast, faint in the center, more evident at the sides.

Downy young not known.

Iris reddish brown; most of maxilla and tip of mandible dark neutral gray; sides of maxilla at base, below the nostril, and the mandibular rami dull greenish olive; tarsus and toes honey yellow; crus and posterior face of tibiotarsal joint mouse brown; claws mouse brown.

Measurements.—Males (7 from Panamá), wing 64.2-69.8 (66.5), culmen from base 16.1-18.5 (17.3), tarsus 22.0-24.2 (23.5) mm.

Females (3 from Panamá), wing 64.3-67.3 (66.0), culmen from base 15.9-17.7 (16.8), tarsus 23.0-25.6 (24.2) mm.

Resident. Found locally in fresh marshes; fairly common near Juan Mina on the Río Chagres; recorded also at Playa Jobo, below Las Lajas, Chiriquí; sight record near Changuinola, Bocas del Toro.

On the early morning of January 8, 1955, as I watched the marsh at the border of the Río Chagres, a short distance below Juan Mina, two of these little rails came walking out at the edge of the floating water plants. The one that I secured on this occasion was the first record for the Isthmus. The following year in eastern Chiriquí on February 24, as I waded through an extensive fresh-water ciénaga back of the coastal sand dunes at Playa Jobo, below Las Lajas, one flushed from low grass growing in the water, and I killed it on the wing. Another was seen on this same occasion. Following this I found these rails fairly common in the marshes bordering the Chagres between Gamboa and Juan Mina, though to be seen only with understanding of their habits. They seem to congregate in small groups in limited areas, and in these are fairly common. In early morning, soon after dawn, they often climb up in the top of clumps of grass growing in the water, and rest there briefly in the

FIG. 57.—Yellow-breasted rail, cocalequita enana, *Porzana flaviventer flaviventer.*

early morning sun. And for an hour or so they may appear in little open areas in the marsh, on muddy shores, or on floating water plants, but then withdraw to heavy cover for the day. Again toward sunset they may appear, but more briefly. The larger white-throated rails, common in these same areas, may drive at them if they approach closely, but the smaller species escapes readily, sometimes running across the floating plants with flapping wings to keep from sinking. None taken in January and February were in breeding condition, though gonads were beginning to develop in some of the males examined. Nothing is known of their nesting.

Eisenmann (Condor, 1957, p. 250) reported two of these rails seen near Changuinola, Bocas del Toro, on June 30, 1956.

From the records available it is evident that this species is widely distributed in Panamá. The series of 10 that I have taken agree in size, and in extent and depth of the deep buff to cinnamon-buff on the forepart of the body, with the typical race of northern South America.

The race *Porzana flaviventer woodi* named from El Salvador, and known now from northern Veracruz in México, and from the Río San Juan in Nicaragua, is smaller, and paler in the colors mentioned.

PORZANA CAROLINA (Linnaeus): Sora; Cocalequita Pasajera

Rallus carolinus Linnaeus, Syst. Nat., ed. 10, vol. 1, 1758, p. 153. (Northeastern Manitoba.)

Breast gray; back olive brown, streaked with black, and lined with white.

Description.—Length 190-200 mm. Adult male, center of crown, forehead, loral area, side of head to eyes, throat and foreneck black; line from fore crown back over eyes, side of head behind eyes, side of neck, and breast light gray; line on either side of black crown, back of neck, and upper back dull buffy brown, changing to light olive-brown on back and scapulars, the whole marked with irregular streaks of black, and lined with white; wings fuscous, edged with dull buffy brown; wing coverts dull buffy brown; lower breast and abdomen white; under tail coverts white, washed with buff; sides and flanks dull black, barred with white.

Females have the black of head and throat reduced, and more white on the back.

Immature birds have still less black on the throat and foreneck.

Measurements.—Males (10 specimens), wing 103.0-109.5 (106.7), tail 43.5-53.0 (47.9), culmen 20.0-22.0 (21.1), tarsus 31.0-33.5 (32.7) mm.

Females (10 specimens), wing 99.5-104.5 (101.1), tail 40.0-49.0 (45.6), culmen 18.0-22.0 (19.5), tarsus 27.0-31.0 (29.2) mm.

Migrant from the north. Fairly common; recorded from October 1 to March 18: Reported from Chiriquí, Veraguas, Bocas del Toro, Canal Zone, eastern Province of Panamá, San Blas; Isla Coiba.

These rails are found in fresh-water marshes, areas of wet lands grown with low sedges and grasses, and along the open banks of lowland streams and drainage ditches. In such localities they range in company with the white-throated rail and like that species are seen walking and skulking under cover. They often fly short distances when approached, but also may crouch and hide. I have found them occasionally climbing about in marsh growth that stood in water about a meter in depth.

In Panamá they are most common on the Caribbean slope.

LATERALLUS ALBIGULARIS (Lawrence): White-throated Rail; Carrasqueadora

FIGURE 58

Small; throat white, with sides of neck and breast reddish brown.

Description.—Length 130 to 150 mm. Adult (sexes alike), above, reddish brown throughout, or (in the race *cinereiceps*) with crown dark gray, and back and wings reddish brown; wing coverts in some individuals plain, in others barred with white; throat white; sides of neck and breast rufous brown; rest of lower surface, including flanks and under tail coverts, white barred with black; in some the center of the breast and abdomen white.

Immature, neck and sides dark gray, with only a slight amount of rufous-brown; center of breast and abdomen white; sides and flanks dusky neutral gray, barred lightly with white.

Downy young, black.

An adult female of the typical form *L. a. albigularis* that I took at El Real, January 22, 1964, had the iris orange-red; base of maxilla below nostril, cutting edge except at tip, and basal three-fourths of mandible greenish neutral gray; rest of basal half of maxilla fuscous black; tip of maxilla and mandible fuscous; front of crus, tarsus, and toes dull yellowish brown; back of crus fuscous black; back of tarsus dull greenish brown; claws fuscous.

This is the most common of the rails in the republic, found in the tropical zone, where it ranges along the wet borders of streams wherever there is cover, and in marshy areas in general. Occasionally there is a glimpse of one as it runs or flies a few meters across some open space, but usually their presence is known from their rattling, chattering calls that are given at any alarm. Though this note is heard regularly it is seldom that the bird is seen in its delivery, so that it was several years before I was certain of the identity of the bird, though frequently the rail calls from a distance of a few meters. The note is a rapid repetition that begins suddenly, is repeated for several seconds, and then terminates more slowly. Often when one calls two or three nearby answer.

In the period of rains these rails range widely away from the marshes in any low cover, but in dry season, though they may come out briefly on higher ground, they are found mainly in lower areas. It is seldom that one is seen wholly in the open, and when they cross trails, or other areas where there is no cover, usually they fly. On floating vegetation they often run with wings flapping to keep from sinking.

As noted in the heading, some individuals have the wing coverts marked with light bars that vary from white to cinnamon-brown. Two distinct races are found in the Republic.

FIG. 58.—White-throated rail, carrasqueadora, *Laterallus albigularis*.

Hellmayr and Conover (Cat. Birds Amer., pt. 1, no. 1, 1942, pp. 375, 376) list the forms of *Laterallus albigularis* as races of *Laterallus melanophaius* (Vieillot), found from southeastern Colombia and Venezuela to northern Argentina and Brazil. The two groups are closely similar in color pattern, but in *melanophaius* the under tail coverts are plain brown without markings, while in *albigularis* this area is barred heavily with black and white. An occasional *albigularis* has some brown markings in the area concerned, varying from a faint cinnamon wash on the tips of a few feathers to a light suffusion of cinnamon brown, that however does not obscure the pattern of barring. This is found in only about 20% of the series of more than

60 specimens that I have handled. It should be added that in extreme examples the cinnamon color extends up over the abdomen, so that it appears to be a tendency toward a rufescent phase rather than an indication of close relationship with the other species.

LATERALLUS ALBIGULARIS ALBIGULARIS (Lawrence)

Corethrura albigularis Lawrence, Ann. Lyc. Nat. Hist. New York, vol. 7, 1861, p. 302. (Atlantic side of the Isthmus of Panamá, along the line of the Panama Railroad.)

Characters.—Top of head reddish brown; side of head similar, or, in some, brighter brown.

Measurements.—Males (14 from Panamá), wing 73.3-81.1 (76.4), culmen from base 17.7-20 (19.2, average of 13), tarsus 27.8-32.3 (30.9) mm.

Females (12 from Panamá), wing 71.0-77.4 (74.2), culmen from base 16.5-18.6 (17.9), tarsus 29.0-31.2 (29.7) mm.

The length of the tail is omitted, as this measurement cannot be made with accuracy.

Resident. Tropical zone, locally common; on the Pacific slope from Costa Rica eastward through Darién; ascending in Chiriquí from sea level to 1,250 meters near El Volcán; recorded also from Boquete; in Coclé taken at El Valle (600 meters); and in Darién from sea level to 600 meters elevation near Cana; on the Caribbean side found from western Colón east to the Colombian boundary; Isla Coiba.

These rails are especially common around Gatun Lake and along the Río Chagres from Gamboa to the bridge on the Trans-Isthmian Highway. I found them present in numbers around Mandinga in the San Blas, where they ranged from marshy spots for some distance out into high grass in open clearings, especially in early morning. In Darién specimens were taken by Festa at the Laguna de Pita, and by W. B. Richardson at El Real. In 1912 Goldman found them abundant around swampy places in the level valley at Cana and collected several. Benson secured others here in 1928. Soon after that date the mines of that area were closed and the whole region was abandoned. In January 1961 I found that the valley was again heavily forested, and so the only rail habitat was in small marshy areas.

On Isla Coiba, there were a few pairs around a small lagoon back of Catival, and others in a marshy spot nearer the sea, both areas in the drainage of the Río San Juan. The three taken do not differ from birds of the mainland.

In laboratory examination of 6 stomachs it was found that approximately 90% of the food was vegetable. In part this was a mass of fiber that was not identified. Mixed with it were seeds of a grass (*Panicum*), sedges (including *Scleria* and *Fimbristylis*), spurge, and *Solanum*. The animal food included spiders, Orthoptera, a variety of beetles, flies, and ants.

The label on a specimen in the British Museum (Natural History) received with the Salvin-Godman collection reads "Veraguas, 1876, Arcé" and is so listed (without the date) by Sharpe (Cat. Birds Brit. Mus., vol. 23, 1894, p. 142). Inasmuch as Arcé at the date in question had transferred his collecting to Chiriquí, the bird probably came from that Province, where this rail is locally common. There are no records from the Pacific slope of Veraguas, as the bird has not been found between eastern Chiriquí (Las Lajas) and eastern Coclé (El Valle). It is also unknown at present from the entire Azuero Peninsula.

Outside of Panamá this race is found north on the Pacific slope to the Gulf of Nicoya in southwestern Costa Rica, and to the south from Antioquia, in western Colombia, to western Ecuador.

In spite of the widespread abundance of this subspecies nothing is recorded of its nesting.

LATERALLUS ALBIGULARIS CINEREICEPS (Lawrence)

Porzana cinereiceps Lawrence, Ann. Lyc. Nat. Hist. New York, vol. 11, nos. 3-4, Feb. 1875, p. 90. (Talamanca, Costa Rica.)

Characters.—Crown and sides of head gray, in contrast with the dark brown of the nape, hindneck, and back.

Measurements.—Males (10 from Nicaragua, Costa Rica, and Panamá), wing 70.0-75.0 (72.3), culmen from base 17.1-19.7 (18.6), tarsus 29.2-32.5 (30.7) mm.

Females (5 from Nicaragua, Costa Rica, and Panamá), wing 67.8-73.8 (71.2), culmen from base 16.4-18.3 (17.3), tarsus 26.8-29.0 (28.3) mm.

Resident. Tropical zone on the Caribbean slope in Bocas del Toro, from Costa Rica east to the Río Calovévora, on the boundary with the Province of Veraguas.

These rails are fairly common near Changuinola and around the western border of Almirante Bay. On the Chiriquí Lagoon they have been recorded on Isla Bastimentos and at Chiriquicito and Cricamola. H. von Wedel secured specimens also at Guabo near Chiriquí Grande. Specimens taken by Benson on the Río Calovévora are of this race, which indicates a range extending into western Veraguas in this river valley. To the north this form ranges on the Caribbean slope to northeastern Nicaragua.

Richmond (Proc. U. S. Nat. Mus., vol. 16, 1893, pp. 528-529), who found these rails common on the Río Escondido, in southeastern Nicaragua, described nests as globular, with a small opening in one side, slightly elevated above the ground in grass, built of grass, and lined with similar materials. Three sets of 3, 4, and 5 eggs in the U. S. National Museum that he collected on May 30, July 18, and August 26, 1892, are subelliptical to slightly oval, with a very slightly roughened shell without gloss. The ground color is light creamy white, marked with small spots of cinnamon and cinnamon-brown, varied to lilac, scattered over the eggs, but more abundant at the larger end. The range of measurement is as follows: 27.3-28.9 × 20.6-21.8 mm. A nest found by Huber (Proc. Acad. Nat. Sci. Philadelphia, vol. 84, 1932, p. 209) at Eden in northeastern Nicaragua, was similar in form and location, and in color and marking of the 3 eggs, which, with measurements of 28.1-32.5 × 20.9-22.0 mm., were slightly larger.

A recently hatched young bird, received from the Gorgas Memorial Laboratory, taken from a nest a little over half a meter from the ground, found near Almirante, March 28, 1962, came preserved in alcohol. The down appears black over the entire body. The bill is pale brownish white, with an irregular band of black around the center, anterior to the nostril.

In an occasional specimen the crown is washed strongly with cinnamon-brown so that the appearance is that of *L. a. albigularis*. On close examination, however the feathers of the loral area, and around and over the eye are gray either wholly or on the partly concealed basal area.

LATERALLUS EXILIS (Temminck): Gray-breasted Rail; Cocalequita Pechiceniza

Rallus exilis Temminck, Nouv. Rec. Planch. Col. Ois., livr. 88, 1831, pl. 523. (Cayenne.)

Small, with gray crown, and a broad reddish brown band on hindneck.

Description.—Length 135 to 145 mm. Adult (sexes alike), crown gray, paler on sides of head, sides of neck, and breast; a broad band of bright reddish brown from the back of the head and the hindneck down to the upper back; back, scapulars, and wing coverts light olive-brown, the wing coverts barred narrowly with white; primaries and secondaries fuscous on inner webs, light olive-brown on outer webs; throat, upper foreneck, and center of abdomen pure white; sides, flanks, rump, and upper and under tail coverts barred narrowly with black and white; tail olive-brown.

Immature birds are said to lack the brown band on the hindneck.
Downy young are not known.

Iris crimson; eyelids clay color; under part of mandible neutral gray; rest of bill dull green; tarsus and toes umber brown; claws dark neutral gray.

Measurements.—Males (2 from Honduras and Nicaragua), wing 72, 72.1; culmen from base 16.5, 17.2; tarsus 22, 26.8 mm.

Females (2 from Isla Coiba and Colombia), wing 74.2, 74.7; culmen from base 16.8, 17.4; tarsus 24.8, 24.8 mm.

Resident. Very rare; Puerto Obaldía, San Blas; Isla Coiba.

The only records for the Republic are of an adult female brought to me alive by a convict on Isla Coiba on January 28, 1956, and of another female, an immature bird, also caught alive in the partly dry channel that passes through the village of Puerto Obaldía, San Blas on March 14, 1963. The one first mentioned was captured when men cleared a tract of marshy ground near the Cativa work camp at the Río San Juan, back of Bahía Damas on the eastern side of the island. The second was taken following similar clearing operations in the coconut groves bordering the village of Puerto Obaldía.

In the latter part of 1961 Mrs. Ricardo Marciaq of Panamá purchased one of these rails alive in the city market but was not able to ascertain where it had been captured. It is probable that it came from Panamá, but this is not certain, since live birds are brought in rather regularly from Colombia. In February 1962 I saw this bird in the collections of living animals at Summit Gardens in the Canal Zone, where it was confined in a small aviary. It showed a trace of albinism in a few scattered feathers over the body.

The species is widely distributed in tropical America but is one that is little known. To the north it has been found in southern Honduras on the Río Segovia and in southeastern Nicaragua on the Río Escondido. In South America it is recorded from northern Colombia, Venezuela, and Trinidad to Ecuador and northern Brazil.

Belcher and Smooker (Ibis, 1935, p. 284) describe a nest found on the Caroni marshes, Trinidad, as "globular, with a large side entrance-hole; it was built of dry coarse grass-blades and weed-stems, and set near the root in the center of a stool of sugar-cane. The three eggs * * * are rather long ovals, smooth-shelled, and with a little gloss; the ground-colour in all is cream, but in two the spotting is of dark brown with underlying pale grey markings, thickest at the big end, while the third has smears of two shades of brown, disposed irregularly over the surface." Schönwetter (Handb. Ool., pt. 6, 1962, p. 346) gives the measurement of 5 (including those from Trinidad described above) as 29.8-32.5 × 22.5-24.0 mm.

GALLINULA CHLOROPUS (Linnaeus): Common Gallinule; Gallineta de Agua

FIGURE 59

Fulica Chloropus Linnaeus, Syst. Nat., ed. 10, vol. 1, 1758, p. 152. (England.)

Frontal shield, and bill (except for the yellow tip) red; toes without lobes.

Description.—Length 290-310 mm. Adult (sexes alike), head and upper neck slate-black; lower neck, breast, and sides slate-gray, the sides with prominent white streaks; upper abdomen and outer under tail coverts white; lower abdomen, central upper and under tail coverts, and tail black; back, rump, lateral upper tail coverts, and ends of tertials and secondaries dull olive-brown; primaries and secondaries fuscous; outer edge of wing, including outer web of outer primary, white.

Immature, paler gray, with throat, sides of head, and tips of breast feathers white.

Downy young, black above, and on the head, with a faint greenish sheen on lower back; somewhat grayish black underneath; throat and sides of head with somewhat elongated, and slightly curled, ends, tipped with silvery white; down covering of head scanty so that skin is visible, particularly on crown and throat.

Iris dark red; tip of bill greenish yellow; remainder, and frontal shield red; tarsus and toes greenish, with a band of red around the crus.

In tropical Panamá the common gallinule, like its relatives elsewhere through the Americas, lives around broad expanses of fresh waters where water hyacinth and other floating plants afford feeding grounds, with taller, denser growths of marsh vegetation adjacent for cover when needed. Though many remain hidden in this taller growth many others move about outside, often in stretches of water that are completely open, where they swim with nodding heads. It is common also to see them walking on muddy shores, or across masses of water plants. Intruders are greeted with clucking or chattering calls, and when alarmed the birds dash to shelter, or rise and fly low over the water. In feeding they dab at the surface to pick out bits of succulent vegetation, which may be shaken to scatter adhering water before they are swallowed. Often the head is completely immersed. They are local in occurrence compared to the more widely distributed purple gallinule.

The two subspecies present as breeding birds in the Isthmus differ slightly in size, and in the extent and depth of brown coloration on the back.

FIG. 59.—Common gallinule, gallineta de agua, *Gallinula chloropus.*

GALLINULA CHLOROPUS CACHINNANS Bangs

Gallinula chloropus cachinnans Bangs, Proc. New England Zoöl. Club, vol. 5, May 17, 1915, p. 96. (Arbuckle Creek, De Soto County, Florida.)
Gallinula chloropus centralis Waldron DeWitt Miller and Ludlow Griscom, Amer. Mus. Nov. no. 25, Dec. 7, 1921, p. 3. (12 miles south of Metapa, central Nicaragua.)

Characters.—Brown of back and wing coverts more extensive, darker, and of a brighter shade, and spread over the greater wing coverts, in some as a slight wash, but in many in an amount equal to that found on the back.

Measurements.—Males (16 from eastern United States and México), wing 167-181 (174.5), tail 64.0-86.0 (71.6), tarsus 49.0-56.5 (52.7) mm.

Females (8 from eastern United States and México), wing 158-174 (166.5), tail 63-71 (66.9), tarsus 48-50 (49.2) mm.

Resident. Found locally in western Bocas del Toro on fresh water ponds and lowland streams where there are borders of marsh growth. One record, possibly of a migrant, for western Chiriquí, on the smaller of the two lakes near El Volcán.

Kennard secured a female near Almirante on February 14, 1926 (Kennard and Peters, Proc. Boston Soc. Nat. Hist., vol. 38, 1928, p. 447), and at about the same time Griscom (Amer. Mus. Nov. no. 293, 1928, p. 1) recorded one taken by Benson (under the name *Gallinula chloropus centralis*), a specimen that I find was collected near Almirante, August 24, 1927. H. von Wedel forwarded several others from near Changuinola taken October 28, 1926, November 17 and December 2, 1927, and July 14, 1928, which were obviously resident birds, a series that Peters (Bull. Mus. Comp. Zool., vol. 71, 1931, p. 301) found to be identical with birds of eastern North America so that he declared the supposed race *centralis* described from Nicaragua one without validity. There is also a specimen in the Havemeyer Collection at Yale, taken at Farm 3 near Almirante by Austin Paul Smith in April 1927. In 1958 near Changuinola I recorded 4 on January 30 and a mated pair on March 4. Eisenmann (Condor, 1957, p. 250) found juvenile birds here on June 30, 1957.

One that I saw on March 6, 1954, on the smaller of the lakes near El Volcán in western Chiriquí may have been a migrant bird from the north.

The race of the West Indies, *G. c. cerceris*, is similar in size to *cachinnans* but has the brown of the dorsal surface grayer and restricted in extent on the wing coverts. Those resident on Cuba and Jamaica are intermediate but slightly nearer *cerceris*.

GALLINULA CHLOROPUS PAUXILLA Bangs

Gallinula chloropus pauxilla Bangs, Proc. New England Zoöl. Club, vol. 5, May 17, 1915, p. 96. (Guabinas, Valle, Colombia.)

Characters.—Differs from *Gallinula chloropus cachinnans* in slightly smaller size and in more grayish brown on the dorsal surface, with this color restricted mainly to the back, only a light wash, or none at all, being found on the wing coverts. The distinctions are slight, but the two groups indicated are apparent when a series of specimens is examined.

Measurements.—Males (8 from Panamá, Colombia, and Venezuela), wing 162-173 (168), tail 64.3-70.0 (68.0), tarsus 50.2-58.8 (55.0) mm.

Females (2 from Colombia), wing 159-167 (163), tail 64.9-67.0 (66.6), tarsus 49.8-55.7 (52.5) mm.

Resident. Found locally on fresh-water lakes; recorded on the Río Chagres from Gamboa to above Juan Mina, and on the Miraflores lakes, Canal Zone.

The first report that may refer to this race was by L. L. Jewel (Auk, 1913, p. 425) who recorded one, but apparently did not preserve it, on January 18, 1911. He does not give the locality, but this may be presumed to be near Gatun as his observations were made mainly in that area.

Gallinules of this species appear to have been rare in central Panamá until recently, as none were reported by the early collectors before Jewel. The formation of Gatun Lake has provided favorable habitat both in the lake and along the Chagres which has allowed these birds to increase. Possibly they had been held down earlier by competition with the more abundant purple gallinule.

On the Chagres and the Miraflores lakes the nesting season appears to begin in December, perhaps in November, and in January young, in size from those recently hatched to others half grown, are common. Pairs of adults are seen regularly swimming in company, and occasionally preening one another's neck feathers. Small young when threatened escape by diving, but may not be able to progress under water because of the submerged plants. If captured they call with high-pitched notes when a parent bird may charge across the water scolding loudly.

These gallinules should be found elsewhere in eastern Panamá, though as yet they have not been reported. The race *pauxilla* ranges in South America from northern Colombia to western Ecuador and western Perú.

PORPHYRULA MARTINICA (Linnaeus): Purple Gallinule; Polla Sultana

Fulica martinica Linnaeus, Syst. Nat., ed. 12, vol. 1, 1766, p. 259. (Martinique, West Indies.)

Brilliant blue and olive-green in the adult and light brown head and back and white breast in the immature stage identify this species from its companion coots and gallinules.

Description.—Length 265-300 mm. Adult (sexes alike), head, breast, sides, and wings deep blue; back, rump, tertials, and tail dull green; abdomen and tibia black; under tail coverts white.

Immature, head, neck, sides, and tibia buffy brown; back, rump, and tail dull brown; wings greenish blue, washed with brown; throat, breast, abdomen, and under tail coverts white.

Downy young, above black, underneath brownish black; crown, sides of head from bill to back of eyes, and throat with somewhat elongated filaments of very pale bluish white.

Iris brown; frontal shield pale bluish white to dull grayish blue; bill red, tipped with greenish yellow to yellow; tarsus and toes light greenish yellow; claws brownish.

Measurements.—Males (6 from Panamá and northern Colombia), wing 178-188 (181.8), tail 65.8-73.7 (69.2), culmen from base of frontal shield 30.0-32.8 (31.5), tarsus 57.6-67.0 (61.7) mm.

Females (5 from Panamá and northern Colombia), wing 166-172 (168.2), tail 56.8-63.3 (60.8), culmen from base of frontal shield 27.2-30.7 (29.0), tarsus 59.0-63.6 (60.1) mm.

Resident. Locally common along lowland rivers, in the backwaters of Gatun and Madden Lakes, and in fresh-water marshes elsewhere.

There is no record for the Pacific slope from western Chiriquí east through Veraguas, Coclé, and the western sector of the Province of Panamá to the Canal Zone.

These handsomely colored gallinules are found amid the floating water plants that border the courses of lowland streams and in fresh-water marsh areas in general. The formation of Gatun Lake has greatly expanded their habitat in the central area of the Canal Zone and is certain to have brought increase in their numbers in this area.

These gallinules are seen during travel in small boats, sometimes as they walk over the aquatic vegetation, but more commonly when they flush from scanty cover to fly a few meters with cackling calls and quickly beating wings. The main impression of color on such occasions is of white from the expanded under tail coverts and of yellow from the dangling legs and feet. When they rise 2 to 3 meters in the air to fly directly and rapidly in more sustained flight, the legs and feet are raised to the line of axis of the body. At times they are seen swimming, but they appear on open stretches of water far less frequently than the common gallinule.

In feeding, in addition to working through the water plants, they climb about in trees, particularly those that grow in water, where wet forests with dense branches stand partly flooded along the streams. In such activities they often go up to 20 meters above the surface.

When the birds are not seen their presence is often known by their clacking or guttural calls, that may be accompanied by cracking sounds made by snapping the bill.

The breeding period is long as eggs or newly hatched young have been recorded in Panamá from March to early November. Nests are shallow platforms made of the marsh vegetation adjacent to the site, usually placed at a slight elevation, that allows a small margin of safety when water levels rise during heavy rains. Gross and Van Tyne (Auk, 1929, pp. 431-446) describe in detail their observations of a nest found along the shore of Barro Colorado Island. The site was concealed in tall grass on a floating island, a few meters from the jungle covered shore. Green grass blades still attached at the base had been woven into a platform 35 centimeters across with a shallow depression to hold the eggs. A runway 3 meters or so long woven from the surrounding grass led to a little platform less than a meter above the water. This was a pathway used to reach and leave the nest, repaired constantly, to keep it in proper shape. The four eggs ranged in measurement from 39.1-42.8 × 28.5-29.8 mm. and in weight from 15.15 to 16.35 grams. They hatched after an incubation period of about 22 days.

The eggs vary from subelliptical to oval, are without gloss, and have the shell very faintly roughened. The color varies from very pale cream color (nearly white) to buff and pale cinnamon-buff, spotted sparingly with dots of cinnamon or rufous-brown, that appear bluish or purplish where covered by a thin deposit of shell. In Florida the usual set of eggs numbers 6 to 8 with an occasional increase to 10, but the number recorded in Panamá is less, being normally 4 or 5. The young remain in the nest a day or so after hatching, and then follow the parent birds in the water.

Food of these gallinules is made up of the insects and spiders available in their watery haunts. The bits of vegetation found in examination of stomachs of birds killed for specimens probably are swallowed by accident with other food items.

The species ranges widely through the tropical zone of the Americas, extending to southeastern United States on the north and northern Argentina on the south without evident differences in size or color.

The species is often called *gallito,* and *cocaleca de la laguna* by country residents.

FULICA AMERICANA AMERICANA Gmelin: American Coot; Gallineta Cenicienta

FIGURE 60

Fulica americana Gmelin, Syst. Nat., vol. 1, pt. 2, 1789, p. 704. (North America.)

Similar to the common gallinule but bill white; toes with elongated, fringing webs or lobes on each joint.

Description.—Length 340-380 mm. Sexes alike; head and neck black; under surface gray; above darker gray, tinged with olive on the back; under tail coverts, and tips of secondaries white.

Small frontal shield dull red; rest of bill white.

Measurements.—Males (10 specimens), wing 182-199 (192), tail 47.0-52.5 (50.2), tarsus 43-50 (46.6) mm.

Females (10 specimens), wing 176-188 (178.8), tail 41.0-54.0 (48.7), tarsus 47-56 (50.6) mm.

Migrant from the north. Common on fresh-water lakes and larger rivers east to central Panamá through the Canal Zone. Recorded from mid-November to the end of March.

During the period of northern winter a few coots appear on the small lakes at Miraflores, in areas of quiet water on Madden and Gatun Lakes, and along the broad expanse of the Río Chagres between Gamboa and Madden Dam. They may come in greater numbers on impounded waters among the banana farms near Changuinola, where on January 30, 1958, I recorded about 400 in one forenoon. I have seen a few on the lakes near El Volcán in Chiriquí, and years ago Arcé secured specimens for Salvin at Laguna del Castillo and Calobre in Veraguas. Karl Curtis informs me that he has found a few at La Jagua, usually in November and December, but that they do not remain for long.

Griscom (Bull. Mus. Comp. Zool., vol. 78, 1935, p. 305) was misinformed when he recorded this species as resident around Laguna de Chiriquí, since though they appear near Almirante, it is only as migrants. I have taken specimens for identification on the Chagres near Juan Mina, Canal Zone, January 8, and near El Volcán, Chiriquí, February 9, 1955.

In Panamá coots range on open waters, often in shallow channels bordered by aquatic weeds, where they swim and dive for food like the ducks that often are present with them. The small, pointed bill, as well as the constantly nodding head, mark them from their duck companions, and the white color of the bill distinguishes them from the gallinules that also may be their companions.

[?**PARDIRALLUS MACULATUS** (Boddaert): Spotted Rail;
Cocalequita Pintada

Rallus maculatus Boddaert, Table Planch. Enl., 1783, p. 48. (Cayenne.)

At Mandinga, San Blas, in the early morning of January 22, 1957, a rail that appeared to be somewhat larger than a sora flushed in fairly open, high grass near the border of the abandoned airfield. The bird rose 5 or 6 meters from the ground, flew swiftly for 75

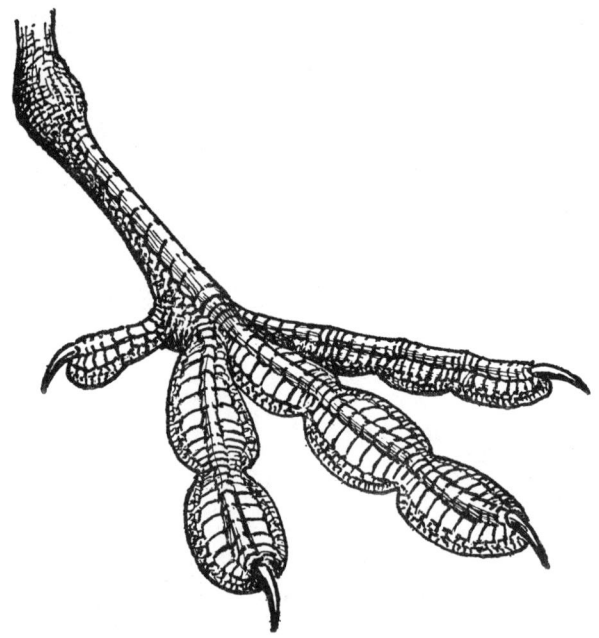

FIG. 60.—Foot of American coot, gallineta cenicienta, *Fulica americana americana*, with lobed toes.

meters or so, and then dropped down on wet, bush-and-grass-grown ground, where it disappeared in the manner usual in this family. On the wing the upper surface of the body appeared black, well-streaked with light gray. I made search in this area on several occasions afterward but did not find the bird again.

It is probable that this was the spotted rail, the only species known to me of the size and marking described that might be found in this area. This species has been recorded in Central America from Mexico, Costa Rica and British Honduras and to the south from northern Colombia. None have been taken to date in Panamá.

In the hand the spotted rail has the throat and under tail coverts white; the rest of the lower surface black, streaked on the neck, and barred elsewhere with white; above blackish on the head and neck, brown mixed with black on the back and wings, streaked narrowly everywhere with white. The wing measures about 120 mm.

LATERALLUS JAMAICENSIS (Gmelin): Black Rail

Rallus jamaicensis Gmelin, Syst. Nat., vol. 1, pt. 2, 1789, p. 718. (Jamaica.)

A black rail is reported by Stephen T. Harty (Cassinia, no. 48, 1964-1965, p. 19) as seen July 6 and 7, 1963, near the International Highway west of Chepo at a point 16.2 miles by auto speedometer from the road circle at the Tocumen Airport. The observation was made in company with George B. Reynard, Philip A. Livingston, Henry Matthews, and Thomas C. Crebbs, Jr. On July 6 two birds called repeatedly so that Reynard was able to make a tape recording, and finally Harty located a globular nest in tall grass that contained 3 fresh eggs. On the following day Matthews had a brief view of a "small dark sparrowlike rail." The eggs, from a photograph submitted to me and the measurements 23.5-24 × 18.5-19 mm. (taken by James Bond) in appearance and size resemble those of the black rail (*Laterallus jamaicensis*). They are distinctly smaller than eggs recorded for *Laterallus albigularis* and *L. exilis*. Those of the yellow-breasted rail *Porzana flaviventer flaviventer*, not yet recorded, may be of similar size or smaller. As the general color of *Porzana flaviventer* is light buffy brown it does not fit the description of the bird that was seen. The area also is not a suitable haunt for the yellow-breasted rail, which is a species of open marshes where grasses stand in shallow water.

On January 4, 1964, with Rudolpho Hinds as assistant, I visited the locality described. We located the spot without difficulty but could not find the rails.

The black rail is recorded by Russell (Amer. Orn. Union Ornith. Mon. 1, 1964, p. 58) in British Honduras, and there are uncertain reports for Guatemala and Colombia.]

Family HELIORNITHIDAE: Finfoots; Zambullidores de Agua

The three species of this family are tropical in distribution, one in Africa, another in southeastern Asia, and the third, the smallest, in the Americas. Structurally, they are allied to rails, but except for museum specimens, are little known as naturalists have had limited opportunity to study them because of their retiring habits. All have close, firm plumage, like that of a duck, and slender, rather elongated bills, with perforate nostrils like those of rails. The feet are webbed at base with the distal joints of the toes lobed, and the tail is long and broad. While they fly readily when approached, more often they dive, as they are truly aquatic in habit.

HELIORNIS FULICA (Boddaert): American Finfoot; Patico de Agua

FIGURE 61

Colymbus fulica Boddaert, Table Planch. Enl., Dec. 1783, p. 54. (Cayenne.)

Like a grebe, but with head and side of neck black; streaked prominently with white behind the eye, and on lower side of neck.

Description.—Length 280 to 305 mm. Adult male, crown and hindneck black, with a white line extending from above eye back to upper neck; back and wing coverts olive-brown; wing feathers fuscous; rump and upper tail coverts brown; tail black, tipped narrowly with white; throat and foreneck white; side of head below eye white, in some washed lightly with buff; a black band at each side of lower foreneck, in some united across the front, separated from the black of the hindneck by a broad white line; a faintly indicated buffy brown band across upper breast and adjacent sides; rest of breast and abdomen white; sides and under tail coverts grayish brown; under wing coverts dark gray.

Adult female, like the male, but with a prominent band of cinnamon brown on the cheeks and adjacent sides of neck.

Immature, like the adult, but with cheeks and sides of neck white.

An adult female, taken on the Río Chagres, at Juan Mina, January 18, 1955, had the iris dark brown; maxilla and side of mandible at base dull red, becoming blackish at the extreme base, and on the tip of the culmen; mandible light horn color on the sides, and light neutral gray at the tip; bare edge of eyelids dull red, forming a narrow ring; lower tarsus, toes, and webs honey yellow; three bands on inner toe, four on the middle toe, five on the outer toe, and two on hind toe dull black; upper third of tarsus dull brownish yellow; a band of dull black on inner side, and on anterior face of tarsus, and also on the posterior half of the outer face.

Measurements.—Males (6 from México, Costa Rica, Nicaragua, and Panamá), wing 138.4-152.0 (141.3), tail 83.0-91.0 (86.7), culmen from base 30.0-33.6 (31.5), tarsus 22.4-24.0 (23.5) mm.

Females (6 from México, Costa Rica, Nicaragua, and Panamá), wing 133.3-142.2 (137.7), tail 78.0-81.5 (80.1), culmen from base 28.5-33.2 (30.3), tarsus 21.7-23.7 (22.7) mm.

Resident. Found locally in the tropical zone on larger bodies of fresh water; recorded from the Río Changuinola and the Changuinola Canal in Bocas del Toro; on Gatun Lake and the Río Chagres in the Canal Zone; Río La Jagua, Panamá (one record); and the Río Tuira at Boca de Paya, Darién (one record).

On the lateral channels and bays bordering the Chagres below Madden Dam these curious birds are fairly common, though easily overlooked because of the broad masses of floating vegetation that furnish them cover. Occasionally they are encountered as they swim in open waters along the shores, when in form they resemble grebes

FIG. 61.—American finfoot, patico de agua, *Heliornis fulica*.

because of the slender bill and neck. When startled they may dive, or may rise, with feet paddling the water for a short distance, and then fly just above the surface to the shelter of water plants where they disappear. Again, they may rise a meter or two in the air and fly swiftly, like a small duck, for a hundred meters or more. When moving slowly in a cayuco so as not to alarm the marsh birds I have had them swim to the shelter of the shore and there remain partly hidden until I approached within a few meters. At such times the dark body merges with the shadows, so that only the white streaks on head and neck are seen. I have observed them swimming in company with small groups of lesser scaup ducks, when, as the ducks take flight, the finfoot may dive, or may rise with them to accompany them for a short distance, but soon to circle back and alight on the water. Once on the surface they swim or fly into the cover bordering the shore.

When I have come quietly in a cayuco into their haunts where the birds remained concealed, I have often induced them to call by striking a paddle on the side of the canoe. The note, resembling the syllable *kow*, in tone closely like the call of the pied-billed grebe, may be given once or may be repeated quickly several times.

On Gatun Lake they frequent sheltered coves, and may be seen in such localities around Barro Colorado Island.

Enrique van Horn, of the staff of the Gorgas Memorial Laboratory, who has accompanied me on much of my work on the Chagres, told me that the nest, built of sticks, placed on a bush or branch over the water, is small in size and flimsy in structure. Soon after hatching the young enter the water where they are carried on the back of the parent, in the manner well known among grebes. The adult when alarmed may dive, when the young cling tightly. As the bird cannot go far with this encumbrance it is soon again on the surface, with the young still in place.

A nest that Enrique Van Horn collected for me on the Río Chilibre near its junction with the Chagres, on June 16, 1963, is made of twigs and dried stems of coarse marsh plants, ranging in diameter from small to pencil size. These formed a flattened platform approximately 180 by 225 mm., with a slight depression that held 3 eggs, buffy white, spotted finely with cinnamon and pale purple rather uniformly over the entire surface. They measure 26.1 × 20.9, 26.8 × 20.1, and 27.3 × 20.7 mm. A second nest, found on July 15, was similar in construction, with measurements of 200 by 250 mm, and held 4 eggs which could not be saved. Both nests were placed in bushes that hung over the water, elevated about a meter above the surface.

Schönwetter (Handb. Ool., pt. 6, 1962, p. 355, pl. 7, fig. 11) describes the eggs as reddish cream, dotted with lilac gray, dark brown and reddish markings, denser around the larger end, with the size range of 27.1-29.3 × 20-20.6 mm.

An early account by Wied (Beitrag. Naturg. Brasilien, vol. 4, pt. 2, 1833, pp. 827-828) states that the young when hatched are naked ("völlig nacktes") and in this condition are carried beneath the wings of the parent. While this statement has been repeated by later authors, so far as I am aware it has not been verified by later observations.

At night I have found the finfoot sleeping on branches a few feet above the water.

In handling them in the flesh, it has been interesting to note the great development of the caudal muscles, in addition to the robust size of those that control the legs. This heavy form in the posterior part of the rather flat body may be noticed in outline when they fly.

In some published accounts this species is called the sungrebe.

Family EURYPYGIDAE: Sunbitterns; Abanicos

These are birds of the American Tropics found locally in forested areas from Tabasco and Chiapas in southern México through Central America and South America to eastern Bolivia and central Brazil. The birds of the north have stronger, heavier bills, and are more subdued in color on the upper surface, with the black bars narrower, less in width than the gray interspaces. While described originally as a distinct species under the name *major* these are now placed as conspecific with the form *helias* of the southern part of the range. In southern Perú birds of this type have the black bars on the rump and upper tail coverts slightly narrower and are recognized as another race, *meridionalis*. The typical subspecies *helias*, found from the Orinoco Valley southward, is quite distinct in more slender bill and in a mixture of buff on the back, where the black bars are wider.

EURYPYGA HELIAS MAJOR Hartlaub: Sunbittern; Abanico

FIGURE 62

Eurypyga major Hartlaub, Syst. Verz. Naturh. Samml. Gesellsch. Mus. Bremen, pt. 1, Vögel, 1844, p. 108. (Colombia.)

Slender in form, with long neck and legs, white throat and abdomen, brown breast and neck; a striking pattern of chestnut, black, and white in the spread wing.

Description.—Length 460 to 475 mm. Adult (sexes alike), head black, with a slender line of white over the eye, and another across the cheeks; neck dull chestnut, barred narrowly with black; upper back like neck but black bars wider; rest of back and tertials brownish gray, barred heavily with black; scapulars spotted with white; rump, upper tail coverts, and base of tail dull black, barred narrowly with white; a band of chestnut bordered with black across center of tail, and another near tip; center and tip of tail gray, banded narrowly with white and pale grayish white; primaries barred widely with chestnut, black, and white; center of secondaries mottled with buff; throat, lower breast, and abdomen white; upper breast dark buff to cinnamon-buff, barred narrowly with black; sides, flanks, and under tail coverts buff, the latter marked finely and irregularly with black.

Young, when hatched, covered with down, with longer filaments thinly scattered over head and body; dark brown above, spotted on the head and streaked on the back and wings with buff and white; buffy brown below, with indistinct darker markings (Bartlett, Proc. Zool. Soc. London, 1866, pl. 9).

Iris red; eyelids yellow edged with brownish; inside of mouth bright orange; maxilla black, brownish at base with tip orange-yellow, and edge of commissure bright orange; mandible bright orange; tarsus and toes bright orange, with front of tarsus and upper surface of toes brown-orange; claws yellow (Deignan, Auk, 1936, p. 188).

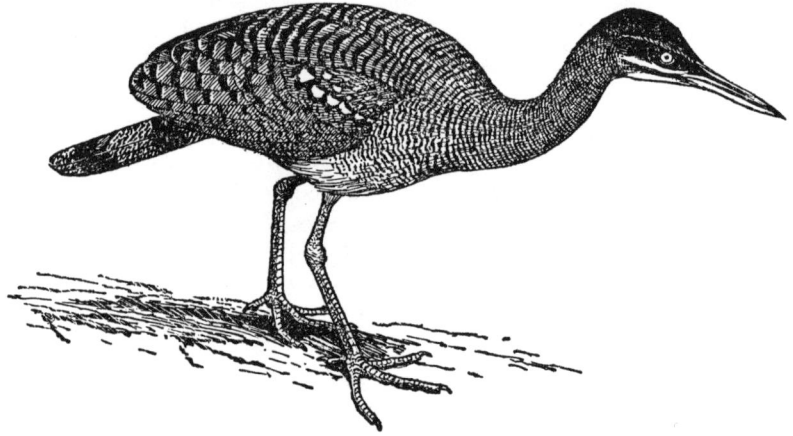

FIG. 62.—Sunbittern, abanico, *Eurypyga helias major*.

Measurements.—Males (7 from Panamá and Colombia), wing 216-230 (223), tail 148-156 (151), culmen from base 61.1-65.1 (62.8), tarsus 54.1-58.0 (55.4) mm.

Females (8 from Panamá and Colombia), wing 218-229 (222), tail 147-155 (150, average of 7), culmen from base 61.1-67.3 (63.4), tarsus 54.6-59.3 (57.1) mm.

Resident. Local, in forests of the tropical and lower subtropical zones; recorded throughout except in the savanna regions of the Pacific slope.

While this is a bird of forested areas it is one that lives around gravel playones, on open-floored quebradas, and along the shores of swift-flowing streams, where it has the protection of shade from the full power of the sun, but open ground on which to move about. It is found in pairs, or at times alone, and it is seldom that more than two are seen together. Since it moves about quietly, often in the cover of bushes, and usually is not wary, when approached it may merely walk aside and hide so that it is often found with some difficulty. Occasionally one may fly into low branches and there remain concealed. As it moves the slender form and long legs and neck often give the impression of a huge sandpiper, a resemblance heightened by its rather somber colors. But this impression vanishes instantly when one begins its display, with the wings and tail fully spread to show their beautiful pattern of black, white and chestnut mingled with light buff, while the bird turns and whirls, in shade or in sun. Then its size seems more than doubled as both wings and tail are broad.

In the field the only note that I have recorded from them is a low trill, but repeatedly in the bird house of the National Zoological Park I have heard a ringing call, *ko wáy,* that has resounded through the building.

They are often found walking over the rocky beds of small streams, and it is here that they secure much of their food. The stomach of one that I examined, taken in Darién where the Río Ucurgantí joins the Chucunaque, held 15 to 20 tiny snails, the elytron of a beetle, and leg bones of a small batrachian. In two taken by Goldman near Gatun on May 16, 1911, one had eaten fragments of a river crab (*Pseudothelphusa* sp.). The other held remains of 2 large spiders, a bug (Heteropteran), moths, 2 large scarabaeids, and another beetle (*Temnochila* sp.). Deignan (Auk, 1936, p. 188) found a shrimp and remains of smaller crustaceans in one taken in Honduras. The bill tip in most museum specimens shows wear from feeding among the stones and hard ground of the usual habitat.

Skutch (Wilson Bull., 1947, p. 38), in Costa Rica, found a bulky nest in a small tree near the bank of a boulder-filled stream, that was built of leaves, stems, and other decaying vegetation, with green moss, and some earth. Two eggs lay in the open cup, which was lined with green leaves. I have seen no description of the eggs of the form of Central America and northwestern South America. Three single eggs of the allied, but quite distinct *Eurypyga helias helias* in the U. S. National Museum collected by R. N. Berryman, Jr., May 10, 1934, June 26, and July 9, 1935, at Guanoco, Sucre, in northeastern Venezuela, have the shell smooth, with a faint gloss, and in ground color vary from tilleul-buff to somewhat darker than pinkish buff. All are spotted sparingly with black, violet-gray, chocolate, and chestnut, mainly around the larger end. They measure 42.8×33.3, 44.0×35.0, and 44.6×33.7 mm.

The species is one of limited habitat and apparently of restricted territorial range so far as individual birds are concerned, that while shy is not especially wary, so that it is vulnerable as settlement encroaches on its haunts. Formerly it was spread widely through the republic, but hunting and casual killing have destroyed it over extensive areas. It has not been reported recently from Chiriquí and southern Veraguas though some may remain in mountain areas, and it has been a good many years since it has been found in the Canal Zone. Some remain in remoter areas in Bocas del Toro, northern Veraguas, Colón, eastern Panamá, Darién, and San Blas, mainly in hill country. C. O. Handley, Jr. found them at a thousand meters and higher on Cerro Malí in 1959, and in 1962 recorded them at similar elevations on Cerro Hoya in western Los Santos.

They are called *primavera* on the Río Tuira; and in Venezuela are known as *tigana,* or locally as *pavito real.*

Order CHARADRIIFORMES

Family JACANIDAE: Jaçanas; Gallitos de Agua

The eight species of this family, found in the tropical and subtropical areas of Africa, southeastern Asia (from India to the Philippine Islands), and America are marked by long, slender legs with the toes tipped with greatly elongated, straight claws, so that these birds walk with ease over the floating plants that carpet the quiet waters of their haunts. In all of the forms the bend of the wing is armed with a sharp-pointed, strong spur, a weapon to be regarded with respect. The wide distribution of the living species indicates a considerable antiquity in geologic time.

In America, where jaçanas range from the lower Rio Grande Valley in Texas through México, the Greater Antilles (except Puerto Rico), Central America, and South America to northern Argentina and Uruguay, two populations are found, superficially so similar that there has been uncertainty as to their status. In the accounts that follow, where their characters are described they are treated as species that may hybridize when they are in contact in the breeding season.

JACANA SPINOSA SPINOSA (Linnaeus): Northern Jaçana; Gallito de Agua Castaño

FIGURE 63

Fulica spinosa Linnaeus, Syst. Nat., ed. 10, vol. 1, 1758, p. 152. (Western Panamá.)

Legs and toes very long in proportion to size of body; back and abdomen chestnut-brown.

Description.—Length 220 to 230 mm. Frontal plate with a central division so that it is 3-lobed. Adult (sexes alike, except in size), head, neck, and upper breast black with a greenish sheen; rest of body

FAMILY JACANIDAE

and under wing coverts, chestnut-brown; primaries and secondaries light greenish yellow, edged with fuscous.

Immature, crown, back, and tertials brownish gray; line behind eye, back of neck, and sides black; rump washed with chestnut; broad line over eye, side of head, and entire under surface white.

Iris dark brown; bill yellow, with base of maxilla pale bluish white; frontal plate orange-yellow to yellow; tarsi and toes dull grayish green; wing spur bright yellow.

Measurements.—Males (7 from Guatemala, Honduras, El Salvador, and Panamá), wing 116.2-120.8 (119.4), tail 37.5-43.5 (40.3), bill from nostril 16.8-19.0 (17.9), tarsus 51.0-57.5 (54.6) mm.

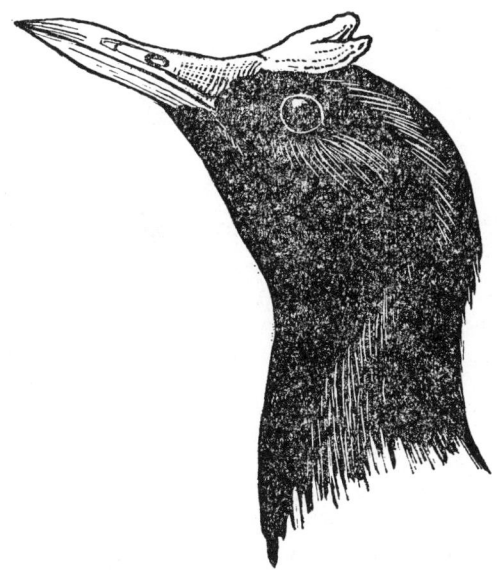

Fig. 63.—Head of northern jaçana, gallito de agua castaño, *Jacana spinosa spinosa.*

Females (7 from Nicaragua and Panamá) wing 130.6-136.6 (134.6), tail 41.6-46.6 (44.1), bill from nostril 19.0-20.4 (19.5), tarsus 55.0-61.8 (58.7) mm.

Resident. Common in the tropical zone of western Panamá, through the lowlands of Chiriquí to extreme western Veraguas (El Zapotillo); wandering casually to the lower subtropical zone (lakes near El Volcán); on the Atlantic side from the Río Sixaola to Almirante in Bocas del Toro.

These brown-backed birds are found in western Chiriquí, and in Bocas del Toro, east to Almirante. They are especially common near

Changuinola and there often come to rain pools on the golf links. On the Pacific slope, in eastern Chiriquí, they mingle with the black-plumaged wattled jacana from Las Lajas and Remedios to the Río Tabasará, and in lesser number in Veraguas to the Río Bubí west of El Zapatillo, an overlap in range of between 40 and 50 kilometers. The two to date have not been found associated on the Caribbean side.

The northern jacana in haunt, habits, and notes is the counterpart of the other species found throughout most of the Republic.

While I have not seen eggs from Panamá, those in a series in the U. S. National Museum from México and Cuba are slightly larger than those of the black form from the Canal Zone, the range in 15 specimens being 29.3-31.2×21.6-24.0 mm. They are also somewhat more heavily marked.

With the large series of these birds now available it is found that populations of the Greater Antilles, México (except for a limited area in the northwest), and southern Central America, formerly regarded as 3 distinct geographic races, are to be merged in one as *Jacana spinosa spinosa*. Specimens from Sinaloa to northern Colima, México, are slightly smaller, so that they are separated as *Jacana spinosa lowei* van Rossem. The northern group, the species *Jacana spinosa* (Linnaeus), has a well-marked central division between the two lateral broader sections in the frontal plate, so that the free upper margin is clearly and definitely three-lobed. The base of the bill is pale bluish or greenish white, and the frontal plate is bright yellow to orange yellow. Birds of the southern species, *Jacana jacana* (Linnaeus), found from western Panamá southward, have only two divisions in the upper margin of the frontal plate and also possess a well-developed lappet on either side of the gape. The frontal plate and the lappet are dark red in color. It should be noted that the lappet is absent in younger juvenile individuals but begins to grow as the frontal plate develops, so that it is present before the bird molts into adult dress. As stated, the ranges meet in western Panamá where the two species now are found together over a space of about 50 kilometers. My own observations in this area of overlap confirm the early reports of Griscom (Bull. Mus. Comp. Zool., vol. 78, 1935, p. 305) who found the two together in the same pools near Remedios, in eastern Chiriquí, "without producing intermediates." However, I have examined several specimens in the British Museum, collected by Arcé in 1869, labeled Calobre, in eastern Veraguas, that appear to be hybrids. Two have maroon backs with trifid frontal lappets, and also a small rictal lappet. Two others with only a tinge of maroon on the back have a small median frontal wattle between the two large ones, and also a rictal wattle. One other, fully adult is completely black on the back, with a small middle frontal wattle, and large ones in the rictal area. All others seen have shown the normal differences described.

Part of the confusion in understanding of the differences that separate the two has been due to individual variability in *Jacana jacana hypomelaena,* the race of the southern species involved. This name is applied to the population found through most of Panamá and northern Colombia, in which the head and body are deep black. It appears that this is a condition of melanism in which the dark pigment conceals the chestnut brown pattern of the back and breast normal in other populations to the south. It is fairly common to find specimens of *hypomelaena* in which a definite wash of brown is evident on the back and wings, often hidden by black tips of the feathers, and an occasional individual in which there are definite chestnut markings on back and breast. As the chestnut pattern is found also in the northern *Jacana spinosa,* these aberrant individuals have been attributed mistakenly to intergradation between the two groups, a supposition supported by specimens of *J. j. hypomelaena* in which the free margin of the frontal plate, through slight distortion in drying, appears to simulate the true central lobe of *J. spinosa*. The clear-cut and striking differences in color of the frontal plate may be the effective factor that separates the two groups during pair formation, and thus maintains the two distinct. I have not seen a supposed intermediate adult specimen that could not be allocated specifically on the characters that I have outlined.

Current acceptance of Todd's designation of "Panama" as type locality for this species (Ann. Carnegie Mus., vol. 10, 1916, p. 219) requires amendment to western Panamá in view of the limited range of this bird in the Republic. The specific name *spinosa* of Linnaeus is based solely on Edwards, Nat. Hist. Birds, 1743, p. 48, pl. 48. Edwards was told that his specimen, "preserv'd a good while in spirits," lent to him by Sir Hans Sloane, "was brought from Carthagena, South America." It seems probable that it came from farther north in Central America rather than from the limited area where this species is found in western Panamá.

JACANA JACANA HYPOMELAENA (Gray): Wattled Jaçana; Gallito de Agua Barbudo

FIGURE 64

Parra hypomelaena G. R. Gray, Gen. Birds, vol. 3, May 1846, pl. 159. (Bogotá, Colombia.)

Similar to the northern jacana in general form, but head, neck, back, and abdomen black.

Description.—Length 210 to 230 mm.; frontal plate with two lobes; a distinct lappet on either side of the mouth at the gape. Adult (sexes alike, except in size), wings as in the northern jacana; entire body and under wing coverts, in most black. Some show a tinge of chestnut on the back, and in a very few this color is sufficiently strong to suggest the markings of the other species.

Immature, crown and back dark brown; side of head, neck, upper back, and sides extensively black, often with a mixture of black on the wing coverts; rump and upper tail coverts black.

Iris dark brown; base of the maxilla, frontal plate, and rictal lappets rather dull red; rest of bill cinnamon to yellow, tinged with slate at the tip; tarsus deep neutral gray, with a tinge of green on the posterior face of the crus; toes and claws dusky brown.

Measurements.—Males (8 from Panamá), wing 115.5-120.1 (117.6), tail 36.3-42.4 (38.8), bill from nostril 17.4-19.4 (18.3), tarsus 53.4-56.8 (55.1) mm.

Females (9 from Panamá), wing 127.0-134.8 (130.7), tail 40.2-44.8 (42.4), bill from nostril 18.5-20.8 (19.7), tarsus 54.8-64.1 (58.7) mm.

Resident. Common in the tropical zone along lowland rivers and in fresh-water marshes from eastern Chiriquí (Las Lajas, Remedios), the Río Indio in extreme northern Coclé (El Uracillo), and western Colón (Chilar and Río Indio) to Colombia. Casual on Isla Coiba.

It is probable that these birds will be found to range much farther west along the rivers of the Caribbean lowlands when field studies have been made in the area from the Valiente Peninsula in Bocas del Toro through northern Veraguas.

The wattled jaçana, like the northern species, primarily is a bird of fresh-water marshes and the borders of the larger lowland streams where shores, bays, and side channels are lined with water-lilies, pondweeds, and other floating aquatic plants. As the small body is light in weight the long toes afford a broad support so that the bird, with nodding head, walks about with ease. Where the plant growth is scanty the wings are fluttered to assist in support in more rapid movement to denser growth. They come frequently to shallow pools in wet pastureland. Once, in the marsh at La Jagua, a pair ranged in the same manner as anis about a bull that fed in water up to its body.

Adults usually are found in pairs, in which the sexes may be distinguished by difference in size, the female being much larger in body than the male. Where the birds are common several pairs may be associated, and with them there are often many of the white breasted young. All feed quietly, picking at the water surface for small insects, or with a quicker dab at a minnow. At any disturbance

FIG. 64.—Wattled jaçana, gallito de agua barbudo, *Jacana jacana hypomelaena*.

the wings may be raised to show the striking, light-colored pattern, and the birds give cackling and grunting calls. Adults often spar with the spread wings raised high, the body horizontal, and the head thrust forward, but seldom seem to come to actual blows, the sharp spurs with which all are armed being a sufficient deterrent. I have noticed this especially where one of a pair in a small group has been killed, when the survivor is constantly driven away when it approaches its companions.

Jaçanas fly easily and in the air present an unusual outline with the neck and feet extended, the latter with a slight curve upward from the linear axis through the head and body. At Juan Mina, when traveling by cayuco along quiet channels, small groups of jaçanas often rise explosively from behind the taller vegetation, with each individual headed in a different direction, but immediately all shift and with chattering calls straggle off together.

They are most abundant in the open lowlands of the Pacific slope. A few, usually, but not always, in the white-breasted immature dress, wander inland along gravel bars exposed in dry season on the larger rivers, and then may be encountered within the open valleys in the hills. I supposed that it was such a wanderer, an adult bird in this instance, that I recorded on Isla Coiba on January 21, 1956.

Four sets of 4 eggs each and one of 3, presented to the U. S. National Museum by Maj.-Gen. G. Ralph Meyer, indicate that this species nests in the main during the rainy season, as these, taken at the Summit Gardens, Canal Zone, from 1940 to 1942, range in date from August 10 to November 26. At Juan Mina, on the Río Chagres, I recorded two broods of 4 young each, on December 14, 1955. Some nest later, as Thomas Gilliard found 4 young recently hatched at Barro Colorado Island March 24, 1937 (Chapman, Life in an Air Castle, 1938, p. 226). And Jackson Abbott has told me of finding a pair with a nest containing 4 eggs in a lily pool at the Summit Gardens on February 15, 1942. General Meyer also reported newly hatched young on May 17, 1941.

The usual nest is a slight depression in a mass of floating vegetation. The eggs, in general, are similar to those of *Jacana spinosa spinosa*, recorded under that species, but average slightly smaller, and viewed as a group are less heavily marked. In form they vary from oval to short subelliptical. The ground color is somewhat brighter than deep olive-buff, marked heavily with irregular, scrawling lines and occasional spots of black, that here and there are modified to dull grayish brown. Measurements of 4 sets are as follows: 27.7-29.7 × 21.0-22.3 mm. A fifth set is somewhat smaller, as indicated by the following dimensions: 23.6-27.5 × 21.0-21.5 mm.

The usual name in Panamá is *gallito de agua,* often abbreviated to *gallito.* In Los Santos they were called *rasca tortilla,* and on the Río Jaqué in Darién they were known as the *lagunero.*

Family HAEMATOPODIDAE: Oystercatchers; Ostreros

The species of this family, true shorebirds in form, are among the largest of the group. All have heavy bodies and strong feet and bills, the latter long, and compressed from side to side at the tip to a chisel form. This is used in prying loose and opening the mollusks that are their principal food. Part of the species recognized are wholly dark in color, and part are blackish on the head and neck, gray or gray-brown on the back and white underneath. As a group they are found worldwide in continental areas, except in regions of heavy cold.

HAEMATOPUS PALLIATUS PITANAY Murphy: American Oystercatcher; Ostrero Blanco

FIGURE 65

Haematopus palliatus pitanay Murphy, Amer. Mus. Nov. no. 194, Nov. 17, 1925, p. 1. (Pisco Bay, Perú.)

A large shorebird with long red to yellow bill, compressed at the tip; sooty black head and neck, grayish-brown back and white underparts.

Description.—Length, 420 to 440 mm. Adult (sexes alike), head and neck sooty black, slightly grayer on the crown; spot on lower eyelid white; back, longer tertials, lesser and middle wing coverts grayish brown; greater wing coverts, and secondaries white except for the black tips; wings and tail sooty black; upper tail coverts, sides of rump, and under parts white; under wing coverts white more or less spotted with sooty black.

A juvenile, half grown, from Isla San José, with the general color pattern of the adult, has the throat covered with gray down, spotted indistinctly with white and darker gray; entire upper surface with feathers tipped narrowly with cinnamon-buff; rump and tail tipped with cinnamon.

Iris yellow; edge of eyelids red; bill red, becoming yellow at tip, and orange at base; tarsus and toes pinkish white to pale flesh color; claws fuscous.

Measurements.—Males (5 from Panamá), wing 141-156 (150), tail 90.6-107.0 (98.7), culmen from base 75.0-81.0 (78.5), tarsus 54.5-58.3 (56.3) mm.

Females (2 from Panamá), wing 157, 158; tail 101.6, 104.0; culmen from base 82.1, 90.0; tarsus 58.0, 61.5 mm.

Resident. Local along the Pacific coast: Archipiélago de las Perlas (recorded from islas San José, Pedro González, Bayoneta, Málaga, Pacheca, Pachequilla, Saboga, Contadora and Rey). Rare elsewhere: Veraguas (specimen in British Museum without definite locality or date taken by Arcé); Los Santos (La Honda); east of Panamá City (Sturgis, Field Book Birds Panama Canal Zone, 1928, p. 54); mouth of Río Majé.

These large shorebirds are found now mainly in the Pearl Islands where they are widely distributed, but nowhere common, on rocky coasts. On the mainland I have seen them on unfrequented sand beaches on the coast of Los Santos and at the mouth of the Río Majé in eastern Panamá near the frontiers of Darién. But only in work in the Pearl Islands have I encountered them regularly. Arcé secured one that is labeled "Veragua," but there are no other records for western Panamá. And the species has not been reported for the long reach of the Caribbean coast.

Fig. 65.—American oystercatcher, ostrero blanco, *Haematopus palliatus pitanay*.

Usually oystercatchers are found in pairs on rock flats near the water, and are wary so that it is necessary to stalk them behind cover to secure specimens. They nest in February and March and then call by day and night, though at other seasons they are vocal mainly when disturbed.

They eat small mollusks, the strong bill with both upper and lower halves compressed at the tip being specially adapted to secure such food. One taken on Isla San José had opercula of the abundant snail *Nerita* and a bit of barnacle in its stomach.

On March 20, 1948, on the beach at La Honda, near the mouth of the Estero Espigadilla, in northern Los Santos, I collected a pair, and by following their tracks in the loose sand located their nest.

The 3 heavily incubated eggs were placed in a slight depression without lining in an open expanse of sand, back of the high water mark, clearly visible at a distance of 15 meters. They are oval in shape, with a slightly roughened shell that is without gloss. The ground color is very pale buff, rather evenly spotted with small irregular marks of fuscous, that appear dull gray to bluish gray where overlaid by a deposit of shell. They measure 57.5 × 37.6, 57.6 × 38.3, and 59.5 × 38.1 mm.

Oystercatchers throughout the world are closely similar in appearance, particularly in the more common color pattern in which the underparts are white. Those of this type of the Old World have the back and rump clear white, while the eye, feet, and tarsi are red. In the New World all have dark-colored backs, only the sides of the rump and the upper tail coverts being white. The eye is bright yellow, and the legs and feet are flesh color or faintly pinkish white. While these are not great differences they are clearcut and are constant, and therefore sufficient to indicate two specific groups *Haematopus ostralegus* for the Old World and *Haematopus palliatus* for the Americas.

As a whole, the white-breasted New World populations are darker colored above along the Pacific coast and lighter in the Atlantic area. The eastern group appears fairly uniform from New Jersey south to Florida, west to Texas and the Yucatán Peninsula, and through the West Indies, on the Guajira Peninsula of northeastern Colombia, and in northern Venezuela. The bird is not known in the Caribbean coastal area from British Honduras, to central Colombia, or along the Atlantic coast from eastern Venezuela to northern Brazil. In the latter country oystercatchers appear on the coast of Pará and range southward to Santa Cruz in southern Argentina. Through this vast area the birds are remarkably uniform. Some from the Bahama Islands have larger bills and have been recognized as a subspecies *H. p. prattii* Maynard, with a range that extends through the Greater and Lesser Antilles and the islands off the north coast of Venezuela. The character, however, is one that is not constant, nor does larger size, alleged in a longer wing, hold, so that the supposed subspecies is one of doubtful value.

In the far south in Argentina, from the east coast of the Province of Buenos Aires to southern Patagonia, oystercatchers average faintly browner above, and are known as *Haematopus palliatus durnfordi* Sharpe.

Along the Pacific coast from Baja California to Guerrero, México, the breeding birds are recognized as *H. p. frazari* Brewster. Compared to *palliatus* these average darker above, have less white on the inner webs of the inner primaries, and the white of upper breast heavily mottled with black, a pattern that in some extends a short distance down the sides. At the Isthmus of Tehuantepec this mottled pattern tends to disappear. Few oystercatchers have been recorded on the Pacific side of Guatemala, there are none known for El Salvador, western Honduras, and Nicaragua, and only two for western Costa Rica. The birds are found regularly only from the Gulf of Panamá south to southern Chile. In this region the population has a clear-cut line between light and dark in the breast pattern like *palliatus,* agrees with *frazari* in restricted white on the inner primaries, but is darker, grayer on the dorsal surface. This may be known as *Haematopus palliatus pitanay,* described from Perú, with a range extended here to include Panamá.

On the Galápagos Islands the birds are much darker than any others in the white-breasted group and have mottled upper breasts, an extensive black pattern on the under wing coverts, and decidedly larger feet. These are *Haematopus p. galapagensis* Ridgway, a population definitely distinct from any others.

Family CHARADRIIDAE: Plovers; Chorlitos

Plovers are birds of worldwide distribution in ice-free areas, related to the sandpipers, snipes, and curlews, but with shorter and somewhat more swollen bills. While several visit Panamá in their migrations only one, the collared plover or *chorlito de collar,* is a resident on the isthmus. Most of the species range the sand beaches of the seashore, but the golden plover in its passage flights comes to open pastures and savannas.

KEY TO SPECIES OF THE CHARADRIIDAE

1. A long, slender crest; throat black.
    Southern lapwing, *Belonopterus chilensis,* p. 383
    Head not crested; throat white.................................... 2
2. A very small hind toe; axillars dark gray to black.
    Black-bellied plover, *Squatarola squatarola,* p. 384
    No hind toe; axillars pale gray or white......................... 3
3. Dorsal surface spotted and barred with white and black, some with golden-yellow; breast mottled with dark gray.
    Golden plover, *Pluvialis dominica dominica,* p. 385
    Dorsal surface plain, or feathers tipped lightly with pale buff or grayish white; breast not mottled.. 4

4. Breast with two prominent black bands.
   Killdeer, *Charadrius vociferus*, p. 390
   Breast with a single black or grayish-brown band.................. 5
5. Bill entirely black, strong and heavy, 19 mm. long or more.
   Wilson's plover, *Charadrius wilsonia*, p. 391
   Bill with orange or yellow at the base, short and more slender........ 6
6. Larger, wing more than 114 mm.; dark brownish gray above; a distinct web between the outer and middle toes.
   Semipalmated plover, *Charadrius semipalmatus*, p. 386
   Smaller, wing less than 105 mm.; light brown above; no web at base of toes........................Collared plover, *Charadrius collaris*, p. 387

BELONOPTERUS CHILENSIS CAYENNENSIS (Gmelin): Southern Lapwing; Teru-teru

Parra cayennensis Gmelin, Syst. Nat., vol. 1, pt. 2, 1789, p. 706. (Cayenne.)

A large plover, with a long, slender crest.

Description.—Length, 290 to 330 mm. Bend of the wing armed with a strong, curved, sharply pointed spur. Adult (sexes alike), forehead, crest, throat, center of upper foreneck, and breast black, with a faint bluish sheen; a narrow line across the back of the forehead, and on the anterior area of the cheeks, dull white; rest of crown grayish brown; rest of head and neck dull buffy gray; back dull greenish gray with a bronzy area on either side; upper tail coverts white; lesser wing coverts, alula, primaries, and outer secondaries black; middle and greater wing coverts white; secondary coverts and inner secondaries dull gray; tail black, with basal half and tip white; abdomen and sides white.

Iris red; bill red on the basal half and black on the tip; tarsus and toes dull red; wing spur red.

Measurements.—Males (5 from Colombia), wing 218-231 (224), tail 92.2-103.0 (97.2), culmen from base 30.0-34.8 (32.7), tarsus 74.3-84.3 (80.8) mm.

Females (5 from Colombia), wing 220-227 (223), tail 89.2-95.5 (92.7), culmen from base 32.6-34.4 (33.4), tarsus 73.0-78.0 (75.7) mm.

Casual visitor. Recorded from the eastern sector of the Province of Panamá (La Jagua, Chepo), and San Blas (Puerto Obaldía).

This is a species of South America, found in open lands, that ranges across Colombia to the lower Río Atrato, and wanders occasionally to eastern Panamá. It was first recorded for the isthmus when Karl Curtis shot one at La Jagua on May 17, 1936 (Griswold, Auk, 1936, p. 457). Curtis informs me that about 1950, toward the end of the dry season, he encountered a flock of about 30 below La Jagua, near the mouth of the Río Chico, and shot two or three that he was unable to retrieve as they fell on mud banks that were not passable. In March 1921, M. J. Kelly, of the Everhart Museum at Scranton, Pa., secured two on a savanna area near Chepo. These, mounted for exhibition for a time, subsequently came in an exchange to the U. S. National Museum.

On August 27, 1934, Wedel shot a female at Puerto Obaldía, San Blas, which was purchased for the Brandt collection, now in the museum at the University of Cincinnati (Brandt, Auk. 1938, p. 288).

The specific name *chilensis* is from *Parra chilensis* Molina of 1782, a name that some have refused, since the description includes a reference to a frontal shield like that of a jaçana. The formal diagnosis describes the short toes and crested head of the plover, and the extended account of habits also is of that species. Many early descriptions are in part composite but are accepted from the action of a reviser who decides the proper allocation of the name. In the present instance the question has been discussed in detail by me (U. S. Nat. Mus. Bull. 133, 1926, pp. 168-169) and by Peters (Bull. Mus. Comp. Zool., vol. 65, 1923, pp. 295-296). In both references *chilensis* is designated as the name to be accepted for the *Belonopterus*.

SQUATAROLA SQUATAROLA (Linnaeus): Black-bellied Plover; Chorlito Gris

Tringa squatarola Linnaeus, Syst. Nat., ed. 10, vol. 1, 1758, p. 149. (Sweden.)

A plover of medium size, with the axillars black.

Description.—Length, 270 to 290 mm. Sexes alike. Breeding dress, face, foreneck, and breast black; forehead, sides of neck, and abdomen white; crown and hindneck grayish, primaries and axillars black; rest of upper surface barred and spotted with brownish black and white.

Winter plumage, above brownish gray, barred and spotted irregularly with white and grayish white; forehead, sides of head, and undersurface white, the cheeks and sides of neck, streaked with dusky; breast streaked and mottled with dusky.

Measurements (from Ridgway, U. S. Nat. Mus. Bull. 50, pt. 8, 1919, p. 73).—Males, wing 178-199 (189.3), tail 68-82 (75.4), culmen 29.5-31.5 (30.4), tarsus 42-51 (45.3) mm.

Females, wing 179-196 (187.5), tail 69-84 (73.7), culmen 27.5-31 (29.5), tarsus 41.5-48.5 (44.7) mm.

Migrant from the north. Locally common along the sea beaches; Isla Coiba; Isla del Rey. A few nonbreeding birds remain through the period of northern summer.

The main migration arrives from the north in September and early October, and most have left on return by April. I have seen them mainly along the Pacific coast, particularly around the shores of Parita Bay. Near Fort Amador, Canal Zone, and on the golf links at Changuinola, Bocas del Toro, they often range on grass, like golden plover. Eisenmann (Wilson Bull., 1951, p. 182) has reported a few non-breeding individuals near Panamá Viejo between June 16 and July 17, from 1948 to 1951, with 13 individuals as the maximum number seen at one time.

In 1956 I found them regularly on the beaches at Isla Coiba, and collected a female on January 12. Though they should be found throughout the Gulf of Panamá a report for Isla del Rey for March 11, 1904 (Thayer and Bangs, Bull. Mus. Comp. Zool., vol. 46, 1905, p. 146), is the only record for the Pearl Islands.

PLUVIALIS DOMINICA DOMINICA (Müller): American Golden Plover; Chorlito Dorado

Charadrius Dominicus P. L. S. Müller, Natursyst. Suppl., 1776, p. 116. (Hispaniola.)

Slightly smaller than the black-bellied plover, darker on the dorsal surface, with pale gray axillars.

Description.—Length, 245 to 260 mm. Sexes alike. Breeding dress, entire undersurface, including side of head black; a broad band of white from the forehead over the eye and down the side of the neck to the side of the upper breast; dorsal surface dusky speckled with buffy-yellow.

Winter plumage, forehead, side of head, and under surface white, streaked with dusky on the side of the head, and mottled with brownish gray on breast and sides; under surface of wings and axillars light gray; upper surface brownish gray, spotted indistinctly with black, white, and dull buff.

Measurements (from Ridgway, l.c., p. 84).—Males, wing 159-183.5 (176.4), tail 60-75 (67.9), culmen 20.5-24 (22.2), tarsus 38.5-45 (41.9) mm.

Females, wing 176-183 (180.8), tail 64-70 (66), culmen 22-23.5 (22.5), tarsus 41-44.5 (43) mm.

Passage migrant. Locally, tolerably common; reported mainly on the Pacific slope toward the end of the dry season when in northward migration; found in flight southward from the middle of August to November.

The golden plover was first recorded from Panamá when T. A. Imhof (Auk, 1950, p. 256) saw a flock of a dozen on the parade grounds at Fort Clayton, Canal Zone on October 4, 1942. Loftin (Carib. Journ. Sci., 1963, p. 65) in 1962 at Panamá Viejo found 2 August 12, another September 23 (statement corrected from that published from data supplied by the author). At Jaqué, Darién, in 1946 I found them regularly from March 15 to April 13, on the airfield and along the river adjacent, and collected the first specimen for Panamá on the date first mentioned. This bird, a male, was in good flesh but was not fat. On the Sabana San José, east of the Río Pacora I recorded them in 1949 on March 22 and 23, and on March 22, 1958, shot one from a flock of a dozen that flew and ran ahead of my jeep. The bird taken on this occasion was a female that was heavy, but with fat that was dry so that it was not difficult to prepare. It appeared that the oily elements normal in such a condition may have been consumed in the first stage of its northward flight from the wintering grounds in Argentina. On April 3, 1955, I recorded a dozen on the mudflats at Panamá Viejo, and on March 2, 1956, saw another flock of similar size on the golf links near Summit, Canal Zone. None that I have observed have been in breeding plumage.

CHARADRIUS SEMIPALMATUS Bonaparte: Semipalmated Plover; Chorlitejo Semipalmeado

Charadrius semipalmatus Bonaparte, Journ. Acad. Nat. Sci. Philadelphia, vol. 5, Aug. 1825, p. 98. (Coast of New Jersey.)

A small plover with a dark grayish brown back and a single dark breast band.

Description.—Length 145 to 160 mm. Breeding plumage, band across center of crown, a narrow line across base of bill, becoming wider on the cheeks, and a broad band across the upper breast black; rest of crown, back, and wing coverts dark grayish brown; primaries and distal half of tail, except tip, black; rest of under surface, tips of primary coverts, and of tail white.

Winter dress, black markings of summer replaced by dark grayish brown.

Measurements (from Ridgway, l.c., p. 117).—Males, wing 114-122.5 (119.4), tail 52-57.5 (54.8), culmen 11.5-13 (12.5), tarsus 21-24 (22.3) mm.

Females, wing 115-127 (119.8), tail 52.5-61 (55.7), culmen 10.5-13.5 (11.9), tarsus 21-23 (21.9) mm.

Migrant from the north. Common along both Atlantic and Pacific coasts: Isla Coiba; Archipiélago de las Perlas (San José, Saboga, Víveros, and Rey islands); Isla Escudo de Veraguas. A few nonbreeding birds are present during the period of northern summer.

These plovers range the sand beaches, sometimes alone, but usually in small groups of half a dozen to a dozen individuals. The ocean front is a regular haunt, but on the larger rivers of the Pacific slope, as on the Chimán and the Jaqué, these plovers regularly come inland to the head of tidewater where the period of low water exposes open bars of sand and gravel on which they may feed. When the tide is in they often take refuge on rocky islets or headlands. At such times they may go back also among the mangroves to rest on exposed roots. A favored place at high tide is on the offshore rocks at Panamá Viejo. At Changuinola, in Bocas del Toro, I have seen them on the golf links, about small pools left by heavy rains.

Some nonbreeding birds remain through June, during the period of northern summer, but when flocks of fair size are recorded after early July, probably they are early arrivals in the fall migration. Large flocks may be encountered in late March and April when the birds are on their way north.

At Puerto Mensabé on the coast of Los Santos on March 26, 1948, two in full plumage, that I assumed to be males, called, sang, and postured as they do on their northern breeding grounds.

CHARADRIUS COLLARIS Vieillot: Collared Plover, Turillo

FIGURE 66

Charadrius collaris Vieillot, Nouv. Dict. Hist. Nat., nouv. éd., vol. 27, Dec. 1818, p. 135. (Paraguay.)

Smallest of the plovers that have a black breast band; bill black, except for the extreme base of the mandible.

Description.—Length, 130 to 145 mm. Adult (sexes alike), forehead, line through eye, including lower eyelid, and under surface, except breast band, white; fore part of crown, line from eye to bill, and breast band black; upper surface from center of crown to upper tail coverts, including ear coverts, and lesser and middle wing coverts, grayish brown, in most with faint tips of dull white to pale cinnamon; usually with a band of cinnamon brown between the black and the gray of crown, and a mixture of the same color on the ear coverts and the side of the neck; greater wing coverts tipped narrowly with white; wings and central tail feathers fuscous; outer tail feathers white.

Juvenile, black band on fore crown much reduced or absent; black band on breast reduced to a spot on either side, broken in the center.

Iris dark brown; bill black, except for a small orange spot on the side of the mandible at the base that extends from side to side across the bare skin between the mandibular rami; tarsus and toes flesh color; claws black.

FIG 66.—Collared plover, turillo, *Charadrius collaris*.

Measurements (from Ridgway, l.c., p. 141).—Males, wing 86-103 (95.3), tail 40-52.5 (45.2), culmen 13-16.5 (14.4), tarsus 24-27 (25.2) mm.

Females, wing 89-102 (94.4), tail 41-48 (42.8), culmen 13-16 (14.6), tarsus 23.5-26.5 (24.9) mm.

Resident. Local; rather rare; found on gravel bars of larger streams, and on sand beaches.

The early specimens of this interesting species were those sent by McLeannan, who collected it in company with Galbreath somewhere on the Caribbean slope along the line of the Panama Railroad. The two specimens concerned, male and female, are in the U. S. National Museum, but as usual with this older material have no definite locality noted on the label. It is probable that they were obtained on the Río Chagres.

The species is one that I have known in other regions, but one that I sought over many miles of beach, mudflat, and stream edge for ten years before I found my first individual on the isthmus. On March 26, 1957, above the head of tidewater on the Río Tonosí in Los Santos, mangrove swallows and black jaçanas drew me to a broad gravel bar in the river bed. Here, presently, two small plovers that at a casual glance I supposed would be the semipalmated rose, but in the same instant it was obvious that they were a lighter, browner gray, and as they alighted I saw that they were my long-sought collared plover. Both were males.

At Changuinola, Bocas del Toro, in January 1958, a few of this species ranged with other shore birds on the golf course after rains. On January 30 I counted six in company. I found others on the outer beach along Tirbi Bight, above Boca del Drago, on February 20, where I believed they were on their breeding grounds, as a male taken here had the testes beginning to enlarge. Apparently they are more common in this area than elsewhere, as Eisenmann (Condor, 1957, p. 252) found 2 pairs at the mouth of the Río San San, farther along on this same stretch of shore.

The flight of these plovers is direct, fairly rapid, and low over open ground or water. Usually after alighting they teeter once or twice, but then walk about slowly, seeming rather inactive. But also they may run quickly with the head down, and then stop suddenly with the head erect but the neck still shortened. In general actions they resemble the snowy plover, but seldom run as far without stopping. On the outer beaches when approached they move back above the crown, where they are inconspicuous among the scattered bits of drift.

The alarm note is a sharp metallic *tsee*. Another common note is a slightly rolling *tur-r-r*. These notes are heard most often during the breeding season. At other periods usually they are silent.

A set of 2 eggs in the U. S. National Museum was collected on September 30, 1926, by E. G. Holt, on the Río Araguaya, below Macaúba, Goias, Brazil. The shell is smooth, without gloss, with the ground color slightly paler than pinkish buff. Small, irregular black spots are scattered over the surface, somewhat less abundantly near the small end. The measurements are 28.3×20.9 and 28.4×21.2 mm. Schönwetter (Handb. Ool., pt. 7, 1963, p. 387) lists the variation in size found in 36 eggs as $26\text{-}31 \times 19.1\text{-}22.5$ mm.

CHARADRIUS VOCIFERUS VOCIFERUS Linnaeus: Killdeer; Chorlito Gritón

Charadrius vociferus Linnaeus, Syst. Nat., ed. 10, vol. 1, 1758, p. 150. (South Carolina.)

A plover with two black bands on the under surface, one on the lower foreneck, the other on the breast.

Description.—Length, 235 to 250 mm. Forehead, line behind eye, collar on hindneck and under surface white; band across anterior edge of crown, extending back over eye, one on malar stripe, one around lower foreneck, and one across breast black; crown, side of head, back, and wing coverts dark grayish brown; rump and upper tail coverts cinnamon-buff; primaries black; primary coverts tipped with white; outer tail feathers cinnamon-buff, banded near the end with black, and tipped with white; 3 central pairs grayish brown, banded with black near the tip.

Measurements (from Ridgway, l.c., p. 100).—Males, wing 154-167 (160.2), tail 88-103 (95.6), culmen 19-23 (20.3), tarsus 33-36.5 (34.6) mm.

Females, wing 147-170 (160.1), tail 90-103 (94.9), culmen 19.5-22 (20.4), tarsus 32-37 (35.2) mm.

Migrant from the north. Fairly common wherever there are open savannas and pasture lands, from sea level to 2,000 meters elevation; Isla San José. Present usually from November to March.

The killdeer is a land plover that is found as frequently in dry pastures as it is around water. Often it ranges alone, except when moving in migration, when several may appear in company. When approached, if at a little distance, these birds may merely turn the back to conceal the striking black and white of the lower surface of the body, or, if near at hand, may run quietly away. When they take wing, flight is usually accompanied by the loud calls in imitation of which they have received their English name.

The majority arrive in November, though a few have been reported earlier in late October, (October 31, Finca Lérida, above Boquete; Oct. 24, 1931, Oct. 27, 1932, Puerto Obaldía, San Blas). Most leave for the north during March, but a few remain until April, my latest date being April 13, 1946, at Jaqué, Darién. Here, a few days earlier (on April 9) one on the old airfield amused me when it settled down, with wings and body moving gently as though it was adjusting eggs against its breast, and then presently stood up and ran away, a realistic performance, but one not at all convincing in view of the vast distance to its northern nesting grounds.

CHARADRIUS WILSONIA Ord: Wilson's Plover; Chorlito Piquigordo

A small plover, with a single breast band, the bill much larger and heavier than in others with similar marking.

Description.—Length, 160 to 180 mm. Breeding dress, male, anterior part of crown, lores, and a band across upper breast black; posterior area of crown, hindneck, back, wing coverts, and tertials grayish brown; side of head and nape in some washed with cinnamon; greater wing coverts tipped narrowly with white; primaries dull black; central tail feathers blackish, outer pairs light gray tipped with white; forehead and underparts, except for breast band, pure white.

Female, similar but dark bands on fore crown, lores, and breast grayish brown, with little or no black.

Winter plumage, like the female in breeding dress, but more grayish brown.

Iris dark brown; bill black; tarsus and toes grayish flesh color; claws black.

These plovers are found in small numbers on sand beaches, usually remote from areas frequented by fishermen and bathers. They are quieter and more retiring than the semipalmated plovers encountered in the same localities, as when approached usually they run back into the loose sand above high tide mark. There, with the breast turned away, the dull gray back forms an effective camouflage so that they are hidden. Often, too, they crouch so that they become completely inconspicuous.

There is much to learn regarding Wilson's plover in Panamá as there are few published records, and in my own studies I have encountered them infrequently. The specimens that I have collected indicate that two geographic races are present.

CHARADRIUS WILSONIA WILSONIA Ord

Charadrius wilsonia Ord, *in* Wilson, Amer. Orn., Ord reprint, vol. 9, 1814, p. 77, pl. 73, fig. 5. (Cape May, New Jersey.)

Characters.—Lighter, grayer on the dorsal surface; middle toe longer, 18 to 20 mm.

Measurements (from Ridgway, l.c., p. 109).—Males, wing 106-121 (116.4), tail 44-50 (47.5), culmen 19.5-21.5 (20.7), tarsus 27.5-30.5 (29), middle toe without claw 18-20 (19.2) mm.

Females, wing 112-121 (117.6), tail 42-50 (46.9), culmen 19-22 (20.8), tarsus 27-31 (28.6), middle toe without claw 18-20 (18.6) mm.

Possibly resident. Status uncertain from present information; recorded on the Caribbean coast of western Colón, Canal Zone, and San Blas.

At Mandinga, San Blas, on February 6, 1957, I found half a dozen Wilson's plovers on a sand bar at the mouth of the Río Mandinga and collected two females. These prove to be the typical subspecies, not previously reported for the republic. A pair recorded on February 10, 1952, near Boca del Río Indio, in the western sector of Colón, I believe to have been the eastern race, but this is not certain as I did not obtain one for a specimen. They were on a sand beach at the mouth of a small stream about 3 kilometers east of the village, and at my approach ran aside to hide, as they do when on their nesting grounds. They have been recorded breeding on Grassy Key off the coast of British Honduras but are little known south of that point.

The only other report for these birds on the Caribbean side of the Isthmus is a sight record by Arbib and Loetscher (Auk, 1935, p. 326) of 21 on August 23, 1934 at the spillway on the Chagres at Gatun.

CHARADRIUS WILSONIA BELDINGI (Ridgway)

Pagolla wilsonia beldingi Ridgway, U. S. Nat. Mus. Bull. 50, pt. 8, June 26, 1919, p. 112. (La Paz, Baja California.)

Characters.—Darker gray on the dorsal surface; middle toe shorter, 17-18 mm., or less.

Measurements (from Ridgway, l.c., p. 112).—Males, wing 115-116 (115.5), tail 45-48.5 (46.7), culmen 19.5-20.5 (20), tarsus 27.5-28 (27.7), middle toe without claw 17-18 (17.5) mm.

Females, wing 113.5-119 (115.5), tail 45-49.5 (47.2), culmen 19.5-21.5 (20.7), tarsus 27-29 (28), middle toe without claw 17.5-18.0 (17.8) mm.

Probably resident. Local in occurrence on the Pacific coast; recorded from Los Santos (La Honda); Canal Zone (Fort Amador); eastern Province of Panamá (near Panama City; mouth of the Río Chico); Isla Coiba; Isla San José; Isla del Rey.

Two males and a female taken March 20, 1948, at La Honda, on the coast of northern Los Santos, were near breeding condition. I believed from their actions that they were on their nesting ground, as when approached they ran back into the loose sands behind high tide mark for concealment. One that I recorded March 16, 1949, on the mudflats at the mouth of the Río Chico, and 4 seen April

2, 1955, on the beach at Fort Amador, probably were migrants. Arbib and Loetscher (Auk, 1935, p. 326) saw several at Panamá Viejo on August 7 and 28, 1934. Hallinan (Auk, 1924, p. 309) collected one near Panama City on August 11, 1907.

A female with undeveloped ovaries was taken on Isla Coiba on January 30, 1956, and another female shot on January 24, 1960, at Manzanillo, on the eastern side of Isla del Rey, was in similar stage. It is possible that the birds may nest on this island as Brown collected 3 near the town of San Miguel on February 29 and March 11, 1904 (Thayer and Bangs, Bull. Mus. Comp. Zool., vol. 46, 1905, p. 146). Morrison secured an immature male, fully grown, on Isla San José, August 2, 1944.

Family SCOLOPACIDAE: Snipe, Sandpipers, and Allies;
Agachadizas, Playeros, y Aliados.

In this, the most abundant group of the true shorebird families, the species in general resemble the plovers, but most have longer, more slender bills, and there is a greater variation in size. None of those found in Panamá nest there, all being migrant from the north. While many are found on inland waters their greatest abundance is along the coasts, where flocks of thousands may be found on muddy shores at appropriate seasons.

KEY TO THE SPECIES OF SCOLOPACIDAE

1. Without a hind toe....................Sanderling, *Crocethia alba*, p. 416
   Hind toe present... 2
2. Bill long and prominently decurved (size large).
   Whimbrel, *Numenius phaeopus hudsonicus*, p. 396
   Bill variable in length, usually straight, if not the curvature only slight and near tip... 3
3. Bill more than 100 mm. long (size large).
   Marbled godwit, *Limosa fedoa*, p. 398
   Bill much shorter, less than 80 mm., usually much less.............. 4
4. Bill more than 40 mm... 5
   Bill less than 40 mm... 9
5. Larger, wing more than 170 mm., tip of bill smooth................. 6
   Smaller, wing less than 160 mm., tip of bill minutely pitted.......... 7
6. Primaries with a striking, contrasted pattern of black and white.
   Willet, *Catoptrophorus semipalmatus inornatus*, p. 406
   Primaries plain brownish black.
   Greater yellowlegs, *Totanus melanoleucus*, p. 400
7. Tail with a chestnut-brown subterminal bar.
   Common snipe, *Capella gallinago delicata*, p. 413
   Tail barred black and white, without chestnut-brown subterminal bar. 8

8. Black bars on tail and upper tail coverts decidedly broader than white ones.
Long-billed dowitcher, *Limnodromus scolopaceus*, p. 413
Black bars on tail and upper tail coverts not wider than white ones, the latter usually decidedly broader.
Short-billed dowitcher, *Limnodromus griseus*, p. 410
9. Primary wing coverts and secondaries with conspicuous white markings. 10
Primary coverts and secondaries not broadly and conspicuously white. 12
10. Bill longer, 30 mm. or more
Bill straight, rump and upper tail coverts prominently barred with black and white..........................Knot, *Calidris canutus rufa*, p. 415
Bill slightly but definitely decurved at the tip, rump and upper tail coverts gray or brownish gray without bars..Dunlin, *Erolia alpina pacifica*, p. 424
Bill shorter, less than 30 mm., lower back or upper tail coverts white... 11
11. Lower back extensively white; tarsi and feet orange to orange-red.
Ruddy turnstone, *Arenaria interpres morinella*, p. 408
Lower back gray to sooty gray, tarsi and feet duller colored, greenish yellow...............................Surfbird, *Aphriza virgata*, p. 407
12. Tail feathers all, or except central pair, white banded with black..... 13
Tail feathers not extensively white barred with black, except for one or two of the outer ones in some species............................ 14
13. Larger; upper tail coverts white, barred somewhat with sooty black, wing more than 145 mm.; tarsus bright yellow.
Lesser yellowlegs, *Totanus flavipes*, p. 399
Smaller; upper tail coverts dark, wing less than 145 mm., tarsus dark olive-green..................Solitary sandpiper, *Tringa solitaria*, p. 400
14. Tail more than 75 mm.; axillars and under surface of outer primaries white or whitish, broadly barred with black or grayish black.
Upland plover, *Bartramia longicauda*, p. 395
Tail less than 70 mm., under surface of outer primaries not distinctly and evenly barred 15
15. With a pronounced buffy color, brightest on lower surface.
Buff-breasted sandpiper, *Tryngites subruficollis*, p. 426
Without evident buff on lower surface, which is white on the abdomen, or wholly white... 16
16. Tarsus more than 35 mm.; legs long and slender, with the bare portion (crus) above the tarsal joint equal to middle toe without claw.
Stilt sandpiper, *Micropalama himantopus*, p. 425
Tarsus less than 35 mm.; legs proportionately shorter and stockier, with the bare portion (crus) above the tarsal joint definitely shorter than middle toe without claw... 17
17. Rump and upper tail coverts gray or greenish gray.
Spotted sandpiper, *Actitis macularia*, p. 402
Rump and upper tail coverts black, sooty, or black and white......... 18
18. Larger, wing more than 115 mm.................................... 19
Smaller, wing less than 105 mm..................................... 21
19. Rump white; tip of maxilla pitted.
White-rumped sandpiper, *Erolia fuscicollis*, p. 421
Rump black or dusky; tip of maxilla smooth........................ 20

20. Tarsus and toes greenish......Pectoral sandpiper, *Erolia melanotos*, p. 423
    Tarsus and toes black.............Baird's sandpiper, *Erolia bairdii*, p. 422
21. No webs between the toes; tarsus greenish gray or yellowish green.
    Least sandpiper, *Erolia minutilla*, p. 420
    A distinct web between the toes; tarsus black....................... 22
22. Bill shorter; in male 17-20 mm., in female 18-22 mm.
    Semipalmated sandpiper, *Ereunetes pusillus*, p. 417
    Bill longer; in male 20.5-23.5, in female 23-28 mm.
    Western sandpiper, *Ereunetes mauri*, p. 419

BARTRAMIA LONGICAUDA (Bechstein): Upland Plover; Correlona

Tringa longicauda Bechstein, *in* Latham, Allg. Uebers. Vögel, vol. 4, pt. 2, 1812, p. 453. (North America.)

A medium-sized sandpiper, buffy-brown in general color, with small head, and long tail, found in open fields and savannas.

Description.—Length, 245 to 260 mm. Crown dusky brown to sooty black, with an indefinite central stripe of pale buff; forehead streaked with white and buff; hindneck buffy, narrowly streaked; back and rump sooty black, with feathers on the upper back bordered with buff; lesser wing coverts sooty black; middle and greater coverts cinnamon-buff to buffy white, barred lightly with black; tertials brownish gray, barred with black; upper tail coverts black, barred with dull cinnamon-buff and pale buff; central tail feathers brownish gray, barred with black; outer ones cinnamon-buff, edged with white and barred with black; primaries and secondaries fuscous, barred narrowly with white; under surface pale buff, darker on the under tail coverts, with the lower foreneck streaked, and the lower breast marked irregularly and narrowly, with sooty black.

Birds in fall migration average deeper buff.

Measurements (from Ridgway, l.c., p. 380).—Males, wing 157-181 (163.3), tail 79-92 (75.6), exposed culmen 26-31 (28.2), tarsus 43.5-49 (46.4) mm.

Females, wing 161-178 (166.6), tail 79-89.5 (84.0), exposed culmen 27.5-32 (29.8), tarsus 47-50.5 (48.5) mm.

(The average measurement for the tail in females through an error in computation is given by Ridgway as 75.6 mm. in the reference cited above.)

Passage migrant. Formerly common, but now rather rare; in southward migration mainly from September to November; in movement northward in March and April (one on May 3).

The only records for western Panamá are of one taken at Divalá, Chiriquí, November 30, 1900, by Brown (Bangs, Auk, 1901, p. 358) and of two from the town of Bocas del Toro, taken by von Wedel, Nov. 18, 1938. Imhof recorded one at Chorrera, western Province of Panamá, October 11, 1942. In the Canal Zone Jewel (Auk, 1913, p. 425) found this species regularly near Gatun in the fall of 1911, when the birds arrived on September 12 and remained until December 8. The following year he saw the first one September 1. Arbib and Loetscher (Auk, 1935, p. 326) recorded one there on August 17, 1933.

On the Pacific side Imhof saw them at Fort Clayton October 14 to 18, 1942, and Hallinan (Auk, 1924, p. 309) secured one at La Boca on October 26, 1915. In 1953 collectors for the Malaria Control Service secured specimens at Albrook Field on October 6 and 21. The bird taken October 6 is in the U. S. National Museum.

Upland plover have been found less commonly in the spring migration. I recorded one on the open savanna at San José, above La Jagua, Panamá, April 7, 1950, and another at the same point on April 11, 1959. There is a specimen in the American Museum of Natural History that was taken at Boca de Cupe, Darién, May 3, 1915.

These birds nest from southern Alaska and southern Manitoba south to Oklahoma and Maryland. They spend the period of northern winter in the pampas region of southern South America.

NUMENIUS PHAEOPUS HUDSONICUS Latham: Whimbrel; Zarapito Trinador

Numenius hudsonicus Latham, Index Orn., vol. 2, 1790, p. 712. (Hudson Bay.)

One of the largest shorebirds, with long, decurved bill; general appearance buffy brown, particularly when flying.

Description.—Length 410 to 450 mm. Crown blackish brown, with a median streak of buffy white; hindneck, dull buffy white, lined heavily with dull grayish brown; back and wings brownish black, with feathers edged and spotted with dull buffy white; rump and upper tail coverts grayer brown, with lighter markings that are distinctly brown; primary coverts tipped lightly with white to produce an indistinct band; primaries and secondaries sooty black, heavily barred on the inner web with buff; tail grayish brown, barred narrowly with dull black, with an edging of pale cinnamon-buff on outer web of outer pair; throat, lower breast, and abdomen white to buffy white; foreneck and upper breast lined heavily with grayish brown, the lines changing to narrow, irregular bars on breast; sides, flanks, axillars, and under tail coverts pale cinnamon-buff, barred heavily with grayish brown.

Measurements (from Ridgway, l.c., pp. 403-404).—Males, wing 231-257 (239.1), tail 88-101 (92.9), exposed culmen 77-93.5 (83.1), tarsus 52-61 (55.7) mm.

Females, wing 240-267 (252.4), tail 92-102 (97.1), exposed culmen 84-95.5 (91.5), tarsus 54-61 (57.9) mm.

Migrant from the north. Found along both coasts of the mainland: Isla Coiba; Archipiélago de las Perlas (Rey, Pájaros, Chapera, Saboga, Cañas, Málaga); Isla Escudo de Veraguas.

The main flight arrives from the north at the beginning of September. Most leave in March and April, with a few nonbreeding birds present during the months of northern summer. Eisenmann (Wilson Bull., 1951, p. 182) has found a few near Panamá Viejo in June and July, and Imhof recorded one here on June 20, 1942; Festa collected one on June 14, 1895, near the mouth of the Río Coconatí, Darién. On June 8, 1953, I recorded 5 near the mouth of the Río Vidal in western Veraguas.

While the whimbrel ranges to some extent on the sand beaches it is most common on mud flats near the mouths of rivers, and in such localities it goes back inland through the coastal swamps. As the tide rises they often seek perches in the mangroves, sometimes as much as 10 meters above the water, and there rest until their feeding grounds again are open. The mudflats at Panamá Viejo are favored haunts where they may be found almost without fail—at low tide spread widely, and when the flats are covered with water on the rocky islets off the beach. Here in December I have seen as many as 100 gathered together. On the Caribbean side of the isthmus they are less common. I have recorded them there in Almirante Bay, at Isla Escudo de Veraguas and at Mandinga. They are recorded along this coast east to Permé, near the Colombian boundary.

At times the whimbrel may come to wet meadows a short distance inland in pursuit of insects, as I found them in such a location at Catival on Isla Coiba. Jewel (Auk, 1913, p. 426) recorded them feeding in the short grass of the clearings around Gatun in 1911, and reported that he saw them catching butterflies, an unusual food for a bird that normally seeks the small crabs of the beaches.

LIMOSA FEDOA (Linnaeus): Marbled Godwit; Aguja Moteada

Scolopax Fedoa Linnaeus, Syst. Nat., ed. 10, vol. 1, 1758, p. 146. (Northeastern Manitoba.)

General appearance of the whimbrel but slightly smaller, with long, slender bill, that curves slightly upward toward the tip.

Description.—Length, 395 to 470 mm. Crown and hindneck dark brownish gray, edged narrowly with buffy white; back, tertials, and rump fuscous-black, with feathers edged and tipped with buffy white; upper tail coverts pale cinnamon-buff, barred narrowly with brownish black; wing coverts, secondaries, and inner primaries cinnamon-buff, the flight feathers tipped, and more or less mottled, with dull black; outer primaries the same, but with outer webs white; outer tail feathers cinnamon-buff, barred lightly with grayish brown; central pairs pale cinnamon-buff, barred heavily with black; throat faintly buffy white; rest of under surface buff to pale cinnamon-buff, lined finely on the foreneck, and barred lightly on the upper breast, sides, flanks, and under tail coverts with dusky brown; under wing coverts cinnamon-buff, nearly immaculate.

In full winter plumage the under surface is plain buff, except for a few faint dusky bars on the sides and under tail coverts.

Measurements (from Ridgway, l.c., p. 185).—Males, wing 221-228 (225.4), tail 77.5-95 (82.9), exposed culmen 92-119 (100.3), tarsus 67-76 (69.4) mm.

Females, wing 212-234 (224.1), tail 79-89 (83.4), exposed culmen 88.5-117.5 (104.8), tarsus 67-76.5 (71.4) mm.

Migrant from the north. Known only from sight records at Panamá Viejo, with one report from Fort Clayton.

The first published record of the presence of this species in Panamá is that of Eisenmann (Auk, 1955, p. 426), who found the marbled godwit at Panamá Viejo on August 11 and 19, 1954, and on September 4 and 11, 1955. In the latter year Maj. F. O. Chapelle recorded these birds on several occasions between April 2 and May 20. I saw 3 there on December 3, 1955. There is an earlier sight record for Fort Clayton, given to me by T. A. Imhof, who saw one November 24, 1942. Dr. Eisenmann informs me that his later records run from April 4 through May and June, and in August and September.

They feed on the open flats at low tide, and then, as the sea rises, come to the rocky offshore islets, often in company with the whimbrel. There is no report of a specimen taken.

The species breeds in the north from central Alberta and southern Manitoba south to Montana and western Minnesota. It is found in winter on the Pacific coast from California to Chile. Others winter from the southern and southeastern coasts of the United States south to México and British Honduras. On the return flight northward they are recorded occasionally in the West Indies. There are no reports as yet from the Caribbean coast of Panamá.

TOTANUS FLAVIPES (Gmelin): Lesser Yellowlegs; Playero Chillón Chico

Scolopax flavipes Gmelin, Syst. Nat., vol. 1, pt. 2, 1789, p. 659. (New York.)

A slender-bodied sandpiper, of medium size, with long, bright yellow legs.

Description.—Length 240 to 250 mm. Breeding plumage, head and hindneck light gray, streaked with dusky brown; back and scapulars brownish gray, spotted irregularly with black and smaller marks of white; rump, upper tail coverts, and tail white barred with grayish black; wing coverts and secondaries brownish gray, edged with white and barred indistinctly with grayish black; primaries black; underneath white with foreneck and upper breast with narrow streaks, and sides, underwing coverts, and under tail coverts with bars of dull black.

Winter plumage, gray above, in some with back and wing coverts spotted lightly with dusky and white; foreneck and chest light gray, lightly streaked.

Measurements (from Ridgway, l.c., p. 338).—Males, wing 149-163 (153.5), tail 61-67 (62.8), exposed culmen 35-38 (36.4), tarsus 45.5-55.5 (50) mm.

Females, wing 149.5-157 (155.8), tail 55-66 (63.2), exposed culmen 30-39 (35.5), tarsus 46.5-52 (50.3) mm.

Migrant from the north. Common on muddy shores, and to a lesser extent along the lower, more open, lowland courses of the larger rivers; Isla Coiba. Present from August to April, rarely later.

A few lesser yellowlegs appear in early August, but the majority arrive later. They are found singly, or a few together, feeding on tidal mud flats, about pools in wet meadows, or less often along the sand and gravel bars on the broad courses of rivers. They range on both coasts, but apparently are attracted only casually to the offshore islands, as my only record in such localities is of one seen on February 2, 1956, on Isla Coiba.

The yellow legs identify this bird and its larger companion, the greater yellowlegs, from other shorebirds. The present species calls quickly when startled, a shrill *whew* or *whew whew*.

TOTANUS MELANOLEUCUS (Gmelin): Greater Yellowlegs; Playero Chillón Grande

Scolopax melanoleucus Gmelin, Syst. Nat., vol. 1, pt. 2, 1789, p. 659. (Chateaux Bay, Labrador.)

Similar to the lesser yellowlegs, but definitely larger; legs bright yellow.

Description.—Length 320 to 340 mm. Differs from the lesser yellowlegs, *Totanus flavipes,* only in decidedly larger size, as the colors in breeding plumage, and in winter, in the two are the same.

Measurements (from Ridgway, l.c., p. 332).—Males, wing 180-198.5 (187.8), tail 71-83 (76.9), exposed culmen 52-61 (55.8), tarsus 57-68 (60.7) mm.

Females, wing 180-197 (188.9), tail 71-83 (76.6), exposed culmen 53.5-58 (55.5), tarsus 55-62.5 (59.4) mm.

Migrant from the north. Common; found on tidal flats, and along the larger streams in the lowlands; casually to such upland localities as the lakes near El Volcán, Chiriquí. Present from August to April.

At Gatun Arbib and Loetscher (Auk, 1935, p. 326) recorded this species from August 22 to 26, 1934. I saw half a dozen at Panamá Viejo on April 3, 1955.

Greater yellowlegs, like the smaller species, are found singly, or in small bands, on attractive feeding grounds. Their greater size usually is evident, as in body they are nearly as large as the willet that often are nearby. Their note in sound is like that of the other yellowlegs but is decidedly louder and also is repeated several times in rapid sequence.

This species may be somewhat the more abundant of the two, as I find that it is recorded more frequently in my field notes.

TRINGA SOLITARIA Wilson: Solitary Sandpiper; Playero Solitario

A small sandpiper that in flight appears dark above, with black wings and white borders on the tail.

Description.—Length, 200 to 215 mm. Breeding plumage, above dark grayish brown; wings black; crown and hindneck streaked indistinctly with whitish; back, scapulars, and wing coverts with many fine spots of white; upper tail coverts blacker, barred with white; lateral tail feathers white, barred with black; central pair black, with white spots on the outer edges of the webs; underneath white; sides of neck, foreneck, and upper breast streaked with grayish brown; eyelids and supraloral streak white; under wing coverts black, barred

narrowly with white; flanks and under tail coverts barred with black.
Fall and winter plumage, similar but grayer above, with streaks on lower surface less distinct.

The solitary sandpiper is the most widely distributed species among the northern migrants of its family that come to Panamá, as it may be found about any small fresh-water pool, and is encountered also along rivers wherever there are open channels. These birds range in suitable places into the lower mountains. As the name indicates, they do not congregate in bands, but in periods of migration, or on especially attractive feeding grounds, they may be found in scattered company.

They tilt the forepart of the body constantly as they walk, whether in water an inch or so deep, or on the shore. When flushed they rise quickly, and fly swiftly, often with a sharp call note. It is common for them to dart away, and then turn to come back and drop again close by.

The two forms of the species are both known in Panamá.

TRINGA SOLITARIA SOLITARIA Wilson

Tringa solitaria Wilson, Amer. Orn., vol. 7, 1813, p. 53, pl. 8, fig. 3. (Pocono Mountains, Pennsylvania.)

Characters.—Blacker, more dusky olive above; a well-defined dark streak on the lores; smaller in size. Wing, males, 121.5-129; females 126-134 mm.

Measurements (from Ridgway, l.c., pp. 358-359).—Males, wing 121.5-129.5 (126.5), tail 50-57 (53.7), exposed culmen 27.0-30.5 (28.8), tarsus 28-31 (29.9) mm.

Females, wing 126-134 (127.8), tail 52-59 (55.4), exposed culmen 28-32 (29.3), tarsus 27.0-32.5 (29.4) mm.

Migrant from the north. Common throughout the mainland around fresh-water pools, and along the rivers. Present from August to April.

There is one record for July 29, 1929, at Permé, San Blas (Griscom, Bull. Mus. Comp. Zool., vol. 72, 1932, p. 322), but the majority arrive from the north after the middle of August. They remain commonly until mid-April, sometimes somewhat later, as I saw them in 1947 on the Río Jaqué, Darién, until April 19. They appear regularly at the lakes at an elevation of 1280 meters near El Volcán in Chiriquí.

This race nests from southeastern Yukon and Labrador, south to eastern British Columbia and eastern Ontario. It is found in winter from northeastern México, Louisiana, and Florida, to Argentina.

TRINGA SOLITARIA CINNAMOMEA (Brewster)

Totanus solitarius cinnamomeus Brewster, Auk, vol. 7, no. 4, Oct. 1890, p. 377. (San José del Cabo, Baja California.)

Characters.—Lighter, more grayish olive above; loral area usually with fine scattered dusky spots, instead of a definite bar; inner web of outermost primary usually mottled with white; spotting on back distinctly buff in birds in fall plumage; larger, wing, males 124-137; females 137-142 mm.

Measurements (from Ridgway, l.c., p. 363).—Males, wing 124-137 (132.2), tail 52.5-59.0 (56.2), exposed culmen 27.5-32.0 (30.2), tarsus 29-32 (30.1) mm.

Females, wing 137-142 (138.7), tail 56-59 (57.6), exposed culmen 29-32 (30.3), tarsus 30-33 (31.7) mm.

Migrant from the north. Rare; one record, a female, taken at the lakes at 1,280 meters, near El Volcán, Chiriquí.

This bird was shot with another of the typical race on March 14, 1955.

This is the western subspecies that nests from central Alaska and MacKenzie to northwestern British Columbia and northeastern Manitoba. It winters mainly in South America, south to central Argentina, so that it may occur with some regularity as a migrant through Panamá.

ACTITIS MACULARIA (Linnaeus): Spotted Sandpiper; Playerito Coleador

FIGURE 67

A small sandpiper. In breeding dress, with round black spots on lower surface; in winter plumage grayish olive-brown above; mainly white below; teeters the body constantly as it walks; flight usually low with quick strokes of the decurved wings.

Description.—Length 160 to 175 mm. Breeding dress, above grayish olive-brown with irregular fine, dusky lines and scattered irregular spots and bars on the dorsal surface; a white line over eye; wing coverts tipped narrowly with white or buffy white, and barred narrowly with black; primaries and secondaries fuscous, the latter, and the inner secondaries, tipped with white; outer tail feathers white, barred with fuscous; under surface white dotted with small, round black spots.

Winter dress, above grayish olive-brown, with indistinct shaft lines of dull black; wing coverts as in breeding plumage; underneath white; with a dark gray wash on the sides of the neck and upper breast; wings and tail as in breeding plumage.

Measurements (from Ridgway, l.c., p. 373).—Males, wing 89-105 (100.5), tail 45-53 (49), exposed culmen 21.5-25.5 (23.6), tarsus 19.5-24 (22.2) mm.

Females, wing 100-109 (104), tail 47-53 (50.4), exposed culmen 21.5-25.0 (23.6), tarsus 21-25 (22.8) mm.

Migrant from the north. Found around water from ocean beaches and mangrove swamps to small streams in the mountains; common from August to May: Isla Parida; Isla Bolaños; Isla Coiba; Isla Canal de Afuera; Isla Cébaco; Isla Iguana; Isla Taboga; Isla Tabo-

FIG. 67.—Solitary sandpiper, playerito solitario, *Tringa solitaria.*

guilla; Isla Uravá; Archipiélago de las Perlas (Pacheca, Saboga, Contadora, Chápera, Rey, Cañas, Bayoneta, Málaga, and San José islands).

In Chiriquí I have found spotted sandpipers regularly near El Volcán and have seen them occasionally near Boquete.

The main flight begins during the first week in August, though an occasional bird may arrive toward the end of July, the earliest report to date being of one taken at Cana, Darién, July 25. The movement northward starts in March, and continues through April, with a few birds still present during the following month. Late dates for specimens include a male in the Havemeyer collection at Yale, taken at Zegla, Bocas del Toro, May 19 (1927), and a male in the U. S. National Museum collected at Portobelo, Colón, May 23 (1911). During the first half of April, near Jaqué, on the coast of Darién, I recorded a considerable flight, evidently in passage from South America, when a hundred or more were seen during single days. On April 11, 1946, soon after dark, at least 200 dropped down on the tar-gravel surface of the old fighter air field. During another flight two evenings later fully 100 appeared about 9:30 p.m. Nonbreeding birds frequently remain far south during the northern summer, so that it may be expected that a few will be recorded during that period in Panamá.

Spotted sandpipers range about water, either salt or fresh, and are found on the coasts on sandy beaches, mudflats, rocky headlands, and mangrove swamps. In the interior they are seen along streams, and around ponds and lakes. They are not gregarious, as though several may be found near one another on attractive feeding grounds, it is only during the height of migration that they join in numbers, and then the flocks appear diffuse. In fact, they are often pugnacious, as one individual often pre-empts one bit of shore, and drives at any other that may appear. Single birds seem in some instances to guard a definite territory where they may be seen daily. Ordinarily, the territorial disputes that I have seen have been merely pursuit and chase, where one bird yielded to another. Occasionally, where two seemed to have asserted definite claims, both stood and pecked hard and steadily at one another for a minute or so. At the end usually both turned and ran off in opposite directions. From a human viewpoint, the apparent pretense seemed to be either that the bout was a draw, or that each felt it was the victor.

They frequent the water's edge, or open areas laid bare by receding water at low tide, moving quickly with the steadily tilting bodies that gives the common Spanish name of *chorlito* or *playerito coleador*, varied sometimes to *meneacola*, of similar meaning. Among English speaking residents around Almirante in Bocas del Toro these birds are called chicken peddy. When flushed they fly rapidly and rather stiffly, with the wings little elevated above the level of the back, and the body usually only a few inches above the water, so that as they move they are mirrored on the surface immediately beneath. Instantly on alighting the teetering motion again begins. In the mangrove swamps it is common to find them at high tide standing on projecting logs, or on small branches, often in the sun, and then they remain quiet without movement, except to preen, until they are approached when teetering may begin before they fly. At other times they may rest quietly for a few minutes to receive the warmth of the early morning sun.

The stomach of one from Portobelo was filled with remains of small crustaceans, with a few bits of ants and a neuropteran. Two others from inland localities in the Canal Zone contained a number of aquatic insects, and a few ants, beetles, and Orthoptera.

Recently this species has been separated into eastern and western subspecies on the basis of a difference in color of the dorsal surface, a distinction that is slight, but one that may be recognized in migrant birds as well as those on their breeding grounds. Both forms come to Panamá, and from the numerous specimens that I have examined are present in equal number. As the two may be distinguished only with birds in the hand and may not be identified in life I have included both in the statement of range given above. The two are similar in size.

ACTITIS MACULARIA MACULARIA (Linnaeus)

Tringa macularia Linnaeus, Syst. Nat., ed. 12, vol. 1, 1766, p. 249. (Pennsylvania.)

Characters.—Dorsal surface grayish brown, with a brownish cast, and a faint metallic gloss; in breeding dress, with under surface more heavily spotted, and the markings more intensely black.

The typical race breeds from California, Montana, Wyoming, and Saskatchewan east to Labrador, and south to southern Nevada, central Texas, northern Alabama, western North Carolina, and Virginia. Specimens in the U. S. National Museum indicate a winter range that covers Central America, through South America to Argentina, the West Indies, and the Bahama Islands. Definite specimen records for this subspecies in Panamá are as follows:

BOCAS DEL TORO: Zegla, May 19, 1927.
HERRERA: Parita, Feb. 13 and 19, 1948.
CANAL ZONE: Miraflores, May 13; Río Indio, near Gatun, Feb. 15; Gatun May 8; and Monte Lirio, Jan. 24; all in 1911.
PANAMÁ: Cerro Azul, Sept. 18, 1953.
DARIÉN: Jaqué, March 17, 1946.
ISLA SAN JOSÉ: Aug. 13 and Sept. 3, 1944.

ACTITIS MACULARIA RAVA Burleigh

Actitis macularia rava Burleigh, Auk, vol. 77, no. 2, Apr. 30, 1960, p. 210. (Lewiston, Nez Perce County, Idaho.)

Characters.—Dorsal surface grayer, with only a faint trace of metallic gloss. In breeding dress, less heavily spotted on the under parts, with the markings less intensely black.

This race breeds from northwestern Alaska, Yukon, and western MacKenzie south to Oregon and Idaho. It is found in winter mingled with the other subspecies south to Perú, Venezuela, and the West Indies.

Definite specimen records for Panamá are as follows:

Los Santos: Guánico Arriba, Jan. 25, 1962.
Canal Zone: Lion Hill, May 1; Río Indio, near Gatun, Feb. 8, 1911.
Colón: Portobelo, May 23, 1911.
San Blas: Mandinga, Jan. 31, 1957.
Darién: Jaqué, Mar. 17 and 27, 1946.

CATOPTROPHORUS SEMIPALMATUS INORNATUS (Brewster): Willet; Playero Aliblanco

Symphemia semipalmata inornata Brewster, Auk, vol. 4, no. 2, Apr. 1887, p. 145. (Larimer County, Colorado.)

Large; gray above, white underneath, with a striking black and white pattern in the wing in flight.

Description.—Length, 340 to 355 mm. Breeding dress, above slightly brownish gray; crown and hindneck streaked, back and scapulars, spotted and barred, with dusky; wing coverts nearly plain; primaries white for basal half, rest dusky black; secondaries white; tail mottled with darker gray; underparts white, with foreneck and upper breast spotted, and sides barred, with dusky; axillars and under wing coverts sooty black.

Winter plumage, above light brownish gray; underneath white shaded on sides, and in some individuals on front of foreneck with pale gray; wings as in breeding dress.

Measurements (from Ridgway, l. c., p. 319).—Males, wing 193-218 (205.2), tail 73-84.5 (79.4), culmen 58-63.5 (59.4), tarsus 57-69 (64.9) mm.

Females, wing 209.5-220 (213.5), tail 74-88 (80.9), culmen 63-65 (64.1), tarsus 66.5-70 (68.3) mm.

Migrant from the north. Common along the Pacific coast; rare on the Caribbean side; Isla Coiba; Isla Cébaco; Isla del Rey, Isla San José. Common from August to April, with numbers of nonbreeding birds remaining through the period of northern summer. All of the hundreds that I have seen have been in plain plumage, with none in barred breeding dress.

T. A. Imhof recorded in his unpublished notes that he saw 35 at Panamá Viejo on June 20, 1942, and Eisenmann (Wilson Bull., vol. 63, 1951, p. 182) from 1948 to 1951 found them here from the latter half of June to the first half of July, with 23 as the maximum number at one time. In 1953 I recorded a dozen at Playa Coronado on June 19, and 3 at Nueva Gorgona on June 23.

Willets are found scattered singly or gathered in small bands on sandy beaches and on the mud flats at the mouths of the larger rivers.

At rest, or as they walk slowly about, they appear gray and white, but as they fly the extensive areas of white in the otherwise black wings, form a striking pattern that serves to identify the species without mistake. Often they give their ringing calls as they take wing. In addition to the numbers usually present at Panamá Viejo I have found them especially common around the Gulf of Parita, and at the mouths of the Chico, Chimán, and Majé rivers. On the larger streams some range inland but not above the limit of the tide. At high water willets often join the whimbrels on perches in the mangroves, to rest until falling water again leaves their feeding grounds bare.

Few range to the offshore islands. I saw them on Isla Coiba in January 1956 and collected one. In the Pearl Islands Morrison shot a female on Isla San José on September 23, 1944, and Brown collected 2 females on Isla del Rey on February 20 and March 2, 1904. I secured a male at the mouth of the Río Cacique on this island on January 27, 1960.

Peters (Bull. Mus. Comp. Zool., vol. 71, 1931, p. 303) has recorded a female *inornatus* taken at Cricamola, Bocas del Toro, on September 19, 1927. Eisenmann (Condor, 1957, p. 252) saw a willet at the mouth of the Río San San on July 3, 1956, in this same province. And Wedel collected one at Puerto Obaldía, San Blas, March 15, 1935. These are the only records at present for the Caribbean side.

The typical race *Catoptrophorus semipalmatus semipalmatus* has been recorded as a migrant visitor south to western Costa Rica, and so may range occasionally to Panamá. It is darker, more brownish gray above and is smaller especially in length of bill and tarsus. In males, the bill ranges from 53 to 58, and the tarsus from 54 to 58.5 mm; and in females, the bill measures from 52.5 to 59, and the tarsus from 51.5 to 58 mm.

APHRIZA VIRGATA (Gmelin): Surfbird; Chorlito de Rompiente

Tringa virgata Gmelin, Syst. Nat., vol. 1, pt. 2, 1789, p. 674. (Prince William Sound, Alaska.)

A heavy-bodied shorebird, with short, greenish-yellow legs; dark gray to dull black above, with white rump.

Description.—Length 230 to 245 mm. Breeding dress, head and neck with feathers dull black centrally, edged widely with dull brownish gray; back dull black, with the feathers edged and tipped with dull white, dull gray, and a few markings of dull buff; wing coverts dark gray; primary coverts and outer secondaries white, forming a distinct white line; rump and upper tail coverts white; tail with central feathers fuscous, the outer ones white tipped with grayish; under surface of body white, heavily marked with triangular spots of dark neutral gray.

Winter plumage, dark brownish gray above with the feathers edged lightly with white; crown streaked indistinctly with fuscous; under surface white; throat with scattered small spots of gray; sides of head and foreneck streaked, and breast with narrow crescentic bars of dark gray.

Iris dark brown; tip of bill black; base of maxilla paler; base of mandible dull orange brown; tarsus and toes greenish yellow; claws black.

Measurements (from Ridgway, l.c., p. 60).—Males, wing 164-183 (170.9), tail 63-69 (65.2), exposed culmen 23-26 (24.2), tarsus 29-30.5 (29.6) mm.

Females, wing 169-181 (176), tail 64-66 (65), exposed culmen 23-26 (24.9), tarsus 29-31.5 (29.6) mm.

Migrant from the north. Rare; one taken at Bahía Piñas, Darién; numerous sight records at Panamá Viejo, Panamá.

This curious shorebird, migrant from its Alaskan nesting grounds south along the Pacific coast as far as Chile, was first reported by Eugene Eisenmann (Auk, 1948, p. 605) from 4 seen at Panamá Viejo, August 14, 1947. Imhof (Auk, 1950, p. 256) found one with turnstones at San Francisco de la Caleta, September 2, 1942, a little farther west on the same beach. And Eisenmann (Auk, 1955, pp. 426-427) recorded others, in part observed by Maj. F. O. Chapelle, May 15, August 11 and 19, October 6 and 16, 1954, and January 22 and June 27, 1955. I found one here January 5, 1964, and another February 21, 1965. There are other sight records for this locality.

The only specimen taken as yet in Panamá is a male in the museum of the University of Miami, collected September 11, 1961, by D. R. Paulson during an oceanographic expedition with A. Glassell on his yacht *Argosy*.

ARENARIA INTERPRES MORINELLA (Linnaeus): Ruddy Turnstone; Vuelvepiedras

Tringa Morinella Linnaeus, Syst. Nat., ed. 12, vol. 1, 1766, p. 249. (Coast of Georgia.)

A heavy-bodied shorebird, with short, orange legs and a broad, heavily mottled, dark band on the breast; in flight the black wings, dark upper back, lower rump and the end of the tail are in prominent contrast with white lower back.

Description.—Length, 225 to 240 mm. Breeding dress, head prominently white, with lores, forehead, cheeks, and fine streaks over crown black; upper back, middle wing coverts and tertials cinnamon, heavily spotted with black; lesser and greater wing coverts grayish brown, the latter tipped prominently with white; lower back and upper tail coverts white; lower rump black; primaries and secondaries fuscous to black; tail white on base, black at tip, edged and tipped with cinnamon and white; throat, sides of lower neck, under side of wing, and rest of under parts white; sides of throat and upper foreneck black, continuous with the broad black band across the lower foreneck and breast.

Winter plumage, differs from the breeding dress in the absence of cinnamon, and with the black replaced by dark grayish brown to fuscous; head with less white.

Iris brown; bill dull black; tarsus and toes yellowish to reddish orange; claws black.

Measurements (from Ridgway, l.c., p. 52).—Males, wing 139.5-155 (145.5), tail 56.5-64 (60), exposed culmen 21.5-24 (22.9), tarsus 22.5-26 (24.5) mm.

Females, wing 144-157.5 (148.6), tail 57-63 (60.4), exposed culmen 21.5-24 (22.9), tarsus 23-25.5 (24.5) mm.

Migrant from the north. Common along both coasts of Panamá; Isla Coiba; Isla del Rey, Isla Saboga.

Turnstones, migrants to Panamá from the far north, are birds of the seashore, where they range on both sand and rock beaches. Usually they are found in little flocks of 3 or 4 to a dozen, often with, or near, other groups of shorebirds. When the tide is low they move along actively, with low, chattering calls, sometimes pecking quickly at the sand, and sometimes, with a quick jerk of the head, flipping over small pebbles to expose what may be hidden beneath—the habit common to them throughout the world from which the common names are taken. At high tide they rest, preen, and doze, often on rocky points, to await the next stage of low water.

The northern migrants appear to arrive in August; most leave for the north in April, though a few nonbreeding birds may be found during the northern summer. T. A. Imhof recorded them in 1942 along the Fort Amador causeway on May 14, June 15, and July 21, and Eisenmann (Wilson Bull., 1950, pp. 182, 183) reported this species July 13, 1950, near Panamá Viejo. There is a specimen in the U. S. National Museum taken near Fort Kobbe on July 24, 1961.

LIMNODROMUS GRISEUS (Gmelin): Short-billed Dowitcher; Agachona Gris Piquicorta

Of medium size, with bill longer than the tarsus; back and rump white; legs rather short, light greenish yellow; tail with white and dark bars of about equal width.

Description.—Length 245 to 260 mm. Breeding plumage, upper surface pinkish cinnamon with crown, hindneck, and back streaked, and scapulars spotted, with black; lesser wing coverts dark grayish brown with paler margins; middle coverts black, margined with cinnamon-buff; greater coverts and secondaries grayish brown, edged and tipped with white; primaries dusky, margined with white; lower back, rump, and upper tail coverts white, with rump spotted, and upper tail coverts barred, with blackish; tail barred with white and black, with the bars and interspaces about equal; sides of head and underparts pinkish cinnamon, mixed with white on breast and abdomen, and spotted with dusky, the spots becoming bars on the sides.

Winter plumage, above gray, darker on the wing coverts, which are margined lightly with white to grayish white; foreneck, chest, and sides gray, mixed somewhat with white; throat distinctly whitish; rest of lower surface white, with sides and under tail coverts barred with dusky; lower back, rump, upper tail coverts, tail, primaries, and secondaries as in breeding dress.

Shorebirds of this genus in heavy body, rather short legs, and long, straight bills, in form resemble the common snipe, but this resemblance. need give rise to no confusion as dowitchers live in the open on sandy beaches and mud flats. And, further, they have the rump and upper tail coverts white, a mark that shows prominently in flight. In feeding they move about quietly, sometimes wading in water nearly to their bodies, while they probe with their long bills, which they may swing from side to side in avocet fashion, often with the head completely immersed. Food is seized readily as the tip of the maxilla may be opened for 5 to 6 millimeters (while the rest of the mouth remains closed) through the operation of muscles at the base of the skull on the flexible bones of the bill. The flight is swift, and when in flocks the band of birds moves in close formation. When tide waters are high dowitchers rest quietly on the upper levels of the beaches or on rocky points. At Mandinga on one occasion I found several standing on timbers beneath an old wharf when no other shelter was near. I have found them in fair numbers on mudflats on the Gulf of Parita, where I have seen as many as 40 in company.

Dowitchers appear as migrants from the north, with two of the three races of the species *griseus* recorded to date. The third, *Limnodromus griseus caurinus*, that nests in Alaska, differs from the other two in darker gray color of the dorsal surface. Its range in southward migration at present is not known with certainty.

Some of the published records are of uncertain allocation as understanding of the characters of the races of *griseus* and of the differences that separate *griseus* and *scolopaceus* until recently has been confused. The characters in general are of such a nature that sight identifications are seldom practicable except as to placement in the genus. The earliest report of these birds is that of Lawrence (Ann. Lyc. Nat. Hist., New York, vol. 7, 1862, p. 479) who lists a dowitcher, under the specific name *griseus*, as one of the birds received from McLeannan, with no explanatory statement. I have not been able to locate a specimen on which this report might have been based. Aldrich (Scient. Publ. Cleveland Mus. Nat. Hist., vol. 7, 1937, p. 58) saw several dowitchers on the mud flats of Montijo Bay, Veraguas, March 29, 1932. Eisenmann (Wilson Bull., vol. 63, 1951, p. 182) recorded 4 seen near Panamá Viejo, June 24, 1951 (which is the only record to date for the months of northern summer). There have been other sight records of uncertain reference.

There is also a report of one banded in Massachusetts on August 24, 1935, taken on the Río Chagres, on September 12, less than a month later.

LIMNODROMUS GRISEUS GRISEUS (Gmelin)

Scolopax griseus Gmelin, Syst. Nat., vol. 1, pt. 2, 1789, p. 658. (Long Island, New York.)

Characters.—Darker gray above; throat only slightly whiter than foreneck and breast.

Measurements (New England specimens, from Pitelka, Univ. California Publ. Zoöl., vol. 50, 1950, p. 38).—Males, wing 133-145 (138.8), culmen 51.2-60.4 (55.1), tarsus 31.5-35.7 (33.7) mm.

Females, wing 136-144 (140.4), culmen 56.4-66.3 (58.8), tarsus 31.3-37.3 (34.3) mm.

Migrant from the north. Local in occurrence and not common; found along the coasts on sandy beaches and mudflats, where it is recorded from September to March; a few nonbreeding birds appear to remain through the period of northern summer.

The first definite record for this subspecies was by Griscom (Bull. Mus. Comp. Zool., vol. 72, 1932, p. 322), who reported a male from Permé, San Blas, taken by Wedel. Through the kindness of Dr. R. A. Paynter, Jr., I have been able to verify the subspecific identification of this specimen as *L. g. griseus* and find that it was collected on October 25, 1929. The gray of the back agrees in dark color with typical *griseus*, being definitely darker than that found in *hendersoni* to which it had been allocated with uncertainty by Pitelka (cit. supra, pp. 44, 49, 79). Three that I collected at Mandinga, San Blas on January 29, and February 6, 1957, and four from Aguadulce, Coclé, January 18 and 19, 1963, also are of the typical subspecies.

LIMNODROMUS GRISEUS HENDERSONI Rowan

Limnodromus griseus hendersoni Rowan, Auk, vol. 49, no. 1, Jan. 4, 1932, p. 22. (Devil's Lake, Alberta.)

Characters.—Similar to *griseus*, but lighter gray on the dorsal surface; also paler on the under surface of the body, with the throat distinctly whiter.

Measurements (Birds from Alberta and Saskatchewan, from Pitelka, l.c., p. 32).—Males, wing 136-150 (143.4), culmen 52.6-61.2 (57.5), tarsus 33.8-39.3 (36.7) mm.

Females, wing 138-152 (145.7), culmen 58.2-65.9 (62.4), tarsus 35.3-41.3 (37.9) mm.

Migrant from the north. Known at present from one record.

A specimen in the American Museum of Natural History, collected at Aguadulce, Coclé, September 11, 1925, by R. R. Benson, is the only record for this race. The bird was listed by Griscom (Bull. Mus. Comp. Zool., vol. 78, 1935, p. 307) as *scolopaceus*, but on examination of the specimen I find that the barring on the tail and upper tail coverts is that typical of the *griseus* group, in which the black and white bars are about equal in width. The specimen is in transition from summer to winter dress, and because of this it requires careful study for definite identification. The few remaining colored edgings on the scapulars and longer tertials are paler, and are buff, rather than the cinnamon of these markings in *L. g. griseus*. The hindneck is slightly brownish, due perhaps to foxing, but on the whole this area is paler as in *hendersoni*.

This is the most southern record reported for this subspecies.

LIMNODROMUS SCOLOPACEUS (Say): Long-billed Dowitcher; Agachona Gris Piquilarga

Limosa scolopacea Say, *in* Long, Exped. Rocky Mountains, vol. 1, 1823, p. 170. (Council Bluffs, Iowa.)

Similar to the short-billed dowitcher but darker gray above and below, and with longer bill.

Description.—Length 245 to 270 mm. Differs from *Limnodromus griseus* in all its races in having the tail and upper tail coverts decidedly blacker, with the white cross bars definitely narrower than the black ones. Compared with *Limnodromus griseus:* Breeding plumage, somewhat darker above, with the markings on the back more reddish brown; lower surface much redder brown; dark markings on foreneck and upper breast in the form of short bars (instead of rounded spots).

Winter plumage, above darker gray; breast and foreneck darker, grayer; throat suffused with gray so that it does not appear solidly white.

Measurements (Alaskan specimens, from Pitelka, l.c., p. 29).—Males, wing 133-144 (138.6), culmen 56.8-68.6 (62.1), tarsus 34.7-41.2 (38.2) mm.

Females, wing 138-151 (143.7), culmen 64.2-76.2 (71.6), tarsus 38.7-44.9 (41.0) mm.

Migrant from the north. Abundance uncertain; known at present from two reports.

At Changuinola, Bocas del Toro, on January 30, 1958, following a heavy rain, dowitchers came with other waders to shallow pools on the golf course. I noted two or three at first and then a band of a dozen. Presently I was fortunate in collecting 3 males, grouped together, all of them of the long-billed form. In feeding these birds walked about poking with their bills at the short grass.

There is a male in the American Museum of Natural History taken on October 27, 1927, at Cocoplum, near the seaward base of the Valiente Peninsula, Bocas del Toro, by R. R. Benson, that also is typical of this species.

The specimen listed by Griscom as *scolopaceus* in his check-list, as indicated above is *L. g. hendersoni*.

CAPELLA GALLINAGO DELICATA (Ord): Common Snipe; Agachadiza

Scolopax delicata Ord, reprint of Wilson, Amer. Orn., vol. 9, 1825, p. ccxviii. (Pennsylvania.)

A long-billed, short-legged snipe of medium size, with dark-colored rump.

Description.—Length, 260 to 275 mm. Sexes alike; above mainly black, with a buff line from the bill down the center of the crown, and another on either side over the eye; feathers of hindneck bordered with cinnamon-buff; back with broad lines of dark buff, and a few bars of cinnamon-buff; wings and wing coverts fuscous, barred with buffy white, the outer web of the outer primary edged with white or cinnamon-buff; rump and upper tail coverts barred with cinnamon-buff; outer tail feathers white, or buffy white, barred with black, with the central pairs black, tipped with cinnamon, barred narrowly with black; under surface white, with foreneck and upper breast mottled with buffy brown and fuscous; under wing coverts, sides, and flanks barred with brownish black; under tail coverts buff, barred with black.

Measurements (from Ridgway, l.c., p. 173).—Males, wing 121-130 (127.1), tail 52-63 (57.1), exposed culmen 57.5-67.5 (62.9), tarsus 27.5-32 (30.4) mm.

Females, wing 117.5-135 (125.2), tail 50-58.5 (54.5), exposed culmen 58.5-73.5 (65.4), tarsus 28-33.5 (30.8) mm.

Migrant from the north. Common locally in boggy ground from the lowlands to high mountain slopes: October to April; most abundant in southward migration from late October to early December.

These are birds of wet meadows, partly dry ciénagas, and other marshy ground where they remain concealed until approached and then rise suddenly, utter a harsh call, and dart away in swift zigzag flight. It is seldom that one is seen before it flies. They are most abundant in swampy lands in the savannas, particularly so east of the Río Pacora, where flights of hundreds come sometimes during November. Most are in passage to points farther south so that only a small number remain after December. The northward flight, which is relatively small, comes during March and early April.

The earliest record for fall is that of Jewel (Auk, 1913, p. 425) for October 7, 1911, near Gatun. T. A. Imhof (manuscript notes) recorded one near Chorrera on October 10, 1942, and collectors for the Malaria Control Service shot one near Pacora on October 16, 1953. Griscom (Bull. Mus. Comp. Zool., vol. 72, 1932, p. 322) listed one taken October 25, 1929, at Permé, in the San Blas. Loftin (Carib. Journ. Sci., 1963, p. 65) caught two in a mist net near Almirante, November 10-11, 1962.

I have found them regularly during February and March near El Volcán, and they come also to the mountain slopes around Boquete. I have one female caught at night by the light of a head lamp at La

Jagua on March 16. My latest record for the season is for March 27 at Laguna de Agua, near El Volcán.

Capella Frenzel, 1801, to replace *Gallinago* Koch, 1816, as the valid name for the snipes follows the Check-list of North American Birds in its fourth edition published in 1931 (continued in the fifth edition of 1957), volume 2 of Peters's Check-list of the Birds of the World of 1934, and other important writings that have appeared in recent years. In 1956 the International Commission of Zoological Nomenclature in its Direction 39 ordered that "Gallinago Brisson, 1760" be placed on the accepted list of generic names. Two years later (Ibis, 1958, pp. 125-127) I ventured to point out that *Gallinago* Brisson did not exist as a generic term, since it is merely the name that Brisson gave for the second species in his genus *Scolopax*, viz, *Scolopax Gallinago*. Obviously it has no validity in the generic sense. While Dr. Ernst Mayr recently (Ibis, 1963, pp. 402-403) has argued that *Capella* has no nomenclatural standing, this is not clear in spite of his argument. It seems desirable to use it here in conformity with current New World practice pending further investigation.

CALIDRIS CANUTUS RUFA (Wilson): Knot; Playero Gordo

Tringa rufa Wilson, Amer. Orn., vol. 7, 1813, p. 43, pl. 57, fig. 5. (New Jersey.)

A short-legged, plump-bodied sandpiper, of medium size, with rather heavy bill.

Description.—Length, 220 to 245 mm. Breeding plumage, narrowly streaked on head and hindneck with black and gray; back mottled heavily with black, white, and cinnamon-buff; rump pale gray barred with black; wing coverts brownish gray, with black shaft lines and narrow white edgings; greater coverts tipped with white to produce a wing bar; flight feathers black on outer web and tip, dark brownish gray on inner web, with ivory-white shafts; tail brownish gray tipped very narrowly with white; line over eye, side of head, breast, sides, upper abdomen, and under tail coverts cinnamon-buff; lower abdomen and under wing coverts white; axillars white, barred with brownish gray. Females are like the males, or may be paler cinnamon on the lower surface.

Winter plumage, crown feathers sooty black centrally, edged widely with dull gray to produce a streaked appearance; hindneck, back, and wings brownish gray, with the feathers margined narrowly with dusky and tipped with grayish white to produce a scalloped appearance; rump white barred with black; under surface white, with the lower neck, breast and sides with slightly elongated spots of dark neutral gray.

Iris dark brown; bill black; tarsi and feet dull black to blackish olive.

Measurements (From Ridgway, l.c. pp. 232-233).—Males, wing 152-174 (162.7), tail 60-66 (62.2), exposed culmen 31-36.5 (33.9), tarsus 29.5-33.0 (31) mm.

Females, wing 155-176 (166.3), tail 57-65.5 (62.3), exposed culmen 32-38 (36.3), tarsus 29.5-33 (31.5) mm.

Migrant from the north; casual in occurrence.

The knot is another of the sandpipers that nest in the tundras of the far north. In winter and in migration it is found from the eastern and southern coasts of the United States south to the southern tip of South America.

The only records for Panamá are two immature males in winter plumage, taken by Wedel, at Puerto Obaldía, San Blas, September 12 and 22, 1934, preserved now in the U. S. National Museum.

CROCETHIA ALBA (Pallas): Sanderling; Playerito Arenaro

Trynga (alba) Pallas, *in* Vroeg, Cat. Rais. Ois. Adumbratiunculae, 1764, p. 7. (Holland.)

Palest in color of the small sandpipers; pure white underneath, with a broad white band in the wing that shows in flight.

Description.—Length, 170 to 180 mm. No hind toe. Winter plumage, broad forehead and undersurface, including under wing coverts, pure white; crown and hind neck pale gray, with narrow streaks of dusky; back darker gray with shaft lines of dusky; rump and upper tail coverts white at sides, blackish in the center, bordered narrowly with white; outer tail feathers light brownish gray, central pair dusky, bordered narrowly with white; lesser wing coverts, primaries, and secondaries dull black; middle and greater coverts brownish black, edged and tipped with white; a broad white mark across primaries and secondaries.

Breeding plumage, basally black above, with the feathers edged with bright cinnamon-buff and grayish white; side of head, throat, neck, and upper breast light cinnamon-buff, dotted with black. This is the plumage from May to August that, in the main, disappears by the end of September. The majority of migrants found in Panamá are in winter dress.

Measurements (from Ridgway, l.c., pp. 308-309).—Males, wing 113-124.5 (119.1), tail 45-55 (50.3), exposed culmen 23-26 (24.7), tarsus 23-25 (23.7) mm.

Females, wing 117-127 (123), tail 47.5-54.5 (52.8), exposed culmen 24-28 (26), tarsus 23-26 (24.7) mm.

Migrant from the north. Fairly common; recorded from August to March.

This species, not included in Griscom's list of 1935, was first recorded by Arbib and Loetscher (Auk, 1935, p. 326) from one seen near Gatun, Canal Zone, on August 7, 1933, and another on August 8, 1934. Imhof (Auk, 1950, p. 256) observed single birds at Fort Amador on September 16 and at Palo Seco on November 8, in the Canal Zone, and a flock of 5 at the mouth of the Río Chico, Panamá, November 17 and 18, all in 1942. In my own work I collected a male from 4 seen at Monagre, on the coast of Los Santos, on March 16, 1948, and saw several at La Honda in the same province on March 20. On February 12, 1961, I recorded four on Venado Beach, Canal Zone. They are found rather regularly in August and September from the Canal Zone west to Los Santos.

In 1956, I saw several on Isla Coiba between January 20 and February 3 and collected two on the latter date. In the Pearl Islands in 1960 I shot one January 17 on Isla Contadora, and saw half a dozen on January 27 at the mouth of the Río Cacique on Isla del Rey. My only record for the Caribbean side is of two seen on February 6, 1957, on a sandy beach at the mouth of the Río Mandinga, San Blas. Eisenmann has informed me of one at Fort San Lorenzo, C.Z., May 13, 1962.

Sanderlings are birds of the beaches, where their common habit is to follow the receding waves to probe in the shifting surface sand for small crustacea, and then to patter quickly back as the water returns. They nest in the tundras around the entire polar area and in migration move south along the seas of the world. In the Americas their flights take them to southern Chile and southern Argentina.

EREUNETES PUSILLUS (Linnaeus): Semipalmated Sandpiper; Playerito Gracioso

Tringa pusilla Linnaeus, Syst. Nat., ed. 12, vol. 1, 1766, p. 252. (Hispaniola, West Indies.)

One of the 3 smallest sandpipers that come to Panamá. This species and the western sandpiper have heavier bills and black legs; the bird of the present account differs from its near relative in shorter bill.

Description.—Length, 140 to 155 mm. Anterior toes with webs. Breeding dress, above brownish gray, with slight edgings of pale cinnamon-buff on crown and back; crown streaked, and back spotted heavily, with black; rump, central upper tail coverts, and central tail feathers blackish; outer rectrices brownish gray, edged narrowly with white; lesser and middle wing coverts brownish gray, with slightly paler borders; greater coverts, primaries, and secondaries dusky, the coverts edged with white; line over eye white, lightly streaked with dusky; loral space and center of forehead to base of bill dusky brown; auricular region streaked with grayish brown; sides of forehead and under surface white, with the breast and anterior half of the sides streaked with dusky.

Winter plumage, above grayish brown streaked, more or less narrowly, with dusky; superciliary, sides of forehead, and undersurface white, with the upper breast streaked lightly with dusky.

Iris brown; bill, tarsus, and toes black.

Measurements (from Ridgway, l.c., p. 211).—Males, wing 88-98.5 (93.9), tail 38-44.5 (41.2), exposed culmen 17-20 (18.6), tarsus 19-21 (20.5) mm.

Females, wing 92-101.5 (96.5), tail 40-44 (41.5), exposed culmen 18-22 (20.3), tarsus 20-22 (20.8) mm.

Migrant from the north. Abundance not certain from the few specimen records at present available; probably of regular occurrence with the great flocks of *Ereunetes mauri*. Some may remain during the period of northern summer.

The most definite character for separation of this species from the western sandpiper is in the length of the bill, this being longer in the latter. Since there is overlap in size between the female of the semipalmated sandpiper and the male of the western, this criterion may be used with certainty only with birds of known sex, which implies a specimen in the hand. In field observations occasionally a bird with a very short bill—shorter than the head—may be accepted as a male of the present species, but such records need to be considered with caution.

A specimen of the present species, collected by McLeannan, in the British Museum that came from the Tweedale collection has a bill length of 18.2 mm. There is no locality data other than Panamá, but it is probable that it is from the Caribbean slope. Bovallius secured a female at Panamá Viejo, February 26, 1882 (Rendahl, Ark. Zool. vol. 12, no. 8, 1919, p. 11). Jewel collected a female (culmen 18.5 mm.) at Toro Point, Canal Zone, on September 4, 1911 (reported by Stone, Proc. Acad. Nat. Sci., Philadelphia, vol. 70, 1918, p. 245). Benson collected one at Aguadulce, Coclé, September 8, 1925 (specimen in American Museum of Natural History). I have identified one taken at Almirante, Bocas de Toro, Oct. 29, 1964. Other reports are sight records, which as explained above may be subject to question.

It is probable that the semipalmated sandpiper is regular in occurrence along the Caribbean coast, and that it comes also along the Pacific in company with the migrant flocks of the western sandpiper.

Loftin (Carib. Journ. Sci., 1963, p. 65) found them abundant at Panamá Viejo from August 12 to October 13, 1962, when he captured and banded 43.

EREUNETES MAURI Cabanis: Western Sandpiper; Playerito Occidental

Ereunetes Mauri Cabanis, Journ. für Orn., vol. 4, 1856 (1857), p. 419. (South Carolina.)

Similar to the semipalmated sandpiper, but with longer bill.

Description.—Length, 140 to 155 mm. Toes webbed; bill thick at base, with tip very slightly decurved. Breeding dress, like the semipalmated sandpiper in general but separated by the much greater extent of the rufous brown markings on the dorsal surface; lower surface more heavily marked, with dark spots and streaks much heavier, and covering more of the lower foreneck, sides, and upper breast.

Winter plumage, similar to that of the semipalmated sandpiper.

Iris brown; bill, tarsus, and toes black.

Measurements (from Ridgway, l.c., p. 216).—Males, wing 91-99 (94.6), tail 37.5-42 (40.2), exposed culmen 20.5-23.5 (22.5), tarsus 20.5-22 (21.2) mm.

Females, wing 90-99.5 (96.4), tail 38-47 (41.7), exposed culmen 23-28 (25.9), tarsus 21-24 (22.1) mm.

Migrant from the north. Abundant locally along the Pacific coast; recorded less commonly from the Caribbean side; Isla Coiba; Isla del Rey. Present, in the main, from August to April; considerable numbers of non-breeding individuals remain through the other months of northern summer.

Small groups of western sandpipers may be found on beaches and mudflats anywhere, while flocks of thousands often congregate at such favorable localities as the mouth of the Río Santa María, at Panamá Viejo, and the mouth of the Río Chico. I have specimens from Alvina near the Río Santa María opposite Parita, Herrera, from El Real, Darién, and from Isla Coiba. There is one in the U. S. National Museum secured at Farfan Beach, Canal Zone, July 21, 1931, and others in the American Museum of Natural History taken at Cocoplum, Bocas del Toro, October 27 and 30, 1927, all collected by Rex Benson. One in the Gorgas Memorial Laboratory was taken at Almirante on October 10, 1964.

EROLIA MINUTILLA (Vieillot): Least Sandpiper; Playerito Menudo

Tringa minutilla Vieillot, Nouv. Dict. Hist. Nat., nouv. éd., vol. 34, Dec. 1819, p. 466. (Halifax, Nova Scotia.)

Differs from the other two species of very small sandpipers by more slender bill and yellowish legs; also is somewhat browner on the back.

Description.—Length, 130 to 145 mm. Bill definitely slender toward the tip; no webs between the toes. Breeding dress, crown with feather centers black, margined narrowly with buffy brown, the brown more cinnamon on the back of the head; an indistinct light line over the eye; hindneck dark gray, lined with buffy brown; upper back and scapulars black, margined and barred irregularly with buff and pale cinnamon; lower back, rump, and central tail feathers black; outer tail feathers light gray, edged narrowly with white; wing coverts dark grayish brown, with the greater coverts tipped narrowly with white; primaries and basal half of secondaries fuscous, with the shafts white; outer ends of secondaries grayish brown tipped with white; foreneck and breast grayish white, narrowly streaked and spotted with dusky; rest of undersurface white.

Winter plumage, above dark grayish brown, with the feathers darker, blacker centrally; less heavily marked on the breast and foreneck; otherwise as in breeding dress. Darker gray above, with the breast more heavily marked than in the semipalmated and western sandpipers.

Iris brown; bill black; legs greenish to yellowish brown.

Measurements (from Ridgway, l.c., p. 295).—Males, wing 82-88 (85.5), tail 35-40 (38.2), exposed culmen 16-19 (17.2), tarsus 16.5-19 (17.7) mm.

Females, wing 83-91 (86.5), tail 35-41 (37.1), exposed culmen 17.5-20 (18.7), tarsus 16-19 (18.1) mm.

Migrant from the north. Common along both coasts; occasional inland in the lowlands, August to April; Isla Coiba; Isla San José; Isla Bayoneta; Isla del Rey.

Least sandpipers begin to arrive from the north during August, with the main flight in September. The northward movement is under way in March and continues into April. My latest record is

April 11 at Jaqué, Darién. It is probable that some remain to near the end of the month.

These birds are found in little flocks, or alone, both on sand beaches and on rock flats and headlands. Also they come inland on the tidal reaches of the rivers, and along the larger channels in the lowlands, where open, muddy shores or gravel bars afford feeding grounds.

EROLIA FUSCICOLLIS (Vieillot): White-rumped Sandpiper; Playerito de Rabadilla Blanca

Tringa fuscicollis Vieillot, Nouv. Dict. Hist. Nat., nouv. éd., vol. 34, Dec., 1819, p. 461. (Paraguay.)

Similar to Baird's sandpiper, but with middle upper tail coverts white.

Description.—Length, 160 to 175 mm. Bill heavier, tip somewhat broadened, with the surface distinctly pitted. Breeding dress, above brownish gray, with the feathers black centrally, those of crown and back edged with buff to cinnamon, and those of hindneck bordered by buff; wing coverts brownish gray, with shaft lines of dusky; greater coverts tipped narrowly with white; outer primaries dusky; secondaries and inner primaries paler edged with white; rump dusky brown, with feathers margined with dull buff; central pair of upper tail coverts dusky black, tipped with white; lateral upper tail coverts white with concealed darker markings; rectrices with central pair black, others dusky brown or gray edged with white; under surface white, with foreneck heavily streaked and spotted, and sides barred, with dusky.

Winter plumage, crown, hindneck, scapulars, and upper back brownish gray, with concealed mottling of black and buff; markings on under surface less in extent and grayer brown.

It is common to find specimens in which details of the markings on the upper tail coverts are not sufficient for identification. The form of the bill described above and under the account of Baird's sandpiper, will serve invariably to separate these two species.

Iris brown; maxilla, except area below nostril, and tip of mandible dull black; maxilla below nostril, and base of mandible brown.

Measurements (from Ridgway, l.c., p. 285).—Males, wing 117-122.5 (119.7), tail 50-53 (51.4), exposed culmen 21-24 (22.7), tarsus 22-24 (23.1) mm.

Females, wing 116.5-124 (120.6), tail 50-54 (51), exposed culmen 21-26 (23.1), tarsus 22-24 (22.8) mm.

Passage migrant from the north. Rare; status uncertain.

The only definite record is that of a specimen in the British Museum (Natural History), received in the Salvin and Godman collection, collected by James McLeannan, and labeled Lion Hill (see Sharpe, Cat. Birds Brit. Mus., vol. 24, 1896, p. 391). Eisenmann (Wilson Bull., 1951, p. 183) quotes Thomas Imhof for a report of 3 seen on June 15, 1942. Loftin (Carib. Journ. Sci. 1963, p. 66) recorded one September 23 and two October 13, 1962 at Panamá Viejo.

The white-rumped sandpiper nests in the tundra regions of the north from northern Alaska to Baffin Island, and winters in southern South America from Paraguay and Brazil to Tierra del Fuego. The Isthmus of Panamá seems to lie to the west of its usual line of migratory flight.

Many individuals may be told from Baird's sandpipers with difficulty, so that sight records, unless supported by specimens, may be open to question.

EROLIA BAIRDII (Coues): Baird's Sandpiper; Playerito Unicolor

Actodromas Bairdii Coues, Proc. Acad. Nat. Sci. Philadelphia, vol. 13, June-Aug. (Dec. 28) 1861, p. 194. (Fort Resolution, Great Slave Lake, MacKenzie District, Northwest Territories.)

Similar to the white-rumped sandpiper, but with all the central upper tail coverts black, so that this area appears dark in flight.

Description.—Length, 170 to 185 mm. Bill more slender than in *E. fuscicollis,* tip not broadened, with surface smooth. Breeding dress, crown, back, and scapulars with the feathers extensively black centrally, bordered by pale buff, buffy white, and, to a lesser degree, cinnamon-buff; wing coverts light grayish brown, edged with grayish white; lesser coverts tipped narrowly with white; primaries dusky; secondaries brownish gray, edged with white; rump and central upper tail coverts dusky; outer ones white, marked with grayish brown near tip; central rectrices dusky; lateral pairs dark gray, margined narrowly with white; foreneck and upper breast grayish white, streaked and spotted heavily with dusky.

Winter dress, dorsal surface, in general, like the summer plumage, but back, rump, scapulars, and lesser and middle wing coverts tipped prominently with white to buffy white; greater coverts edged with buff and tipped rather widely with white to form a distinct band; crown and hindneck edged with buff; upper breast feathers with dusky central mottling, washed with light buff; rest of under surface white.

Iris brown; bill, tarsus, and toes black.

Measurements (from Ridgway, l.c., p. 281).—Males, wing 114-122 (118.7), tail 48-53 (51.1), exposed culmen 20.5-23 (21.7), tarsus 20-23 (21.1) mm.

Females, wing 119-126 (122.3), tail 49-54 (51.7), exposed culmen 21.5-24 (22.8), tarsus 20-23 (21.4) mm.

Passage migrant from the north. Status uncertain; reported definitely only during southward flight.

Baird's sandpiper is another species that nests in the far northern tundras, from northeastern Siberia to Greenland, and winters in South America. Griscom (Bull. Mus. Comp. Zool., vol. 78, 1935, p. 307) included the species with the statement "Canal Zone on migration (once)." Hellmayr and Conover (Cat. Birds Amer., pt. 1, no. 3, 1948, p. 190) say "a few records from Panama," with no details of occurrence. The only other definite report is of sight records by Imhof (Auk, 1950, p. 256), who recorded these birds regularly from September 19 to October 28, 1942, at rain pools on the grass grown parade grounds at Fort Amador (Pacific side) and Fort Davis (Caribbean side), in the Canal Zone. I have seen no specimens from Panamá.

EROLIA MELANOTOS (Vieillot): Pectoral Sandpiper; Playerito Pectoral

Tringa melanotos Vieillot, Nouv. Dict. Hist. Nat., nouv. éd., vol. 34, Dec. 1819, p. 462. (Paraguay.)

Of medium size, with foreneck and breast gray, washed with buff, and streaked heavily with dusky in a solid pattern, in sharp contrast with the white throat, lower breast, and abdomen.

Description.—Length, 220 to 235 mm. Breeding dress, feathers of upper surface heavily black centrally, with those on crown and upper back, edged with buff and cinnamon-buff, and on hindneck and sides of neck, bordered widely with buff; tertials edged broadly with buff and cinnamon-buff; wing coverts dusky bordered with buff and cinnamon-buff; lower back, rump, and upper tail coverts plain black; outer primaries black; inner primaries and secondaries dark gray, the latter bordered with white; central tail feathers black; outer pairs brownish gray, edged lightly with white; upper foreneck to upper breast grayish buff, lined narrowly with dull black, the whole sharply cut off from the white of the throat, lower breast, and abdomen; under tail coverts white, with shaft lines of dusky.

Winter plumage, similar, but with the cinnamon markings on the upper surface reduced or absent, and foreneck and upper breast grayish white.

Iris brown; base of bill dull greenish yellow, tip black; legs greenish yellow.

Measurements (from Ridgway, l.c., pp. 270-271).—Males, wing 137-146 (139.8), tail 59-65 (62.4), exposed culmen 26-29.5 (28.4), tarsus 27-30 (27.7) mm.

Females, wing 119.5-130 (125.8); tail 51-60 (55.3); exposed culmen 24-29 (25.8), tarsus 24-26.5 (25.8) mm.

Passage migrant from the north. Fairly common in southward flight in fall, mainly in October, seen less often in September; rare in spring.

There are sight records near Gatun on August 30 and September 1, 1934 (Arbib and Loetscher, Auk, 1935, p. 326), and at Fort Amador on September 16, 1942 (Imhof, MSS field notes). Hasso von Wedel secured specimens at Puerto Obaldía, San Blas, on September 25 and October 2 and 15, 1931, November 15, 1932, September 16 and 17, 1933, and September 21, 1934 (data from skins in the Herbert Brandt collection at the University of Cincinnati). There is a skin in the U. S. National Museum, forwarded by the Malaria Control Service, that was taken on the Pacific side of the Cerro Azul, Province of Panamá, on October 11, 1955. There are numerous other records for October. The only reports during the northward flight are of one seen by C. O. Handley, Jr., May 30, 1959, on the old airstrip at Mandinga, San Blas, and others noted by Eugene Eisenmann, April 28, at Puerto Pilón, Colón, and on May 11 at Coco Solo, Canal Zone, both in 1961.

In migration these sandpipers usually are found in fresh-water marshes or wet meadows and also come to pools of water left by rains on such open areas as parade grounds or golf links. Most of the reports to date have come from the Canal Zone. Hellmayr and Conover (Cat. Birds Amer., pt. 1, no. 3, 1948, p. 194) have recorded one from Francés, in Chiriquí, but this seems to be in error, as Emmet Blake informs me that there is no specimen from that place in the Chicago Natural History Museum.

EROLIA ALPINA PACIFICA (Coues): Dunlin; Correlimos Común

Pelidna Pacifica Coues, Proc. Acad. Nat. Sci. Philadelphia, vol. 11, 1861, p. 189. (Simiahmoo, Washington.)

The dunlin is a short-legged bird, slightly larger and heavier in body than the spotted sandpiper, with a bill decidedly longer than the head, rather heavy, and slightly, but noticeably, curved downward near the tip.

Description.—Length, 200-220 mm. In winter dress gray above, with a grayish wash on the breast.

In the brighter breeding plumage the lower breast and abdomen are black.

Measurements (from Ridgway, l.c., pp. 262-263).—Males, wing 108.5-125.5 (115.9), tail 42-57 (52), culmen 31-41 (35.6), tarsus 23-28 (25.2) mm.

Females, wing 114-125 (117.4), tail 44.5-56 (53), culmen 34-42 (38.3), tarsus 25-27 (26) mm.

Migrant from the north. Rare; status uncertain.

In the New World the dunlin nests in Alaska, northern Canada, and Greenland and winters regularly along the coasts from southeastern Alaska to Sonora and from Massachusetts to Florida and Texas. There is one record for Momotombo, western Nicaragua (Sharpe, Cat. Birds Brit. Mus., vol. 24, 1896, p. 611). I have seen sandpipers on three occasions that I identified as this species, one December 3 and another December 28, 1955, at Panamá Viejo, and five at the mouth of the Río Chico, March 5, 1956. Since Panamá is so far beyond the recorded range I include these as not wholly definite, pending the capture of specimens.

MICROPALAMA HIMANTOPUS (Bonaparte): Stilt Sandpiper; Chorlito Patilargo

Tringa himantopus Bonaparte, Ann. Lyc. Nat. Hist. New York, vol. 2, 1826, p. 157. (Long Branch, New Jersey.)

Slender, larger than the spotted sandpiper, with very long yellowish-green legs and slender, straight bill that is decidedly longer than the head.

Description.—Length, 195 to 210 mm. Breeding dress, crown dusky black, edged with grayish white and buffy white; hindneck streaked with dusky and grayish white; a light superciliary somewhat streaked with dusky; back and scapulars mixed black and gray, with scattered edgings of buff; rump and upper tail coverts white barred with black; primaries black; wing coverts and secondaries dark gray, the latter tipped with white; tail gray, with white base and white tips on outer pairs; underneath white, with throat plain, foreneck and upper breast streaked, and lower breast, abdomen, and under tail coverts evenly barred with dusky; side of the head behind the eye cinnamon-rufous.

Winter dress, upper surface plain brownish gray; superciliary stripe white; under parts white, with the lower foreneck, sides of neck, upper breast, and under tail coverts narrowly and rather indefinitely streaked with gray.

Iris brown; bill black, somewhat brownish basally; legs dull yellowish green.

Measurements (from Ridgway, l.c., p. 206).—Males, wing 116-135 (124.4), tail 45-53 (51.1), exposed culmen 35.5-41 (38.5), tarsus 36-43 (39.9) mm.

Females, wing 120-137 (127), tail 44-58 (51.5), exposed culmen 36-44 (39.9), tarsus 39.5-45 (42.9) mm.

Passage migrant from the north. Rare.

This interesting sandpiper breeds in tundra areas from northern Alaska and far northern Ontario south to the northern edge of the forests, and spends the northern winter season in southern South America.

The stilt sandpiper was first recorded in Panamá from 2 seen by Arbib and Loetscher, August 22 and 26, 1934 (Auk, 1935, p. 326). Eisenmann noted 3 on the Gatun Dam spillway August 28, 1958. The only other reports are of one that I observed on the mud flats at the mouth of the Río Chico, March 5, 1956, and one that I collected from 4 seen at La Jagua, Panamá, March 24, 1964.

The species is one that may be expected to occur rarely in its migrations. It is recorded in Guatemala and Nicaragua to the north, and in Colombia and Ecuador to the south.

Stilt sandpipers frequent tidal flats and other muddy shores, sometimes coming to open pools. It is common for them to wade in water so deep that it nearly reaches the body, and to feed with head and neck immersed.

TRYNGITES SUBRUFICOLLIS (Vieillot): Buff-breasted Sandpiper; Chorlito Canelo

Tringa subruficollis Vieillot, Nouv. Dict. Hist. Nat., nouv. éd., vol. 34, Dec. 1819, p. 465. (Paraguay.)

Rather small, with short bill; yellowish legs; buffy underneath from bill to tail.

Description.—Length, 190 to 205 mm. Adults, upper surface in general grayish buff, the feathers with black centers; edge of wing white, narrowly barred with black; greater wing coverts grayish brown, tipped with buff; primary coverts darker, with a subterminal spot of black, and a narrow tip of white; primaries grayish brown, black at end, tipped with white; secondaries with outer webs grayish brown at base, dusky at tip, inner webs white, with the tips mottled with black and buff; rump and upper tail coverts black, tipped with cinnamon-buff; middle rectrices dusky, tipped with buff, the outer pairs grayish brown, black toward the end, tipped and edged with deep buff, that becomes narrowly white distally; underneath mainly light pinkish cinnamon, edged with white to buffy white; throat, abdomen, and under tail coverts pale buff; axillars and main under wing coverts white; under primary coverts grayish buff, tipped with white, with irregular lines and subterminal spots of black; inner web of remiges with irregular spots of black toward the tips.

Iris brown; base of maxilla deep olive gray; rest of bill black; tarsus brownish orange (yellow ocher to olive-ocher), shading to grayish buff on the upper part (the crus); toes olive-buff to honey yellow; nails black.

Measurements (from Ridgway, l.c., p. 227).—Males, wing 129-136 (132.1), tail 58-63 (60.6), exposed culmen 19.5-20.5 (19.9), tarsus 30-37 (32.1) mm.

Females, wing 122-132 (127.2), tail 54-62 (57), exposed culmen 17.5-19.5 (18.4), tarsus 29-31 (29.5) mm.

Passage migrant from the north. Rare.

The only specimen record is that of Jewel (Auk, 1913, p. 426), who collected one in a dry pasture near Gatun on October 18, 1911. He saw another at the same place on March 29, 1912. Dr. Eisenmann has recorded this species at Coco Solo, and at Balboa, Canal Zone, on September 28, 1958.

The buff-breasted sandpiper is another that nests in the tundras of the far north, from northern Alaska to northern MacKenzie, and migrates south to Argentina for the period of northern winter.

On their wintering grounds in the far south I have found single birds with other sandpipers, but remaining somewhat apart, on muddy shores. More often they were in small flocks that ranged over alkaline barrens amid scattered herbaceous growth. They are active and quick in their movements, and are constantly in motion. Their distinct buffy color distinguishes them from the other small sandpipers, as does the slender neck, small head, and short bill, a profile that suggests that of a pigeon.

Family RECURVIROSTRIDAE: Avocets and Stilts; Avocetas y Cigüeñuelas

The few living species of this family of shorebirds are widespread through temperate and tropical regions of the world. All are of moderate size, and all stand on tall legs, those of the stilt, the only species of the group in Central and South America, being especially long and slender. Both avocets and stilts range in marshlands and along muddy shores, usually in companies that remain together during the nesting season. Their food is obtained from water and mud, that of the stilt by probing. Avocets often walk through shallows with the bill sweeping like a scythe back and forth over the surface of the mud.

HIMANTOPUS MEXICANUS (Müller): Black-necked Stilt; Viuda

FIGURE 68

Charadrius Mexicanus, P.L.S. Müller, Natursyst. Suppl., 1776, p. 117. (México.)

Legs very long and slender; black above, white underneath.

Description.—Length, 345 to 365 mm. Adult male, crown, sides of head, hindneck, upper back, and wings black, with a slight sheen of greenish blue; forehead, spot behind eye, central portion of both eyelids, central and lower back, rump, upper tail coverts and entire undersurface pure white; tail pale gray; under wing coverts dull black, with a few white markings on the edge of the wing.

Female, similar but lower hindneck, upper back, and scapulars brownish black.

Immature, black of crown duller; hindneck and upper back grayish brown to brownish black.

Iris red; bill black; legs and feet pinkish red; claws black.

Resident. Found locally along channels in the mangroves, on tidal mudflats, and around lowland pools. Part of those present in the dry season may be migrants from elsewhere.

The first report of the species is that of Lawrence (Ann. Lyc. Nat. Hist. New York, vol. 8, 1863, p. 12) who listed it as received from McLeannan without comment. Jewel (Auk, 1913, p. 425) secured one at the Gatun Dam on November 11, 1911, a bird that had been present there for a week. Griscom (Bull. Mus. Comp. Zool., vol. 69, 1929, p. 155) recorded a female taken by Benson at El Real, Darién, in 1928, and another (l.c., vol. 72, 1932, p. 322), a male, collected by Wedel, at Permé, San Blas. These are the only published records of specimens that I have seen.

In my own field studies I found an adult and a full grown immature bird on April 4, 1948, at the mouth of the Río Chico, Panamá, and in the following year on March 16, I shot a bird there that still had part of the juvenile plumage on the back of the neck. Others were seen there on March 24. On March 5, 1956, I found between 50 and 60 at this point, the largest assemblage that I have recorded in

Panamá. Some of those seen have been encountered along a channel that is bordered by mangroves, but most have been out on the open flats. T. A. Imhof in his notes recorded them here on November 17, 1942. I was told that in the rainy season they spread back around pools in the savannas. My only record here away from the coast is of two at a fresh-water pond on the eastern side of the Río La Jagua

FIG. 68.—Black-necked stilt, viuda, *Himantopus mexicanus*.

on March 21, 1958. The birds are well known, and it is my supposition, from those in partial immature dress that I have seen, that they nest here.

My only record in other areas is of one flushed on March 23, 1960, from a roadside pool west of Puerto Vidal, Veraguas, a short distance from the Río Tabasará.

Family PHALAROPODIDAE: Phalaropes; Falaropos

The phalaropes in general form resemble their cousin plovers and sandpipers but differ in the possession of lobes that broaden the toes and a feather covering that is dense and strongly water repellant, like the plumage of gulls. Both are developments for a truly aquatic life as phalaropes are adept swimmers.

The tarsus in all is strongly compressed from side to side. Males are smaller and duller in color than females. The three species nest in the north and in winter move into the Southern Hemisphere, where two range in flocks at sea, and the third is found along shores and inland in southern South America.

KEY TO THE SPECIES OF PHALAROPODIDAE

1. Bill shorter, about as long as head, broad, slightly expanded toward the tip; base of bill with nostrils definitely separated from the frontal feathering.
   Red phalarope, *Phalaropus fulicarius,* p. 430
   Bill longer than head, slender and attenuate, with the nostrils close to the frontal feathers... 2
2. Smaller, with much smaller legs; tarsus less than 24 mm.; bill more slender, especially at the tip, and shorter, not more than 25 mm.
   Northern phalarope, *Lobipes lobatus,* p. 432
   Larger, with longer, heavier legs; tarsus more than 28 mm.; bill heavier, particularly toward tip, and longer, not less than 28 mm.
   Wilson's phalarope, *Steganopus tricolor,* p. 431

PHALAROPUS FULICARIUS (Linnaeus): Red Phalarope; Pollito de Mar Rojizo

Tringa Fulicaria Linnaeus, Syst. Nat., ed. 10, vol. 1, 1758, p. 148. (Northeastern Manitoba.)

A small, swimming shorebird, with heavy bill that is slightly expanded toward the tip.

Description.—Length, 200 to 210 mm. Nostril separated from the anterior margin of the feathers on the forehead by a definite space of 2 mm. or more; tarsus short, about equal to middle toe. Summer plumage (male definitely duller than female), crown, hindneck, and loral area slaty black; throat somewhat gray; upper back dull black; scapulars and upper tail coverts black, edged broadly with buff; wing coverts dark gray edged lightly with white; primary coverts and inner secondaries with broad white tips and edgings; primaries, rest of secondaries, and tail slaty black; under wing coverts and sides white; entire under surface vinaceous-brown.

Winter plumage (sexes alike), head, neck, and entire under surface white; occiput and region around eye slate; upper surface light gray. In changing plumage the white of the under surface often is mixed with brown.

Measurements (from Ridgway, l.c., p. 419).—Males, wing 119-130 (125.2), tail 59-70.5 (62.9), culmen 18.5-23 (21.9), tarsus 19.5-21.5 (20.7), middle toe 19.5-21.5 (20.5) mm.

Females, wing 129.5-139 (135.1), tail 63-71 (66.4), culmen 21.0-24 (22.5), tarsus 20-22.5 (22.0), middle toe 19-21.5 (20.4) mm.

Migrant from the north. Occurrence uncertain.

Red phalaropes nest in the far north and winter at sea, chiefly in the Southern Hemisphere, where they are common off both coasts of South America. Their main migrations, which include many thousands of individuals, are also offshore. They may be expected at sea on the Pacific side, perhaps casually in the outer Gulf of Panamá. The only record to indicate this at present is one by Robert Cushman Murphy who informs me (in litt.) that he saw two about 5 p.m. on November 19, 1956, when the ship's position at noon had been at lat. 8°55′ N., long. 88°50′ W., a point far to the west of the Gulf of Panamá.

In Spain this species is called *falaropo picogrueso*.

STEGANOPUS TRICOLOR Vieillot: Wilson's Phalarope; Pollito de Mar Tricolor

Steganopus tricolor Vieillot, Nouv. Dict. Hist. Nat., nouv. éd., vol. 32, Sept. 1819, p. 136. (Paraguay.)

Largest of the phalaropes; rump white, wing nearly plain.

Description.—Length, 215 to 230 mm. Tarsus decidedly longer than middle toe. Breeding dress (male duller than female), crown and upper back gray; hindneck white; wing coverts and lower back brownish gray; upper tail coverts and side of rump white; primaries and secondaries fuscous brown; tail brownish gray; sides of head black; sides of neck, of upper back, and much of scapulars rufous; foreneck and upper breast pale cinnamon; rest of under surface white.

Winter dress, crown and sides of neck light gray; hindneck and back brownish gray; underneath white.

Immature birds have the wing coverts slate gray margined with pale buff and white.

Measurements (from Ridgway, l.c., pp. 431-432).—Males, wing 116-125 (121.1), tail 48-54 (51.2), culmen 28-31 (30.5), tarsus 28.5-33 (30.1), middle toe 22-25 (24) mm.

Females, wing 130-137.5 (132.6), tail 52.5-65 (55.9), culmen 31-36 (33), tarsus 30.5-33 (31.7), middle toe 24.5-26.5 (25.3) mm.

Migrant from the north. Several sight records indicate casual occurrence.

The Wilson's phalarope, in addition to following the sea, comes to fresh and brackish waters regularly during its migrations between its summer home in fresh-water marshes of the western United States and Canada, and its wintering grounds, which are mainly in southern South America.

Eugene Eisenmann informs me that he observed this species at Puerto Pilón, Colón, and at the Gatun spillway in the Canal Zone, on August 28, 1958. It was found also at Coco Solo, Canal Zone, September 28, 1958. Arbib and Loetscher (Auk, 1935, p. 326) reported one seen at Gatun several times from August 22 to 26, 1934.

LOBIPES LOBATUS (Linnaeus): Northern Phalarope; Pollito de Mar Boreal

Tringa lobata Linnaeus, Syst. Nat., ed. 10, vol. 1, 1758, pp. 148, 824. (Northeastern Manitoba.)

Smallest of the phalaropes, with slender, pointed bill.

Description.—Length, 170 to 190 mm. Posterior border of nostril nearly in contact with frontal feathering; tarsus short, about equal to middle toe; lateral membrane of toes broad and prominent. Breeding dress (males decidedly duller than females), head, hindneck, and upper back dark gray; rest of upper surface blackish slate, lined with buff; middle wing coverts tipped lightly with white; primary coverts and inner secondaries broadly margined with white; wings dull black; tail dull brown, the central rectrices blackish; neck, including sides, cinnamon; upper breast, including adjacent sides dark gray, with a slight mixture of this color on the cinnamon foreneck; throat and rest of under surface white, with sides indistinctly lined with light gray.

Winter plumage, occiput and side of head from eye back over ear coverts slate gray; back mainly gray, edged more or less with white; head, except as indicated, and entire lower surface white. In September and October some of the buff markings of the summer dress may be present.

Measurements (from Ridgway, l.c., pp. 424-425).—Males, wing 102-109 (105.1), tail 46-50 (48.3), culmen 21-23 (22), tarsus 18-20 (19.2), middle toe 18-20.5 (19.5) mm.

Females, wing 105-116 (110.2), tail 48.5-52.5 (50.2), culmen 20-24 (22.4), tarsus 18.5-21 (19.8), middle toe 18-20 (19.1) mm.

Migrant from the north. One record in the Gulf of Panamá.

The northern phalarope nests in the far north in both New and

Old Worlds and spends the winter season at sea, ranging far south in southern oceans.

Eugene Eisenmann informs me that on May 1, 1961, while on a trip in the lower Bay of Panamá he observed two flocks of at least 300 birds in the area between Isla Chame and Isla Otoque. As the launch cruised among them for some time he noted that most were in breeding dress.

In Spain this bird is known as *falaropo picofino*.

Family STERCORARIIDAE: Skuas and Jaegers; Gaviotas Salteadoras

These are the predatory robber gulls that on their nesting grounds kill and eat smaller avian companions, as well as small mammals. When at sea, off their nesting grounds, they are scavengers on dead fish and other animals and also harass gulls and other birds to force them to drop or regurgitate food that they have taken. As this falls the robber may seize it expertly in the air. The smaller jaegers nest in the north, while the skuas that reach Panamá breed in the Antarctic. They are seen most often in the Gulf of Panamá.

Members of this family differ from gulls and terns in the possession of a horny cere on the base of the bill.

KEY TO THE SPECIES OF STERCORARIIDAE

1. Larger, wing 380 mm. or more; bill strong and heavy, more than 45 mm. long.
   Skua, *Catharacta skua*, p. 433
   Smaller, wing not more than 370 mm.; bill smaller, more slender, less than 40 mm. long.. 2
2. Wing 350 mm. or more; depth of bill at base slightly more than width; adult with elongated central tail feathers twisted toward tip.
   Pomarine jaeger, *Stercorarius pomarinus*, p. 435
   Wing less than 345 mm.; depth of bill at base about equal to width; adult with elongated central tail feathers flat and straight................ 3
3. Horny cere (supranasal saddle) decidedly longer than distal section of bill (dertrum); adult with middle rectrices less than 235 mm.
   Parasitic jaeger, *Stercorarius parasiticus*, p. 436
   Horny cere not longer than dertrum; adult with central rectrices more than 240 mm. long........Long-tailed jaeger, *Stercorarius longicaudus*, p. 437

CATHARACTA SKUA Brünnich: Skua; Salteador Grande

FIGURE 69

Catharacta skua Brünnich, Orn. Borealis, 1764, p. 33. (Iceland.)

Gull-like in form, of large size, with a prominent white area in each wing.

Description.—Length, 520 to 560 mm. Above dark grayish brown, streaked, particularly on head and neck, with pale cinnamon; under surface mainly cinnamon to cinnamon-rufous.

FIG. 69.—Skua, salteador grande, *Catharacta skua*.

Measurements (from Murphy, Oceanic Birds S. Amer., vol. 2, 1936, p. 1011).—Wing 370-412 (380.4), tail 131-158.4 (144.8), culmen 48.9-56.1 (52), tarsus 60.6-71.5 (67.5) mm.

Migrant from the far south. Recorded in the western area of the Gulf of Panamá.

My first observation of skuas was on February 7, 1944, in crossing to Isla San José when I saw two in the Bay of Panamá about 5 to 6 kilometers outside Balboa Harbor, and another in the gulf 25 kilometers or so off the island. One turned to pursue a laughing gull, buffeted it about without making it disgorge, and then flew on its way. On February 6, 1956, on the return journey from Isla Coiba, I saw between 15 and 20 at sea offshore between Punta Mala and a point to the northward where Otoque and Boná were barely in sight. All were flying low among the terns and other sea birds. On March 17, 1962, a few kilometers north of Isla Iguana, a skua appeared and finally swung in toward the launch on which I was traveling. I shot it at long range, but it continued so far before falling that we were not able to find it, since the waves were fairly high. On February 9, 1963, I saw another that came along side the MV *Pelican* between Isla Iguana and Isla Boná.

It is probable that these were the race *Catharacta skua chilensis* (Bonaparte), described in Conspectus Generum Avium, vol. 2, Feb. 1, 1856 (Oct. 1, 1857), p. 207, with the type locality Chile, which nests from Arauco Bay, Chile, south along the coast to Tierra del Fuego, and ranges north along the Pacific coast regularly to Perú, and casually to southern California. I was interested, however, in 1956 to have a brief distant view of one that was definitely lighter in color, which suggested that another of the several races may be found also. No specimens have been collected.

STERCORARIUS POMARINUS (Temminck): Pomarine Jaeger; Salteador Pomarino

Lestris pomarinus Temminck, Man. Orn., 1815, p. 514. (Arctic regions of Europe.)

Largest of the 3 jaegers; adult with elongated central tail feathers twisted toward the tip.

Description.—Length, 460 to 495 mm. Bill higher than wide at base. Light-colored phase, crown, lores, malar region, and upper surface (except hindneck) sooty gray; hindneck and lower surface white, except for lower abdomen and under tail coverts which are like the back.

Dark phase, dark sooty gray throughout.

Many are in an intermediate stage in which the lower surface in general is white with foreneck, upper breast, sides, flanks, lower abdomen and under tail coverts lined, barred and spotted with sooty gray.

Measurements (from Ridgway, l.c., p. 682).—Males, wing 349-374 (361.9), tail 172-243 (207.9), culmen 38-43.5 (40.4), tarsus 48-54 (52) mm.

Females, wing 351-370 (359.7), tail 128-205.5 (182.2), culmen 38-44 (40.2), tarsus 50-55 (52.1) mm.

Tarsus pale bluish gray on upper part in life; lower part and feet blackish brown.

Migrant from the north. Known from sight records in Colón harbor, and in the Gulf of Panamá.

Griscom (Amer. Mus. Nov. no. 282, 1927, p. 3) on March 13, 1927, in company with Maunsell Crosby, recorded several at Colón. In later comment (Bull. Mus. Comp. Zool., vol. 78, 1935, p. 308) he wrote that these jaegers sometimes enter Colón harbor where they live on garbage and rob the many laughing gulls. Eisenmann has given me a record of several seen at Coco Solo on April 28, 1961. Murphy has seen them in late November (1956) parasitizing the laughing gulls in the Gulf of Panamá. On February 8, 1963, I saw one with fully developed tail from the MV *Pelican* when off Isla Iguana. Certain other reports appear uncertain.

No specimens have been collected.

This species is of heavier form than the others of the genus, and in the adult is distinguished by the form of the elongated central rectrices which are broad at the tip, in addition to having the plane of the web rotated or twisted toward the free end.

STERCORARIUS PARASITICUS (Linnaeus): Parasitic Jaeger; Salteador Parásito

Larus parasiticus Linnaeus, Syst. Nat., ed. 10, vol. 1, 1758, p. 136. (Coast of Sweden.)

Adult with slender, pointed central tail feathers projecting from 12 to 100 mm.

Description.—Bill heavier; length of horny cere (supranasal saddle) from base decidedly more than the length of the distal, hooked section (dertrum). Length, adult 450 to 470 mm.; immature 420 to 440 mm. Adult, light phase, upper surface and under tail coverts sooty gray, slightly darker on the crown, somewhat paler on the lower hindneck; a brownish gray band across lower foreneck and upper breast; a buffy white band across hindneck; under surface, except as described, white.

Dark phase, sooty gray above, blacker on crown, wings, and tail; brownish gray on lower surface.

Immature, in light phase, head and neck streaked, and lower surface more or less barred and spotted, with dusky brown. In dark phase, underparts barred with grayish white.

Adult, tarsi and feet black. Immature, tarsi bluish gray, with ends of toes and webs black.

Measurements (from Ridgway, l.c., p. 688).—Males, wing 301-340 (320), tail 164.5-235 (188.9), culmen 28-35 (31.2), tarsus 39.5-45.5 (41.9) mm.

Females, wing 317-341 (323.7), tail 176-226 (199.7), culmen 29-34.5 (31.8), tarsus 39-45 (42.1) mm.

Visitor from the north. Known from one taken on the coast of the Comarca de San Blas, and a few sight records.

A male in the Herbert Brandt Collection at the University of Cincinnati was collected by Wedel on November 27, 1934, at Puerto Obaldía, San Blas. One was seen by Robert Cushman Murphy near Isla San José, February 21, 1941 (see Wetmore, Smithsonian Misc. Coll., vol. 106, no. 1, 1946, p. 34). Another was recorded in Colón harbor Feb. 9, 1927, by Griscom (Amer. Mus. Nov. no. 282, 1927, p. 3).

STERCORARIUS LONGICAUDUS Vieillot: Long-Tailed Jaeger; Salteador Rabudo

Stercorarius longicaudus Vieillot, Nouv. Dict. Hist. Nat., nouv. éd., vol. 32, Sept. 1819, p. 157. (Northern Europe.)

Adult with central tail feathers projecting 80 to 150 mm. or more.

Description.—Bill smaller; horny cere (supranasal saddle) shorter, not more than length of distal segment of bill (dertrum). Length adult 520 to 570 mm., immature 410 to 460 mm. Adult, crown, including loral and orbital regions sooty black; rest of head and hindneck yellowish white; rest of upper parts brownish gray; wings and tail dull black; abdomen, flanks and under tail coverts gray; rest of undersurface white.

Immature, undersurface and upper tail coverts barred more or less extensively with brownish gray.

A few birds in dark phase have been reported in life, but this color stage, if correctly identified, must be rare, as no specimens of it have been collected.

Tarsus light bluish gray, toes and webs black; immature, only distal end of toes black.

Measurements (from Ridgway, l.c., p. 696).—Males, wing 295-327 (309.1), tail (to end of middle rectrices) 263-350 (299), culmen 27-31.5 (28.6), tarsus 38-44 (41.1) mm.

Females, wing 305-317 (313.3), tail (to end of middle rectrices) 238-350 (295), culmen 27.5-30 (28.8), tarsus 40-42.5 (41.8) mm.

Visitor from the north. Status not certain.

The only record is of one seen by L. Griscom and M. Crosby in Colón harbor on February 9, 1927 (Griscom, Amer. Mus. Nov. no. 282, 1927, p. 3).

Adults of the two smaller jaegers usually may be separated on the length of the central tail feathers; and a small bird in dark phase plumage may be accepted as *S. parasiticus,* since this type of coloration in *S. longicaudus* is not yet firmly established by a specimen. Field identification of immature individuals is uncertain unless chance may give a clear view of the leg color, black in *parasiticus* and bluish gray in *longicaudus*. With birds in the hand the two may be separated by close scrutiny of the size of the bill—heavier in *parasiticus,* slightly more slender in *longicaudus*. It is probable that both species come occasionally along the coasts so that I have included them on the basis of sight records, which are not wholly certain.

Family LARIDAE: Gulls and Terns; Gaviotas y Gaviotines

The two groups of aquatic habit included in this family, while allied structurally, differ so clearly in carriage and action that they are distinguished at a glance by any one reasonably familiar with them. The gulls are larger and are more robust, wider-winged birds that in flight carry the strong, rather heavy bill with its hooked tip pointed forward in line with the long axis of the body. While they may snatch at food on the surface of the water, it is not their regular habit to dive. All the species found in Panamá are migrant from the north or south. Terns as a group are small, with slender bodies, and narrow, pointed wings. As they fly over the water in search of food the slender, straight bill is pointed down at an angle, and the birds habitually feed by plunging, often going beneath the surface. Only the royal tern, of those found in Panamá, has the body size of the smaller gulls. At least two species, the noddy and the sooty tern, come to nest on the rocky islets of Los Frailes off Punta Mala. Probably a third, the bridled tern, may breed there also. Other kinds are found as migrants. While both gulls and terns range along the coasts, some of them come inland on larger bodies of fresh water.

FAMILY LARIDAE 439

KEY TO THE SPECIES OF LARIDAE

1. Culmen with tip distinctly decurved; the curving end of the maxilla overhanging the end of the mandible; tarsus relatively longer (Gulls). 2
Culmen with tip not decurved, more nearly straight throughout its length; end of maxilla not overhanging that of mandible; tarsus relatively shorter (Terns)... 8
2. Tail truncate or slightly rounded................................. 3
Tail definitely forked... 7
3. Under surface white, or washed and mottled with grayish brown; back plain gray, or grayish brown; bill not completely black............ 4
Entire body plain mouse gray; bill completely black.
    Gray gull, *Larus modestus*, p. 440
4. Size large, wing more than 410 mm.
    Herring gull, *Larus argentatus smithsonianus*, p. 441
Size smaller; wing less than 390 mm............................. 5
5. Bill small, exposed culmen less than 35 mm.; tarsus less than 45 mm.
    Franklin's gull, *Larus pipixcan*, p. 445
Bill larger; exposed culmen 40 mm. or more; tarsus more than 45 mm. 6
6. Tarsus and feet light-colored; bill light-colored, at least at base; if immature, upper tail coverts spotted with grayish brown.
    Ring-billed gull, *Larus delawarensis*, p. 441
Tarsus, feet, and bill dark; if immature, upper tail coverts plain white or grayish white, without spots........Laughing gull, *Larus atricilla*, p. 442
7. Large; wing more than 390 mm.; bill slender, exposed culmen more than 45 mm...................Swallow-tailed gull, *Creagrus furcatus*, p. 446
Small; wing less than 300 mm.; exposed culmen less than 30 mm.
    Sabine's gull, *Xema sabini*, p. 447
8. Head smooth, not crested... 9
Back of head with feathers elongated in a definite crest................ 15
9. Toes partly webbed, the webs extending only to the bases of the outer toe joints; outer tail feathers broad and rounded at tip.
    Black tern, *Chlidonias niger surinamensis*, p. 448
Toes fully webbed, the webs extended on the outer toe joints; outer tail feathers narrowed and pointed at tip............................ 10
10. Size small; wing not more than 180 mm..Least tern, *Sterna albifrons*, p. 457
Larger; wing more than 200 mm.................................. 11
11. Bill relatively short and heavy, with greatest depth equal to about one third length of exposed culmen; tarsus longer than middle toe with claw.
    Gull-billed tern, *Gelochelidon nilotica aranea*, p. 449
Bill relatively longer and more slender, with greatest depth definitely less than one third length of exposed culmen; tarsus shorter than middle toe with claw... 12
12. Back and wings light gray....Common tern, *Sterna hirundo hirundo*, p. 452
Back and wings dark sooty brown, sooty gray, or black.............. 13
13. Tail rounded; body and wings dark sooty or grayish brown.
    Brown noddy tern, *Anous stolidus*, p. 461
Tail deeply forked.. 14

14. Back brownish gray; with hindneck white to pale gray.
    Bridled tern, *Sterna anaethetus nelsoni*, p. 454
    Back and hindneck black.................Sooty tern, *Sterna fuscata*, p. 455
15. Bill black, with yellow or whitish tip; smaller, wing less than 310 mm.
    Sandwich tern, *Thalasseus sandvicensis acuflavidus*, p. 459
    Bill orange or red; wing more than 350 mm........................ 16
16. Bill orange to orange-yellow; feathers on back of head more elongated and definitely pointed; tail forked for one-fourth of its length; smaller, wing less than 400 mm........Royal tern, *Thalaseus maximus maximus*, p. 458
    Bill red; feathers on back of head less elongated, more rounded at tip, and blended in a smooth crest; tail less deeply forked; larger, wing more than 400 mm..................Caspian tern, *Hydroprogne caspia*, p. 451

LARUS MODESTUS Tschudi: Gray Gull; Gaviota Garuma

Larus modestus Tschudi, Arch. Naturg. vol. 9, pt. 1, 1843, p. 389. (Lurín, south of Lima, Perú.)

Slightly larger than the laughing gull; body uniform gray, with a prominent white border on the posterior edge of the wing.

Description.—Length, 420 to 450 mm. Plain gray; anterior half of crown, forehead, and throat grayish white; primaries and secondaries black, with the inner primaries lightly, and the secondaries broadly, tipped with white; tail with a subterminal band of black, and a narrow tip of white.

Iris brown; bill black; tarsus and toes black.

Measurements (from Murphy, Oceanic Birds S. Amer., 1936, p. 1049).—Males, wing 314-337 (329.2); tail 117-131 (124), culmen 40-43 (41.8), tarsus 48-55 (53.2) mm.

Females, wing 299-328 (318.7), tail 116-122 (119.6), culmen 37-41 (39.6), tarsus 46-51 (48.7) mm.

Visitor from the south. Casual in the Gulf of Panamá.

According to Eisenmann (Trans. Linn. Soc. New York, vol. 7, 1955, p. 32), Robert Cushman Murphy has reported this species in Panama Bay near the entrance to the Canal. On February 6, 1956, on the return from Isla Coiba, about 5 kilometers south of Isla Otoque, I saw 3 grayish gulls, lighter on forepart of the head and with a conspicuous white border on the posterior edge of the wing. It is not always easy to identify birds flying at a distance from the deck of a crash boat travelling at rapid speed, and at the time I thought that they were Heermann's gulls, *Larus heermanni*, from the north, and so recorded them (Smithsonian Misc. Coll., vol. 134, no. 9, 1957, p. 33). I believe, however, that it is more probable that they were *Larus modestus*, a species that ranges regularly to central Ecuador and has been reported casually along the Pacific coast of Colombia.

LARUS DELAWARENSIS Ord: Ring-billed Gull; Gaviota de Pico Anillado

Larus Delawarensis Ord, *in* Guthrie, Geogr., 2d Amer. ed., 1815, p. 319. (Delaware River, below Philadelphia.)

A dark ring around the bill near the end; legs yellowish; smaller than the herring gull.

Description.—Length, 460 to 530 mm. Adult, back, scapulars, and wings light gray; body and tail otherwise white; outer primaries black, the two outermost tipped with white.

In winter plumage, head and hindneck streaked with brownish gray.

Immature, above grayish brown; under parts white mottled with grayish brown; a narrow black subterminal tail bar.

Measurements (from Ridgway, l.c., p. 625).—Males, wing 365-389 (378.1), tail 143-161 (150.8), culmen 42-45.5 (44.3), tarsus 54-61 (56.5) mm.

Females, wing 334-372 (362.4), tail 132-150 (141.8), culmen 37-41.5 (39.5), tarsus 47-54 (50.9) mm.

Migrant from the north. Casual wanderer.

There is record of one banded as a nestling on Little Galloo Island in Henderson Harbor, Lake Ontario, Jefferson County, N. Y., on June 14, 1953, by Allan S. Klonick, that was found dead (without feathers) at Boca del Río Grande, Coclé, on July 11, 1954. Eugene Eisenmann has reported ring-billed gulls seen along the sea wall in Panamá City, November 9 and 26 and December 4, 1962.

The species comes south regularly along the coast of México, and has been reported from one sight record from El Salvador. It appears to be of casual occurrence in Panamá.

LARUS ARGENTATUS SMITHSONIANUS Coues: Herring Gull; Gaviota Argentea

Larus Smithsonianus Coues, Proc. Acad. Nat. Sci. Philadelphia, vol. 14, no. 6, June (Aug. 1), 1862, p. 296. (Eastern and western coasts of North America.)

Adult with a subterminal spot of red on lower mandible; legs flesh-colored; larger than the ring-billed gull.

Description.—Length, 560-625 mm. Adult, back, scapulars, and wings pale gray; head, neck, rump, tail, and entire underparts white; outermost primaries black with white toward the tips.

Winter dress, head and hindneck streaked with dusky.

Immature, mainly grayish brown, with head and neck streaked with whitish; rest of upper surface spotted irregularly with grayish buff; wings and tail blackish.

Measurements (from Dwight, Bull. Amer. Mus. Nat. Hist., vol. 52, 1925, p. 182).—Males, wing 405-460 (433.8), tail 151-190 (175.2), culmen 49-62 (57), tarsus 60-74 (67.8) mm.

Females, wing 397-422 (410.6), tail 154-178 (165.3), culmen 47-53 (50.1), tarsus 57-66 (62.1) mm.

Migrant from the north. Present in small number during the period of northern winter.

The herring gull recorded at Bocas del Toro, on December 10, 1933, by Griscom (Bull. Mus. Comp. Zool., vol. 78, 1935, p. 308) had been banded as an immature bird in New Hampshire in July of the same year. Hofslund (Bird-Banding, vol. 30, 1959, p. 113) has reported another, banded as an immature bird at Knife Island, Lake Superior, off the mouth of Knife River, Lake County, Minn., June 8, 1957, that was "caught on fish hook," in the bay at Bocas del Toro, February 7, 1958. Another banded in Wisconsin in July 1930, was found near Panama City the following December. Eugene Eisenmann has reported one seen off San Francisco de la Caleta, near Panamá Viejo on December 4 and 20, 1962. In 1963, I recorded one on January 30 in the entrance of the Canal at Colón, and another on February 9 near Balboa. The herring gull comes south regularly during the northern winter along both coasts as far as southern México, in small numbers farther south. It is found most often in the Caribbean area.

LARUS ATRICILLA Linnaeus: Laughing Gull; Gaviota Reidora

Figure 70

Larus Atricilla Linnaeus, Syst. Nat., ed. 10, vol. 1, 1758, p. 136. (Bahama Islands.)

In flight, adult with outer half of wing wholly black; tail white. Immature, wing like adult; tail with black subterminal band and indistinct light tip; middle toe with claw definitely shorter than culmen.

Description.—Length 380 to 425 mm. Adult, in summer dress, head black, with a white spot on eyelid; back, scapulars, and wings dark gray; hindneck, tail, and undersurface white; outer primaries black distally, with small inconspicuous white tips, except on the outermost; innermost primaries and secondaries gray, tipped with white.

Winter plumage, similar, but head and upper foreneck white, spotted and mottled with brownish gray on the occiput and sides of the head.

Immature, above, mainly grayish brown; tail light gray at base, dull black at end, tipped obscurely with white; underneath grayish brown except for the abdomen, which is paler.

Measurements.—Males, wing 316-348 (332.7), tail 121-135 (127.6), culmen 40-43 (41), tarsus 47-53 (50.4), middle toe 34.5-38 (36) mm.

FIG. 70.—Right wings of two gulls to show pattern of marking. Upper: Franklin's gull, gaviota de Franklin, *Larus pipixcan*. Lower: Laughing gull, gaviota reidora, *Larus atricilla*.

Females, wing 311-331 (322), tail 116-125.5 (120.2), culmen 38-40 (39.1), tarsus 46-51.5 (48.1), middle toe 32.5-35 (33.5) mm.

Migrant from the north. Found along both coasts, abundant in the Bay and Gulf of Panamá; common on Gatun Lake, and casual on other larger bodies of water inland. Recorded regularly at Isla Coiba, and occasionally around other offshore islands. Nonbreeding individuals remain through the period of northern summer.

The main influx from the north comes in October and November, and during succeeding months the birds are widely spread. Molt into the breeding plumage begins in late February and continues through the middle of March. By the end of March birds that display the black head of the summer dress are common. Flocks in full plumage evidently are in northward flight by early April. Though there is great reduction in their number at this time, scores remain in Panamá through the months of northern summer. Scattered birds, all in nonbreeding plumage, may be found in their usual haunts through this period, with flocks congregated in favorable localities where food is attractive. As an example, on May 11, 1953, I observed 50 or more widely scattered high in air over Albrook Field, evidently hawking for flying insects, probably termites.

The greatest concentrations during the winter months are in the Gulf of Panamá, where they range down to Punta Mala and shift about with changes in wind and tide. Many join the pelicans, cormorants, and frigatebirds as they feed on the great schools of sardinelike fishes. When these appear gulls may be observed in flight toward them from considerable distances. After feeding small groups may raft in fairly close formation, but it is more common to find them spread singly, or 2 or 3 together, over wide spaces of the sea. As passing launches disturb them, or as the waves increase, they rise and straggle off, flying into the wind. Such groups fly regularly and easily if disturbed on the darkest nights, seemingly without being troubled by the lack of light. Flocks that may number 1500 to 2000 birds appear regularly in the Bay of Panamá from the entrance of the Canal around to Panamá Viejo.

Laughing gulls cross the Isthmus through Gatun Lake and also appear at times on such smaller bodies as the Miraflores lakes and water impoundments in the old banana farms near Changuinola. They come also with regularity over the wide reaches of the Chagres above Gamboa toward Madden Dam, but the lake above does not seem attractive, probably through its lack of easily accessible food. Once in early January I saw 4 walking over short cut grass opposite the old Balboa railroad station, but this appears to be unusual.

In launch travel during March, when anchored in some protected bay, at sunrise I have seen flocks of up to 200 or more swing in suddenly from the sea, turn and gyrate wildly for several minutes in wind currents high in air, and then disappear. On one trip in the little steamer *Pirre,* while crossing the Gulf of San Miguel toward the mouth of the Tuira, an immature gull with a band on one leg appeared among the following flock and came repeatedly close at hand. The numerous records in Panamá of birds banded between

Maine and Florida on the eastern coast of the United States, indicate a heavy mortality among first year birds, as only 2 among 64 had lived beyond the first winter. The reports of these returns cover the entire range in the Republic.

The laughing gull is probably the principal species concerned in the account of Lionel Wafer (Voy. and Descript. Isthm. Amer., 1699, p. 121) whose observations made in 1681 are as follows: "There are a great many Sea-Gulls and Sea-Pies on that Coast; both of them much like ours, but rather smaller. The Flesh of both these is eaten commonly enough, and 'tis tolerable good Meat, but of a Fishy Tast, as Sea-fowl usually are. Yet to correct this Tast, when we kill'd any Sea-Gulls, Sea-Pies, Boobies, or the like, on any Shore, we us'd to make a Hole in the hot Sand, and there bury them for eight or ten Hours, with their Feathers on, and Guts in them: And upon dressing them afterwards, we found the Flesh tenderer, and the Tast not so rank nor fishy."

LARUS PIPIXCAN Wagler: Franklin's Gull; Gaviota de Franklin

Figure 70

Larus Pipixcan Wagler, Isis von Oken, vol. 24, heft 5, (May) 1831, col. 515. (México.)

Middle toe with claw about equal in length to culmen. In flight, adult, wing appears light gray to white, with a prominent subterminal black band and white tip, tail white. Immature, wing wholly dark at tip like laughing gull; markings on back of head blacker, more definite; tail with subterminal black band and distinct white tip.

Description.—Length 330-380 mm. Adult, in summer dress, head and upperneck slaty black; a white spot on eyelid; back, scapulars, and wings neutral gray, with tertials and secondaries broadly tipped with white; 5 outer primaries with a subterminal black band, and white tip, bordered above by white of central part of wing; tail white, with middle rectrices tinged with gray; lower neck (front and back), rump, upper tail coverts, and lower surface white.

Winter dress, head and neck white, with back and side of head dusky gray.

Immature, like winter adult, but outer primaries black like laughing gull; tail with a broad black subterminal bar and distinct white tip. Differs from laughing gull in smaller size, particularly of bill.

Measurements (from Ridgway, l.c., p. 642).—Males, wing 280-295 (289.6), tail 97-109 (103.9), culmen 30-34 (32.6), tarsus 38-42.5 (40.8) middle toe 31.5-33 (32.4) mm.

Females, wing 270-293 (282), tail 94-105 (99.7), culmen 30-34.5 (32.5), tarsus 39-41 (39.9), middle toe 31.5-34 (32.2) mm.

Migrant from the north. Fairly common along both coasts; recorded on Gatun Lake.

Adult Franklin's gulls, easily identified by the prominent black and white markings on the end of the wing, are observed with fair regularity among the hundreds of laughing gulls along the coasts, but I have yet to detect one among the flocks that range the open Gulf of Panamá. It is probable that their pattern of migration is like that of the related species, but at present there is no definite information on this. Some nonbreeding individuals remain in Panamá through the period of northern summer. They are seen occasionally on Gatun Lake, but have not been recorded elsewhere in the interior.

The only specimen I have examined is an immature bird in the U. S. National Museum, taken at Panamá City by Dr. George Suckley, on December 28, 1855. There is a further record of one banded in South Dakota in June 1940 that was found on the Pacific coast of Panamá in the vicinity of the Golfo de Montijo on July 8 of the following year. In my own observations I have seen these birds at Panamá Viejo, recording 15 to 20 on December 28, 1955, one at the Miraflores Locks December 29, 1963, and have found an occasional one among the many laughing gulls at Fort Amador.

CREAGRUS FURCATUS (Néboux): Swallow-tailed Gull; Gaviota Rabihorcado

Larus furcatus Néboux, Voy. "Venus," Atlas, Zool., Ois., 1846, pl. 10. (Galápagos Archipelago.)

A large, gray-backed gull, with dark head, and forked tail.

Description.—Length 550 to 600 mm. Tail deeply forked. Adult, in breeding dress, head and neck slate gray, with a white spot on the forehead at the base of the bill, and a smaller one on the feathers adjacent to the side of the lower mandible; back, rump, and lesser wing coverts gray, with the scapulars edged with white; outer webs of primaries black; inner webs, rest of wing coverts, secondaries, and tail white; sides of breast and lower foreneck pale gray; rest of under surface white.

Nonbreeding dress, head white, streaked with gray; space around eyes and over ears grayish black.

Immature, brown above; head white streaked as in nonbreeding dress of adult; below white.

Iris brown; edge of eyelids and edge of gape bright red; tip of bill greenish; base black; tarsus and toes pink.

Measurements (from Murphy, l.c., p. 1086).—Males, wing 405-433 (414.8); tail 184-202 (191.1), culmen 47-55 (52), tarsus 45-55 (52.1) mm.

Females, wing 393-414 (404.1), tail 181-197 (189.7) culmen 49-52 (50.9), tarsus 47-54 (51) mm.

Visitor from the south. Casual.

The only record is that of Robins (Condor, 1958, p. 302) who recorded one seen at a deep reef northwest of Bahía Piñas, July 18, 1957. I have found no basis for the statement by Swarth (Occas. Papers California Acad. Sci., vol. 18, 1931, p. 66) that "one or two stragglers have been found on the coast of Panamá."

The fork-tailed gull breeds at the Galápagos Islands, and after the breeding season it is found at sea as far as the coasts of Ecuador and Perú. It nests also on Isla de Malpelo, approximately 500 kilometers west of Buenaventura, on the coast of Colombia, and about 400 kilometers due south of Isla Coiba.

XEMA SABINI (Sabine): Sabine's Gull; Gaviota de Sabine

Larus sabini J. Sabine, Trans. Linn. Soc. London, vol. 12, pt. 2, 1819, p. 522, pl. 29. (Sabine Islands, near Melville Bay, west coast of Greenland.)

A small gull, with a deeply forked tail.

Description.—Length, 300 to 350 mm. Adult, summer dress, head slate-colored, with a narrow black ring around the neck; back, lesser wing coverts, secondaries, scapulars, and tertials dark gray; outer webs of outer primaries black, tipped with white; inner primaries, tips of secondaries, tail, upper tail coverts, and under parts white; edge of wing black.

Winter dress, head and neck mainly white, with occiput, nape, and auricular region brownish gray.

Immature, grayish brown above, with feathers edged with dull white to grayish buffy white; tail white, with a broad subterminal band of black, and a white or grayish tip.

Measurements (from Ridgway, l.c., p. 664).—Males, wing 265-286 (277.2), tail 114.5-130 (122.4), culmen 25.5-28.5 (27.4), tarsus 31.5-34.5 (33.1) mm.

Females, wing 260-276 (267.5), tail 111-114.5 (112.2), culmen 25-27 (26.2), tarsus 30-32 (31.5) mm.

Migrant from the north. Casual.

The only reports are those of Robert Cushman Murphy (Vert. SCOPE, Nov. 7-Dec. 16, 1956, p. 137, mimeograph, and *in litt.*) who says that this species was seen occasionally southward to the latitudes of Panamá but far at sea between long. 88° and 100° W.

In 1941, during the cruise of *Askoy*, however, he saw 8 Sabine's gulls close along the coast of southern Darién, and later, on May 11, 1941, he collected two to the southward in Bahía Cuevita, below Cabo Corrientes, on the northwestern coast of Colombia.

The species nests in the far north, and in migration moves south off the Pacific coast of America as far as Perú.

CHLIDONIAS NIGER SURINAMENSIS (Gmelin): Black Tern; Gaviotín Negro

Sterna surinamensis Gmelin, Syst. Nat., vol. 1, pt. 2, 1789, p. 604. (Surinam.)

A small tern; adult in breeding dress, black on head and lower surface; immature and winter adult, tail dark gray (white, or mainly white, in other terns); bill, tarsi, and feet black.

Description.—Length, 230 to 250 mm. Adult, breeding dress, entire head and under surface back across abdomen sooty black; anal region and under tail coverts white; back, rump, wings, and tail dark gray.

Winter dress and immature birds, anterior half of crown, fore neck, and under surface white; spot on either side of breast dusky; rest of upper surface as in summer.

Measurements (from Ridgway, l.c., p. 533).—Males, wing 192-213 (203.2), tail 73-87.5 (79.8), culmen 26-29.5 (27), tarsus 14.5-16 (15.4) mm.

Females, wing 191-215 (199.6), tail 73.5-82 (77.8), culmen 25.5-27 (26.2), tarsus 14-16.5 (15.6) mm.

Migrant from the north. Common along the coast, and in the Gulf of Panamá; ranges regularly over Gatun Lake, and other larger inland bodies of open water.

The flight from the north comes in September and continues through October. Northward movement appears to begin in April and to extend well into May. On May 13, 1953, at sunrise I found many passing toward the north across the dry savannas near Río Hato in the Province of Coclé on a course that would carry them over the low divide to the Caribbean west of the Canal Zone. Two that I shot, male and female, were in worn plumage and were molting the wing and tail feathers but did not show any of the black body plumage of the nesting season. Considerable numbers of nonbreeding birds in immature dress remain in Panamá through the period of northern summer, when they are found especially in tidal areas on the lower courses of rivers of the Pacific side. In June 1953 I recorded many on the lower Río San Pablo, below Soná, where they moved back and forth with the tides from the head of the Gulf of Montijo. Hundreds more ranged the shallow waters of the head of the Gulf itself between Isla Leones and Isla Verde. They come inland also when rains fill the channels in the swamps of the La Jagua marshes.

A principal haunt here at the northern edge of their wintering area is in the Gulf of Panamá, where I have found them regularly as far down as Punta Mala and also to the eastward toward Colombian waters. They range in flocks of 30 or 40 to 200 or more, sometimes rafting in fairly close formation, sometimes spread over wide areas. A floating board or stick may have one or two standing on it, and a log of driftwood may support several. They join other larger birds in hovering over the great schools of sardines to snatch at the smaller ones as the rush of predatory fish below drives them to break at the surface. I have seen black terns at various points in the Archipiélago de las Perlas, but they are found more commonly in the open sea. It is interesting to compare this winter habit with that of their breeding grounds, which lie entirely in fresh waters inland.

GELOCHELIDON NILOTICA ARANEA (Wilson): Gull-billed Tern; Gaviotín Piquigordo

Sterna aranea Wilson, Amer. Orn., vol. 8, 1814, p. 143, pl. 72, fig. 6. (Cape May, New Jersey).

A tern of medium size with strong, heavy bill like that of a gull; tail notched, not deeply forked.

Description.—Length, 330 to 355 mm. Bill short and stout. Adult, breeding plumage, crown and nape black; back, wings, and tail light gray; entire under surface white.

Winter dress, head and neck white, with the auricular region and a crescent in front of the eye dusky gray; otherwise as in summer.

Measurements.—Males (9 from Maryland, Virginia, Bahamas, Cuba, Haiti, and Veracruz), wing 285-304 (295), tail 108-122.8 (113.7), culmen from base 38.2-42.5 (39.7), tarsus 29.5-32.7 (30.8) mm.

Females (8 from Virginia, Florida, Alabama, Bahamas, and Haiti), wing 286-297 (292), tail 105.6-118.8 (110.4), culmen from base 35.6-40.6 (38.2), tarsus 28.3-31.9 (30.5) mm.

Migrant from the north. Fairly common in the Gulf of Panamá; one report from the Caribbean coast.

The first record of this tern is found in 2 skins in the American Museum of Natural History, an immature male and another male, apparently adult in winter dress, taken by Rex Benson near Aguadulce, Coclé, September 24, 1927. In crossing from Balboa to Isla San José on February 7, 1944, I observed several hundred feeding over the sea from 50 to 15 kilometers off the island. Other sight records are for occasional birds seen near Panamá Viejo, where Eisenmann (Wilson Bull., 1951, p. 182) reported one, considered to be a nonbreeding, summering individual, on July 16, 1950, and I have recorded others April 3 and December 18, 1955. With this scanty information it was of considerable interest to me to find gull-billed terns fairly common in January 1963 over the channels and mud flats of the Bahía Parita area below Aguadulce, Coclé. January 16 and 17 I shot five from small groups coursing in a strong wind at Gallo and on January 25 recorded 40 resting in a close flock at low tide, on a sandspit on the shore of the bay. Two of those taken had eaten shrimp, two others fiddler crabs, and the fifth a small fish. As this is the general area where Benson secured his specimens it appears that this tern may be regular here in occurrence.

The record for the Atlantic side is of one seen by Eugene Eisenmann, August 28, 1958, near Coco Solo, Canal Zone. (I know of no basis for the statement by Hellmayr and Conover, Cat. Birds, Amer., pt. 1, no. 3, 1948, p. 299, that includes the Caribbean side of Panamá in the winter range.) The race *aranea* breeds along the Atlantic coast from southeastern Maryland and Virginia to eastern Florida, the Bahamas, and the Virgin Islands, and is found in winter from the Gulf coast of the United States south along Central America, to northern South America.

The gull-billed tern as a species ranges throughout the world, except in the colder regions and the islands of the central Pacific. While all are closely similar in appearance, several races are recognized, two of them in North America, viz, the one discussed above and a western one, *Gelochelidon nilotica vanrossemi* Bancroft (described in Trans. San Diego Soc. Nat. Hist., vol. 5, Dec. 10, 1929, p. 284; type locality Salton Sea, Imperial County, California). Its known breeding grounds are on islands in Salton Sea and along the coast of Sinaloa, with other records not wholly definite from the head of the Gulf of California (Isla Monteague), and the coast of Sonora (Bahía Tóbari). This subspecies is separated from *G. n. aranea* by slightly larger size, stronger, heavier bill, and slightly longer tarsus. The following measurements are taken from specimens in the Museum of Comparative Zoology and the U. S. National Museum.

Measurements.—8 males, wing 287-295 (291.4), tail 102.5-119.0 (111.6), culmen from base 41.4-46.5 (43.8), tarsus 32.0-35.2 (33.2) mm.

3 females, wing 287-298 (292), tail 98.7-115.0 (104.4), culmen from base 42.9-44.5 (43.6), tarsus 32.9-33.3 (33.1) mm.

Wing and tail measurements are difficult to ascertain, since many specimens show much wear, even breakage in the slender tips of the longer feathers. Also, immature birds in their first winter do not appear to develop full bill and tarsus size until they have been for some time on the wing.

The specimens now known from Panamá (including the two collected by Benson) all agree in size with the race *aranea*. It appears, therefore, that these birds, like the laughing gull, in southward migration cross in part to winter on the Pacific side of Panamá.

HYDROPROGNE CASPIA (Pallas): Caspian Tern; Gaviotín Piquirrojo

Sterna caspia Pallas, Novi Comm. Acad. Sci. Petrop., pt. 1, 1770, p. 582, pl. 22. (Caspian Sea, southern Russia.)

Differs from the royal tern in red bill, tail only slightly forked, and elongated crest feathers rounded, with the free ends smoothly blended.

Description.—Length, 480 to 540 mm. Adult (sexes alike) in breeding dress, crown including upper half of lores and side of head immediately behind eye, black; rest of upperparts light gray, becoming white on upper tail coverts, and pale grayish white on tail; line on lower eyelid, and under surface, including under wing coverts, white; inner webs of primaries dark gray.

Winter plumage, crown, including forehead and side of head, dusky black streaked with white.

Immature, upperparts paler, with a few dusky spots; crown with more white.

Iris dark brown; bill deep red, with the tip orange or yellowish orange; legs and feet black.

Measurements.—(from Ridgway, l.c., p. 462).—Males, wing 400-422 (411.1), tail 130-150 (137.9), exposed culmen 65-75 (69.4), tarsus 40.5-46 (43.2) mm.

Females, wing 404-423 (416), tail 135-148 (140.2), exposed culmen 64-70 (67.5), tarsus 40-44 (42.4) mm.

Migrant from the north. One record at Aligandí, San Blas.

The Caspian tern breeds locally throughout the Northern Hemisphere. In the New World in winter it is found from central California, the Gulf of Mexico, and North Carolina, south along both coasts of México, and in the Greater Antilles east to Haiti. To the southward it is regular in northern Colombia along the Caribbean coast and on the lower Río Magdalena but is not reported elsewhere in South America.

The only record for Panamá is of a bird banded by L. Tyler on South Limestone Island, Georgian Bay, southeastern Ontario, on June 11, 1955, that was found wounded at Aligandí, San Blas, on the evening of November 12 of that year. It died the following morning, according to the report forwarded by Dr. Alcibíades Iglesias.

It seems probable that the species may come in small numbers along the eastern coast of the San Blas, as it is recorded from Puerto Colombia and Cartagena, Colombia. The red bill is the most definite mark of the species during flight.

In Spain the Caspian tern is known as *pagasa piquirrojo.*

STERNA HIRUNDO HIRUNDO Linnaeus: Common Tern; Gaviotín Común

Sterna Hirundo Linnaeus, Syst. Nat., ed. 10, vol. 1, 1758, p. 137. (Sweden.)

Gray above, with the back of the head and shoulder black.

Description.—Length, 290 to 320 mm. Outer tail feathers with outer web dark, and inner web white. Breeding dress, crown and nape black; rest of upper surface light gray; outer primaries with outer web black; outer webs of others gray; lower surface white.

Winter plumage, forepart of crown white; space around eye, rest of crown and nape black; lesser wing coverts dusky; otherwise as in summer. In many the silvery gray of the outer webs of the primaries wears thin to show black beneath.

Immature, like winter adults, but tertials with a dusky subterminal bar, and white tip.

Measurements. (from Ridgway, l.c., p. 494).—Males, wing 256-273 (265.6), tail 128-174 (148.9), culmen 33-39 (37.2), tarsus 18-20.5 (19.2) mm.

Females, wing 235-273 (257.7), tail 132.5-161.5 (147.4), culmen 32-40.5 (35.7), tarsus 17.5-20 (18.9) mm.

Migrant from the north. Fairly common on both coasts; occasional on Gatun Lake and other large inland waters.

The main flight from the north appears to come in October and

November, and the return northward is mainly in April. Numbers of nonbreeding individuals, in immature (or winter) plumage, remain through the months of northern summer. In 1953, on June 11, I collected one on the lower Río San Pablo, near Guarumal in southern Veraguas. Others were recorded later in this month at Riomar, Playa Coronado, and Nueva Gorgona along the Pacific coast and on the Río Chagres above Gamboa in the Caribbean drainage. Eisenmann (Condor, 1957, p. 252) recorded them in Almirante Bay, Bocas del Toro, June 29, 1956. There are numerous other summer records. These terns range regularly through Gatun Lake, and less commonly over the broad reaches of the Chagres between Gamboa and Juan Mina.

In 32 records for Panamá of birds banded on their northern nesting grounds the majority were marked in Ontario, with others from Michigan, Wisconsin, Minnesota and Illinois. Only four came from east coast colonies in Massachusetts, New York and Maryland. Of the total returns 30 are of birds that died during their first winter.

Common terns range alone or in small groups, usually in flight a few meters above the water, which they scan with bills pointed downward. When small fishes appear they dive instantly in attempt to seize them. Near Isla Taboga in December I have recorded flocks of 30 to 40 resting in company on calm water, and off the Balboa entrance of the Canal I have seen 20 or more crowded together on the base of a buoy. Near Punta Mala I have observed one in company with black terns, resting on a stick of driftwood 5 kilometers or so offshore. And in Almirante Bay I have seen them with royal terns standing on snags stranded in shallow water. One that I shot here February 20, 1958, was in very badly worn plumage on the wing coverts and the whole upper surface.

[It is probable that *Sterna paradisaea* Pontoppidan, the Arctic tern, *gaviotín ártico,* which includes the eastern Pacific in its migrations from northern breeding grounds may come casually into offshore Panamanian waters. The nearest record to date is an adult female in the British Museum (Natural History) taken during the St. George Expedition on October 4, 1924, "at sea 300 m. S. of Panama." As the ship was en route to Isla Gorgona this would have been approximately 200 kilometers from the coast of Colombia. The species has been found in considerable numbers at sea off Perú and Chile, and is reported casually on the coast of the latter country.

The Arctic tern differs from the common tern in grayer color on the ventral surface and in the shorter tarsus, which measures 13.5 to 16. mm.]

STERNA ANAETHETUS NELSONI Ridgway: Bridled Tern; Gaviotina Monja

Sterna anaetheta nelsoni Ridgway, U. S. Nat. Mus. Bull. 50, pt. 8, June 26, 1919, pp. 487 (in key), 514. (Zihuatanejo, Guerrero, México.)

In life, in general appearance like *Sterna fuscata*, but dark gray on the back, and with a grayish white ring on the hindneck.

Description.—Length, 375-400 mm. Adult, crown, hindneck, and a heavy line through the lores to the eye deep black; base of hindneck grayish white, forming a distinct collar; upper back, rump, and upper tail coverts dark gray; wing coverts, tertials, and middle of back dark grayish brown; primaries, primary coverts, and secondaries black; tail feathers white basally; outer pair with outer web white and inner web dusky toward tip; forehead, and sides of crown back past the eyes, and under surface white, with the breast and abdomen tinged strongly with pale gray.

Immature, crown and upper hindneck dusky, with the feathers bordered with plain gray; back, rump, and upper tail coverts grayish brown, barred indefinitely with grayish white; wings dusky, with the coverts edged with grayish white; under surface white, tinged very slightly with gray on the lower breast and abdomen.

Iris brown; bill, tarsi, and feet black.

Measurements (from Ridgway, l.c., p. 514).—Males, wing 260-274 (267.7), tail 163-178 (170), exposed culmen 41.5-44.0 (42.0), tarsus 20.0-21.5 (20.7) mm.

Females, wing 260-270 (265), tail 169-170 (169.5), exposed culmen 36.0-40.5 (38.2), tarsus 20 mm.

Believed to nest on Los Frailes, off Punta Mala.

The first record of this tern for Panamá was an immature female sent to me by Charles L. Fagan, wireless operator on the Grace Line S.S. *Santa Elisa,* a bird that came aboard his ship at midnight on September 24, 1922, when the ship was abeam of Punta Mala. To date this is the only specimen recorded for Panamanian waters.

On February 6, 1956, as the Air Force crash boat on which I returned from Isla Coiba passed the two rocks of Frailes del Sur, scores of terns appeared over the sea, with hundreds more over the larger of the two islets. They continued in numbers near the boat as far as Isla Iguana, and occasional individuals were noted north nearly to Isla Otoque. A few that came near were identified as the present species, but I believe now that part were *Sterna fuscata crissalis.* None were seen when I had passed on the trip outward on January 6, so that I believed that those observed on the return voyage had come in recently from the sea.

Apparently these terns may follow a breeding schedule that is not based on a 12-month annual cycle, as on a trip on the launch *Sea Raider* with Capt. Richard E. Parker, on February 25 and 26, 1957, that I made especially to look for them, no terns were found.

Robert Cushman Murphy (Nat. Hist., 1938, p. 177) in September 1937 found numbers of bridled terns around Cabo Marzo and the Octavia Rocks, on the Coast of Chocó, a short distance south of the Panamanian boundary. Robins (Condor, 1958, p. 302) recorded them in July 1957 from Punta Garachiné to beyond Bahía Piñas. And Dennis R. Paulson, on the yacht *Argosy,* saw a number south of Isla San José September 7, and others near Bahia Piñas, September 12, 1961.

It is probable that the race *Sterna anaethetus recognita* Mathews, which has nested in Caribbean waters on islands off British Honduras, and at a number of islands in the West Indies, will be found eventually on the northern shore of Panamá. It differs from *S. a. nelsoni* in having the under surface of the body pure white and, with the wing ranging from 251 to 263 mm., averages slightly smaller.

STERNA FUSCATA Linnaeus: Sooty Tern; Gaviotín de Dorso Negro

Medium size; black above, white below.

Description.—Length, 340 to 390 mm. Adult, line from gape to around eye and entire upper surface black; forehead, side of fore crown back above eye, and undersurface white, tinged faintly with gray on posterior area; outer rectrix white basally and on outer web; inner web black at tip.

Immature, in first plumage, above, including side of neck, wings, and tail sooty black; wing coverts, back, rump, and tail tipped with dull buff or white; under surface dusky gray; abdomen partly white; flanks and under tail coverts tipped with dull cinnamon-buff.

Iris dark brown; bill black; tarsus and toes dusky black.

This is a tern of worldwide range in tropical and subtropical seas that is little known in Panamá. Two races are recorded, one on the Pacific side of the Isthmus and one on the Atlantic.

STERNA FUSCATA FUSCATA Linnaeus

Sterna fuscata Linnaeus, Syst. Nat., ed. 12, vol. 1, 1766, p. 228. (Hispaniola.)

Characters.—More distinctly white on the lower surface, with the gray wash faint, and only on the abdomen and under tail coverts.

Measurements (from Murphy, l.c., p. 1123).—Males (from Bahamas, Fernando Noronha, Rocas, South Trinidad, and St. Helena), wing 285-310 (300), tail 162-177 (168.8), exposed culmen 42-47.6 (44.5), tarsus 22.1-25.2 (23.6) mm.

Females (from Bahamas, Fernando Noronha, South Trinidad, and St. Helena), wing 292-306 (297.1), tail 152-185.5 (171.3), exposed culmen 41.2-43 (42.3), tarsus 22-24 (23) mm.

Accidental in occurrence.

Inclusion of the typical race is based on two specimens that I have examined in the British Museum (Natural History), both well-marked examples of this subspecies. One was sent by Arcé to Salvin, who recorded it as from "Santiago de Veragua." As the locality is inland, and in the Pacific lowlands, the birds must have been a wanderer, perhaps storm-blown, as so often happens with these birds. The second was forwarded to Salvin by McLeannan and has no locality data other than "Panamá." Presumably it is from the Caribbean side since that is where this collector obtained nearly all of his birds.

All published records are based on these two skins. Griscom, and Hellmayr and Conover, recorded the Santiago bird under the name *crissalis* through the assumption that it would be the Pacific race because of the locality.

STERNA FUSCATA CRISSALIS (Lawrence)

Haliplana fuliginosa var. *crissalis* Lawrence, Proc. Boston Soc. Nat. Hist., vol. 14, 1871 (Apr. 1872), p. 285. (Isla Socorro, Islas Revilla Gigedo, México.)

Characters.—Similar to *Sterna f. fuscata,* but with underparts more strongly gray, a color that extends forward on the breast.

Measurements.—Males (five from Tres Marías, Socorro, and Panamá), wing 278-292 (287), tail 135-174 (150), exposed culmen 40.0-43.5 (41.5), tarsus 21.0-24.0 (22.6) mm.

Females (7 from Tres Marías, Galápagos, and Panamá), wing 271-298 (286), tail 124-174 (153), exposed culmen 41.0-43.5 (41.8), tarsus 21.0-23.0 (22.1) mm.

Breeds on Islas Frailes del Sur, off Punta Mala; ranges the adjacent waters of the Gulf of Panamá and the open sea.

My second visit to the rocky islets known as Los Frailes off Punta Mala was made on the launch Barbara II with Captain George Edgington. We came out of a rough overnight anchorage at Isla Iguana on the morning of March 18, 1962, with a strong wind blowing. As we approached Los Frailes del Sur I made out circling terns, and to my surprise as we came nearer these proved to be the sooty, instead of the bridled tern that I had expected, an identification easily evident since a number of the dark-plumaged immature individuals were on the wing flying among the adults. The birds circled swiftly in the strong wind, ranging out for some distance. On watching we noted that occasionally a group came to the lee of the rocky islets where the sea was a bit quieter, so that Captain Edgington circled in this area. Shooting was difficult because of the bucking of the launch in the rough water, while the force of the wind made the birds fly so wildly that only occasionally one came within 60 meters when a successful shot was due more to chance than to skill in marksmanship. I secured 3 adults and 1 juvenile in due course before the birds would no longer come near, so that we turned away to head through the rough sea for a sheltered anchorage at Playa Venado on the southern end of the Azuero Peninsula. It was my estimate that there were approximately 100 pairs of the terns around the larger of the two islets of the Frailes del Sur. Young birds, so far as I could tell, were all on the wing, and the 3 adults taken, two males and a female, were all past breeding. On the return journey from the Veraguas coast 12 days later we passed the Frailes before dawn so that I had no other opportunity for observations.

This is the only specimen record to date for this race of the sooty tern in Panamanian waters. Their breeding on Los Frailes apparently is not based on the 12-month cycle of the calendar year, since none were present when I visited these rocks at the end of February 1957.

Dennis R. Paulson, traveling on the yacht *Argosy*, A. Glassell owner, recorded one seen resting on a bit of driftwood off Isla Pedro González, September 7, 1961.

STERNA ALBIFRONS Pallas: Least Tern; Charrancito

Sterna albifrons Pallas, *in* Vroeg, Cat. Adumbr., 1764, p. 6. (Maasland, Netherlands.)

Smallest of the terns.

Description.—Length 210 to 230 mm. Adult, breeding dress, forehead, sides of crown back to level of eyes, and entire under surface white; a narrow line from lores around eye, crown, and upper hindneck black; rest of upper surface, including tail, light neutral gray; outer webs of outermost primaries slate black, with inner webs white.

Winter plumage, lores, forehead, and crown grayish white; a crescent mark around back of head, extended forward to eyes blackish. In breeding season bill yellow, usually tipped with black; tarsus and feet orange-yellow; in winter, bill blackish; legs and feet dull yellow.

Measurements (from Ridgway, l.c., p. 522).—Males, wing 163-178 (168.1), tail 70-93 (81.2), culmen 26-31 (28.8), tarsus 14-15.5 (14.5) mm.

Females, wing 160-167 (162.9), tail 61-85.5 (72.9), culmen 25.5-30 (27.5), tarsus 14-16 (14.7) mm.

Migrant from the north. Status uncertain.

The only report for this species is a sight record by Eugene Eisenmann, who saw 3 at Coco Solo, Canal Zone, on August 28, 1958, in company with larger terns.

Two races may be concerned in this species should it be found regularly in Panamá, the subspecies *antillarum,* paler gray above, of the eastern United States, and one darker gray, found in the western Mississippi Valley. The latter has been recognized as a distinct subspecies, *S. a. athalassos,* but its separation from the subspecies *browni* of California and southward is not certain.

THALASSEUS MAXIMUS MAXIMUS (Boddaert): Royal Tern; Gaviotín Real

Sterna maxima Boddaert, Table Planch. Enlum., 1783, pl. 58. (French Guiana.)

Largest of the terns found regularly in Panamá, larger than the laughing gull; with orange or yellow bill.

Description.—Length, 460 to 530 mm. Feathers on back of head elongated, pointed, forming a crest. Adult, in breeding dress with crown and crest deep black; otherwise as in nonbreeding plumage.

Nonbreeding plumage, forehead, lores, and forepart of crown white; rest of crown and space around eye streaked with black; crest sooty black; back and wings light gray; tail pale gray centrally, with lateral feathers darker; primaries in fresh plumage silvery gray on the surface of the outer web, black underneath, with the gray disappearing with wear to leave the feathers dull black.

Iris dark brown; bill orange to yellowish orange; tarsus and toes black.

Measurements (from Ridgway, l.c., p. 468).—Males, wing 360-382 (371), tail 147.5-192 (171.9), exposed culmen 59-68 (64.1), tarsus 29.5-34.5 (31.8) mm.

Females, wing 357-393 (374); tail 130-196.5 (167.5), exposed culmen 57.5-67 (62.7), tarsus 30-34.5 (32.6) mm.

Migrant from breeding grounds outside Panamanian waters. Common on both coasts, with individuals present throughout the year; found regularly over Gatun Lake.

The royal tern is known to breed on the Pacific coast from San Diego Bay and Baja California to Sonora and the Islas Tres Marías; in Atlantic waters along the shores of Texas and Louisiana, on Cayos Arcas in the Bahía de Campeche, and from Maryland to Georgia, the Bahamas, on scattered West Indian islands south to the Grenadines, on Curaçao and Bonaire, and at Islas Los Roques and Las Aves, Venezuela. Many range to Panamanian waters in the resting period of their life cycle, the majority found there having the light colored crown that indicates nonbreeding dress. While they seem most abundant in the period of Northern Hemisphere winter, the information available does not indicate a clearcut schedule of migratory movements, as they are fairly common at all seasons. It is possible that this is due to their arrival and departure in Panamá from both northern and tropical centers, where breeding comes at different periods of the year. They are found in greatest number along the Pacific coast and in the Chiriquí Lagoon.

Frequently royal terns are seen fishing over the open sea in small groups of 3 to 6 or so, and at other times they are found in flocks that rest on sand beaches. I have seen 20 together at La Honda on the coast of Los Santos in late March, 30 to 40 at Venado Beach, and 25 to 30 at the Río Chico in February. Many come to Isla Coiba where as many as 50 may congregate in Bahía Damas. Here frigatebirds sometimes pursued them, but the terns seemed to have little difficulty in avoiding these attacks. There are usually a number about the Pacific entrance of the Canal, and a few come regularly to Gatun Lake. At sea they often rest on floating logs or boards, and in the Chiriquí Lagoon it is common to see them perched on poles standing in shallow water.

There is much variation in size among them, some of the females being quite small.

THALASSEUS SANDVICENSIS ACUFLAVIDUS (Cabot):
Sandwich Tern; Gaviotín Patinegro

FIGURE 71

Sterna acuflavida Cabot, Proc. Boston Soc. Nat. Hist., vol. 2, 1847 (1848), p. 257. (Tancah, Quintana Roo, México.)

A crested tern of medium size, with slender black bill tipped with yellow.

Description.—Length, 320 to 355 mm. Adult, in nesting season with crown and crest black; at other times crest, nape, and narrow space around eye dull black; back of crown gray bordered with white; forehead, forecrown, lores, and lower hind neck white; rest of upper surface light gray; primaries in fresh plumage with outer webs silvery gray, which disappears with wear, leaving this area black; tail white to light gray centrally; tip gray to dark gray; under surface white.

Iris brown; bill black, with yellowish tip; tarsus and toes black.

Measurements (from Ridgway, l.c., pp. 476-477). —Males, wing 259-302 (278.2), tail 122-130 (126.2), exposed culmen 52-54.5 (53.3), tarsus 25-27 (26) mm.

Females, wing 270-294 (283.5), tail 99-121 (111.8), exposed culmen 49.5-53.0 (50.9), tarsus 25-26 (25.5) mm.

Fig. 71.—Head of Sandwich tern, gaviotín patinegro, *Thalasseus sandvicensis acuflavidus*.

Migrant from the north. Fairly common along the Pacific coast to the Gulf of Panamá; recorded from Permé, San Blas, on the Caribbean side; found occasionally over Gatun Lake.

This species is seen with fair regularity along the Pacific coast, mainly in the Gulf of Panamá. While most of the reports have been in the months of northern winter, some nonbreeding individuals may be found throughout the year. I shot one on June 11, 1953, opposite Isla Verde at the head of Golfo Montijo, and Imhof (Auk, 1950, p. 256) has recorded one July 31, 1942, on the coast of Coclé, below Río Hato.

My notes include records of 2 near Isla Cébaco, March 20 and 29, 1962. On March 16 and 17, 1958, at Riomar, on the coast near

San Carlos, in extreme west Panamá Province, 40 or more came along shore in late afternoon in pursuit of a school of minnows. I took 3 here. They appear at times at Farfan Beach and off the causeway near Fort Amador, in the Canal Zone, and also at Panamá Viejo. I have seen one over the wide arm of the Río Chagres opposite Gamboa, and there is record of one on Gatun Lake at Barro Colorado Island.

The only report for the Caribbean coast is of one taken by Wedel at Permé, San Blas, on November 30, 1929. Griscom in recording this (Bull. Mus. Comp. Zool., vol. 72, 1932, p. 322) wrote, "I am aware of only one previous capture . . . in Panama," a statement that I have been unable to verify.

ANOUS STOLIDUS (Linnaeus): Brown Noddy; Cervera
FIGURE 72

A tern of medium size, dusky brown throughout.

Description.—Length, 360 to 385 mm. Adult, plain grayish brown to sooty brown, somewhat lighter on under surface; nape paler, with

FIG. 72.—Brown noddy, cervera, *Anous stolidus*.

a gray wash on the back of the head that becomes progressively lighter over the crown to the forehead, which may be nearly white.

Immature, usually with less gray on the crown.

Iris dark brown; bill black; tarsi and toes fuscous; claws black.

These are terns of the oceans that nest on small islands and range over the open sea. Two of the recognized subspecies are recorded from Panamanian waters, where, however, they are little known.

ANOUS STOLIDUS STOLIDUS (Linnaeus)

Sterna stolida Linnaeus, Syst. Nat., ed. 10, vol. 1, 1758, p. 137. (West Indies.)

Characters.—General color lighter, and browner; crown paler gray, becoming definitely white on the forehead; average size slightly smaller.

Measurements (from Ridgway, l.c., p. 547).—Males, wing 261.5-273 (268.1), tail 139-148 (144), exposed culmen 41-44.5 (43.4), tarsus 23.5-25.5 (24.4) mm.

Females, wing 259-266 (263.3), tail 137.5-140 (138.2), exposed culmen 39.5-42 (40.5), tarsus 23-24.5 (23.6) mm.

The only records are of a male in the American Museum of Natural History, taken by R. R. Benson at Cocoplum, Bocas del Toro, November 2, 1927, and of an immature male in the Herbert Brandt Collection secured by Wedel at Puerto Obaldía, San Blas, August 10, 1934.

The nearest breeding colony that has been recorded is at Serrana Bank in the Caribbean northeast of Isla de San Andrés.

ANOUS STOLIDUS RIDGWAYI Anthony

Anous stolidus ridgwayi Anthony, Auk, vol. 15, no. 1, 1898, p. 36. (Isla Socorro, Islas Revilla Gigedo, México.)

Characters.—General color darker, with the crown darker gray; bill somewhat heavier through the gonydeal angle.

Measurements.—Males (4 from Cocos Island), wing 279-292 (286), tail 155-167 (163), exposed culmen 40.2-42.5 (41.3), tarsus 25.0-26.9 (25.8) mm.

Females (6 from Clipperton Island), wing 265-281 (270), tail 146-162 (154), exposed culmen 38-42 (39.6), tarsus 24-24.5 (24.1) mm.

Apparently breeds on Los Frailes. Status uncertain.

Mrs. Sturgis (Field Book Birds Panama Canal Zone, 1928, p. 105) has written that she saw many noddies flying off Isla Chepillo, in Panamá Bay, in March 1926. Fleming (Emu, vol. 49, Jan. 1950, p. 177) recorded a noddy in the Gulf of Panamá, resting on floating drift, on July 20, 1948. The only other report is from an interesting photograph, given to me by Harry L. Peck of Tonosí. This was made on May 6, 1949, by a party from the Gorgas Memorial Laboratory during a journey by launch to the southern end of the Province of Los Santos. The picture shows a swarm of terns leaving one end of the larger rock of Frailes del Norte south of Punta Mala. Though the birds were at a distance, there is no question that those near at hand are brown noddy terns. It is also evident that they seemed to be at a nesting ground. It appears, therefore, that in addition to the sooty terns that I found at Los Frailes del Sur, two other species, the bridled tern and the brown noddy, may come to breed on these two groups of rocks.

The records cited are placed under the name *ridgwayi* in accordance with current usage. No specimens from Panamanian waters are available, but those that I have examined from Cocos Island appear darker over the body and darker gray on the crown than our series from along the west coast of México that represent the typical population of *ridgwayi*. In fact, the few seen from Cocos in darker color show a definite approach to the race *galapagensis* that nests at the Galápagos. Birds from Clipperton Island to the north of Cocos also are somewhat different from the Mexican series.

Murphy (Nat. Hist., vol. 41, 1938, p. 177) has reported many brown noddies around Cabo Marzo and Octavia Rocks on the coast of Colombia, a short distance south of boundary with Panamá, and there is record of one taken at Isla de Malpelo, Colombia. In the collections of the British Museum (Natural History) I have examined a noddy of this group taken on June 13, 1925, by naturalists on the St. George Expedition at a point approximately 350 kilometers west of Isla de Malpelo.

Family RYNCHOPIDAE: Skimmers; Rayadores

The members of this family in general form of wings and body resemble large terns, but in detail differ widely. The bill, compressed laterally from base to tip to a knifelike form, has the lower mandible considerably longer than the upper. This curious development allows a peculiar habit of feeding in which the birds fly low with the breast barely above the water, the head slightly lowered, and the mouth opened wide so that the lower mandible cuts below the surface to pick up small fish and crustaceans. It is this habit that gives them the spanish name of *rayador,* varied sometimes to *arador,* or plowman, as they seem to draw lines over the surface. Another peculiarity is found in the eye, in which the pupillar opening, when contracted, forms a vertical slit, like that in the eye of a cat (see Wetmore, Proc. Biol. Soc. Washington, 1919, p. 195.) Three species are known, one in the Americas, another in tropical Africa, and the third in southeastern Asia.

RYNCHOPS NIGRA Linnaeus: Black Skimmer; Rayador
FIGURE 73

Like a large tern in form, with a laterally compressed, knifelike bill, in which the lower mandible is much longer than the upper.

Description.—Length, 410 to 460 mm. Adult, in breeding plumage, sooty black above; wing coverts somewhat browner; secondaries tipped narrowly with white; tail dark gray edged with white; forehead and lower surface white; under wing coverts pale gray.

Postbreeding adults and immature, browner above, with a white, or grayish white band on the hindneck.

FIG. 73.—Head of black skimmer, rayador, *Rynchops nigra*.

The black skimmer in the north is mainly a bird of ocean beaches and salt-water inlets, but in South America it also ranges widely along the larger rivers. As the few reports for Panamá come from both coasts, two geographic races probably are represented, though only one from the Caribbean side to date has been verified by a specimen.

RYNCHOPS NIGRA NIGRA Linnaeus

Rynchops nigra Linnaeus, Syst. Nat., ed. 10, vol. 1, 1758, p. 138. (Coast of South Carolina.)

Rynchops nigra oblita Griscom, Ibis, ser. 13, vol. 5, no. 3, July 1, 1935, p. 545. (Laguna Acapám, Pacific coast of Guatemala.)

Characters.—White edgings on secondaries broader; tail more extensively white; underwing coverts usually white, though in some tinged with gray; somewhat smaller.

Measurements.—Males, wing 364-401 (380), tail 112.0-128.1 (120.4), culmen 63.7-73.8 (69.5), tarsus 30.8-37.8 (34.8) mm.

Females, wing 331-362 (342), tail 102.6-112.8 (108.4), culmen 51.8-64.8 (56.4), tarsus 26.6-33.7 (30.1) mm.

Presumed to be migrant from the north. Casual in occurrence.

Griscom (Ibis, 1935, p. 545, and also in his check-list) gives a sight record for the Pacific coast of Veraguas, which must have been made in the early part of 1924 during a trip out from the Wilcox camp on the Río San Lorenzo, west of the entrance of the Golfo de Montijo. He refers also to "skimmers seen but not collected" by Arcé, a report that may have been a slip of the pen, as I have not found any authority for such a record.

In recent years nesting colonies of the black skimmer that have been found on the western coast of México, in Sonora, Sinaloa, and Nayarit, are the evident source of the birds reported in the nonbreeding season south to El Salvador. Griscom, on the basis of a small series of these northern migrants taken on the coast of Guatemala, described a race *oblita*. Recent studies indicate that the Pacific populations do not differ from those of the Atlantic area so that the proposed form is a synonym of typical *nigra*.

RYNCHOPS NIGRA CINERASCENS Spix

Rynchops cinerascens Spix, Avium Spec. Nov. Bras., pt. 2, 1825, p. 80, pl. 102. (Rio Amazonas, Brazil.)

Characters.—Differs from typical *nigra* in lesser extent of the white edgings on the ends of the secondaries; tail, in adult, with dark colors predominating, especially on the inner webs of the feathers; under wing coverts neutral gray in the adult, sometimes almost white in immature birds.

Measurements.—Males, wing 380-416 (392), tail 111.5-130.3 (113.7), culmen 75.0-87.7 (86.6), tarsus 32.2-38.5 (34.8) mm.

Females, wing 333-375 (353.7), tail 100.3-119.0 (108.8), culmen 59.4-66.8 (64.0), tarsus 28.4-31.5 (30.2) mm.

Casual in occurrence on the Caribbean coast.

A male in the American Museum of Natural History, taken by R. R. Benson at Cocoplum, Bocas del Toro, October 28, 1927, is a typical example of this race. Eugene Eisenmann has informed me that on June 28, 1952, in company with John Bull he saw two skimmers flying at Fort San Lorenzo on the mouth of the Río Chagres. These are the only records.

The subspecies *cinerascens* of northern South America is common on the larger rivers of northern Colombia including the Río Atrato. It is probable that these birds wander from time to time into Panamanian waters.

INDEX

(Spanish vernacular names are printed in *italics*.)

Abanico, 369
abbreviatus, Buteo albonotatus, 198
Accipiter bicolor bicolor, 174, 190
    ruficaudus, 215
    striatus velox, 174, 194
    superciliosus fontainier, 173, 192
    superciliosus superciliosus, 194
Accipitridae, 171, 172
Actitis macularia, 394, 402
    macularia macularia, 405
    macularia rava, 405
Actodromas Bairdii, 422
acuflavida, Sterna, 459
acuflavidus, Thalasseus sandvicensis, 440, 459
acuta, Anas, 130, 140
aequatorialis, Penelope purpurascens, 298, 302
aequinoctialis, Buteogallus, 230
affinis, Aythya, 130, 148
    Fuligula, 148
Agachadiza, 393, 413
Agachona gris piquicorta, 410
Agachona gris piquilarga, 413
agami, Agamia, 78, 95
    Ardea, 95
Agamia agami, 78, 95
Águila blanca y negra, 244
Águila crestuda negra, 240
Águila moñuda, 246
Águila de penacho, 241
Águila pescadora, 256
Águila solitaria, 238
Águilas, 171
Aguja moteada, 398
Ajaia ajaja, 122, 127
ajaja, Ajaia, 122, 127
    Platalea, 127
alba, Crocethia, 393, 416
    Scolopax, 125
(alba), Trynga, 416
Albatros cabecigris, 32
Albatros errante, 33
Albatros galapagüeño, 34
Albatroses, 31
Albatross, Galápagos, 32, 34
    Gray-headed, 32
    Wandering, 32, 33
Albatrosses, 31

albifrons, Sterna, 439, 457
albigularis, Corethrura, 353
    Laterallus, 339, 351
    Laterallus albigularis, 353
albonotatus, Buteo, 174, 197
    Buteo albonotatus, 198
albus, Eudocimus, 122, 125
Alcatraz, 51
alia, Rupornis magnirostris, 216
alius, Buteo magnirostris, 216
americana, Anas, 146
    Fulica americana, 339, 363
    Mareca, 129, 146
    Mycteria, 120
americanus, Daptrius americanus, 259, 276
    Falco, 276
Amaurolimnas concolor guatemalensis, 339
Ánade real, 139
Anas acuta, 130, 140
    americana, 146
    autumnalis, 132
    bicolor, 131
    clypeata, 145
    collaris, 150
    cyanoptera septentrionalium, 130, 144
    discors, 130, 141
    discors discors, 142
    discors orphna, 144
    dominica, 150
    moschata, 134
    platyrhynchos platyrhynchos, 130, 139
    viduata, 130
Anatidae, 129
anatum, Falco peregrinus, 260, 280
Anhinga, 69
Anhinga anhinga anhinga, 72
    anhinga leucogaster, 69
    anhinga minima, 72
Anhingidae, 69
Anous stolidus, 439, 461
    stolidus galapagensis, 463
    stolidus ridgwayi, 462
    stolidus stolidus, 462

Anseriformes, 129
antarcticus, Podiceps, 27
   Podilymbus podiceps, 27
anthracinus, Buteogallus, 174, 230, 231, 232
   Buteogallus anthracinus, 235
   Falco, 235
antillarum, Podilymbus podiceps, 26
Aphriza virgata, 394, 407
Aramidae, 334
Aramides axillaris, 339, 346
   cajanea, 339, 341
   cajanea cajanea, 344, 347
   cajanea latens, 345
   cajanea morrisoni, 345
Aramus guarauna, 335
   guarauna dolosus, 338
   guarauna guarauna, 337
   pictus dolosus, 338
aranea, Gelochelidon nilotica, 439, 449
   Sterna, 449
Ardea, 78
   Agami, 95
   caerulea, 91
   cayennensis, 102
   cocoi, 78, 81, 82
   crythromelas, 113
   Egretta, 88
   exilis, 113
   herodias, 78, 80
   herodias fannini, 82
   herodias herodias, 80, 82
   herodias lessonii, 81
   Hoactli, 99
   Ibis, 93
   lentiginosa, 112
   lineata, 106
   pileata, 97
   ralloides, 95
   striata, 86
   Thula, 89
   violacea, 101
   virescens, 84
Ardeidae, 78
Ardeola, 95
Arenaria interpres morinella, 394, 408
arguta, Rupornis magnirostris, 213
argutus, Buteo magnirostris, 213
Astur mirandollei, 264
Asturina nitida costaricensis, 201
   ruficauda, 215
athalassos, Sterna albifrons, 458
atratus, Coragyps, 154
   Coragyps atratus, 161

atricilla, Larus, 439, 442
audubonii, Caracara plancus, 273
   Polyborus, 273
aura, Cathartes, 154, 161
   Cathartes aura, 165
   Vultur, 165
australis, Rhynchortyx cinctus, 333
autumnalis, Anas, 132
   Dendrocygna autumnalis, 129, 132
Aves del trópico, 48
Avetoro pasajero, 112
Avocetas, 427
Avocets, 427
axillaris, Aramides, 339, 346
Aythya affinis, 130, 148
   collaris, 130, 150
azarae, Buteogallus urubitinga, 230

Bairdii, Actodromas, 422
bairdii, Erolia, 395, 422
balzarensis, Geranospiza caerulescens, 255
   Ischnosceles caerulescens, 253, 255
bancrofti, Nyctanassa violacea, 101
Bandurria común, 126
bangsi, Buteogallus anthracinus, 234, 235, 236
   Urubitinga anthracina, 236
Bartramia longicauda, 394, 395
beldingi, Charadrius wilsonia, 392
   Pagolla wilsonia, 392
Belonopterus chilensis, 382
   chilensis cayennensis, 383
bendirei, Falco columbarius, 290
bicolor, Accipiter bicolor, 174, 190
   Anas, 131
   Dendrocygna bicolor, 129, 131
   Sparvius, 190
bidentatus, Harpagus bidentatus, 184, 186
Bittern, American, 79, 112
   Least, 79, 113
blakei, Buteo nitidus, 174, 199
Boba blanca, 63
Boba borrega, 60
Bobas, 55
Bobwhite, 316
   Crested, 311
bonapartei, Nothocercus, 6
Boobies, 55
Booby, Blue-faced, 56, 60
   Blue-footed, 56, 61
   Brown, 56
   Red-footed, 55, 63

borealis, Buteo jamaicensis, 215
Botaurus lentiginosus, 79, 112
    pinnatus, 113
Bougainvillii, Carbo, 65
bougainvillii, Phalacrocorax, 65
brachypterus, Colymbus dominicus, 28
    Podiceps dominicus, 28, 31
brachyurus, Buteo, 174, 202
brasiliensis, Cathartes, 157
    Coragyps atratus, 157
brevirostre, Tigrisoma salmoni, 112
brewsteri, Egretta thula, 91
browni, Sterna albifrons, 458
brunneiventris, Tinamus major, 12
brunnescens, Penelope purpurascens, 302
Bubulcus, 95
    ibis ibis, 78, 92, 93
buffoni, Circus, 272, 273
Buitres Americanos, 153
bulleri, Diomedea, 33
burrovianus, Cathartes, 154
    Cathartes burrovianus, 168
Busarellus nigricollis nigricollis, 173, 227
Buteo albicaudatus hypospodius, 174, 195
    albonotatus, 174, 197
    albonotatus abbreviatus, 198
    albonotatus albonotatus, 198
    brachyurus, 174, 202
    Harrisi, 226
    jamaicensis, 174, 206
    jamaicensis borealis, 215
    jamaicensis calurus, 208
    jamaicensis costaricensis, 201, 206
    magnirostris, 174, 211
    magnirostris alius, 216
    magnirostris argutus, 213
    magnirostris griseocauda, 216
    magnirostris insidiatrix, 214, 215, 217
    magnirostris magniplumis, 216
    magnirostris petulans, 214, 215, 216
    melanoleucus, 244
    nitidus blakei, 174, 199
    platypterus platypterus, 174, 204
    swainsoni, 174, 208
Buteogallus aequinoctialis, 230
    anthracinus, 174, 230, 231, 232
    anthracinus anthracinus, 235
    anthracinus bangsi, 234, 235, 236
    anthracinus rhizophorae, 237

Buteogallus anthracinus subtilis, 237
    gundlachii, 231, 234
    urubitinga, 173, 229
    urubitinga azarae, 230
    urubitinga ridgwayi, 231
    urubitinga urubitinga, 232
Butorides striatus, 79, 84
    striatus patens, 86, 87, 88
    striatus robinsoni, 88
    striatus striatus, 86
    virescens, 79, 83
    virescens maculatus, 85, 86, 88
    virescens margaritophilus, 86
    virescens virescens, 84
Buzo, 25

Cacao, 276
cachinnans, Falco, 260
    Gallinula chloropus, 358
    Herpetotheres, 259
    Herpetotheres cachinnans, 260
caerulea, Ardea, 91
    Florida, 79, 91
caerulescens, Ischnosceles, 173, 253
    Ischnosceles caerulescens, 254
    Sparvius, 253
Cairina moschata, 129, 134
cajanea, Aramides, 339, 341
    Aramides cajanea, 334, 347
    Fulica, 344
Calidris canutus rufa, 394, 415
californicus, Podiceps caspicus, 31
caliginis, Nyctanassa violacea, 101, 103
calurus, Buteo jamaicensis, 208
Camanáy, 61
cancrivora, Urubitinga anthracina, 235
Cancroma Cochlearia, 116
    maculata, 85
Capella, 415
    gallinago delicata, 413
capnodes, Crypturellus soui, 21
Caracara, 259, 271
Caracara plancus, 259, 271
    plancus audubonii, 273
    plancus cheriway, 273
    Red-throated, 259, 276
    Yellow-headed, 259, 274
Caracaras, 259
Carancho, 259, 271
Carbo Bougainvillii, 65
Carnifex naso, 266
carolina, Porzana, 339, 350
carolinensis, Falco Haliaëtos, 256
    Pandion haliaetus, 256
    Pelecanus occidentalis, 51

carolinus, Rallus, 350
Carrao, 334, 335
Carrasqueadora, 351
Casmerodius albus egretta, 78, 88
caspia, Hydroprogne, 440, 451
    Sterna, 451
castaneiceps, Tinamus major, 10
castigatus, Odontophorus gujanensis, 321
castro, Oceanodroma, 43
Catharacta skua, 433
    skua chilensis, 435
Cathartes aura, 154, 161
    aura aura, 165
    aura meridionalis, 165
    aura ruficollis, 161, 166
    aura teter, 165
    brasiliensis, 157
    burrovianus, 154
    burrovianus burrovianus, 168
    burrovianus urubitinga, 171
Cathartidae, 153, 154
Catoptrophorus semipalmatus inornatus, 393, 406
    semipalmatus semipalmatus, 407
caudatus, Scolopax, 126
    Theristicus caudatus, 122, 126
cayanensis, Falco, 186
    Leptodon cayanensis, 172, 186
cayannensis, Parra, 383
cayennensis, Ardea, 102
    Belonopterus chilensis, 383
    Mesembrinibis, 122
    Nyctanassa violacea, 102
    Tantalus, 122
centralis, Gallinula chloropus, 358, 359
Centropelma micropterum, 24
cerceris, Gallinula chloropus, 359
Cerceta ala-azul, 141
Cerceta colorado, 144
Cernícalo, 291
Cervera, 461
Chachalaca, Gray-headed, 293, 305
Chamaepetes unicolor, 293, 303
chapmani, Herpetotheres cachinnans, 263
    Odontophorus guianensis, 319
Charadriidae, 382
Charadriiformes, 372
Charadrius collaris, 383, 387
    Dominicus, 385
    Mexicanus, 428
    semipalmatus, 383, 386
    vociferus, 383

Charadrius vociferus vociferus, 390
    wilsonia, 383, 391
    wilsonia beldingi, 392
    wilsonia wilsonia, 391
Charrancito, 457
cheriway, Caracara plancus, 273
    Falco, 273
Chicuaco, 86
chihi, Plegadis, 124
chilensis, Belonopterus, 382
    Catharacta skua, 435
    Parra, 384
chimachima, Milvago chimachima, 276
Chimango, 274
Chlidonias niger surinamensis, 439, 448
Chloropus, Fulica, 357
chloropus, Gallinula, 339, 357
chlororhynchus, Puffinus pacificus, 42
chocoensis, Ortalis cinereiceps, 306, 307
Chondrohierax uncinatus uncinatus, 172, 188
Chorlitejo semipalmeado, 386
Chorlito canelo, 426
Chorlito de rompiente, 407
Chorlito dorado, 385
Chorlito gris, 384
Chorlito gritón, 390
Chorlito patilargo, 425
Chorlito piquigordo, 391
Chorlitos, 382
chrysostoma, Diomedea, 32
Ciconia mycteria, 120
Ciconiidae, 119, 120
Ciconiiformes, 78
Cigüeñas, 119
Cigüeñuelas, 427
cinctus, Odontophorus, 330
    Rhynchortyx, 311
    Rhynchortyx cinctus, 330
cinerascens, Rynchops nigra, 465
cinereiceps, Laterallus albigularis, 354
    Ortalida, 307
    Ortalis, 293, 304, 305
    Ortalis cinereiceps, 306, 307
    Porzana, 354
cinnamomea, Tringa solitaria, 402
cinnamomeus, Totanus solitarius, 402
Circaëtus solitarius, 238
Circus buffoni, 272, 273
    cyaneus hudsonius, 173, 251
clypeata, Anas, 145
    Spatula, 129, 145
Cocaleca cabecicastaña, 346

Cocaleca gris, 341
Cocalecas, 338
Cocalequita enana, 348
Cocalequita pasajera, 350
Cocalequita pechiceniza, 355
Cocalequita pintada, 364
Cochlearia, Cancroma, 116
Cochleariidae, 114
Cochlearius cochlearius, 115
　cochlearius cochlearius, 116
　cochlearius panamensis, 115, 117, 118
　cochlearius zeledoni, 115
　zeledoni panamensis, 118
Coco blanco, 125
cocoi, Ardea, 78, 81, 82
Cocolino, 229
Cocos, 122
Codornices, 310
Codorniz, 311
Codorniz norteña, 316
colchicus, Phasianus, 333
Colinus cristatus, 311
　cristatus leucotis, 313
　cristatus mariae, 315
　cristatus panamensis, 314
　cristatus sonnini, 313
　leucopogon, 313
　leucotis panamensis, 314
　virginianus, 316
collaris, Anas, 150
　Aythya, 130, 150
　Charadrius, 383, 387
coloratus, Odontophorus melanotis, 325, 326
columbarius, Falco, 260, 288
　Falco columbarius, 289
Colymbus dominicus brachypterus, 28
　fulica, 366
　podiceps, 27
Coot, American, 339, 363
Coots, 338
Coragyps atratus, 154
　atratus atratus, 161
　atratus brasiliensis, 157
cordatus, Milvago chimachima, 259, 274
Corethrura albigularis, 353
Corethrura Gautemalensis, 339
Cormorant, Olivaceous, 65
　Peruvian, 65
Cormorants, 64
Corocoro, 122
coronatus, Harpyhaliaetus, 239
Correlimos común, 424

Correlona, 395
costaricensis, Asturina nitida, 201
　Buteo jamaicensis, 201, 206
　Leucopternis albicollis, 173, 217
　Leucopternis ghiesbreghti, 217
Cracidae, 293
Crake, Uniform, 339
Crax rubra, 293
　rubra griscomi, 298
　rubra rubra, 293
Creagrus furcatus, 439, 446
crissalis, Haliplana fuliginosa, 456
　Sterna fuscata, 456
cristatus, Colinus, 311
　Tetrao, 311
Crocethia alba, 393, 416
Crypturellus soui, 6, 17
　soui capnodes, 21
　soui modestus, 17, 20, 23
　soui panamensis, 17, 18, 20, 21, 22
　soui poliocephalus, 17, 18, 22, 24
Crypturus modestus, 20
　soui harterti, 22, 23, 24
　soui panamensis, 22
Crypturornis soui poliocephalus, 22
crythromelas, Ardea, 113
Cuervo de aguja, 69
Cuervo marino, 64, 65
Cuiscui, 211
Curassow, Central American, 293
Curassows, 293

dabbenena, Diomedea exulans, 34
dactylatra, Sula, 56, 60
　Sula dactylatra, 60
Danzarina, 43
Daptrius americanus americanus 259, 276
　americanus guatemalensis, 279
deiroleucus, Falco, 260, 281
delawarensis, Larus, 439, 441
delicata, Capella gallinago, 413
　Scolopax, 413
Dendrocygna autumnalis autumnalis, 129, 132
　autumnalis fulgens, 134
　bicolor bicolor, 121, 131
　viduata, 129, 130
dialeucos, Odontophorus, 311, 327
diodon, Harpagus, 186
Diomedea bulleri, 33
　cauta salvini, 33
　chrysostoma, 32
　exulans, 32, 33
　exulans dabbenena, 34

Diomedea irrorata, 32, 34
Diomedeidae, 31, 32
discors, Anas, 130, 141
    Anas discors, 142
dolosus, Aramus guarauna, 338
    Aramus pictus, 338
dominica, Anas, 150
    Oxyura, 130, 150
    Pluvialis dominica, 382, 385
Dominicus, Charadrius, 385
dominicus, Podiceps, 25
    Podiceps dominicus, 31
Dowitcher, Long-billed, 394, 413
    Short-billed, 394, 410
Duck, American comb, 129, 137
    Black-bellied tree, 129, 132
    Fulvous tree, 129, 131
    Masked, 130, 150
    Muscovy, 129, 134
    Ring-necked, 130, 150
    White-faced tree, 129, 130
Ducks, 129
Dunlin, 394, 424
durnfordi, Haematopus palliatus, 381

Eagle, Crested, 172, 246
    Harpy, 172, 249
    Solitary, 173, 238
Eagles, 171
Egret, Cattle, 78, 93
    Common, 78, 88
    Snowy, 78, 89
Egretta, 91
    ruficollis, 92
    thula brewsteri, 91
    thula thula, 78, 89
Egretta, Ardea, 88
egretta, Casmerodius albus, 78, 88
Elanoides forficatus, 172
    forficatus forficatus, 176
    forficatus yetapa, 175
Ereunetes mauri, 395, 418, 419
    pusillus, 395, 417
Erolia alpina pacifica, 394, 424
    bairdii, 395, 422
    fuscicollis, 394, 421
    melanotos, 395, 423
    minutilla, 395, 420
erythromelas, Ixobrychus exilis, 113
erythrorhynchos, Pelecanus, 51
etesiaca, Sula leucogaster, 58
Eudocimus albus, 122, 125
Eurypyga helias helias, 371
    helias major, 369
Eurypygidae, 369

excisa, Sula nebouxii, 63
    Ardea, 113
    Ixobrychus, 79, 113
    Ixobrychus exilis, 113, 114
    Laterallus, 339, 355
    Rallus, 355
extimus, Micrastur mirandollei, 264, 265
exulans, Diomedea, 32, 33

Faisán común, 333
Faisana, 293, 305
Faisanes, 310
Falaropos, 429
falcinellus, Plegadis falcinellus, 122, 124
Falcinellus, Tantalus, 124
Falco americanus, 276
    anthracinus, 235
    cachinnans, 260
    cayanensis, 186
    cheriway, 273
    columbarius, 260, 288
    columbarius bendirei, 290
    columbarius columbarius, 289
    deiroleucus, 260, 281
    femoralis femoralis, 260, 287
    femoralis septentrionalis, 288
    guianensis, 246
    Haliaëtos carolinensis, 256
    hamatus, 182
    hudsonius, 251
    jamaicensis, 206
    magnirostris, 211
    meridionalis, 223
    nigricollis, 227
    peregrinus, 283
    peregrinus anatum, 260, 280
    Plancus, 271
    plumbeus, 177
    rufigularis petoensis, 260, 283
    rufigularis rufigularis, 286
    sparverius sparverius, 260, 291
    uncinatus, 188
    Urubitinga, 232
    velox, 194
Falcon, Aplomado, 260, 287
    Bat, 260, 283
    Laughing, 259, 260
    Orange-breasted, 260, 281
    Peregrine, 260, 280
Falconidae, 259
Falconiformes, 153
Falcons, 259
fannini, Ardea herodias, 82

fasciatus, Harpagus bidentatus, 172, 184
fedoa, Limosa, 393, 398
Fedoa, Scolopax, 398
femoralis, Falco femoralis, 260, 287
Finfoot, American, 366
Finfoots, 365
flavipes, Scolopax, 399
  Totanus, 394, 399
flaviventer, Porzana flaviventer, 339, 348
  Rallus, 348
Florida caerulea, 79, 91
fontainier, Accipiter superciliosus, 173, 192
Forest-falcon, Barred, 259, 268
  Collared, 259, 266
  Slaty-backed, 259, 264
Forest-falcons, 259
forficatus, Elanoides, 172
  Elanoides forficatus, 176
frantzii, Nothocercus bonapartei, 14
  Ortalida, 308
  Ortalis cinereiceps, 307, 308
  Tinamus, 14
frazari, Haematopus palliatus, 381, 382
Fregata magnificens, 73
  magnificens lowei, 77
  magnificens rothschildi, 77
  minor palmerstoni, 77
  minor ridgwayi, 77
Fregatidae, 72
Frigatebird, Magnificent, 73
Frigatebirds, 72
fulgens, Dendrocygna autumnalis, 134
fulica, Colymbus, 366
  Heliornis, 366
Fulica americana americana, 339, 363
  cajanea, 344
  Chloropus, 357
  martinica, 360
  spinosa, 372
Fulicaria, Tringa, 430
fulicarius, Phalaropus, 430
Fuligula affinis, 148
furcatus, Creagrus, 439, 446
  Larus, 446
fuscata, Sterna, 440, 455
  Sterna fuscata, 455
fuscicollis, Erolia, 394, 421
  Tringa, 421
fuscipennis, Tinamus major, 6, 10, 12

Gabán, 120

galapagensis, Anous stolidus, 463
  Haematopus palliatus, 382
galapagoensis, Oceanites gracilis, 45
galeata, Numida meleagris, 334
Galliformes, 293
Gallina de Guinea, 333, 334
Gallinago, 415
Gallinago, Scolopax, 415
Gallinazo, 157
Gallineta cenicienta, 363
Gallineta de agua, 338, 357
Gallinula chloropus, 339, 357
  chloropus cachinnans, 358
  chloropus centralis, 358, 359
  chloropus cerceris, 359
  chloropus pauxilla, 359
Gallinule, Common, 339, 357
  Purple, 339, 360
Gallinules, 338
Gallito de agua barbudo, 376
Gallito de agua castaño, 372
Gallito del monte fajeado, 327
Gallito del monte jaspeado, 311, 316
Gallito del monte menor, 330
Gallito del monte pechicastaño, 325
Gallito del monte pechinegro, 328
Gallito del monte pintado, 322
Gallitos de agua, 372
Gannets, 55
Garceta azul, 91
Garceta blanca, 89, 91
Garcilla bueyera, 93
garrula, Ortalis, 306, 307
Garza blanca, 88
Garza enana, 113
Garza paleta, 122, 127
Garza pechiblanca, 92
Garza pechicastaña, 95
Garza real, 97
Garza tigre oscura, 109
Garza tigre rayada, 106
Garzas, 78
Garzón cenizo, 80
Garzón moreno, 82
Garzón soldado, 120
Garzota cuchara, 114, 115
Gautemalensis, Corethrura, 339
Gavilán acanelado, 223
Gavilán andapié, 226
Gavilán azul, 221
Gavilán bidente, 184
Gavilán blanco, 217
Gavilán cabecigris, 186
Gavilán cangrejero, 232
Gavilán caracolero, 180

Gavilán cenizo, 220
Gavilán cola corta, 202
Gavilán de ciénaga, 227
Gavilán de paso, 204
Gavilán gris, 199
Gavilán negro, 197
Gavilán pantalón, 190
Gavilán piquidelgado, 182
Gavilán piquiganchudo, 188
Gavilán plomizo, 177
Gavilán rayado, 222
Gavilán sabanero, 251
Gavilán tejé, 195
Gavilán tijereta, 175
Gavilancito de paso, 194
Gavilancito enano, 192
Gavilanes, 171
Gaviota argentea, 441
Gaviota de Franklin, 445
Gaviota de pico anillado, 441
Gaviota de Sabine, 447
Gaviota garuma, 440
Gaviota rabihorcado, 446
Gaviota reidora, 442
Gaviotas, 438
Gaviotas salteadoras, 433
Gaviotín común, 452
Gaviotín de dorso negro, 455
Gaviotín negro, 448
Gaviotín patinegro, 459
Gaviotín piquigordo, 449
Gaviotín piquirojo, 451
Gaviotín real, 458
Gaviotina monja, 454
Gaviotines, 438
Gelochelidon nilotica aranea, 439, 449
  nilotica vanrossemi, 450
Geranospiza, 253
  caerulescens balzarensis, 255
Godwit, Marbled, 393, 398
Golondrina de mar chica, 45
Golondrina de mar menuda, 45
Golondrina de mar negra, 47
gracilis, Oceanites, 43, 45
  Thalassidroma, 45
granti, Sula dactylatra, 61
Grebe, Least, 25, 28
  Pied-billed, 25
Grebes, 24
griscomi, Crax rubra, 298
grisea, Procellaria, 36
griseocauda, Buteo magnirostris, 216
griseus, Limnodromus, 394, 410
  Limnodromus griseus, 411
  Puffinus, 35, 36

griseus, Scolopax, 411
Gruiformes, 334
Guala, 168
Guan, Black, 293, 303
  Crested, 293, 298
Guanáy, 65
Guans, 293
Guaraguao, 206
guarauna, Aramus, 335
  Aramus guarauna, 337
  Scolopax, 337
guatemalensis, Amaurolimnas concolor, 339
  Daptrius americanus, 279
guerilla, Micrastur ruficollis, 270
guianensis, Falco, 246
  Morphnus, 172, 246
Güichichí, 132
Guineafowl, 333
Guinea-hen, 334
Guiño, 253
gujanensis, Odontophorus, 311, 316
  Tetrao, 316
Gull, Franklin's, 439, 445
  Gray, 439, 440
  Herring, 439, 441
  Laughing, 439, 442
  Ring-billed, 439, 441
  Sabine's, 439, 447
  Swallow-tailed, 439, 446
Gulls, 438
gundlachii, Buteogallus, 231, 234
guttata, Ortyx, 322
guttatus, Odontophorus, 311, 322

Haematopodidae, 378
Haematopus ostralegus, 381
  palliatus, 381
  palliatus durnfordi, 381
  palliatus frazari, 381, 382
  palliatus galapagensis, 382
  palliatus pitanay, 379
  palliatus prattii, 381
Halcón Azulado, 287
Halcón cazamurciélagos, 283
Halcón de paso, 288
Halcón del monte Collarejo, 266
Halcón del monte rayado, 268
Halcón gateador, 264
Halcón pechicastaño, 281
Halcón peregrino, 280
Halcones, 259
Halcones del monte, 259
Haliplana fuliginosa crissalis, 456
Halocyptena microsoma, 42, 43, 45

hamatus, Falco, 182
  Helicolestes, 172, 182
Harpagus bidentatus bidentatus, 184, 186
  bidentatus fasciatus, 172, 184
  diodon, 186
Harpía, 249
Harpia harpyja, 172, 249
Harpyhaliaetus, 239
  coronatus, 239
  coronatus solitarius, 239
harpyja, Harpia, 172, 249
  Vultur, 249
Harrisi, Buteo, 226
harrisi, Parabuteo unicinctus, 173, 226
harterti, Crypturus soui, 22, 23, 24
Hawk, Barred, 173, 222
  Bicolored, 174, 190
  Black-collared, 173, 227
  Broad-winged, 174, 204
  Crane, 173, 253
  Gray, 174, 199
  Greater Black, 173, 229
  Harris's, 173, 226
  Large-billed, 174, 211
  Lesser Black, 174, 232
  Marsh, 173, 251
  Pigeon, 260, 288
  Plumbeous, 173, 221
  Red-tailed, 174, 206
  Savanna, 173, 223
  Semiplumbeous, 173, 220
  Sharp-shinned, 174, 194
  Short-tailed, 174, 202
  Sparrow, 260, 291
  Swainson's, 174, 208
  Tiny, 173, 192
  White, 173, 217
  White-tailed, 174, 195
  Zone-tailed, 174, 197
Hawk eagle, Barred, 173, 241
  Black, 173, 240
  Black-and-white, 172, 244
Hawks, 171
heermanni, Larus, 440
helias, Eurypyga helias, 371
Helicolestes hamatus, 172, 182
Heliornis fulica, 366
Heliornithidae, 365
hendersoni, Limnodromus griseus, 412
herodias, Ardea, 78, 80
  Ardea herodias, 80, 82
Heron, Agamí, 78, 95
  Black-crowned night, 79, 99
  Boat-billed, 114, 115

Heron, Capped, 78, 97
  Cocoi, 78, 82
  Great Blue, 78, 80
  Green, 79, 83
  Little Blue, 79, 91
  Striated, 79, 86
  Tricolored, 79, 92
  Yellow-crowned night, 79, 100
Herons, 78
Herpetotheres cachinnans, 259
  cachinnans cachinnans, 260
  cachinnans chapmani, 263
  cachinnans queribundus, 263
  sociabilis, 180
Heterocnus mexicanus, 79, 103, 106
Heterospizias meridionalis meridionalis, 173, 223
  meridionalis rufulus, 225
himantopus, Micropalama, 394, 425
  Tringa, 425
Himantopus mexicanus, 428
hirundo, Sterna hirundo, 439, 452
Hoactli, Ardea, 99
hoactli, Nycticorax nycticorax, 79, 99
hudsonicus, Numenius phaeopus, 393, 396
hudsonius, Circus cyaneus, 173, 251
  Falco, 251
Huraña, 100
Hydranassa tricolor ruficollis, 79, 92
Hydrobatidae, 42, 43
Hydroprogne caspia, 440, 451
hyperorius, Theristicus caudatus, 127
hypomelaena, Jacana jacana, 375, 376
  Parra, 376
Hypomorphnus, 230
hypopius, Rhynchortyx cinctus, 330, 333
hypospodius, Buteo albicaudatus, 174, 195

Ibis, Ardea, 93
ibis, Bubulcus ibis, 78, 92, 93
Ibis, Cayenne, 122
  Glossy, 122, 124
  White, 122, 125
  White-throated, 122, 126
  Wood, 120
Ibises, 122
Ictinia misisippiensis, 179
  plumbea, 172, 177
inornata, Symphemia semipalmata, 406
inornatus, Catoptrophorus semipalmatus, 393, 406

insidiatrix, Buteo magnirostris, 214, 215, 217
Rupornis magnirostris, 215
intercedens, Nothocercus bonapartei, 15
interstes, Micrastur ruficollis, 259, 268
Irol, 208
irrorata, Diomedea, 32, 34
Ischnosceles caerulescens, 173, 253
    caerulescens balzarensis, 253, 255
    caerulescens caerulescens, 254
    caerulescens livens, 254
    caerulescens niger, 253, 255
Ixobrychus exilis, 79, 113
    exilis erythromelas, 113
    exilis exilis, 113, 114

Jabiru, 120
Jabiru mycteria, 120
Jacamillo, 130
Jaçana, Northern, 372
    Wattled, 376
Jacana jacana hypomelaena, 375, 376
    spinosa lowei, 374
    spinosa spinosa, 372
Jaçanas, 372
Jacanidae, 372
Jaeger, Long-tailed, 433, 437
    Parasitic, 433, 436
    Pomarine, 433, 435
Jaegers, 433
jamaicensis, Buteo, 174, 206
    Falco, 206
    Laterallus, 365
    Oxyura, 152
    Rallus, 365
Jorrálico, 103

kelsalli, Oceanodroma tethys, 44
    Thalassidroma tethys, 44
Killdeer, 383, 390
Kite, Cayenne, 172, 186
    Double-toothed, 172, 184
    Everglade, 172, 180
    Hook-billed, 172, 188
    Plumbeous, 172, 177
    Slender-billed, 172, 182
    Swallow-tailed, 172, 175
Knot, 394, 415

Lapwing, Southern, 382, 383
Laridae, 438, 439
Larus argentatus smithsonianus, 439, 441
    atricilla, 439, 442

Larus delawarensis, 439, 441
    furcatus, 446
    heermanni, 440
    modestus, 439, 440
    parasiticus, 436
    pipixcan, 439, 445
    sabini, 447
latens, Aramides cajanea, 345
Laterallus albigularis, 339, 351
    albigularis albigularis, 353
    albigularis cinereiceps, 354
    exilis, 339, 355
    jamaicensis, 365
    melanophaius, 352
lentiginosa, Ardea, 112
lentiginosus, Botaurus, 79, 112
Leptodon cayanensis cayanensis, 172, 186
    cayanensis monachus, 188
lepturus, Phaethon, 51
lessonii, Ardea herodias, 81
Lestris pomarinus, 435
leucogaster, Anhinga anhinga, 69
    Pelecanus, 58
    Plotus, 69
    Sula, 56
    Sula leucogaster, 58
leucolaemus, Odontophorus, 311, 328
Leucophoyx, 91
leucopogon, Colinus, 313
Leucopternis albicollis costaricensis, 173, 217
    ghiesbreghti costaricensis, 217
    plumbea, 173, 221
    princeps, 173, 222
    princeps zimmeri, 222, 223
    schistacea, 237
    semiplumbea, 173, 220, 222
leucotis, Colinus cristatus, 313
lherminieri, Puffinus, 35, 37
    Puffinus lherminieri, 37
Limnodromus griseus, 394, 410
    griseus griseus, 411
    griseus hendersoni, 412
    scolopaceus, 394, 413
Limosa fedoa, 393, 398
    scolopacea, 413
Limpkin, 334, 335
lineata, Ardea, 106
lineatum, Tigrisoma lineatum, 79, 106, 109, 112
livens, Ischnosceles caerulescens, 254
lobata, Tringa, 432
lobatus, Lobipes, 430, 432
Lobipes lobatus, 430, 432

longicauda, Bartramia, 394, 395
  Tringa, 395
longicaudus, Stercorarius, 433, 437
Loomelania melania, 42, 43, 47
lowei, Fregata magnificens, 77
  Jacana spinosa, 374
loyemilleri, Puffinus lherminieri, 38

macularia, Actitis, 394, 402
  Actitis macularia, 405
  Tringa, 405
maculata, Cancroma, 85
maculatus, Butorides virescens, 85, 86, 88
  Pardirallus, 364
  Rallus, 364
magnificens, Fregata, 73
magniplumis, Buteo magnirostris, 216
magnirostris, Buteo, 174, 211
  Falco, 211
major, Eurypyga helias, 369
  Tetrao, 6
  Tinamus, 6, 15
Mallard, 130, 139
Mareca americana, 129, 146
margaritophilus, Butorides virescens, 86
mariae, Colinus cristatus, 315
markhami, Oceanodroma, 48
marmoratum, Tigrisoma lineatum, 108
marmoratus, Odontophorus gujanensis, 319, 327
  Ortyx, 319
Martinete, 83
martinica, Fulica, 360
  Porphyrula, 339, 360
mauri, Ereunetes, 395, 418, 419
maxima, Sterna, 458
maximus, Thalasseus maximus, 440, 458
melania, Loomelania, 42, 43, 47
  Procellaria, 47
melanoleucus, Buteo, 244
  Scolopax, 400
  Spizastur, 172, 244
  Totanus, 393, 400
melanophaius, Laterallus, 352
melanotis, Odontophorus erythrops, 311, 323, 325
melanotos, Erolia, 395, 423
  Tringa, 423
meridionalis, Cathartes aura, 165
  Falco, 223
  Heterospizias meridionalis, 173, 223

Mesembrinibis cayennensis, 122
mesonauta, Phaethon aethereus, 49
Mexicanus, Charadrius, 428
mexicanus, Heterocnus, 79, 103, 106
  Himantopus, 428
  Tigrisoma, 103
Micrastur mirandollei, 259, 264
  mirandollei extimus, 264, 265
  ruficollis guerilla, 270
  ruficollis interstes, 259, 268
  semitorquatus, 263
  semitorquatus naso, 259, 266
  semitorquatus semitorquatus, 268
Micropalama himantopus, 394, 425
micropterum, Centropelma, 24
microsoma, Halocyptena, 42, 43, 45
Milvago chimachima chimachima, 276
  chimachima cordatus, 259, 274
Milvus yetapa, 175
minima, Anhinga anhinga, 72
minutilla, Erolia, 395, 420
  Tringa, 420
mira, Ortalis cinereiceps, 306, 309
  Ortalis garrula, 309
mirandollei, Astur, 264
  Micrastur, 259, 264
misisippiensis, Ictinia, 179
modestus, Crypturellus soui, 17, 20, 23
  Crypturus, 20
  Larus, 439, 440
monachus, Leptodon cayanensis, 188
  Sparvius, 188
morinella, Arenaria morinella, 394, 408
Morinella, Tringa, 408
Morito, 124
Morphnus guianensis, 172, 246
  taeniatus, 248
morrisoni, Aramides cajanea, 345
moschata, Anas, 134
  Cairina, 129, 134
murphyi, Pelecanus occidentalis, 55
mycteria, Ciconia, 120
  Jabiru, 120
Mycteria americana, 120

naso, Carnifex, 266
  Micrastur semitorquatus, 259, 266
nebouxii, Sula, 56
  Sula nebouxii, 60, 61
nelsoni, Sterna anaethetus, 440, 454
niger, Ischnosceles caerulescens, 253, 255
nigra, Rynchops, 464
  Rynchops nigra, 464

nigricollis, Busarellus nigricollis, 173, 227
Falco, 227
Noddy, Brown, 439, 461
Noneca, 161
Nothocercus bonapartei, 6
    bonapartei frantzii, 14
    bonapartei intercedens, 15
Numida meleagris galeata, 334
Numididae, 333
Numenius phaeopus hudsonicus, 393, 396
Nyctanassa violacea, 79, 100
    violacea bancrofti, 101
    violacea caliginis, 101, 103
    violacea cayennensis, 102
    violacea violacea, 101
Nycticorax nycticorax hoactli, 79, 99

oblita, Rynchops nigra, 464, 465
Oceanites gracilis, 43, 45
    gracilis galapagoensis, 45
Oceanodroma castro, 43
    markhami, 48
    tethys, 42, 43
    tethys kelsalli, 44
    tethys tethys, 44
Odontophorus cinctus, 330
    dialeucos, 311, 327
    erythrops melanotis, 311, 323, 325
    guianensis chapmani, 319
    guianensis panamensis, 319
    gujanensis, 311, 316
    gujanensis castigatus, 321
    gujanensis marmoratus, 319, 327
    guttatus, 311, 322
    leucolaemus, 311, 328
    melanotis coloratus, 325, 326
    rubigenis, 330, 333
    smithians, 328
    smithianus, 328, 329
    spodiostethus, 330
    strophium, 328
    Veraguanensis, 322
    veraguensis, 322, 323
Oestrelata phaeopygia, 35
olivacea, Ortalis garrula, 307
olivaceus, Pelecanus, 65
    Phalacrocorax olivaceus, 65
ornatus, Spizaetus ornatus, 244
orphna, Anas discors, 144
Ortalida cinereiceps, 307
    Frantzii, 308
Ortalis cinereiceps, 293, 304, 305
    cinereiceps chocoensis, 306, 307

Ortalis cinereiceps cinereiceps, 306, 307
    cinereiceps frantzii, 307, 308
    cinereiceps mira, 306, 309
    garrula, 306, 307
    garrula mira, 309
    garrula olivacea, 307
    ruficrissa, 306
    struthopus, 307
    vetula, 306
Ortyx guttata, 322
    marmoratus, 319
Osprey, 256
ostralegus, Haematopus, 381
Ostrero blanco, 379
Ostreros, 378
Oxyura dominica, 130, 150
    jamaicensis, 152
Oystercatcher, American, 379
Oystercatchers, 378

pacifica, Erolia alpina, 394, 424
Pacifica, Pelidna, 424
pacificus, Puffinus, 35
Pagolla wilsonia beldingi, 392
Painos, 42
palliatus, Haematopus, 381
palmerstoni, Fregata minor, 77
panamensis, Cochlearius cochlearius 115, 117, 118
    Cochlearius zeledoni, 118
    Colinus cristatus, 314
    Colinus leucotis, 314
    Crypturellus soui, 17, 18, 20, 21, 22
    Crypturus soui, 22
    Odontophorus guianensis, 319
Pandion haliaetus carolinensis, 256
Pandionidae, 256
papa, Sarcoramphus, 154
Papa, Vultur, 154
Parabuteo unicinctus harrisi, 173, 226
paradisaea, Sterna, 453
parasiticus, Larus, 436
    Stercorarius, 433, 436, 438
Pardela chica, 37
Pardela del Pacífico, 42
Pardela sombría, 36
Pardelas, 35
Pardirallus maculatus, 364
Parra cayennensis, 383
    chilensis, 384
    hypomelaena, 376
patens, Butorides striatus, 86, 87, 88
Patico de agua, 366
Pato calvo, 146
Pato crestudo, 137

Pato cuchara, 145
Pato de collar, 150
Pato pechiblanco, 148
Pato rabudo, 140
Pato real, 134
Pato tigre, 150
Patos, 129
pauxilla, Gallinula chloropus, 359
Pava cimba, 298
Pava negra, 303
Pavón, 293
Pavones, 293
Pavos reales, 310
Peacocks, 310
Pelecanidae, 51
Pelecaniformes, 48
Pelecanus erythrorhynchos, 51
    Leucogaster, 58
    occidentalis carolinensis, 51
    occidentalis murphyi, 55
    olivaceus, 65
    Sula, 63
Pelican, Brown, 51
Pelícanos, 51
Pelicans, 51
Pelidna Pacifica, 424
Penelope purpurascens, 293
    purpurascens aequatorialis, 298, 302
    purpurascens brunnescens, 302
    purpurascens purpurascens, 302
Perdiz de arca, 6
Perdiz de rastrojo, 17
Perdiz serrana, 14
peregrinus, Falco, 283
petoensis, Falco rufigularis, 260, 283
Petrel, Black, 43, 47
    Dark-rumped, 35
    Galápagos, 43
    Graceful storm, 43, 45
    Least, 43, 45
Petrel de Rabadilla oscura, 35
Petreles, 35
Petrels, 35
    Storm, 42
petulans, Buteo magnirostris, 214, 215, 216
phaeopygia, Oestrelata, 35
    Pterodroma, 35
    Pterodroma phaeopygia, 35
Phaethon aethereus mesonauta, 49
    lepturus, 51
Phaethontidae, 48
Phalacrocoracidae, 64

Phalacrocorax bougainvillii, 65
    olivaceus olivaceus, 65
Phalarope, Northern, 430, 432
    Red, 430
    Wilson's, 430, 431
Phalaropes, 429
Phalaropodidae, 429, 430
Phalaropus fulicarius, 430
Phasianidae, 310
Phasianus colchicus, 333
Pheasant, Ring-necked, 333
Pheasants, 310
pileata, Ardea, 97
pileatus, Pilherodius, 78, 97
Pilherodius pileatus, 78, 97
pinnatus, Botaurus, 113
Pintail, 130, 140
pipixcan, Larus, 439, 445
Piquero moreno, 56
Piqueros, 55
pitanay, Haematopus palliatus, 379
plancus, Caracara, 259, 271
Plancus, Falco, 271
Platalea Ajaja, 127
platypterus, Buteo platypterus, 174, 204
    Sparvius, 204
platyrhynchos, Anas platyrhynchos, 130, 139
Playerito arenaro, 416
Playerito coleador, 402
Playerito de rabadilla blanca, 421
Playerito gracioso, 417
Playerito menudo, 420
Playerito occidental, 419
Playerito pectoral, 423
Playerito unicolor, 422
Playero aliblanco, 406
Playero chillón chico, 399
Playero chillón grande, 400
Playero gordo, 415
Playero solitario, 400
Playeros, 393
Plegadis chihi, 124
    falcinellus falcinellus, 122, 124
Plotus leucogaster, 69
Plover, American golden, 382, 385
    Black-bellied, 382, 384
    Collared, 383, 387
    Golden, 382
    Semipalmated, 383, 386
    Upland, 394, 395
    Wilson's, 383, 391
Plovers, 382
plumbea, Ictinia, 172, 177
    Leucopternis, 173, 221

plumbeus, Falco, 177
Pluvialis dominica dominica, 382, 385
podiceps, Colymbus, 27
    Podilymbus, 25
    Podilymbus podiceps, 27
Podiceps antarcticus, 27
    caspicus californicus, 31
    dominicus, 25
    dominicus brachypterus, 28, 31
    dominicus dominicus, 31
    dominicus speciosus, 31
Podicipedidae, 24, 25
Podicipediformes, 24
Podilymbus podiceps, 25
    podiceps antarcticus, 27
    podiceps antillarum, 26
    podiceps podiceps, 27
poliocephalus, Crypturellus soui, 17, 18, 22, 24
    Crypturornis soui, 22
Polla sultana, 360
Pollito de mar boreal, 432
Pollito de mar rojizo, 430
Pollito de mar tricolor, 431
Polyborus, 272
    Audubonii, 273
pomarinus, Lestris, 435
    Stercorarius, 433, 435
Porphyrula martinica, 339, 360
Porzana carolina, 339, 350
    cinereiceps, 354
    flaviventer flaviventer, 339, 348
    flaviventer woodi, 350
prattii, Haematopus palliatus, 381
princeps, Leucopternis, 173, 222
Procellaria grisea, 36
    melania, 47
Procellariidae, 35
Procellariiformes, 31
Pterodroma, 35
    phaeopygia, 35
    phaeopygia phaeopygia, 35
Puffinus, 35
    griseus, 35, 36
    lherminieri, 35, 37
    lherminieri lherminieri, 37
    lherminieri loyemilleri, 38
    lherminieri subalaris, 41
    pacificus, 35
    pacificus chlororhynchus, 42
    tenuirostris, 36
purpurascens, Penelope, 293
    Penelope purpurascens, 302
pusilla, Tringa, 417
pusillus, Ereunetes, 395, 417

Quail, Banded wood, 311, 330
    Black-breasted wood, 311, 328
    Marbled wood, 311, 316
    Rufous-breasted wood, 311, 325
    Spotted wood, 311, 322
    Tacarcuna wood, 311, 327
Quails, 310
queribundus, Herpetotheres cachinnans, 263

Rabijunco, 49
Rail, Black, 365
    Gray-breasted, 339, 355
    Gray-necked wood, 339, 341
    Rufous-crowned wood, 339, 346
    Spotted, 364
    White-throated, 339, 351
    Yellow-breasted, 339, 348
Rails, 338
Rallidae, 338
ralloides, Ardea, 95
Rallus carolinus, 350
    exilis, 355
    flaviventer, 348
    jamaicensis, 365
    maculatus, 364
Rascón castaño, 339
rava, Actitis macularia, 405
Rayador, 464
recognita, Sterna anaethetus, 455
Recurvirostridae, 427
Rey gallinazo, 154
rhizophorae, Buteogallus anthracinus, 237
Rhynchortyx cinctus, 311
    cinctus australis, 333
    cinctus cinctus, 330
    cinctus hypopius, 330, 333
ridgwayi, Anous stolidus, 462
    Buteogallus urubitinga, 231
    Fregata minor, 77
    Urubitinga, 231
robinsoni, Butorides striatus, 88
Rostrhamus, 184
    sociabilis sociabilis, 172, 180
rothschildi, Fregata magnificens, 77
rubigenis, Odontophorus, 330, 333
rubra, Crax, 293
    Crax rubra, 293
rufa, Calidris canutus, 394, 415
    Tringa, 415
ruficauda, Asturina, 215
ruficaudus, Accipiter, 215
ruficollis, Cathartes aura, 161, 166
    Egretta, 92
    Hydranassa tricolor, 79, 92

ruficrissa, Ortalis, 306
rufigularis, Falco rufigularis, 286
rufulus, Heterospizias meridionalis, 225
Rupornis magnirostris alia, 216
  magnirostris arguta, 213
  magnirostris insidiatrix, 215
Rynchopidae, 463
Rynchops nigra, 464
  nigra cinerascens, 465
  nigra nigra, 464
  nigra oblita, 464, 465

sabini, Larus, 447
  Xema, 439, 447
salmoni, Tigrisoma, 79, 109
Salteador grande, 433
Salteador parásito, 436
Salteador pomarino, 435
Salteador rabudo, 437
salvini, Diomedea cauta, 33
Sanderling, 393, 416
Sandpiper, Baird's, 395, 422
  Buff-breasted, 394, 426
  Least, 395, 402
  Pectoral, 395, 423
  Semipalmated, 395, 417
  Solitary, 394, 400
  Spotted, 394, 402
  Stilt, 394, 425
  Western, 395, 419
  White-rumped, 394, 421
Sandpipers, 393
Sarcoramphus papa, 154
Sarkidiornis sylvicola, 129, 137
saturatus, Tinamus major, 6, 10, 11, 12
Scaup, Lesser, 130, 148
schistacea, Leucopternis, 237
  Urubitinga, 237
scolopacea, Limosa, 413
scolopaceus, Limnodromus, 394, 413
Scolopacidae, 393
Scolopax alba, 125
  caudatus, 126
  delicata, 413
  Fedoa, 398
  flavipes, 399
  Gallinago, 415
  griseus, 411
  guarauna, 337
  melanoleucus, 400
semipalmatus, Catoptrophorus semipalmatus, 407
  Charadrius, 383, 386

semiplumbea, Leucopternis, 173, 220, 222
semitorquatus, Micrastur, 263
  Micrastur semitorquatus, 268
septentrionalium, Anas cyanoptera, 130, 144
septentrionalis, Falco femoralis, 288
serus, Spizaetus tyrannus, 173, 240
Shearwater, Audubon's, 35, 37
  Sooty, 35, 36
  Wedge-tailed, 35, 42
Shearwaters, 35
sheffleri, Urubitornis solitaria, 239
Shoveler, 129, 145
Skimmer, Black, 464
Skimmers, 463
Skua, 433
skua, Catharacta, 433
smithians, Odontophorus, 328
smithianus, Odontophorus, 328, 329
smithsonianus, Larus argentatus, 439, 441
Snakebirds, 69
Snipe, 393
Snipe, Common, 413
sociabilis, Herpetotheres, 180
  Rostrhamus sociabilis, 172, 180
solitaria, Tringa, 394, 400
  Tringa solitaria, 401
  Urubitornis solitaria, 173, 238
solitarius, Circaëtus, 238
  Harpyhaliaetus coronatus, 239
Somormujos, 24
sonnini, Colinus cristatus, 313
Sora, 339, 350
soui, Crypturellus, 6, 17
  Tinamus, 17
sparverius, Falco sparverius, 260, 291
Sparvius bicolor, 190
  caerulescens, 253
  monachus, 188
  platypterus, 204
Spatula clypeata, 129, 145
speciosus, Podiceps dominicus, 31
spinosa, Fulica, 372
  Jacana spinosa, 372
Spizaetus ornatus ornatus, 244
  ornatus vicarius, 173, 241
  tyrannus serus, 173, 240
  tyrannus tyrannus, 241
Spizastur melanoleucus, 172, 244
spodiostethus, Odontophorus, 330
Spoonbill, Roseate, 122, 127
Spoonbills, 122

squatarola, Squatarola, 382, 384
    Tringa, 384
Squatarola squatarola, 382, 384
Steganopus tricolor, 430, 431
Stercorariidae, 433
Stercorarius longicaudus, 433, 437
    parasiticus, 433, 436, 438
    pomarinus, 433, 435
Sterna acuflavida, 459
    albifrons, 439, 457
    albifrons athalassos, 458
    albifrons browni, 458
    anaethetus nelsoni, 440, 454
    anaethetus recognita, 455
    aranea, 449
    caspia, 451
    fuscata, 440, 455
    fuscata crissalis, 456
    fuscata fuscata, 455
    hirundo hirundo, 439, 452
    maxima, 458
    paradisaea, 453
    surinamensis, 448
Stilt, Black-necked, 428
Stilts, 427
stolidus, Anous, 439, 461
    Anous stolidus, 462
Storks, 119
striata, Ardea, 86
striatus, Butorides, 79, 84
    Butorides striatus, 86
strophium, Odontophorus, 328
struthopus, Ortalis, 307
subalaris, Puffinus lherminieri, 41
subruficollis, Tringa, 426
    Tryngites, 394, 426
subtilis, Buteogallus anthracinus, 237
Sula, Pelecanus, 63
sula, Sula, 55
    Sula sula, 63
Sula dactylatra, 60
    dactylatra dactylatra, 60
    dactylatra granti, 61
    leucogaster, 56
    leucogaster etesiaca, 58
    leucogaster leucogaster, 58
    nebouxii, 56
    nebouxii excisa, 63
    nebouxii nebouxii, 60, 61
    sula, 55
    sula sula, 63
    sula websteri, 64
Sulidae, 55
Sunbittern, 369
superciliosus, Accipiter superciliosus, 194

Surfbird, 394, 407
surinamensis, Chlidonias niger, 439, 448
    Sterna, 448
swainsoni, Buteo, 174, 208
sylvicola, Sarkidiornis, 129, 137
Symphemia semipalmata inornata, 406

taeniatus, Morphnus, 248
Tantalus cayennensis, 122
    Falcinellus, 124
Teal, Blue-winged, 130, 141
    Cinnamon, 130, 144
tenuirostris, Puffinus, 36
Tern, Black, 439, 448
    Bridled, 440, 454
    Caspian, 440, 451
    Common, 439, 452
    Gull-billed, 439, 449
    Least, 439, 457
    Royal, 440, 458
    Sandwich, 440, 459
    Sooty, 440, 455
Terns, 438
Teru-teru, 383
teter, Cathartes aura, 165
tethys, Oceanodroma, 42, 43
    Oceanodroma tethys, 44
Tethys, Thalassidroma, 44
Tetrao cristatus, 311
    gujanensis, 316
    major, 6
Thalasseus maximua maximus, 440, 458
    sandvicensis acuflavidus, 440, 459
Thalassidroma gracilis, 45
    Tethys, 44
    tethys kelsalli, 44
Thericticus caudatus caudatus, 122, 126
    caudatus hyperorius, 127
Threskiornithidae, 122
Thula, Ardea, 89
thula, Egretta thula, 78, 89
Tiger-bittern, Banded, 79, 106
    Bare-throated, 79, 103
    Salmon's, 79, 109
Tigrisoma lineatum lineatum, 79, 106, 109, 112
    lineatum marmoratum, 108
    mexicanus, 103
    salmoni, 79, 109
    salmoni brevirostre, 112
Tigua, 28
Tijereta de mar, 73
Tijeretas de mar, 72
Tinamidae, 5, 6

Tinamiformes, 5
Tinamou, Great, 6
    Highland, 6, 14
    Little, 6, 17
Tinamous, 5
Tinamus frantzii, 14
    major, 6, 15
    major brunneiventris, 12
    major castaneiceps, 10
    major fuscipennis, 6, 10, 12
    major saturatus, 6, 10, 11, 12
    major zuliensis, 11
    soui, 17
Totanus flavipes, 394, 399
    melanoleucus, 393, 400
    solitarius cinnamomeus, 402
tricolor, Steganopus, 430, 431
Tringa Fulicaria, 430
    fuscicollis, 421
    himantopus, 425
    lobata, 432
    longicauda, 395
    macularia, 405
    melanotos, 423
    minutilla, 420
    Morinella, 408
    pusilla, 417
    rufa, 415
    solitaria, 394, 400
    solitaria cinnamomea, 402
    solitaria solitaria, 401
    squatarola, 384
    subruficollis, 426
    virgata, 407
Tropicbird, Red-billed, 49
Tropicbirds, 48
Trynga (alba), 416
Tryngites subruficollis, 394, 426
Turillo, 387
Turnstone, Ruddy, 394, 408
tyrannus, Spizaetus tyrannus, 241

uncinatus, Chondrohierax uncinatus, 172, 188
    Falco, 188
unicolor, Chamaepetes, 293, 303
urubitinga, Buteogallus, 173, 229
    Buteogallus urubitinga, 232
    Cathartes burrovianus, 171
Urubitinga, Falco, 232
Urubitinga anthracina bangsi, 236
    anthracina cancrivora, 235
    ridgwayi, 231
    schistacea, 237
Urubitornis solitaria sheffleri, 239
    solitaria solitaria, 173, 238

vanrossemi, Gelochelidon nilotica, 450
Vaquero, 260
velox, Accipiter striatus, 174, 194
    Falco, 194
Veraguanensis, Odontophorus, 322
veraguensis, Odontophorus, 322, 323
vetula, Ortalis, 306
vicarius, Spizaetus ornatus, 173, 241
viduata, Anas, 130
    Dendrocygna, 129, 130
violacea, Ardea, 101
    Nyctanassa, 79, 100
    Nyctanassa violacea, 101
virescens, Ardea, 84
    Butorides, 79, 83
    Butorides virescens, 84
virgata, Aphriza, 394, 407
    Tringa, 407
virginianus, Colinus, 316
Viuda, 428
vociferus, Charadrius, 383
    Charadrius vociferus, 390
Vuelvepiedras, 408
Vultur Aura, 165
    harpyja, 249
    Papa, 154
Vulture, Black, 154, 157
    King, 154
    Turkey, 154, 161
    Yellow-headed, 154, 168
Vultures, American, 153

websteri, Sula sula, 64
Whimbrel, 393, 396
Widgeon, American, 129, 146
Willet, 393, 406
wilsonia, Charadrius, 383, 391
    Charadrius wilsonia, 391
woodi, Porzana flaviventer, 350

Xema sabini, 439, 447

Yaguaso colorado, 131
Yellowlegs, Greater, 393, 400
    Lesser, 394, 399
yetapa, Milvus, 175
    Elanoides forficatus, 175

Zambullidores de agua, 365
Zarapito trinador, 396
zeledoni, Cochlearius cochlearius, 115
zimmeri, Leucopternis princeps, 222, 223
Zorro de agua, 99
zuliensis, Tinamus major, 11